A Journey Through European and International Taxation

EUCOTAX Series on European Taxation

VOLUME 73

Series Editors

Introduction

EUCOTAX (European Universities Cooperating on Taxes) is a network of tax institutes currently consisting of thirteen universities: WU (Vienna University of Economics and Business) in Austria, Katholieke Universiteit Leuven in Belgium, Université Paris-I Panthéon-Sorbonne in France, Universität Osnabrück in Germany, Libera, Eötvös Loránd University in Budapest in Hungary, Università Internazionale di Studi Sociali in Rome University of Lodz and University of Warsaw in Poland, in Italy, Fiscaal Instituut Tilburg at Tilburg University in the Netherlands, Universitat de València in Spain, Uppsala University in Sweden, Universität St. Gallen in Switzerland, and Georgetown University in Washington DC, United States of America. The network aims at initiating and coordinating both comparative education in taxation, through the organization of activities such as winter courses and guest lectures, and comparative research in the field, by means of joint research projects, international conferences and exchange of researchers between various countries.

Contents/Subjects

The EUCOTAX series covers a wide range of topics in European tax law. For example tax treaties, EC case law, tax planning, exchange of information and VAT. The series is well-known for its high-quality research and practical solutions.

Objective

The series aims to provide insights on new developments in European taxation.

Readership

Practitioners and academics dealing with European tax law.

Frequency of Publication

2-3 new volumes published each year.

The titles published in this series are listed at the end of this volume.

A Journey Through European and International Taxation

Liber Amicorum in Honour of Peter Essers

Edited by

Carla De Pietro
Cees Peters
Eric Kemmeren

Wolters Kluwer

Published by:
Kluwer Law International B.V.
PO Box 316
2400 AH Alphen aan den Rijn
The Netherlands
E-mail: lrs-sales@wolterskluwer.com
Website: www.wolterskluwer.com/en/solutions/kluwerlawinternational

Sold and distributed by:
Wolters Kluwer Legal & Regulatory U.S.
920 Links Avenue
Landisville, PA 17538
United States of America
E-mail: customer.service@wolterskluwer.com

ISBN 978-94-035-3197-7

e-Book: ISBN 978-94-035-3207-3
web-PDF: ISBN 978-94-035-3217-2

Editors

Carla De Pietro works as an Associate Professor at the Fiscal Institute Tilburg of Tilburg University, the Netherlands. She is also the Academic Director of the master's programme in International Business Taxation at Tilburg University, the Netherlands. She is an approved expert on the UNDP ExpRes Roster, a consultant deployment mechanism at the United Nations within the framework of the United Nations Development Programme to realize the Sustainable Development Goals.

Cees Peters works as an Associate Professor at the Fiscal Institute Tilburg of Tilburg University, the Netherlands. His work received recognition with the granting of the 'Jaap van den Berge Literatuurprijs' in 2019 for its contribution to the development of tax law in the Netherlands. Cees is currently serving as the Head of the Department of Tax Law at Tilburg Law School.

As of 2002, **Eric Kemmeren** is Professor of International Taxation and International Tax Law at the Fiscal Institute Tilburg of Tilburg University, the Netherlands. As of 1992, he is of counsel to Ernst & Young Belastingadviseurs LLP, Rotterdam, the Netherlands, and as of 2007, he is Deputy Justice of the Arnhem Court of Appeals (Tax Division), the Netherlands.

Prof Dr Peter H.J. Essers

Contributors

Philip Baker is a visiting professor at Oxford University, United Kingdom, and King's counsel at Field Court Tax Chambers, Gray's Inn.

Niels Bammens is Professor of Tax Law at KU Leuven, Belgium and of counsel to EY Tax Consultants (FSO Tax, Brussels). He can be contacted at niels.bammens@kuleuven.be.

Katia Cejie is Full Professor in Fiscal Law at the Department of Law in Uppsala University, Sweden and a member of the Board of Advanced Tax Rulings in Sweden. She holds the Chair of the Centre for Tax Law and is the CEO of Skatterättsligt Forum AB. She is also the editor of the tax law journal *SkatteNytt* and a member of IFA and EATLP. In 2019, she received the Distinguished Teaching Award of Uppsala University, Sweden. She is engaged in both EUCOTAX/Wintercourse and the Tax Moot Court Competition (Leuven).

Daniel Deak, DSc (Hungarian Academy of Sc.), specializes in international taxation and EU law. He was the founding president of the Hungarian branch of IFA and is a member of the EATLP scientific committee. He has been active in academia for almost fifty years. Also showing an interest in social sciences and theology, he is one of the editors of two Hungarian periodicals devoted to distributing progressive theology worldwide.

Prof Dr Joachim Englisch holds a chair for public law and tax law at Münster University, Germany. His current research focuses on International and European tax law covering both direct and indirect taxation. Dr Englisch has continuously advised the OECD and the EU Commission on tax matters for more than a decade, and he has given expert advice also to national governments, NGOs and MPs.

Ricardo García Antón is Assistant Professor in International Tax Law and European Tax Law at Tilburg University, the Netherlands. From 2015 to 2018, he was a research associate and postdoctoral research fellow at IBFD Academic (Amsterdam, the Netherlands). He was educated at the University of Seville, Spain, where he graduated in

Law in 2002. He received his Ph.D. from the European University Institute, Italy, in 2015 on a thesis about the interplay of the preliminary reference procedure and direct taxation.

F. Alfredo García Prats is Professor of Financial and Tax Law at the University of Valencia, Spain. He holds the Jean Monnet Chair on EU Tax Law and Policy. He is Director of the ETICCs Research Group (Group of Studies on International, Comparative and Constitutional Tax). He has been serving as an advisor to the Ad Hoc Group of Experts on International Cooperation in Tax Matters of the United Nations for thirteen years and has served as a senior counsel of the Legal Department of the International Monetary Fund. Nowadays, he is of counsel at the Montero-Aramburu Law Firm.

Daniel Gutmann is Professor of Tax Law at the Sorbonne Law School (University Paris-1, France), where he is the Director of a research centre in taxation (Sorbonne-Fiscalité-Finances Publiques). He wrote numerous articles in tax matters and is the author of books on taxation of businesses (*Droit fiscal des affaires*, Lextenso, 14th ed., 2023) and on the methodology of tax law interpretation (*Sources et ressources de l'interprétation juridique. Etude de droit fiscal*, Lextenso, 2023). He has succeeded Peter Essers as Chairman of the Academic Committee of EATLP (European Association of Tax Law Professors) until 2023. He is also a partner at CMS Francis Lefebvre.

Hans Gribnau is Full Professor of Tax Law at Tilburg University, the Netherlands. His recent publications deal with topics such as tax governance, corporate social responsibility, cooperative compliance, tax transparency, reciprocity, trust, ethics and tax in the history of ideas. Hans is a guest lecturer for tax ethics in Oxford University's MSc in Taxation, and in the Doctoral Programme in International Business Taxation of the Vienna University of Economics and Business (WU), Austria. Most of his English publications are available at http://ssrn.com/author=441648.

Johanna Hey is Professor of Tax Law and Director of the Institute for Tax Law at the University of Cologne, Germany. She serves as a member of the Advisory Board of the German Federal Ministry of Finance and chairs the Deutsche Steuerjuristische Gesellschaft (German Tax Law Association).

Peter Hongler is Professor of Tax Law at the University of St. Gallen, Switzerland. Peter Hongler was educated at the Universities of Bern (MLaw 2008) and Zurich (Dr iur. 2011), Switzerland. As assistant to Prof. Dr Madeleine Simonek, he conducted research at the Universities of Zurich and Lucerne, Switzerland. Besides, he was a guest researcher at the Institute for Austrian and International Tax Law at the Vienna University of Economics and Business, Austria and Post-Doc Research Fellow at the IBFD in Amsterdam. In the last few years, he has been a guest professor/visiting fellow at various institutions around the world. Moreover, he is experienced in advising political bodies on tax policy matters.

Prof. Dr Adolfo Martín Jiménez is Professor of Tax Law at the University of Cadiz, Spain, Vice-chairman of the International Fiscal Association Permanent Scientific Committee and former chairman of the European Association of Tax Law Professors.

Dr Hab. Ziemowit Kukulski is Associate Professor at and Head of the Tax Law Department, Faculty of Law and Administration, University of Lodz (Poland); and Head of the Centre of Tax Documentation and Studies, University of Lodz (Poland).

Steffen Lampert is Professor of Public Law, Finance Law and Tax Law at the University of Osnabrueck, Germany. His main fields of research are international and European tax laws.

Michael Lang is Head of the Institute for Austrian and International Tax Law at WU Vienna, Austria and Director of the postgraduate LLM Programme in International Tax Law and of the Doctoral Programme in International Business Taxation at that university. Email: michael.lang@wu.ac.at.

Hanna Litwińczuk is Ordinary Professor at the Faculty of Law and Administration of Warsaw University, Poland. Hanna's main fields of research and teaching are direct taxation, especially business taxation, as well as accounting law, international and EU tax law. She is a member of the European Association of Tax Law Professors (EATLP) and the International Fiscal Association (IFA). She is a member of the Supervisory Board of the Polish branch of IFA.

Guglielmo Maisto is Professor of International and Comparative Law at the Università Cattolica del S. Cuore, Piacenza, Italy.

Giuseppe Marino is Full Professor of Tax Law and Theory and Practice of International Tax Law at the Faculty of Law of the University of Milan, Italy; Member of the Tax Committee of the BIAC at the OECD; Member of the Italian Government Commission for the 2023 Tax Reform; Former Deputy Member of the Academic Committee of the EATLP; General Reporter at EATLP 2014; and Director of *Diritto e pratica tributaria* and *Rivista di diritto tributario internazionale*.

Giuseppe Melis is Full Professor of Tax Law at LUISS Guido Carli University, Rome, Italy. He has Ph.D. in Tax Law and MSc in International Tax Planning. He is also the Director of the Master in Tax Law at LUISS Business School, Member of the Council of the Italian branch of the International Fiscal Association, tax lawyer and tax accountant. He is the author of two monographs, one handbook and over two hundred articles, among which seventy are in A-Class Reviews.

Prof. Dr Hab. Dr h.c. Włodzimierz Nykiel is Professor at and Former Head (2007–2022) of the Tax Law Department, Faculty of Law and Administration, University of Lodz (Poland); Chief Specialist at, Founder and Former Head (1997–2022) of the Centre of Tax Documentation and Studies, University of Lodz (Poland); Former Rector (2008–2016) of the University of Lodz (Poland); Former Member of Parliament (2015–2019) at the Sejm of the Republic of Poland.

Bruno Peeters is Full Professor of Tax Law, Faculty of Law, University of Antwerp, Research Group Business and Law, DigiTax Centre of Excellence and Antwerp Tax

Academy, Belgium; Assessor of the Section Legislation of the Belgian Council of State; and Lawyer (Tiberghien Lawyers).

Alessio Persiani is Contract Professor of European and International Tax Law at the Università Europea di Roma, Italy. He earned his Ph.D. in Corporate Tax Law at the LUISS Guido Carli University in Rome, Italy. He published articles on tax law matters in both national and international journals. He regularly takes part in international projects in the tax field involving the LUISS Guido Carli University, Italy, including the 'Eucotax – Wintercourse' and the 'International and European Tax Moot Court Competition'.

Pasquale Pistone is Academic Chairman of IBFD (the Netherlands); Full Professor of Tax Law at the University of Salerno, Italy; Holder of a Jean Monnet ad Personam Chair in European Tax Law and Policy at WU Vienna, Austria.

Sylvie de Raedt is Tax Law Professor, Faculty of Law, University of Antwerp, Research Group Business and Law, Belgium; Research Manager of the DigiTax Centre of Excellence, University of Antwerp, Belgium; Academic Coordinator of the Customs and Excises Educational Program, University of Antwerp, Belgium; Member of the Management Committee of Antwerp Tax Academy; and Member of the Editorial Board of *Tijdschrift voor Fiscaal Recht*.

Eugenio Ruggiero is an expert in corporate law, tax and pension fund legislation, areas in which he has authored several articles and publications. He is currently Adjunct Professor of Corporate Law and Private Comparative Law at LUISS Guido Carli University in Rome, Italy. For the past twenty-five years, together with Giuseppe Melis, he has been leading and coordinating the participation of LUISS Guido Carli University, Italy in the EUCOTAX programme (European Universities COoperating on TAXes).

Marilyne Sadowsky is Associate Professor, Sorbonne Law School (Université Paris 1 Panthéon-Sorbonne, France).

Wolfgang Schön is Director at the Max Planck Institute for Tax Law and Public Finance and Honorary Professor at the University of Munich, Germany.

Roman Seer is a fulltime University Professor at the Ruhr-University of Bochum, Germany. He is the Director (and Founder) of the Institute of Tax Law and Tax Procedure Law of the Ruhr-University, Bochum, Germany. Moreover, he is currently the Chairman of the Academic Committee of the European Association of Tax Law Professors (EATLP).

Dr Małgorzata Sęk is Assistant Professor at the Tax Law Department, Faculty of Law and Administration, University of Lodz (Poland); and Deputy Head of the Centre of Tax Documentation and Studies, University of Lodz (Poland).

István Simon is Head of the Fiscal and Financial Law Department at Eötvös Loránd University (ELTE) Faculty of Law Budapest, Hungary, since 2004. He studied Law

(1984-1989) and Sociology (1985-1990) at ELTE, and Sociology of Law at the International Institute for the Sociology of Law Oñati, Gipuzkoa, Spain (LLM 1991-1992), and his Ph.D. thesis was on banking regulation (2003, ELTE). He is Member of the European Association of Tax Law Professors (2011) and its Academic Committee (2017-2023), Member of the Budapest Bar (1994), EU tax arbitrator (2010).

Rita Szudoczky is an Associate Professor at the Institute for Austrian and International Tax Law at the WU Vienna, Austria, where she has been teaching and researching International and EU Tax Law since 2014. She completed her habilitation in 2022 on the topic of the principles of the international tax regime and obtained the title of *venia docendi*. Since the beginning of her activities at the WU, Rita has been a staff member of the EUCOTAX programme supervising the master theses of the WU students participating in the programme.

Professor Bertil Wiman is Professor Emeritus of Fiscal Law at Uppsala University, Sweden. He was until 2022 Director of the research foundation Uppsala Center for Tax Law. His primary research interests are domestic, EU and international aspects of corporate taxation. He has been a visiting professor at numerous non-Swedish universities. Wiman is a founding member of the European Association of Tax Law Professors (EATLP) and has also served as its Treasurer and Chairman. He has been Vice President of IFA and Chairman of the Swedish IFA Branch. He is chairing the Swedish organizing committee for the IFA Congress in Stockholm 2027.

Diheng Xu is Assistant Professor of Tax Law at the Fiscal Institute Tilburg, Tilburg University, the Netherlands. Diheng Xu received her Ph.D. from the Fiscal Institute Tilburg, Tilburg University, the Netherlands, in 2016. She did her postdoctoral research at New York University Law School and was also a research fellow at Singapore Management University Center for Excellence in Taxation. Her research interests are international tax law, corporate tax law and Chinese tax law.

Summary of Contents

Table of Contents

Preface

Peter Essers started working at the Tilburg University in 1984 which adds up to forty years of loyal service to academic life. During these years, Peter performed many functions for the benefit of the Fiscal Institute Tilburg and the university in general. He served, for example, as the Head of Department of the Institute and as the Dean of Tilburg Law School. Peter somehow managed to combine these responsibilities with his role as a senator for the Christian-democratic party for sixteen years.

One of the characteristic aspects of Peter's academic life is probably that he combined an excellent reputation within the Netherlands with a well-respected standing abroad. The result of this quality is that Peter is not receiving just one Liber Amicorum but two instead. There is a present from his exhaustive group of Dutch academic friends[1] and a gift from his broad circle of international friends. This book is therefore basically the second honour in favour of Peter.

The title of this Liber Amicorum is *A Journey Through European and International Taxation*. It is after all another characteristic of Peter's academic life that he made a great contribution to the internationalization of research on taxation. This includes, for example, his tireless commitment to the development of the EATLP (European Association of Tax Law Professors) including his role as the chairman of the Academic Committee.

Most of all, Peter was, however, one of the founding fathers, together with Eric Kemmeren, of the EUCOTAX network (i.e., European Universities COoperating on TAXes) back in 1993. The objective of this programme was to create a permanent structure in order to stimulate the instruction in and research on European aspects of tax law. It is fair to say, thirty-one years later, that this network has truly contributed to an invaluable exchange of ideas between both students and researchers.

The yearly highlight of this EUCOTAX network is without a doubt the Wintercourse. This project has given a countless number of students from, by now, twelve different countries the possibility to perform a comparative research. The beauty of this project, however, is that it is not just about the research as such. It is also a truly

1. *Essersbundel* (S. Dusarduijn, T. van Kempen and T. Stevens eds, Wolters Kluwer 2024).

European endeavour to create mutual understanding between all of these students of their different cultural backgrounds. As such, it is a truly European journey that corresponds with Peter's commitment to a model of unity in diversity within the European Union. Moreover, it is also the proof of the fact that the success of the European project critically depends on personalities with diplomatic skills like Peter's.

In a way, the thirty-two chapters in this Liber Amicorum are the result of Peter's journey through European and international taxation. As a matter of fact, it is actually very telling how Peter's friends are painting a very accurate picture of his academic personality. The various chapters give a wonderful overview of his research interests during his academic life. There are chapters on history of taxation, politics of taxation, general notions of taxation, European tax law and international tax law. It is therefore only natural to group the book into these five parts to make these thirty-two gifts an easy-to-read book.

Being the joint editors of this Liber Amicorum, we would like to express our sincere gratitude to all contributors. The cooperation was flawless in the usual cooperative spirit between Peter's friends. Moreover, we would like to thank Loet L'Herminez and Pieter de Vleesschauwer for their tireless editorial work for this book. It was a pleasure to work with these two talented students who already have a professional attitude towards a project like this one.

We truly wish that Peter and all the other readers of this book will enjoy the wide variety and the academic rigor of the chapters. Moreover, we truly hope that this Liber Amicorum will serve as a homage to Peter's contribution to academic life. Thank you very much Peter!

Carla De Pietro / Cees Peters / Eric Kemmeren
Tilburg

PART I History of Taxation

CHAPTER 1
Writing Tax History

Wolfgang Schön

§1.1 HISTORY AND TAXATION

'History and Taxation' is the title of a collected volume published in 2022 by the *International Bureau for Fiscal Documentation* and edited by *Peter Essers*. This book convenes the contributions submitted for the 2021 (virtual) Congress of the *European Association of Tax Law Professors*.[1] The subtitle that was chosen by *Peter Essers*, who also acted as General Reporter for this Congress, reads: *The Dialectical Relationship Between Taxation and the Political Balance of Power*. The book delves deeply into fiscal history on a comparative basis, testing the interaction between politics and taxation and comparing the different trajectories taken by European (and some non-European) countries with a special focus on the differences between democratic and dictatorial states. In his General Report, which emerged from a large number of country reports and thematic reports prepared for this venture, *Peter Essers* reached the conclusion that 'the effects of taxation on the political balance of power, and vice versa, are always interlinked with other phenomena, such as wars, crises, religious developments and inequalities in society'.[2]

This Congress book is one of the most prominent examples of a contemporary movement among tax law academics to immerse themselves in the historical aspects of taxation. Other major projects – some of which have been running for many years – include the 'Tax History Conferences'[3] which were initiated by the unforgotten *John*

1. Peter Essers (ed.), *History and Taxation: The Dialectical Relationship Between Taxation and the Political Balance of Power*, 20 EATLP International Tax Series (2022).
2. Peter Essers, *General Report*, in: Peter Essers (ed.), *History and Taxation: The Dialectical Relationship Between Taxation and the Political Balance of Power*, 20 EATLP International Tax Series 35 (2022).
3. The papers submitted for these conferences have been published as *Studies in the History of Tax Law*, Vols 1-10 (2002-2020) with Bloomsbury.

Tiley more than twenty years ago, and the 'Arbeitskreis Steuergeschichte'[4] established by *Ekkehart Reimer* and his colleagues at the University of Heidelberg and supported by the German Branch of the International Fiscal Association.

But lawyers are not alone in this venture. More and more scholars coming from different disciplinary backgrounds share this evolving interest in fiscal history: Economists, political scientists and sociologists have joined lawyers in competing with proper historians when tax history has to be written. And it should not be overlooked that practitioners and judges have made and are still making valuable contributions to this field.[5] Some of them devote their time to write on tax history after retirement.[6] There is an abundant production of monographs, collected volumes, journal articles and handbooks which cover more and more dimensions of taxation from a historical vantage point.

Against this background, it seems sensible to take stock of the existing movements and to compare the approaches taken by the different disciplines. What research questions do they pursue and what research methods do they apply? It is hoped that *Peter Essers* to whom these thoughts are dedicated might find this approach interesting.

§1.2 THE CHALLENGES OF WRITING TAX HISTORY

§1.2.1 The Blind Men and the Elephant

Taxation is a strange subject to study. On the one hand, it is immensely technical even for lawyers and accountants, and it is therefore hard to fully grasp its meaning and its impact without immersing oneself deeply into the fine-grained wording of the relevant statutes and statistics. On the other hand, taxation is essential for the functioning of the state, for the interaction between the individual and the government and for the stability of the fabric of any society. Taxation is linked to the political foundations of states, a link that becomes visible in 'iconic events'[7] in their history ('no taxation without representation'), but it is also denounced as one of the most opaque and hermetic functions of administration. It is an 'evolutionary universal' in the sense of *Talcott Parsons*,[8] meaning that modern societies cannot do without taxation. And, at the same time, the fiscal system is important for the economic well-being of a community, defining the borderline between the public and the private sector and supporting or constraining the economic activities of individuals. Thus, taxation works

4. https://www.steuergeschichte.de/.
5. *See*, most recently, Parthasarathi Shome, *Taxation: History, Theory, Law and Administration* (Springer 2021).
6. Examples include: J. Harvey Perry, *A Fiscal History of Canada – The Postwar Years* 85 Canadian Tax Paper (1989); Walter Mathiak, *Das preußische Einkommensteuergesetz von 1891 im Rahmen der Miquelschen Steuerreform* (Duncker & Humblot 2011); Stephen Pierpoint, *The Success of English Land Tax Administration 1643-1733* (Palgrave Macmillan 2018).
7. Essers, *supra* n. 1, at VI.
8. Talcott Parsons, *Evolutionary Universals in Society*, 29 American Sociological Review 339 (1964) DOI: 10.2307/2091479; Parsons does not mention taxation as such, but his focus on the emergence of democracy, bureaucracy and the money system naturally leads to the inclusion of taxation into this picture.

as a focal point for research from different perspectives. What does this mean for the study of fiscal history?

Taking a closer look, students of taxation from different disciplines seem to resemble the 'blind men'[9] in the famous Indian parable about the proverbial elephant of whom all scholars and scientists can only touch and grasp a small part. Historians will be more able than other scholars to identify taxation's place in general history, including *longue durée* political and social developments.[10] Economists will be particularly adept at studying the fiscal and economic features of taxation over time, ranging from 'number crunching' in historical perspective[11] to the application of economic theories on human behaviour. Political scientists have learned how to test their hypotheses on the workings of political systems in the tax area, trying to draw generalizable conclusions from comparing historical trajectories. Sociologists care about issues of social stratification; in recent years, much of their work in the fiscal area has focused on inequality. Lawyers are best equipped to study the institutional foundations of taxation, i.e. statutes, court practice and administrative features of taxation. They also examine the creation of the international tax treaty network which belongs to the most esoteric features of taxation.[12] But this does not mean for any of these groups that their interest does not reach further than their traditional field of expertise: Lawyers nowadays care more than ever about the political and economic dimensions of taxation. Economists work heavily on social issues like taxation and equality, while sociologists and political scientists have started to make themselves familiar with the institutional nitty-gritty of the fiscal state,[13] including highly technical features like international taxation.[14] And proper historians do not shy away from statistics and regressions anymore.

9. 'A group of blind men heard that a strange animal, called an elephant, had been brought to the town, but none of them were aware of its shape and form. Out of curiosity, they said: "We must inspect and know it by touch, of which we are capable". So, they sought it out, and when they found it they groped about it. The first person, whose hand landed on the trunk, said, "This being is like a thick snake". For another one whose hand reached its ear, it seemed like a kind of fan. As for another person, whose hand was upon its leg, said, the elephant is a pillar like a tree-trunk. The blind man who placed his hand upon its side said the elephant, "is a wall". Another who felt its tail, described it as a rope. The last felt its tusk, stating the elephant is that which is hard, smooth and like a spear.' For a short history and references with regard to the parable of the blind men and the elephant and its Indian origin, *see*: https://en.wikipedia.org/wiki/Blind_men_and_an_elephant.
10. Outstanding examples are: Martin Daunton, *Trusting Leviathan: The Politics of Taxation in Britain 1799-1914* (Cambridge University Press 2007); Ralf Banken, *Hitlers Steuerstaat: Die Steuerpolitik im Dritten Reich* (De Gruyter 2018).
11. For a classic example *see*: Glenn W. Fisher, *The Worst Tax? A History of the Property Tax in America* (University Press of Kansas 1996).
12. *See* Sunita Jogarajan, *Double Taxation and the League of Nations* (Cambridge University Press 2018); Michael Lang & Ekkehart Reimer (ed.), *The History of Double Taxation Conventions in the Pre-BEPS Era* (IBFD 2020).
13. Isaac William Martin et al., *The New Fiscal Sociology: Taxation in Comparative and Historical Perspective* (Cambridge University Press 2010).
14. Thomas Rixen, *The Political Economy of International Tax Governance* (Palgrave Macmillan 2008).

§1.2.2 What Is the 'Reality' of Taxation?

The complexity of the topic becomes even more evident when we try to define the 'reality' of taxation which scholars would like to understand. What is the substance of a tax system at any given time in any given country? Lawyers would show a tendency to focus on the relevant statutes or other legal texts which inform them about the fiscal powers of the rulers and the administration on the one hand and about the fiscal obligations and individual rights of the taxpayers on the other hand. But this traditional approach to writing the 'legal history' of taxation is subject to two criticisms which come from different viewpoints and lead to different outcomes:

(1) The most prominent German 'tax historian' of the twentieth century, *Fritz Karl Mann*, published his comprehensive study on the modern history of taxation in 1937 under the title 'Steuerpolitische Ideale'[15] ('*tax policy ideals*'). For him, the main challenge of researching tax history was – according to the preface to this book – to identify the middle ground between the theoretical writings of ancient tax scholars (which bear testimony to much thoughtfulness but had a lamentably low impact on the political reality of their day) and the day-to-day operations of politicians and administrators (which had a clear impact on the everyday life of taxpayers but which do not provide an understanding of the larger developments of taxation over time). In his view, '*tax policy ideals*', representing the dominant *zeitgeist* in matters of taxation, are the right target for exploring tax history as these *ideals* can be understood both as elements of social and political reality and as expressions of theoretical thinking.[16]

(2) The most prominent French 'tax historian' of the twentieth century, *Gabriel Ardant*, published his large-scale, two-volume 'Histoire de l'Impôt' ('*history of taxation*') in 1971.[17] Unlike *Fritz Karl Mann*, *Gabriel Ardant* was not a full-time academic but a former *Inspecteur des Finances*, one of the highest officials of the French administration. For him, the practical implementation of the fiscal system counted more than anything else – even beyond the details of tax statutes and tax rulings. He reminds the reader of the necessity to always check 'reality' by the following anecdote which he had found in the archives:

> At the end of the reign of Louis XIV an intendant, answering a request by one of his colleagues, indicated how he would proceed with the tax base of the head tax. He added: Above all, don't tell the General Comptroller, as the procedure which I apply runs contrary to the instructions, but I did not find another solution.

15. Fritz Karl Mann, *Steuerpolitische Ideale* Vorwort & V-VII (Jena 1937).
16. Mann, *supra* n. 15, at VI: '*Es musste versucht werden, jene Mittelschicht zwischen Wirklichkeit und Lehre, zwischen den Handlungen der Staatsmänner und der Buchdruckerschwärze zu erfassen, die wir als eine der stärksten Triebkräfte der Geschichte anerkennen*'.
17. Gabriel Ardant, *Histoire de l'Impôt Livre I* (Fayard 1971); Gabriel Ardant, *Histoire de l'Impôt Livre II* (Fayard 1972).

Ardant adds his personal take on this anecdote:

> Whenever we do not possess such documents – this is the general case even for relatively recent periods – reality will escape us.[18]

These two references clearly show the difficulty: to write meaningful tax history one has to be as general as possible (to identify the larger philosophical, political and social factors driving tax history) while also being as specific as possible (to show the reality of the fiscal state as taxpayers and tax officials experienced it in their time).

§1.2.3 Qualitative and Quantitative Research in Taxation

Another special feature of taxation is its precarious stance between qualitative and quantitative aspects. On the one hand, it is very clear that all taxation boils down to numbers. The tax base is a number, the tax rate is a number and the revenue flowing from taxation can be expressed as a number as well. The same quantitative approach can be employed for studies regarding the unequal treatment of taxpayers depending on their wealth and income or the size of the public sector when compared to the gross domestic product of a country. Thus, it makes no sense to form judgments on taxation without having a sufficient grasp of the underlying statistics. This makes economists and social scientists using quantitative methods also particularly strong in the area of fiscal history. When we deal with the relationship between the private sector and public sector or when we try to measure tax effects on inequality, we are lost without quantitative research. On the other hand, the best numbers cannot tell us anything about the historical 'truth' without detailed knowledge about the institutional framework behind them, an object of research that particularly lawyers and historians are trained for.

But there are overlaps. More and more research by social scientists is devoted to attempts to use quantitative methods in areas which were previously fully occupied by qualitative research. A recent example is the use of the 'Tax Introduction Dataset (TID)' developed by *Philip Genschel* and *Laura Seelkopf*, two social scientists from Germany who have mapped a comparative history of taxation by focusing on the sequence of the respective introductions of the six most prominent tax types[19] in each examined country.[20] This dataset is clearly a very helpful starting point as it helps to avoid entrenched 'biases' on the development of modern taxation and provides a fresh

18. Ardant, *supra* n. 17, at 17: '*Vers la fin du règne de Louis XIV un intendant, répondant à une demande d'un de ses collègues, indique comment il procède à l'assiette de la capitation. Il ajoute: surtout ne le dites pas au Contrôleur général, car le procédé qu'j'emploie est contraire aux instructions, mais je n'ai pas trouvé d'autre solution.*

    Lorsque nous ne possédons pas de tels documents – c'est le cas général même pour de périodes relativement rapprochées – la réalité nous échappe.'
19. Personal Income Tax, Corporate Income Tax, Inheritance Tax, Goods and Services Tax, Value Added Tax, Social Security Contributions.
20. Philip Genschel & Laura Seelkopf, *Global Pathways to Modern Taxation*, in: Philip Genschel & Laura Seelkopf (eds), *Global Taxation* (OUP 2022).

starting point for historical tax research. On the basis of the TID, other authors have explored new hypotheses on historical trajectories of taxation.[21] But they would not deny that the 'full picture' will always require some qualitative input as well in order to understand the legal background and the historical setting of the legislation in question.

§1.2.4 Scholarly and Political Aims of Writing Tax History

Taxation is a highly political issue. Competing concepts for tax policy can prove decisive in general elections. This is not only a historical fact but can be experienced on current basis. In France, increases in environmental taxation led to the initiation of the *gilet jaunes* movement which challenged the administration of *Emmanuel Macron* in a fundamental fashion. In the United Kingdom, the announcement of sharp tax reductions with no proper fiscal compensation for the public sector led to *Liz Truss* losing her job as Prime Minister within a few weeks after acceding to that position. Tax history evolves as we speak, and none of us can distance himself or herself from being part of an existing political community. All scholars who try to write up the history of taxation cannot escape being human beings who pay taxes themselves, thereby forming their own private opinions on which tax policy should be implemented.

Against this background, one should always ask oneself to what extent writing tax history is informed by current political debates. Is it even conceivable that tax history is 'weaponized' to gain ground in political struggles on contemporary fiscal issues? In this respect, one would have to distinguish between two possible positions: A more scholarly view would not deny the weight of historical arguments for current political decision-making, but one would not put it in the foreground of the research. A more political view would try to 'read' history in a fashion that strongly supports the current worldview of the writer. While this perspective is not illegitimate per se, readers should always bear its character in mind.

To give two examples of a more scholarly and a more political approach to a similar issue:

(1) In his book *Les Batailles de l'Impôt: Consentement et résistances de 1789 à nos jours*,[22] the French author *Nicolas Delalande*, a historian with Sciences Po in Paris, explores the interaction between the taxpayer and the state under the perspective of 'consent', meaning the democratic participation of taxpayers in the production of revenue mechanisms. For him, not only major foundations of democracy, like confidence in the state, but also the never-ending story of the resistance of taxpayers deserve scholarly examination. The main research

21. This is how most contributions to the collected volume employ the TID with respect to specific research issues (*see, e.g.*, Junko Kato & Miki Toyofuku, *Democratization and Tax Innovation*, in: Philip Genschel & Laura Seelkopf (eds), *Global Taxation* 141 et seq. (OUP 2022); Per F. Andersson, *Political Institutions and Income Taxes*, in: Philip Genschel & Laura Seelkopf (eds), *Global Taxation* 178 et seq. (OUP 2022).
22. Nicolas Delalande, *Les Batailles de l'Impôt: Consentement et résistances de 1789 à nos jours* (Seuil 2011).

question of this book is to identify the requirements that enable a state to make financial demands on its citizens without running into political turmoil and fundamental resistance.

(2) In their book *La Révolte Fiscale – L'Impôt: histoire, théories et avatars*, French authors *Victor Fouquet and Jean-Baptiste Noé* strongly dismiss redistributive and incentivizing elements in taxation right from the start.[23] They explicitly try to employ fiscal history to provide a justification for a fundamental downsizing of the state at large, reducing the fiscal system to a narrow financial source for some basic administrative functions. While this book is an entertaining read as well, the basic political message is clear at the outset, and the reader will know how to assess the authors' findings.[24]

§1.3 THE STATE AND THE INDIVIDUAL

One of the recurring features of tax history – whether written by historians, economists, political scientists, sociologists or lawyers – is the well-known fact that taxation is (next to military draft) the most prominent lien between the individual and the state. (Nearly) all inhabitants of a state are obliged to pay taxes, and this is by far the most important sacrifice they provide for the government and its manifold emanations. As there exists *per definitionem* no specific consideration for this unrequited payment, there is a natural inclination of taxpayers to reject the financial demands of the state. Thus, issues of coercion, consent and confidence play a major role in the history of taxation. It seems fair to say that the history of taxation is to a large extent a history of the complicated and fraught relationship between the state and the individual.

Taking stock of current historical research on taxation in this perspective, there seem to be three major strands of thinking which deserve being mentioned.

§1.3.1 Consent and Democracy

In the first place, the necessity of 'consent' by individuals to be subject to fiscal obligations has been one of the mainstays of historical research in taxation for a long time. The above-mentioned book edited by *Peter Essers* on 'History and Taxation' is built around the notion that taxation and democracy are deeply interrelated[25] and that much of the individual history of nations can be explored and explained by looking into this 'link' between the individual and the government. This is where all disciplines involved in writing tax history meet on common ground. Lawyers look into the

23. Victor Fouquet & Jean-Baptiste Noé, *La Révolte Fiscale – L'Impôt: histoire, théories et avatars* (Calmann Levy, 2019).
24. Another example for this approach is Richard J. Joseph's book *The Origins of the American Income Tax: The Revenue Act of 1894 and Its Aftermath* (Syracuse University Press 2004) which employs a detailed description of the enactment of the first US Federal Income Tax to justify its existence vis-à-vis political pressure for its abolition.
25. Essers, *supra* n. 1, at 3 et seq.

constitutional requirements of tax legislation.[26] Historians identify the links between taxation and major movements towards democracy.[27] Political scientists research the role of taxation within political systems vis-à-vis their citizens. And, economists working in political economy or public choice study the interaction between rulers (being political entrepreneurs) and citizens when it comes to building consent around envisaged fiscal policies.

A major example in this respect is the above-mentioned book by *Nicolas Delalande* which puts the concept of 'consent' front and centre of the research. Starting from the French Revolution, which was built on the convention of the *Etats Généraux* by Louis XVI in order to allow the king to lay new taxes, the issue of democratic participation in tax matters has never left French politics.[28] A striking counterexample has been described by *Michael Littlewood* in his book *Taxation Without Representation*,[29] a fascinating study on the evolution of the tax system of Hong Kong. While the citizens of this special economic and political zone never had any meaningful democratic influence on Hong Kong's tax legislation, the local government succeeded in introducing and maintaining a highly efficient and business-friendly tax system.

A completely different approach is taken by political economists hailing from the 'public choice' school of thought. A prominent example of this methodological approach building on findings by *James Buchanan* and *Geoffrey Brennan* is provided by *Margaret Levi* in her book *Of Rule and Revenue*[30] published in 1988. In her view, any 'ruler' is primarily interested in enlarging their sphere of power by extending their access to private means. This initial situation leads to a constant bargaining between the ruler and the taxpayers – a process which involves the establishment of institutions like Parliaments. In the author's view, democratic institutions have a two-sided nature: They ensure the necessity for the ruler to seek the 'consent' of taxpayers and they channel the ruler's demands to the people. Reading this book raises the reader's awareness of both the constraints and the benefits of starting out with a strong theoretical hypothesis: The historical account becomes more selective but simultaneously less chaotic when compared to 'pure' historical accounts free of any systematic background theory.

§1.3.2 Tax Rebellions

Pivotal events in the history of many nations are 'tax rebellions', i.e., events when large parts of the population have decided to not comply with their fiscal obligations and to

26. Wolfgang Schön, *Taxation and Democracy* 235-303 (Tax Law Review, Volume 72 2019).
27. A brilliant example for this kind of approach is Andreas Thier's *Steuergesetzgebung und Verfassung in der konstitutionellen Monarchie: Staatssteuerreformen in Preußen 1871-1893* (Vittorio Klostermann 1999), which disentangles the interaction between tax legislation and the franchise under the Prussian census system.
28. Nicolas Delalande, *Les Batailles de l'Impôt: Consentement et résistances de 1789 à nos jours* (Seuil 2011).
29. Michael Littlewood, *Taxation Without Representation: The History of Hong Kong's Troublingly Successful Tax System* (Hong Kong University Press 2010).
30. Margaret Levi, *Of Rule and Revenue* (University of California Press 1988).

reject the financial demands of the state. While some of these 'tax rebellions' floundered, many of them proved to represent turning points in the history of the relevant communities. Thus, it comes as no surprise that much has been written about tax rebellions from different angles. Two books show the range of approaches which we find in this area.

David F. Burg's monumental volume one, '*A World History of Tax Rebellions*' presents itself as an '*Encyclopedia of Tax Rebels, Revolts, and Riots from Antiquity to the Present*'.[31] And, indeed, everything can be found in this colourful book, starting from tax rebels under Hammurabi and ending with the fuel-tax protests in several European countries around the year 2000. The author is a freelance historian deeply impressed by the fact that his home country – the United States – grew out of a tax rebellion but has somehow become accustomed to the existence of a highly complicated and demanding tax system. By scrolling through this book, the acknowledgement of the ubiquity of tax rebellions in time and space gives the reader a hunch that the notion of the tax rebellion as a safety valve in the relationship between state and taxpayers will never go away.

A completely different book has been recently published by two prominent economists, *Michael Keen* and *Joel Slemrod*. In *Rebellion, Rascals, and Revenue: Tax Follies and Wisdom Through the Ages*,[32] the authors' aim is to identify common structures behind apparently completely different historical events:

> For it is a theme of the book that, when it comes to designing and implementing taxes, our ancestors were addressing fundamentally the same problems that we struggle with today.[33]

They examine ancient tax concepts and practices from an efficiency point of view, which allows them to go far beyond anecdotal evidence and assess historical policies in the light of modern methodology. In the end, they formulate 11 '*Pillars of Tax Wisdom*'[34] which they consider to hold true for the future.

§1.3.3 Tax Evasion and Tax Avoidance

While – historically speaking – tax evasion and tax avoidance are as old as tax itself, writing tax history with a focus on these concepts is a rather recent phenomenon. This is an 'emerging topic' in the best sense, which may well be driven by the current debate on fiscal issues surrounding presumed large-scale tax avoidance by multinational companies and – in some countries – by pervasive tax evasion by rich individuals and a comprehensive black market for goods and services. But one should account for the difference between tax evasion and tax rebellion: While tax evasion has a clandestine character and runs contrary to the general expectations in a society, tax rebels come

31. David F. Burg, *A World History of Tax Rebellions: An Encyclopedia of Tax Rebels, Revolts, and Riots from Antiquity to the Present* (Routledge 2004).
32. Michael Keen & Joel Slemrod, *Rebellion, Rascals, and Revenue: Tax Follies and Wisdom Through the Ages* (Princeton University Press 2021).
33. Keen & Slemrod, *supra* n. 32, at XVI.
34. Keen & Slemrod, *supra* n. 32, at 375 et seq.

forward, identifying themselves as being critical of the government and pressing publicly for a better tax system or even a better state.

A good example of this line of research is the collective volume '*Histories of Tax Evasion, Avoidance and Resistance*'[35] edited by *Korinna Schönhärl, Gisela Hürlimann* and *Dorothea Rohde*. In their preface to this volume, the editors clarify that they do not only aim at filling a gap in contemporary tax research but also want to highlight the relevance of tax avoidance and tax evasion for society as a whole as tax avoiders and tax evaders contribute to inequality and expose the lack of solidarity within the social fabric.[36]

§1.4 SOCIETY AND INEQUALITY

It goes without saying that quite a few recent examples of writing tax history look into the impact of the tax system on the social fabric of a country. The biggest topic in this respect is equality. As there exists a growing perception that inequality is rising all over the world and as taxation is regarded to be a major instrument in order to reduce the gap between the rich and the poor, it comes as no surprise that authors from different disciplinary backgrounds have decided to explore the interaction between tax and equality. Two recent publications deserve being mentioned as they show very different approaches to this topic.

In '*Das Versprechen der Gleichheit*'[37] ('*The Promise of Equality*'), Berlin-based historian *Marc Buggeln* tries to understand the progress of progressive taxation in Germany from the times of the German Empire in the late nineteenth century to today's Federal Republic of Germany. While he accepts the premise that progressive taxation fosters burden-sharing in a community and implements certain redistributive goals, he highlights that it also contributes to an enlargement of the state as such, including its capacity to go to war. It turns out that hardly any emanation of the state is not affected by this discourse, as matters of equality cannot be discussed in isolation and always are embedded in the larger discourse on the role of the state in general.

A different approach is taken by political scientists *Kenneth F. Scheve* and *David Stavasage* in their book '*Taxing the Rich*'[38] which tries to pin down the extension of progressive taxation by focusing on war and the necessity for the 'rich' to provide compensatory sacrifices for the many lives lost by the 'poor' in battle. It is not – so they say – the move towards democracy and an enlargement of the franchise which drives tax increases for the wealthy. It is the simple necessity to reach something close to 'equal treatment' between the upper and the lower social classes, given the hugely different kinds of sacrifices made by people in wartime.

35. Korinna Schönhärl et al. (eds), *Histories of Tax Evasion, Avoidance and Resistance* (Routledge 2023).
36. Korinna Schönhärl et al., *The Ability and Intention of Not Paying Taxes in History*, in: Korinna Schönhärl et al. (eds), *Histories of Tax Evasion, Avoidance and Resistance* (Routledge 2023).
37. Marc Buggeln, *Das Versprechen der Gleichheit: Steuern und soziale Ungleichheit in Deutschland von 1871 bis heute* (suhrkamp taschenbuch wissenschaft 2022).
38. Kenneth Scheve & David Stavasage, *Taxing the Rich: A History of Fiscal Fairness in the United States and Europe* (Russell Sage & Princeton University Press 2016).

§1.5 TIME FOR COOPERATION

In the preface to their book on 'Rebellion, Rascals and Revenue', economists *Michael Keen* and *Joel Slemrod* humbly express the hope that 'real historians will forgive our blundering over their terrain'.[39] What sounds like an excuse should be further developed into an invitation to cooperate. Lawyers and historians, economists and sociologists, practitioners and theorists, political scientists and even politicians should find fora and formats to tackle the history of taxation from all necessary angles. '*History never repeats itself*', *Mark Twain* famously said, '*but it does often rhyme*'. And why should the sound of tax coming from the past be interpreted by soloists only? Sometimes, only the performance of a whole orchestra – composed of all kinds of winds – can give the audience the full experience.

39. Keen & Slemrod, *Rebellion, Rascals, and Revenue: Tax Follies and Wisdom Through the Ages* XVIII (Princeton University Press 2021).

CHAPTER 2

Twenty-Five Years of EATLP

Bertil Wiman

§2.1 INTRODUCTION[1]

Peter Essers has been my friend since the 1990s. I cannot recall when I first met him, but we got involved in several mutual projects. Soon a mutual trust and understanding developed of the kind that stands firm not only in good times but also in difficult times. He invited me and my university to participate in EUCOTAX and in Wintercourse.

His engagement in international cooperation on tax research and studies is great. He was one of the founders of EUCOTAX and Wintercourse. To honour him, I have chosen to describe the development of the European Association of Tax Law Professors (EATLP). Peter has done invaluable services to EATLP, not least as the chairman of the Academic Committee.

It sounds good to have twenty-five years of EATLP years as a title, but when has EATLP reached that age? The general assembly at the EATLP congress in Luxemburg was the 25th, as the first general assembly took place at our first congress in Stockholm in 1999. However, it also means that in 2024, EATLP will have existed twenty-five years, almost at the same time as we will celebrate Peter Essers.

My presentation is based on my recollection of what happened, especially in the early days. Thus, there is ample room for mistakes. I have read old communications, protocols, old notes, and so on. I was not only the first treasurer but also the chairman of the Executive Board for a period. During other periods of the EATLP existence, my engagement has been as any member, i.e., not directly involved in the real inside work of the EATLP.

In a press release dated 29 June 1999, it was stated the following:

1. My contribution is based on my presentation honouring former EATLP chairman Adolfo Martin Jiménez at EATLP congress in Luxembourg 10 June 2023.

> Association of European Tax Professors founded
>
> At a meeting of 80 professors of tax law from 16 European countries at the Stockholm School of Economics, it was decided to found an Association of European Tax Professors.

This is the press release issued by Professor Manfred Mössner at the University of Osnabrück, at the end of June 1999. Manfred was instrumental in establishing the EATLP. Formally, the EATLP was founded at a general assembly at the Stockholm School of Economics. I was one of the founding members and also a member of the first Executive Board. I would like to provide a description of the EATLP through my lenses. It is only twenty-five years ago, but when I study the work we did then, it also provides an interesting display of the technical advances society has made with respect to communications, payment systems, etc. The Internet did barely exist, fax and regular telephones were still important, cell phones did exist, were expensive to acquire, and not to mention, it was relatively expensive to make international calls even within the European Union. Equally, cross-border payments were expensive. Facebook, etc., did not exist. Internet was at a very early stage. We did not use PowerPoint but overhead projectors. No GDPR. But we did have artificial intelligence ☺.

The possibilities for students to study at other European Universities as part of their national degree had started but were far from as developed as they are now. The same is true for EU-funded research. I could go on, but the developments over the last twenty-five years in all these areas have been tremendous, and going back and reading our communications, etc., from the late 1990s between us involved certainly bear proof of this. The European Union has been instrumental in providing many improvements benefitting us in our daily lives, for which we should be very grateful.

It was not easy to have international programmes and exchanges before the EATLP. Looking at my alma mater, Uppsala University, and our international law programmes, they were few. We had established a programme with the University of Minnesota in 1983 that actually still runs in its fortieth year. Our students could take courses in maritime law at Oslo University, and there were minor academic exchanges with, e.g., King's College in London. But I would say the establishment of the EU programmes in the early 1990s, Sokrates/Erasmus, triggered many new exchanges of different types. There were clusters of law faculties providing common programmes. And I think the EUCOTAX cooperation, headed by Tilburg University and Peter Essers, started from that framework in 1993.

In Germany, two separate academic initiatives were taken. Professor Joachim Lang at Cologne together with Professor Dieter Birk at Münster started the Academic Committee on European Taxation, ACET. In Osnabrück, Professor Manfred Mössner took the initiative to create an association for European tax professors. It was felt, not least from many of us from other countries that participated in both initiatives, that it would be more efficient and timesaving to have only one organization. It was decided to amalgamate the two initiatives. The decision was made at a conference in Osnabrück called 'Meeting of European Professors of Tax Law' in early June 1998.

I remember that at the conference, the discussion on teaching tax law at universities in Europe displayed some of the cultural differences among us. The moderator asked the panel whether it was common in their respective countries that persons left national tax agencies to work for private firms. The Italian panel member provided an extensive and lengthy answer. Next, our colleague from Finland, Professor Edward Andersson, got the same question, whether it was common to leave the tax agency and work for private firms. Andersson simply replied: 'yes'. After fifteen seconds, laughter broke out as we realized he would not say anything more.

It was decided that I should organize a conference on the subject Taxation of Small and Medium Sized Enterprises at the Stockholm School of Economics. It took place in 1999 from late Thursday afternoon, 10 June, and ended with a lunch reception on Saturday, 12 June 1999. It was pretty much the same format and length that we still have. We started Thursday with the tax professors meeting, the continuation of Professor Mössners initiative, and the first general assembly was held starting at 6 pm.

It was a beautiful, sunny day, and we discussed the wording of the draft articles of incorporation. The draft had been prepared by a smaller group and then further developed by the founding members. Of course, as could be expected when eighty law professors discuss draft articles, there were a lot of discussions on both major and minor issues, linguistic issues, the location of commas, etc. After a while, I think many of us were pretty bored with the discussion on the wording, looking out at the wonderful sunny evening.

However, I had secretly organized for the student choir to come on a surprise visit after forty-five minutes. Suddenly, the doors to the aula opened, and around thirty singing students entered down two aisles and performed their programme. After that beautiful performance, no one was interested in continuing the discussion. The assembly was soon concluded. It shows that after all, despite all our fears, tax law professors are human beings.

The programme for Friday and Saturday was the continuation of the programme by Professor Dieter Birk, i.e., what was then called the Academic Committee of European Tax Law.

Professors Mössner and Birk shared many responsibilities for the Stockholm programme, which was good as it was an amalgamation of their respective initiatives. The social events were also important, and Friday evening started with a buffet reception at the City Hall, hosted by the mayor of Stockholm. It was followed by a boat tour starting from the City Hall, going through the locks and out into the harbour of Stockholm. It was a beautiful ride sponsored by the International Bureau of Fiscal Documentation (IBFD).

Being in Stockholm at the beginning of June meant very short nights. As the boat came to its destination around 11 pm, Professor Kees van Raad later told me that the Dutch delegation went to have a beer, awaiting the darkness. At 1 am, as the sun started to be visible again, they realized there would not be a real night. And a Portuguese professor told me he thought he had missed breakfast as the sun reached his eyes in the hotel room. He had forgotten to close the curtains. Embarrassed, he found himself in the hotel reception at 3 am, alone with a sleepy receptionist. This is a reminder that Europe stretches from north of the Arctic Circle to Africa.

§2.2 CONCERNS WHEN ESTABLISHING EATLP

Creating a new organization involved many deliberations. We wanted to have a structure that gave the organization a chance to survive over time and to be sustainable from that point of view. I will point to a few of these tools we thought were essential.

The first issue was limits on the length of terms for boards and committees and age limits. In order to have as many academics involved over time, some precautions were necessary. The two essential organs of the EATLP are the Executive Board and the Academic Committee. We decided that the term for members of these organs should be for three years with a possibility to be re-elected one time, thus maximizing the service to six years. This allowed for a reasonable turnover of academics involved in the EATLP.

In addition, we thought it would be appropriate to have an upper age limit to serve in the different functions. That is why Article 16 of our Articles requires that members of the Executive Board and the Academic Committee have to resign from the general assembly after the year they reach the age of 70.

We were concerned by examples of other organizations where a few persons could be in control for many years, making the organizations not very dynamic. I think the example set by EATLP has proven to be successful. The restriction to two consecutive terms and the age limit has ensured that tasks are rotated among the many members.

Our first chairman Manfred Mössner was thorough in making sure that the organization would survive in the long run, and he was very diplomatic in his approach to different issues. *Geographic* diversity was a key element, which is why we have the tradition of over time having all parts of Europe represented in the Board. Looking back at the composition of the Executive Board, I think it is fair to say that overall, there has been geographic diversity.

And congresses have been allocated to many different countries. So far, sixteen different countries have hosted a congress. Of those having had two congresses, which are six countries, it is only Portugal where the venue was twice in the same city, but at two different universities. The Board has done a good job in making sure that all countries represented in the EATLP can also host a congress. However, delicate issues do arise. I recall that there was a push for having St. Petersburg as a venue around ten years ago. However, the annexation of Crimea showed not only the political risks but also the concern whether a congress could at all be safely organized. In retrospective, I am glad we did not choose that alternative. And there have been other issues. In Istanbul, in 2014, Professor Billur Yalti organized a wonderful congress at Koc University. However, while we had our congress, there were political demonstrations in the city centre that affected our congress, not least with respect to transportation. In the end, it worked out well, but it shows that there are many aspects to take into account when finding a venue for EATLP congresses.

The EATLP has been successful as regards geographical diversity. Gender diversity is a different issue. There was no woman in the first Executive Board. Among the founding members, there was only one woman, Professor Maria Teresa Soler Roch from Alicante. She was also the only woman in the first Academic Committee.

However, very soon, Maria Teresa also became a member of the Executive Board. There has also at times been criticism of there being too few women in panels, etc. In the beginning, it was quite natural, as the number of academic women active in tax law was relatively low. Now, the number of women involved in the EATLP has increased. The current Executive Board has a chairwoman, Cecile Brokelind, and in addition, Madeleine Simonek is a member. At least, the EATLP has improved in this respect.

As regards the composition of the Academic Committee, all European countries having members are involved. In the beginning, sixteen countries were represented, and now the number of countries is twenty-four. Furthermore, there is both a member and a deputy member from each country, and they shall normally not be from the same university. In principle, it meant that at the start of EATLP, we had sixteen countries and thirty-two universities represented.

When I study the persons represented in the Academic Committee, it has been clear that many very knowledgeable professors have been members. Stating names is always risky; those not named can be insulted. So, I restrict myself to the Nordic countries. The first Academic Committee had Professors Peter Melz (Stockholm, Sweden), Aage Michelsen (Aarhus, Denmark), Kari S. Tikka (Helsinki, Finland) and Frederik Zimmer (Oslo, Norway). They were all outstanding scholars. The same can be said about the rest of the first Academic Committee. Of course, over time, more junior academics have been members of the Academic Committee. That was also the intention to get younger persons involved in order for the EATLP to be sustained over time.

§2.3 HOW TO DEFINE A PROFESSOR OF TAX LAW

It is, of course, fundamental for an organization for tax law professors to know who is a professor of tax law. It was not easy. I wish we could have used the methodology of US Supreme Court Justice Potter Stewart when he stated that he could not define pornography, but he knew what it was when he saw it. That method does not work in defining a tax law professor. They come in all shapes!

Considerable thinking was devoted to this issue. Article 5 of the Constitution states the following:

> Membership of the Association shall be open to individuals who bear the title of ordinary, extra-ordinary, associate, honorary or retired professor of tax law, and other individuals *who have achieved distinction in the field of tax law and* fulfil an equivalent academic function *in teaching and supervising doctoral candidates* at a University in a European country. *In the case of a researcher of a high international reputation the Executive Board with the consult of the Academic Committee may in the latter case make exceptions.*

The words in italics have been added later and reflect some of the difficulties. It was clear that membership required that you were a professor of tax law and not a professor of economics. While law and tax are fairly clear terms, it was more difficult with the term ‘professor’ as academic practice differs in various countries. In some countries, one can bear the title of professor without really being involved in teaching, research and supervising Ph.D. candidates. In other countries one is doing just that without being able to call oneself a professor. For instance, in Sweden, a person carrying the academic title 'docent' is carrying out such duties while not being titled professor. In other countries, the use of the title 'professor' was much more relaxed.

In any case, at the beginning, long discussions on how to compare the different systems in various countries took place. I assume by now, practices on who can become a member of the EATLP have been fairly well established.

Then, pretty soon, it also became clear that there were individuals doing high-level research in tax, while not formally being a professor, but having an outstanding international reputation. It would almost be ridiculous if such a person would not be eligible for membership. Therefore, there was a need for the possibility for the Executive Board to make exceptions.

§2.4 FINANCES

The EATLP started without any money. In the early communications within the Board, I described myself as a very poor treasurer. How true was not this statement? So we had to build resources.

Membership fees were one source. I think originally it was EUR 50, later lowered to EUR 30. Now it is EUR 100 depending on the mode of payment. Reading the reminder from this spring on membership fees, I get a flashback. Even though it is easier now to make cross-border payments, especially within the European Union, there are still issues. Back then, the cost for making a cross-border payment was relatively high. Single Euro Payments Area (SEPA)-payments have lowered the cost. And professors are professors, absentminded; they forget to pay. This has always put an unduly pressure on IBFD to keep track of payments and send out reminders. With respect to Sweden, I persuaded a Swedish research foundation to pay for all Swedish members, which made administration so much easier. Only one payment and no one forgot. Perhaps an example other countries can follow?

In order to build resources, I had learned from the IFA experience that congress fees could be utilized. However, we also thought that the IFA congress fees were too high for academics and wanted to make sure that academics could afford to attend. In that respect, I think EATLP has been successful. The registration fee for the 2023 congress as a member is EUR 190, and so much is included in this fee.

In the beginning, we had nothing in our bank account and could not afford to have a congress that incurred a loss. The lessons from the 2001 IFA congress in San Francisco showed the necessity to build funds. That congress took place soon after 11 September, the terrorist attacks on the World Trade Center in New York, and many cancelled their participation. IFA was lucky that the congress took place in the USA, with an IFA Branch that could absorb the losses. To a large extent, IFA US had to pay hotels, venue, catering because less than half of the expected delegates actually came. From Sweden there were very few showing up. People were scared of flying. I was that academic year visiting professor at Georgetown University in Washington D.C., and on my flight from Washington to San Francisco, there were only a few passengers. For security reasons, we had to be seated the entire first and last hour of the flight.

My tactics to build disaster funds were simple. When determining the congress fee, we conservatively assumed a relatively few number of participants. Breakeven could, e.g., be set at 80 participants, and if more registered (which we did expect), the additional participants would result in a profit. It was a successful strategy.

The allocation of responsibilities, costs and efforts for sponsoring between the local congress organizer and the central organization is always very delicate. If all financial responsibilities are on EATLP and not the local organizer, you can be sure that the dinners, lunches, tours, etc., will be really nice as the costs are borne by the central organization, but the gratitude of the participants goes to the local organizer. We were sometimes struggling with such issues.

It has turned out to be efficient to have a Dutch-speaking treasurer, or at least someone being supported by a Dutch-speaking person. The minutes from the general assembly 2002 in Lausanne reveal the problems of having the accounting in Dutch, a Swedish treasurer and an Austrian auditor.

After me as treasurer came for a year Michael Lang, then Daniel Gutmann (Dick Schonis supported as Financial Coordinator), Ana Paula Dourado (Dick still being coordinator), before we started to only have Dutch-speaking treasurers, Henk van Arendonk and now Bruno Peeters.

§2.5 THE EXECUTIVE BOARD AND THE ACADEMIC COMMITTEE

The task of chairing the Academic Committee is extremely important. EATLP has been very lucky in that respect. Professor Kees Van Raad was the first chair. He set the tone of having very high ambitions and worked hard on making sure that the congresses were academically well prepared. Kees realized that in having in essence only one day for the discussion of the main topic, one had to be very tough in moderating. Many of us vividly remember when Kees, in order to make sure that panels stuck to the allotted time limit, set his alarm clock to three minutes. It was quite difficult to continue talking once the alarm went off. Those that tried were not successful.

Kees was followed by Michael Lang, Peter Essers, Daniel Gutmann and now Roman Seer. EATLP has really attracted outstanding academics for this most important function.

The first Executive Board consisted of Manfred Mössner as chairman and our president. Other members were Hubert Hamaekers, the director of the IBFD and acting as ex officio member and secretary of the Board, Kees Van Raad as chair of the Academic Committee, myself as treasurer and Claudio Sachetto as member. As the EATLP was founded in 1999, all members of the Board started at the same time. If everyone in the Board sat for six years, the entire Board would be replaced at the same time. That would not be so smart. Manfred had a lottery to make sure that the whole Board would not resign at the same time. Claudio had to resign first, then me, and last Manfred.

Presidents of the EATLP have been Manfred Mössner, Kees van Raad, Bertil Wiman, Wolfgang Schön, Adolfo Martin Jimenez and at last a chairwoman, Cécile Brokelind.

§2.6 THE IMPORTANCE OF IBFD

Hubert Hamaekers and the IBFD were instrumental not only in the creation of the EATLP but also for the long-term survival of the EATLP. Hubert not only made sure the IBFD sponsored the first congress in Stockholm (as well as previous events, e.g., in Osnabrück) but also provided a permanent secretariat at IBFD. His academic successors at IBFD, Han Kogels and IBFD Academic Chairmans Frans Vanistendael and Pasquale Pistone, have continued to strongly support EATLP. They have also been ex officio Secretary General of the EATLP Executive Board. Without them, EATLP would not be what it is. They have been important for the well functioning of the EATLP.

I would also like to mention Joke Straver, Herman Rösslau, Adina Moldova and the current administrator Yolanda Arbon. I worked very closely with Joke when I was treasurer. It was the start of a new organization. She was very pragmatic, found solutions and was always eager to help. She was not alone at IBFD providing support, but without her, not much would have happened. This supportive and helpful tradition continues, represented now by Yolanda!

The indirect financial support by the IBFD in providing for both a secretariat and a secretary general, now being Pasquale, is instrumental for EATLP. Do not be fooled by the fact that EATLP in its budget allocates a yearly amount to IBFD. It does not cover the real costs.

§2.7 HAS EATLP REACHED ITS GOALS?

In my opinion, EATLP has been a great success. Article 2 of our constitution provides the goals:

1. The objects of the Association shall be to contribute to the development of European tax law and to the development of academic teaching and research programmes on European, international, domestic and comparative taxation.
2. The Association shall pursue its objects through cooperation not only with academic institutions but also with other non-profit organizations with similar objects, in particular with the International Bureau of Fiscal Documentation in Amsterdam.

In addition, Article 3 states the following:

The Association shall pursue its objects by:

a) supporting the organization of the Annual Congress and other scientific meetings;
b) supporting scientific research projects;
c) assisting members in developing undergraduate and postgraduate tax curricula at Universities throughout Europe;

d) presenting the opinion of the Association to institutions of the European Union and parliaments, governments and tax authorities of European countries.
e) supporting exchange programmes for professors and students of tax law; and
f) all other means conducive to its objects.

I think we can tick all of these boxes. Of course, the annual congresses are clearly visible, providing a three-day programme. However, the output is not only the congress where the research is conducted by general and national reporters, and topical issues are actively discussed. If we assume that each national reporter spends at least 3 weeks, 120 hours, a general reporter and a topical reporter 8 weeks, 320 hours, each congress entails only in those preparations more than 4,000 hours. This roughly equals one person working full-time more than two and a half years.

Not only is it of tremendous value to have it discussed and published. The academic research on the issues starts with the preparations by the Academic Committee. It has resulted in many academic seminars and other activities in the respective countries. Add to this all other preparations, and the fact that normally there are around 200 participants on a congress spending 1.5 day on the academic part of the congress. All in all, the EATLP stimulates an immense load of research and debate.

The publications from our yearly congresses are very important for many reasons. It seems as if there is one publication from every congress except for the year 2000. It is impressive that EATLP has been able to continue to publish these valuable congress books. There was a backlog for some years, but now the books come within a reasonable time after the congress. Again, thanks to the hard work by reporters, the Secretary General and the Academic Committee.

EATLP has also been a respected party to the European Union. We were represented in the EU Joint Transfer Pricing Forum by Professor Adolfo Jimenez, who together with Georg Kofler very much contributed to the Forum. Historically, Ana Paula Dourado represented EATLP in the EU Platform for Tax Good Governance (aggressive tax planning and double taxation). Now, Edoardo Traversa and Johanna Hey are representing the EATLP in the Platform.

My experience from the Platform is that it was only Ana Paula and I who could speak academically freely. Everyone else represented an organization with a specific agenda. But, the EATLP did not provide any guidelines on what standpoint we should take. I am convinced that we contributed to the discussions in the Platform being lively. We could often be critical on proposals from the Commission without having to be too diplomatic.

EATLP has also been the academic hub through which many research projects, other academic cooperations and projects has started. There are so many that it is impossible to name them. And I would only be aware of a few. One example: Professor Tanja Bender from Leiden University and I presented at the Paris Congress in 2005 a survey on the requirements for obtaining a Ph.D. in various EU countries. It showed substantial differences. Given that it was twenty years ago, and much has happened since then, perhaps it could be worthwhile to do a new survey.

In 2006, we had the first Ph.D. seminar on comparative tax law, a tradition that has continued and now is held every second year in Uppsala. Now, Professor Katia

Cejie is responsible. In the same coordinated package, we have similar seminars on EU tax law at Wirtschaftsuniversität in Vienna and on international tax law at Leiden University. Professor Jérôme Monsenego at Stockholm University organizes a seminar on transfer pricing in conjunction with the Uppsala seminar. Every second year, around twenty-five Ph.D. candidates are admitted to these seminars.

The poster programme at the congresses is a useful tool for promoting young researchers and enabling them to establish their own networks. Some will be so successful that they receive the European Doctoral Tax Thesis Award, EATTA. The Doctoral Tax Thesis Award is a joint venture of the EATLP and the European Commission. So many successful academics have enjoyed the poster programme and the Award. For example, the host of the Luxembourg congress in 2023, Professor Werner Haslehner, received the award in 2010.

An organization without members will die. In that vein, it is comforting to know that membership levels are rising. Even during the pandemic, EATLP managed to attract more than 40 new members, and now it totals 340 members. And the new members are young. That is very promising for the future.

§2.8 CONCLUSION

I am proud that the EATLP has not only survived twenty-five years but also developed and continued to engage more and more researchers and academics. There is an absolute maximum of members, as one has to be a professor of tax law to be invited. However, there are no such restrictions as to the academic involvement in EATLP.

The friendship and networking facilitated by the EATLP have resulted in many other networks, such as the one our current chairwoman Cécile Brokelind has founded together with friends and colleagues, Group for Research on European and International Taxation (GREIT) (Board Prof. Dr Cécile Brokelind, Prof. Dr Ana Paula Dourado, Prof. Dr Pasquale Pistone, Prof. Dr Dennis Weber). This is just one example where I assume that the EATLP has provided the framework for establishing other networks enabling research in tax law.

But what makes EATLP unique is that it does not depend on the contribution and efforts of specific individuals. The persons involved and assuming different responsibilities within EATLP will change over time.

Much of what I have described with respect to EATLP is equally true for the outstanding achievements by Peter Essers with respect to EUCOTAX and especially Wintercourse. He has been responsible for those programmes for three decades. I am very grateful to Peter for inviting me to participate. Through him, I have got to know not only his colleagues and staff in Tilburg but also the entire Wintercourse society, a wonderful collection of academics from thirteen universities in two continents. Thank you, Peter!

CHAPTER 3

Taxing Wartime Profits: Belgian Measures at the End of World War II

Niels Bammens

§3.1 INTRODUCTION AND OVERVIEW

In 2012, Peter Essers published a fascinating book about the Dutch tax system in World War II.[1] It describes the changes made to that system by the occupiers (some of which still resonate to this day) and the role played by the tax authorities in the persecution of Jews, as well as the evolution of case law and academic research in matters of taxation, and the aftermath of the war. It is an original and intriguing work that does not shy away from uncomfortable truths.

As a modest tribute to that research, the present contribution discusses a number of interesting tax laws that were introduced in Belgium immediately after the end of World War II. The chapter starts with a brief discussion of the Gutt Operation, an ambitious plan to avert financial catastrophe in post-war Belgium. That plan included a tax proposal that was never implemented, but it paved the way for the three tax measures that are discussed in the remainder of this chapter: a special tax on profits from goods and services provided to the enemy, an additional tax on exceptional income and profits derived during the war, and a (moderate) tax on capital.

§3.2 BACKGROUND: THE GUTT OPERATION AND ACCOMPANYING TAX MEASURES

Due to the monetary policies that were implemented during the war to finance occupation costs, Belgium was faced with a considerable monetary overhang. According to contemporary estimates, the total amount of cash in circulation increased from

1. Peter Essers, *Belast Verleden* (Kluwer 2012).

approximately BEF 28 billion at the end of 1939 to approximately BEF 113 billion in August 1944.[2]

That overhang, in combination with dramatic price increases due to food shortages and the rampant black market during the war, created a risk of financial disaster. In order to stabilize prices and protect purchasing power, an ambitious post-war monetary plan was drawn up. Named after Camille Gutt, the Minister of Financial and Economic Affairs in the Belgian government in exile (the Pierlot government), the so-called Gutt Operation included a scheme to withdraw all existing banknotes and exchange them up to a fixed maximum.[3]

In particular, a legislative order that was published on 7 October 1944 provided that banknotes with a value of BEF 100 or more lost their status as legal tender as from 9 October 1944 (notes in smaller denominations and coins were not targeted by the measure).[4] The Belgian National Bank was tasked with emitting new currency, and Belgian residents were able to exchange old banknotes for new, up to BEF 2,000 per household. Any amount declared in excess of that threshold was deposited in a special account opened in the name of the owner of the notes.

In addition, all current accounts held with Belgian banks were temporarily frozen.[5] 40% of the amounts held in those accounts and of the amounts declared in excess of BEF 2,000 that were deposited in special accounts was declared 'temporarily unavailable'. The objective was to release those funds gradually, taking account of the economic and monetary circumstances.[6] Ultimately, it would take five years before the funds were released to the owners.[7] The other 60% was 'permanently blocked' and was later transformed into a forced loan ('*muntsaneringslening*'/'*emprunt de l'assainissement monétaire*').[8]

Another objective of the Gutt Operation was to tax excessive wartime profits.[9] In order to achieve that objective, Gutt proposed to introduce a general tax on the increase

2. Statement of the Government, Official Gazette 7 October 1944, 379.
3. The Gutt Operation appears to have inspired other governments' plans for post-war monetary reform, such as the policy implemented in the Netherlands by Piet Lieftinck ('*Tientje van Lieftinck*') (see Herman Van der Wee & Monique Verbreyt, *A Small Nation in the Turmoil of the Second World War: Money, Finance and Occupation. Belgium, Its Enemies, Its Friends, 1939-1945* 436 (Leuven University Press 2009); *see also* Peter Essers, *supra* n. 1, at 468).
4. Legislative order of 6 October 1944, Official Gazette 7 October 1944, 386. Note that the scheme was introduced by a legislative order, rather than by a law. Legislative orders (in Dutch: '*besluitwet*'; in French: '*arrêté-loi*') were laws that were adopted by the Belgian government during World War I and World War II when the Belgian parliament was unable to convene.
5. A number of limited exceptions applied: withdrawals were possible up to a limit of either 10% of the balance of the account on 8 October 1944; the actual account balance on 9 May 1940; or, if it concerned an enterprise's account, BEF 1,000 per employee.
6. Report to the Regent, Official Gazette 7 October 1944, 383.
7. Kim Oosterlinck & Eugene N. White, *La Politique du Moindre Mal: Twice-Occupied Belgium*, in *Paying for Hitler's War: The Consequences of Nazi Hegemony for Europe* 191 (Jonas Scherner & Eugene N. White eds, Cambridge University Press 2016).
8. Law of 14 October 1945, *Official Gazette* 28 October 1945.
9. Report to the Regent, Official Gazette 7 October 1944, 383: '*De rechtvaardigheid zal een bezonder zware deelneming eischen van de oorlogswoekeraars, zoomede van al degenen die door de omstandigheden begunstigd werden en door een passende belasting zullen moeten getroffen*

in wealth between 9 May 1940 and 9 October 1944.[10] That increase would be made subject to graduated rates: 70% on the amount between BEF 0 and BEF 200,000; 80% on the amount between BEF 200,000 and BEF 350,000; 90% on the amount between BEF 350,000 and BEF 500,000 and 100% on the amount over BEF 500,000. Nevertheless, reductions were applied to ensure that modest increases in wealth were not unduly targeted.[11]

An interesting feature of the proposed tax concerned the burden of proof: while the burden of proof as regards the post-war amount of a taxpayer's wealth was on the tax authorities, it was up to the taxpayer to demonstrate the amount of that wealth in 1940. Interestingly, the explanatory memorandum to the draft bill suggested that it was necessary to reverse the burden of proof because tax fraud was so rampant before the war that no reliable estimates of wealth were available.[12] The draft bill nevertheless recognized that meeting that burden of proof could be difficult in practice and therefore provided for a number of legal presumptions. For instance, taxpayers that did not demonstrate how much cash they had available in 1940 were presumed to have owned banknotes for an amount equal to six months' wages as reported in their income tax return, with a maximum of BEF 100,000.[13]

When the draft bill was introduced in Parliament, it was met with fierce criticism. One of the main points of criticism was that the tax was discriminatory because taxpayers with a modest capital, such as small entrepreneurs, could not be expected to have evidential documentation available (given that keeping financial records was not very common at the time), while taxpayers with a substantial capital were generally able to demonstrate the pre-war origin of that capital. Although there was some merit in that argument, there may also have been a hint of hypocrisy in the diatribes that moneyed opinion makers levelled against the tax.[14] Ultimately, the criticism contributed to the Pierlot government losing a vote of confidence and resigning in February 1945.[15]

worden. De opzit van dit besluit kan doelmatig bijdragen tot het innen van deze belasting en het toepassen van de maatregelen welke ten opzichte van het vijandelijk eigendom getroffen werden of dienen getroffen.'

10. Draft bill of 20 December 1944, Parliamentary Documents 1944-45, 30, 1.
11. Draft bill of 20 December 1944, Art. 21.
12. Explanatory memorandum to the draft bill of 20 December 1944, Parliamentary Documents 1944-45, 30, 5: '*Wij staan hier tegenover een omkeering van den bewijslast. Dit is een belangrijke, doch gewettigde afwijking van het gemeenrecht. Zij zou niet noodig zijn indien, vóór den oorlog, de aangiften voor de inkomstenbelastingen getrouw de samenstelling van de fortuinen hadden weergegeven. Zulks was evenwel niet het geval. Ontduiking heerschte op ruime schaal, ondanks de inspanning van het Bestuur van Financiën dat niet voldoende gewapend was om ze te verijdelen. De buitensporige afmetingen van deze belastingontduiking hebben den aard van het redmiddel ingegeven.*'
13. Draft bill of 20 December 1944, Art. 14.
14. Van der Wee & Verbreyt, *supra* n. 3, at 434.
15. *Ibid.*, at 423.

§3.3 THE EYSKENS/DE VOGHEL MEASURES: THREE TAXES ON WARTIME PROFITS

After the resignation of the Pierlot government, a new government, headed by Achille Van Acker, was quickly installed (the Van Acker I government). Van Acker wanted to continue the monetary policies implemented by Camille Gutt but was adamantly opposed to Gutt's wealth tax. When Gutt was asked by Van Acker to stay on as Minister of Finance, he refused, making it clear that he would not return without his wealth tax.[16]

When Gaston Eyskens was appointed as Minister of Finance in the Van Acker I government, he did not reintroduce the draft bill for the Gutt wealth tax. Instead, he devised his own plan for taxing wartime profits, a plan that consisted of three separate tax measures. Those measures were later implemented by Franz De Voghel, the Minister of Finance in the Van Acker II government.[17] The measures were introduced in three separate laws, all of which were approved in Parliament in October 1945:

- the law of 15 October 1945 on the introduction of a special tax on profits from goods and services provided to the enemy;[18]
- the law of 16 October 1945 on the introduction of an additional tax on exceptional income and profits derived during the war;[19]
- the law of 17 October 1945 on the introduction of a tax on capital.[20]

Those three laws will be discussed in the sections below.[21]

§3.4 SPECIAL TAX ON PROFITS FROM GOODS AND SERVICES PROVIDED TO THE ENEMY

The first tax measure introduced by Eyskens/De Voghel was a special tax on profits from trading with the enemy. According to the explanatory memorandum, the introduction of the tax was necessary as a matter of fairness and public morality: the

16. Hélène Van Praag, *L'assainissement monétaire au lendemain de la Seconde Guerre mondiale*, 60 Revue de la Banque (Supplément historique) 3, 28 (1996).
17. The Van Acker I government (February 1945-August 1945) fell within six months, while the Van Acker II government (August 1945-March 1946) lasted less than eight months. Post-war Belgium saw a succession of governments that fell fairly quickly due to political crises that found their origin in World War II, such as the 'royal question' (i.e., the question whether Leopold III could return to the throne despite allegations that his actions during World War II had been unconstitutional).
18. Official Gazette 28 October 1945, 7247 (the original title of the law was '*Wet van 15 oktober 1945 tot invoering van een speciale belasting op de winsten voortvloeiend uit leveringen en prestaties aan den vijand*').
19. Official Gazette 28 October 1945, 7252 (the original title of the law was '*Wet van 16 oktober 1945 tot invoering van een extra-belasting op de in oorlogstijd behaalde exceptioneele inkomsten, winsten en baten*').
20. Official Gazette 28 October 1945, 7260 (the original title of the law was '*Wet van 17 oktober 1945 tot invoering van een belasting op het kapitaal*').
21. For further details, analysis, and a discussion of case law, *see* Dirk Deschrijver, *Inkomstenbelastingen 1919-2020. Buitengewone en tijdelijke heffingen* (Knops Publishing 2021).

government considered it unfair and immoral that war profiteers had realized significant profits while the rest of the country had suffered during the war. For that reason, the government considered it necessary to tax those profits.[22] The explanatory memorandum further stated that wartime profits arose from two sources: on the one hand, profits were realized by providing goods and services to the enemy; on the other hand, profits were derived by dint of the difficult economic circumstances created by the occupation (particularly due to food shortages). According to the government, it was necessary to take away the full amount of profits of the first category. Since persons who supplied goods or services to the enemy contributed to the enemy's war effort, it was considered fair, from a moral and financial perspective, that those profits return to the community.[23] That was the objective of the law discussed in this section. The second category of profits (i.e., exceptional profits derived during the war but not from trading with the enemy) was targeted by another tax that was not quite as burdensome (and which is discussed in §3.5 below).

The material scope of application of the tax on profits from dealing with the enemy was defined as the income, profits and remunerations derived between 10 May 1940 and 31 December 1944 by:

(a) entities, individuals or juridical persons in the enemy's service, as well as by individuals or juridical persons commandeered by the enemy;
(b) enterprises that had been the subject of a measure of provisional administration if the income was derived due to goods or services provided to the entities and persons referred to in (a);
(c) individuals and juridical persons if the income was derived due to any goods or services provided to entities and persons referred to in (a) or (b).[24]

While the scope of the tax appears to be very broad, the explanatory memorandum adds some nuance. It points out that common retail transactions and services of everyday life provided to civilians or military personnel of enemy nationality were not in scope, unless it concerned suppliers which were granted a monopoly or special assignment by the enemy.[25]

22. Explanatory memorandum to the draft bill on the introduction of a special tax on profits from goods and services provided to the enemy, Parliamentary Documents 1944-45, 118, 1. It is worth quoting this passage entirely as it expresses how strong the calls for justice (and perhaps retribution) were in those days: '*De oorlogsbelasting en de andere, gedurende meer dan vier jaar besetting, aan België opgelegde uitgaven, alsmede de massale en gestadige opeischingen van den bezetter hebben den financieelen toestand van den Staat diep geschokt. Anderdeels hebben oorlogswoekeraars en tusschenpersonen vaak gewetenloos aanzienlijke en tevens gemakkelijk verdiende winsten verwezenlijkt. … Wil men dat de belastingpolitiek rechtvaardig zij en dat het krediet van den Staat kunne hersteld worden, dan moeten de dank zij de oorlogsomstandigheden verkregen winsten massaal en onverwijld getroffen worden. Het gaat hier ten andere om een quaestie van openbare moraliteit. Tekortkoming op dit gebied zou het gezag van den Staat ernstig schokken en de gemeenschap die in de massa reeds zoo wreed werd beproefd in den loop van de bezetting, al het gewicht van ons financieel herstel op de schouders leggen.*'
23. Explanatory memorandum, Parliamentary Documents 1944-45, 118, 2.
24. Article 1, law of 15 October 1945.
25. Explanatory memorandum, Parliamentary Documents 1944-45, 118, 3.

The tax was due at a flat rate of 100%, and it also applied if the goods or services were provided through an intermediary, unless the provider of the goods or services demonstrated that he was not aware of the ultimate destination of the goods or services. Moreover, in cases of requisitioning, the tax was only due insofar as the income exceeded a 'normal' amount of income.

The law expressly provided that no credits for dependents could be applied to the tax and that the tax could not be deducted as a business expense.[26] Finally, the law contained severe penalties for cases of non-compliance and very long prescription periods (an assessment period of ten years and a collection period of thirty years).[27]

The law further introduced a legal presumption that certain assets of persons subject to the special tax were considered to derive from taxable income (i.e., from trading with the enemy). Those assets included banknotes and deposits held in bank accounts on 9 October 1944, as well as the assets declared in accordance with the legislative order of 6 October 1944 (*see* §3.2). The taxpayer could rebut that presumption by demonstrating that the assets had a different origin (e.g., an inheritance). At the same time, the law acknowledged that many taxpayers that were liable to the special tax did not keep financial records. For practical reasons, the law therefore contained a number of legal presumptions concerning such taxpayers' assets on 10 May 1940. For instance, taxpayers that did not demonstrate how much cash they had available in 1940 were presumed to have owned banknotes for an amount equal to six months' wages as reported in their income tax return, with a minimum of BEF 25,000 and a maximum of BEF 100,000.[28]

Interestingly, the law included two provisions to deal with potential cases of double taxation. First, a number of Belgian taxes (including the schedular taxes that applied at the time) that had already been paid could be deducted from the liability due under the special tax insofar as those other taxes applied to the income in question. Second, the law contained a mechanism to prevent double taxation for qualifying income that was derived abroad: in such a case, the liability under the special tax was reduced by the amount of tax paid on that income under an 'analogous' foreign tax.[29]

§3.5 ADDITIONAL TAX ON EXCEPTIONAL INCOME AND PROFITS DERIVED DURING THE WAR

The law of 16 October 1945 introduced an additional tax on exceptional income derived during the war. As noted above, this law concerned wartime profits that did not derive from trading with the enemy but that were derived by dint of the difficult economic circumstances created by the occupation, such as food shortages.

26. Article 6, law of 15 October 1945.
27. Articles 9 and 12, law of 15 October 1945.
28. Article 5, law of 15 October 1945.
29. Article 14(3), law of 15 October 1945: '*De speciale belasting verbonden aan in het buitenland behaalde en aangeslagen belastbare inkomsten wordt verminderd met de som welke de belastingplichtige bewijst definitief op dezelfde inkomsten te hebben betaald uit hoofde van een belasting analoog met die gevestigd bij deze wet*'.

To an extent, the provisions of the law are similar to those of the law of 15 October 1945, but there are some important differences. In particular, the tax introduced by the law of 16 October 1945 applied on the basis of graduated tax rates (rather than at a flat rate of 100%), and it applied only to the excessive portion of the qualifying income (i.e., the portion of the income that was higher than the normal income that could be derived in a similar, pre-war tax year). It thus appears that the legislator considered that it was not necessary to tax these types of wartime profits quite as severely as the profits derived from trading with the enemy.

The tax applied to the exceptional income derived between 1 January 1940 and 31 December 1944, a period that was considered a single tax period for purposes of the tax.[30] The taxable income for purposes of the tax was broadly defined and included not only profits from business activities but also salaries, income from liberal professions and commissions. According to the explanatory memorandum, it was necessary to use a broad definition to ensure that all persons who benefited from food shortages and black market transactions could be taxed. Interestingly, the definition of taxable income also included income from gambling, not so much because the legislator expected that such income could effectively be taxed, but rather to prevent that war profiteers could argue that the profits from their wartime activities originated in gambling winnings.[31]

Similarly to the law of 15 October 1945, a legal presumption applied according to which certain assets of persons subject to the special tax were considered to derive from taxable income (which, again, included the assets declared in accordance with the legislative order of 6 October 1944).[32]

As noted, the tax only applied to the excessive portion of a taxpayer's qualifying income. That excessive portion was defined as the portion of the taxable income that exceeded the total amount of such income that the taxpayer had derived in the five years before the start of the war.[33] In other words, the legislator assumed that any wartime income that exceeded the 'normal' income that was earned in a corresponding pre-war period of five years was derived from wartime profiteering. Of course, such excessive income could have, in part, derived from trading with the enemy in which case it was already subject to the special tax on profits from dealing with the enemy (*see* §3.4). In order to avoid double taxation, such income was exempt from the additional tax on exceptional income and profits derived during the war.[34]

30. Article 1, law of 16 October 1945.
31. Explanatory memorandum to the draft bill on the introduction of an additional tax on exceptional income and profits derived during the war, Parliamentary Documents 1944-45, 119, 4-5: '*Ten slotte heeft de drift van het spel zich vooral bij een minderheid onder de oorlogsprofiteurs ontwikkeld; § 1 vermeldt dan ook onder littera f), onder de belastbare winsten, elke winst voortkomend van de gezamenlijke spelverrichtingen waartoe de belastingplichtige zich gedurende het belastbaar tijdperk heeft overgeleverd ... De Administratie maakt er zich natuurlijk geen illusies over dat het de – overigens veeleer onwaarschijnlijke – winsten verwezenlijkt bij casinospelen of wedrennen zou kunnen opsporen, maar de tekst van littera f) laat toe te vermijden dat de oorlogsprofiteurs aanvoeren dat hun verrijking voortkomt van dergelijke winsten*'.
32. Article 2, law of 16 October 1945.
33. Article 4, law of 16 October 1945.
34. Article 10, law of 16 October 1945.

The tax liability was calculated on the basis of a graduated rate structure. The portion of the taxable income up to BEF 100,000 was subject to a rate of 70%; the portion between BEF 100,000 and BEF 200,000 was subject to a rate of 80%; the portion between BEF 200,000 and BEF 1,000,000 was subject to a rate of 90%; and the portion exceeding BEF 1,000,000 was subject to a rate of 95%.[35]

Similarly to the law of 15 October 1945, the law provided that other Belgian taxes already levied from the qualifying income could be deducted from the liability due under the additional tax and that international double taxation was avoided by allowing for the deductibility of analogous foreign taxes.[36] Finally, the law of 16 October 1945 expressly stated that the proceeds of the additional tax were used to settle the loan that was created as part of the Gutt Operation (*see* §3.2).

The application of the special tax under the law of 15 October 1945 and the additional tax under the law of 16 October 1945 gave rise to an enormous amount of legal challenges, leading to drawn-out legal proceedings and a severe judicial backlog. In September 1952, over 16,000 administrative appeals were pending with the tax authorities, while 3,694 appeal cases were pending before the Brussels Court of Appeal, 1,774 before the Liège Court of Appeal and 501 before the Ghent Court of Appeal.[37] The legislator decided to intervene in 1945 by introducing a special reconciliation procedure to deal with these challenges more efficiently.[38] Nevertheless, a considerable amount of challenges were pursued up to the level of the Supreme Court, with proceedings lasting several decades after the end of the war.[39]

Remarkably, a 2020 law extended the possibility to issue new or additional tax assessments under the laws of 15 and 16 October 1945 until 31 December 2021. According to the Parliamentary Documents, that extension was necessary because it could be expected that a number of disputes relating to those taxes would still be unresolved in 2021.[40] However, the Minister of Finance later pointed out that the tax authorities were not aware of any such pending cases in 2021.[41]

§3.6 TAX ON CAPITAL

The law of 17 April 1945 introduced a one-time tax on the capital of natural and juridical persons on the date of 9 October 1945. Similarly to the law of 16 October 1945 (*see* §3.5), the law of 17 October 1945 expressly stated that the proceeds of the capital tax were used to settle the loan that was created as part of the Gutt Operation.[42]

35. *Ibid.*
36. Article 13(2), law of 16 October 1945.
37. Explanatory memorandum to the law on the temporary introduction for some taxes and tax periods of a reconciliation procedure in income tax matters, Senate 1952-53, 78, 1.
38. Law of 24 Jul. 1953, Official Gazette 20 August 1953.
39. For example, Supreme Court 21 April 1967, Arr. Cass. 1967, 1018; Supreme Court 17 September 1968, Arr. Cass. 1969, 68; Supreme Court 2 September 1971, Arr. Cass. 1972, 1; Supreme Court 4 April 1975, Arr. Cass. 1975, 846; Supreme Court 7 Jun. 1984, Arr. Cass. 1984, 1320.
40. Parliamentary Documents 2020-21, Doc. 55, 1577/001, 90.
41. Vr. & Antw. Kamer, 55, 073, 112 (No. 499, Van Hees).
42. Article 1, law of 17 October 1945.

The tax was introduced because the government expected that the proceeds from the special tax on profits from goods and services provided to the enemy (*see* §3.4) and the additional tax on exceptional income and profits derived during the war (*see* §3.5) would not be sufficient to meet the short-term needs of its post-war monetary policy. For that reason, all taxpayers were asked to make a sacrifice in proportion to their fortune.[43]

At the same time, the government observed that the tax should be moderate, and for that reason, a fixed tax rate of 5% was applied.[44] The explanatory memorandum acknowledged that progressive tax rates would better serve the requirements of distributive justice, but it was felt that the application of progressive rates would lead to evasion.[45] However, the law took some account of the ability to pay concerns as a basic exemption of BEF 40,000 applied, with additional exemptions being available for married taxpayers and for dependent children.[46]

In principle, the tax applied to the entirety of a taxpayer's assets on 9 October 1944, including immovable property and movable investments held by natural persons. The tax also applied to the capital of Belgian companies. Interestingly, companies could pay the tax by increasing their capital by 5% and issuing new shares to the Belgian government in order to settle the capital tax liability.[47] The government then sold those shares, either by way of a share repurchase or on the secondary market. In cases where a Belgian company that was subject to the tax held shares in another Belgian company subject to the tax, a mechanism to avoid double taxation applied.[48]

§3.7 CONCLUSIONS

The Belgian experience at the end of World War II illustrates the difficulties that arise when taxes are introduced to fund post-war financial reconstruction. Imposing additional tax burdens on a population still reeling from the war is a bitter pill to swallow, and legislators tend to be aware that such measures are likely to be unpopular and controversial, particularly if they apply without distinction to all taxpayers.[49]

---

43. Explanatory memorandum to the draft bill on the introduction of a tax on capital, Parliamentary Documents 1944-45, 120, 1: '*Van alle belastingplichtigen zal een offer moeten worden gevraagd, naar verhouding van hun fortuin*'.
44. *Ibid.*
45. *Ibid.*, at 2.
46. Article 13, law of 17 October 1945.
47. On that mechanism, *see* Dirk Deschrijver, *De wet van 17 oktober 1945 tot de invoering van een belasting op het kapitaal en het vennootschapsrecht*, Algemeen Fiscaal Tijdschrift 5, 22 (2023).
48. Article 6, law of 17 October 1945.
49. The Belgian government was acutely aware of this risk when introducing the 5% capital tax presumably because the earlier experience with Gutt's proposed capital tax was not easily forgotten: '*Het schijnt onnoodig hier over de verdiensten en de bezwaren van dien vorm van heffing te redetwisten. De Regeering heeft geen keuze van middelen. Zij kan er niet aan denken de reeds zeer zware belastingen op de inkomsten, de handelsverrichtingen en het verbruik nog uitermate te verhoogen. Massale en onmiddellijke overplaatsing van groote bedragen kan trouwens alleen door middel van een heffing op het kapitaal bereikt worden*' (Explanatory memorandum to the draft bill on the introduction of a tax on capital, Parliamentary Documents 1944-45, 120, 1).

As noted in §3.2, the fierce criticism on Camille Gutt's proposed wealth tax contributed to the resignation of the Pierlot government. The Eyskens/De Voghel proposals, by contrast, were not met with such hostility.[50] It appears that a moderate wealth tax, in combination with two taxes that were ostensibly targeted at those who had profited from the war, was more palatable for the population (and its representatives) coming to terms with Belgium's post-war financial reality.

In 1962, the tax authorities published an overview of the proceeds from the special tax on profits from goods and services provided to the enemy (discussed in §3.4) and the additional tax on exceptional income and profits derived during the war (discussed in §3.5).

According to that overview, 50,565 tax returns were issued in relation to the special tax for a total tax liability of BEF 13,260 million.[51] However, the overview also indicates that refunds and reliefs were granted for a total amount of BEF 9,016 million (i.e., 68 % of the total tax liability). According to the tax authorities, that considerable amount could be explained by a variety of reasons. In many cases, for instance, the tax was assessed on the basis of the legal presumption as regards the provenance of certain assets (*see* §3.4). If a taxpayer succeeded in rebutting that presumption, a revision of the assessment was necessary. Moreover, a significant number of tax claims were irrecoverable due to the insolvency of the taxpayer (generally because the taxpayer's assets had already been confiscated for the payment of criminal penalties).[52] The tax authorities finally pointed out that the total revenue would ultimately be even lower due to pending challenges and relief for double taxation to be granted. Taking those factors into account, the tax authorities estimated that the special tax would ultimately generate an amount of BEF 1,353 million (i.e., approximately 10% of the total tax liability).

As regards the additional tax, the overview indicated that 193,394 tax returns were issued for a total tax liability of BEF 27,132 million.[53] In this context as well, a considerable amount was refunded and relieved, i.e., BEF 12,769 million (47% of the total tax liability). Taking account of relief for double taxation to be granted, the tax authorities estimated that the total tax to be collected would amount to BEF 9,813 million (36% of the total tax liability).[54]

50. Which is not to say that these laws were passed without any resistance. *See*, for instance, the lively discussions in the reports of the parliamentary meetings of 16 August 1945 (No. 46, 691), 24 August 1945 (No. 53, 803) and 29 August 1945 (No. 57, 863).
51. Bulletin der Belastingen 1962, No. 390, 1693.
52. *Ibid.*, 1695.
53. *Ibid.*, 1699.
54. The 1962 overview did not include information on the proceeds from the tax on capital (discussed in section 6). According to Van Houtte, that tax had generated net revenue of BEF 31,944 million in 1964 (Jean Van Houtte, *Beginselen van het Belgisch belastingrecht* (Story-Scientia 1979, 96)). He further states that the special tax had generated net revenue of BEF 3,180 million in 1964 and the additional tax net revenue of BEF 13.514 million. Presumably those figures (which were based on information provided by the tax authorities) are higher than the 1962 estimates because not all pending challenges and requests for relief had yet been resolved in 1964.

Based on those figures, the taxes do not appear to have been an unqualified success. In addition, there was some resentment among taxpayers because the tax authorities tended to be fairly assertive in applying the mechanisms offered by the laws of 15 and 16 October 1945, which led the legislator to curtail those mechanisms in 1953.[55]

55. Law of 19 March 1953, Official Gazette 1 April 1953, 1.

CHAPTER 4

Lessons from the Negotiations of the Franco-Dutch Convention Signed in 1949

Marilyne Sadowsky

What happens during the negotiation of an international tax treaty? This is an essential question, as it helps us to understand the meaning of the text by clarifying the intentions of the contracting parties. However, it remains difficult to answer, as this phase in the drafting of treaties is so little known. To find out, the public must have access to various economic and diplomatic archives, the consultation of which varies from country to country. These archives are accessible in France,[1] but they are subject to specific disclosure rules.

When I was invited to write and honoured to be able to contribute to the liber amicorum offered to Professor Peter Essers, whom I admire both intellectually and humanely, the choice of this topic was an obvious one. I met Peter twenty years ago when I was an assistant on a comparative law programme, the Wintercourse. Over the years, I have been lucky enough to share many moments of friendship with Peter and numerous discussions on history and politics in general. As history is one of his passions, it seemed natural to write about an unpublished political and historical subject that links our two countries. I therefore decided to consult the French economic and diplomatic archives relating to the negotiations of what appears to be the first Franco-Dutch tax treaty, signed in Paris on 30 December 1949.

1. I would like to thank the staff of the Economic and Financial Archives Department of the Ministry of the Economy and Finance (Service des archives économiques et financières (SAEF)) for their help with this research, as well as the staff of the Diplomatic Archives Center of the Ministry of Europe and Foreign Affairs (Centre des archives diplomatiques). All the documents referred to in this chapter are contained under the reference: SAEF, B 54226 Netherlands. Those relating to the diplomatic archives, or to another SAEF number (B 0067907), will be expressly mentioned.

Why take this old example when we know that the convention currently applicable between France and the Netherlands is more recent?[2] First of all, it should be noted that this agreement is one of the oldest in the French treaty network.[3] Against this backdrop, it was interesting to see how the first links between France and the Netherlands were forged around this tax treaty in the context of historic negotiations conducted in the absence of an international model, such as that of the OECD. How did these negotiations proceed in the absence of a common framework? How were they pursued during the occupation at the time of World War II? Did state practice influence the development of the OECD model? Conversely, did the work of the League of Nations – which was still in its infancy – influence these bilateral negotiations? This research allows us to answer all these questions, as well as to understand the duration and progress of these negotiations. The negotiations lasted twenty-three years, since the Netherlands' intention to enter into talks with France dates back to 22 January 1931, whereas the text came into force on 22 May 1954 and lasted through the war.

The central question was therefore to understand how the negotiations were conducted in the absence of a common international model, and what the intentions of the contracting parties were when they entered into the treaty. While it is taught today that international tax treaties are based on international, regional or national models, this teaching could not have been given in the 1920s, when the first international tax treaties were being negotiated, at a time when the League of Nations was looking for an international model. This is the case with the Franco-Dutch convention, the negotiations for which were officially opened on 22 January 1931 in a letter from the Minister of Foreign Affairs to the French Minister of Finance announcing the following: 'The Minister of the Netherlands has informed me that his government wishes to conclude with us a convention governing tax matters. He adds that the Dutch Government suggests that we propose a text.'[4] History will tell us that it was not the French but the Dutch who produced this first text, which gave rise to two conventions signed on 30 December 1949. These texts, the ratifications of which were exchanged at The Hague on 21 May 1954, were intended, on the one hand, to eliminate double taxation in respect of income tax and to settle certain other questions relating to taxation and, on the other hand, to avoid double taxation resulting from the application of extraordinary

2. The current agreement on income and wealth tax was signed in Paris on 16 March 1973. This agreement came into force on 29 March 1974 and was amended by a rider dated 7 April 2004, which came into force on 24 July 2005.
3. In this respect, one document refers to a Franco-Dutch convention dated 8 February 1927, which settled the question of tax advantages granted to French and Dutch nationals, without the text being reproduced. In this regard, *see*: Ministry of National Economy and Finance, Directorate General of Registration, Estates and Stamps, Financial Administration Coordination Department, Communication made on behalf of the Minister on 11 June 1947, Follow-up given on 16 June 1947.
4. Minister of Foreign Affairs, Sub-Directorate for Administrative Affairs and International Unions, Letter from the Minister of Foreign Affairs to the Minister of Finance (Direct Tax Department), 22 January 1931.

taxes on wealth or on the increase in wealth established in France and the Netherlands.[5] Very few comments have been made on the agreement relating to wealth, so we will not repeat them here. In any event, although these texts are no longer in force, they will have been the first building block not only in the Franco-Dutch treaty relationship but also in the development of the OECD model.

This chapter will solely focus on the treaty negotiations and will seek to establish a reality rather than a myth.[6] Many other issues have arisen since the text came into force in 1954, such as the adaptation of tax treaties to national reforms,[7] the interpretation of the concept of permanent establishment,[8] similar interpretations between treaties[9] and the special tax rules applicable to colonies.[10] While these issues are all interesting, these few lines will not suffice to analyse them in depth, although we will make a few references to them. This research will have enabled us to draw some lessons from these lengthy treaty negotiations conducted before (§4.1) and after (§4.2) 1945.

§4.1 CONVENTIONAL NEGOTIATIONS BEFORE 1945

The negotiations on this agreement between France and the Netherlands prior to 1945 were divided into two periods. The first period extended from the proposal made by the Netherlands to conclude a tax treaty on 22 January 1931 to 3 September 1939, the date on which France and Great Britain declared war on Germany and the Netherlands wished to remain neutral. This period was marked by difficulties in reaching agreement (§4.1.1). The second period began with this declaration of war and, a few months later, Germany's invasion of the Netherlands, prolonging negotiations during the occupation (§4.1.2).

5. In France, the national solidarity tax was introduced by the ordinance of 15 August 1945, while in the Netherlands, the extraordinary taxes on wealth and increases in wealth were enacted by the laws of 19 September 1946 and 11 July 1947.
6. In this regard, *see*: Yariv Brauner, *Tax treaty negotiations: Myth and Reality*, University of Florida Levin College of Law, Legal studies Research Paper Series no. 22-15.
7. When corporation tax was introduced in France in 1948, the question arose as to whether a branch in Amsterdam of a société anonyme established in Paris constituted a permanent establishment within the meaning of the convention. *See* Letter from the Banque de Paris and Netherlands to the Director General of Taxes, Coordination, 2nd Office, 25 July 1955 and Letter from the Director General of Taxes to the Director of Tax Affairs at the Ministry of Finance in The Hague, 26 September 1955. The same was true of the Netherlands, which in the 1960s wished to modify its corporate tax system along the lines of the German model in order to eliminate economic double taxation and stimulate capital markets. *See* Letter from Mr Van den Berge, Dutch State Secretary for Tax Affairs, to Mr Giscard d'Estaing, French State Secretary for Finance, 17 February 1961.
8. An agreement in principle was reached between France and the Netherlands on this issue in 1957. *See*: Letter from Mr Van Den Tempel to Mr Blot, Director General of Taxes, 20 August 1957.
9. In reality, many similar interpretations have been rejected as being difficult to transpose to the Franco-Dutch relationship either because they put one contracting state at a disadvantage compared to the other or because they are not in line with the work of the OEEC Tax Committee, which was conducted at the same time as the Franco-Dutch convention was being applied.
10. The archives mainly contain documents relating to the Netherlands Indies and Surinam for the Netherlands, and Algeria and Indochina for France.

§4.1.1 The Difficulty of Reaching Agreement

On 22 January 1931, the Dutch Department of Foreign Affairs announced its wish to conclude a convention with France on tax matters. Two months later, the French authorities responded favourably to this initiative on condition that they completed talks on the same issues with other countries.[11] In fact, it was not until 28 April 1932 that France declared its readiness to enter into talks when the final text with the United States was adopted and only the Franco-British draft remained under discussion.[12] Initially, the Netherlands wanted to propose a double taxation agreement with the Netherlands Indies, intended to have its main effect in Indochina, before discussing a general negotiation on double taxation. The aim was to put an end to double taxation between the Netherlands Indies and French Indochina. For the French authorities, this was not possible, as the French colonies had their own specific tax legislation that was distinct from that of metropolitan France. Thus, a tax treaty could not be applicable to both the colonies and mainland France.[13] This context reflects uncertainty as to the real objective of the negotiations at the time they were initiated.

This hesitation continued for a few more years, as negotiations were then limited to the double taxation of airline profits. The idea was to propose the conclusion of a special agreement exempting certain profits from the operation of air navigation services in France and the Netherlands from income tax.[14] Two preliminary drafts had been presented before finally being abandoned by the Dutch authorities when the draft general agreement for the avoidance of double taxation of 18 August 1937 was presented, incorporating the principle of the exclusive taxation of maritime or air navigation companies in the State of the operator's tax domicile in its Article 6 paragraph 1.[15] At the time, the Ministry of Foreign Affairs was negotiating a convention on establishment which appeared to be more advantageous for the Netherlands than for France, and the question arose of compensation for the advantages thus granted in the context of the tax convention negotiations. For France, it was essential to give the tax treaties to be signed with Denmark and Romania the necessary balance to avoid unilateral waivers. The only way to do this was to pursue negotiations on tax and administrative assistance in parallel. It therefore seemed essential to France to conclude agreements aimed at discouraging tax evasion with countries likely to serve as havens for French capital. To this end, France has stated its position on administrative

11. Directorate General of Registration, Domains and Stamps, Letter from the Director General to the Minister of Finance, Control no. 3 A.M., Letter dated 28 April 1932.
12. Ministry of Finance, Communication made on behalf of the Minister on 28 December 1934, 3 am, Continuation given on 14 February 1935 by the Conseiller d'Etat, Director General, Mr Trochon.
13. *Ibid. Eod. Loc.*
14. Dispatch dated 25 June 1935 from the Netherlands Legation to the French Minister of Foreign Affairs.
15. Provided that the ships and aircraft were flying the flag or had the nationality of that State. In this regard, *see*: Ministry of Foreign Affairs, Letter from the Minister of Foreign Affairs to the Minister of Finance, General Secretariat, 2nd Office, 24 December 1937.

assistance in the Franco-Swedish agreement.[16] The 'bargaining chip' in the balance of power was therefore the need to conclude a convention on administrative assistance in combating tax fraud with the countries concerned. The opening of talks on double taxation was conditional on a formal commitment from the Dutch government to negotiate such an agreement on the prevention of tax fraud at the same time. In order to obtain concessions on this point, France planned to point out the advantages that the Netherlands would derive from the convention on establishment and the agreement on double taxation.[17]

When the draft Franco-Dutch convention was sent to the French authorities on 18 August 1937, the Netherlands was aware that the text did not contain a tax assistance clause. They were therefore keen to make it clear that this should not lead the French authorities to conclude that the Royal Government was opposed to the principle of mutual administrative assistance. Their difficulty was in fact that, at the time, the law did not allow action to be taken against banks in order to force them to provide information about the personalities of depositors.[18] For the French State, this argument did not seem decisive as it was always possible to ask Parliament to amend existing laws, especially as the Dutch authorities had asked France to restrict the law of 29 June 1872 on income tax on securities in respect of companies. In this context, the Finance Department would refuse to open negotiations on double taxation without the parallel opening of negotiations on administrative assistance. If this were the case, it would mean that there was no quid pro quo for the advantages granted to Dutch companies. As for content, and in the absence of a model, the draft contained sixteen articles covering the definition of tax domicile, the taxes covered, the taxation of different types of income, equal treatment of domestic and imported products and most-favoured-nation treatment, territorial application and entry into force. For its part, the Final Protocol provided details on students, dividends and bonuses, the avoidance of double taxation, diplomatic and consular officials and the competent authorities in the event of interpretation and application.

In order to start to negotiate, it became necessary to obtain documents setting out the legislation of the contracting parties and the means of action or investigation granted to their administrations. In February 1938, the Netherlands Legation sent to the French authorities a summary of Dutch taxes on income, profits and capital in a League of Nations document entitled 'Taxation of Foreign and Domestic Enterprises', specifying that only one difference applied to the Netherlands Indies, where foreign legal entities were not subject to capital tax.[19] In July 1938, the means available to the Dutch

16. Minister of Finance, Control, Financial Administration and Expenditure Department, Letter from the Minister of Finance to the Minister of Foreign Affairs, Sub-Directorate for Administrative Affairs and International Unions, Letter dated 20 January 1937.
17. Ministry of Finance, Communication made on behalf of the Minister, 23 December 1936, 3 am, on 4 January 1937.
18. Minister for Foreign Affairs, Sub-Directorate for Administrative Affairs and International Unions, Letter from the Minister for Foreign Affairs to the Minister for Finance (General Secretariat), 18 August 1937.
19. Minister for Foreign Affairs, Sub-Directorate for Administrative Affairs and International Unions, Letter from the Minister of Foreign Affairs to the Minister of Finance (Secretariat General, 2nd Office), 11 February 1938.

authorities to monitor the correct collection of income and wealth tax were also communicated.[20]

By 17 June 1939, the negotiations had not yet really gotten under way, as at the time the Dutch government wrote to 'resume negotiations, if possible, in The Hague', on the outstanding tax issues between the two countries.[21] To this end, it was proposed that the talks should take place between 18 and 23 July 1939.[22] Although the French government was prepared to meet, it was unable to travel to the Netherlands at such short notice. Aware of the passage of time and in order to allow the resumption of negotiations, France agreed not to make this conditional on reaching an agreement in principle on tax assistance measures, specifying, however, that these questions should not be excluded from the negotiations. As a result, and subject to the same provision, France saw no disadvantage in granting a deferment in favour of Dutch companies' subject in France to income tax on securities and movable capital.[23]

In the meantime, the registration authorities submitted their observations on 5 August 1939.[24] The first difficulty arose from rules inspired by Dutch legislation which had no equivalent in French law, or from rules that were too general, leading to the taxation of individuals but not of companies. Then, concerning indirect taxes (e.g., French production and armament taxes), it fell outside the scope of the double taxation agreements previously concluded with foreign States. Finally, as regards the scope of application of certain provisions to the overseas territories, the method involved first settling this question between the metropolitan territories of the two countries before subsequently extending all or part of the provisions to the colonial territories.

On 9 August 1939, the Dutch Legation informed the French Ministry of Foreign Affairs that it was prepared to examine the problem of mutual assistance on the basis of the 1937 draft proposed by the Dutch government, it being specified that this draft reserved the question of fiscal assistance 'under the same conditions' as the agreement concluded by France with Switzerland in 1937. Mutual assistance was also an issue for the Netherlands, as it was a condition for France to grant a reprieve to Dutch companies that owed money to the French Treasury. This first period was therefore characterised by the difficulty of the contracting parties to reach an agreement. This reluctance to enter into real negotiations lasted throughout the occupation.

20. Minister for Foreign Affairs, Sub-Directorate for Administrative Affairs and International Unions, Letter from the Minister of Foreign Affairs to the Minister of Finance (Secretariat General, 2nd Office), 6 July 1938.
21. Ministry of Foreign Affairs, Note of 17 June 1939.
22. Letter from the Minister for Foreign Affairs to the Minister for Finance (Cabinet Office), 10 July 1939.
23. Financial Administration Control Department, Letter from the Minister of Finance to the Minister of Foreign Affairs (Sub-Directorate for Administrative Affairs and International Unions), 21 July 1939.
24. Ministry of Finance, Communication made on behalf of the Minister on 24 July 1939, Action taken on 5 August 1939 by the Director General of Registration, Estates and Stamps.

§4.1.2 Negotiations During the Occupation

In 1939, a number of documents show that negotiations continued during the occupation since France refused to grant any deferment to Dutch companies in debt to the French Treasury and operating in France until the Netherlands had taken a firm position on administrative assistance.[25] On 15 April 1940, the French Minister of Finance gave his opinion on the draft of 18 August 1937, stating that the proposed provisions would mainly benefit Holland, which had more companies operating in France than there were French companies operating in its territory. It therefore seems normal to him that in return significant advantages should be requested, namely the adoption of measures to facilitate the fight against tax fraud. For France, a convention aimed at eliminating double taxation is only justified if it includes administrative assistance provisions, which the Dutch draft does not. This problem should not be overlooked in any negotiations that may be opened.[26] With regard to the content of the project as a whole, while the Minister made the same observations as those made by the General Directorate of Registration in August 1939, other remarks were made as the necessity to remove from the list of French taxes of the business tax ('contribution des patentes'), the withdrawal of the texts of the statutory auditors and liquidators, or the clarification of some articles. Lastly, comments on the Final Protocol suggested the inclusion of a special provision on dividends and directors' fees in the convention. The same applies to the progressive nature of certain taxes, such as the general French income tax or several Dutch taxes,[27] in order to ensure that the state of domicile has a minimum level of taxation, as is already provided for in the Franco-Swiss treaty, which sets an overall minimum tax.

On 10 May 1940, Germany invaded the Netherlands, resulting in the occupation of both contracting parties until victory on 8 May 1945. There are no documents in the French economic archives between 15 April 1940 and 22 December 1942, the date on which Dr Kuntze from the German Embassy's economic services submitted a draft decree on measures to be taken to avoid double taxation between France and the Netherlands to the Minister, in order to obtain comments on this text from the French Ministry of Finance.[28] The 1942 draft contained 9 articles and was intended to apply in particular to taxes levied from 1 January 1940. The French comments on this text were highly critical.[29] Generally speaking, the translated text is rather difficult to read due to incorrect turns of phrase and the use of inappropriate terms. In reality, the text repeats elements that were discussed in 1937, drawing heavily on the Franco-German convention, but with two differences. First, the method differs because a decree is not a treaty.

25. Ministry of Finance, Direct taxation department, Communication made on behalf of the Minister on 22 August 1939, Follow-up given on 12 September 1939 by Director General J. Watteau.
26. Letter from the Minister of Finance to the President of the Council, Minister of Foreign Affairs, 15 April 1940.
27. These include income tax, tax for municipal funds and defence tax I.
28. Ministry of Finance, Note for the Directorate General of Registration, 2nd Office, no. 3 A.M., 22 December 1942.
29. Ministry of Finance, Financial Administration Coordination Department, Continuation given on 23 January 1943.

It does not allow for an in-depth article-by-article study discussed by technical delegations and, above all, exposes States to the risk of going back on the tax advantages granted to nationals of the other State. A legislative discussion was required, especially as the French political organisation of the time did not allow the Minister of Finance to issue decrees. Second, the new text does not take the same form as the previous double taxation agreements, which were all more or less of the same type. This remark is interesting because it suggests the existence of a standard model that would already be the fruit of bilateral negotiations. In this respect, France proposes to use the text of one of the conventions currently in force between France and foreign countries, or even the 1937 draft with the Netherlands, as a basis for discussions. In particular, certain provisions are ill-conceived, and some measures should be scrapped, as they make no sense in themselves. Overall, no provision for administrative assistance appeared, which was one of the conditions for opening negotiations. The draft decree needs to be supplemented by provisions on mutual assistance based on Articles 17 and 23 of the Franco-Swedish agreement.[30]

This period of occupation also reveals the difficulty of finding the right interlocutors since it was necessary for the Germans to appreciate the importance of the economic interests at stake in these negotiations, on both the Dutch and French sides. At the time, no organisation was in a position to provide this information due to the abolition of the post of French sales representatives in The Hague and the closure of the Dutch Chamber of Commerce in Paris.[31] Apart from a few lists of companies[32] or the total amount of business transacted in 1938 alone by Dutch or French companies in France and Holland, nothing could be provided.[33] This period also marked a change in the tax legislation then applicable in the Netherlands, with the introduction of a series of very heavy taxes and strict controls on foreign companies with their main establishment in Holland.[34] During the occupation, a tax on profits of the 'industrial and commercial profit' type was introduced in 1940, at a rate of 31.5%. To this was added very strict legislation aimed at limiting the distribution of profits, making it impossible to distribute a dividend of more than 6%. On 4 May 1942, three new ordinances introduced a German-inspired system in Holland, as companies had to bear a corporation tax (Körperschafstseuer),[35] a business tax (Gewerbesteuer)[36] and an income tax

30. Ministry of Finance, Directorate General of Direct Taxation, Communication made on behalf of the Ministers on 22 December 1942, Follow-up given on 3 February 1943 by the Director General.
31. Note for the Financial Administration Coordination Department, 1 June 1943.
32. This includes a list of the main French or Dutch companies with holdings in Dutch or French companies, a list of the main French companies with establishments in Holland (agencies, offices, branches, factories or buildings), and lists of Dutch insurance companies operating agencies in France.
33. Note for the head of the department for the coordination of financial administrations, 2ème Office, 27 May 1943.
34. Note concerning the tax regime for companies in Holland and the question of double taxation in dealings with that country, 4 June 1943.
35. This tax was progressive, reaching a rate of 50% very quickly. Depreciation and reserves could only be applied in accordance with the principles of strict regulations, which applied to all profits, whether distributed or not.

falling into the general income tax class (Vermögensteuer).[37] In addition, dividend tax, which had been abolished for Dutch companies, remained in force at a rate of 15% for dividends received by foreign companies that did not pay the Körperschafsteuer. Finally, the tax regime for patent licences was to be eased since patent royalties subject to French tax were also subject to the Körperschafsteuer. In this context, it seemed urgent to rethink the patent royalty regime and to finalise an agreement on double taxation of dividends.

During this period, the archives also show that the taxpayer contacted the tax authorities. The first difficulty was the lack of elimination of double taxation in the Franco-German treaty and in the planned treaty between France and Holland. The public limited company Saint-Gobain, Chauny and Cirey drew up a list of its holdings in Holland to demonstrate the existence of such double taxation.[38] The second difficulty related to disputes already initiated with the tax authorities during this period. For example, the Dutch company 'Van Berkel's Patent Maatschappij', which was liable for French tax on income from transferable securities in respect of assets owned or operated in France, was unable to provide the information needed to accurately determine the taxable portion of its capital because its administration office had been bombed, and had to reconstitute its archives as a result of this destruction. Lastly, during the occupation, a number of taxpayers saw their titles despoiled. After the war, it was therefore necessary to carry out a census of Dutch securities and to invite the Allies to see how this census was carried out.[39] This long and tedious task meant that a blacklist of looted securities had to be drawn up. It was actually in the post-war period that this work was carried out with the Allied forces. This is what French diplomatic archives tell us.[40]

§4.2 CONVENTIONAL NEGOTIATIONS AFTER 1945

The German capitulation took place a few days after the liberation of the Netherlands, on 5 May 1945. There are no documents in the archives for 1945 and 1946. The first note is dated 23 April 1947, and concerns the Dutch government's willingness to enter into talks with the French administration with a view to negotiating agreements to avoid double taxation on income and capital tax.[41] It was when this freedom was regained in the discussions that an agreement was reached (§4.2.1). The history of

36. This tax was levied for the benefit of the municipalities, at a much lower rate than the Körperschafsteuer.
37. Income tax was 5% of the social security capital.
38. Ministry of Finance, Note for the Directorate General of Registration, Domains and Stamps, 12 July 1943 and Note on the holdings of Compagnie de Saint-Gobain in Holland, 4 May 1943.
39. Letter from the General of the Army, French Commander-in-Chief in Germany, to the General Commissioner for German and Austrian Affairs, entitled 'Census of Dutch titles', 21 July 1947.
40. Diplomatic Archives, Europe – Netherlands, 1949-1955, FR MAE 198QO, State Secretary for German and Austrian Affairs, Telegram on the census of Dutch securities held in Germany, 1 July 1949.
41. Ministry of Finance, Note for the Directorate General of Registration, Estates and Stamps, 23 April 1947.

these talks offers a number of lessons (§4.2.2), which will be enriched by an analysis of other conventional negotiations.

§4.2.1 The Agreement Reached

When negotiations resumed, a first difficulty was linked to the elimination of double taxation on securities due to the Dutch delegation's proposal to tax income from securities in the creditor's country of domicile, with the abolition or reduction of withholding tax in the other country. This principle had always been deliberately rejected during discussions on the various treaties signed by France, as it had the disadvantage of placing the burden of refunds on the tax authorities. Indeed, French companies that pay income tax on securities on behalf of shareholders are generally unaware of the domicile of their shareholders, unless registered shares exist, which implies a posteriori imputation by way of restitution that cannot be left to the responsibility of the company in order to avoid fraud.[42] Furthermore, there are fears of evasion when French taxpayers fictitiously place their securities on the heads of Dutch nationals. These fears are to be feared in a safe haven country like the Netherlands, whose banking system has always been geared towards importing foreign capital, just like Luxembourg and Switzerland.[43] In this context, it would be necessary to require proof of a declaration of income in Holland and of their taxation in this territory at a tax equal to or higher than the refund claimed. France succeeds in demonstrating that the system suggested by the representatives of the Dutch administration is not favourable to France, and better account should be taken of the rules contained in the agreements with Sweden and the USA, which are in fact similar to the Franco-Belgian and Franco-Italian agreements. If the Dutch delegation does not support the French position, France proposes either to allow double taxation to continue in this particular case, as is already the case with Switzerland and England, or to settle this practical difficulty on the basis proposed by France as a condition for concluding the convention.

These observations were also to be found in the French comments on the 1947 draft, repeating the text and remarks made during the 1937 talks.[44] On the one hand, certain measures should be adopted, such as excluding Algeria from the scope of the agreement. On the other hand, certain provisions do not call for comment, as they are, in fact, inspired by other conventions. This is the case for Article VII, which limits the taxation of Dutch companies with a permanent establishment in France to the foreign securities income tax schedule, inspired by Article 4 of the Franco-Swedish Convention of 24 December 1936 or for Articles X and XI on royalties, inspired respectively by Article 7 of the Franco-American Convention of 25 July 1939 and Article 10 of the Franco-Swedish Convention. Finally, certain provisions are to be deleted by the Dutch

42. Central Direction, 1st Office, Directorate General of Registration, Domains and Stamps, Note for the Minister, Financial Administration Coordination Department, 2nd Office, 6 June 1947.
43. *Ibid. Eod. Loc.*
44. Ministry of National Economy and Finance, Directorate General of Registration, Domains and Stamps, Department for the Coordination of Financial Administrations, Communication made on behalf of the Minister on 11 June 1947, Measures taken on 16 June 1947.

delegation, such as the method of eliminating double taxation on dividends by restitution in favour of an offset of the tax withheld at source against the tax levied in the beneficiary's domicile, as well as the provisions that appear contrary to the law.[45]

The final draft convention was finalised on 27 November 1948.[46] Some reactions to the Dutch suggestions were emerging. On the one hand, France did not wish to add the concept of commissioners ('commissaires') to Article XI, which deals with directors and managers of joint-stock companies. This would exacerbate the ambiguity of the term 'director' ('directeur'), whereas, in France, public limited companies were administered exclusively by a Board of Directors. It is therefore proposed to refer in this article only to the directors of joint-stock companies, unless the corresponding translation of the term 'administrators' is indicated. Thus, on the Dutch side, the term 'administrators of joint stock companies' ('administrateurs de sociétés par actions') would include all persons legally responsible for administering such companies, and, on the French side, this formula would also include members of supervisory boards who manage public limited companies governed by German law which may exist in the departments of Haut-Rhin, Bas Rhin and Moselle. Two other modifications were made by the French representatives, verbally accepted by the Dutch delegation: the substitution in §1 of Article II of the term 'overseas territories' for the word 'colonies' and the extension of the scope of Article V, which allows profits indirectly transferred to a subsidiary headquartered in the other country to be reincorporated into the taxable profits of a parent company established in one of the two countries, as well as the reverse situation. Attached are the letters to be exchanged at the time of signature of the two agreements on income tax and wealth tax,[47] and a list of the information which the administrations of the two countries agree to provide to each other, either automatically or on request, in accordance with Article XXII of the agreement on double taxation in respect of income tax or Article VIII with respect to wealth tax. A verbal agreement having been given by the Dutch authorities on these last changes by the French representatives, the two convention texts were transmitted by a letter of the same day to the French Minister of Foreign Affairs.[48] The final draft of the exchange of letters shows how the States make mutual concessions and gives a very precise example of the information that France and the Netherlands have authorised each other to exchange.[49]

45. Article XXIII effectively grants natural persons domiciled for tax purposes in the Netherlands the same rights as French nationals with regard to benefits. It thus allows subjects of countries that have not signed a reciprocity agreement with France to benefit from advantages reserved for French nationals, which is contrary to Art. 44 of the Law of 22 March 1924. *See* Ministry of National Economy and Finance, Directorate General of Registration, Domains and Stamps, Financial Administration Coordination Department, Communication made on behalf of the Minister on 11 June 1947, Action taken on 16 June 1947.
46. Letter from the Minister of Finance and Economic Affairs to the Dutch Ambassador, 27 November 1948.
47. Suggestions relating to wealth tax were also rejected by the French authorities, with the agreement of the Dutch authorities, due to the existence of technical difficulties in maintaining them and the maintenance of double taxation which the text seeks to avoid.
48. Minister of Finance and Economic Affairs to the Minister of Foreign Affairs, Directorate of Administrative and Social Conventions, 27 November 1948.
49. Exchange of letters dated 30 December 1949.

The convention was signed in Paris on 30 December 1949. Some difficulties remained before the French Parliament passed the law authorising the President of the Republic to ratify the agreement. In fact, the income tax treaty left open the question of double taxation of income from securities. This problem, which arose during the negotiations, could not be resolved, and France proposed to the Netherlands to remedy it through special negotiations in October 1950.[50] In fact, the two countries agreed to delay the entry into force of the convention in order to include a rider to deal with this issue at the suggestion of the Dutch Director General of Tax Affairs, Mr Van Den Berge.[51]

France wanted a system to eliminate the double taxation of securities in the State of source and in the State of the creditor's domicile, allowing the tax levied in the first State to be offset against the tax levied in the second. The Netherlands had refused this proposal before the war for technical reasons. France then reiterated its proposal, taking the Franco-Swedish Convention as an example, to establish the principle of exclusive taxation in the State of the creditor's tax domicile, which the Dutch finally accepted.[52] A rider, dated 24 July 1952, specifies its application for the first time to income from securities paid as from 1 January 1951, without any tax refund.[53] Retroactive effect is therefore granted,[54] and a fairly complex refund procedure was set up depending on whether the income was received before or after 1 September 1954,[55] in order to put all holders on an equal footing. On several occasions, the French Budget Ministry has urged Parliament to adopt these texts as quickly as possible in order to offer French nationals substantial tax relief while at the same time granting the French Treasury the benefit of a transfer of income and significant additional foreign exchange reserves.[56] The desire for rapid entry into force was also apparent on the Dutch side.[57] All the more so as the Queen of the Netherlands had ratified these texts in 1953.[58] Ratifications of the two conventions relating to income and wealth were exchanged at The Hague on 21 May 1954, thus ending twenty-three years of negotiations.

---

50. Letter from Mr Certeux to Mr W. H. Van Den Berge, Director General of Taxes at the Ministry of Finance in The Hague, 17 August 1950.
51. Ministry of Finance, Letter from Jean Moréau, Head of Office, to the Dutch Minister of Finance, 3 June 1952.
52. This principle also applies to the taxation of income from loans, deposits, deposit accounts and other receivables, unless there is a permanent establishment. On this point, *see*: Letter from the Secretary of State for the Budget to the Minister for Foreign Affairs, Administrative and Social Affairs Department, Administrative agreements, 3 June 1952.
53. In this respect, *see* Art. 6 of the rider.
54. Letter from the Secretary of State for the Budget to the Minister for Foreign Affairs, Directorate of Administrative and Social Affairs, Conventions, 11 September 1952.
55. State Secretariat for the Budget, General Tax Directorate, 2nd Office, Notice relating to the application of the provisions of the Franco-Dutch double taxation agreement concerning income from securities, 10 September 1954.
56. *See* in particular: Ministry for the Budget, Letter from Jean Moréau to the Chairman of the National Assembly's Finance Committee, 31 March 1953.
57. Letter from the Acting Director General of Tax Affairs, Mr A.J. Van Den Tempel, to the Director General of Taxes, Ministry of the Budget, 16 July 1953.
58. Letter from the Secretary of State for the Budget to the Chairman of the Finance Committee of the National Assembly, 13 August 1953.

§4.2.2 Lessons from History

Five key lessons can be drawn from the history of these negotiations.

The first lesson is that the States have followed a method for negotiating. First of all, it should be pointed out that France imposed its method before entering into talks since it first wanted to make progress on the other bilateral agreements under discussion before entering into talks on the Franco-Dutch agreement. So, it was when the final text of the agreement with the United States was being adopted, and negotiations were continuing with Great Britain, that France announced its intention to enter into talks with the Netherlands. Second, as regards the method applicable to exchanges between the two countries, it is clear that the negotiations should begin with an exchange of summaries of the respective legislation and the means of action or investigation granted to the administrations of the two States. In this case, the Dutch delegation had already drawn up a draft text in 1937, even before exchanging these summaries in 1938. Concerning the timing of transmission by France, the documents remain silent. That did not stop the first comments on the 1937 project, which came late, in the summer of 1939 and again in the summer of 1940. It is also clear that the period of occupation modified the talks since a new text dating from 1942, in the form of a decree, was proposed to the original contracting parties by the Germans. In this respect, we note Germany's difficulty in conducting talks without real knowledge of the economic interests of both countries and, consequently, the influence of German law on the discussions and on the desired legislation for the two countries. In the Netherlands, this influence goes as far as reproducing the German tax system. The end of the war allowed negotiations to resume freely, as they had been before the start of the conflict, culminating in an exchange of letters on 30 December 1949 which sealed the final agreement. Entry into force was delayed by the desire of both countries to conclude a rider, dated 24 July 1952, to settle matters that had not been agreed during the negotiations. In this respect, the rider technique enables us to go back over elements of the negotiations that were not successful when the final agreement was reached. This explains the delay between the signing of the text in 1949 and its entry into force in 1954, the ratification having been rushed through by the Dutch since the text had already been ratified by the Queen of the Netherlands. Subsequently, a rider was to amend the treaty regarding the taxation of dividends, but the French and Dutch tax systems had undergone such far-reaching tax reforms in the 1960s that it was finally decided to renegotiate a new agreement. This treaty signed in 1973 and currently in force is clearly based on the OECD model.[59]

The second lesson is the existence of a 'bargaining chip'. Throughout these negotiations, the question of administrative assistance was taken by France as a central element in obtaining several things from the Netherlands in the name of reciprocity. In fact, this was one of France's main concerns. The priority was to conclude mutual tax

59. The negotiations for the 1973 convention contain the OECD model in force at the time, and the discussions show that its content was discussed, article by article. For a comparison of the changes between the 1949 and 1973 Conventions, *see*: SAEF, B 0067907, Senate, Report on behalf of the Finance Committee by Gustave Heon, no. 113, pp. 2-5.

assistance agreements with countries likely to offer a haven for French capital, such as the Netherlands.[60] However, for Léon Blum, then President of the Council, the subject of mutual assistance to combat tax fraud could not succeed on the basis of separate, give-and-take negotiations but rather on the basis of overall action and 'a psychological or political fact of a general nature', which could only be supported by the League of Nations, as a form of duty of international solidarity.[61] However, France has always reiterated the requirement for administrative assistance in these bilateral negotiations, calling for the introduction of assistance measures equivalent to those set out in Articles 17 to 19 of the Franco-Swedish Convention of 23 August 1937.[62] While this request has apparently been taken on board by Dutch minister Jonkheer Loudon, who indicated that he would recommend these conclusions to his government,[63] no progress had been made in this area. In this context, France has tirelessly used this argument to reject several Dutch requests in the absence of progress on this issue and to refuse a request for information from the Dutch authorities.[64] The balance of power was therefore not easy to strike. France even pointed out the intransigence of the Dutch position on the issue of mutual administrative assistance, and this attitude certainly played a part in the long time it took to get the first exchanges going. Concessions must be reciprocal, and this reciprocity also results from the establishment of a relationship that will lead to a final agreement. There is a psychological aspect to these exchanges, as States need to be reassured as the discussions progress on the elements they consider essential to the negotiation. It will be recalled that when the negotiations resumed in the summer of 1939, France agreed not to make the discussions conditional on the conclusion of an agreement in principle on the question of administrative assistance, without however renouncing it. At that time, France did not expressly note in the Dutch correspondence any 'appeasement' regarding the subject of these concerns. Taking into account the concerns of the other State was already part of the process of drawing up the joint agreement. If concessions are to be reciprocal, each party must find something to gain and the country's economic situation must be such as to enable the co-contractors to offer the necessary quid pro quos, which the economic crisis at the time did not necessarily allow.[65] Moreover, the advantages granted to the Netherlands by the establishment agreement with France have also been weighed in the balance, showing that the balance to be struck at the time of negotiation is in reality global, even beyond the tax balance alone. Finally, it sometimes appears that there is an imbalance of power, with the provisions being more or less favourable to one of the countries, with figures to back this up. If the balance of income is not balanced between the two countries, this situation often leads the country in an

60. Diplomatic Archives, Letter from the Minister for Foreign Affairs to Mr Léon Blum, President of the Council of Ministers (Minister's Office), 7 September 1936.
61. Diplomatic Archives, Letter from Léon Blum to the Minister of Foreign Affairs, 12 September 1936.
62. Communication made on behalf of the Minister of Finance, dated 23 July 1938.
63. Letter from the Minister of Foreign Affairs to the Minister of Finance, 20 July 1938.
64. Ministry of National Economic Affairs and Finance, Communication made on behalf of the Minister on 7 January 1948, Follow-up given on 5 February 1948 by General Manager Rampon.
65. Diplomatic Archives, Letter from the Minister for Foreign Affairs to Mr Spinasse, Minister for the National Economy, 16 September 1936.

unfavourable position to demand other compensatory measures to offset the losses. For example, the determination and calculation of a withholding tax rate are based on the desire to correct such an imbalance.[66]

The third lesson is the importance of word choice in an international context. It was during the period of occupation that this lesson first became apparent. Indeed, France was quick to point out difficulties of interpretation in the 1942 draft, arising directly from the use of a word that did not have the same acceptance in the two contracting countries. In the Netherlands, for example, the term 'statutory auditors' ('commissaires') has a broader meaning, encompassing both statutory auditors and non-executive directors. In addition, certain words need to be clarified, such as the notion of 'remuneration', in order to determine whether remuneration for the duties of statutory auditors includes directors' fees. This is an important issue, as the Netherlands has a specific tax regime for directors' fees. The same applies to the expression 'normal residence', which in reality refers to 'domicile for tax purposes', which should therefore be replaced by the concept of 'principal place of residence' and the cases in which it can be assimilated with domicile for tax purposes should be clarified. Thus, Articles 1 and 2 of the 1942 draft assimilate the concept of fiscal domicile with that of 'permanent residence' (Article 1) and that of 'normal residence' (Article 2), in an indiscriminate manner, whereas it is a question of defining strictly identical situations, and the French Ministry of Finance indicates that the term 'permanent residence' seems the most appropriate to retain.[67] Article 4 of the 1942 draft defines the notion of tax domicile as 'the place where the taxpayer has a dwelling under conditions that allow it to be concluded that he wishes to keep it'. While this was the same definition as that contained in the Franco-German treaty (Article 13), it was suggested that it would be preferable to replace it with that contained in the Franco-Belgian (Article 1), Swedish (Article 14), Swiss (Article 14) and Romanian (Article 16) agreements. Under these treaties, the tax domicile of an individual is the place of normal residence, understood as a permanent home. Those who have their permanent residence in one of the two States appear to have their tax domicile in these States. The concept of normal residence should be deleted, especially since it contains a translation error since it is defined as 'a stay in a place or in a country under conditions which lead to the conclusion that the person wishes to remain there only temporarily', whereas this definition should rather be read as 'a stay in a place or in a country under conditions which lead to the conclusion that the person *does not remain* there only temporarily'.[68] Lastly, certain definitions appear too restrictive, such as that used for 'taxpayer', which restricts the application of the text to nationals of both countries, whereas previous French treaty texts gave it a broader scope.

66. These discussions were developed in the post-1954 negotiations and were the reason for the suspension of the negotiations begun in March 1961. *See*, for example: SAEF, B 0067907, Minister for Finance and Economic Affairs, General Tax Directorate, International Relations Department, Note for the Minister, For the attention of Mr Delignières, 17 December 1963.
67. Ministry of Finance, Communication made on behalf of the Minister on 22 December 1942, Continuation given on 3 February 1943.
68. We underline, *see*: *ibid.*, at 5.

The fourth lesson concerns the influence of the work of the League of Nations on these bilateral negotiations, since the work of the Tax Committee was held in parallel with the participation of France and the Netherlands. Indeed, when bilateral tax negotiations between these two countries began in 1931, the Council of the League of Nations had just been set up. One of its tasks was to prepare model bilateral or collective agreements,[69] and it was already working on a plurilateral agreement, which was not favoured by the French Finance Minister,[70] who preferred to multiply bilateral agreements with a view to standardising them.[71] It was within this framework that, in 1933, a first draft convention was published for the allocation of industrial and commercial income between States for tax purposes,[72] revised in 1935 to serve 'as a model in negotiations for the conclusion of bilateral conventions'.[73] This limitation to industrial and commercial income perhaps explains why the negotiations on the Franco-Dutch convention between 1935 and 1937 were restricted to the double taxation of the profits of one category of business, namely air navigation companies. A little later, in 1937, the League of Nations invited governments to express their views on signing an agreement to prevent tax evasion, particularly with regard to income from movable capital.[74] Here again, it is interesting to note that a few months after this request in an international context, France and the Netherlands reached an initial draft agreement. Although no direct reference is made to the Mexico 1943 and London 1946 models, it is clear that after the treaty came into force, and in order to adapt the treaty to the tax reform in the Netherlands, the work of the OEEC Tax Committee in March 1961 was explicitly mentioned since it was proposed to wait for the sessions of this international work before progressing with the bilateral negotiation of a new rider.[75] The negotiations on the 1973 convention also clearly stated the need to revise the convention due to the ageing of the text caused by the evolution of tax systems and by the use of the OECD Model Convention, which was at the time increasingly used since it had been adopted and recommended in 1963.[76] In reality, these international sessions enable the contracting parties to meet and pursue any bilateral talks that may be held at the end of these international discussions.

---

69. This committee was set up by a resolution of 14 December 1928. On this subject, see: Diplomatic Archives, Societies of Nations, Letter from the Secretary General to the Minister of Foreign Affairs, 1 March 1929.
70. Diplomatic Archives, Ministries of Foreign Affairs, Note for the French Service of the League of Nations, 16 November 1931.
71. Diplomatic Archives, Financial Administration and Expenditure Control Department, 2nd Office, no. 4 A.M., Letter from the Minister of Finance to the Minister of Foreign Affairs, 11 May 1934.
72. League of Nations, Fiscal Committee, Report to the Council on the work of the fourth session of the Committee, held in Geneva from 15 to 26 June 1933, pp. 3 et seq.
73. League of Nations, Revised Draft Convention for the Avoidance of Double Taxation of Industrial and Commercial Undertakings, C.L. 166. 1935. II A, 29 October 1935.
74. League of Nations, Tax Evasion and Double Taxation, C.L. 31. 1937. II. A, 18 February 1937.
75. Letter from Van den Berge to Mr Giscard d'Estaing, Secretary of State for Finance, concerning the revision of the Franco-Dutch agreement of 30 December 1949, 17 February 1961.
76. SAEF, B 0067907, National Assembly, Report on behalf of the Foreign Affairs Committee by M. Caro, First Ordinary Session 1973-1974, p. 2.

The fifth and final lesson is conventional imitation, in particular, the influence of bilateral state practice on the development of a bilateral or international model. With regard to the bilateral model, in the absence of an international model serving as a common basis for all negotiations, States were in fact imitating other bilateral agreements already concluded, of which there were few at the time. Thus, when the Franco-German convention was being drafted in the 1930s, the sales representative in Berlin asked the French Minister of Foreign Affairs for information on other French conventions with Belgium, Italy and the United States in preparation for the negotiations.[77] In fact, these inspirations can be used to build a basis for discussion, drawing inspiration from or departing from the examples chosen, depending on the interests involved. This led to the emergence of standard models, the fruit of bilateral negotiations. Besides, some comments were rejected on the grounds that the new text did not reproduce the same form as previous double taxation agreements, revealing the existence of standard models. When drafting and exchanging views between the two countries, it is very common for one or other of the States to take a third-party treaty provision as a reference. A letter from a French sale's representative notes that the agreement between Belgium and the Netherlands, which was signed on 20 February 1933 and came into force on 1 January 1936, is very similar to the Franco-Belgian agreement of 16 May 1931.[78] On the subject of administrative assistance, France has repeatedly cited the Franco-Swedish and Franco-Swiss agreements as examples. In this respect, a note from the French legation dated 16 August 1938 states that this question is reserved 'under the same conditions' as the agreement concluded by France with the Swiss government in 1937.[79] These influences are evident in the 1937 and 1942 drafts, as references are made to certain provisions of the Franco-Belgian, Franco-Italian and Franco-German conventions. This imitation also limits differences in interpretation. During the talks on the double taxation of the profits of air navigation companies, it was suggested that the term 'operation of air navigation' should follow the definition contained in the Franco-British treaty, which was inspired by the treaties signed in the application of Article 5 of the law of 29 April 1926 concerning maritime navigation companies.[80] Even more surprisingly, the Dutch authorities have asked France for the contents of letters exchanged with Norway in order to interpret the concept of permanent establishment applicable to insurance companies. On the French side, it seemed difficult to refuse the Netherlands this communication, despite its confidential nature, concerning an agreement 'of which they are already aware the existence and no doubt the scope'.[81] States are therefore privy to confidential documents relating to bilateral agreements that do not concern them.

77. Diplomatic Archives, Sales representative to the French Embassy in Berlin, Letter to the Cabinet of the Minister for Foreign Affairs, 2 May 1933.
78. Note no. 40.011, from Henry Bouchet – sales representatives – to the Minister for Trade and Industry, 29 August 1935.
79. Note from the Netherlands legation regarding a note from the French legation, 9 August 1938.
80. Ministry of Finance, Letter from the Minister of Finance to the Minister of Air, Directorate of Civil Aeronautics, n°10725, 2ème Bureau, n°3 A.M., 24 December 1935.
81. Communication from the State Secretariat for Finance and Economic Affairs, 26 December 1955.

As far as the international model is concerned, it is clear that the practice of States, particularly those that signed the first international tax treaties, has influenced the development of a model. The work of the League of Nations at that time clearly shows how bilateral tax treaties and the evolution of tax systems fed into and advanced international discussions.[82] At the time of the Franco-Dutch talks, when no international definition of tax domicile had yet been given, the 1937 draft text already proposed one,[83] which was partly taken up in the convention signed in 1949.[84] The same applies to the structure of the first draft of 1937, which already included only 16 articles and a final protocol, including the definition of tax domicile, but also articles relating to the taxes covered, the taxation of different types of income, equality of treatment, most-favoured-nation status and scope of application. It was even proposed to remove the question of dividends from the Final Protocol and insert it directly into the convention, which included other articles on the avoidance of double taxation and diplomatic and consular officials. Today, these headings are reminiscent of the structuring elements of the OECD Model Convention. Even the concept of a minimum tax for the state of domicile was discussed. In addition, many of the principles of the 1949 convention were taken up in the 1973 convention.[85] In this context, there is no doubt that this Franco-Dutch bilateral experience, as well as all the others, helped to build the OECD model that we know today.

82. *See* the reports to the Council on the work of the Tax Committee's sessions published between 1928 and 1937: Diplomatic archives, League of Nations, Economic and financial issues, Double taxation and tax evasion, no. 1305, 1929-1937.
83. Article 1 §2 of the draft of 18 August 1937 defined it as follows: 'For the purposes of this Convention, the tax domicile of individuals shall be the place of their normal residence understood to mean their permanent home, and that of companies, which constitute a distinct legal entity, shall be the place of the effective registered office.'
84. Article 2 §4 of the convention signed in 1949 defines it as follows: 'The tax domicile of individuals is at the place of their normal residence, understood as a permanent dwelling place, or, failing that, at the place where they have their principal place of abode. That of legal persons or groups of individuals without legal personality is at the place of their effective management (...).'
85. SAEF, B 0067907, Minister for the Economy and Finance, Note for the Minister, Sub-Directorate III E, Office III E I, n°1295/73, 13 November 1973.

PART II Politics of Taxation

CHAPTER 5

Value Imperialism and Global Tax Policy: A Plea for a Meta Regime

Peter Hongler[*]

§5.1 INTRODUCTION

Personally, I know Peter Essers from our engagement in the EUCOTAX Wintercourses organized by Tilburg University and led by Peter and Eric Kemmeren. These annual seminars, held in various places in Europe, are always a great opportunity for our students (and for us professors!) to exchange ideas and learn from different cultures and tax systems.

Being confronted with other cultures also shows us that sometimes we are quite apart from each other when it comes to our values. Value differences are not something that should concern us but something that we need to consider when we discuss international policy options. Peter has often, during many of our very enjoyable lunch meetings, emphasized how important it is to understand other opinions and critically reflect on whether our own position still holds after being scrutinized.

For the purpose of the present chapter, when I refer to values, I am primarily addressing our understanding of how societies should be organized, i.e., what kind of societies we consider to be just and fair. Of course, the present chapter focuses mainly on our tax-related values and the role our tax system should play in achieving our ideal picture of our societies.

The goal of the present chapter is to demonstrate the role of values in international tax policy and how international tax policy might impact domestic value agreements. By international tax policy, I mean policies that are based on decisions of international organizations such as the OECD, the G20, or the UN.[1] For such purpose,

* The author would like to thank Nelly Stöckl for her help in finalizing this chapter.
1. I will not discuss domestic policy decisions that might also have an impact on other tax systems.

we use the term 'value imperialism' to describe a situation in which a society such as a state is forced to agree on a certain societal value (e.g., the size of the state) based on a decision of an international organization. This means that fiscal values are transferred from one state to another state without a genuine agreement. I will later describe in more detail what I mean by fiscal or tax-related values.

§5.2 PRAGMATISM AND THE USE OF VALUES

Before outlining some examples and also before discussing ways to limit value imperialism, it is important to make some theoretical remarks on the objectivity of values. In order to do so, I find pragmatism a rather persuasive way of looking at morality and the question of how we should design our societies.

Pragmatism, in simplified terms, tells us that the value discussion is not a discussion that should and can be based on objective criteria. We should rather focus on how we can improve a society and how we can justify our moral decisions.[2] We should also accept that the agreed values differ in various cultures and even within the same culture, and that none of the approaches is the true and only right one.

The underlying idea is an epistemological one, according to which there is no (eternal) truth, or as Rorty famously held, that: 'we see knowledge as a matter of conversation and of social practice, rather than as an attempt to mirror nature'.[3] Therefore, it is derived from social practice and not an absolute truth of what is considered to be right from a moral perspective and what is considered to be a just society. There is no 'the' right moral behaviour or 'the' right societal design.

It is also important to understand that what a value means and whether a value is considered right also depend on each person's perspective and social experience. In short, our own values are contingent upon a broad variety of social factors. They are in particular contingent on our own experience of life. If we want to approach international tax policy in a neutral manner, we need, therefore, to waive some of our own positions that seem to us the only way forward.

In the following, we will take the view of moral pluralism and follow the position that there are various value agreements possible, and none of them is objectively true.

---

2. This is the wrong place to outline in detail what pragmatism is. As in many other fields of philosophy, a rather comprehensive outline can be found in the Stanford Encyclopedia of Philosophy (*see* Catherine Legg & Christopher Hookway, *Pragmatism*, The Stanford Encyclopedia of Philosophy (Summer 2021 Edition), https://plato.stanford.edu/archives/sum2021/entries/pragmatism/).
3. Richard Rorty, *Philosophy and the Mirror of Nature*, 171 (Princeton University Press 1979).

§5.3 THE IMPACT INTERNATIONAL TAX POLICY HAS ON TAX-RELATED VALUES

§5.3.1 What Are Tax-Related Values?

This brings us, of course, to the question of what fiscal or tax-related values are. Here, we can simply assess the most common theories of political justice for 'fiscal' references. Let me provide three very important examples:

(1) The size of the state: it is well known that the tax-to-GDP ratio differs significantly among various states.[4] In liberal democracies, this difference depends on the political will to have a larger or smaller state. As an example, a state may decide to introduce paid maternity leave for one year or only three months. The former is fiscally more expensive than the latter. Of course, it would be too easy to argue that states can simply decide upon the size of the state. In particular, in developing states, this is not true, and a low tax-to-GDP ratio might not be due to lack of a political will but due to fiscal limitations. The latter means that the state is unable to increase the tax-to-GDP ratio above a certain threshold, e.g., above 20%. Nevertheless, in the developed world, the size of government is to a large extent a political decision, as is the introduction of new or higher taxes to finance such state projects.

(2) The level of distribution: each state has a different level of distribution. Therefore, it is not just the amount of fiscal revenue that differs but also how much is redistributed. Therefore, the difference between the market income and the after-tax/after-distribution income can differ significantly. How much the difference should be is a democratic decision.

(3) The culture of punishment: another important value relevant from a tax perspective is the culture of punishment. There are significant differences in how countries punish their citizens in case of criminal behaviour. Also, in tax matters, punishment might differ significantly. For instance, tax evasion might be punished with jail in some states, while in others, it might result in a fine only.

§5.3.2 The Impact of International Tax Policy Decisions

As outlined and analysed by others, there are sometimes waives of sovereignty-enhancing and sovereignty-constraining developments in international tax politics.[5] Since the financial crisis, we have seen various developments that have constrained the

4. *See Tax-to-GDP ratios*, OECD (6 December 2021), https://www.oecd.org/coronavirus/en/data-insights/tax-to-gdp-ratios.
5. On this topic *see*, for instance, Rasmus Corlin Christensen & Martin Hearson, *The New Politics of Global Tax Governance: Taking Stock a Decade after the Financial Crisis*, 26 Rev. Int'l. Pol. Econ. 1068, 1068-1088 (2019) DOI: 10.1080/09692290.2019.1625802.

sovereignty of states from a fiscal perspective. The sovereignty-constraining developments are also the interesting ones in order to better understand how domestic value-based decisions are limited through international tax policy.

Looking back to the last three decades of international tax policy, we find some examples in which internationally agreed[6] value decisions also had an impact on domestic tax systems (i.e., cases of value imperialism). The following are the most obvious examples:

- The work of the OECD on Harmful Tax Regimes had an impact on domestic legislation, as many states were forced to change their domestic tax regimes.[7]
- The work on mutual administrative assistance has forced states to abolish their domestic secrecy laws and align procedural requirements with international requirements (often soft law).[8]
- BEPS Action 5 has required states to implement a spontaneous exchange of tax rulings and to align their patent boxes with the modified nexus approach. This was considered to be the minimum standard within the BEPS project.
- Pillar 2 will require many things from countries. In order not to lose tax revenue, states will introduce a QDMTT, an IIR, and a UTPR. Moreover, states are de facto forced to change their tax incentives into subsidy-like incentives like QRTCs or at least MTTCs. States might, of course, also choose genuine subsidies.

Over the past decades, there has been a clear tendency that international tax policy has more and more of a limiting impact on the design of our domestic tax system and our societal decisions, i.e., how we want to structure our societies. International tax policy is no longer a mere coordinative regime but a regime with a harmonization effect.

Historically, the impact was limited to the alignment of the domestic tax systems with tax treaties. For instance, states might partly use the same definition of a permanent establishment in domestic law as in Article 5 OECD MC or states might domestically implement a 183-day rule as provided for in Article 15 paragraph 2 OECD MC. So, decisions of the OECD, for instance, concerning the OECD MC have had a minimal impact on domestic law in general and value-based societal decisions in particular. However, as outlined, this has changed.

6. By using the term 'agree', we do not necessarily mean that there has been a genuine explicit agreement among states but that some representatives at an international organization have agreed to a certain policy.
7. *See most recently Harmful Tax Practices – Peer Review Results, Inclusive Framework on BEPS: Action 5*, OECD (Update as of June 2023), https://www.oecd.org/tax/beps/harmful-tax-practices-consolidated-peer-review-results-on-preferential-regimes.pdf; *see also Harmful Tax Practices – 2018 Progress Report on Preferential Regimes, Inclusive Framework on BEPS: Action 5*, OECD (29 January 2019), https://www.oecd-ilibrary.org/docserver/9789264311480-en.pdf?expires=1695243576&id=id&accname=guest&checksum=920E3081C2DEDB09B467E87469BC3DEA.
8. A famous example is that Switzerland was forced to allow group requests and not just information requests in which the identity of the affected person is clear.

§5.3.3 Degree of the Impact

If we look at these developments, they have a different degree of impact on the fiscal self-determination of states. Prima facie, all of the above decisions de facto limit the leeway of domestic policymakers. It is fair to admit, however, that the forced abolishment of a specific harmful tax regime is, for instance, not a core element of the fiscal state. The global minimum tax, however, restricts a core part of the democratic fiscal competence (i.e., whether a society wants to tax corporations or not) and seems, therefore, more problematic.

In some instances, the impact on fiscal self-determination could be (untechnically speaking) offset by the infringement a certain policy has on other states. For instance, being forced to abolish the banking secrecy might be justified because the banking secrecy led to an infringement of other states' sovereignty, as states were not able to tax their residents as they were hiding their wealth and income abroad.[9] Such infringements seem more justified than others. Although, historically, this was seen as very controversial, as the level of privacy is an important element of a state-government relationship, and thus, it should be up to the people to decide upon secrecy laws.[10]

The same could be true for international policies aiming at challenging beggar-thy-neighbour measures.[11] Maybe this was the case with respect to some of the harmful regimes - especially regimes that ringfenced foreign from domestic income. In some cases, the main goal of these regimes might indeed have been to harm other states. Therefore, an international policy that has a limiting effect on what other states can legislate domestically might be justified if it aims at abolishing beggar-thy-neighbour policies.

To conclude, the more essential the values are for a specific society, the more problematic a forced transfer of values through international policies becomes. For instance, forcing another state to comply with administrative standards such as the exchange of information procedure might be less interfering than forcing a state to change its income tax rates or force a state to introduce a corporate income tax. Forcing a state to abolish harmful tax regimes might also be less problematic than forcing a state to introduce very strict penalties for tax evasion. Moreover, as mentioned, some international measures might be justified to protect other state's interests.

9. Peter Hongler, *Justice in International Tax Law*, 498 et seq. (IBFD 2019).
10. For a historical overview from a Swiss perspective, *see* Stefan Tobler, *Der Kampf um das Schweizer Bankgeheimnis* (NZZ Libro 2019).
11. Beggar-thy-neighbour policies are defined as policies that aim at harming other states. This term is traditionally used to qualify some of the most harmful trade measures. *See, e.g.*, Richard E. Baldwin & Simon J. Evenett, *Beggar-thy-Neighbour Policies During the Crisis Era: Causes, Constraints, and Lessons for Maintaining Open Borders*, 28 Oxf. Rev. Econ. Pol. 211, 211-234 (2012) DOI: 10.1093/oxrep/grs015.

§5.4 MEASURES AGAINST VALUE IMPERIALISM

In the following, we will analyse what kind of measures could help to mitigate the risk of unjustified value imperialism and the protection of domestic value-based decisions by the legitimate bodies in a society.

A first approach would be to assess how we ensure in a domestic setting that the majority does not, in an illegitimate form, impose values on the minority of the people. If we look at our domestic systems, we indeed face the challenge as well of aligning various values in our tax system. For instance, some might be in favour of more distribution, while others might support less distribution. However, domestically, we indeed have a democratic process that helps us to agree in a pluralistic society on a set of principles according to which we want to design our societies. In this way, we consider the decisions of the legislator as legitimate, although personally, we might not agree.

Therefore, the first option would be to enhance the democratic process at an international level and, by doing so, reduce the risk of value imperialism. This is also a claim regularly found in tax law literature, and we will deal with it in the following section 5.4.1. Moreover, we could also improve the legal framework in which international tax policy decisions are made (section 5.4.2), or we could try to limit international tax policy decisions to the necessary minimum (section 5.4.3). These three options will be addressed separately in the following sections.

§5.4.1 Inclusiveness and Democracy

An obvious measure against value imperialism would be to strengthen the inclusiveness of the international decision-making body and to make it genuinely democratic. Here, I would, of course, completely agree with Peter's conclusion that we need more Habermas (and less Machiavelli), and this will help to steer the international tax regime in the right direction.[12] Peter writes, for instance, that: 'In the end, a true dialogue with national parliaments and citizens will be necessary.'[13]

So, it is not just that we should enhance deliberations at an international level but also that we should enable a better dialogue between international policymakers and domestic parliaments. Actually, Peter has probably created a whole 'Tilburg School' which highlights the importance of deliberation and democratic approval to achieve legitimate tax policy decisions both at a domestic and at an international level.[14]

I would unconditionally agree that it is important that tax policy decisions are based on a genuine democratic process and not just based on the consent of the elites

12. Peter Essers, *International Tax Justice Between Machiavelli and Habermas*, 68 Bull. Int'l. Tax'n. 54, 54-66 (2014) DOI: 10.1017/9781780684734.012.
13. *Ibid.*, 65.
14. *See in particular* Cees Peters, *On the Legitimacy of International Tax Law* (IBFD 2014). *See also* Ricardo Garcia Anton, *The 21st Century Multilateralism in International Taxation: The Emperor's New Clothes?*, 8 World Tax J. 147, 147-192 (2016). However, at the time of the publication, the latter author was not yet affiliated with Tilburg. Of course, the 'Tilburg School' is still fragmented.

– at least in democratic states such as the Netherlands or my home country Switzerland. Moreover, we should also understand the constant dialectical relationship between taxation and the political balance of power in a domestic setting.[15] However, the more I think about the topic at an international level, the more I believe that such dialogue and true democratic approval are just very highly unlikely to happen in the near future at a global level, and therefore, we should not necessarily aim for it.[16]

Of course, we are not talking about direct democracy but at least an indirect and representational approval of decisions of international organizations such as the OECD or the UN. It seems even very unlikely to achieve such an indirect approval of international policy decisions. Would it be consensus based? If yes, we will not see a lot of progress. Would it be majority based? It seems very unlikely that states would agree on a majority-based system, and moreover, many questions would need to be solved – we would need detailed regulation to achieve a fair deliberative process: who presides over the negotiations? Who is competent to participate? Who is competent to propose new ideas? etc.

Moreover, countries which form part of the international tax debate have different domestic legislative approval procedures, and some might even be considered undemocratic. Nevertheless, they participate and should participate in global tax policy negotiations. As a consequence, international policy decisions are contingent on the level of domestic democracy, and we are far from achieving a global system that consists only of democratic states. This is another reason why we will not achieve genuine democratic approval of international tax policy decisions, and the ideal dialogue between national parliaments and international tax policymakers might be impossible to achieve.

It is also not surprising that other fields of law are facing similar limitations. The international trade law system is also blocked and will unlikely develop more democratically in a multilateral form. However, we will see a lot more plurilateral agreements, i.e., trade agreements not at a global level but at a sublevel among a few states focusing on specific industries. It seems also unlikely that we will see the incorporation of a strong global tax body in the next months, but we will see a lot more tax-related agreements among various groups of countries. There are many existing examples – e.g., the AEOI Agreement, the CbCR Agreement, or the upcoming Pillar 1 Agreement are all agreements that are or will only be signed by a limited number of states. This will be further outlined in the following sections.

Of course, there are small steps that can be taken in order to improve the decision-making process. For instance, we should not speak of '*agreement*' if there is none, and we should not speak of '*equal footing*' if there is not a voting process indeed achieving an equal footing.[17] Moreover, of course, the dialogue should be transparent; i.e., we should understand who was in favour of which proposal and which country

15. *See* Peter Essers, *General Report on History and Taxation: The Dialectical Relationship Between Taxation and the Political Balance of Power*, 20 EATLP Int'l Tax Ser. 3, 3-38 (2022).
16. Even just genuine, open and transparent Habermasian deliberation seems impossible to achieve at an international level.
17. United Nations, General Assembly, Promotion of inclusive and effective international tax cooperation at the United Nations, A/78/235, 26.7.2023.

suggested a specific solution. We should enable processes that create accountability for the involved delegates.[18] Currently, there is no accountability at all at an international level.

But apart from these small steps forward, I doubt that we will achieve a true dialogue between national parliaments and international policymakers in the near future with a clear institutional setting. I would even doubt whether global negotiations, which are similar to domestic democratic negotiations, are normatively something we want to achieve.[19] Yes, I am not a cosmopolitan, neither from a substantive perspective nor from a procedural perspective. So, we are likely facing an unrealistic utopia in that we will anyway not achieve a true dialogue, and we will not see a substantially more democratic and inclusive spirit in international tax negotiations in the near future. Of course, it is a different story that some individual states might, within a small group, agree on more integration and more democratic processes beyond the domestic setting. This is, for instance, the case in the EU. However, this does not fundamentally change the institutional setting of international tax policymaking.

In these circumstances of strong de facto limitations, it is helpful to broaden the perspective and assess other means that would help to improve international tax policymaking besides the decision-making processes. Therefore, we will, in the following, outline two other ideas which might not have received the necessary attention. The focus is again on measures that would avoid what we have called value imperialism.

§5.4.2 The Importance of Legalization and the Importance of Dispute Resolution

One way of reducing unjustified value imperialism, or at least mitigating its effects, would be to legalize the international tax law framework. This means that the international tax regime would more intensively be based on a legally structured regime, and this does not mean that we necessarily need a very strong international organization. Such legalization can include not only more rules, more precise rules, but also, in general, a clear definition of the existing legal obligations.[20] It can also include more delegations, i.e., the transfer of traditional domestic competences to an international body; however, it does not necessarily mean more centralization. Enhanced legalization of the international tax regime seems helpful to reduce unintended value imperialism since it could again ensure a reduction of imperialistic policies through checks and balances.

18. *See e.g.*, Irma Mosquera Valderrama, *Global Tax Governance: Legitimacy and Inclusiveness: Why It Matters*, Leiden (30 June 2023), https://scholarlypublications.universiteitleiden.nl/access/item%3A3628031/view.
19. *See my own normative position* Hongler, *supra* n. 9, at 343 et seq.
20. *See for details* Kenneth W. Abbott et al., *The Concept of Legalization*, 54 Int'l. Org. 401, 401-419 (2000) DOI: 10.1162/002081800551271.

Prima vista, with the global minimum tax, we have reached the maximum level of precision and legal obligations. Non-compliance with the Model Rules means harsh economic consequences, and the rules to be compliant with are extremely detailed. However, an important part is still missing: judicial control. An important element towards the legalization of international tax law would indeed be an actual judicialization.[21]

In the past decades, we have delegated (although not officially) significant competences, both legislative and executive, to the OECD and G20. However, judicial control of both legislative and executive actions is missing.[22] What do we mean by judicial control? Most tax scholars focus on the need for dispute resolution as an instrument to mitigate double taxation and avoid overlapping jurisdictions in general. However, from an institutional perspective, judicial control is necessary to ensure that the provided rules are followed by countries on a truly equal footing.

What is particularly important is that in areas where there seems to be an intense impact on nationally defined values, as outlined above, the international regime must foresee interstate judicial protection. This is currently not the case at all. Therefore, the international tax regime should contain a dispute resolution mechanism to solve interstate disputes in case international tax policy decisions have a significant impact on national values in particular and domestic tax regimes in general. To be more concrete, the following are examples that would require judicial control to mitigate the level of value imperialism:

- The peer-review process for harmful tax regimes needs to be subject to an appeal process.
- The peer-review process for the IIR, the UTPR, and the QDMTT should be subject to an appeal process. The same is true for the question of whether a domestic QRTC or an MTTC is indeed in line with the requirements in the Model Rules and the related documents.
- Lastly, the question of whether a country is compliant with the obligations derived from the Convention on Mutual Administrative Assistance in Tax Matters or with any other convention on mutual assistance should be subject to an appeal process.

§5.4.3 Minimalism

A third way to avoid value imperialism through international tax policy would be to focus only on the necessary areas of cooperation and to reduce the need for global solutions to a minimum. The fewer international policy decisions are needed at a global level, the less impact there is on domestic societal decisions. So, what are the necessary areas of cooperation?

21. We rely here heavily on Judith Goldstein, Miles Kahler, Robert O. Keohane & Anne-Marie Slaughter, *Introduction: Legalization and World Politics*, 54 Int'l. Org. 385, 385-399 (2000) DOI: 10.1162/002081800551262.
22. *See already* Hongler, *supra* n. 9, at 244 et seq.

The ultimate goal of international tax policy should be to ensure that states are able to tax what happens within their territory. This requires, for instance, that we achieve sufficient transparency through administrative assistance so that states become aware of what is going on in their territory. But it also requires that the international tax regime enables states to tax what happens in their territory. Here, of course, the current permanent establishment definitions seem to limit several states from taxing digital services.[23]

If, of course, there is a wish for further integration, states are free to sign double tax treaties or further integrative agreements such as fully fledged non-discrimination treaties, investment treaties or all-encompassing mutual assistance agreements (e.g., including joint audits and spontaneous exchange of information). One reason for the failure of the most recent projects is that the OECD, under the guidance of Pascal Saint-Amans, has aimed at global solutions, ignoring the fact that global solutions are not necessary even in very specific areas such as the taxation of the digital economy.

Therefore, international tax policy should be more differentiated and should have several layers. There is a core element (i.e., the meta regime) that needs to be open to everyone and that should ideally be followed by everyone. However, the international tax regime should ensure that states can opt for further integration.

§5.4.4 Intermediate Conclusion: Focus on a Meta Regime Instead of Strong Global Institutions

It seems very unlikely that we see a major institutional development in the next years in the form that an international organization will indeed provide for a genuine democratic body, allowing the international tax regime to progress in a highly legitimate form. If we see the creation of a new international tax body, it will very likely not satisfy the needs of a true democratic decision-making process. I suggest that focusing on different angles is more effective instead of improving the negotiation framework.

It would be more effective for the purpose of avoiding value imperialism to design a meta regime at a global level. Such a meta regime would contain the most essential rules required to ensure the fiscal self-determination of states and to ensure that states are indeed on an equal footing. This, in particular, means cross-border transparency accessible to all states. Moreover, such a regime should provide for a sufficiently strong and legalized institution to ensure that states can agree on further integration on a true equal footing. Such enhanced integration does not need to happen at a global but, for instance, at a regional level.

It does not mean that states must agree on further integration, but they can in a regulated manner if they wish to. Potential further-reaching tax-related agreements, however, do not need to be global agreements, but groups of states can agree to a further level of tax integration. We can call these agreements plurilateral agreements.

23. Although digital service taxes have proved to be a way out of double tax treaty obligations. They also enable taxation in the market state without amending Art. 5 OECD MC and the respective treaty provisions.

Plurilateral agreements are industry-specific under the umbrella of the WTO, but the term could also have a place in the tax regime as it could describe agreements by two or more states regulating a specific area of the international tax regime.[24] The following could be considered plurilateral tax agreements (some of them exist already):

- Mitigations of double taxation using bilateral or multilateral tax treaties.
- Cross-border mutual assistance beyond the necessary element of cross-border transparency (e.g., joint audits and spontaneous exchange of information). Of course, some of these rules are part of the Convention on Mutual Administrative Assistance in Tax Matters.
- Reduction of harmful tax regimes following the rationale of Action 5 and the 1998 report through an international binding instrument.
- Reduction of harmful income tax regimes through an international binding instrument.
- Non-discrimination agreements containing all or parts of the fundamental freedoms within the EU. As an example, the free-movement agreement between Switzerland and the EU contains a free movement of workers provision with a significant impact on the tax systems.
- Implementation agreement of Pillar 1.
- Implementation agreement of Pillar 2.[25]
- The Multilateral Convention to Implement Tax Treaty Related Measures to Prevent BEPS.
- States might even agree to apply a formulary allocation system in the sense of BEFIT within the EU.
- States could agree on an arbitration convention for tax matters.

The meta regime would then regulate these agreements but only the most essential parts. It would, for instance, clarify under what circumstance a country can become a member of any of these agreements and whether some benefits could be granted to developing countries without reciprocal obligations. But also, and this is the key element, states can agree that a certain agreement shall be subject to judicial control (and not just an arbitrary peer-review process). Such judicial control, as mentioned, would be limited to interstate disputes – e.g., whether a regime is harmful under an agreement prohibiting harmful corporate income tax regimes or whether a QRTC is indeed a QRTC under a Pillar 2 agreement.

Of course, it makes a lot more sense to place such a meta regime under the auspices of the UN instead of the OECD. Such a meta regime would be less imperialistic than the current global governance structure, but it does not require that global policymaking become genuinely democratic. States could voluntarily agree on further integration, and if they do, there is a dispute resolution mechanism that makes the system less arbitrary.

24. Garcia Anton, *supra* n. 14, at 147-192.
25. The OECD does not see a need to sign such an implementation agreement. However, the current implementation chaos could have been avoided by the use of multilateral agreements to implement the QDMTT, the IIR and the UTPR.

Of course, states could individually or together with other states use legitimate economic power[26] to force other states to agree on some of the above conventions. This is what is currently done, for instance, under the EU standard of tax good governance, i.e., combining the signing of a trade agreement with some minimum tax standard (e.g., signing the Convention on Mutual Administrative Assistance in Tax Matters). However, a meta regime, including judicial protection, would ensure that compliance with these agreements is reciprocal and not arbitrary or one-sided.

§5.5 CONCLUSION

Why am I concerned with value imperialism? The main reason is that it undermines democratic decision-making, and here Peter would very likely agree.[27] Living in a country with a strong history of direct democracy, it is problematic to see that unelected officials of international organizations can decide how a domestic tax regime is structured. The Pillar 2 proposal has been the most extreme form due to the brutality of the UTPR.

Therefore, it would indeed be the first choice – following the Tilburg School! – to transform global tax policymaking into a genuinely democratic process and to ensure a true dialogue with national parliaments in order to mitigate value imperialism. However, as it was outlined[28] above, this is simply not realistic, so we need to look for other solutions to mitigate the problem of value imperialism.

I suggest designing a meta regime, which would, on the one hand, be minimalistic as it would only contain the necessary tools to achieve fiscal self-determination of states. This, in particular, means that cross-border transparency is key, at least the most essential form of exchange of information on request, and likely an automatic exchange of bank-related information.

On the other hand, such a meta regime would enable states to agree individually or in larger groups to sign further tax-related agreements but under the umbrella of such a meta regime. We have listed a variety of tax-related agreements that could be placed under the umbrella of such a meta regime. A key element would be a judicial control element to ensure that treaty obligations are fulfilled reciprocally. Currently, the international tax regime is not balanced, as international organizations such as the OECD have gained strong de facto legislative (and also executive) powers, but there is no judicial control. The idea would be that states could agree to use a global dispute resolution mechanism to ensure a fair and systematic application of tax-related treaty obligations. Of course, such a mechanism would not be mandatory for all tax-related agreements, but it is part of a meta regime, so states could opt for some tax-related agreements to be subject to such interstate dispute resolution.

26. We are not able to deal with the question of legitimate economic power in the course of the present chapter, but it is also not necessary for the purpose of the chapter. Of course, here we should refer to Essers, *supra* n. 12, at 54-66.
27. *See already* Hongler, *supra* n. 9, at 348.
28. *See* §5.4.1.

CHAPTER 6

(Re)considering the Legitimacy of International Tax Standards: A Proposal for (Re)formulation*

F. Alfredo García Prats

§6.1 INTRODUCTION

In 2014, Peter Essers published an article in the *Bulletin for International Taxation* titled 'International Tax Justice Between Machiavelli and Habermas', which summarized the Klaus Vogel lecture given by Professor Essers in 2013 at the Institute for Austrian and International Tax Law.[1] In this article, prof Essers rightly pointed out that 'the choices in the field of international tax law have to be made, explained and justified by responsible politicians and policymakers' (p. 54). Now that new agents and organizations seem concerned with the so-called new paradigms of international taxation, it is important to take into consideration some elements that help to understand both: (a) how international (tax) rules were and are developed, signed and implemented, and (b) how States incorporate them into their respective domestic tax systems.

Globalization and the new international business models in the era of digitalization enabled the development of tax strategies by some taxpayers, mainly multinationals, that reported to them a significant reduction of their accumulated tax burden. This process led to an unfair and asymmetric distribution of the tax charges among taxpayers, as a result of the asymmetries, lack of coordination and insufficient

* The present chapter has been developed as a part of the Research Project 'La necesaria actualización de los sistemas tributarios ante los retos del S. XXI (XXITAX). Proyecto Prometeo 2021-041 of the Generalitat Valenciana.

1. Peter Essers, *International Tax Justice Between Machiavelli and Habermas* 68 Bulletin for International Taxation 54 (2014) DOI: 10.1017/9781780684734.012.

attention by developers of international tax standards, and the incapability to tackle this unfair result by unilateral actions.

In such an increasingly interconnected global economy, the development of international tax rules has become a subject of significant concern and debate. As a result, a major attention to the need of coordination among corporate income tax systems of different States emerged, and several initiatives were taken to improve and implement the necessary measures to deal with the new challenges.

At the end, globalization entails the need to seek supranational answers to questions that had traditionally been formulated and developed at a purely internal level as regards tax matters.

The move towards greater coordination and development of international tax rules and structures being necessary, the actual evolution of international taxation standards demands knowing whether, why, and, if in the affirmative, how the new international tax standards, rules, models and recommendations that derive from the new tax paradigms have been developed or are being developed fulfilling certain minimum levels of legitimacy.

New business models' scenarios and the implications of the new digital era convey the formulation of standards that depart from a traditional, purely domestic unilateral standard. Global solutions have to be searched, and are being searched, to tackle more efficiently and in a more coordinated way with gaps, asymmetries, loopholes and insufficient and inefficient control of certain tax planning strategies of some taxpayers, mainly multinational enterprises. In this sense, claims of appropriateness, adequacy, representativity, and technical expertise have been argued by different authors and organizations to improve the legitimate expectations of different States and stakeholders on the outcomes, and efforts have been made to enlarge the original representativity at the discussions developed so far.[2]

The effort being necessary, there is a need to verify how this coordination and formulation of the new paradigms are achieved at the international level. Moreover, it is important to analyse what are the mechanisms used by different countries to ensure domestic tax legitimacy.

In order to ask these questions, it is important to consider:

(a) what is the scope and the extent of the competences assumed or to be assumed by international and supranational bodies and organizations;
(b) which process or procedure has been used to grant and recognize such attribution of competences at a domestic level; and
(c) what is the verification of the proper use of such mandate and the legitimation strategies developed by international organizations to guarantee an accepted and efficient result.

2. G20 Bali Leaders' Declaration. 15-16 November 2022. G20/OECD Roadmap on Developing Countries and International Taxation. OECD Report for the G20 Finance Ministers and Central Bank Governors. October 2022. UN. U.N. General Assembly, 'Promotion of Inclusive and Effective International Tax Cooperation at the United Nations', A/78/235 (26 July 2023).

Several authors have contributed significantly to the analysis of the legitimacy standards in international tax law.[3] The exercise is needed in order to identify potential areas of improvement of the system as a whole, assuming that it is possible to consider the international tax order as a system.

In order to do so, it is important to clarify what is the meaning being given to 'legitimacy' of international tax standards and to verify the mechanisms used by countries to respect domestic tax legitimacy concerns. This short chapter, which is the first of a series, intends to focus on the analysis of the legitimacy of international tax standards from a domestic/constitutional perspective. Instead, from an international legal perspective, it is considered more appropriate to speak about legitimacy strategies to improve the foundations of these new standards from decision-making process and the international tax fairness – both inter-nations' and inter-taxpayer's perspectives.

Deeper comparative research is needed to verify to which extent domestic legitimate bodies have respected their constitutional functions as regards the fulfilment of their respective democratic or constitutional standards.

§6.2 THE NEED FOR A RECONSIDERATION OF THE INTERNATIONAL TAX SYSTEM

As a result of the liberalization of the world economy after the 1980s, most of the countries lost the traditional 'full' sovereignty in tax matters. Despite the fact that the exercise of taxing powers is retained at the core of the State sovereignty, the need to adapt tax systems, and specially corporate income taxes, to the liberalization of the economy, the legal requirements derived from recognized and protected cross-border economic freedoms, or the market conditions, led States and other stakeholders to a tax competition – a 'race to the bottom'. This was due to the lack of parallel regulatory competition standards and minimum tax requirements of effective or nominal taxation. As a result, the protection of the domestic tax base as regards corporate income tax could not be effectively and solely ensured by the implementation of purely domestic measures, and a certain coordination at a supranational or international level was

3. Linda Brosens & Jasper Bossuyt, *Legitimacy in International Tax Law-Making: Can the OECD Remain the Guardian of Open Tax Norms?* 12 World Tax Journal 313 (2020). Rasmus C. Christensen et al., *At the Table, Off the Menu? Assessing the Participation of Lower-Income Countries in Global Tax Negotiations* (ICTD 2020). Alfredo García Prats, *The Legitimacy of AEOI and Measures Other than AEOI*, in *New Exchange of Information Versus Tax Solutions of Equivalent Effect* 13 IBFD 133. Jennifer Gronau & Henning Schmidtke, *The Quest for Legitimacy in World Politics – International Institutions' Legitimation Strategies*, 42 Review of International Studies 535 (2016) DOI: 10.1017/s0260210515000492. Irma J. Mosquera Valderrama, *Legitimacy and the Making of International Tax Law: The Challenges of Multilateralism*, 7 World Tax Journal (2015). Irma J. Mosquera Valderrama, *Output Legitimacy Deficits and the Inclusive Framework of the OECD/G20 Base Erosion and Profit Shifting Initiative*, 72 Bulletin for International Taxation 160 (2018). I. Ozai, *Institutional and Structural Legitimacy Deficits in the International Tax Regime*, 12 World Tax Journal 53 (2022). K. Blanchard, *UPTR: An Undemocratic Vehicle to Force GLOBE Compliance*, 109 Tax Notes International 6 March 2023, p. 1219.

sought. The financial crisis that started in 2008 led States and international organizations to reconsider the previous tax standards, forcing a reinforcement of administrative (and judicial) assistance in tax matters in front of the bank secrecy and other traditional guarantees and barriers to effective cross-border cooperation.

Three main areas of action claimed the need to reconsider traditional tax standards:

(a) the fight against bank secrecy for tax purposes;
(b) the reconsideration of (harmful) tax competition; and
(c) the need to tackle base erosion and profit shifting by more stringent international tax rules.

The actions taken against these concerns led to some reconsideration, reconfiguration and update of traditional international tax standards. In order to achieve this, different levels of coordination measures were suggested, considering the consensus, the support and the theoretical legal foundations that needed to be maintained to ensure efficiency and timely reaction of the measures. Some tax literature had already started, however, to question whether it would have been necessary to establish certain standards of coordination, decision-making processes and new consensus models.[4]

The reaction against base erosion and profit shifting developed a substantial amount of efforts and changes at an international level, but it did not finish with the outcomes of the BEPS action plan. On the contrary, in order to prevent the development of unilateral mechanisms to tackle the insufficient consensus about action 1 of the BEPS project – Tax Challenges Arising from Digitalization – a proposal that incorporated a two-pillar solution was presented by the OECD.

The proposal was developed within the realms of the so-called Inclusive Framework and may lead to significant changes in: (a) the taxation of MNEs, (b) the distribution of taxing rights among jurisdictions, and (c) the reconsideration of tax competition policies, instruments and measures. In the development of the new international tax standards, the G20 took the political lead, and the OECD served as the intellectual provider of the solutions.

This double mechanism has been partly criticized, considering that the settings for the development of the new standards and measures were taken without an adequate role and representativity of the States and jurisdictions that finally are to be committed with the outcomes of the proposals and debates.[5]

4. M. Zagler, *International Tax Coordination: An Interdisciplinary Perspective on Virtues and Pitfalls* (Routledge 2010).
5. Rasmus C. Christensen et al. *At the Table, Off the Menu? Assessing the Participation of Lower-Income Countries in Global Tax Negotiations* (ICTD 2020).

§6.3 THE 'NEW' PARADIGMS OF INTERNATIONAL TAXATION

There are a few elements that result from the new international tax landscape that deserves specific attention from the perspective of legitimacy.

§6.3.1 A New Multilateral Approach

On the one hand, it is important to consider that the new international approach towards certain cross-border tax issues is taken from a multilateral perspective, overcoming the traditional bilateral approach based on models that guided the development of bilateral international tax rules almost exclusively until recently.

Multilateralism generates important concerns regarding the legitimacy of the outcome, especially when it leads to a 'one-size-fits-all' solution that does not take into account the peculiarities and needs of certain groups of States and stakeholders.

On the one hand, the generation of the texts requires the signatory members to identify the level of commitment to the outcomes. A weak consensus on the content, extent and effects of the multilateral proposals may lead to some ineffective outcome. A strong consensus but with important leeway, exceptions, options or alternatives to the commitment may lead to a multilateralism *à la carte*. The MLI has generated an important level of consensus despite the fact that the options and reserves result in different outcomes at a bilateral level. Recently, the July 2023 UN proposal opens the possibility of consensus to a three-approach alternative, with a very different binding effect and scope.

Additionally, the generation of truly multilateral solutions requires important analysis about which institutions are attributed the function of suggesting, initiating, developing and reaching the international consensus on the new measures and proposals. This is the area that has concentrated the biggest efforts of both the international community and the tax literature to claim for a reinforcement of the legitimacy of the new emerging standards.

The formulation of the new paradigms is the result of the collaboration between different international actors that play an important role. The political support at the highest level has turned out tax concerns as one of the major economies and world political leaders' consensus leading to very interesting initiatives to reshape international taxation.

§6.3.2 The International Players and Stakeholders and Their Respective Mandates

The G-7 and the G-20 have played an important role in the needed political support for reaching a global agreement on the need to tackle the challenges that domestic corporate tax systems faced in front of specialized preferential tax regimes and complex tax strategies of MNEs. The political agreement at the highest level at G-7 and G-20 summits was reinforced by the so-called Inclusive Framework, developed to open the debate, if not the political initiative, to ensure a sufficient ground of international commitment to the measures foreseen to be developed for the implementation of the outcomes reached. Despite that important and very relevant international consensus, some groups, such as the G-24, formed by different countries from Africa, Asia and Central and South America, have presented some alternatives for the debate and for the potential consensus and outcomes.

The OECD has continued playing a main political and technical role in the design, formulation and development of the new international tax standards, *executing* the political agreements reached at the international level by the G-7 and G-20 group of States. In order to gain greater representativeness, the OECD led the creation of the Inclusive Framework (IF) founded on inclusiveness, coordinated approach and transparency, which has enabled the broadening of representativeness of the groups discussing and elaborating the standards, rules, recommendations and guidelines.

Not to forget the increasing relevance of the European Union as a true international tax player. The European Union, despite the fact of the full competence of the Member States in direct taxation matters, has played a significant role in supporting, complementing, implementing and, thus, forcing the reach of important consensus about the new international tax framework.

Other bodies and institutions, such as the IMF, the Global Forums and the Platform for Collaboration on Tax, have played an assisting role in the development of consensus and administrative guidance.

Last but not least, there is a need to mention the increasingly relevant role to be played by the UN. Departing from its traditional, limited action, that suited as a complement and adaptation role of the OECD works, during the last few years has demanded a greater recognition and responsibility, requesting the creation of an intergovernmental body to deal with international tax rules to contribute to a better delineation of the taxing rights and tax governance standards, taking into account the special needs and budgetary concerns of developing countries.

A proper legitimacy analysis of the functions of the international actors requires to verify their mandates to perform their functions and competences, as well as the decision-making process that is being used to reach the international consensus in those international organizations.

§6.3.3 The Legal Status of the Outcomes Generated by the 'New' International Tax Organizations

Connected with that analysis, it is important to analyse the content and type of outcomes that are produced by the international organizations. The implications for domestic legitimacy and the requirements to verify its fulfilment vary depending on the type of outcome, its legal binding effect, and its extent or scope. This analysis needs to be made together with the study of the extent and the content of the mandates given to the international organizations and bodies.

Historically, some international organizations restricted their role in income and corporate tax matters with the formulation of model conventions that States, in the exercise of its full tax sovereignty, could use to prevent double taxation and international tax avoidance and evasion. In order to prevent dissenting views of the Model among jurisdictions, the international organizations reinforced their role as soft-law makers, through the development of the Commentaries to the Model Conventions and other non-legally binding instruments. However, since the reaction against harmful tax competition, international organizations were also concerned on the need to generate unilateral effective reactions and not only on the suggestion of bilateral international tax measures.

The BEPS action plan reinforces the role of international organizations as authentic international rule makers, initially with the MLI and then with the proposed new multilateral treaty to implement the UTPR rule. Moreover, it broadens the goals of certain international organizations, especially the OECD, fostering certain domestic tax rules, approaches and models, and changes their traditional role, thus penetrating the traditional sphere of domestic Parliaments with the detailed formulation of domestic tax measures (for instance, as regards the development of measures that implement Pillar II).

An analysis of the legitimacy of the international organizations should also seek to verify the mandate given to international organizations to see to which extent they have been enabled to formulate not only models and soft-law pieces in a variety of forms but also if they received a proper and legitimate mandate to limit, restrict and condition the exercise of taxing powers that originally correspond to national Parliaments. This action is mainly developed through the formulation of detailed rules and administrative guidance *to be implemented* at a domestic level by States without significant room of manoeuvre to decide whether to implement or not, and little room to amend or adapt its implementation. Despite the fact that its implementation is not mandatory per se, lack of proper or coordinated implementation with the international tax standards may result in some undesired results.

§6.3.4 International Tax Paradigms and Tax Fairness

Another point of interest is the analysis of the outcome of the new paradigms from the fairness point of view, from both the inter-taxpayer's and the inter-nations' equity perspective.

From the inter-taxpayer's equity perspective, the proposals of Pillar I and Pillar II may result in a trial international tax system:

(a) one applicable to major multinationals, subject to both Pillar I and Pillar II;
(b) another one applicable to multinationals with a turnover exceeding 750 million euros;
(c) and the third, classical system updated after BEPS 1.0, applicable to the rest of the taxpayers.

Therefore, the implications of the new understanding of the arm's-length principle, the new extended permanent establishment thresholds, or the update of double tax conventions – with the PPT or LOB clauses as a minimum standard – may be different for the different groups of taxpayers, thus creating a different level playing field, generating different risks and opportunities for different taxpayers and putting at risk the inter-taxpayer's equity perspective.

From the inter-nations' perspective, it is to be seen whether the outcome of the minimum effective (corporate) tax enshrined with the GloBE proposal will fulfil the requirement of taxes being allocated where activities take place and value is created, or, on the contrary, if the use-it-or-lose-it principle may create an undesired result of allocation of taxes to a different jurisdiction. Moreover, it is to be seen how to reconcile the underlying principles of value-creation allocation and the single-tax principle (tax wherever, but tax at least once).

In that respect, the broadening of objectives to be displayed by international tax standards corners the fight against base erosion and profit shifting in favour of a broader fight against tax competition, thus hampering the legitimate expectations of certain States after the consensus reached under BEPS action plan number 5 – harmful tax practices. This new approach places some States at a comparative competitive disadvantage to attract foreign investments since they are deprived of the tax policy instruments that are traditionally used (tax incentives, privileged tax regimes, etc.).

The issue should be deeply considered since this may turn into favouring alternative public aid mechanisms to attract foreign investment, thus placing States in different positions regarding the availability of such means. And, at the same time, it generates important concerns about the international mechanisms that should be put in place to control not only tax incentives but also State aids and other public economic policies, broadly considered, considering the EU model or reinforcing the WTO control mechanisms. In other words, if there is a need to control tax incentives and grants from an international position, a similar need should request the same legitimacy concerns as regards any similar type of subsidies and government grants.[6]

§6.4 THE MEANING OF LEGITIMACY

§6.4.1 Input and Output Legitimacy and Legitimation Strategies

Tax literature has approached the legitimacy concerns regarding the new international tax paradigms from different perspectives, but mainly focusing on the justification of the right to rule by international organizations establishing the 'new international tax order'.[7] The majority of authors distinguish between input legitimacy and output legitimacy, some others adding the throughput legitimacy.

Input legitimacy refers to the standard settings in decision-making process. It refers to the analysis of the participation process in the formulation and elaboration of (international) rules. The main criticism in that regard refers to the unequal participation and involvement of countries in the formulation and discussion of the new

6. Mindy Herzfeld, *Pillar 2, State Aid, and Industrial Policy*, 112 Tax Notes International 329 (2023).
7. *Supra* n. 3.

international tax standards. The input legitimacy questions and verifies the domestic legitimacy standard in terms of democratic guarantee of the tax rules. The authors mainly confirm that international setting-rule standards cannot be judged against some ideal democratic (domestic) institution, and at the same time consider it incorrect to enable only democratic countries to participate in the decision-making process at the international level. However, some improvements can be made as regards the decision-making process at the international level, what is defined as legitimation strategies by part of the international literature, and improvement of legitimate domestic mandate, control, approval and implementation - more than a simple rubberstamp mechanism - should also be stressed, what I mainly consider a domestic legitimation issue of the new international tax standards.

On the contrary, output legitimacy pays attention to the outcomes of process, analysing their acceptance, tolerance and support, which makes compliance easier. Some authors consider that efficiency and effectiveness of the solutions being provided can be checked under this approach. This analysis also enables the outcomes under the fairness and equality principles.

Despite the position of the majority of the literature questioning the legitimacy of international tax standards, efforts to analyse the legitimacy of these standards should be revisited and completed for two main reasons.

First, it is more accurate to identify at international level *legitimation strategies* or legitimacy aspirations to convince the constituencies of legitimation of the right to rule of international institutions than to consider that international law contains legitimacy requirements. Negotiation power and capacity to reach consensus among the constituency - mainly the States - play a very important role in the development of international tax law and also in the formation of international soft law. Nevertheless, it is important to identify some alternatives to improve strategies, mainly from a top-down approach, that reinforce representativity and the decision-making process that helps compliance with the outcome.

On the other hand, legitimacy constraints and analysis force the international community to identify international tax values that should be considered when developing the justification of the new decision-making rules. Good governance practices are to be taken into account when considering legitimacy concerns, as they developed internationally and were influenced by Western-European democracies' tradition and practices as developed in their domestic tax systems. Additionally, international (customary) law formulates a considerable bunch of criteria to settle the new international tax parameters, especially when referring to the legal position of taxpayers, such as the full respect for human rights as enshrined under international law.

While considering that the discussions around the decision of the UN to create a global intergovernmental tax body under the framework of the United Nations are initially linked to input legitimacy concerns, the impact on output legitimacy should not be underestimated. The critics that signal the risk of having different international bodies making diverging proposals on the update of international tax rules should bear in mind that the reaction of the UN, and of the G34 group to a similar extent, should bear in mind that the reaction reflects the critical position of many countries that do not show enthusiasm around the outcomes of the process started by the OECD and the Inclusive Framework, despite its global initial acceptance, before its development and regulation came into the debate. It is precisely in the regulation of the principle agreed - the devil is in the details - where the legitimacy concerns arise since the initial international or global consensus needs to be developed taking into consideration the interests, voices and positions of all the countries having agreed.

§6.4.2 Domestic/Constitutional Legitimacy

Second, it is more appropriate to discuss legitimacy concerns from the domestic perspective of each of the countries concerned in the formulation, verification and implementation of the new international tax standards. The new standards and paradigms do not solely affect international relations but have a direct impact on the domestic tax systems, formulating new rules, eliminating certain tax figures (taxes) already implemented, or forcing to change domestic tax measures already in place - that had already been verified according to the settled governance standards/tax competition standards. Since tax is a matter that initially corresponds to the core of the State and the Parliament is normally the main actor in comparative constitutional law, it would be necessary from this legitimization perspective (from a comparative perspective):

- First, to analyse the existence and extension of the mandate given to the representatives of each State in order to enable them to participate, negotiate and sign the agreements.
- Second, to verify the mechanisms of control of such a mandate and, in the alternative, the verification of the agreement and implications of such agreement in the tax policy/tax system of the State concerned.
- Third, to verify which elements have to be automatically implemented at the domestic level.

As a result of the changes derived from the potential implementation of new international tax standards - Pillar I and Pillar II measures, exchange of information mechanisms, etc. - decisions taken by international (tax) organizations do not only affect or influence international legal rules (tax treaties, conventions, instruments and so on) but also affect, influence and have an impact on domestic tax rules, whose competences initially correspond and are attributed to the domestic legislator. Automatic acceptance of the outcomes at a domestic level without a minimum intervention of the national Parliaments may endanger the legitimacy of the whole process, and the lack of specialization or technical capacity of Parliament members cannot be upheld as a valid counterargument to dismiss their constitutional role.

Therefore, there is a need to incorporate into the domestic traditional debate and analysis of legitimacy regarding the tax system the content and implications of the new supranational and international acts, declarations and statements that have a direct influence on the development of domestic tax systems.

Some of them have already had a clear legal impact on domestic tax systems, such as the mandatory amendments derived from the automatic exchange of information requirements formulated at the international level – Common Reporting Standards – that forced some countries to change domestic legislation or even constitutional framework.

Some other instruments should also be carefully considered. The first ones are the political commitments made – and signed – by representatives of States before international bodies – such as the ones giving support to the G20 statements regarding the minimum effective corporate tax rate, to delineate their legal consequences if any. Second, there is a need to properly and accurately distinguish the legal effects and constraints derived from a variety of instruments that have been traditionally considered in unity under the denomination of soft law (such as reports, recommendations, guidelines, model rules, and best practices). It is necessary to properly clarify which effects they produce and distinguish them depending on whether their focus is on the clarification and development of international law (tax treaties) or when their object and purpose is to interpret and modulate domestic tax law.

In a parallel line of research, the legitimacy of domestic tax law requires to investigate the extent of minimum standards when agreed at an international level and whether they affect or have an impact on domestic legislative decisions. From this perspective, it is clear that the domestic legitimacy of the new international tax standards should improve and must improve by reinforcing the mechanisms that clarify the mandate given to the international organizations as such. Moreover, it has to be verified the extent of such a mandate, the accountability of the representatives of the States before the (national) Parliament, and the control of such Parliament on the position of the State before the international organization and on the measures to be implemented. Otherwise, the internationalization may not simply deprive the Parliaments of their legitimate constitutional functions.

This is not an impediment but an additional requirement to the efforts of improving legitimacy strategies at the international level by international organizations. Movements towards improvement have been developed in the last few years, but it is obvious that there is room for development. A potential division between input and output legitimacy could clarify the respective positions of different international organizations. This could be done by attributing a leading role in the decision-making process to the institutions more respectful of the representativity of the different States at the international level. At the same time, the output legitimacy could be ensured, maintaining the final decisions of the process in the hands of the institutions with demonstrated technical capability and knowledge to provide the necessary normative outcomes. Those should be produced in line with the extent of the mandate given to international organizations and the appropriate solutions that respond to a sufficient international consensus. Mechanisms for improving coordination, transparency and procedural rules for ensuring the participation of States and stakeholders on equal footing should be considered. These technical improvements would certainly reinforce the political support at the highest level that requests the update of the international tax paradigms for the twenty-first century.

CHAPTER 7

Citizens' Initiatives in Tax Matters: A Glimpse of EU Law and French Constitutional Law

Daniel Gutmann

§7.1 INTRODUCTION

The debate about the relationship between taxation and democracy has considerably gained in intensity in recent years due to the conjunction of several trends: international agreements reached at the level of the OECD and the Inclusive Framework are being transposed in many countries without serious control exercised by domestic parliaments; the content of tax legislation borrows more and more accounting concepts and rules that have been set up by organisations without any kind of democratic legitimacy; the European Union behaves very much as a follower of initiatives conceived in a broader forum; and, last but not least, modern democracies are becoming increasingly fragile, both because of a rising lack of interest of citizens in the participation in the democratic process and because of the growing importance of extremist political parties with little culture of political debate.

Against this background, the emergence of new forms of citizenship is particularly interesting to observe, in particular in a legal field such as taxation, where most constitutional systems protect taxpayer consent as a fundamental value. Among these new forms of institutionalised citizenship, the idea that citizens could play an active role, independently from Parliament or in support of legislative authorities, is slowing catching on and producing concrete results. This is the topic that I would like to address in this short contribution to the *Liber Amicorum* for Peter Essers.

The choice of this topic comes as no surprise for anyone who is familiar with Peter Essers' writings, activities and personality. In addition to his activities in the Dutch Senate, Peter is deeply engaged in research on the legitimacy of taxes from a historical and legal perspective. His writings on these matters are exceptionally well documented and display truly humanist qualities that should serve as an example for current and future generations of tax lawyers. In particular, his ability to deal with extremely technical topics without losing sight of the essential, namely the need to make sure that taxation respects and enhances the fundamental rights of the citizens, is a source of inspiration for us all. Besides, and if I may introduce a personal note in this chapter, I would like to say how much I owe Peter in many respects, not all of them of a legal nature. As a newcomer in the international tax arena at the beginning of the 2000s, I had the privilege to meet Peter regularly at the EUCOTAX Wintercourse and to learn a lot from his way of coordinating together with Eric Kemmeren a challenging program with constant benevolence towards his colleagues and students. As a member of the European Association of Tax Law Professors, I also attended several congresses chaired by Peter in his capacity as chairman of the Academic Committee and admired his way of making sure that everyone could have a say and contribute to the international dialogue between academics. When I succeeded him in his position, I did nothing but try to walk in his footsteps. I even praised him for offering me an entire year free of work: this was before the 2021 Congress of the association on 'History and Taxation: the Dialectical Relationship between Taxation and the Political Balance of Power'.[1] Peter was the general reporter, and I soon understood that everything would be so perfectly handled by him that I would have nothing to do but approve his scientific choices which drove to a hallmark congress of the European Association of Tax Law Professors. For all these reasons, this chapter is only a very small gift compared to what I received from Peter.

As mentioned above, the topic of this chapter is about citizens' initiatives in tax matters. It finds its roots in an apparent theoretical paradox: while a democratic deficit is often deplored in tax matters, this diagnosis drives most authors to call for a renewed role of Parliament but rarely for an increase in direct participation of citizens.

A lot has been written on the need to provide national parliaments with more significant resources in terms of expertise, in order to allow them to exercise their legislative function in a highly technical field.[2] At the EU level, there is also a lot of literature on the ways by which more democracy could be introduced in the tax legislation process through exceptions to the unanimity principle or through greater powers given to the European Parliament.[3] However, there is much less literature on

1. The congress book has been published by IBFD, EATLP International Tax Series, Vol. 20, 2022.
2. Just to give examples drawn from the French experience, it is worth mentioning that a recent report published by two members of Parliament suggests to improve the level of information of expertise of the finance committee and the foreign affairs committee of both chambers of Parliament in tax matters, particularly with respect to ongoing negotiations at international level: *see* Éric Coquerel & Jean-René Cazeneuve, *Rapport d'information No. 1538 sur les différentiels de fiscalité entre entreprises,* Proposal No. 11 (Assemblée Nationale, 19 July 2023). Interesting proposals may also be found in a book written by a former Director of tax legislation at the Ministry of Finance (Michel Taly, *Les coulisses de la politique fiscale,* PUF, 2016) and in another parliamentary report of 2018 (Bénédicte Peyrol, *Rapport d'information No. 1236 sur l'évasion fiscale internationale des entreprises*).
3. A complete survey of current issues and literature may be found in *The Power to Tax in Europe, Swedish Studies in European Law,* Vol. 14 (Johan Lindholm & Anders Hultqvist eds, Hart Publishing, 2023). A French Ph.D. thesis has also been devoted recently to these questions: Marie

the idea that direct taxpayer participation in the legislating process could be one of the ways to improve the current situation.[4] This can be explained by the intrinsic shortcomings of participatory democracy: citizens' lack of understanding of the technical aspects of the subject, political bias in the voting process independently of the topic at stake, etc.

The relative lack of interest in literature about citizens' initiatives in tax matters may also be explained by the scarcity of the legal means by which citizens can actually play a role in this process. However, scarcity does not coincide with vacuum. Citizens' initiatives are handled by specific rules of EU law which may apply to taxes. Besides, some national constitutions may provide a possibility to organise referenda in tax matters: while this seems to be very rare, this exists in France.

Here are two examples to set the scene.

On 11 July 2023, the European Commission published an 'implementing decision' on the request for registration of the European Citizens' Initiative (hereinafter referred to as 'ECI') entitled 'taxing great wealth to finance the ecological and social transition'.[5]

A few months earlier, on 25 October 2022, the French Constitutional Court had to deal with a draft law submitted by more than one-fifth of the members of Parliament which aimed at organising a referendum on the creation of an additional contribution on the windfall profits derived by large corporations. The Court came to the conclusion that the content of this draft legislation did not meet the constitutional requirements that allowed to proceed with the referendum, but it did not rule out the possibility of a referendum being held in tax matters.[6]

These examples are very different, in particular with respect to the role played by citizens in the legislative process. While the ECI provides European citizens with a possibility to invite the Commission to initiate a process which will then follow the ordinary course of EU legislation, the French Constitution organises a more complex process. As we will *see* below,[7] Parliament members must be supported by a sufficient number of voters within a certain time frame, and if this is the case, there is still a possibility for Parliament to examine the draft law without any referendum being organised. It is only in the absence of such Parliament action that a referendum must be organised by the President of the Republic.

Notwithstanding the significant differences between the European and French mechanisms, there is a common feature in these two examples, which is the direct involvement of citizens at some point of the legislative process. Let me therefore

---

Hemery, *Citoyenneté fiscale et droit de l'Union européenne. De la protection européenne du contribuable national au consentement de l'impôt européen* (th. Paris-Est Créteil, 2023).

4. *See*, however, for instance, Ariel Jurow Kleiman, *Reaction Paper to 'Tax Limits and the Future of Local Democracy'*, 133 Harvard Law Review 1884 (2020); also, from an economic perspective, Benno Torgler, *Direct Democracy Matters: Tax Morale and Political Participation: Proceedings. Annual Conference on Taxation and Minutes of the Annual Meeting of the National Tax Association*, 95 National Tax Association 50 (2002).
5. Decision C(2023) 4751 final. One of the members of the citizens' committee for this proposal is the famous French economist Thomas Piketty.
6. French Constitutional Court (*Conseil constitutionnel*), Decision n° 2022-3 RIP, 25 October 2022.
7. *See* §7.2.

provide for some background explanation of these two examples and some comments on their legal characteristics.

§7.2 EUROPEAN CITIZENS' INITIATIVES AND TAXATION UNDER EU LAW

The ECI has been introduced in EU law by the Lisbon Treaty. As a 'fact sheet on the European Union' published in 2023 by the European Parliament puts it, the ECI 'is an important instrument of participatory democracy in the EU'. The legal basis of the ECI is to be found in Article 11(4) of the Treaty on European Union (TEU) which provides that 'not less than one million citizens who are nationals of a significant number of Member States may take the initiative of inviting the European Commission, within the framework of its powers, to submit any appropriate proposal on matters where citizens consider that a legal act of the Union is required for the purpose of implementing the Treaties'. In accordance with Article 24(1) of the Treaty on the Functioning of the European Union (TFEU), several regulations have been enacted to implement this procedure.[8]

In short, the ECI works in the following way: a citizens' committee must be created by at least seven people who decide to support the proposal and collect statements of support from EU citizens. This committee must register the initiative with the European Commission which has to decide whether the procedural requirements have been met and whether the proposal falls within the framework of the Commission's powers to submit a proposal for a legal act. The latter condition is logical: since the ECI is nothing else but an invitation to the Commission to submit a proposal, it is essential to check from the outset that the content of the proposal can indeed be the subject of a future legal act of the EU. Once the registration process has ended, the organisers can start collecting statements of support. An ECI will be successful only if within twelve months from registration, one million statements of support have been gathered from at least one-quarter of the Member States, with an additional requirement that for each Member State, there is a sufficient number of statements.[9] After these statements have been checked by national authorities and the initiative has been submitted to the Commission, the group of organisers is given the opportunity to present the initiative at a public hearing held by the European Parliament which then assesses the political support for the initiative. The Commission is also expected to make up its mind on the proposal, and it must 'set out in a communication its legal and political conclusions on the initiative, the action it intends to take, if any, and its reasons for taking or not taking action'.[10] Lastly, the European Parliament must scrutinise the actions taken by the Commission in response to the initiative. This short description of the ECI procedure shows that it offers the possibility to EU citizens to stimulate the decision-making process at the EU level. Citizens are not called to vote in

8. Regulation (EU) nos 211/2011 and 2019/788.
9. Regulation (EU) 2019/788, Art. 3 and annex I.
10. Regulation (EU) 2019/788, Art. 15.

any way on the proposal, but their support can be the starting point of a future directive or other legal act.

Experience shows that for the time being, there is a very low number of successful ECIs,[11] none of them related to taxation.[12] However, this does not mean that no ECI has been launched in tax matters. One was about VAT: 'Green VAT - An EU Green VAT to stimulate sustainable and eco-friendly products and services.' It has been registered by the Commission[13] but only collected 4,379 statements of support after one year. Another one was entitled 'Ending the aviation fuel tax exemption in Europe'[14] and collected 75,301 statements of support, which was again not enough. Lastly, an ongoing ECI is about the creation of a European 'excess wealth tax' that would contribute to the Union's own resources. According to its organisers, the revenue generated by this tax would make it possible to amplify and perpetuate European ecological and social transition and development cooperation policies.

This last proposal raises interesting issues with respect to the legal possibility of the European Commission to start legislative action on such a topic. Is there really a legal ground allowing EU legislation on wealth taxation? According to the text of the proposal, enacting a European wealth tax perfectly falls within the scope of Article 115 TFEU because 'national differences in the taxation of the ultra-rich are likely to fuel increased tax competition within the Union and create distortions in the internal market'. Another point along the same line, which reveals the technical and political skills of the organisers, is that the proposal does not rely on Article 115 TFEU only. By inviting the Commission to propose an amendment to the rules regarding the EU's own resources,[15] the proposal offers a complementary legal ground available for legislative action, namely Article 311(3) TFEU. More broadly, the implementing decision published by the Commission even mentions that the text of the initiative makes a reference to the aims of the Union as they appear in Article 3 TEU: the Union's aim is indeed to 'promote the well-being of its peoples',[16] 'combat social exclusion [and]

11. In order to understand this, *see* M. Ballesteros, E. Canetta and A. Zaciu, *European Citizens' Initiative – First Lessons of Implementation, Study Requested by the Committee on Petitions and by the Committee on Constitutional Affairs of the European Parliament*, PE 509.982, 2014.
12. The Fact Sheet mentioned above indicates that nine initiatives have reached the requisite number of signatures: Right2Watger, One of Us, Stop Vivisection, Ban Glyphosate, Minority SafePack, End the Cage Age, Save Bees and farmers, Stop-Finning – Stop the Trade and Save Cruelty-Free Cosmetics.
13. ECI (2021) 000011.
14. ECI (2019) 000009. Interestingly, this ECI was coupled with a petition filed before the European Parliament in accordance with Art. 227 TFEU which provides that 'any citizen of the Union, and any natural or legal person residing or having its registered office in a Member State, shall have the right to address, individually or in association with other citizens or persons, a petition to the European Parliament on a matter which comes within the Union's fields of activity and which affects him, her or it directly'. It gave rise to several exchanges of views with the European Commission which, in the end, considered that the citizens' message had been heard, as part of the Fit for fifty-five package included a removal of the current tax exemption of aviation in the context of the revision of energy taxation in the EU. The description of the petition and the Commission replies can be found in the European Parliament Committee on Petitions' Notice to members of 22 July 2022, CM\1261450EN.docx.
15. Notably Decision 2020/2053 of 14 December 2020.
16. Article 3(1) TEU.

promote social justice and protection'.[17] Against this background, the Commission's implementing decision states that 'no part of the initiative is manifestly outside the scope of its powers under which it may submit a proposal for a legal act of the Union for the purpose of implementing the Treaties'.[18]

This conclusion deserves some observations. First, the question of whether national differences in the taxation of the 'ultra-rich' effectively distort the internal market is not easy to answer in an objective manner. Second, one may wonder to what extent Article 3 TEU should come into play when it comes to deciding whether EU institutions can legislate on tax matters. The aims set out in this provision are so incredibly broad that virtually any legal action in any tax field could be connected to them. Third, one may wonder whether enacting EU legislation on wealth taxation in the name of social justice is compatible with the principle of subsidiarity of EU law which rules out Union intervention when an issue can be dealt with effectively by Member States themselves. By endorsing the possibility of a purely European wealth tax, the Commission implicitly seems to suggest that the objective of social justice through personal taxation cannot be 'sufficiently achieved'[19] by the Member States themselves and that tax justice is to be pursued globally rather than locally. This may be true to a certain extent but probably goes far beyond the dominant view among many Member States. Lastly, the goal to increase the Union's own resources does not seem to suffice to bypass the requirements of Article 115 TFEU regarding legislation in the field of direct taxes.

The stakes are clear. On the one hand, it is certainly desirable to foster direct participation of European citizens in the legislative process of the EU. On the other hand, this political objective should not drive the European Commission to uphold an overly bold interpretation of the articles of the Treaties regarding the material field of EU legislation.[20]

Similar questions regarding the extent to which citizens' interventions in the legislating process are admissible have arisen in the French constitutional context.

§7.3 REFERENDUM, TAXATION AND FRENCH CONSTITUTIONAL LAW

As mentioned in the introduction of this chapter, the recourse to referendum in tax matters seems to be extremely rare in comparative law, with the notable exception of Switzerland. In several countries, there is even a constitutional ban to organise a referendum on a tax- or budget-related proposal.[21]

17. Article 3(3) TEU.
18. Implementing decision, point 6.
19. Borrowing the wording of Art. 5(3) TEU.
20. One can note, however, that the Commission seems to limit itself to checking that the proposal submitted by the organisers of the ECI is not 'manifestly outside the scope of its powers'. This seems to suggest that the control exercised in the preliminary phase of the ECI would require further analysis if the ECI would be successful.
21. *See* in particular Art. 75 of the Italian Constitution, Art. 42(6) of the Danish Constitution and Art. 115. 4(b) of the Portuguese Constitution.

The debate on the possibility to use referendum in tax matters has nevertheless gained importance in France recently when a significant number of members of Parliament submitted to the Constitutional Court a proposal with a view to organising a referendum on the creation of an additional contribution on the windfall profits derived by large corporations.

The legal background of this proposal is the following. Article 11 paragraph 1 of the French Constitution provides that the President of the Republic, acting on a proposal from the Government during the sessions or on a joint proposal from the two Assemblies, may submit to a referendum 'any draft law concerning the organisation of the public authorities, reforms relating to the nation's economic, social or environmental policy and the public services that contribute to it'. This is the 'classical' procedure of the referendum in the French Constitution which has existed for decades.

Another form of referendum, called 'shared-initiative referendum',[22] has been introduced in the French Constitution by a constitutional law of 23 July 2008 which entered into force on 1 January 2015. It is described in Article 11 paragraph 3 of the Constitution which states that 'a referendum on any of the matters referred to in the first paragraph may be held on the initiative of one fifth of the members of Parliament, supported by one tenth of the electors entered on the electoral rolls. This initiative shall take the form of a draft law and may not have as its object the repeal of a legislative provision that has been in force for less than one year'.[23]

The Constitutional Court is tasked with controlling that the object of the referendum meets the requirements established by Article 11. It must also check that no provision of the draft law is contrary to the Constitution.

If the Constitutional Court comes to the conclusion that the draft law complies with the Constitution, a period of nine months is opened during which one-tenth of the electors (amounting to approximately 4.8 million individuals in France) must express their support, possibly by electronic means.

Assuming that the draft law indeed gets sufficient support, the referendum does not automatically take place. In principle, it is up to the chambers of Parliament to examine the draft law. It is only if the two chambers of Parliament have not examined the draft law within a period of six months that the President of the Republic must organise the referendum.

In the case which gave rise to the decision of 25 October 2012, the draft law established a tax on windfall profits[24] which was supposed to apply to corporations with a turnover exceeding EUR 750 million. The tax was intended to be provisory until 2025. The Constitutional Court therefore had to decide whether the establishment of such a tax could be regarded as a 'reform relating to the nation's economic, social or environmental policy'.

22. *Référendum d'initiative partagée* in French.
23. The implementation rules of Art. 11 of the Constitution are laid down by an 'organic law' of 6 December 2013.
24. Windfall profits were defined in the draft law as profits in excess of 1.25 times the average taxable profits for 2017, 2018 and 2019.

The question was a hard one, as the preparatory work of the constitutional act which broadened the scope of the referendum to such reforms was very ambiguous.[25] Academic literature was also quite divided regarding the question of whether tax legislation falls within the scope of Article 11 of the Constitution.[26]

In the end, the Court came to a negative conclusion. After having considered the features of the proposed tax, the Court considered that 'its sole effect is to add to the State budget through the introduction until 31 December 2025 of a measure that merely increases the existing level of taxation on the profits of certain companies. It does not therefore concern, within the meaning of Article 11 of the Constitution, a reform relating to the nation's economic policy'. The Court also took the view that the draft law's object was not related to any other substantive matter listed in Article 11 of the Constitution. This was the end of the story for this particular tax.

Several lessons can be drawn from this decision. First, a minor amendment of a tax legislation does not constitutive a 'reform'. As the official commentary of the Court's decision puts it, a reform is a 'sufficiently important modification of the structure of taxes'.[27] Second, a revenue-raising contribution does not by itself relate to 'economic policy'. Third, however, the Constitutional Court did not rule out that a tax reform could be related to the nation's economic policy.[28] One can therefore think that a future draft reform related to taxation will pass the 'economic policy test' if it bears on structural features of the French tax system or if it aims at changing the behaviour of economic actors. For instance, a carbon tax with an explicit behavioural objective could probably be connected to the 'economic policy' or to the 'environmental policy' of the nation.[29]

The balance reached by the Constitutional Court between a systematic refusal and a conditional acceptance of referendum in tax matters leaves a lot of space open for discussion of hypothetical cases. In 2018, for instance, a discussion took place (outside Parliament) on the question of whether a referendum could be organised in order to restore the wealth tax in its form prior to Mr Macron's election in 2017 as French President (namely as a comprehensive tax on all assets owned by high net-worth taxpayers, not only on immovable property). Would a change in the base of a specific tax be regarded as a 'reform'? Bets are on! And assuming that it would, would it relate to the nation's 'economic or social policy'? Here again, one might hesitate. There is no doubt that wealth taxation triggers important economic events, insofar as it deters

25. This concept of 'reform relating to the nation's economic, social or environmental policy' appeared in the French Constitution after a constitutional revision of 4 August 1995.

26. *See* Romain Rambaud, *Le Conseil constitutionnel n'écarte pas les lois fiscales du champ du référendum, L'Actualité Juridique. Droit Administratif* 2023, pp. 40 et seq. and the literature cited.

27. In France, every decision of the Constitutional Court is accompanied by the publication on the Court's website of a commentary which is drafted by the legal department of the Court. This commentary is a precious tool to understand the actual meaning and scope of the Court's decisions.

28. This point is also clarified by the decision's commentary on the website of the Court.

29. Along this line, *see* Martin Collet, *Référendum d'initiative partagée (RIP) et fiscalité: l'impôt peut-il être un outil de politique économique, Revue française de droit administratif* 2022, pp. 1177 et seq.

natural persons with high net worth from establishing their tax residence in France and stimulates transfers of residence abroad in order to avoid taxation. However, the incidental (and accepted) economic effects of the wealth tax are not to be confused with the 'economic policy' of the nation. Would it, however, be possible to argue that a net wealth tax has to do with 'social policy'? This is a more open question. Wealth taxation is undisputedly designed to achieve more equality between taxpayers and is one tool among many to organise redistribution of wealth among them. However, failing a clear definition of 'social policy', the solution cannot be held certain.

These interpretation issues around the notions of 'economic policy' and 'social policy' reveal a fundamental ambiguity as to the desirable scope of the referendum. Clearly, if those concepts are interpreted broadly, and if future proponents of referenda use their open texture in a clever strategic way, the scope of the referendum in tax matters will increase considerably. If any tax that has something to do with social equity or redistribution is deemed to belong to 'social policy', there is virtually no limit to tax referenda. If any tax that has something to do with the protection of the environment (for instance, the creation of a new tax credit for expenses incurred by individuals in low-energy consumption devices) is deemed to belong to 'environmental policy', the conclusion is identical.

In 2022, some members of Parliament suggested changing the wording of Article 11 of the Constitution so as to clarify that 'tax policy' falls within its scope.[30] This proposal, which has not been discussed (yet) by Parliament, would help solve part of the interpretation issues described above, but the desirability of such an evolution is obviously subject to discussion.

§7.4 CONCLUSION

The description of the EU and French state of positive law regarding citizens' direct participation in the tax legislation process drives to similar questions and observations.

To date, European Citizens' Initiatives and referenda play a marginal role in EU law and French constitutional law on tax matters. However, the potential of these instruments is high, and it is pretty clear that legal arguments are available to develop them. The extent to which they will be used in the future highly depends on the audacity of the Commission on the one hand and on the Constitutional Court on the other hand.

We live in interesting times in which traditional patterns of EU law and constitutional law are being questioned. The longstanding idea that EU tax legislation should remain exceptional and that only a narrow interpretation of Articles 113 and 115 of the TFEU should prevail is challenged. The debate about whether the European institutions have exceeded their powers in tax matters has never been as intense as it is today. Legal inventiveness to justify the EU's initiatives in tax matters is also at an all-time high, as demonstrated by the use of Article 122 TFEU to justify the introduction

30. This proposal is an amendment (no. 2) to a constitutional draft law (no. 291) presented on 6 October 2022 at the National Assembly by a significant number of left-wing members of Parliament.

of a temporary solidarity contribution on the energy sector.[31] Against this background and in light of the implementing decision taken by the Commission about the European excess wealth tax ECI, the future of ECIs in tax matters pretty much depends on the interpretation of the articles of the EU treaties which deal with the material scope of EU law. Let us hope that the importance of participatory democracy will not be instrumentalised to strengthen, albeit indirectly, the Commission's prerogatives in tax matters. If the current balance of powers between Member States and EU authorities is found to be unsatisfactory by the former, let us have a democratic debate on the need to change it, but let us not distort the meaning of the existing EU legislation.

In domestic law too, things are changing. Parliament is no longer the sole master of tax legislation and cannot ignore the importance of a growing number of competitors: international and EU institutions on the one hand and citizens on the other hand.

This evolution is partly due to the globalisation of the tax legislation process and to the need to give back some direct power to citizens. It is also the outcome of a fundamental technological move. There was a time when it was necessary for the people's representatives to meet in person in order for a collective will of citizens to materialise. Those days are gone. Citizens can, by moving a finger on a screen, express their support or rejection of a given idea without having to meet physically. Digital technologies are therefore depriving Parliament of its logistical legitimacy, so to speak.

At this point, one must probably come back to the roots of democracy and ask fundamental questions. Do we believe that a true debate in Parliament is worth more than a 'debate' on social networks? Do we believe that tax legislation is done in a better way by Parliament than by individuals and why? Is the particularly technical character of tax legislation compatible with participatory democracy and to what extent? Is there a risk that increasing the use of referendum in tax matters would jeopardise budgetary balance and how could this risk be prevented?

This is just a short sample of the many questions that arise when one starts thinking about the development of participatory democracy in tax matters. As always, when legal academics sense that a major change is about to occur, they are torn between their natural conservative tendency and their concern to keep pace with the evolution of society without upsetting fundamental institutional balances. Everything is a matter of balance, a fundamental lesson from Peter Essers.

31. Council Regulation (EU) 2022/1854 of 6 October 2022 on an emergency intervention to address high energy prices.

CHAPTER 8

Ten Years into the BEPS Project: A Snapshot of Legitimacy and Justice in International Tax Lawmaking

Rita Szudoczky

§8.1 INTRODUCTION

Peter Essers is a pioneer in many ways in our field of science and has always been ahead of his time writing about topics that became headlines several years later in international tax literature and tax policy. Therefore, it is not a surprise that the topic of this chapter, which Peter started to research more than a decade ago, is one of the most momentous subjects of current international tax discourse. The EUCOTAX program, Peter's signature academic project that he and Eric Kemmeren initiated thirty years ago and that gave several generations of enthusiastic, ambitious and talented international tax professionals to the world, benefitted much from his foresight. Many of the general topics of the past EUCOTAX Wintercourses uncover Peter's fingerprint and, in particular, his interest in tax policy and topics on the fringe of taxation and other disciplines like political science, political history, philosophy and economy. 'Tax Planning and Corporate Social Responsibility' (2008/09), 'Principle of Equality in Taxation' (2009/10), 'Taxation and Global Mobility' (2012/13), 'Fairness and Taxation' (2013/14), 'Impact of the Digital Economy on Taxation' (2014/15), 'Tax Autonomy in an Era of Conflicting Political Goals' (2017/18), 'Sustainable Taxation and Developing Countries' (2018/19); 'Taxpayers' Rights in the 21st Century' (2021/22), 'Legitimacy and Tax Rules' (2022/23) and 'Tax Reforms Between Success and Failure – Past, Present, Future' (2023/24); these are some of the topics that we, the EUCOTAX staff, and our students were working on in the past years and decades. It has been a real pleasure and an exceptional privilege to work with Peter – alongside all the other excellent colleagues – in the EUCOTAX program and learn from his forward-looking thinking, his belief in the importance of research and his ability to make tax policy-oriented research accessible and doable for students.

In this chapter, I would like to revisit Peter's article on 'International Tax Justice Between Machiavelli and Habermas',[1] which he published in 2014 based on the Klaus Vogel Lecture that he delivered in 2013 at the Vienna Institute for Austrian and International Tax Law that is now my academic home. In the article, Peter examined the question of how international tax justice is determined in the (then) existing political, institutional, governance and social structure and to what extent international tax justice is shaped in a democratic process based on a true dialogue between all stakeholders. He concluded, *inter alia*, that: (i) the concept of international tax justice is mainly determined by supranational organizations, like the G8, G20, OECD, and European Union, and these organizations lack sufficient democratic legitimacy, and, in addition, they do not represent all relevant countries and citizens; (ii) national parliaments and citizens are not sufficiently involved in the process; (iii) the development of the concept of international tax justice is not based on a true dialogue between all stakeholders, and the debate is polluted by power play and deception. He emphasized that to ensure the legitimacy and effectiveness of the measures proposed by the G20, OECD and the European Union, it is important that these measures are not imposed unilaterally on countries and taxpayers, but they are a result of true democratic deliberations and a decision-making process with and within these countries along the ideas of Habermas' deliberative democracy.

What follows is an examination of the question of what has changed with regard to legitimacy, democracy and justice in the domain of international taxation since 2013 when the BEPS Project had just started. What have been the changes or improvements, if any, to the governance structure and decision-making procedures in international tax law that help attain tax justice? Far from a comprehensive examination, it is a rather selective – and likely – subjective selection of relevant developments as well as their assessment in international tax literature where the critical sounds are far more numerous now than ten years ago when Peter formulated his insightful criticism.

§8.2 REPRESENTATION AND PARTICIPATION OF STATES IN INTERNATIONAL TAX LAWMAKING

Peter's first criticism concerns the international organizations that play the leading role in international tax standard-setting and norm-shaping, and specifically, the deficient legitimacy of these organizations in terms of both representation and democratic decision-making. In short, the criticism relates to the input legitimacy of international tax lawmaking. Input legitimacy is defined as 'that quality of a rule which derives from a perception on the part of those to whom it is addressed that it has come into being in accordance with right process'.[2]

1. Peter Essers, *International Tax Justice Between Machiavelli and Habermas*, 68 Bulletin for International Taxation 2 (2014) DOI: 10.1017/9781780684734.012.
2. Thomas M. Franck, *Legitimacy in the International System*, 82 The American Journal of International Law 705, 706 (1988) DOI: 10.2307/2203510.

Since 2013, there have been important changes as far as the relevant institutional players in international tax law are concerned. While at that time the OECD was the undisputed quasi-legislator in international tax law, in 2016, the OECD/G20 Inclusive Framework on Base Erosion and Profit Shifting ('Inclusive Framework') was set up, taking over the role of developing new international tax standards and monitoring the implementation of measures recommended under the first round of the BEPS Project. The creation of the Inclusive Framework was a response to the growing criticism that the OECD as an exclusive club of rich countries, which was not representative of all the countries to which international tax standards set by the OECD apply, dominated the shaping of the international tax system. This led to biases in substantive tax standards in favour of developed countries at the detriment of developing countries, in particular, with regard to tax standards governing the interstate allocation of taxing rights.[3] The Inclusive Framework is regularly described in the OECD and Inclusive Framework documents as a forum where all countries interested in joining the BEPS Project can participate on an 'equal footing'.[4] Currently, the Inclusive Framework has more than 140 members and became, in fact, the core policy- and norm-setting body in international taxation. The creation of the Inclusive Framework has thus remedied to a certain extent the problem that the relevant organizations in international tax lawmaking (OECD and G20) were not representative of all the countries which were subject to the international tax regime.[5] However, being formally represented in the relevant organization 'on an equal footing' does not necessarily ensure substantive equality in terms of participation in the decision-making.

Many words have been spoken in recent years in academic commentary on the Inclusive Framework's flaws of legitimacy. It has been pointed out that the participation of developing countries in international tax policy through the Inclusive Framework was initially confined to implementation while having been left out of the agenda-setting.[6] Even if developing countries were fully part of the agenda-setting and

3. From the abundance of academic literature, *see*, for example, Irma J. Mosquera Valderrama, *Legitimacy and the Making of International Tax Law: The Challenges of Multilateralism*, 7 World Tax Journal (2015); Tarcísio D. Magalhães, *What Is Really Wrong with Global Tax Governance and How to Properly Fix It*, 10 World Tax Journal (2018); Linda Brosens & Jasper Bossuyt, *Legitimacy in International Tax Law-Making: Can the OECD Remain the Guardian of Open Tax Norms?*, 12 World Tax Journal (2020); Ivan Ozai, *Two Accounts of International Tax Justice*, 33 Canadian Journal of Law and Jurisprudence 317 (2020); Yariv Brauner, *Agreement? What Agreement? The 8 October 2021, OECD Statement in Perspective*, 50 Intertax (2022) DOI: 10.54648/taxi2022001; Cees Peeters, *The Legitimacy of the OECD's Work on Pillar Two: An Analysis of the Overconfidence in a 'Devilish Logic'*, 51 Intertax (2023) DOI: 10.54648/taxi2023057; Werner Haslehner, *The Costs of Pillar 2: Legitimacy, Legality, and Lock-In*, 51 Intertax (2023) DOI: 10.54648/taxi2023066; Sigrid Hemels, *Tax autonomy from a Member State Perspective: are we faced with a democratic deficit?*, Working paper for the 17th GREIT Conference, Maastricht University 5-6 October 2023 (forthcoming in the next volume of the GREIT book series).
4. *See* https://www.oecd.org/tax/beps/about/.
5. At the same time, the African Group Input to the Secretary-General's Report on Promotion of Inclusive and Effective International Tax Cooperation at the United Nations points out that the Inclusive Framework still excludes over a third of the world's countries, including most least developed countries (LDCs), *see* para. 10 at: https://financing.desa.un.org/sites/default/files/2023-03/African%20Group_Input%20Tax%20Report.pdf.
6. Ivan Ozai, *Two Accounts of International Tax Justice*, 33 Canadian Journal of Law and Jurisprudence 317, 319 (2020) DOI: 10.1017/cjlj.2020.8.

decision-making in the Inclusive Framework, structural inequalities, asymmetries in power as well as the difficulty in changing the entrenched international tax concepts and principles that tend to favour developed countries prevent them from effectively pursuing their own agenda and interest in international tax policy decisions.[7] In addition, the fact that developing countries have less experience and less technical capacities in international tax negotiations, coupled with the lack of financial and human resources, renders the equal participation of developing countries in international tax decisions illusory.

Overall, the diagnosis provided by academia is that the current international tax system displays serious deficits in input legitimacy, that is, participatory or democratic legitimacy[8] as well as throughput legitimacy which refers to governance processes, that is, accountability, transparency, inclusiveness and responsiveness.[9] Contrarily, Ruth Mason as a dissenting voice in the choir of criticism pointed out that the BEPS Project did have positive effects on international tax law to the extent that it 'changed participants, institutions, agenda, norms, and forms of international tax cooperation',[10] which may well be characterized as transformative. At the same time, she observed that the greatest change brought about by BEPS with regard to participation is the growing weight of emerging economies (BRICS) in international tax discussions and decisions, while smaller and poorer countries are still incapable of influencing the latter.[11]

As to the solutions for the legitimacy problems of international tax law stemming from its institutional structure, academia offers a range of suggestions. Ideas for creating an international tax organization or global tax body with universal membership and supranational legislative and enforcement powers have been present in international tax discussions for a long time.[12] The discussion intensified during the second round of the BEPS Project that envisaged the most substantial reform of the international tax system in its hundred-year history, thus increasing the stakes as to the question who should be in charge of such reform. Some recent proposals would set up the global tax body within the UN;[13] others propose setting up a whole new organization for this purpose.[14] Contrarily, other commentators warn against constructing another formal legal coercive structure aimed at enforcing ostensibly rational technical

7. Ozai, *supra* n. 6, at 321; Tarcísio D. Magalhães, *What Is Really Wrong with Global Tax Governance and How to Properly Fix It*, 10 World Tax Journal 500, 508-510 (2018).
8. Tarcísio D. Magalhães, *What Is Really Wrong with Global Tax Governance and How to Properly Fix It*, 10 World Tax Journal 500, 527 (2018).
9. Linda Brosens & Jasper Bossuyt, *Legitimacy in International Tax Law-Making: Can the OECD Remain the Guardian of Open Tax Norms?*, 12 World Tax Journal, 351 (2020).
10. Ruth Mason, *The Transformation of International Tax*, 114 The American Journal of International Law 353, 381 (2020) DOI: 10.1017/ajil.2020.33.
11. Mason, *supra* n. 10, at 383.
12. *See*, for example, Vito Tanzi, *Is There a Need for a World Tax Organization?*, In: *The Economics of Globalization: Policy Perspectives from Public Economics* 173-186 (Cambridge University Press 1999).
13. Reuven Avi-Yonah & Haiyan Xu, *Evaluating BEPS: A Reconsideration of the Benefits Principle and Proposal for UN Oversight*, 6 HBLR 185, 210 (2016).
14. Natalia Quiñones, *Beyond the 2-Pillar Solution: A Case for a Global Income Tax and the Creation of the International Tax Organization*, 51 Intertax, 324, 331 (2023).

principles in international tax relations, as such approach would merely replicate the legitimacy deficits of the current system.[15] Instead, along the lines of Habermas' deliberative democracy promoted by Peter in his 2014 article, this proposal advocates for a bottom-up approach whereby an international tax regime is built on discursive practices of decision-making at all levels of international tax governance. In order to ensure the legitimacy of such regime, it is crucial that mechanisms of political participation and dialogue are developed beyond the border of the nation state, aiming at the democratization of the global system of tax governance.[16] Yet another string of arguments consider that regional forums could provide an alternative institutional arrangement for developing countries as it may be easier to align the interest and cooperate within a smaller group and then effectively represent such interest towards developed countries.[17] Creatively and differently from others, Alison Christians suggests that international tax governance should take the form of a 'lottocracy', that is, a system of democratic governance by lottery.[18] This would mean that those entrusted with leadership in international tax governance matters would not be appointed by the OECD or its member countries but chosen by a lottery from a pool of candidates by way of chance. According to Christians, 'selection by lot could improve decision-making, reduce the entrenchment of historical factions, and instill a sense of legitimacy in a process that involves a worldwide polity'.[19]

§8.3 THE UN'S PLEA FOR AN ENHANCED ROLE IN INTERNATIONAL TAX LAWMAKING

Apart from the clash of opinions in academia, we are witnessing an actual institutional battle between the UN and the OECD for the leading role in international tax lawmaking. This can be seen as a direct consequence of the new form of tax competition that emerged in the second round of the BEPS Project: 'competition for revenue' as coined by Hugh Ault.[20] While the pretense under which the current fundamental reform of the international tax system is carried on is the need to find solutions for the taxation of the digitalized economy, it is evident that the reform was necessitated by the long-term dissatisfaction of many countries with the prevailing allocation of taxing rights between residence and source which overly limits the taxing right of source countries over the international tax base and thus their share from global tax revenues. Competition for revenue results in an institutional row as developing countries and emerging economies feel that they cannot participate on an

15. Magalhães, *supra* n. 8, at 531 et seq.
16. Magalhães, *supra* n. 8.
17. Ozai *supra* n. 5, at 320.
18. Allison Christians, *A Wish for the Future of International Tax Cooperation*, Tax Notes International (2022).
19. Christians, *supra* n. 18.
20. Hugh. J. Ault, *Tax Competition and Tax Cooperation: A Survey and Reassessment*, in: *International Taxation in a Changing Landscape*, in: *Liber Amicorum in Honour of Bertil Wiman* 1-14 (Kluwer 2019).

equal footing in the decision-making on substantive international tax standards under the current institutional setting of the Inclusive Framework.

The latest development in this row is the Report issued in August 2023 by the Secretary General of the UN on the 'Promotion of inclusive and effective international tax cooperation at the United Nations'.[21] The Secretary General Report concluded that the substantive aspect of inclusive and effective international tax cooperation is not met by the guidance and standards issued by the OECD – more precisely, the Inclusive Framework and the Global Forum on Transparency and Exchange of Information for Tax Purposes – as the latter are not effectively implemented by all jurisdictions partly because they do not respond to their needs and priorities and partly because they are beyond their capacities.[22] This can be traced to procedural issues that prevent developing countries from full participation in the agenda-setting and decision-making process.[23] As regards the UN, the Report concluded that the UN Committee of Experts on International Cooperation in Tax Matters does not meet the procedural criterion of universal participation by right without preconditions, as it is a body consisting of experts acting in their personal capacities and not representing governments. In other words, it is not an intergovernmental forum where countries could participate in the norm-shaping process. Apart from this, the Report found that the agenda-setting process in the UN Tax Committee is open and the decision-making processes are transparent, and, therefore, other aspects of inclusive and effective international tax cooperation are met by the UN Tax Committee. There are reasons to suspect that this may not be a fully unbiased and objective assessment, taking into account the numerous shortcomings that Brosens and Bossuyt identified with regard to the processes of the UN Tax Committee.[24]

Having regard to the conclusion that neither the OECD nor the UN meets the defined criteria of inclusivity and effectiveness, the Report suggests enhancing the UN's role in tax-norm shaping and rule-setting and making it an intergovernmental forum for fully inclusive and more effective tax cooperation.[25] Three options are provided for achieving this goal: (i) a multilateral convention on tax, (ii) a framework convention on international tax cooperation and (iii) a framework for international tax cooperation. The first two options would involve legally binding commitments for the participating countries, while the last one would mean a coordination function for the UN. None of these options are surprisingly new or truly innovative and all of them have featured previously in academic or tax policy discussions.[26] Academic commentary has

21. Report of the Secretary-General, Promotion of inclusive and effective international tax cooperation at the United Nations (A/78/235), 08/08/2023 issued as a response to the UN General Assembly resolution on 'Promotion of inclusive and effective tax cooperation at the United Nations' (A/RES/77/244) 30/12/2022.
22. *Supra* n. 21, at para. 41.
23. *Supra* n. 21, at para. 42.
24. Brosens & Bossuyt, *supra* n. 9, at 368.
25. Report of the Secretary-General, Promotion of inclusive and effective international tax cooperation at the United Nations (A/78/235), 08/08/2023, para. 49.
26. As regards a framework agreement, *see*, for example, Abdul M. Chowdhary & Sol Picciotto, *Streamlining the Architecture of International Tax Through a UN Framework Convention on Tax Cooperation*, 21 Tax Cooperation Policy Brief (2021). As regards non-binding international tax

added, in the meantime, more flesh to one or the other options, as demonstrated by Peter Hongler's plea for a meta regime.[27] Such a meta regime would be constituted through a framework agreement (option (ii)) not requiring a strong global body or elaborated quasi-democratic procedures but rather only an institutional structure that enables the international tax regime to develop 'in a more fragmented but Darwinian manner'. Part of the meta regime would be a minimum level of transparency among the members, a common institutional and procedural framework that allows the members to develop tax-related international agreements, a mechanism of allowing the non-reciprocal application of certain tax-related agreements and dispute resolution for interstate disputes in the form a judicial forum.[28]

What is not clear from the UN Secretary General Report is to what extent and how any of the three options address and remedy the deficiencies in inclusiveness and effectiveness that have been identified as the problems of the existing institutional arrangements for international tax cooperation. The options presented in the Report are legal instruments of varying degrees of bindingness (at least the first two of them). The Report does not say anything about their adoption, voluntariness of joining the instruments, the procedures instituted under the agreements, forms of decision-making, voting rights, guarantees of equal participation in decision-making and agenda-setting and guarantees that the participating states concerns are addressed by the instruments. Overall, the options presented have not much to do with improving input legitimacy, inclusiveness and democratic participation in international tax cooperation. They are not solutions for the problems that have been identified. In this regard, it must be noted that merely transferring the locus of international tax cooperation from the Inclusive Framework to the UN will not change anything if the underlying governance structure remains essentially the same. The dynamics, the diverging interests and the power relations will remain the same whether the tax cooperation is conducted under the aegis of the UN or the Inclusive Framework. It is true that the UN works based on a one-country–one-vote system (as opposed to the Inclusive Framework's consensus-based decisions), but this alone will not be sufficient to guarantee the democratic participation of all countries in the decision-making. Moreover, according to many, such system raises significant challenges to effective decision-making in international tax matters that should be carefully considered in the debate.

In order to find real solutions for inclusiveness and effectiveness, the conversation should not primarily be about legal instruments but procedures that address the underlying inequalities in governance and ensure substantive equality, i.e., equal participation and equal voice for all countries involved in international tax cooperation. Moreover, inclusiveness should not – significantly – compromise efficacy and efficiency in tax cooperation; in other words, input and output legitimacy should be

cooperation, *see*, for example, David H. Rosenbloom et al., *The Unruly World of Tax: A Proposal for an International Tax Cooperation Forum* 15 Florida Tax Review 57 (2014).

27. Peter Hongler, *Plea for a Meta Regime! (and Why the UN Should Be the Governing Body)*, GLOBETAXGOV (12 October 2023), https://globtaxgov.weblog.leidenuniv.nl/2023/10/12/plea-for-a-meta-regime-and-why-the-un-should-be-the-governing-body/#_ftnref4.
28. Hongler, *supra* n. 27.

balanced against each other when rethinking the current institutions and procedures for international tax cooperation.

§8.4 THE (LACK OF) ROLE OF NATIONAL PARLIAMENTS IN INTERNATIONAL TAX LAWMAKING

The second line of criticism formulated by Peter ten years ago regarding the legitimacy of international tax lawmaking was that national parliaments and citizens were not sufficiently involved in the process. In this regard, not only has the situation not improved but probably deteriorated. This stems from the fact that the extent of tax coordination and harmonization at the international and supranational levels has greatly increased since 2013 precisely due to the BEPS Project, while no steps have been made to involve national parliaments to a greater extent in these processes. The BEPS Project resulted in a growing number of tax rules, even those destined to be implemented in domestic laws, being decided at the global level in the OECD or the Inclusive Framework. These organizations consist of government officials who negotiate with their peers on behalf of their states. Although it can be said that the government officials represent the elected government of their states that has been voted into power by the people of their states, these indirect mechanisms of representation do not ensure sufficient legitimacy for the decisions taken at the OECD or Inclusive Framework.[29] The legitimacy deficit is amplified by the fact that national parliaments are increasingly relegated to a rubberstamping function when it comes to the approval of tax norms agreed upon at the international level.[30] This is related, on the one hand, to the fact that a national parliamentary control that is subsequent to a global agreement reached between 130-plus countries after years of negotiation and following an endorsement by the highest international political forum (G20) can hardly be more than a formality. The pressure of the existence of a global agreement and the need for coordinated implementation, which is heavily stressed by the OECD in connection with all the global agreements, do not leave room for meaningful deliberations, debates and possible deviations in national parliaments.[31] On the other hand, the lack of expertise of parliamentarians in international tax law and the high complexity and technicality of the tax rules that form part of the global tax deals agreed upon in the Inclusive Framework also result in a minimal role of parliamentary control over these rules.[32] Undoubtedly, the distance between rule-making in tax law and the citizens and

29. Brosens & Bossuyt, *supra* n. 9, at 560 et seq.
30. Brosens & Bossuyt, *supra* n. 9; Sam van der Vlugt, *The Principle of Legality of Taxation as a General Principle of EU Law: National and Supranational Differences of Interpretation and Potential Difficulties* 32 EC Tax Review 214, 226-227 (2023) DOI: 10.54648/ecta2023027.
31. Bertil Wiman, *Klaus Vogel Lecture 2022: Who should be in the driver's seat in developing international tax norms – civil servants or national parliaments?,* 77 Bulletin for International Taxation 157 (2023), at 159; Sigrid Hemels, *Tax autonomy from a Member State Perspective: are we faced with a democratic deficit?,* Working paper for the 17th GREIT Conference, Maastricht University 5-6 October 202, s. 6.
32. Brosens & Bossuyt, *supra* n. 9, at 371; Hemels, *supra* n. 31, s. 6.5.

businesses that eventually pay taxes continuously widens.[33] People have less and less influence over the adoption of the tax rules which they are subjected to questioning whether the age-old principle of 'no taxation without representation' has any meaning left in the era of international tax lawmaking by global and supranational organizations.

With regard to the implementation of the global agreements reached in the Inclusive Framework, it is a noteworthy tendency that these agreements are implemented in the European Union at the supranational instead of the national level. In particular, the EU seeks to ensure the coordinated implementation of the relevant measures in the Member States via the adoption of EU law – a harmonizing directive – thereby turning the OECD-originated soft law into EU hard law. This is the case with regard to the most important anti-avoidance measures that resulted from the first round of the BEPS Project and have been included in the Anti-Tax Avoidance Directive[34] as well as the two-pillar solution addressing the tax challenges of digitalization of the economy, the second pillar of which has been transformed into the GloBE Directive.[35] From the point of view of democratic legitimacy, the question can be asked whether the insertion of the supranational level between the international and the national changes anything with regard to the legitimacy of the process, either to the better or the worse. As is well known, the EU as a quasi-federal polity with strong competencies at the supranational level has its own issues with democratic legitimation and is itself characterized by a democratic deficit. This results from, *inter alia*, the limited role of national parliaments in the adoption of EU law and, in the field of taxation, the absence of the European Parliament as a co-legislator. The latter is confined to a mere consultative role when legislating in tax matters based on either Article 113 or Article 115 of the Treaty on the Functioning of the European Union (TFEU). Does this mean that the inclusion of the EU in the process of international tax lawmaking aggravates the concerns with regard to democratic deficiency? This is probably not the case as the national parliaments of the Member States would not have a greater role in the shaping of international tax norms at global level even if the EU were left out of the process of implementation. The EU – more precisely, representatives of the European Commission – take part in the work of the OECD and the Inclusive Framework; however, they do not replace the Member States and especially not the national parliaments of the Member States, which have never been there. The EU Directive adopted by the relevant ministers in the Council still has to be transposed to the national law of the Member States, which means that it passes through national parliaments. Although the transposition of binding EU law into national law does not enable a meaningful and substantive discussion in the Member States' parliaments, the situation is not different – as discussed above – with the global tax deals agreed upon in the Inclusive Framework despite the fact that the latter are not binding. Finally, national parliaments

33. Brosens & Bossuyt, *supra* n. 9, at 342; van der Vlugt, *supra* n. 30, at 228.
34. Council Directive (EU) 2016/1164 of 12 July 2016 laying down rules against tax avoidance practices that directly affect the functioning of the internal market, OJ L 193, 19.7.2016, pp. 1-14.
35. Council Directive (EU) 2022/2523 of 14 December 2022 on ensuring a global minimum level of taxation for multinational enterprise groups and large-scale domestic groups in the Union, OJ L 328, 22.12.2022, pp. 1-58.

do have a limited role in the EU legislative procedure through the 'yellow card' procedure[36] where they can express their opinion on the compatibility of the European Commission's proposal (i.e., the draft directive implementing the global agreement) with the principle of subsidiarity. The existence of this procedure may induce national parliaments to examine the proposal more in detail and have a debate on its content going beyond issues of subsidiarity. It is also worth noting that although the European Parliament has no decision-making power in tax matters, debates on taxation do take place in the Parliament and experts are invited to give testimony at hearings of the relevant committees of the EU Parliament. These are steps in the right direction of enhancing the deliberative democratic nature of tax lawmaking in the EU. Overall, the EU's involvement in the implementation of international tax norms does not worsen democratic legitimacy, whereas it does not considerably improve it either. For the latter to happen, the EU should deal with its own democratic deficits in the first place and then use its voice to promote positive changes in the decision-making processes of international tax organizations.

Peter suggested in his 2014 article that national parliaments and citizens must be seriously involved in the making of international tax policies and rules as this would be a precondition for securing international tax justice. This advice is as pertinent nowadays as it was ten years ago. We can, however, ask the question whether it is 'only' international tax justice that is infringed by the lack of democratic participation of those who are subjected to the international tax rules or perhaps a binding legal norm too. Having regard to the Court of Justice's recent recognition of the principle of legality of taxation as a general principle of EU law,[37] this question is justified.[38] Even if the Court's definition of the principle is not complete, it may give grounds to argue that the deficiencies of international tax lawmaking with regard to democratic participation are problematic not only as a matter of political legitimacy and justice but also as a matter of law.[39]

As is apparent, the suggestions that Peter made ten years ago with the aim of improving and enhancing international tax justice are just as valid today as they were back then. International tax policymakers would need to listen and follow up on them at this turning point in international taxation as the success of the ongoing and future reform of the international tax regime largely depends on the legitimacy and just nature of the procedures through which the reform is adopted.

36. *See* Title 2, Art. 12 Treaty on the European Union and Protocols 1 and 2 to the Treaty on the European Union and the Treaty on the Functioning of the European Union.
37. CJEU, 8 November 2022, Joined cases C-885/19 P and C-898/19 P, *Fiat Chrysler Finance Europe v. European Commission*, ECLI:EU:C:2022:859, para. 97.
38. Similarly, Hemels, *supra* n. 31, s. 5.
39. Admittedly, as Sam van der Vlugt pointed out, the general EU law principle of legality of taxation in the meaning recognized by the Court in the *Fiat* case differs from most of its national constitutional law counterparts, as it lacks the democratic element, that is, the requirement that the statute which provides for a tax is to be adopted through a democratic procedure, *see* van der Vlugt, *supra* n. 30.

CHAPTER 9

The Desired and the Actual Role of Public Consultations in Tax Lawmaking in Poland

Włodzimierz Nykiel, Ziemowit Kukulski & Małgorzata Sęk

§9.1 TERMINOLOGY

In Polish legislation, case law and literature, the term 'social consultations' (*konsultacje społeczne*) is more frequent than the term 'public consultations' (*konsultacje publiczne*), but in both cases, the meaning generally remains equivalent to the one associated with 'public consultations' in international literature.

There are no legal definitions of social consultations and public consultations in Polish law, and no clear distinction is made. However, academic debate on the issue remains open. One of the leading experts in the field, P. Kuczma, defines social consultations as '... activities initiated as part of a formalized procedure by public authorities in order to obtain non-binding public opinion on planned legal solutions and intended political decisions'.[1] In his opinion, public consultations are one of the varieties of social consultations and '... are conducted only at the stage of the governmental legislative process'.[2] P. Kuczma refers to the fact that the term '*konsultacje publiczne*' can be specifically found in the Work Regulations of the Council of Ministers.[3] Especially paragraph 36 section 1 of this Resolution, which will be discussed further below, shapes the scope of its meaning.

But a broader analysis of Polish literature shows that the term 'public consultations' is also used, with various meanings, including the one similar or identical to that

1. Paweł Kuczma, *Model ogólnokrajowych konsultacji społecznych w Polsce* 39-40 (TNOiK 2018).
2. Paweł Kuczma, *Model ogólnokrajowych konsultacji społecznych w Polsce* 50 (TNOiK 2018).
3. Resolution number 190 of the Council of Ministers of 29 October 2013 Work Regulations of the Council of Ministers (Uchwała Nr 190 Rady Ministrów z dnia 29 października 2013 r. Regulamin pracy Rady Ministrów), consolidates text Official Gazzette Monitor Polski of 2016, item 1006.

of 'social consultations'.[4] For the sake of clarity for international readers, the term 'public consultations' or 'consultations' will be adopted below.

§9.2 FUNCTIONS AND BENEFITS

The essence of consultation lies in obtaining opinions, positions and even proposals on matters that directly or indirectly concern consulted entities located outside the system of public authorities and acting towards them as social partners.[5]

Various functions of public consultations are distinguished.[6]

The development of participatory democracy, as advocated by the contemporary literature on the state system, requires the increase of the role of citizens in the functioning of the state.[7] One of the practices of participatory democracy consists in the use of public consultations in lawmaking processes. For this reason, the participatory function of consultations is considered the most important, primary and conditioning of other functions.[8]

Since the bidirectional flow of information (from public authorities to citizens and from citizens to these bodies) is at the very heart of consultations, the information function is mentioned. As the Latin word 'consultatio' means deliberation, consideration, inquiry, and the word 'consulto' – to carefully consider, to deliberate[9] – it is crucial that consultations involve an element of dialogue, exchange of opinions and careful consideration of expressed opinions and are not limited to one-sided storytelling of the legislative power (and/or executive power).

Due to the importance of consultations for lawmaking, a lawmaking function is also distinguished, alongside an optimization/rationalization function. Consultations enable correction of errors included in draft legislation and introduction of new solutions better suited to the realities of those concerned. Consultations provide the lawmakers with information on how the discussed legislation is assessed by the public or parties concerned, but the decision ('the last say') remains with the legislative power, so the foundations of representative democracy are not undermined.

Consultations combine the elements of direct and representative democracy – the final decision belongs to the legislative power, but it is preceded by the collection of public opinion.[10]

---

4. *See, e.g.*, Joanna Woźniczko, *Konsultacje społeczne jako narzędzie partycypacji publicznej* 7, 18 (Kancelaria Senatu 2019).
5. Cezary Kosikowski, *Zasięganie opinii i korzystanie z ekspertyz oraz przeprowadzanie konsultacji społecznych i dokonywanie uzgodnień w procesie tworzenia prawa i jego kontroli – rzeczywistość czy fikcja?* 108 Przegląd Legislacyjny 1 (2006); Dagmir Długosz & Jan Jakub Wygnański, *Obywatele współdecydują. Przewodnik po partycypacji społecznej* 23 (Forum Inicjatyw Pozarządowych 2005).
6. *See* Paweł Kuczma, *Model ogólnokrajowych konsultacji społecznych w Polsce* 51-55 (TNOiK 2018).
7. Paweł Kuczma, *Model ogólnokrajowych konsultacji społecznych w Polsce* 445-448 (TNOiK 2018).
8. Włodzimierz Nykiel, *Konsultacje społeczne a stanowienie prawa podatkowego*, in *Wyzwania współczesnej polityki prawa. Pani Profesor Małgorzacie Król uczniowie i przyjaciele* 180 (Sylwia Wojtczak & Joanna Wyporska-Frankiewicz eds., C.H. Beck 2022).
9. Kazimierz Kumaniecki, *Słownik Łacińsko-Polski* 120-121 (PWN 1967).
10. Martin Bozek, *Konstytucyjne podstawy partycypacji społecznej i formy jej realizacji w samorządzie terytorialnym* 103 Przegląd Sejmowy 5 (2012); Roman Marchaj, *Samorządowe konsultacje społeczne. Propozycje de lege ferenda* 66 Samorząd Terytorialny 7-8 (2020).

Continuous dialogue between the sovereign people and their elected representatives is one of the founding principles of democracy.[11] In Poland, the representatives exercising legislative power are not bound by any instructions of the electorate, but they need to continue dialogue with the people also during the term of office, and consultations are one of the means thereto. Consultations are part of a broader concept of public participation. Other legally institutionalized elements of participatory democracy include (in Poland) petitions, public hearings, citizens' legislative initiatives and referendums.[12] Public participation includes a variety of practices enabling citizens to influence public affairs and to get engaged in shaping public policies[13] and legal frameworks.

Public participation contributes to a better understanding of the needs of the public. Participation generally improves the transparency and credibility of decision-making process. Hence, it may increase the level of acceptance of newly adopted legislation and facilitate its implementation. It reduces the perceived gap between the legislative (and executive) power and the people.

However, in the case of consultations, the above positive effects will depend on how the outcome of consultations is utilized. The submitted opinions need to be carefully considered and not disregarded without proper explanation.

§9.3 LEGAL CONTEXT

The Polish Constitution[14] does not include the 'right to public consultations'.

However, as has been emphasized by the Constitutional Court, consultations are a 'legal phenomenon' that has its roots, among others, in the Preamble, which states that the Constitution as the basic law of the state is founded on, *inter alia*, 'social dialogue'. The Constitutional Court included social dialogue among the 'basic principles organizing the life of the state community'.[15] Moreover, under Article 20 of the Constitution, 'dialogue and cooperation between social partners' is included among the foundations of a social market economy which is the economic system of Poland.

Inclusion of social partners in the legislative process also serves two important pillars of a democratic state of law, namely legal certainty and citizens' trust in law.[16]

11. Sławomir Patyra, *Konsultacje społeczne w procesie przygotowania rządów projektów ustaw – zarys problemu* 497 Studia Iuridica Lublinensia 22 (2014).
12. Joanna Woźniczko, *Konsultacje społeczne jako narzędzie partycypacji publicznej* 3 (Kancelaria Senatu 2019).
13. Joanna Woźniczko, *Konsultacje społeczne jako narzędzie partycypacji publicznej* 3 (Kancelaria Senatu 2019).
14. The Constitution of the Republic of Poland of 2 April 1997, Official Gazette *Dziennik Ustaw* of 1997, no. 78, item 483; available in English at https://www.sejm.gov.pl/prawo/konst/angielski/kon1.html (10 October 2023).
15. PL Constitutional Court: judgment K18/04 (11 May 2005). *See also* Marek Piechowiak, *Komentarz do preambuły*, in *Konstytucja. Tom I. Komentarz Art. 1-86* 147-148 (Marek Safjan ed., C.H. Beck 2016).
16. Sławomir Patyra, *Konsultacje społeczne w procesie przygotowania rządów projektów ustaw – zarys problemu* 499 Studia Iuridica Lublinensia 22 (2014).

According to Article 2 of the Constitution, Poland 'shall be a democratic state ruled by law and implementing the principles of social justice'. The right to public consultations is also derived from Article 4 of the Constitution which states that the supreme power is vested in the nation, and the nation shall exercise such power directly or through their representatives.[17]

Besides, under Article 11 of the Treaty on European Union,[18] participation (dialogue, consultations, exchange of opinions) belongs to the EU (normative not purely political) principles of democracy. Hence, consultations are a component of the EU-wide concept of democracy.

In Poland, the legal regulation of public consultation is assessed as rather general and superficial.[19] It is also dispersed. Provisions of various legal instruments, from generally binding to internally binding, state which issues may or shall be consulted and with whom, making a distinction between mandatory and optional consultations.[20]

The adoption of laws is subject to the provisions of the Constitution and the regulations of the Sejm and Senate.

Pursuant to Article 34 section 2 of the Rules of Procedure of the Sejm of the Republic of Poland,[21] a bill is accompanied by a justification. Pursuant to section 3 of this article: 'The justification should also present the results of consultations and provide information on the presented variants and opinions, in particular if the obligation to seek such opinions results from provisions of an act.' Initiators of a bill are obliged to conduct the legally required consultations before they exercise their legislative initiative, with the noticeable exception of Sejm committees and groups of Sejm deputies. In the case of committee and deputies' bills for which no consultations have been held, the Marshal of the Sejm, before submitting it for first reading, refers the bill for consultation in the manner and on the terms specified in separate acts (Article 34 section 3). Thus, for committee and deputies' bills, consultations are only ordered to the extent they are mandatory under provisions of a separate act.

Government bills are more extensively covered by consultations. A distinction is made between arrangements (in particular inter-ministerial), public consultations and opinions on a draft government document, the latter two fitting the concept of

17. Joanna Woźniczko, *Konsultacje społeczne jako narzędzie partycypacji publicznej* 9 (Kancelaria Senatu 2019); Martin Bozek, *Konstytucyjne podstawy partycypacji społecznej i formy jej realizacji w samorządzie terytorialnym* 90 Przegląd Sejmowy 5 (2012).
18. Consolidated version OJ EU C 202, 7 June 2016, pp. 13-46.
19. Sławomir Patyra, *Konsultacje społeczne w procesie przygotowania rządów projektów ustaw – zarys problemu* 508 Studia Iuridica Lublinensia 22 (2014).
20. Joanna Woźniczko, *Konsultacje społeczne jako narzędzie partycypacji publicznej* 9 (Kancelaria Senatu 2019).
21. Resolution of the Sejm of the Republic of Poland of 30 July 1992 on the Rules of Procedure of the Sejm of the Republic of Poland (*Uchwała Sejmu Rzeczypospolitej Polskiej z dnia 30 lipca 1992 r. Regulamin Sejmu Rzeczypospolitej Polskiej*), consolidated version Official Gazette *Monitor Polski* of 2021, item 481.

consultations. Under paragraph 36 section 1 of the Resolution of the Council of Ministers of 29 October 2013 on Work Regulations of the Council of Ministers:[22]

> The applicant authority, taking into account the content of the draft act or draft regulation, as well as taking into account other circumstances, including the importance of the draft and the expected socio-economic effects, the degree of its complexity and its urgency, presents the draft for public consultations, and may refer the draft to social organizations or other interested entities or institutions in order to present their position, taking into account the guidelines for conducting public consultations, if they were established by the Council of Ministers or its subsidiary body.

Under paragraph 38 section 2:

> In cases specified in separate regulations, the draft government document is submitted for opinion to the entities indicated in these regulations, in particular the draft which provisions concern issues covered by the scope of activities of the joint commission of the government and representatives of local government, churches and social partners or other entities, shall be submitted to the relevant joint committee for an opinion.

As expected, public consultations are excluded when the government prepares binding instructions (guidelines and recommendations) for the negotiation of tax treaties. No consultations are held during the process of negotiation and signing of a tax agreement, which results from the specificity of international agreements as sources of law. This is in opposition to the obligation to consult governmental bills containing domestic tax law provisions.

In Poland, there are no mandatory consultations regarding the general assumptions, goals and guiding principles of the new tax provisions being drafted, including the ones developed by the government. This is criticized in the literature because consultations at such an early stage would increase the recipients' influence on the lawmaking processes and reduce taxpayers' uncertainty about the future law. R. Mastalski points out that 'the participation of representatives of specific social groups in the legislative process cannot be overestimated, especially at the early stage of preparation of draft legal acts, i.e., the assumptions of these drafts, or even more specific theses'.[23] In Poland, this participation takes place only after the bill itself has been drafted.

In some instances, consultation of drafts is mandatory, in other cases, optional. The right to participate in mandatory consultations (or to provide an opinion) on draft laws is granted to several dozen entities of various natures, depending on the subject matter and including: public authorities, e.g., the National Council of the Judiciary, the Inspector General for Personal Data Protection, professional self-governments, e.g., tax advisors, legal advisors, social partners, e.g., trade unions, employer organizations, churches and religious associations, other entities, e.g., the Supervisory Board of the

22. Resolution no. 190 of the Council of Ministers of 29 October 2013 on the Work Regulations of the Council of Ministers (*Uchwała Nr 190 Rady Ministrów z dnia 29 października 2013 r. Regulamin pracy Rady Ministrów*), consolidated version Official Gazzette *Monitor Polski* of 2016, item 1006.
23. Ryszard Mastalski, *Tworzenie prawa podatkowego a jego stosowanie* 67 (Wolters Kluwer 2016).

Social Insurance Institution.[24] The right to consult, the issues covered and the formal and temporal aspects of involvement are provided not in a single act but in numerous acts devoted to these entities, their legal status, composition and competencies.[25]

C. Kosikowski observes that the consulted entities may be directly or indirectly concerned by the matter under consultation.[26]

Within the framework of social dialogue, mandatory consultations generally involve social partners or entities representative of persons concerned rather than individual citizens. The general public may also be involved, but it is a rare occurrence.[27]

The personal scope of consultations, implemented in the concepts of entitled entities and persons concerned, heavily affects the actual significance and potential of consultations. However, the quality of consultations does not lie in the number of participants but in the substantive value of their submissions and in their potential impact on the draft legislation.[28] In this context, the participation of organizations is especially valuable.

§9.4 PRACTICE

In Poland, the quality of the process of creating tax law itself and of its results, i.e., tax laws, is often unsatisfactory for both substantive and formal reasons.[29]

An assessment of the practice of conducting social consultations, seeking opinions and expert opinions regarding tax law, was presented several years ago by C. Kosikowski.[30] He wrote about the engagement of social partners in performing opinion-giving and consultative functions, but he also pointed out that 'these activities generally do not have a major impact on increasing the rationality of law-making and improving its quality, although it should be otherwise'.[31] This assessment remains valid today, and the situation has even deteriorated. The analysis of the Polish legislative practice in recent years proves that the importance of public consultations in the field of tax law has been, unfortunately, decreasing. As a matter of fact, as in other

---

24. *See* Paweł Kuczma, *Model ogólnokrajowych konsultacji społecznych w Polsce* 360-361 (TNOiK 2018).
25. Sławomir Patyra, *Konsultacje społeczne w procesie przygotowania rządów projektów ustaw – zarys problemu* 500 Studia Iuridica Lublinensia 22 (2014).
26. Cezary Kosikowski, *Zasięganie opinii i korzystanie z ekspertyz oraz przeprowadzanie konsultacji społecznych i dokonywanie uzgodnień w procesie tworzenia prawa i jego kontroli – rzeczywistość czy fikcja?* 108 Przegląd Legislacyjny 1 (2006).
27. Joanna Woźniczko, *Konsultacje społeczne jako narzędzie partycypacji publicznej* 17 (Kancelaria Senatu 2019)
28. Roman Marchaj, *Samorządowe konsultacje społeczne. Propozycje de lege ferenda* 74 Samorząd Terytorialny 7-8 (2020).
29. Włodzimierz Nykiel, *Konsultacje społeczne a stanowienie prawa podatkowego*, in *Wyzwania współczesnej polityki prawa. Pani Profesor Małgorzacie Król uczniowie i przyjaciele* 184 (Sylwia Wojtczak & Joanna Wyporska-Frankiewicz eds, C.H. Beck 2022).
30. *See* Cezary Kosikowski, *Ustawa podatkowa, geneza, ewolucja i stan prawny, tworzenie, kontrola, wykładnia, wykonywanie* 111-115 (Lexis Nexis 2006).
31. Cezary Kosikowski, *Ustawa podatkowa, geneza, ewolucja i stan prawny, tworzenie, kontrola, wykładnia, wykonywanie* 114 (Lexis Nexis 2006).

fields, consultations of tax drafts seem to be treated as a formal nuisance rather than a valuable tool for the improvement of future legislation. During the governmental drafting process, consultations tend to be primarily carried out when and to the extent they are obligatory.[32]

In practice, attempts are even made to avoid or limit consultations without (formally) breaking the procedures, but violating the principles of parliamentarism and moral standards.[33] The most frequently used method is the submission of draft tax laws by members of the parliamentary majority, which eliminates the need for prior extensive consultations with social partners. Recently, the number of such drafts has increased significantly.[34]

There are many indications that a number of bills submitted by members of the Sejm majority were created in the Ministry of Finance or at least in close cooperation with the Ministry. During the meetings of the Sejm Public Finance Committee, questions clearly addressed to a deputy representing the applicants are often answered without any delay by a representative of the Ministry of Finance, while the deputy asked remains silent. Transcripts from the meetings of the Public Finance Committee provide insights on the frequency of such situations.[35]

The Constitutional Tribunal emphasizes that consultations need to be real and not just formal.[36] In practice, even though consultations are carried out, their importance might be substantially reduced by treating them as a mere formality and not giving enough attention to their results. Such consultations are not genuine, but simulated or facade. An example of the merely formal treatment of consultations is setting such short deadlines for submitting comments that a deeper analysis of the drafts becomes impossible.[37] Another practice is ignoring the opinions expressed in the consultations and merely stating in the justification to the draft that the opinion is incorrect without providing detailed explanations for such assessment. Despite an obligation to provide reasons for disregarding an opinion, the explanations are sometimes very brief and superficial. The disregarding of sensible opinions, not corresponding with the views of the drafters, heavily weakens the institution of consultations, discouraging the entitled entities from future participation.

32. Sławomir Patyra, *Konsultacje społeczne w procesie przygotowania rządów projektów ustaw – zarys problemu* 509 Studia Iuridica Lublinensia 22 (2014).
33. Włodzimierz Nykiel, *Konsultacje społeczne a stanowienie prawa podatkowego*, in *Wyzwania współczesnej polityki prawa. Pani Profesor Małgorzacie Król uczniowie i przyjaciele* 186 (Sylwia Wojtczak & Joanna Wyporska-Frankiewicz eds., C.H. Beck 2022).
34. Włodzimierz Nykiel, *Konsultacje społeczne a stanowienie prawa podatkowego*, in *Wyzwania współczesnej polityki prawa. Pani Profesor Małgorzacie Król uczniowie i przyjaciele* 186 (Sylwia Wojtczak & Joanna Wyporska-Frankiewicz eds., C.H. Beck 2022).
35. Włodzimierz Nykiel, *Konsultacje społeczne a stanowienie prawa podatkowego*, in *Wyzwania współczesnej polityki prawa. Pani Profesor Małgorzacie Król uczniowie i przyjaciele* 186 (Sylwia Wojtczak & Joanna Wyporska-Frankiewicz eds., C.H. Beck 2022).
36. PL Constitutional Court: judgment K 13/03 (18 January 2005).
37. Michał Wilk, *Potrzeba wprowadzenia Karty Praw Podatnika w Polsce* 98-99 Kwartalnik Prawa Podatkowego 1 (2018).

Another problem is that consultations are carried out regarding an early wording of the draft, which may be seriously amended in the course of parliamentary discussion. A good practice would be to more frequently organize public hearings as an opportunity to comment on the altered version of the bill.

Inevitably, the role of consultations is limited in case of acts consenting to the ratification of international tax agreements[38] and acts implementing EU tax directives.

Results of consultations (if held at all, which is not the followed practice due to the lack of mandatory character) may not lead to any alterations in already negotiated and signed international agreements. The negotiated text of an international agreement on tax matters cannot be unilaterally changed. However, consultations could potentially result in the agreement not being ratified in the end if an act consenting to ratification is not passed because of strong public opposition expressed during consultations and taken into account by the parliament.

Under Article 95a sections 2 and 3 of the Rules of Procedure of the Sejm of the Republic of Poland, when submitting a draft act, the Council of Ministers shall declare whether it is a draft act implementing European Union law. In the case of other bills (i.e., those from other initiators), the Marshal of the Sejm, before submitting the bill for first reading, shall decide whether it is a bill implementing EU law. The justification attached to a bill submitted by the Council of Ministers must contain a table of compliance of the draft provisions with the provisions of EU law (Article 34 section 4a of the Rules of Procedure of the Sejm of the Republic of Poland). Poland as an EU Member State is obliged to implement EU legislation, and public views expressed in the consultation process (which generally does not differ from the one concerning other bills) should not undermine this obligation. However, it is very important that the need to transpose EU law is not used by the drafters and promoters of a tax bill as a mere (false) pretext to introduce changes which actually are not required by EU law.[39] During consultations, such a practice may be discovered and exposed.

§9.5 IMPROVEMENTS NEEDED

The quality of consultations is correlated with the general quality of exercising public authority in a jurisdiction.[40]

38. Ratification of a tax international agreement and its termination require prior consent granted by statute – Art. 89 in connection with Arts 84 and 217 of the Constitution.
39. The introduction of mandatory disclosure rules (MDRs) is an example of such a practice where the implementation of EU law seems to be used as a façade, under the pretext of which additional, original ideas of the Polish Ministry of Finance, going well beyond what is required by EU law, are also introduced (*see* Krzysztof Koślicki, *Polski fiskus chce wiedzieć za duzo*, Prawo.pl (10 October 2023). https://www.prawo.pl/podatki/raportowanie-schematow-podatkowych-w-polsce-i-ue-tajemnica,350277.html). Interestingly, Polish MDR legislation was considered so complicated that the Ministry of Finance issued a public ruling. Between 21 December 2019 and 7 January 2020, consultations were held on the draft public ruling of over seventy pages, giving interested parties very little time to analyse the draft and express their opinion.
40. Joanna Woźniczko, *Konsultacje społeczne jako narzędzie partycypacji publicznej* 12 (Kancelaria Senatu 2019).

Avoidance of consultations or shortcomings in the process of conducting them undermines confidence in the tax lawmaking process and reduces acceptance and perceived legitimacy of its products – new laws. It also leads to the adoption of defective or imperfect tax legislation, including provisions which require changes shortly after their adoption or entry into force.

The need to increase the role of consultations in Poland was noticed at the European Union level.[41] The Council Recommendation of 9 July 2019 on the 2019 National Reform Programme of Poland and delivering a Council opinion on the 2019 Convergence Programme of Poland states:

> The quality of new and revised legislation, and a stable and predictable business environment are of high importance for sustaining favourable economic conditions and supporting the increase in private investment. The unstable regulatory framework and other barriers to the expansion of firms are negatively affecting investment activity and productivity. Establishing an effective dialogue with all stakeholders would help improve the quality of legislation and – by limiting the number of revisions needed – would contribute positively to the stability of the business environment. Therefore, strengthening the role of consultations of social partners and public consultations – by ensuring a sufficient length of time for consultations, improving the uptake of the stakeholders' opinions gathered in the process, and minimising the number of laws exempted from consultations – would substantially help to minimize the administrative burden resulting from frequent changes in the law, increase investment and promote sustainable economic growth in the long term ... Legal certainty and trust in the quality and predictability of regulatory, tax and other policies and institutions are important factors for the investment environment.[42]

For the sake of developing participatory democracy also in the crucial sphere of taxation, the introduction of a statutory regulation of taxpayer's right to consultations should be advocated in Poland. Formal and substantive quality of tax law, as well as the transparency and confidence in the legislative process, could greatly improve thereby. Thoroughly conducted consultations strengthen the legitimacy of tax laws and their acceptance.[43]

The right to consultation should be included in the Tax Ordinance[44] or – if ever adopted – in the Act on Taxpayer's Charter of Rights.[45] Consultations on draft tax law

---

41. Włodzimierz Nykiel, *Konsultacje społeczne a stanowienie prawa podatkowego*, in *Wyzwania współczesnej polityki prawa. Pani Profesor Małgorzacie Król uczniowie i przyjaciele* 187 (Sylwia Wojtczak & Joanna Wyporska-Frankiewicz eds., C.H. Beck 2022).
42. Council Recommendation of 9 July 2019 on the 2019 National Reform Programme of Poland and delivering a Council opinion on the 2019 Convergence Programme of Poland, Official Journal EU C 301, 5 September 2019, pp. 123-128.
43. Joanna Woźniczko, *Konsultacje społeczne jako narzędzie partycypacji publicznej* 24 (Kancelaria Senatu 2019).
44. Act of 29 August 1997 Tax Ordinance (*Ustawa z dnia 29 sierpnia 1997 r. Ordynacja podatkowa*), consolidated version Official Gazette *Dziennik Ustaw* of 2022, item 2651, amended.
45. A draft Act on Taxpayer's Charter of Rights, drafted by Włodzimierz Nykiel and Małgorzata Sęk, was twice submitted to the Sejm by a group of opposition deputies: on 26 April 2019 (*see Poselski projekt ustawy – Karta Praw Podatnika*, Sejm RP of the Eighth Term, print no. 3458 (4.2.2020) https://www.sejm.gov.pl/Sejm8.nsf/druk.xsp?nr=3458), and again (due to the new Sejm term of office) on 8 January 2020 (*see Poselski projekt ustawy – Karta Praw Podatnika*, Sejm

provisions should be mandatory, and the list of entitled entities should be wide and adequately represent taxpayer's interests. Parliamentary bills should also be covered. Moreover, government assumptions of draft tax law provisions should be published and consulted and not only drafts already composed. The establishment of expert consultative bodies for the specialist field of tax law could also be considered, following the EU example.

RP of the Ninth term, print no. 137 (10.10.2023) http://www.sejm.gov.pl/Sejm9.nsf/druk.xsp?nr=137). The draft puts an emphasis on the proper process of tax lawmaking, also extending the role of public consultations.

PART III General Notions of Taxation

CHAPTER 10
Cameleon Taxation

Daniel Deak

An institution can be a chameleon subject to changes in its appearance and behaviour, depending on the circumstances. Such an institution can also be a type of tax. A tax can be called a chameleon if it can hardly be categorised for lack of characteristics that would be typical.

One such tax is the Hungarian local business tax (HIPA),[1] which is charged on turnover but from which significant expenditure items are deductible for tax purposes. It can be seen as either a turnover tax (an indirect tax) or a profit tax (a direct tax). The analysis shows below that the distinction between direct and indirect taxes is not self-evident, not only concerning the Hungarian business tax, but such taxes can occur worldwide.

§10.1 LOCAL TAXES AND LOCAL BUSINESS TAX

Taxation in Hungary is divided between the central and local levels. Although central taxes constitute the state budget's revenue, local taxes are levied and collected by local governments, even if the latter are increasingly deprived of their powers and financial resources. The introduction and setting of a level of local taxes are, within certain legal limits, left to the discretion of each municipality.

Local taxes include:

- property taxes, namely building taxes and land taxes;
- taxes of a municipal nature, such as the communal tax and the tourist tax; and
- local business tax.

1. For its effective version, *see* Act C of 1990, Chapter IV (sections 35-40/M).

HIPA is the most widely applied local tax. The tax is levied on all business activities carried out permanently or temporarily on the territory of the respective local government. The local business tax is payable by any entrepreneur who has a registered office or place of business on the local government's territory (permanent character) or temporarily performs business activities in the municipality for more than thirty days.

HIPA is based on net turnover less the purchase value of goods sold, the value of services supplied, the cost of materials, the value of subcontracted services, and the direct cost of research and experimental development. There are relief measures and exemptions linked to different circumstances. The maximum rate of HIPA is 2 % of the taxable amount, but this varies from municipality to municipality.

§10.2 OCCURRENCE OF BORDERLINE SITUATIONS

HIPA is generally not considered a tax equivalent to income tax under a double taxation convention. However, there are Hungarian double taxation conventions (e.g., those with Poland or Albania) explicitly listing HIPA as falling within the scope of the respective treaty Article 2.[2] However, concerning those conventions which do not mention local business tax, Hungarian administrative and judicial practice is steady in that HIPA cannot be classified as a type of income tax.[3]

The Hungarian authorities had a different view on HIPA in the *KÖGÁZ* case before the Court of Justice of the EU (CJEU), when the Hungarian administrative authorities explicitly argued that HIPA is a direct tax; i.e., it cannot be compared to the harmonised value added tax (VAT).[4] A similar problem had already arisen in the *IRAP* case, where the question was whether the Italian tax could compete with the harmonised VAT.[5] According to the practice developed by CJEU, VAT can be identified by taking into account four criteria: (i)-(ii) a wide range of taxable persons and taxable

---

2. Poland-Hungary double tax convention, signed at Budapest on 23 September 1992, promulgated by Act XCV, Art. 2 (3)(v); Albania-Hungary double tax convention, signed at Tirana on 14 November 1992, Art. 2 (3)(v).
3. Based on the resolution of the Ministry of Finance No. 28208/2001 (31.10.2000), the local tax authority, in a decision, intends to retroactively enforce the local business tax with late payment surcharges and penalties on the export sales of the business establishment, which had already been taxed in Germany, since, according to the resolution of the Ministry of Finance, the Hungarian local business tax is not an income tax. However, on a case-by-case basis and the basis of reciprocity, Hungary is willing to grant exemptions from the payment of HIPA to non-resident companies, as with Deutsche Lufthansa AG. Pénzügyi Közlöny, 1994/17.
4. Joined Cases C-283/06 *KÖGÁZ*, 312/06 *OTP Garancia Biztosító* (2007), ECR I-8463, ECLI: EU:C:2007:598. An Advocate General did not hear the case, and the documents of hearings (the parties' observations), which would reveal the Hungarian Government's position, are not in the public domain. For further explanation, *see* Daniel Deak, *A Case Study on Initiating Disputes in Fiscal Law Matters: The Example of Hungarian Local Trade Tax, ECJ – Recent Developments in Direct Taxation* (M. Lang, J. Schuch, C. Staringer (eds), Linde 2007).
5. C-475/03 *Banca popolare di Cremona* (2006), ECR I-9373, ECLI:EU:C:2006:629. Daniel Deak, *Hungarian Local Trade Tax in the EU Context,* Fiscalità Internazionale, Issue 2 (March-April 2007).

transactions are concerned, (iii) the tax liability is proportional to the turnover and (iv) the tax burden is transferable.[6]

Borderline problems can also arise in the case of corporate income taxation, mainly if the taxation of profits (concerning its rate or due date) depends on whether the owners have distributed profits. In the *Burda* case, the German corporate tax system was characterised by the fact that if the owners distributed profits, the corporate tax rate was lower on distributed earnings than on accumulated ones (the corporate tax policy was to encourage distribution).[7]

Concerning the Greek corporate tax on earnings at issue in *Athinaïki*, however, the lower tax burden is not related to distributed profits but to accumulated ones (the tax rate is lower for accumulated profits, and complete corporate tax is still payable *subsequently* if profits are distributed). These circumstances show that the Greek corporate tax policy was designed to encourage accumulation.[8] The lower tax burden associated with retained earnings has been or is being applied elsewhere, typically in capital and technology importer countries (Hungary has had two years of split corporate tax rates,[9] and in Estonia, corporate income tax can still be deferred until the profits are distributed).

A legal application problem arises when, while distributing profits, the non-Greek shareholder's interest is to show withholding tax due to the payment of dividends (like Amstel's Greek subsidiary). However, the local financial administration insists that the Greek (or Estonian or Hungarian) tax under discussion is considered corporate tax, applicable upon profit distribution. Similarly, the Portuguese government argued against withholding tax on dividends in the *Epson* case, considering the profit distributed from the capitalised company profit as the subject of capital turnover taxation.[10] Notably, cross-border withholding taxation is prohibited by the relevant Parent-Subsidiary Directive.

Since one can argue in the above cases that a subsidiary is obliged to calculate and deduct a tax to be withheld on the dividend payment from shareholders and pay it to the Treasury, a tax on the company itself can be established, the burden of which can then be passed on to the owner. There is the question of whether the tax relating to the event of the payment of dividends is a corporate tax or a withholding tax and whether the corporate tax can be passed on to the recipient when the burden of corporate tax is effectively borne by the recipient from whose payment the corporate tax is deducted. The question arises as to whether a transferable corporate tax on distribution remains a direct tax.

Another argument in favour of recognising the indirect tax nature of the tax is that:

6. *Banca popolare di Cremona*, Para. 28; joined Cases C-283/06 *KÖGÁZ*, 312/06 *OTP Garancia Biztosító*, Para. 37.
7. C-284/06 *Burda* (2008), ECR I-4571, ECLI:EU:C:2008:365.
8. C-294/99 *Athinaïki Zythopoiia* (2001), ECR I-6797, ECLI:EU:C:2001:505.
9. Daniel Deak, *Supplementary Corporate Tax in Hungary: Confusion for Foreign Investors*, 11 Tax Notes International, 23 (1995).
10. C-375/98 *Epson* (2000), ECR I-04243, ECLI:EU:C:2000:302.

- the withholding tax is levied on a transaction and not on aggregate income;
- pass-through of a corporation is made;
- personal exemptions or discounts are not eligible;
- nor can expenses be recognised.

It is also sometimes a legal policy argument that, while income is typically subject to in personam taxation, usually at progressive rates, considering the taxpayer's ability to pay, turnover is subject to *in rem* taxation since the state levies the tax on turnover.[11] This picture can be confused if personal taxation is not generally applied to income but to the revenue consumed, thus considering private expenditure (expenditure tax). In this case, progression might be eliminated from the system, making the ability to pay irrelevant.

With the expansion of the digital economy, the problem of excess profits of multinationals has become more acute, which may be due to the characteristics of the digital market and to tax minimisation manoeuvres of cross-border multinationals. Taxing the profits of large digital corporations is difficult or impractical, and the use of digital services taxes has become widespread. A taxing state can tax the extraordinary earnings of these companies through the taxation of well-understood sales revenue (apart from the problem of whether, in the absence of a permanent establishment, the source country has a taxing title, and if so, what it would be). Interestingly, it is also doubtful whether direct or indirect taxation can be established in each case for such taxes on services.

The situation is similar to the proposed directive on the digital services tax,[12] which essentially taxes the extra profits of large digital companies. However, formally, it is a tax on transactions, and the tax base is turnover. Quite similarly, concerning many sectoral special taxes (most of which are levied on turnover and paid at progressive rates) that the Hungarian government has applied in several waves to date, it is often unclear whether they are indirect or direct taxes.

Going further, the classification of HIPA raises problems in applying the GLoBE (global base erosion) rules arising from Pillar II of the BEPS 2.0 programme. To calculate the source country's minimum tax, the official guidance issued by OECD defines not only the corporate profit tax but also a tax equivalent to the corporate income tax. Still, HIPA is not considered compatible with corporate income tax according to the criteria.[13]

11. Richard A. Musgrave & Peggy B. Musgrave, *Public Finance in Theory and Practice* 215 (McGraw-Hill 1973).
12. Proposal for a Council Directive on the common system of a digital services tax on revenues resulting from the provision of certain digital services, COM/2018/0148 final, Brussels, 21 March 2018.
13. *OECD/G20, Base erosion and profit shifting project; Two-pillar solution to address the tax challenges arising from the digitisation of the economy*; Paris, Oct. 2021; *OECD/G20, Base Erosion and Profit Shifting Project, Tax challenges arising from the digitisation of the economy - Commentary to the global anti-base erosion Model Rules (Pillar Two); Inclusive Framework on BEPS* (OECD Publishing, 11 March 2022). Concerning the interpretation of Art. 4 of the GloBE Model Rules, para. 32 of the Commentary sets out a very narrow scope of taxes creditable to a regular corporate income tax, which the Hungarian HIPA does not seem to fit into. It is a different matter that, during the negotiations on the relevant EU Directive (Council Directive

§10.3 DIRECT AND INDIRECT TAXES FROM THE PERSPECTIVE OF THEORIES OF JUSTICE

When studying the taxation of consumption and considering the relationship between direct and indirect taxes, it is helpful to start with the role played by these two basic types of tax in society. More specifically, it is necessary to explore how they are related to distributional issues and, more specifically, to theories of justice. How the great thinkers of the Enlightenment thought about the case still shapes thinking about justice today. The most comprehensive approach to justice today is that of John Rawls, who goes back to John Locke's conception of justice in his analysis.

While Locke's treatise on good government discusses property, a conception of justice appropriate to a bourgeois social order unfolds. He who cultivates the land and generally creates high value by his labour deserves to be the landowner and enjoy the fruits of his or her work. Private property ownership will lead to social differences facilitated by market competition.

Still, all who are diligent enough should enjoy the fundamental opportunity to work and the freedoms that accompany it (first proviso). The limit to the inevitable differences that will arise from the exercise of private property is that the enrichment of one citizen should not be accompanied by the oppression of another and the worsening of his or her situation (second proviso).[14]

In Rawls' theory of justice, the underlying concepts of income redistribution can be grouped around four branches: allocation, stabilisation, income transfer, and the functions that flow from distributive justice in general. The first part of the distributive justice branch can be associated with progressive inheritance and income taxation to ensure, within certain limits, the realisation of fundamental freedoms and equal opportunities, while the logic of the second part requires that there be sufficient tax revenue, which in turn can best be achieved through the application of proportional consumption taxation. The latter is preferable to income taxation in terms of the logic of the second part (of the branch of distributive justice) since it is easier to achieve justice through a tax linked to elementary consumption than through income taxation, which many consider to be artificial. Proportional taxation of consumption is naturally adapted to the order of the market economy: on the one hand, there is less interference in the market economy, and, on the other hand, proportional taxation of goods ensures perfect equality in the abstract.

The two parts of the distributive function can be reconciled with the two fundamental principles of justice: the guarantee of basic freedoms and the principle of

2022/2523 EU, 22.12.2022. OJ L 328, 1), the Hungarian government filed a non-public pledge to the EU authorities concerning the possible recognition of HIPA when calculating the source country's minimum tax.

14. The formulation of the clauses attributed to him does not come directly from Locke, but the formulas were developed by the literature that expounded on him. John Locke, 'An Essay Concerning the True Original, Extent, and End of Civil Government', in: Peter Laslett, *John Locke: Two Treatises of Government* (ed. With an introduction and notes; student ed., Cambridge University Press, 1960 [1689]). For the first proviso, *see* Book II, Chapter V of the property, § 27 (287-288), § 33 (291); for the second: § 36 (292-293).

differentiation. The explanation of progressive inheritance and income taxation, on the one hand, and proportional consumption taxation, on the other hand, is essential at the level of the theory of justice, and only then is it possible to look at traditional tax policy principles (such as the principles of benefit and sacrifice or the doctrine of the ability to pay).[15]

Distributive justice theory concerns the distinction between income and consumption (direct and indirect) taxation. Progressive personal income taxation is necessary to ensure fundamental freedoms. Still, since the capitalist economy is competitive, sales taxation, which allows for minimal state intervention compared to progressive personal income taxation, is indispensable.

These are the two basic, and not confusable, strands of taxation from the point of view of distributive justice. In practice, however, taxation has not succeeded in developing pure forms of taxation that could lead to purely direct or indirect taxes.

In the context of proportional consumption taxation, Rawls attaches particular importance to the veil of ignorance, meaning that the information available to parties is never complete. According to David Elkins, Rawls focuses on the methodological advantages of freedom of choice but pays less attention to the material consequences.[16] Hence, Rawls' theory is of little relevance to tax policy options, and the question of how to distinguish between direct and indirect taxes cannot be raised in the context of this theory.

David Elkins fails to consider that Rawls' proportional taxation of consumption is explained in the context of the differentiation principle,[17] which justifies the Rawlsian conception, if not at the level of tax policy, then at the level of social philosophy. When Hobbes favours a consumption tax (1651), it is a self-evident proposal before inventing the comprehensive distribution of personal income.[18] Income taxation in Great Britain was introduced in 1799, overcoming several political obstacles and undergoing numerous modifications. In its modern form, it appeared in 1970 (Income and Corporation Tax Act).

Compared with direct and indirect taxes, examining the effects of economic policy alone is insufficient, although this is the subject of much of the literature. John Stuart Mill shows that, in addition to the lack of economic development and liberalism, psychological reasons also played a part in the difficulty of spreading direct taxes.[19] While Mill analyses the effects of tax policy, he does not address the nature of indirect or direct taxes and thus subordinates legal doctrine to tax policy. Tax law dogmatics is

15. In developing the two principles of justice, Rawls draws on John Locke's conception. John Rawls, *A Theory of Justice* (Belknap, revised ed. 1991), 1999, 245-247.
16. David Elkins, *Consumption Taxation in Rawls' Theory of Justice*, 29 Cornell Journal of Law & Public Policy 799 (2020).
17. *Ibid.*, 858.
18. Thomas Hobbes, *Leviathan (Leviathan or the Matter, Form & Power of a Common-Wealth Ecclesiastical and Civil), ed. with an Introduction and Notes by J. C. A. Gaskin* 229 (Oxford University Press 1998).
19. John Stuart Mill, *Principles of Political Economy, with Some of Their Applications to Social Philosophy* 431-432 (John W. Parker, West Strand, London, 1848; Volume ii, Book v, Chapter vi, as reproduced by Hein Online).

still a neglected area, although it can be of enormous practical importance for interpreting the law.

§10.4 PROGRESSIVE CONSUMPTION TAX

A consumption tax is levied in proportion to the revenue, and the tax burden can be passed on. In the 1950s, the literature began the career of an expenditure tax, which, although directed at consumption, is a tax on income, i.e., a direct tax.[20] A characteristic feature of this tax is progressive rates, even if the taxed object is consumption.

The thesis of Nicholas Kaldor, considered a classic on the topic, is that progressive taxation promoting redistributive justice need not necessarily be seen as contrary to economic efficiency, provided that the tax progression is established on expenditure (consumption) and not on income in its entirety.[21] The traditional income tax need not arbitrarily discriminate between the objects of consumption. Still, it interferes with the earning activity, or more precisely, with whether the taxpayer works, engages in business, or saves.[22]

Several conceptual and measurement problems arise when looking for a tax base that is well measured, and that satisfactorily assesses one's spending power, regardless of one's actual spending.[23] Kaldor points out that Mills' proportional taxation is the more contingent and less perfect form of fairness since what matters is not how much a taxpayer spends in a given period but how much his or her spending power is, regardless of his or her actual spending.[24]

It can occur that a progressive consumption-based tax is introduced without referring to the ability to pay. If the ability to pay or spend is measured as to how much money a person has, no difference is considered between the stock of wealth and the income flow. However, measuring the ability to pay based on stock or flow is two different approaches. Whether the income recorded in a given time is derived from capital or labour is irrelevant to assessing someone's ability to pay.

The distinction between capital and income is relevant mainly in competitive capitalism in the nineteenth century. A rigid separation is no longer appropriate, although the fact that capital and income are two fundamental sources of livelihood remains relevant and suggests that it is also reasonable to subject capital and income

20. This type of tax was recommended in the 1990s by many Western experts for transition economies, for whom the incentive to save was significant in constructing a capitalist market economy. For example, Croatia also introduced a personal income tax on consumption in 1994, which was still phased out in 2000. Sandra Švaljek, *The 200 Tax Reform in Croatia: Causes and Consequences*, 56 Ekonomski Pregled 12 (2005). *See also*: Charles E. McLure Jr., *The U.S. Debate on Consumption-Based Taxes: Implications for the Americas*, 29 University of Miami, Inter-American Law Review 1-2 (1997-1998).
21. Nicholas Kaldor, *An Expenditure Tax* (Routledge 2003, first published by Allen & Unwin 1955), 15. *See supra* n. 17, at 15.
22. Kaldor, *ibid.*, 24.
23. The ability to pay and spend (purchasing power) can be assessed as the same but simultaneously different since the ability to pay is not necessarily reflected in spending (purchasing power), but wealth is always available.
24. Kaldor, *supra* n. 21, at 29-30.

(or passive and active income) to tax separately and progressively.[25] The comprehensive income tax is developed considering fairness, while a consumption-based tax can be assessed according to its effectiveness.

Concerning the traditional progressive personal income tax, high spending capacity can be shown for some individuals even if income is accumulated but not spent. Therefore, that income is taxable whether or not the income is spent, which distorts economic judgment and is unfair. An expenditure tax would only affect actual spending to remedy this anomaly.

Unlike sales taxes, the financial burden of a consumption tax proposed by Nicholas Kaldor cannot be passed on. Kaldor's tax is an income tax, although a personal income tax is reduced to consumption, including actual spending. Corporate profits may also be subject to a Kaldor-type consumption-oriented tax. In such a case, accumulated profits are exempt from taxation, and pass-through is possible, but only indirectly when the company prices the higher expenditure.

As Peggy and Richard Musgrave described, the traditional approach to taxing consumption is regressive simply because consumption expenditure as a percentage of income tends to fall as there is a move up the income scale. Therefore, throughout history, income taxation has been identified with progressive taxation and sales taxes with regressive ones. However, nothing in the logic of the two tax bases makes this necessary. This situation has arisen because income taxes have evolved within the framework of personal taxation, while consumption taxes have captured the impersonal or property tax.[26]

Applying a personal consumption tax would break this constraint and allow consumption to be taxed individually and progressively. In such a case, the line between direct and indirect taxation would not be blurred, but it would become possible to tax consumption under personal income taxation. There is, of course, no technical obstacle to this.

Kaldor is not simply describing personal income taxation reduced to consumption but also attributing the characteristics of progressiveness. In this way, it is possible to use a form of income taxation that is less disruptive to market circulation. At the same time, a personal tax is also capable of at least limited enforcement of distributive justice

International harmonisation is more of a problem because the world has been based on progressive taxation of total income (changes in consumption rights and wealth) for about a hundred years. A radical consumption tax reform would have to be implemented globally, but there is no political will. A shift from income taxation to consumption would also lead to significant inequalities. In particular, pensioners, who paid a lot of income tax during their working lives, would now be taxed again on their consumption, even though their income is low.[27]

25. *Ibid.*, 30-33.
26. Richard A. Musgrave & Peggy B. Musgrave, *supra* n. 11, at 404-405. Joseph Pechman similarly describes the situation: Joseph A. Pechman, *The Rich, the Poor, and the Taxes They Pay* 216-217 (Routledge, Apple Books, 1986).
27. Pechman, *ibid.*, at 224.

§10.5 COMPREHENSIVE OR CONSUMPTION-BASED INCOME TAX?

Consumption taxes generally take the form of flat-rate sales taxes or value added taxes. Like expenditure taxes (consumption-based income taxes), these transaction taxes are also levied based on consuming goods (or services). Sales and value added taxes are levied on less than the total consumption base. Services such as medical and hospital care provided by state and local governments, public transport, financial services provided by banks and savings institutions, or travel abroad are typically excluded from the tax base.[28]

Income and expenditure taxes may be subject to progressiveness. However, since an income tax also affects the return on savings, it imposes a higher burden on future consumption than an expenditure tax.[29] Taxation on expenditures, therefore, seems preferable because it does not tax capital income and, therefore, cannot distort it. At the same time, both an expenditure tax and a comprehensive income tax distort the decision to earn labour income insofar as high taxation may encourage workers to choose leisure rather than additional work.

An argument favouring traditional income taxation is that taxing comprehensive income is more effective than taxing expenditures because it also affects the benefits associated with wealth, such as power, prestige, and security. Furthermore, from a distributive justice perspective, it is interesting to note that since expenditure taxes are not levied on capital income, nontaxation leads to wealth accumulation and thus increases social inequality.

Comprehensive income taxation increases the number of people who enjoy welfare because if progressive taxation transfers income from the rich to the poor, the welfare of the latter increases. At the same time, the former feels withdrawal much less being rich. Indeed, the marginal utility of the income withheld is lower for a poor person than for the rich.[30]

Those favouring comprehensive income taxation argue that the efficiency claims of expenditure taxation are exaggerated.[31] Because of the nontaxation of savings, wages must be taxed more heavily. Thus, the efficiency gains of expenditure taxation are offset by the higher tax burden on wages through income taxation.

The opposite view is also possible: an income tax that taxes savings, in fact, also taxes the income from the labour that generated the savings, i.e., it taxes diligence and skill, which leads to inefficiency.[32] Ultimately, the crucial issue is not the choice between the various types of taxes but their impact on society, regardless of their form.

There is an alternative to the distinction between conventional income tax and a consumption-based tax: an income tax that considers the whole life cycle. In lifetime income taxation, the tax is also paid annually, but on the average gain over the

28. Michael J. Graetz, *Implementing a Progressive Consumption Tax*, 92 Harvard Law Review 8 (1979) DOI: 10.2307/1340462.
29. Joseph Bankman & David A. Weisbach, *The Superiority of an Ideal Consumption Tax over an Ideal Income Tax*, 58 Stanford Law Review 1413 (2006).
30. *Ibid.*, 1420-1421.
31. *Ibid.*, 1455.
32. *Ibid.*, 1455-1456.

estimated lifetime, following William Vickrey's theory of income averaging.[33] Consumption-based taxation is very similar to income averaging because consumption-based income taxation also considers lifetime. This feature is because even if the capital income is not taxed, it will still be spent at some point when the capital owner does pay an expenditure tax on his or her consumption.

Both averaged income taxation and consumption-based income taxation are conditional: they depend on market perfection, consistently rational decisions, and the availability of relevant information. However, there is no market perfection. The findings of market participants are not always reasonable, and since the lifetime allowance is based on an estimate, the relevant information may not be complete. According to Daniel Shaviro, considering these components of reality, the thesis that an ideal consumption-based income tax is superior to a comprehensive income tax cannot be accepted.[34]

§10.6 CONCLUDING REMARKS: HOW CAN INDIRECT TAXES BE DETERMINED?

Concerning HIPA, local governments tax sales (i.e., turnover), but it could be argued that because of the deduction opportunities, the objective is essentially to tax profits locally. HIPA seems to be an unfortunate construct, or it could be argued that it is a fiscal chameleon. Indeed, as has been shown, depending on the context, it can be classified as a direct tax (e.g., in the *Kögáz* case) or an indirect tax (e.g., concerning Article 2 of a double tax treaty).

A lesson to be learnt from comparing direct and indirect taxes can be that even in cases where it is apparent at first glance whether a tax is indirect or direct, later in its application, there might be confusion about how to classify one or the other. Therefore, it is safe to venture that HIPA might be by no means the only one in identifying chameleon taxation. The chameleon's nature is not only a puzzle but can also cause difficulties in daily implementation.

The confusion surrounding the categorisation of HIPA arises from the unclear criteria for distinguishing between indirect and direct taxes. One may speculate that their distinction can theoretically not even be completed. Whether a state applies an indirect or a direct tax in given circumstances should be a matter of practical considerations. Immanuel Kant warns[35] that welfare policy is not a matter of principle but merely a choice between options dictated by the contingencies of the material world.

33. William Vickrey, *Averaging of Income for Income-Tax Purposes*, 47 Journal of Political Economy (1939) DOI: 10.1086/255390.

34. Daniel Shaviro, *Beyond the Pro-consumption Tax Consensus*, 60 Stanford Law Review 745 (2007).

35. 'Wohlfahrt aber hat kein Princip, weder für den, der sie empfängt, noch der sie austheilt (der eine setzt sie hierin, der andere darin): weil es dabei auf das Materiale des Willens ankommt, welches empirisch und so der Allgemeinheit einer Regel unfähig ist.' Immanuel Kant, *Der Streit der Facultäten in drei Abschnitten* 86 (Friedrich Nicolonius 1798).

A bourgeois society must guarantee fundamental human rights and protect human dignity (see the first Rawls' condition). At the same time, it must be liberal, guaranteeing freedom of differentiation (see the second Rawls' condition).

Suppose that tax policy fails to express this fundamental distinction. In that case, it is not tax policy that is essentially to blame, but the economic and fiscal policy of the state in question that is pregnant with compulsions and is in the crossfire of lobby forces. So, tax policy is only part of the problem.

CHAPTER 11

Developing Sustainable Corporate Tax Governance

Hans Gribnau

§11.1 INTRODUCTION

Today's world is changing rapidly and companies are contributing to it. Think of the big tech companies that have dramatically changed the way we communicate and behave. Some corporations are larger than small states, and they influence society and the everyday lives of countless people – not just their employees – and the environment in no small measure. Stakeholders, however, perceive that companies often pay too little attention to their environmental impact. Other stakeholders' concerns and expectations are frequently neglected as well.

In addition, many policy goals that governments pursue and try to achieve through good public governance cannot be achieved without the help of the business community; combating further global warming is a pregnant example (climate). Sustainable development has become an important driver of government policies. This is, however, far too complex a problem to be solved solely by governments. Cooperation between government, businesses and society is urgently needed.

Unsurprisingly, sustainability is also high on the corporate governance agenda and translated into their 'Environmental, Social & Governance' (ESG) policies. Taxes are crucial to sustainable development. This requires corporations to gear their governance towards sustainability; it requires sustainable corporate tax governance.

This chapter starts with depicting some views on a number of crises the present-day world is facing. Taxes and corporations play a notable role in each of these crises. A look at history will then show that this is not new to the world. Next, various developments in the field of corporate tax governance will be briefly analysed along two dimensions: paying a fair share of taxes and transparency.

§11.2 MANY CRISES, FEATURING TAXATION AND CORPORATIONS

In his recent very rich book *The Crisis of Democratic Capitalism*, the *Financial Times'* chief economics commentator Wolf argues for the 'need for substantial change if core Western values of freedom, democracy, and the Enlightenment are to survive'.[1] He discusses the causes of the rising inequality, increasing personal insecurity, and slowing economic growth, after the global financial crisis, and more especially after the Great Recession of 2007-2009. Economic globalization changed global and political power relations. Democracies were impacted too: there is a shift away from liberal democracy to illiberal democracy. Demagogic autocrats, like Trump and Johnson, have undermined international cooperation and the rule of law. Climate change, immigration, and more recently COVID-19 and Russia's evasion of Ukraine (February 2022) were added to today's challenges.

According to Wolf, many of these issues are created or exacerbated by elites' mismanagement of major issues such as globalization. Meritocratic well-off, well-connected and well-educated individuals, political business and political establishment and media elite all have put self-interest ahead of the common good. This elitist failure resulted in popular distrust of the institutions which are essential to democratic capitalism, that is, a healthy balance between liberal democratic and market capitalism. Consequently, trust in democracy is corroded as people feel that their country is not being governed for them but for a narrow elite 'who reap most of the gains, and when things go wrong, are not just shielded from loss but impose massive costs on everybody else'.[2]

Wolf points at well-known concerns such as increasing inequality in both wealth and incomes,[3] the extraordinary rise in top incomes of corporate management and in the financial sector in a number of countries, the erosion of rule of law which should underpin democracy and capitalism but is captured by the wealthy and powerful.[4] Importantly, Wolf discusses the role of taxation in these developments: tax avoidance and evasion by the rich has put the cost of maintaining public infrastructure entirely on less well-off working people and small local businesses.

Taxation is indeed one of the drivers here. The wealthy play a dominant role in shaping tax policy. They have captured the democratic system to create favourable tax codes that, for example, facilitated base erosion and profit shifting. This refers to an often voiced more general concern. Powerful lobbies advocating wealthy and corporate taxpayers' interests often successfully attempt to redirect public policy and influence legislation which are often formed according to their needs.[5] It should, however, be a

1. Martin Wolf, *The Crisis of Democratic Capitalism* xviii (London: Allen Lane 2023).
2. Wolf, *supra* n. 1, at 7. Cf. Rana Foroohar, *Don't Be Evil: The Case Against Big Tech* (Allen Lane, 2019), 13.
3. Wolf, *supra* n. 1, at 88.
4. *Ibid.*, at 168.
5. Alan Dignam & Michael Galanis, *The Globalization of Corporate Governance* 134 (New York/London: Routledge, 2016). *See also* Yascha Mounk, 'How Populist Uprisings Could Bring Down Liberal Democracy', *The Guardian*, 4 March 2018 and Sheldon S. Wolin, *Democracy Incorporated: Managed Democracy and the Specter of Inverted Totalitarianism* (Princeton/Oxford: Princeton University Press, 2008).

mistake to see authorities as a kind of puppets since they are oftentimes willing to cooperate with businesses to advance their own agendas; for example, they engage in (harmful) tax competition which serves their policy economic policy agenda. For example, the U.K. Government stressed its aim to create 'the most competitive corporate tax regime in the G20' in 2010.[6]

As a result, many less-educated and less well-off members of society feel abandoned by the elite and losing control to forces operating at an international level, such as the European Union. Of course, when the outcomes of the political process become less legitimate in the eyes of large parts of the people, this impacts trust in democracy adversely. People who feel economically insecure are attracted to demagogues which causes the leaders the rise of populism which indicates 'a move toward political extremes'.[7] Hampered economic growth failed indeed to distribute wealth, fuelling distrust and polarization in society and politics. The wealthiest members of society not doing their part is a crucial source of social distrust. 'Generalized resentment', especially among members of the middle and the working classes, 'has fueled the rise of the extreme right in Europe'.[8]

Wolf is of course not the first to point at the tax system as part of a larger set of major problems the world faces today. Piketty's analysis showed the rise of extreme inequality of income and wealth since the 1970s tax reform by Margaret Thatcher and Ronald Reagan, while the regressive tax system resulted in lower tax revenue.[9] The increase in economic inequality hampered economic growth, but extreme economic inequality also impacts society, say critics like Piketty. Society can hardly function well 'with such extreme divergence between social groups'.[10] When government collects less tax, there is less money to spend on public goods and services. This includes cuts in public services and welfare programs but also subsidies for schools, sports clubs, community centres, schools and the like that are important elements of a healthy civil society. This may 'undermine confidence in government, which makes it more difficult to raise taxes significantly'.[11]

Decreasing revenue has another effect. Public services deteriorate further as the affluent elites increasingly rely on private services. They become less willing to support public services and facilities they no longer use with their taxes. And since the rich secede from public places and services, the public realm 'where citizens of different walks of life encounter one another' and a sense of community is hollowed out, Sandel

6. U.K. Government, *The Corporate Tax Roadmap* 9 (2010), https://assets.publishing.service.gov.uk/government/uploads/system/uploads/attachment_data/file/193239/Corporation_tax_road_map.pdf.
7. Wolf, *supra* n. 1, at 195.
8. Pierre Rosanvallon, *The Society of Equals* 275 (Cambridge (Mass.) & London: Harvard University Press, 2013). Adrian Wooldrigde, *The Aristocracy of Talent: How Meritocracy Made the Modern World* 335 (Allen Lane, 2021) points at the Yellow Jackets Protests in France.
9. Thomas Piketty, *Capital in the Twenty-First Century* 302 (Cambridge (Mass.) & London: The Belknap Press of Harvard University Press, 2014).
10. Piketty *supra* n. 9, p. 297.
11. Piketty *supra* n. 9, p. 491.

argues.[12] Thus, the increasing gap between rich and poor undermines the solidarity (and redistribution) that democratic citizenship requires. Sandel, pointing at the need for a 'broad equality of condition' if democracy is to thrive,[13] echoes Piketty's concern that rising inequality also adversely impacts confidence in democracy (public opinion data confirm this concern[14]).

Unsurprisingly, for Piketty, taxes make society possible and may well enhance social cohesion. This view calls to mind the German philosopher Peter Sloterdijk's statement that 'taxes are the central moral phenomenon of our civilization'.[15] Taxation's foundational character implies a shared responsibility for the integrity of the tax system for those who are shaping and affected by it. Consequently, the various actors bear a shared (though not an equal) responsibility. Since responsibility comes with power, the more powerful parties involved, such as states and multinational corporations, bear more responsibility. States, being the primary responsible actors, are indeed cooperating to improve the international tax system.[16] Here, I focus on the responsibility of multinational corporations.

§11.3 SUSTAINABLE DEVELOPMENT AND TAXATION

Many of the problems just mentioned concern in fact sustainability issues which appear to be closely connected to the design of tax systems that makes everybody pay their fair share. Sustainability or sustainable development is a big thing nowadays. The concept is made more concrete in the United Nations' Sustainable Development Goals (SDGs). They were formulated in the resolution 'Transforming our world: the 2030 Agenda for Sustainable Development' adopted by the United Nations General Assembly on 25 September 2015. The agenda has three intertwined and balancing dimensions of sustainable development – 'the economic, social and environmental'. To achieve sustainable development, five 'p's' are guiding: 'people, planet, prosperity, peace and partnership'.[17] This last 'p' points to an important governance aspect. Sustainable development requires global cooperation by states with stakeholders and the private sector (business community) as crucial partners. SDG 17 ('Partnerships for the Goals') advocates a strong commitment to global partnership and cooperation. Sustainable

12. Michael Sandel, *Justice: What's the Right Thing to Do?* 267 (New York: Farrar Straus and Giroux 2009).
13. Michael Sandel, *The Tyranny of Merit* 192 (London: Allen Lane 2020).
14. Roberto Stefan Foa & Yascha Mounk, *The Danger of Deconsolidation: The Democratic Disconnect*, 27(3) Journal of Democracy 5 (2016) DOI: 10.1353/jod.2016.0049.
15. Peter Sloterdijk, *Die nehmende Hand und die gebende Seite* 141 (Berlin: Suhrkamp Verlag, 2010). *See* Hans Gribnau, 'Why Social Responsible Corporations Should Take Tax Seriously', in Karina Kim Egholm Elgaard et al. (eds.), *Fair Taxation and Corporate Social Responsibility* 103-159 (Copenhagen: Ex Tuto Publishing, 2019).
16. Cooperation should be beneficial to all parties involved; *see* Tsilly Dagan, *Globe: 'The Potential Costs of Cooperation*, 51(10) Intertax 638 (2023) DOI: 10.54648/taxi2023059. *See also* Cees Peters, *The Legitimacy of the OECD's Work on Pillar Two: An Analysis of the Overconfidence in a 'Devilish Logic*, 51(8-9) Intertax 554 (2023) DOI: 10.54648/taxi2023057.
17. A/RES/70/1, *Transforming our world: the 2030 Agenda for Sustainable Development, Resolution adopted by the General Assembly on 25 September 2015*, https://sdgs.un.org/documents/ares701-transforming-our-world-2030-agen-21254.

development is indeed too complex to be solved and handled by governments alone. Clearly, it should not be about global partnership and cooperation only. Cooperation is needed between public agencies and the people and organizations affected, and more generally, society (including NGOs). As Essers reminds us, however, this kind of (inter)national cooperation inevitably implies a tension with democracy and the rule of law (which fall under SDG '16 Peace, justice and strong institutions'[18]) which should be carefully handled.[19] Apart from being partners, firms have their own duty to focus on sustainable development.

The seventeen SDGs address major global issues, including poverty and hunger, climate action, affordable and sustainable energy, industry, innovation and infrastructure, life in water and on land, inequality, sustainable cities and communities, and more. The SDGs entail a call for 'action by all countries, poor, rich and middle-income to promote prosperity while protecting the planet'.[20] Thus, sustainability is a comprehensive concept regarding sustainable development of all countries which is restricted to concern for the environment and reducing energy consumption.

Taxes provide states with the revenue needed to attain SDGs (budgetary function); paying taxes is thus a sustainability issue. The tax system itself can also be used to attain different SDGs. Here, too, governance requires ensuring policy coherence; this is not easy given the enormous complexity of the tax system and its sometimes counterproductive behavioural incentives. For example, an unbalanced system of tax incentives can lead to redistribution 'upwards', as with tax incentives to promote the use of electric vehicles to reduce carbon emissions (SDG 13 'Climate Action'). The same goes for a possible reduction in the VAT rate for fruits and vegetables to reduce diabetes, heart disease and obesity (SDG 3: 'Good health and well-being'), and more generally for a reduced VAT rate. The legislator employing the budgetary, (re)distributive and regulatory functions of the tax system to promote SDGs should of course respect fundamental rights and the principles of the rule of law (see SDG 16).[21]

§11.4 CORPORATIONS AND TAXATION

This chapter advocates sustainable corporate tax governance. Interestingly, history might teach us a lesson, or rather, since it does not repeat itself, offer us some valuable insights. Roman history provides a nice example of the disruptive impact of the connection between the unchecked power of corporations and taxation on society and the rule of law.

The Roman Republic (509 BC–27 BC) did not have a large administrative bureaucracy. Many duties of government were contracted out to private enterprise (to govern its rapidly expanding imperium). Tax collecting was one of the main activities,

18. *See* https://www.un.org/sustainabledevelopment/peace-justice/.
19. Peter Essers, 'International Tax Justice Between Machiavelli and Habermas', in Bruno Peeters et al. (eds.), *Building Trust in Taxation* 235-265 (Cambridge: Intersentia, 2017).
20. United Nations, *The Sustainable Development Agenda*, https://www.un.org/sustainabledevelopment/development-agenda/.
21. Klaus Tipke, *Die Steuerrechtsordnung. Volume I* (Cologne: Verlag Dr. Otto Schmidt, 2000).

'a significant source of revenue' of these private organizations, the *societas publicanorum* ('society of publicans').[22] These companies participated in tenders for tax-collecting rights (and other public duties) in a particular region or province. These government contractors were well organized and adept at lobbying the Roman government. The corporate executives of the companies, which collected taxes for private gain, grew into a very wealthy management class. This kind of elite enrichment contributed to growing income and wealth (and political power) inequality and ensuing polarization between rich and poor.[23]

Thanks to the successful *societates*, the Roman Republic saw a steady increase in revenue. However, as the corporations, created 'to promote the good of the commonwealth',[24] grew in size and power, the problem of fraud and corruption became a serious risk for the Republic. Moreover, their greed when collecting taxes and the widespread use of slaves were increasingly met with criticism. Moreover, the systematic importance of the *societates* to the Roman state led them to have great political power. In the eighteenth century, Montesquieu denounced these tax collectors: they were rapacious and corrupt without any judicial oversight while ravaging the provinces of the Roman Republic. And when they were also allowed to sit on (legal) courts, it had disastrous moral consequences. Persons being both tax collector and judge eroded the legal system: 'when judgments were transferred to tax-collectors, virtue, police, laws, magistracy, and magistrates were no longer'.[25] More recently, Badian tends to agree with Montesquieu: that the publicans (and in particular the tax collectors of the imperial Republic) – turned to the wrong purposes and were perhaps responsible for the downfall of the Roman Republic.[26]

Perhaps unsurprisingly, in the early Roman Empire, the successor of the Roman Republic, emperors gradually replaced the corporations by a salaried civil service. In due course, the power of the *societates* waned.[27] By the second century AD, the *societates* had given way to a more centralized imperial bureaucracy which performed public duties including tax collection.

This story of early Roman tax collection practice is a striking example of tax governance failure. Public and private interests were intertwined as tax collecting was privatized. Corporations engaged in tax practices which were evidently not sustainable. They abused (privatized) duties of government and their political clout for private gain at the expense of large parts of the people. Corporate tax behaviour thus undermined the sustainability of the legal system and society. They contributed to income and wealth (and political power) inequality, polarization between rich and poor and undermined public morality and the legal system. These developments were

22. William Magnuson, *For Profit: A History of Corporations* 37 (New York: Basic Books, 2022).
23. Walter Scheidel, *The Great Leveller: Violence and the History of Inequality from the Stone Age to the Twenty-First Century* 71-79 (Princeton: Princeton University Press, 2018).
24. Magnuson, *supra* n. 22, at 37.
25. Montesquieu, [1748], *The Spirit of the Laws, Anne M. Cohler, Basia C. Miller, and Harold F. Stone (Transl. and eds.),* XI, 18 Cambridge: Cambridge University Press 183 (1989).
26. E. Badian, *Publicans and Sinners* 85 (Ithaca: Cornell University Press, 1983).
27. Carolyn Webber & Aaron Wildavsky, *A History of Taxation and Expenditure in the Western World* 123 (New York: Simon and Schuster, 1986).

at odds with – the 'society' dimension of – sustainable development as we would call it today. Companies are nowadays expected to assume responsibility for sustainable development, which comprises a wide set of issues as the SDGs show. This requires sustainable corporate governance of which tax is an integral part.

§11.5 CORPORATE TAX GOVERNANCE

§11.5.1 Corporate Tax Governance, CSR and Sustainability

Like all citizens, corporations benefit from public goods funded by tax revenue. Healthy institutions, good infrastructure and macroeconomic environment, highly educated people (employees) and consumers with great purchasing power enable businesses to thrive. Corporate economic (and political) 'power depends on the state in innumerable ways depends on the state in innumerable ways: for contracts, subsidies; for promoting opportunities at home and abroad'.[28] In this sense, taxes are due to pay for the costs of the benefits accepted by (corporate) citizens provided by the state and society.

Moreover, governments cannot achieve sustainability without the help of companies. Large multinationals play a crucial role here, e.g., because of their ecological footprint and global value chains that cross national borders.[29] Firms thus have their own duty to focus on sustainable development, which includes the payment of a fair share of tax. Tax should be an integral part of a corporation's sustainability strategy. Companies' tax governance should therefore be geared towards sustainable taxation. Corporate tax governance, as part of corporate governance, concerns the way in which management and supervisory bodies exercise their duties and responsibilities with regard to taxation within a company and the communication and accountability. The primary responsibility rests with the board. Stakeholders expect board members to address sustainability concerns through the corporate governance system of a business. About fifteen years ago, Erle wrote: 'tax cannot stay in the splendid isolation in which its technical nature has historically placed it'.[30] This statement has lost none of its topicality, on the contrary.

First of all, 'the philosophical and ethical principles' will have to be formulated.[31] The company's purpose is to guide in this respect. The purpose of the company cannot be separated from moral considerations, Charkham argues. 'The purpose of the company, is to provide ethically and profitably the goods and services people need and

28. Wolin, *supra* n. 5, at 136.
29. Beate Sjåfjell, *Sustainable Value Creation Within Planetary Boundaries – Reforming Corporate Purpose and Duties of the Corporate Board*, 12(15) Sustainability 6245 (2020) DOI: 10.3390/su12156245. More than two-thirds of world trade occurs through global value chains; World Trade Organization, *Technological Innovation, Supply Chain Trade, and Workers in a Globalized World: Global Value Chain Development Report 2019* 1 (WTO: Geneve, 2019).
30. Bernd Erle, 'Tax Risk Management and Board Responsibility', in Wolfgang Schön (ed.), *Tax and Corporate Governance* 209 (Berlin/Heidelberg: Springer-Verlag, 2008).
31. KPMG, *Tax in de Boardroom. A Discussion Paper* 12, 2004.

want.'[32] For a long time, many boards seemed, however, to aim at maximization of shareholder value, which was translated into aiming at the highest possible profit after tax through tax minimization. But we may observe a shift here. Acting in the best interests of the company allows management to take the interests of other stakeholders than shareholders more seriously. Such a pro-social purpose 'is eminently legal' – since 'directors have very wide latitude'.[33]

The Sustainable Development Goals embody a variety of stakeholders' interests. They 'lay out a coherent road map – widely embraced by the business community – for building a just and sustainable world'.[34] They are ways of taking into account companies' economic, social and environmental impact. Companies are therefore increasingly thinking in terms of concepts such as 'Governance, People, Planet & Prosperity', in which their strategic objectives are anchored in their 'Environmental, Social & Governance' (ESG) policy. Moreover, (institutional) investors are increasingly assessing companies on their ESG policy and performance.

The SDGs which are primarily to be pursued by governments therefore also require a sustainability commitment from companies. They will have to take ESG seriously. But what actually is ESG?[35] ESG comprises three complementary dimensions. 'Environmental' (E) concerns the impact of a company on nature and the environment, such as greenhouse gas emissions, pollution, and freshwater supply. In this regard, the amount of, e.g., carbon taxes, plastics taxes companies pay, and the amount of green subsidies and incentives, they receive is relevant. 'Social' (S) refers to human and labour rights issues which include the interaction with stakeholders such as employees and communities in which the company operates and supply chain responsibility towards suppliers and customers. In this respect, a company's tax policy could, for example, include a whistleblower's policy. Finally, 'Governance' (G) refers to a variety of issues that relate to the proper governance of corporations, e.g., the structure and the composition of the board of directors, leadership style and culture within a company, executive remuneration, shareholder rights, (internal and external) risk management, transparency, corporate lobbying, anti-corruption measures and the relationship with and involvement with stakeholders.[36] A company's engagement with stakeholders on their expectations with regard to its tax management, its relationship with the tax authorities and its lobbying activities on tax are relevant factors. E, S and G are each referred to in sustainability reports translated into more concrete criteria,

32. Jonathan Charkham, *Keeping Better Company: Corporate Governance Ten Years On*, 2nd ed. 2 (Oxford: Oxford University Press, 2005).
33. Rebecca Henderson, *Reimagining Capitalism: How Business Can Save the World* 36 (Penguin 2020).
34. *Ibid.*, 27.
35. Elizabeth Pollman, *The Making and Meaning of ESG*, European Corporate Governance Institute – Law Working Paper No. 659/2022 (31 October 2022), https://ssrn.com/abstract=4219857.
36. Andreas Rasche et al., 'Corporate Sustainability – What It Is and Why It Matters', in Andreas Rasche et al. (eds.), *Corporate Sustainability Managing Responsible Business in a Globalised World*, 2nd ed., 4-5 (Cambridge: Cambridge University Press, 2023).

the so-called ESG 'metrics', that ensure measurability and comparability.[37] Consequently, taking also the economic dimension into account, sustainable value creation requires creating values in ecological, social and economic terms.[38]

Corporate tax governance must reflect the shift towards more sustainable and responsible business practices. Sustainability is an extension of corporate social responsibility (CSR) and can be seen as broadening and updating it. Social responsibility follows from the contract between society and business, the essence of which is that 'companies shall not pursue their immediate profit objectives at the expense of the longer-term interests of the community'.[39] The purpose of many companies nowadays includes the CSR and sustainability elements 'People, Planet and Profit/Prosperity' (from which logically follows a fourth P – 'Paying a fair share'), which companies' tax policy must therefore be in line with.[40] Value creation in this 'triple bottom line' must lead to more sustainable business practices. Consequently, companies' tax policy and tax strategy should focus on sustainability.

Cooperations, as powerful tax actors, have a special responsibility for the integrity of the tax system.[41] Tax minimization does not fit in with that. This is recognized in the Dutch Corporate Governance Code. Principle 1.1.1. says, among other things, that when developing the strategy for long-term value creation, the board will in any event pay attention to 'vii. paying a fair share of tax to the countries in which the company operates'.[42]

Corporate governance's moral dimension should thus impact the form and content of a company's tax governance. Taxation, corporate governance, CSR and sustainability should be connected. Indeed, companies are putting tax on the ESG agenda.[43] The sustainability assignment then calls for 'sustainable (or good) tax governance'. The company, as a responsible (corporate) citizen, must deal with its tax obligations as a contribution to a sustainable society.

§11.5.2 Fair Share and Transparency

Sustainability requires taxpayers to pay a fair share of taxes. This is in line with the CSR principle that companies voluntarily accept ethical obligations on top of legal and

37. *See* Financial Accounting Standards Board, *FASB staff Educational paper – Intersection of Environmental, Social, and Governance Matters with Financial Accounting Standards* (March 2021), https://fasb.org/.
38. Florian Lüdeke-Freund & Stefan Schaltegger, 'Business Model Innovation for Sustainability', in Rasche et al. (eds.), *supra* n. 36, at 395-400.
39. Adrian Cadbury, *Corporate Governance and Chairmanship: A Personal View* 160 (Oxford: Oxford University Press, 2002).
40. Eelco van der Enden & Bronte C. Klein, *Good Tax Governance ... Govern Tax Good* (2020), https://papers.ssrn.com/sol3/papers.cfm?abstract_id=3610858.
41. Hans Gribnau, *The Integrity of the Tax System after BEPS: A Shared Responsibility*, 10 Erasmus Law Review 1(2017), https://papers.ssrn.com/sol3/papers.cfm?abstract_id=3026295.
42. Corporate Governance Code Monitoring Committee, *The Dutch Corporate Governance Code* 11 (2022), https://www.mccg.nl/publicaties/codes/2022/12/20/dutch-corporate-governance-code-2022.
43. Cf. the Dutch employers' organization VNO-NCW's Tax Governance Code 1 (May 2022), https://www.vno-ncw.nl/taxgovernancecode#documents.

economic obligations towards society.[44] Of course, they have a right to arrange their tax affairs in such a way as to achieve a favourable tax treatment within the limits set by the law. Sustainable social responsibility, however, entails the ethical obligation to go 'beyond compliance' with the law which is at odds with complying with the (tax) law in a minimalist way.[45] Good tax governance should ensure responsible tax behaviour. Paying a fair share is the substantive element of good tax governance; the second, procedural, element is transparency.[46] Transparency enables internal and external stakeholders to hold a company to account with regard to its tax policy and actual tax behaviour.

Accessible and adequate tax information can lead to a better understanding of companies' tax behaviour (and the tax system) and is a precondition for a better-informed and more nuanced public debate. Transparency has an educational function because it allows stakeholders to gain more insight into the complex, highly technical (corporate) taxation and to discuss this with companies. But it is not a one-way street, as Gutmann emphasizes. Corporations should also want to be educated themselves 'about societal perspectives, concerns, needs etc.'[47]

Tax complexity implies, however, that reporting inevitably has a certain degree of complexity: overly simple, one-dimensional information can mislead stakeholders. Being open and transparent towards society shows the people in the company that you actually do what you say. In addition, those doing the right thing benefit because 'it makes it harder for others to hide in the shadows, and focuses the attention of scrutineers'.[48]

Transparency can be voluntary but also mandatory. Think of the mandatory country-by-country reporting to the tax authorities (only). Other stakeholders also insist on (public) transparency for their assessment of companies' tax sustainability performance. In Europe, the public country-by-country reporting directive has been in force since 9 December 2021.[49] This mandatory provision of information probably does not contain sufficiently detailed tax data to enable a proper analysis of the tax

44. Archie B. Carroll, *The Pyramid of Corporate Social Responsibility: Toward the Moral Management of Organizational Stakeholders*, Business Horizons 39, 48 (July-August 1991) and Archie B. Carroll, *Corporate Social Responsibility: Perspectives on the CSR Construct's Development and Future*, 60(6) Business & Society 1258, 1278 (2021) DOI: 10.1016/0007-6813(91)90005-g.
45. Hans Gribnau, *Corporate Social Responsibility and Tax Planning: Not by Rules Alone*, 24(4) Social & Legal Studies 225, 250 (2015), http://papers.ssrn.com/sol3/papers.cfm?abstract_id=2610090.
46. On 'substantive' and 'procedural good tax governance', *see*: H.J.L.M. Gribnau & A.-G. Jallai, *Good Tax Governance: A Matter of Moral Responsibility and Transparency*, 5(1) Nordic Tax Journal 70, 88 (2017), https://papers.ssrn.com/sol3/papers.cfm?abstract_id=3021914 and Ave-Geidi Jallai, *Good Tax Governance: International Corporate Tax Planning and Corporate Social Responsibility – Does One Exclude the Other?, PhD thesis* 161-170 (Tilburg University, Tilburg, 2020).
47. Daniel Gutmann, *Corporate Groups in the Age of Communication*, 154, 155 European Taxation (April 2023).
48. Jeremy Hirschhorn, *Tax in a Transparent World* 11 (2019), https://www.ato.gov.au/Media-centre/Speeches/Other/Tax-in-a-Transparent-World/.
49. Willemien Netjes & Dominik Freyer, *Tax Transparency Is Here to Stay: An Analysis of the Public CbCR Directive*, 50(8 & 9) Intertax 1 (2022) DOI: 10.54648/taxi2022060.

behaviour of multinationals. Responsible (sustainable) tax governance entails for companies to go 'beyond compliance' in this respect as well.

Various initiatives have been developed to make corporate tax governance more sustainable. Some of these will now briefly be dealt with. As for corporations, the B Team sees paying taxes as a social responsibility for a sustainable society. The B Team, a group of internationally active companies, published its 'Responsible Tax Principles' in February 2018.[50] In doing so, the B Team aims to restore trust between business and the public – which believes that companies value short-term profit (and shareholder value) over long-term sustainability. Taxes are an important means of achieving the SDGs, and this includes compliance with the letter and spirit of the law.[51] Given the often diverging visions and expectations of stakeholders, it will not be easy to reach a consensus on what exactly constitutes good tax governance. 'In particular, stakeholders will have different expectations on what measures should be in place within an MNE to ensure that taxes are managed ethically.'[52] Responsible tax behaviour plays a role in both obligations and entitlements. For example, the B Team has a separate principle 'Seeking & Accepting Tax Incentives'. Transparency is the procedural element of good tax governance. The importance of transparency is recognized by the B Team. Rightly so, the B Team also wants to be transparent about the manner of lobbying and advocacy among tax policymakers.[53]

In the spring of 2022, the Dutch employers' organization VNO-NCW published its Tax Governance Code.[54] Tax is not seen as 'a cost factor only, but as a means for social economic cohesion, sustainable growth and long-term prosperity'. More than 40 multinationals in the Netherlands pledged to comply with the letter, the intent and the spirit of the tax legislation of the countries in which they operate, and not to use tax havens for tax avoidance. They will also be transparent about, for example, their tax strategy and publish how much tax they pay per country and what financially material tax incentives they use. This code is based on the 'comply or explain' principle.

There are also investors that draw up reporting standards and thus contribute to consistent and uniform reporting. This can be an individual (very) large investor such as Norges Bank Investment Management (officially 'Government Pension Fund Global'), one of the largest investors in the world. This fund adheres to three principles: 1) taxes should be paid where economic value is generated, 2) the company's tax arrangements are the responsibility of the board, and 3) public country-by-country reporting is a core element of transparent tax disclosure. These principles are then

50. The B Team, *A New Bar for Responsible Tax. The B Team Responsible Tax Principles* (2018), https://bteam.org/our-thinking/reports/responsibletax-2. Responsible tax governance is deemed particularly important for companies operating in developing countries (at 13).
51. *See*, for example, OECD, *Guidelines for Multinational Corporations* 60 (Paris: OECD 2011).
52. The Conference Board/B team/European Business Tax Forum, *Best Practices for Good Tax Governance* 10 (2022), https://ebtforum.org/good-tax-governance/.
53. Jallai, *supra* n. 46, at 35-37. *See also* Anne Van de Vijver, *Morality of Lobbying for Tax Benefits: a Kantian perspective,* 1 Journal of Business Ethics 57 (2022) DOI: 10.1007/s10551-021-04911-3.
54. VNO-NCW, *supra* n. 43.

(briefly) elaborated along two lines: 'A. Implement appropriate and prudent tax policies' and 'B. Report transparently on corporate value generation'.[55]

Investor organizations are another example: they (sometimes) link taxes to companies' sustainability policies. For example, the Dutch Association of Investors for Sustainable Development (VBDO) has developed a Tax Transparency Benchmark (2014) in collaboration with Oikos, which is nowadays implemented by VBDO and PwC, to make performance in this area transparent and improve it. This benchmark consists of six principles for good tax governance – each elaborated into a number of more concrete indicators.[56] In recent years, companies have shown (sometimes strong) progress on a number of principles, but ESG fiscal reporting in particular is still underdeveloped.[57]

More recently, the Global Reporting Initiative (GRI), which develops global standards for (voluntary) sustainability reporting, released the 'GRI 207: Tax standard' in 2019 after extensive stakeholder consultation.[58] GRI 207 emphasizes that any obligation in the field of transparency and, more generally, tax governance should be accompanied by a system of independent monitoring.

§11.6 CONCLUSION

Governments and society, including the business community, bear responsibility for a sustainable development – elaborated in SDGs and ESGs. Taxes are crucial for sustainable development. Both public and corporate tax governance show an increasing focus on sustainability. A closer look at tax corporate tax governance developments (including tax reporting, transparency) confirmed this picture. Some recent initiatives by multinationals and investor organizations to promote sustainable and socially responsible tax behaviour were briefly dealt with. Tax indeed entered the corporate sustainability scene but is still looking for what role to play.

55. NBIM, *Tax and Transparency*; https://www.nbim.no/en/the-fund/responsible-investment/principles/expectations-to-companies/tax-and-transparency/.
56. *See* VBDO/PwCNL, *Principles for Good Tax Governance*, https://www.vbdo.nl/.
57. VBDO, *Tax Transparency Benchmark* 12 (2021), https://www.vbdo.nl/.
58. Global Reporting Initiative, *GRI 207: Tax Standard*; https://www.globalreporting.org/standards/gri-standards-download-center/gri-207-tax-2019/. *See also* Gurpinder Singh & Ave-Geidi Jallai, *Tax Transparency and GRI 207: Sustainability Reporting Meets Tax Reporting*, 51(3) Tax Management International Journal 1 (2022).

CHAPTER 12

Recognition of Inflation in Income Tax Law

Roman Seer

§12.1 INTRODUCTION

Peter Essers is a tax generalist who does not avoid questions of detail regarding domestic, European and global taxation. Therefore, the celebrator deserves a contribution which links a general problem with the concrete design of tax law. What is taxable income and in what way it may be taxed is a legal burden decision that must be made in the economic context. With the supply chain disruption caused by the pandemic and especially with Russia's belligerent invasion of Ukraine, the comfortable decade of low inflation[1] has come to an abrupt end for the time being. In Germany, the inflation rate measured by the consumer price index has ranged during the last year between 6.1% and 8.8% (arithmetic mean in the period August 2022-July 2023: 7.67%).[2] In the Netherlands, inflation has risen to an average inflation rate of 11.62% in 2022.[3] During 2023, the inflation rate in the Netherlands has diminished in July to 4.58%.[4] For Europe, the harmonised inflation rate (HICP Europe) has been 6.12% in May.[5] Though the inflation rates are recently moving back from their peak in 2022, it is quite unsure if this development will continue in the future. Thus, the discussion

1. https://de.statista.com/statistik/daten/studie/1046/umfrage/inflationsrate-veraenderung-des-verbraucherpreisindexes-zum-vorjahr: In the period between 2010 and 2020, inflation rates in Germany fluctuated between 0.5% and 2.2% (arithmetic mean: 1.25%).
2. https://de.statista.com/statistik/daten/studie/1045/umfrage/inflationsrate-in-deutschland-veraenderung-des-verbraucherpreisindexes-zum-vorjahresmonat.
3. https://de.statista.com/statistik/daten/studie/213055/umfrage/inflationsrate-in-den-niederlanden/statisticContainer.
4. https://www.inflation.eu/de/inflationsraten/niederlande/inflation-niederlande.aspx.
5. https://www.inflation.eu/en/inflation-rates/europe/inflation-europe.aspx. The HICP-index is not identical with the current inflation-index (CPI) which is the main inflation indicator in most countries.

about the effects of the so-called *cold tax progression* (hidden/silent tax progression) is at least in the German economic literature still ongoing.[6]

§12.2 NOMINAL VALUE PRINCIPLE VERSUS ABILITY-TO-PAY PRINCIPLE

The German income tax law has always followed the nominal value principle. The German Federal Constitutional Court (*Bundesverfassungsgericht* (BVerfG)) considers it to be a constitutionally justified legislative system decision and a 'supporting' regulatory principle, which also claims validity in income tax law.[7] In its decisions, the Court emphasises particularly the clarity and manageability of the law, i.e., legal certainty. Older decisions of the German Federal Fiscal Court (*Bundesfinanzhof* (BFH)) even considered the nominal value principle to be constitutionally unreviewable.[8] Without backing up its statement with economic-empirical evidence, the Federal Administrative Court (*Bundesverwaltungsgericht* (BVerwG)), for example, regarded the nominal value principle as a tool that itself directly contributes to monetary stability as a fundamental, indispensable principle of our legal and economic order.[9]

The unrestricted approval of the nominal value principle by the courts has been criticised in German jurisprudence for some time. Above all, a violation of taxation according to economic performance is stated.[10] Klaus Tipke vividly described the nominal value principle in his *Steuerrechtsordnung* as an economic 'fair weather principle' and classified it – as apparently also the Austrian Constitutional Court (*Verfassungsgerichtshof* (VerfGH)) did later[11] – as a merely technical principle serving the purpose of tax simplification.[12] This is to be agreed. The nominal value principle is not an outflow of the ability-to-pay principle but is in tension with this fundamental principle.[13] The principle of taxation according to actual ability to pay asks about economic realities. It is a *real value principle and not a nominal value principle.*[14] Fictitious profits do not generate economic capacity; this principle presupposes the existence of real income. Therefore, income tax law must not simply ignore the

6. *Pars pro toto in ifo* Schnelldienst, 2/2023, Vol. 76, 15 February 2023.
7. BVerfG 19 December 1978 – 1 BvR 335/76 et al., BVerfGE Vol. 50, p. 57 (p. 77); BVerfG 7 July 2010 – 2 BvL 14/02 et al., BVerfGE Vol. 127, p. 1 (p. 31) – Official Collection of Decisions.
8. BFH 27 July 1967 – IV 300/64, Bundessteuerblatt (BStBl.) Part III 1967, p. 690 (Federal Gazette); *see also* BFH 27 June 1996 – VIII B 102/95, marginal no. 5 (juris data base), with further references.
9. BVerwG 3 Oct. 1972 – I C 36.68, BVerwGE Vol. 41, p. 1 (p. 5) – Official Court Decision Collection.
10. For example, *see* J. Lang, *Die Bemessungsgrundlage der Einkommensteuer*, Habilitation, Otto Schmidt Verlag, 1981/88, p. 176.
11. VerfGH 3 March 2017 – G 3-4/2017-9, ECLI:AT:VFGH:2017:G3:2017, marginal no. 5.2 (https://www.ris.bka.gv.at).
12. Klaus Tipke, *Die Steuerrechtsordnung*, vol. I, 2nd ed., Otto Schmidt Verlag 2000, p. 513.
13. Roman Seer, *Geldwert und Steuern, Steuer und Wirtschaft* (StuW, journal) 2019, p. 212 (213).
14. Tipke, *supra* p. 512; Christoph Gröpl, *Das Nominalwertprinzip im Steuerrecht, Festschrift für Kußmaul* (Book of Honour), Erich Schmidt Verlag 2022, p. 411 (p. 417); Victor Thuronyi, *Tax Law Design & Drafting*, Vol. I, 1996, p. 439; Kevin Holmes, *The Concept of Income*, Diss., IBFD 2001, p. 342.

phenomenon of monetary devaluation but must - as far as practically possible - normatively capture it.[15]

§12.3 INCOME TAX RATE AND ABILITY-TO-PAY PRINCIPLE

The progressive income tax rate has historically been justified by the ability-to-pay principle. According to the urgency of the income components for the free development of the person and his or her dignified existence, the tax is to be progressively structured as the tax base increases.[16] It would mean an equal relative loss of satisfaction of needs if, with rising income, a growing proportion of income were covered by the tax.[17] Initially, this also corresponded to the view of the German Federal Constitutional Court.[18] However, the prevailing view is that only proportional taxation can be derived from the ability-to-pay principle, while a progressive tax rate is justified solely based on its redistributive purpose in line with the welfare state principle.[19] The original German income tax scale of 1958 corresponded at that time to the idea of the sacrifice theory, aimed to tax 95% of taxable persons at a proportional rate of 20%, with only the top 5% subject to progressive taxation.[20] Proportional taxation was supposed to be the *norm*. Accordingly, the upper proportional zone (the top tax rate) is only set at a level corresponding to twenty-one times (!) the average income.[21] For a long time, however, the German legislator did not shift the rate brackets - regardless of creeping inflation. The tariff threshold for the end of linear progression had remained virtually unchanged for decades since 1958.[22] Since then, significant changes have only taken place in the increase of the basic tax-free allowance (Grundfreibetrag)[23] and the gradual reduction of the top tax rate to 42% (as of the 2005 assessment period for taxable income over EUR 52,152). However, the progression zone was not adjusted to the development of the monetary value, but conversely even further compressed. This was done on the one hand in favour of lower incomes (through a significant increase in the basic tax-free

15. Seer, *supra* p. 212 (p. 213).
16. Fritz Neumark, *Grundsätze gerechter und ökonomisch rationaler Steuerpolitik*, 1970, p. 177.
17. *See also* Moris Lehner, *Abzug des Grundfreibetrages von der Bemessungsgrundlage oder von der Steuerschuld*, StuW 1986, p. 59 (p. 62); from a merely economic perspective, Hinterberger/Müller/Petersen, *'Gerechte' Tariftypen bei alternativen Opfertheorien und Nutzenfunktionen*, Finanz-Archiv (Journal), Vol. 45 (1987), p. 45.
18. BVerfG v. 24 June 1958 - 2 BvF 1/57, BVerfGE Vol. 8, p. 51 (p. 68) - Official Court Decision Collection.
19. Tipke, *supra* p. 403; Hey, in Tipke/Lang (founder), *Steuerrecht*, 24. Edition, Otto Schmidt Verlag 2021, marginal no. 8.802.
20. German Federal Government, *Bundestags-Drucksache* (parliamentary printout) 3/260, p. 37, p. 43.
21. Clemens Esser, *Die neuen Einkommensteuertarife 2000 bis 2005*, Institut Finanzen und Steuern (Ifst)-Schrift Vol. 383, 2000, p. 19.
22. Then DM 110,040, top tax rate 53%, *see* Tax Amendment Act 1958 of 18 July 1958, *Bundesgesetzblatt* (BGBl.) Teil I 1958, p. 473 (p. 492: Annex to § 32a dEStG) - German Federal Law Gazette.
23. Urged by BVerfG 25 Sep. 1992 - 2 BvL 5/91, BVerfGE Vol. 87, p. 153 (p. 172) - Official Court Decision Collection. With this decision, the BVerfG declared the former amount of the basic tax-free allowance (until 1995: only EUR 2,871 p.a.) to be unconstitutional and obliged the tax legislator to leave the subsistence needs determined by social welfare law tax free.

allowance) and on the other hand in favour of high incomes (through a significant reduction in the top tax rate).[24] If even average earners are already caught by the progression due to a lack of adjustment of the rate limits and the progression zone ends at 1.5 times average earnings[25] instead of 21 times, this certainly no longer has anything to do with a decreasing marginal benefit of taxpayers who are taxed progressively. But the welfare state principle can also no longer justify the 'cold growth' of average earners into the tax progression by any redistribution purpose.

§12.4 ADJUSTMENT OF THE TAX RATES TO INFLATION

Since 1955, the German Income Tax Act has contained a progressive formula tariff instead of a graduated tariff. The difference is that a formula tariff can express the tax amount in a complex mathematical formula (here, a second-degree polynomial), whereas the other tariff forms only have linear relationships available.[26] The advantage of a formula tariff with a linear-progressive tariff zone is that it avoids possible performance inhibitions at the step entries. If there is only an increase in nominal income without an increase in purchasing power, the taxpayer has not become more efficient in real terms. If, despite this, an additional tax burden arises due to the progression, this violates the ability-to-pay principle.[27] Furthermore, the inflation-related hidden (silent) tax progression is also problematic with regard to the principle of democracy. The considerable tax increase[28] brought about by it is not based on any explicit decision by the legislator. Rather, a tax burden is 'secretly' created, which in its amount and distribution was not originally intended by the legislator.[29]

For this reason, there have long been strong calls in the German literature to put the tax scale 'on wheels'.[30] However, only the regular increase of the basic tax-free

24. The latter effect was, however, relativised again by the introduction of a second proportional top tax rate of 45% (from the 2007 assessment period, the rate jumped from 42% to 45% at EUR 250,000 at that time – 'tax of the rich', *see* Tax Amendment Act 2007 of 19 July 2006, BGBl. I 2006 [German Federal Law Gazette], p. 1652 [p. 1654]).
25. The average gross earnings of a full-time employee in Germany in 2018 amounted to EUR 3,880 per month (approx. EUR 48,000 p.a.), according to https://de.statista.com/statistik/daten/studie/237674/umfrage/durchschnittlicher-bruttomonatsverdienst-eines-arbeitnehmers-in-deutschland.
26. Siegel, *supra* section 32a EStG n. 5 (February 2021).
27. Henriette Houben, *Reformüberlegungen zur Bemessung der Einkommensteuer*, Deutsche Steuerjuristische Gesellschaft (DStJG), Annual Meeting (2013: Erneuerung des Steuerrechts), Vol. 37 (2014), p. 321 (p. 323), Seer, *supra* p. 212 (p. 214); Gröpl, *supra* p. 411 (p. 417); Holmes, *supra* p. 342.
28. For example, Christiana Djanani & Thimo Grossmann, *Kalte Progression aufgrund fehlender Inflationskorrektur außertariflicher Abzüge und Höchstbeträge bei der Einkommensteuer*, StuW 2015, p. 33 (p. 50) estimate for the year 2013 the secret tax increase attributable to the tariff including the basic tax-free allowance at approximately EUR 6.6 billion.
29. Ralph Brennecke & Frank Klanberg, *Auswirkungen alternativer Vorschläge zur Einkommensbesteuerung in einer inflationären Wirtschaft*, FinArch. Vol. 33 (1974), p. 73 (p. 89); *see also* Friederike Knaupp, *Der Einkommensteuertarif als Ausdruck der Steuergerechtigkeit*, Dissertation, Utz Verlag 2004, p. 61.
30. *Pars pro toto* Volker Stern, *Der Tarif muss auf Räder – Heimliche Steuererhöhungen vermeiden*, Karl-Bräuer-Institut des Bundes der Steuerzahler, Vol. 95, 2002 (short version in Deutsche Steuerzeitung [DStZ, Journal] 2003, pp. 29-302).

allowance remained, as well as a decision of the German Bundestag to have the federal government prepare a *tax progression report* on the effect of the cold tax progression in the tax scale every two years.[31] Since then, the Government has presented a total of five tax progression reports. Only as a result of these reports has the German legislator, since the 2016 assessment period, complied with the demand to avoid 'cold tax progression' by making annual changes to the tax scale contained in section 32a(1) of the German Income Tax Act through tariff measures. These adjustments have shifted the tax brackets to the right by various percentages each year. The most recent adjustments were made by the so-called Tax Relief Act 2022[32] and the Inflation Compensation Act 2022.[33] This shifted the tax rate to the right by 7.2% for 2023 and by 6.3% for 2024.

In contrast to the German tax law design, the income tax tariffs of the Netherlands have a quite simple structure. The Netherlands is following the concept of an analytic income tax base with different tax rates for different kinds of income. The Individual Income Tax Law of 2001 (*Wet op de Inkomstenbelasting 2001*) divides the taxable income into three categories known as 'boxes'.[34] This box-tax system differs between earned income (especially from work) and owner-occupied dwellings (box 1) and income from substantial shareholding of at least 5% of the subscribed capital of the corporation (box 2) and income from savings and investments (box 3). Box 2 and box 3 income are taxed by proportional rates of 26.9% (box 2) and 32% (box 3).[35] For the design of a proportional tax rate, the problem of a silent progression is irrelevant, in general.[36] Only the tax tariff of box 1 has a progressive structure as a 'slice tariff (*schijventarief*)'. With effect from 1 January 2020, the Income Tax Law of the Netherlands[37] provides a simple two-bracket rate system.[38] For 2023, the tax rate is 36.93% for income up to EUR 73,030, with any amount above that threshold taxed at 49.50%. The rate of the first tax bracket includes the state social security contribution (27.65%) up to a maximum amount of EUR 37,150 (2023). Up to this threshold, the income tax rate is therefore in fact 9.28%. After Article 10.1 NL Income Tax Act (*Wet IB*), the tax brackets of box 1 have to be annually adjusted to the inflation which is measured by the consumer price index (CPI). For this purpose, the average of the CPI of the eighteenth to the seventh month before the beginning of the tax year (calendar

31. Decision by the German Bundestag, 172nd session, 29 March 2012, Stenographic Report, Plenary Minutes 17/172, p. 20267, p. 20272.
32. BGBl. I 2022 (German Federal Law Gazette), p. 749.
33. BGBl. I 2022 (German Federal Law Gazette), p. 2230.
34. Enacted by the income tax act (*Wet op de Inkomstenbelasting 2001*) of 11 May 2000, Staatsblad von het Koninkrijk der Nederlanden - Stb. (Official Gazette) 2000, p. 215.
35. The tax rate has increased from 31% (2022) to 32% (2023).
36. Only specific tax base allowances or tax deductible amounts may trigger the effect of an indirect silent ('cold') tax progression; regarding box 3, *see* later under §12.6.
37. Article 2.10 Wet inkomstenbelasting (Wet IB) 2023.
38. Marnix Veldhuijzen, *Netherlands – Individual Taxation – Country Tax Guides* (last reviewed 20 May 2023), IBFD Tax Research Platform.

year) has to be compared with the average of the CPI of the thirtieth to the nineteenth month before the beginning of the tax year (calendar year).[39]

The Dutch system of an *automatic* adjustment of the tax rate to the rate of inflation is superior to the *discretionary* system in Germany. It makes a big difference whether the parliament decides on the adjustment every year in a discretionary manner[40] or whether it has to repeal the automatic adjustment stipulated in the law by means of a corrective law in order to deviate from it. From a constitutional point of view, however, one cannot deny parliament the right to decide anew on the question of adjustment.[41]

§12.5 ADJUSTMENT OF ALLOWANCES, TAX DEDUCTIONS, EXEMPTION LIMITS AND LUMP SUMS

'Silent' tax increases which are caused by inflation in the absence of legislative action are not only limited to progressive tax rates but also extended to the tax base items. For the individual concerned, the inflation-related exceeding of exemption thresholds is particularly noticeable when the rise in the price level suddenly leads to the fact that previously tax-exempt parts of income are now fully taxed (in the sense of an 'either or').[42] But 'frozen' allowances also cause tax increases that amplify over time. The same applies to non-refutable deduction lump sums in contrast with lump sums which leave the taxpayer the possibility of itemising expenses. In the absence of inflation adjustments, the last mentioned lump sums merely lose their function of administrative simplification over time.

Since the child benefit, subsistence minimum and child care decisions of the German BVerfG,[43] the legislature has been forced to exempt the family subsistence minimum in the assessment basis of income tax at the current level in coordination with social welfare law. Since then, it has also complied with this at regular intervals. In contrast to these fiscal purpose exemptions, the adjustment of social or incentive purpose exemptions is within the legislature's scope. The same applies to simplification exemptions and the lump sum for income-related expenses within the meaning of section 9a German Income Tax Act, in particular the employee lump sum of EUR 1,230. However, if such amounts are not adjusted over a period of years, they fail to achieve

39. For example, the tax bracket has been increased from EUR 69,398 in 2022 to EUR 73,030 in 2023 (= adjustment of 5.23%). Even the threshold for the social security contribution has been adjusted from EUR 35,473 (2022) to EUR 37,148 (2023).
40. *See* BGBl. I 2022 p. 2230, *supra.*
41. Lang, *supra* p. 179; Hechtner, *supra* p. 132 (p. 143); *see also* Thuronyi, *supra* p. 443.
42. On the effects of inflation on exemption limits, allowances and lump sums for deductions, *see* Rolf Wiswesser, *Einkommens- und Gewinnbesteuerung bei Inflation*, Dissertation, Peter Lang Verlag 1997, p. 34.
43. BVerfG 29 May 1990 – 1 BvL 20/84 et al., BVerfGE Vol. 82, p. 60; BVerfG 12 June 1990 – 1 BvL 72/86, BVerfGE Vol. 82, p. 198; BVerfG 25 September 1992 – 2 BvL 5/91, BVerfGE Vol. 87, p. 153; BVerfG 10 Nov. 1998 – 2 BvR 1057/91 et al., BVerfGE Vol. 99, p. 216; BVerfG 10 November 1998 – 2 BvL 42/93, BVerfGE Vol. 99, p. 246; BVerfG 10 November 1998 – 2 BvR 1220/93, BVerfGE Vol. 99, p. 268; BVerfG 10 November 1998 – 2 BvR 1852/97 et al., BVerfGE Vol. 99, p. 273 – Official Court Decision Collection.

their administrative simplification effect, as shown by the valuation exemption for low-value assets in the amount of DM 800 (later EUR 410), which was frozen for decades in accordance with section 6 paragraph 2 German Tax Act. The legislator also has a significant discretion when it comes to mixed expenses related to private living. Therefore, the lump sum of EUR 0.30 for travel between home and the first place of work (section 9 paragraph 1 sentence 2 no. 4 German Income Tax Act) does not have to be adjusted to inflationary developments. It is also ultimately a question of administrative simplification if the legislator leaves the lump sum for disabled persons according to section 33b German Income Tax Act unchanged for decades because the proof of extraordinary burdens according to section 33 German Income Tax Code remains unaffected.

In the German Tax Code, we cannot find any position which is automatically adapted to inflation increases. Even the constitutionally protected allowances for child maintenance costs as well as the associated child support payments by the state are indexed by the Consumer Price Index (CPI)-Rate. It remains still in a discretional decision of the Government if and to which extent the amounts will be adapted by CPI-Rates. The findings of the updated subsistence level report are only indicators for this decision.

In contrast, in the Netherlands, personal allowances are recognised not in the tax base or – like in Germany – integrated in the tariff as a zero-tax bracket (*Grundfreibetrag*) but as a *tax credit* (*heffingskortingen*). The most relevant tax credits are the following: personal allowances are covered by a *general tax credit* (Article 8.10 Wet IB) which melts off depending on the income.[44] A similar technique is used for an *employment tax credit* (Article 8.11 Wet IB) which relieves substantially all employed and self-employed persons with low and middle income.[45] A *senior citizen credit* (Article 8.17 and Article 8.18 Wet IB) serves the same purpose and is available to taxpayers who are at least 66 years and 10 months old.[46] All these tax credits are automatically indexed by the CPI (*see* Article 10.1 paragraph 1 Wet IB).

§12.6 TAXATION OF INVESTMENT INCOME

In view of the creeping inflation, those who earn income from the transfer of financial capital must spend part of it to maintain the real earning power of their asset base. In

44. In 2023, the tax credit amounts to EUR 3,070 up to an income of EUR 22,660. Does the income of box 1 exceeds this threshold EUR 22,661, the tax credit is to be reduced by 6.095% of the income of box 1 that exceeds EUR 22,660. The effect is that the tax credit will be EUR 0 if the income of box 1 amounts to EUR 73,030 and more.
45. In 2023, the tax credit rises up to a maximum level of EUR 5,052 at a threshold of EUR 37,697 income and is melting off up to an income of EUR 115,294 by using a factor of 6.51% for the part of the income which exceeds EUR 37,697.
46. In 2023, the senior tax credit amounts to EUR 1,835 (for singles: EUR 2,313). From an aggregated income of EUR 40,488 on the tax credit is lowered of 15% of the exceeding income. The effect is that the tax credit will be EUR 0 if the aggregated income of the senior amounts to EUR 53,122 (for a single senior: EUR 55,908). If a senior is still working as an employee or self-employer, the employment tax credit is accounted by a special (reduced) scheme.

this respect, the capital gain does not reflect a genuine growth in economic performance.[47] The amount of monetary devaluation that has occurred is rather merely an investment for the loss of real purchasing power. To the extent of the inflation rate, the capital gain represents economically only a kind of *demonetisation premium*.[48] By not allowing this demonetisation premium to be deducted, the current law taxes an inflation-related fictitious gain and violates the *objective net principle*, which is to be understood as the actual principle.[49] From an economic point of view, it contains a *wealth tax in disguise*,[50] which is not changed by the system of special flat-rate taxation according to section 32d EStG.

Depending on the amount of the nominal capital yield and the inflation rate, the burden on the real yield can easily be significantly above 100%. With regard to safe euro bonds, it can be seen that since 2011 the real interest rate has only been negative, and the taxation of the nominal interest rate successively leads to the *effective consumption of assets*. The final withholding tax of 25% is therefore unsuitable to bring about a typifying compensation for inflation by lowering tax rates - even for high incomes.[51] This is even more true in combination with the savers' lump sum of EUR 1,000 according to section 20 paragraph 9 German Tax Act, which makes the flat-rate tax degenerate into a gross income tax with increasing income.

The German Federal Constitutional Court had also justified the fading out of inflation in capital income with the previous separation between taxable income and the non-taxable changes in capital stock at the asset level.[52] This argument has become obsolete due to the expansion of income from capital assets to include the unlimited taxation of capital gains since 2009. Since capital gains are now fully recognised, irrespective of the holding period of the capital assets sold, the taxable capital gain includes an *inflation-related fictitious gain* that grows exponentially with the investment period.[53] However, insofar as the taxpayer finances his capital assets by borrowing, *inflation-related debtor gains* (*dummy losses*) arise on his liabilities side because of the merely nominal repayment obligation.[54] Inflation then only impacts the disparity between capital assets and the related debts.[55] However, this effect is negligible *de lege lata* because the debt interest associated with the debts is not deductible, contrary to section 9 paragraph 1 sentence 3 no. 1 German Income Tax

47. Tipke, *supra* p. 512.
48. F.W. Wagner, *Warum die 'Lücken' der Besteuerung von Veräußerungsgewinnen bestehen bleiben sollten*, Zeitschrift für Wirtschaftspolitik (ZfWp), Vol. 56 (2007), p. 55 (p. 59): *Geldentwertungsprämie*.
49. The objective net principle requires an elimination of fictitious profits, *see* Guido Weber, *Inflationsberücksichtigung in der Einkommensteuer*, Dissertation, Nomos Verlag 2011, p. 93.
50. Florian Kleinmanns, *Besteuerung inflationbedingter Scheingewinne im System des deutschen Einkommensteuerrechts und ihre verfassungsrechtliche Rechtfertigung*, Dissertation, Nomos Verlag 2009, p. 25.
51. *See already* Joachim English, *Verfassungsrechtliche und steuersystematische Kritik der Abgeltungssteuer*, StuW 2007, p. 221 (p. 228).
52. BVerfG 19 December 1978 - 1 BvR 335/76 et al., BVerfGE Vol. 50, p. 57 (p. 80) - Official Court Decision Collection.
53. Kleinmanns, *supra* p. 20.
54. Kleinmanns, *supra* p. 51; Weber, *supra* p. 51.
55. Weber, *supra* p. 51.

Code, and is compensated by the savers' lump sum under section 20 paragraph 9 sentence 1 German Income Tax Code.

A similar problem urges the taxation of box 3 income in the Netherlands. When box 3 was created as of 2001, the legislator set the flat-rate return at *four percent*. This percentage has not been dependent on the actual return on assets during the year. The idea has been to allow a global but acceptable way to align with the returns that taxpayers should be able to achieve on average in practice.[56] The legislator presumed that this has been a realistic yield which is attainable without having much risk if viewed over a longer period of time. The Dutch Supreme Court (*Hoge Raad*) has accepted this 'robust' and therefore 'somewhat rough' flat-rate system, in general, with the well-known argument of the legislature's wide margin of discretion in the field of tax law.[57] However, the Court limited this discretion by applying Article 1 of the First Protocol (FP) to the European Convention of Human Rights (ECHR), the *protection of property*. In the view of Article 1 FP ECHR, the box 3 – system would be contrary to the fundamental property right if the assumed four percent return would no longer be feasible for private investors and taxpayers without an excessive burden.[58]

Under the circumstances of a capital market with zero or even negative interests, the presumption of a return of riskless attainable 4% return on the capital did not fit any longer. Thus, the Dutch legislator abandoned the basis of the low-risk return from 2017 on and substituted it by a link with an average distribution of box 3 assets between savings and investments (*asset mix*).[59] The taxation in box 3 has been based afterwards on a weighted notional yield on net assets. The Dutch Supreme Court has set further limits on the legislator's discretion to design tax rules with a fictitious income and reduced the tax assessments on the basis of the actual achieved return.[60] Besides the above-mentioned fundamental right of the protection of property (Article 1 of FP ECHR), the Court has additionally applied Article 14 ECHR with the prohibition of discrimination and the *proportionality test*.[61] From the view of the Court, the new flat-rate system of a deemed asset mix has contravened these fundamental rights of the taxpayer because the new system has distanced even further from an income that could reasonably be assumed to have actually been enjoyed by the individual taxpayer. The new system has disproportionately limited the freedom of property disposal by

56. Parliamentary Papers (*Kamerstukken*) II 1999/2000, 26 727, No. 7, p. 263.
57. Hoge Raad 3 April 2015 – 13/04247, ECLI:NL:HR:2015:812 (case of the taxyear 2010); Hoge Raad 10 June 2016 – 14/05020, ECLI:NL:HR:2016:1129 (case of the taxyear 2011).
58. Hoge Raad 3 April 2015 (footnote 77), under 2.3.2.; Hoge Raad 10 June 2016, *supra* under 2.4.1.3.
59. The waiver of the approach of an without much risk achievable return of investment has had primarily budgetary reasons, *see* Parliamentary Papers (*Kamerstukken*) II 2015/2016, 34302, no. 3, pp. 9/10 and 20; 2016/2017, 34552, no. 6, Annex 783311, pp. 7 and 9 to 12.
60. Hoge Raad 24 December 2021 – 21/01243, ECLI:NL:HR:2021:1963 (case of the taxyears 2017 and 2018); the box 3 tax amounts for 2017, EUR 12,705 and for 2018, EUR 11,969 though the actual achieved return has been only EUR 6,612 in 2017 and EUR 3,528 in 2018.
61. Hoge Raad 24 December 2021, *supra* under p. 3.3.3.; about procedural issues of legal protection in similar cases, *see* Essers, *De Hoge Raad als Deus ex Machina in het Box 3-Drama*, Weekblad Fiscaal Recht (WFR) 2022, p. 223.

imposing a relatively heavy financial burden on the choice not to engage in risky capital investments.[62]

After this decision, the legislator has tried to approximate the box 3 - scheme closer to the actual return of investments of the taxpayers. Therefore, in 2023, the focus has shifted to the actual allocation of the taxpayer's capital, emphasizing its real-world investment strategies. Cash and savings have a deemed return of 0.36%; other assets have a deemed return of 6.17%. From these returns, a fictitious debt return of 2.57% will be subtracted to calculate the total deemed return.[63] Regardless of these amendments, from a German law perspective, the box 3 - taxation still has the character of a mere *target income tax*. It is a wealth tax in a robe of an income tax. Not much better than the German income tax on private investments, box 3 does not recognise the Dutch system, and it also does not know any reduction of the deemed yield by the inflation rate.

§12.7 TAXATION OF REAL ESTATE INCOME

The box 3 - taxation system of the Netherlands also includes investments in real estate rentals. Therefore, it seems to be quite tax neutral if the taxpayer invests in stocks or in real property. In the German tax law, this is not the case. In contrast to capital investments, value-preserving expenses on rented real estate are tax deductible: either as immediately deductible maintenance expenses according to section 9 paragraph 1 sentence 1 German Income Tax Act or via the deductible depreciation for wear and tear on subsequent production costs of the rented building according to section 9 paragraph 1 sentence 3 German Income Tax Act in conjunction with section 7 paragraph 4 German Income Tax Act. Furthermore, inflation-related fictitious losses or debtor's gains regularly arise on the liabilities side of the income from renting and leasing by taking out real estate loans. The related debt interests are fully deductible as income-related expenses (unlike in the case of income from capital assets). The inflation-related fictitious gain is thus limited to the balance between the property values and the related debts when the properties are sold.

In addition, income from private asset transactions is limited to disposals within a holding period of a maximum of ten years pursuant to section 22 no. 2 in conjunction with section 23 paragraph 1 no. 1 German Income Tax Act. In this context, units used for residential purposes by the owner are even completely exempted from taxation according to section 23 paragraph 1 no. 1 sentence 3 German Income Tax Act. The increases in value in the last decade, which were significantly above the rate of inflation, have led to a (real) *untaxed increase in net assets*, just as in the case of real

62. Article 5 para. 2 *Wet IB* has divided the capital into two asset-classes. The riskless investment-class I has had a deemed yield of –0.1% and the risky investment-class II a deemed yield of + 5.53% (2022). The scheme assumed further that as higher the capital is, as more will be spent in risky investments: Up to EUR 50,650 = 67% is assigned to class I (33% to class II), from EUR 50,650 on and up to EUR 962,350 = 21% is assigned to class I (79% to class II), above EUR 962,350 = 100% is assigned to class II. A capital up to EUR 50,650 (2022) respectively EUR 57,000 (2023) is tax free (Art. 5 para. 5 *Wet IB*).
63. *See* Veldhuijzen, *supra* under 1.5. Investment income.

estate held for longer than ten years. It would be in line with the ability-to-pay principle to tax it when it is realised (irrespective of a ten-year period).

However, the capital gain would have to be appropriately transferred to the acquisition or production costs of the replacement asset in the case of reinvestment, in order to consider the increase in land and construction prices in the meantime to avoid a fictitious taxation of profits. Due to that, the currently only limited recognition of gains from the sale of real estate might be seen as a *simplification exemption*. Ultimately, there remains a need to eliminate the inflation-related fictitious gain on the sale of real estate not used for own residential purposes only within ten years. The aforementioned reinvestment rule could take this need into account.

§12.8 FINAL REMARKS

The first step to recognize inflation in the income tax law is to 'put' the tax tariff-brackets 'off the ground'. In this respect, the income tax of the Netherlands can be a model for countries like Germany to link it automatically to the CPI. The same should be the case for allowances which have the function to map the minimum subsistence level in the income tax law. The last step would be to recognize the inflation rate during the determination of the net income. Since the indexation of all assets and economic burdens is hardly practicable, the tax exemption of a return on equity in the amount of the inflation rate remains as an alternative (so-called *inflation allowance*).[64] One can also speak of the 'indexation of equity' with this proposal. Similar to this way is the interest-adjusted taxation; well-founded income is only taxed to the extent that it exceeds the normal market interest rate (in relation to the equity capital invested).[65] The *protective interest* deducted from the tax base avoids the taxation of inflation-related fictitious profits insofar as the market interest rate is regarded as an indicator of inflation. However, the market interest rates are not identical with the inflation rates, so that the inflation allowance has a more targeted effect in this respect. But the aim of a protective interest rate is not only to adjust for inflation but also to achieve *financing neutrality*. From the entrepreneurial point of view, it should be as decision-neutral as possible to finance the enterprise by using equity capital or by borrowing. From this perspective, it could be the best choice to instal measures of interest deductions.

64. Clemens Esser, *Ertragsbesteuerung und Geldentwertung – das Problem des 'Scheingewinns'*, Institut Finanzen und Steuern (ifst), Vol. 374, 1999, p. 58.
65. Wiswesser, *supra* p. 236; Weber, *supra* p. 60.

CHAPTER 13

The Notion of Income from Capital: Twenty Years Later

Johanna Hey

§13.1 THE EATLP CONGRESS 2003 IN COLOGNE: MAIN FINDINGS

Twenty years ago, Peter Essers chaired the EATLP Congress on the Notion of Income from Capital together with Arie Rijkers in Cologne. The debate was very fundamental. Joachim Lang[1] and Manfred Rose[2] on the one side and Wolfgang Gassner[3] on the other side argued about the meaning, purpose and content of the ability-to-pay principle, about the lifetime notion of income versus the technical principle of the annual levy of income tax and the section principle (*Abschnittsprinzip*), the distinction between the real value principle and nominal value principle, the net principle and the simplifying effect of taxing fictitious income.

Peter Essers and Arie Rijkers declared their support for income taxation based on the ability-to-pay principle. There would simply be no other equally suitable principle. Dutch pragmatism possibly allowed them to avoid German/Austrian rigorism when they formulated:

> The reality and existence of the ability-to-pay-principle does not depend on the description or definition of scientists. Scientists do not choose principles. They

1. Joachim Lang, *The Influence of Tax Principles on the Taxation of Income from Capital*, in *The Notion of Income from Capital* 3 et seq. (Peter Essers & Arie Rijkers eds., IBFD 2005).
2. Manfred Rose, *Economic Aspects of Taxation of Income from Capital*, in *The Notion of Income from Capital* 53 et seq. (Peter Essers & Arie Rijkers eds., IBFD 2005).
3. Wolfgang Gassner, *The Influence of Tax Principles on the Taxation of Income from Capital—A Response*, in *The Notion of Income From Capital* 33 et seq. (Peter Essers & Arie Rijkers eds., IBFD 2005).

> choose us. Scientists don't have to develop principles. These principles develop themselves. Tax scientists ought to make this development visible and palpable.[4]

From the principle of equal taxation of income according to the ability-to-pay principle follows the ideal of a comprehensive income tax.[5] However, at this time already, the real tax world was far apart from the ideal global income tax. Some of the contributions read like a swan song to the synthetic income tax since special regimes for the taxation of capital income, namely interest and dividends, had already been established in many European countries by the early 2000s.[6] There may be good reasons for distinguishing between labor and capital income, but splitting income into different types has significant drawbacks with which all States struggle.[7]

§13.2 WHAT IS DIFFERENT IN 2023?

§13.2.1 Final Withholding Taxes All Over the Place

Today, there is not a country left in the European Union where income from capital is taxed progressively as part of the global income tax base.[8] In Germany, the imputation system for dividend income was already replaced in 2000/2001 by a partial exemption system. This was followed by the introduction of a final withholding tax with a flat rate of 25% for interest, dividends and investment income in 2008, whereby a differentiation is made between investments held as business assets and investments held as private assets for the taxation of dividend income. Only the former are subject to the gross taxation of the final withholding tax, while the latter are subject to the partial exemption method, which includes only 60% of the dividend into the personal income tax base and at the same time allows deducting 60% of the expenses. This creates an incentive to transfer shares to business assets. Different sub-schedules within the capital income schedule give rise to tax planning activities. Therefore, Peter Essers and Arie Rijkers had rightly pointed out that both should be taxed alike.[9]

---

4. Peter Essers & Arie Rijkers, *General Report*, in *The Notion of Income from Capital* 334 no. 2 (Peter Essers & Arie Rijkers eds., IBFD 2005).
5. Peter Essers & Arie Rijkers, *ibid.*, at 286.
6. Dual Income Taxes in Scandinavia, also known as the Nordic Dual Income Taxes, which were implemented in the early 1990s, *see* Peter Birch Sørensen, *Dual Income Taxes: A Nordic Tax System*, EPRU Working Paper Series 2009-10, 2 (2009). In regard to the Austrian final withholding tax (*KESt*), a flat tax of 22% applied since 1994, *see* Bernd Genser, *Austria's Steps Towards a Dual Income Tax*, 2.288 ZBW (1995); the Netherlands operated a "fixed amount scheme," implemented in 2001, *see* Henk van Arendonk, *Fixed Amount Taxation with Respect to Income from Capital in Personal Income Taxation*, in *The Notion of Income From Capital* 110 (Peter Essers & Arie Rijkers eds., IBFD 2005). The Dutch system stood out because it taxes a fictitious return.
7. *See*, for example, the recent comparison (Elisabeth Steinhauser & Sandra Müller-Thomczik, *Die Verlustberücksichtigung bei Kapitaleinkünften in Deutschland als Vorbild für Österreich?—Eine vergleichende und normative Analyse mit Implikationen für Reformdiskussionen*, 2 StAW 169 (2022)) between Austrian and German restrictions on loss-offsetting for capital income, where it is difficult to say which system is more restrictive and leads to more severe distortions.
8. EU Commission, *Taxation of Household Capital in the EU Member States: Impact on Economic Efficiency, Revenue & Redistribution*, 130 Discussion Paper 1, 52 et seq. (2020).
9. Essers & Rijkers, *supra* n. 4, at 335 no. 7.

§13.2.2 Automatic Exchange of Information

At the same time, the major challenges of the enforcement of taxing income from capital due to its elusiveness have been mitigated by the implementation of the worldwide automatic exchange of information on capital income. When the 25% final withholding tax on capital income was proposed in Germany in 2007, the comparison between the highest tax bracket of the personal income tax (45%) and the low tax burden of "effortless" income from capital was hotly debated as an equity and tax justice problem. The German Minister of Finance at that time referred to the difficulties of collecting tax on capital with the slogan "better 25% of x, than 50% of *nix* (= nothing)." Today, this argument loses its persuasive power more and more. Although it is unclear how well it actually works in practice,[10] the Multilateral Competent Authority Agreement on Automatic Exchange of Financial Account Information (MCAA)[11] changed the situation fundamentally. In theory, it is impossible to hide capital abroad any longer.

§13.2.3 Inflation and Negative (Real) Interest

The argument that the enforcement problems cannot be solved in any other way than through the low final withholding tax is—at least for the time being—no longer even necessary. The low personal income taxation of dividends and capital gains results from the pre-taxation at the corporate level[12] and, therefore, does not require a justification at all. The low taxation of non-pre-taxed interest income is a—highly imperfect[13]—response to inflation and negative real interest rates. On the contrary, it is difficult to justify that interest is taxed at all.

So far, the biggest change since the EATLP Congress of 2003 is of factual nature. In 2003, it was conceivable neither that the European Central Bank's key interest rate would be negative for years 2013-2021 nor that we would see the worst inflation of the post-war period beginning in 2022. In this context, the main problem in the phase of negative nominal interest rates was the treatment of so-called custodian fees. As long as real income instead of fictitious income is used as a computational basis, the interest income of savers is zero. Therefore, the problem is at least not exacerbated by the capital income tax. However, the intervention of the tax is particularly problematic if—as has been the case since mid-2022—while interest is paid again, it lags far behind

10. Vokhid Urinov, *Developing Country Perspectives on Automatic Exchange of Tax Information*, 1 LGD 1, 11 et seq. (2015); Leo Ahrens & Fabio Bothner, *The Big Bang: Tax Evasion after Automatic Exchange of Information under FATCA and CRS*, 25.6 NPE 849, 862 (2020) DOI: 10.1080/13563467.2019.1639651.
11. OECD, *Multilateral Competent Authority Agreement on Automatic Exchange of Financial Account Information*, 2014.
12. *See* Claudio Sacchetto & Laura Castaldi, *Relationship Between Personal Income Tax on Income from Capital and Other Taxes on Income from Capital (Corporate Income Tax, Wealth Tax, Inheritance and Gift Tax and Real-Estate Tax)*, in *The Notion of Income From Capital* 94 et seq. (Peter Essers & Arie Rijkers eds., IBFD 2005).
13. Roman Seer, *Geldwert und Steuern: Inflation und Niedrigzins als Herausforderungen für den Steuergesetzgeber*, Steuer und Wirtschaft 2019, 212, 224.

inflation. In this case, the tax exacerbates the problem of wealth loss due to negative real interest rates. Even though inflation momentum has weakened[14] in recent months and the ECB's key interest rate has been raised by 3.5% since July 2022, various indicators point to a clearly negative real interest rate in the long term (Figure 13.1).[15]

Figure 13.1 Interplay: Inflation/ECB Key Interest Rate/Real Interest Rate[16]

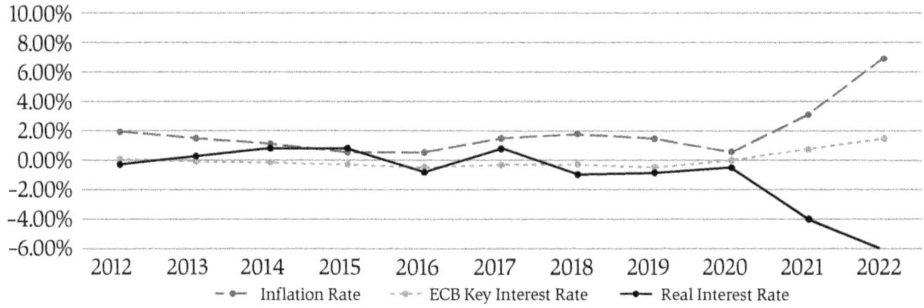

§13.3 INFLATION: THE UNSOLVED PROBLEM OF THE TAXATION OF INCOME FROM CAPITAL

So far, the tax system provides no systematic answers, though Peter Essers and Arie Rijkers rightly saw an important role in inflation accounting.[17] The effects of inflation affect the entire tax system; particularly problematic are the taxation of capital gains accrued over a long period of time on the one hand and, on the other hand, the taxation of nominal interest.

Nevertheless, the nominal value principle is not fundamentally called into question. A comprehensive inflation adjustment is complex and would have to capture not only inflation losses on the creditor side but also inflation gains on the debtor side. Therefore, the nominal principle is acceptable as long as inflation is moderate. According to the case law of the German Federal Constitutional Court, the tax legislator is not constitutionally obliged to take inflation into account when taxing interest income.[18] However, this statement cannot be set in absolute terms. Rather, it depends on the extent of inflation and the negative real interest rate in particular. In countries

14. Annual inflation down to 5.3% in the euro area, down to 6.1% in the EU, and by 6.5% for Germany, *see* Eurostat (July 2023).
15. Tobias Adrian & Nassira Abbas, *Low Real Interest Rates Support Asset Prices, but Risks Are Rising*, IMF (January 27, 2022). The authors indicate a negative real interest rate amounting to −1.5% for Germany for 2031.
16. *Sources: Inflationsrate in Deutschland von 1992 bis 2022*, Statistisches Bundesamt (September 8, 2023); *Key ECB Interest Rates*, European Central Bank (September 8, 2023); *Realzinssätze Banken DE / Neugeschäft / Einlagen privater Haushalte, vereinbarte Laufzeit von über 2 Jahren*, Deutsche Bundesbank (September 8, 2023).
17. Essers & Rijkers, *supra* n. 4, at 325; in detail Ian Roxan, *Influence of Inflation*, in *The Notion of Income From Capital* 223 et seq. (Peter Essers & Arie Rijkers eds., IBFD 2005).
18. Bundesverfassungsgericht (Federal Constitutional Court) of 19.12.1978—1 BvR 335/76, BVerfGE 50, 108.

with high double-digit inflation rates (like Latin America[19] or now in Turkey[20]), it is essential to take inflation into account systematically. This point has not been reached in the Eurozone.

If inflation is corrected only punctually, the risk of new discrimination arises.[21] This would be particularly true if capital gains would be indexed only for private investors but not for entrepreneurs. However, instruments can be mirrored to special needs. Thus, a roll-over relief allows an inflation-adapted reinvestment for businesses but is not sufficient for the generic private owner of real estate. Here, a possible solution aside from indexing the historical price could be to tax only the difference between the book value and the historical cost of acquisition.

Regarding interest, the only correct reaction to negative real interest is to completely exempt interest income from taxation. The German tax legislator did not want to go that far and only reacted by increasing the saver's allowance from EUR 801 to EUR 1,000 from 2023 onwards.[22] However, the expropriating effect of inflation is not a phenomenon limited to small savings, nor can this be justified as a disguised wealth tax.[23] Inflation and negative real interest rates initially have the effect of a wealth tax on financial capital, irrespective of the taxation of interest. However, regardless of one's position on a wealth tax, it cannot be justified to subject it only to financial capital while exempting real capital. Ian Roxan's statement at the Cologne EATLP Congress, i.e., that the effect of taxes and inflation does not create an equity problem,[24] holds true only for the group of capital asset owners all similarly affected by inflation but not with comparison to other assets. Thus, a non-inflation-adapted capital income tax leads to severe distortions of investment decisions.[25]

§13.4 LACK OF PRINCIPLE IN THE CAPITAL INCOME SCHEDULE

§13.4.1 Net or Gross Taxation

The saver's allowance and, in particular, its recent increase illustrate the imperfect system of modern capital income taxation in Germany. With the introduction of the

19. *See* on the global adjustment of the tax base in these countries, Roxan, *supra* n. 17, at 234 et seq.
20. Refet S. Gürkaynak et al., *Exchange Rate and Inflation under Weak Monetary Policy: Turkey Verifies Theory*, Economic Policy 1, 5 (2023) DOI: 10.1093/epolic/eiad020. For the viability of the arrangements made to counter the negative effects of inflation on accounting and taxation in Turkey, *see* Naim Varol, *Inflation Accounting in Terms of Tax Legislation and Accounting Standards in Turkey*, 93 J. Acct. and Fin. 19, 23 et seq. (2022).
21. Essers & Rijkers, *supra* n. 4, at 336.
22. Jahressteuergesetz 2022 (JStG 2022) of 16.12.2022, BGBl. I 2022, 2294 (2301). Denmark increased the threshold for applying a beneficial tax rate for dividends from DKK 57,200 to DKK 58,900 in 2023, *see Tax rates*, Danish Ministry of Finance (September 8, 2023). Lithuania increased the threshold for applying a beneficial tax regime for interest from EUR 180,492 to EUR 202,188, *see Personal Income Tax*, State Tax Inspectorate under the Ministry of Finance of the Republic of Lithuania (September 8, 2023). In regard to similar measures in other European countries back in 2003, *see* Roxan, *supra* n. 17, at 232.
23. In regard to this effect of an after-tax rate of return below inflation, *see* Roxan, supra n. 17, at 238.
24. Roxan, *supra* n. 17, at 226.
25. *Ibid.*

final withholding tax, the legislator has switched to gross taxation. This is seen as a consequence of the imposition of withholding tax on the level of the financial institutions, which are obliged to withhold tax at source;[26] it is supposed to be compensated by the withholding tax rate of 25%, which is lower than the progressive rate of up to 45%. However, it is unsystematic that gross taxation applies even if the taxpayer makes use of the assessment under the favorable tax treatment test[27] because their personal tax rate is below 25%. One may consider gross taxation a necessary consequence of the withholding requirement at source, yet it bears no justification in the assessment procedure.

The saver's allowance (previously EUR 801, now increased to EUR 1,000) is intended to partially take into account capital income-related expenses.[28] However, a distinction must be made at this point. As far as interest income from savings deposits is concerned, there are generally no income-related expenses since most savings accounts in Germany are free of charge. It is, therefore, easier to justify the tax exemption as a compensation for inflation. But—as previously noted—this is not sufficient as soon as the real interest rate is negative because, in this case, interest may not be taxed at all,[29] regardless of the amount of the savings deposits. Otherwise, the income tax turns into a disguised wealth tax.

The lump-sum saver's allowance has to be seen as more differentiated when it comes to dividend income. The custody account fees incurred rarely exceed EUR 100 for small investors but increase with the size/amount of the securities and the frequency of orders. Moreover, the saver's allowance of EUR 1,000 may still cover most management fees. However, in cases of debt financing, applying the lump sum quickly becomes insufficient.[30] Furthermore, in this case, the low withholding tax reflects the income at the level of the distributing company and therefore does not represent a privilege compared to the regular progressive income tax rate. Here, gross taxation lacks any justification. If shares are held as business assets, section 3c paragraph 2 German Income Tax Act (GITA) allows the deduction of 60% of the expenses. However, in view of the fact that the partial tax exemption of dividends (section 3 number 40 GITA) is only of a technical nature, the deduction of 100% of the expenses related to the participation should be allowed.

26. Section 43 para. 1 sentence 1, section 44 para. 1 GITA.
27. Section 32d para. 6 GITA.
28. Section 20 paragraph 9 sentence 1 GITA.
29. *See also* Rose, *supra* n. 2, at 72, not as a correction of inflation but as a consequence of a lifetime point of few.
30. Here, section 32d para. 2 number 3 GITA provides a tax assessment option under the normal progressive tax rate regime which allows for offsetting financing expenses. This only applies under the condition that the taxpayer holds a minimum participation of 25% or if the taxpayer holds a participation of at least 1% in the corporation and where he or she is able to exert a significant entrepreneurial influence on its economic activities through professional activity on its behalf.

§13.4.2 Treatment of Capital Gains and Losses: Restrictive Deductibility of Capital Losses

Even more serious is the shift from the synthetic income tax as it led to the abandonment of the basic income tax principle of netting profits and losses within the newly created capital income schedule.

It is in the nature of schedular taxation that no offsetting of losses is possible between different schedules. Losses from the 25% capital income schedule cannot be offset against regular profits taxed progressively at up to 45%.[31] Within the individual schedules, however, unlimited compensation must be possible. Nevertheless, from its conception in 2008 onwards, loss-offsetting possibilities from share transactions were limited to gains from the sale of shares. Offsetting with positive interest and dividend income is not possible. The only conceivable justification is that taxpayers can influence their tax burden by choosing when to realize losses[32] in a way of cherry-picking losses and not gains, which is why loss-offset restrictions within the capital income schedule are widely used internationally. Judith Freedman correctly pointed out at the Cologne EATLP Congress that such restrictions violate both principles of horizontal equity and vertical equity because taxpayers with smaller equity portfolios are less able to offset losses with capital gains.[33] Against the backdrop of repeated complaints about the low level of share ownership in Germany and discussions about measures to improve the attractiveness of share investments, especially for small investors, the restriction on loss-offsetting mechanisms is all the more incomprehensible. However, after the invention of the capital gains schedule, the legislator even tightened the rules for offsetting losses against capital gains. Since 2020, losses from trading derivatives, which can be offset only from gains from derivatives, are now further limited to be deducted only up to EUR 20,000. A higher loss can be carried forward.[34]

The Federal Tax Court rightly asserted a violation of the equal treatment clause[35] by the loss-offsetting limitations within the capital income schedule and appealed to the Federal Constitutional Court. Once capital gains are comprehensively taxed, capital losses have to be offset fully against these gains.[36]

§13.5 THE EUROPEAN UNION'S IMPACT

§13.5.1 The Notion of Capital Income as Part of Member State's Sovereignty

Up until now, the Member States have made mistakes in the design of capital income taxation "on their own account." Starting with the Savings Directive,[37] which was

31. Section 20 para. 6 sentence 1 GITA.
32. Judith Freedman, *Treatment of Capital Gains and Losses*, in *The Notion of Income from Capital* 211 (Peter Essers & Arie Rijkers eds., IBFD 2005).
33. Freedman, *ibid.*, at 212.
34. Section 20 para. 6 sentence 5 GITA.
35. Bundesfinanzhof (Federal Tax Court) of 17.11.2020—VIII R 11/18, BStBl. II 2021, 562. Pending before the Bundesverfassungsgericht (Federal Constitutional Court) under reference 2 BvL 3/12.
36. Essers & Rijkers, *supra* n. 4, at 336 no. 15.
37. Council Directive (EC) 2003/48 of June 3, 2003 on taxation of savings income in the form of interest payments, OJ L 157/38, 26.6.2003.

replaced in 2014 by the automatic exchange of information,[38] the Union has set only the framework for enforcement. The establishment and functioning of the internal market does not require harmonization of the substantive tax law on capital income since the competition-distorting enforcement deficits have been eliminated. The approximation of substantive tax law has primarily taken place by way of negative or silent harmonization. In a decades-long learning process, the Member States have adapted their dividend taxation[39] to the requirements of the European Court of Justice[40] without the need for a Directive. The formerly applicable imputation systems, which were limited to distributions by domestic companies, have disappeared.[41] In principle, distributions by domestic and foreign corporations, as well as domestic and foreign shareholders, are now treated equally.

§13.5.2 Capital Income Taxation and Capital Expense Deduction: How Does DEBRA Interplay with the Taxation of Income from Capital?

With the DEBRA-proposal,[42] the Commission intervenes—albeit only indirectly—in the capital income taxation of individuals for the first time. The Directive's objective of eliminating the debt-equity bias is to be welcomed without reservation. It is even more relevant than before because the debt-equity bias has been further exacerbated by the final withholding tax. Despite the fact that only dividend income is subject to corporate income tax, the German final withholding tax does not differentiate between interest and dividend income. The supposed equal treatment leads to a preferential treatment of debt-capital payments. The notional equity capital interest deduction under Article

38. Council Directive (EU) 2014/107 of December 9, 2014 amending Directive 2011/16/EU as regards mandatory automatic exchange of information in the field of taxation, OJ L 359/1, 11.3.2011 (DAC 2: automatic exchange of financial account information).
39. Malcolm Gammie, *Non-discrimination and the Taxation of Cross-Border Dividends*, 2.2 WTJ 162, 170 (2010); Christoph Maier & Deborah Schanz, *Convergence of Dividend and Capital Gains Taxation in the European Union from 1990 to 2015*, 44.12. Intertax 913, 916 (2016) DOI: 10.54648/taxi2016086. This also led to a reduction of (partial) imputation systems and the prevalence of shareholder relief systems, *see* Leonie Fischer, Jessica M. Müller & Christoph Spengel, *The Distorting Effects of Imputation Systems on Tax Competition in the EU*, 51.3 Intertax 196, 197 (2023) DOI: 10.54648/taxi2023021.
40. Case C-35/98, *Staatssecretaris van Financiën v. B.G.M. Verkooijen*, 6.6.2000, ECLI:EU:C:2000:294; Case C-315/02, *Anneliese Lenz v. Finanzlandesdirektion für Tirol*, 15.7.2004, ECLI:EU:C:2004:446; Case C-319/02, *Petri Manninen*, 7.11.2004, ECLI:EU:C:2004:484; Case C-292/04, *Wienand Meilicke, Heidi Christa Weyde and Marina Stöffler v. Finanzamt Bonn-Innenstadt*, 6.3.2007, ECLI:EU:C:2007:132; Case C-513/04, *Mark Kerckhaert and Bernadette Morres v. Belgische Staat*, 14.11.2006, ECLI:EU:C:2006:713; Case C-262/09, *Wienand Meilicke and Others v. Finanzamt Bonn-Innenstadt*, 30.6.2011, ECLI:EU:C:2011:438; Case C-375/12, *Margaretha Bouanich v. Directeur des services fiscaux de la Drôme*, 13.3.2014, ECLI:EU:C:2014:138.
41. Leonie Fischer, Jessica M. Müller & Christoph Spengel, *The Distorting Effects of Imputation Systems on Tax Competition in the EU*, 51.3 Intertax 196, 197 (2023) DOI: 10.54648/taxi2023021.
42. Proposal for a Council Directive (EU) on laying down rules on a debt-equity bias reduction allowance and on limiting the deductibility of interest for corporate income tax purposes, COM(2022) 216 final, 11.5.2022.

4 DEBRA would eliminate the pre-tax burden on dividend income, although, unlike a dividend deduction system,[43] only on a fictitious basis.

However, first of all, it is not evident as to why this decision should be made uniformly for all Member States by the EU tax legislator. Furthermore, DEBRA would force Member States to make more far-reaching adjustments. DEBRA only relates to corporate income tax but would have to be extended to the personal income tax for reasons of equal treatment. Far more serious is the accompanying measure of the partial limitation to interest deduction (Article 6 DEBRA) for interest on borrowed capital. It is inconsistent with the ability-to-pay principle[44] and the net income principle. The non-deductibility of the interest expense at the borrower's level would need to correspond with a tax exemption of the interest income at the lender's level in order to avoid new distortions.

§13.6 INSPIRATION INSTEAD OF UNIFORMITY

The deduction of a notional interest on equity proposed by DEBRA is an element of consumption-based taxation as it has been discussed at the Cologne EATLP Congress.[45] However, even though most Member States went at least halfway in this direction, some—like the Nordic countries—more than others,[46] it represents a landmark decision interrelated with the tax system as a whole, having a serious impact on its distributional effects,[47] and also with possible consequences for inheritance taxation.[48] Notwithstanding the theoretical superiority of consumption-based income taxation from the point of view of efficiency and inflation neutrality, this decision must remain with the Member States. A Directive forcing Member States into such a consumption-based tax would not be advisable, if only for reasons of unanimous amendment. Flexibility is needed in particular with regard to the fiscal implications of a dual income tax or any other form of a consumption-based taxation. In view of the omnipresent shortage of skilled workers, there may also be economic policy reasons not to tax labor income more heavily than capital income in the future. Finally, it is more than uncertain that the EU tax legislator will be able to transform the imperfect capital income tax schedule into a systematically thought-out dual income tax. So far, the EU tax legislator has lacked clear guiding principles, at least in the area of direct taxation. The combination of a partial ban on interest deductions, a conceivable compromise

43. Kevin Buchanan, *The Dividend Paid Deduction Proposal: Separating Myth from Reality*, 28 Tax Notes 97, 99 (1985).
44. Eric Kemmeren, *Editorial: Taxing Interest in the Debtor State as an Alternative to DEBRA*, 32.3. EC Tax Review 44, 55 (2023) DOI: 10.54648/ecta2023010.
45. Rose, *supra* n. 2.
46. Dual income taxes, *see* Sørensen, *supra* n. 6.
47. Gerorg Kofler, *Steuerrecht: Einkommen—Einkünfte—Einkunftsermittlung: Gutachten zum 19. ÖJT* 28 et seq. (Manz Verlag, vol. IV/1, 2015).
48. Anna-Maria Andernwald, *Der steuerverfassungsrechtliche Rahmen der Nettovermögensteuer in Österreich*, Steuern und Wirtschaft (2023), 158.

between a consumption-based income tax and a comprehensive business tax, does cast doubt.[49]

The non-harmonized tax systems of the Member States are a source of inspiration. Organizations like the EATLP allow a scientifically based comparison. Peter Essers stands for this like no other. I hope for many more encounters.

49. Eric Kemmeren, *Editorial: Taxing Interest in the Debtor State as an Alternative to DEBRA*, 32.3. EC Tax Review 44, 54 (2023) DOI: 10.54648/ecta2023010 Roland Ismer, *Editorial: A Zebra or a Donkey? The European Commission's Proposal for a Debt-Equity Bias Reduction Allowance (DEBRA)*, 31.4 EC Tax Review 164, 168 (2022) DOI: 10.54648/ecta2022017; *Statement on the European Commission's Proposal for a Directive on a Debt-Equity Bias Reduction Allowance (DEBRA)*, Academic Advisory Board of the Federal Ministry of Finance (August 17, 2023).

CHAPTER 14
The Ability-to-Pay Principle in Hungarian Context

István Simon

§14.1 INTRODUCTORY REMARKS

The function of tax law is to provide those rules under which a political community finances common institutions and goals. Meeting fiscal needs involves the distribution of scarce resources, and conflict may arise between private and public interests. An important element of public life is to minimise the occurrence of conflicts and correct harms produced by conflicts. As the ethologist Vilmos Csányi writes, human cultures are functional rule systems, meaning that cultures are rule systems of behaviour. The rules are never neutral; these are defined by the dominant participant in the political community. The human being is the only existing creature that is able to solve the problem of aggression – i.e., to compel other individuals to hand over scarce resources – via rules that substitute for the dominant actor. Humans have properties that make the operation of this rule system possible. Two of these are submissive behaviour and the ability of construction, in other words, to create secondary and tertiary representations based on language, thanks to the human capacity for abstraction. Csányi calls such functionally integrated representations ideas. For instance, ownership and freedom are ideas.[1] Coming to our subject, the ability-to-pay principle is an idea according to the thoughts summarised above, in that it integrates the thoughts about fair taxation. The meaning of the ability-to-pay principle, like other tax principles, is historically and culturally context-dependent, defined by a political community and, in our days, to a certain extent in an EU and global framework. This is why the 2021 congress topic – history and taxation – of the European Association of Tax Law Professors has had

1. Vilmos Csányi, *Az emberi természet: humánetológia* 180-182, 214-217 (Vince Kiadó, Budapest 1999).

substantial significance. The main line of enquiry was to clarify the dialectical relationship between taxation and the political balance of power, as the subtitle of the congress book shows.[2] The topic was initiated by the general reporter, and editor of the book, Peter Essers. Who decides over taxation and in what way? This is the question of the so-called input legitimacy. My conclusion on the subject has been that the consent concept – that consent of the taxpayers is the source of legitimate tax laws – is an ideal type, and it only existed in practice in unique circumstances. It had political significance in some periods, like in the Northern American British colonies in the second half of the eighteenth century and, since World War II, as theory and practice, in all those countries where the political system has been based on universal, equal and secret suffrage. In a wider, global and European context, the issue of democratic decision-making on taxation also raises questions today – the direct link between voters as principals and their representatives has been stretched to the end. The other side of the coin – besides input legitimacy – is the result of the decision, the quality of procedural and substantive tax law, the issue of output legitimacy. One can raise the question, together with Frans Vanistendael, of whether fiscal justice is progressing.[3] It leads us to the subject matter of this chapter, the meaning of the ability-to-pay principle in the Hungarian context.

Before going into some details, it is necessary to clarify some basic elements of the terminology as they are understood in this chapter. First, ability-to-pay, faculty and capability principles are synonyms.[4] Second, the ability-to-pay principle applies to both natural persons and legal entities. Third, the ability-to-pay principle is a yardstick for direct and indirect taxes. Therefore, fourth, the ability-to-pay principle is the benchmark for the sum of all taxes paid by natural persons and legal entities as tax subjects or simply as the bearers of the tax burden. In other words, the ability-to-pay principle is a yardstick for the complete income and wealth of natural and legal persons.

§14.2 THE HUNGARIAN CONSTITUTIONAL FRAMEWORK OF TAX LEGISLATION

The ability-to-pay principle is defined in the Hungarian Fundamental Law. Before going into the details of this principle, the structure of the Constitution and two elements of the constitutional basis of tax legislation must be clarified. The Fundamental Law has four structural elements. The first part, titled National Avowal, serves as a preamble for the Constitution. The second part – Articles A)-U) – titled Foundations, embraces the basic properties of the country, among others the name of the country, its symbols, the rule of law clause, and the connection to the European Union. The third

2. *History and Taxation: The Dialectical Relationship Between Taxation and the Political Balance of Power* (Peter Essers ed., IBFD-EATLP Amsterdam 2022).
3. Frans Vanistendael, *Is Fiscal Justice Progressing? Bulletin for International Taxation* 526-540 (IBFD 2010).
4. For example, Richard Musgrave, *The Theory of Public Finance: A Study in Public Economy* 94 (McGraw-Hill, New York 1959); Stephen G. Utz, *Tax Neutrality: Whittier Law Review* Vol. 23, no. 4, 867-950, 867-869 (Summer 2002); Edwin Seligman, *The Income Tax* 3-22 (MacMillan, New York 1914).

part, titled Freedom and Responsibility, defines the fundamental rights and obligations - Articles I.)-XXXI.) - including the taxation clause (Article XXX.). The fourth part - titled The State, Articles 1)-56) - regulates the competences of the state organs and also contains articles on public finances.

The two elements of the Constitution mentioned that are relevant to tax legislation are the so-called rule of law clause and the principle of legality (*nullum tributum sine lege*). The content of the rule of law clause in both the previous and the recent constitutions was interpreted and therefore defined by the Constitutional Court. Several composite elements of the rule of law clause - such as the prohibition of retroactive legislation, legal certainty and clarity of legal norms - were worked out by the Court. The principle of legality of taxation is derived from two articles of the Constitution. One of them states that the rules on fundamental rights and obligations are to be defined exclusively by the acts of the Országgyűlés, as the unicameral National Assembly is named. The other is the taxation clause (Article XXX), which defines taxation as a fundamental obligation. Therefore, taxes can be constituted almost exclusively by Acts passed by the Országgyűlés, apart from fees and local taxes. The Constitutional Court had a major role in working out the constitutional law dogmatics of tax legislation from the transition in 1990 onwards. Now, the competence of the Court is limited regarding public finance legislation until the public debt decreases to 50% of Hungary's GDP. As the equality and non-discrimination principles and fundamental rights are the limits of tax legislation, it must be added that the Fundamental Law defines them and also the fundamental rights that are in substance equal to those defined in the EU Charter of Fundamental Rights.

§14.3 THE ABILITY-TO-PAY PRINCIPLE AS DEFINED IN THE FUNDAMENTAL LAW

The ability-to-pay principle is defined in Article XXX of the Fundamental Law as follows:

> (1) Everyone shall contribute to covering common needs according to his or her capabilities and to his or her participation in the economy.
> (2) For persons raising children, the extent of their contribution to covering common needs must be determined while taking the costs of raising children into consideration.

Article XXX embraces three standards. These are the ability-to-pay principle ('capabilities'), the participation in the economy principle, and the family allowance principle. The participation in the economy principle is an innovation of the Fundamental Law. It gives a constitutional basis for taxation independently of the taxpayer's ability to pay, such as environmental taxes and the payment obligation of VAT subjects. The family allowance principle is a subjective fundamental right ensured by the Fundamental Law.

The Fundamental Law orders in its Article 40 that the basic rules for taxation are to be enacted in a cardinal act, being one that requires a two-thirds majority vote by the representatives present. These rules are in Chapter 8/A of the Stability Act,[5] among which are four rules that limit the tax legislative competence of the simple majority Országgyűlés regarding the distribution of tax burden; this way formulates some aspects of the ability-to-pay principle. These are the tax wedge limiting rule, meaning that the fiscal burden cannot increase above 50% of the employment cost, the flat tax rule for individuals' active income, the rules on family allowance and the flat tax rule for corporate tax law. In addition, the Act states that the social security payroll tax (paid by the employer) does not grant social security rights to the employee.[6]

The purpose of the ability-to-pay principle under Hungarian law is to ensure the fulfilment of taxation according to the principle of social justice, as can be read in the legislative explanatory memorandum of the Fundamental Law. The previous Constitution, as amended in 1989, gave the constitutional basis for taxation as solely the principle of ability to pay ('according to income and wealth'), and its explanatory memoranda also defined the legislative purpose of the ability-to-pay principle, as equity in taxation. That means that taxation under the Hungarian constitutional system will meet the condition of the ability-to-pay principle if it has met the condition of social justice or equity in the previous wording. Therefore, one must first clarify the concept of (social) justice as far as the context requires it.

§14.4 THE CONCEPT OF JUSTICE AND THE ABILITY-TO-PAY PRINCIPLE

Reading the literature on justice, one realises that, in substance, justice equals equality, and in modern times, the main issue is the divergence between the formal equality of taxpayers and the inequality of their material positions. The basic tension is between private property and solidarity via taxation. Seligman wrote more than a century ago that our ideals of justice in taxation, as well as the theories on taxation, change as the social conditions and the economic base change.[7] His concept is rather materialistic; however, it is true that the concept of justice changes over time, or more exactly the prevailing view changes over time. The two leading and opposite intellectual positions on the subject in the second half of the last century may be marked by names such as John Rawls and Robert Nozick.[8] Rawls takes a communitarian while Nozick an individualistic position. These two intellectual positions, in different forms and intensity, have existed since the beginning of the modern era, and their roots may go deeper.

The context does not allow us to follow the history of the concept of justice and distributive justice. Rather, it seems appropriate to recall some thoughts on equality

5. Act CXCIV of 2011 on the Economic Stability of Hungary.
6. 36-38. § of Stability Act.
7. Edwin Seligman, *Essays in Taxation, 1* Ch. 1 (MacMillan and Co., New York, 1895).
8. Robert Nozick, *Anarchy, State and Utopia* (Blackwell, Oxford 1999 (reprinted)); John Rawls, *The Theory of Justice* (Harvard University Press, Boston 1971).

and inequality of taxation with a perspective of what kind of problem was offered a solution.

Sonja Dusarduijn and Hans Gribnau have offered a solution of how a structured way of thinking can be developed on tax justice in a democratic rule of law state. They define three types of justice relevant to taxation. These are legal justice, economic justice, and tax justice. In their concept, legal justice in substance equals the concept of rule of law, legality, and the existence of fundamental rights that was outlined above as the constitutional framework of tax legislation in Hungary. In their definition, economic justice is distributive justice in the narrower sense, meaning the distribution of income and wealth. Tax justice - as part of distributive justice - is the term applied in tax relations and equals the ability to pay.[9] Distributive justice - as these authors also mention - has a wider meaning and is named social justice, which includes the distribution of other goods of society besides material resources, among others, cultural goods.[10] Samuel Fleischacker states that distributive justice has existed as a theory for not more than two hundred years since its real meaning is the legally guaranteed right for distributing income from the rich to the poor, meaning that it is not an issue of charity but law.

The literature on distributive justice frequently commences the discussion of the topic with Aristotle. He says that justice seems somehow to be equality.[11] Aristotle's interest in justice and equality came from his presupposition that harm to this rule is one of the causative factors of social upheavals, revolutions and changes in the form of government.[12] Equality is a central term for Aristotle, and he distinguishes between arithmetic and geometric equality. The first is based on the equality in numbers (e.g., one citizen, one vote), the latter on value and therefore requires proportionality as the means of expressing equality and at the same time difference.[13] For Aristotle, inequality means injustice. He made a distinction between universal and partial justice, and inside the latter also defined two categories, namely commutative (or corrective) and distributive justice. The concept of distributive justice for Aristotle applies to the justification of distribution of advantages - such as offices or newly acquired land - among the members of the political community. Aristotle analysed 158 constitutions[14] and derived the conclusion that the criterion of distribution in different states was merit. However, depending on the form of government, different meanings of merit were utilised. In a democracy, the status of a free citizen qualified as merit; in an

9. Sonja Dusarduijn & Hans Gribnau, *Balancing Conflicting Conceptions of Justice in Taxation* in *Tax Justice and Tax Law: Understanding Unfairness in Tax Systems* (Dominic de Cogan & Peter Harris (eds), Hart, Oxford 2020).
10. Pierre Bourdieu, *A társadalmi egyenlőtlenségek újratermelődése* (Gondolat, Budapest 1978); Samuel Fleischacker, *A Short History of Distributive Justice* (Harvard University Press, Cambridge, MA 2004).
11. Arisztotelész, *Eudémoszi etika* VII. book 9, MEK https://mek.oszk.hu/05700/05709/05709.htm#5.
12. Péter Takács, *Az ókori politikai bölcselet vázlata* in Katalin Egresi et al., *Államelmélet* 12., 17. (Széchenyi Egyetem, Győr 2016).
13. Aristoteles, *Politika* V. book 1. MEK https://mek.oszk.hu/04900/04966/04966.htm.
14. János Sarkady, *Bevezetés* in Aristotelés, *Az Athéni állam – Pseudo-Xenophón: Az athéni állam* 7-17 (Akadémia, Budapest 1954).

oligarchic state, noble status or wealth; while in an aristocratic political system, virtue was the decisive form of merit.[15] One can derive the conclusion that the actual political balance of power gave the bases of qualification (merit) and in this way the basis of distributive justice. Aristotle offers a solution to the problem of citizens' equality or rather inequality; however, the criterion (i.e., merit) for qualification is abstract and flexible and depends on the form of dominance (form of government) and the value judgements and interests it carries. Aristotle answered the question of how to differentiate in a way that meets the standard of equality, according to merit. Public finances in ancient Athens were based on customs, indirect taxes, and fees. Only one direct tax existed, the eisphora, which was an asset tax on land. However, it was an extraordinary tax type and was levied only in times of need. The one-time common sense was that services to the public, whether personal (soldiering) or material (taxation), shall be the burden of the wealthy. The same word (*τέλ.ख*) referred to both taxes and the wealthier class.[16]

In respect of taxation, a usual starting point of the discussion of fair taxation is Adam Smith's maxim of proportionality.[17] Having offered this principle, Smith devised an answer to the question as follows: how can the inequalities – among the post-feudal circumstances of equality – be handled in a way that results in equality in taxation, i.e., that, according to his concept, the market-based income proportions are not modified. There are two ways of understanding his maxim; one of them is the so-called benefit and the other is the ability-to-pay approach. They do not correspond directly to the above-mentioned individualistic and communitarian theories in terms of redistribution. They differ from each other on the basis of the relationship between the individual and the state and in the relationship between the tax payment on the one hand and services provided by the state on the other or, more plainly, the two sides of the budget.[18] As an example, we can mention the Italian De Viti di Marco, who, on the basis of the benefit principle, argued in favour of a progressive tax rate.[19] As he wrote, while in the case of the ability-to-pay method, a few pay for many, in the case of the benefit principle, everyone pays for oneself.[20]

John Stuart Mill solved the issue of setting aside the exchange concept included in the contractarian benefit theories by applying a state concept, in which the functions of the (narrow) state, the existence of the state itself, give the justification for taxation. He also offered an answer to the equality inequality question via his equal sacrifice

15. Aristotle, *The Nicomachean Ethics*, 5th ed. 145-146 (Kegan Paul, Trench, Trubner & Co., London 1893).
16. Hans van Wees, *Ships and Silver, Taxes and Tribute: A Fiscal History of Archaic Athens* 86 (Bloomsbury, London 2013); Matthew R. Christ, *The Evolution of the Eisphora in Classical Athens. The Classical Quarterly* 53-69 New Series, Vol. 57, No. 1 (May 2007) DOI: 10.1017/s0009838807000043.
17. Adam Smith, *An Inquiry into the Nature and Causes of the Wealth of Nations* Book V, Chapter II, Part II, https://www.econlib.org/library/Smith/smWN.html?chapter_num=36#book-reader.
18. Musgrave, *supra* n. 4, at 62.
19. Musgrave, *supra* n. 4, at 72-73.
20. Quoted by Alessandro Petretto, *The Modern Theory of Regulation as an Inheritance of De Viti de Marco's Cooperative State* 9, Working Paper No. 21/2014, 1-23 (Università degli Studi di Firenze).

theory, which gives a basis for linear taxation that does not modify primary income distribution.[21] This equal sacrifice model of the ability-to-pay principle was transformed into the equal marginal sacrifice version, which emerged as the 'correct' solution as it has immediate fairness appeal, according to Musgrave.[22]

Richard Musgrave formulated the ability-to-pay principle by applying its two components, horizontal and vertical equity.[23] It is important to note that he applied the terms 'equality' and 'equity' as synonyms, which sometimes causes confusion.[24] Musgrave's formula embraces the solution to the question of how equality as horizontal equity and inequality as vertical equity can be considered. The concept was born in the Second World War era when the welfare state was invented.

It is important to emphasise in this context that income is relevant but not the sole index of ability to pay, and income tax is a strongly relevant element of the tax system but not the sole tax type and is not the only tax burden borne by taxpayers.

§14.5 THE CONCEPT OF TAX AND THE COORDINATES OF ABILITY-TO-PAY PRINCIPLE IN THE CONSTITUTIONAL COURT JURISPRUDENCE

When discussing the concept of the ability-to-pay principle, one cannot avoid pointing out that the concept of tax in Hungarian law – according to the legislative practice and the jurisprudence of the Constitutional Court[25] – embraces all the three goals of taxation:[26] financing the state, redistribution, and regulation.

As a starting point, it is important to see how the Constitutional Court defined its own role in three landmark decisions regarding tax cases. First, the Court denied its involvement in tax policy decisions; therefore, it refused to take the preliminary norm control of tax bills.[27] Second, since the early 1990s, the Court utilised the wide margin formula, meaning that the Országgyűlés has a wide discretionary power regarding fiscal legislation.[28] Third, although the Fourth Modification of the Fundamental Law repealed prior decisions of the Court, as of 1 April 2013, the Court decided that if the Fundamental Law regulates a fundamental right without almost any modification to how the Constitution provided it, the Fundamental Law shall keep the principles worked out by the Constitutional Court under the Constitution.[29] The wording of the ability-to-pay principle in the text of the Fundamental Law differed, though in

21. Richard Musgrave 1959, at 90; Richard Musgrave, *A Brief History of Fiscal Doctrine*, in *Handbook of Public Economics* Vol. 1, 1-59, p. 18 (A.J. Auerbach & M. Feldstein eds, North-Holland 1985).
22. Richard Musgrave, *Horizontal Equity, Once More* Vol. XLIII. No. 2 113-122, 115-116 (National Tax Journal 1990) DOI: 10.1086/ntj41788830.
23. Musgrave, *supra* n. 4, at 160.
24. Richard Musgrave 1985, 16. Richard Musgrave 1990, 114-115.
25. For example, Constitutional Court decisions: 31/1998. (VI. 25.) V.; 440/D//2001. (V.12.) III.1.; 657/B/2005. III. 2.1.
26. Reuven S. Avi-Yonah, *The Three Goals of Taxation* 1-28 (Tax L. Rev. 60, no. 1 2006).
27. Constitutional Court decision 620/B/1992.
28. For example, Constitutional Court decisions: 61/1992 (XI. 20.), 620/B/1992, 182/B/1992; 281/B/1992, 978/B/1993, 424/B/1994, 140/B/1995, 178/B/1995.
29. Constitutional Court decision 6/2016. (III. 11.) [22].

substance remained the same; therefore, any analysis based on the previous practice of the Court is valid today.

In 2009, the Court stated that the ability-to-pay principle is a special equality principle derived from 70/I. § of the Constitution, the wording of which was that everyone must pay taxes according to their income and wealth, i.e., according to the ability to pay.[30] Before that statement and later as well, the Court solved cases by applying the general anti-discrimination clause, 70/A. §, in several cases when the question was about similarities and differences in taxation. However, the Constitution – unlike other states' constitutions, like Germany's – embraced the special standard calibrated for taxation: the ability-to-pay principle that has the inherent meaning of handling the same phenomena equally and the different ones differently, and it is expressed via the terms of vertical and horizontal equity.

The question is how the basic coordinates of the ability-to-pay principle can be outlined on the basis of the Constitutional Court's jurisdiction. In the scope of vertical equity, the two extreme points – subsistence minima taxation and confiscation – and the question of progressivity were raised before the Court. As the Court decided, the Constitution did not prohibit the taxation of subsistence minima; there has been no tax-free threshold,[31] and differentiation via a progressive tax rate was not unconstitutional.[32] That latter wording also means that a linear tax rate is also inside the constitutional frame. Although it did not arise in the Court's practice, there is a consensus in the academia that the regressive rate structure is unconstitutional. For the question of disproportionality, the Court decided in a property tax case – in which the yearly local tax to be paid was higher than the market value of the land – that a maximum of 20% of the market value of property as tax base should be the tax rate.[33] Similarly, in the public employees' severance payment case, the 98% rate was considered as confiscatory.[34]

In the scope of horizontal equity, the Court decided upon differentiation by tax types (e.g., different business tax regimes for sole entrepreneurs and companies)[35] and within a tax type (e.g., differentiation between employees' income and sole entrepreneurs' income on the basis of risk-taking).[36] In a landmark decision, the Court decided that 'it is the scope of authority of the legislator to decide to create different rules for different groups of entrepreneurs and their taxable activities. This power is limited by the Constitution to ensure that the regulation shall not result in discrimination within the same selected group of entrepreneurs, within the same scope of activity'.[37] The interpretation of the same scope of activity in this case has been a very narrow standard, and the decision made a distinction between providing a loan and its

30. Constitutional Court decision 127/2009. (XII. 17.) IV. 2.
31. Constitutional Court decision 85/B/1996.
32. Constitutional Court decision 1558/B/1991.
33. Constitutional Court decision 1531/B/1991.
34. Constitutional Court decision 184/2010. (X. 28.) Abh and ECHR Case of *Gáll v. Hungary* (2013).
35. Constitutional Court decision 54/1993. (X. 13.).
36. Constitutional Court decision 191/B/1992, similarly: Constitutional Court decision 12/2023. (VII. 13.) Abh.
37. Constitutional Court decision 57/1995 (IX. 15.).

functional equivalent, leasing. As a consequence of the concept of this judgment, sectoral taxes and extraordinary sectoral taxes are in accordance with the Fundamental Law.

In the jurisdiction of the Constitutional Court, both individuals and legal entities fall under the ability-to-pay principle.[38] Similarly, the Court of Justices of the European Union also referred in its judgment to the ability-to-pay principle, applying it to the Hungary-based corporation Vodafone Hungary Ltd. in 2020.[39]

Issues regarding the ability-to-pay principle in the context of indirect taxes were seldom in the practice of the Court. The nature of indirect taxes and their legal construction leaves little space for constitutional challenge; the taxpayer (tax subject) does not bear the tax burden, and it is difficult to calibrate the tax burden to the capacity of the person who bears the tax (the consumer). In one of its decisions, the Court stated that 70/I. § of the Constitution – i.e., the ability-to-pay principle – does not exclude the right of the state to constitute other tax types besides the income taxes, including turnover taxes, wealth taxes, duties, customs duties, contributions and fees.[40] In another case, the issue was that the sale of basic childcare goods falls under the normal VAT rate. The petitioners argued that it is discriminative and in conflict with the stated purpose of supporting children set out in the Constitution. The Court denied the petition, stating that the consumer is not a tax subject and is not obliged to purchase and pay tax. Therefore, the constitutional standard prescribed in 70/I. § in the case of VAT is that the tax rate shall be the same for everyone. However, the Court made an important statement closing this part of the judgement: the tax system as a whole must meet the 70/I. § standard.[41] Reading the two judgments, the conclusion is that the burden to be borne by both natural persons and legal entities as a whole must meet the principle of ability to pay as it was defined in 70/I. § of the Constitution and now in Article XXX of the Fundamental Law.

However, the issue is not unambiguous in the Hungarian jurisprudence. As a former justice of the Court explained in a study, the Constitutional Court does not observe the proportionality of the tax system as a whole since it has no mandate for that. The Court has the mandate to observe the constitutionality of single tax statutes in the form of abstract and concrete norm control only, and not the capabilities (the tax burden-bearing capacity) that must be observed in the context of proportionality.[42]

§14.6 FLAT TAX FOR PERSONAL INCOME: A SUMMARY IN THE CONTEXT OF ABILITY TO PAY

The constitutional ability-to-pay principle is based on the concept of social justice under Hungarian law. Following the decisions of the Constitutional Court, a picture of

38. Constitutional Court decision 8/2007. (II. 28.).
39. C-75/18 *Vodafone Hungary v. NAV*.
40. Constitutional Court decisions 66/2006. (XI. 29.) III. 3. and 61/1992. (XI. 20.).
41. Constitutional Court decision 127/2009. (XII. 17.) V. 2.
42. Éva Tertyánszkiné Vasadi, *A magyar Alkotmánybíróság pénzügyi tárgyú döntései*. In *Formatori iuris publici*. (szerk. Hajas Barnabás & Schanda Balázs). PPKE JÁK 483 (Szent István Társulat, Budapest 2006).

the basic structural elements of the principle can be created, namely equal sacrifice and equity, horizontal and vertical. Under this system, progressive and linear (flat) tax rates can be defined. As referred to above, the Constitutional Court interpreted the ability-to-pay principle as a benchmark for the whole tax system. However, the application of the wide margin formula means that the Court put freedom before equality and formal equality before material equality.[43] The legislator therefore has a wide margin of appreciation in formatting tax policy, similar to other states. After 2010, there was a tax reform. I would like to consider one of its element, the personal income flat tax rate, from the perspective of taxpaying capacity.

Individual income taxation cannot be analysed without taking the effect of indirect taxes into account, especially VAT and the excise tax. Individual taxation must be observed from at least two dimensions: income and savings. Although the proportion of those individuals who cannot cover an unexpected bill for cc 200 euro because of their lack of such savings decreased from 75% to 35% between 2013 and 2019,[44] the economic effects of the pandemic and the war in Ukraine increased this figure again; however, it is just around the deprivation level. The statistical distribution of financial savings shows that a significant part of society has no meaningful savings. The reason is that the level of active income is very low in absolute and in European relative terms. Although the official subsistence level calculation was abandoned for methodological reasons, the meaningful data from 2010 is worth mentioning. The net national average wage (5th decile in the gross wage statistics published by the tax authority) was one and a half times more than the subsistence minima, and the 8th decile net wage was three times more than subsistence. The last decade brought a measurable salary increase, and the flat income tax rate complemented by the childcare allowance eased the life of the employed and politically active so-called middle class (cc 5th-10th decile earners), but recently the effect of inflation has diminished the real salary. As such, there has been very little scope for progressive taxation of employment income. That was one of the reasons for the tax reform after 2010, which meant in substance the introduction of the flat tax rate and childcare allowance for active individual income; that proportional rate had existed for passive incomes since the introduction of the personal income tax in 1988.

The tax reform attracted criticism.[45] The substance of the critics in respect of personal income taxation was that the abolition of the second bracket of the income tax rate was against tax fairness since it favours the wealthier taxpayer against the needy. Although, more than a decade ago, I proposed to create a tax-free threshold for the subsistence and a progressive two-rate structure in a way that would take into account the effect of indirect taxes, in the light of the above-written statistical data, I do not agree with the critics. Evaluating the income tax policy measures, it is especially important to consider the levels of household savings, the levels of official salaries described above, the effect of VAT on taxpayers' ability to pay and also the fact that the

43. Béla Pokol, *Jogelmélet* 87-90 (Századvég, Budapest 2005).
44. Central Statistical Office: Standard of Living of Households 2020; https://www.ksh.hu/docs/hun/xftp/idoszaki/hazteletszinv/2020/index.html.
45. For example, Dániel Deák, *Alkotmány és adójog* (HVG-Orac, Budapest 2016).

one-time legislation was based on the concept that no one should be in a worse position than existed before the reform. In this context, one must consider the structure of the whole tax system and its properties, among them the significant measure of tax evasion and tax avoidance. According to estimates, 20-33% of the tax base remained untaxed between 1990 and 2009.

CHAPTER 15
The Taxation of Pension in Italy

Eugenio Ruggiero

§15.1 INTRODUCTION

Pension systems are built in order to provide for retirement income, so that individuals may have a source of income to support them when age may not allow them to find such support with their working activity. The existence of such source of income responds to both: (i) a public and collective interest, as, if people do not have income when they stop working, that will put a strain on society; and (ii) a private interest, as people generally wish to maintain a somehow stable standard of living throughout their lives, and that may only happen if they are able to maintain a stable amount of income.

Public pension systems are most commonly public, mandatory, and unfunded; i.e., contributions of active members to the system are not invested but immediately used to pay benefits of retirees (so-called *pay-as-you-go* systems). Although those schemes are often contributory, financing gaps might be closed from the State's budget, especially from taxes. States may also provide unconditional minimum pensions irrespective of earlier contributions.

In addition to public pension systems, there are supplementary pension arrangements, which generally complete and integrate the public pensions (in order to have higher levels of income at retirement) or, in some cases, they may be used to even substitute public pensions. Supplementary pension schemes are more commonly private, contributory (as regards both employers and employees), funded (and growing also through capitalization of investments), and voluntary. A distinction may also be made between arrangements whereby the contributions are fixed and the benefits entirely related to the level of contributions and related investment return ("defined contribution" arrangements) and those where the future benefits are fixed (typically by reference to remuneration and length of service) and the contributions vary as necessary in order to finance those benefits ("defined benefit" arrangements).

Following the described distinction, pension arrangements may be broadly classified according to a "three-pillar" approach:

(a) the first pillar: basic public pensions;
(b) the second pillar: employment-related (or "occupational") pensions; and
(c) the third pillar: personal individual private savings and annuity schemes for use after retirement.

Pension arrangements of the second and third pillar are the ones that are generally referred to as "supplementary pension schemes."

The combination of public and private interests underlying the setting up of pension systems, and the very long time horizons through which such interests have to be dealt with, provide for a fundamental role to be played by taxation in imposing or encouraging savings, either at a collective level or at an individual level, whereas such savings will then be used to finance the payment of pensions.

In principle, the operation of pension systems may identify three possible stages where taxation may apply along the course of the pension cycle, i.e.: (a) the contributions paid to the pension scheme, (b) the income earned by the pension scheme (if any such accumulation is envisaged), and (c) the pension benefits paid by the pension scheme. Tax usually applies on only one or two of these stages.

In this respect, the main taxation models of pension schemes may be described as follows:

(1) E-E-T model (Exemption-Exemption-Taxation), which is characterized by the tax exemption both of the contribution payments and of the income earned by the pension scheme (if any) and by the taxation of the benefits paid to the beneficiary;
(2) E-T-T model (Exemption-Taxation-Taxation), which is characterized by the exemption of contribution payments and by the taxation of both the income earned by the pension scheme (if any) and the benefits paid to the beneficiary;
(3) T-E-E model (Taxation-Exemption-Exemption), characterized by the taxation of the contribution payments and the exemption both of the income earned by the pension scheme (if any) and of the benefits paid to the beneficiary.

In this chapter, we shall briefly review how and to what extent the Italian pension system and the applicable taxation system comply with such models, also having regard to the circumstance that, given the time horizons under which a full pension cycle is completed for each individual, labor mobility will put further strains on such systems, as the single stages of the pension cycle may occur under different legal and tax systems.

§15.2 OUTLINE OF THE ITALIAN PENSION SYSTEM

The Italian pension system may be described as a "two-pillar" system, consisting of a public compulsory scheme and of a private supplementary pension system. All employees must adhere to the public pension scheme (indeed, such mandatory participation is provided for all those performing any working activity),[1] whereas the private pension system is mainly based upon collective bargaining,[2] and participation is entirely voluntary.[3]

The public pension system is a defined benefit system, guaranteeing at least a minimum pension regardless of the amounts of the contributions paid by the employee or by the employer, although the final amount of pension to which beneficiaries are entitled to depends to a large extent on the amount of contributions that were paid over time. It operates as a "*pay-as-you-go*" system: current pensions are financed by the contributions of current workers; any deficit is covered by public expenditure. The obvious consequence is that any such "*pay-as-you-go*" system will be heavily influenced by demographic factors, as its equilibrium will mainly depend on the existing relationship between the number of current workers (paying contributions) and the number of retirees (receiving pension benefits).

The private pension system, however, is a defined contribution system, operating through funding coming from the employees and, generally, from the employers as well.[4] The private pension system also includes individual pension plans provided by specialized intermediaries such as insurance companies, banks and asset management companies. The individual pension plans enjoy the same tax treatment as collective pension schemes.[5]

1. The Italian public pension system underwent several reforms in the last thirty years, due to the difficulties in reaching long-term balanced budgets. Starting from the 1990s (mainly through Law No. 335 of 1995 and then with further adjustments over the years), pension coverage (and duty to pay pension contributions) was gradually extended not only to employees but also to any other form of lending labor, retirement age was gradually increased and the amount of accruing pension benefits was adjusted to be consistent with the contributions paid by each beneficiary (rather than to the salaries received in the last years of their working life).
2. Until the 1990s, there was no express regulation of private pensions in the Italian legal system, as it was deemed to be a matter within the scope of collective bargaining by trade unions. In parallel with the public pension reforms, it was felt that a more thorough legislation of supplementary pension schemes should be required. The first law on private pensions dates back to 1993, with Legislative Decree No. 124 of 1993, the backbone of which still stands, despite the reforms occurred over time (mainly with Legislative Decree No. 47 of 2000, which mainly dealt with tax matters; then with Legislative Decree No. 252 of 2005, which carried an overall review of the private pension system; and, more lately, with Legislative Decree No. 147 of 2018, which implemented the EU Directive No. 2016/2341 (so-called IORP II Directive) mainly dealing with the governance of supplementary pension schemes).
3. Article 3 of Legislative Decree No. 252/2005 states that supplementary pension schemes (pension funds) are mainly established by collective bargaining, whereas Art. 1, para. 2, expressly states that participation to pension funds is "free and voluntary."
4. Article 2, para. 2, of Legislative Decree No. 252/2005 states that any supplementary pension scheme for employees must be funded and operating through defined contributions (defined benefits may only be envisaged in pension funds operating for self-employed workers).
5. Article 13 of Legislative Decree No. 252/2005.

The tax structures for the public pension system and the private pension system operating in Italy are framed according to the following description concerning each single phase of the pension cycle: the contribution phase, the accumulation or investment phase, and the payment of pension phase.

§15.2.1 Outline of the Taxation of Public Pensions

The public pension system is taxed under a pure E(xemption)-E(xemption)-T(axation) framework:

- Pension contributions (both the employer's and the employee's) are totally exempt from taxation.[6]
- The public pension schemes and any returns on their investments are not subject to any taxation (or, in special cases, to very limited taxation).
- The payment of pensions envisages income for the pension recipients, subject to the personal income tax.[7]

§15.2.2 Outline of the Taxation of Private Pensions

The private pension system may instead be described as an E-R-RTE framework (Exemption-Reduced Tax-Reduced Taxation and Exemption).[8] The basic understanding of this framework is that any financial component entering the pension cycle will only be taxed once, in either one of the three phases of the pension cycle; hence, if a component is taxed during the contribution phase (e.g., because there is contribution exceeding the deductible limit), then it will not be taxed in either of the following investment phase or the payment of pension phase:

- Pension contributions are exempt from taxation: they are totally deductible for the employer; they are deductible up to a set ceiling for the employee (an annual deductible amount of EUR 5,164.54, with some increases in some special cases).[9]
- Returns on the investments of the private pension schemes are taxed at a reduced rate (20% on the accrued return) compared to the rate of taxation of similar financial investments (26% on the cash return of investments).[10]
- The payment of private pensions is subject to income tax for the pension recipients at a special rate between 15% and 9% depending on the number of years the private pension has accumulated, except that the component of the pension corresponding to the financial returns, which were already taxed (at a

6. Article 51, para. 2(a), of Law No. 917/1986 (the general Income Tax Code), states that public pension contributions are excluded from employment income.
7. Article 49 of the Income Tax Code qualifies pensions as taxable income (the same way as employment income) and submits it to regular progressive taxation.
8. The taxation of private pensions and of private pension schemes is regulated in Legislative Decree No. 252/2005 (which operates as a Code for private pensions).
9. Article 8, para. 4, of Legislative Decree No. 252/2005.
10. Article 17 of Legislative Decree No. 252/2005.

reduced rate) when accumulating with the pension scheme, is exempt from any further taxation.[11] It is worth noticing that the 15% tax rate (which may then become as low as 9%) is much lower than the minimum tax rate applying to personal income tax (23%).[12]

§15.2.3 An Overview of the Differences in Taxation of Public and Private Pensions

The differences between the tax treatment of the public pension system and the private pension systems may be explained on the following bases:

- As for the circumstance that there is total tax relief for contributions to public pension schemes, whereas there is a limited tax relief for contributions to private pension schemes, this may be explained by the fact that contributions to public pension schemes are mandatory, whereas contributions to private pension schemes are voluntary. As mentioned, participation in a private pension scheme is entirely voluntary; it may be connected to a particular employment, but it may not be automatically consequent to that employment.
- As for public pension schemes being totally tax exempt, whereas private pension schemes are taxed (although at a reduced rate), one should consider the structural difference in the accumulation mechanisms. Public pension schemes operate as "pay-as-you-go" systems, whereas private pension schemes are "funded" systems. In "pay-as-you-go" systems, there is hardly any financial component in the formation of the pension position, and this accounts for the nontaxation of the pension scheme. Indeed, it is to be considered that, since the financial returns on funded private pension schemes are taxed at a reduced rate (compared to taxation of any other financial investment) and they are no longer subject to any further taxation when they are paid out as pension to the pension recipient, the system of taxation of private pensions may, in this respect, turn out to be more favorable than the system of taxation of public pensions. In fact, when public pensions are paid out, the entire amount will be subject to progressive personal income taxation. In this view, the more the public pension system is to address and to be transformed into a "funded" system (capitalization of defined contributions), the more taxation mechanisms should equalize the ones applied to private pension schemes.
- As for the payment of private pensions being subject to income tax for the pension recipients at a special rate between 15% and 9%, whereas public pensions are taxed at the ordinary progressive tax rate (between 23% and 43%), that may only be explained as a measure of incentive to encourage employees to voluntarily adhere and participate in private pension schemes.

11. Article 11, para. 6, of Legislative Decree No. 252/2005.
12. Article 11 of the Income Tax Code.

Whether that measure of incentive is completely rational, according to principles of equality or to ability to pay principles, is a matter which has never been brought to the attention of the Italian Constitutional Court.

§15.2.4 Other Characteristics of Public and Private Pensions

As private pensions are deemed to be supplementary to public pensions, private pension schemes generally adapt their pension vesting requirements to the ones in place for public pensions.[13] The public pension system envisages "old-age" pensions to be received when achieving the final retirement age (generally, at the age of 67), and "elderness" (or "anticipated") pensions may be received when fulfilling set requirements in terms of age and in terms of years of employment and participation to the public pension scheme (generally requiring that the age of the future pension recipient plus the years of participation adds up to no less than 100). Such public pension requirements will also apply to private pensions, which will then be vested when the age for receiving public pension is reached, with the further requirement of having participated in the private pension scheme for at least five years.

Both public pensions and private pensions are perfectly portable, substantially and tax-wise, at least from a domestic and from an EU point of view.

The public pension system is run by public entities operating under the supervision of the Ministry of Labor.

Private pension schemes may be "collective" or "individual."

Collective pension schemes arise out of collective bargaining, which may take place at a national level, at a regional level or at the firm level. They are generally set up as private not-for-profit entities (associations or foundations) whose members are the participating employees and employers (if the latter were part of the collective bargaining). The management of the collective pension scheme is entrusted to a board of directors that must be formed by an equal number of representatives of the employees and of the employers.

Individual pension schemes may be set up through collective investment schemes promoted and managed by banks, asset managers or insurance companies or through special insurance contracts.

Tax-wise, individual pension schemes are treated the same way as collective pension schemes for all phases of the pension cycle.

§15.3 A CLOSER LOOK AT THE TAXATION OF PUBLIC AND PRIVATE PENSIONS

Following is some greater detail as to the tax regulation of public and private pension schemes.

13. Article 11, para. 2, of Legislative Decree No. 252/2005.

§15.3.1 Tax Treatment of Contributions

Employees' and employers' contributions to the public pension system are totally exempt from taxation, both for the employees (public pension contributions are not considered to be income)[14] and for the employers (public pension contributions are considered to be tax-deductible labor costs).[15]

Contributions to private pension funds are exempt from taxation as well, within a maximum amount. Such maximum amount is equal to EUR 5,164.57 annually.[16] This maximum amount includes both employers' contributions and employees' contributions; as a matter of fact, the employer's contributions to private pension funds are regarded as part of the employee's income for tax purposes: they will be summed up to the employee's contributions and, together with such contributions, their tax relief will be subject to the above-described limits. Hence, if the total amount of contributions paid to the pension fund (including both the employer's and the employee's) exceeds that maximum amount, the relevant surplus will be considered income for the employee and be subject to regular taxation. However, as mentioned, once those contributions exceeding the maximum deductible amount turn into pension payments, those corresponding pension payments will be totally tax exempt.[17]

One important thing to consider is that whenever a collective pension scheme exists to which the employee may participate, then the contribution to the pension scheme may be further increased by allocating in favor of the pension fund the employee's right to the so-called *liquidation bonus*.[18] The so-called liquidation bonus applies to any employment relationship, and it is deferred remuneration accruing every year (about 7% of the annual salary for each year of employment), which will only be paid out to the employee when his or her employment contract is terminated, for whatever reason.[19] Hence, during the course of the employment, the liquidation bonus is a debt of the employer toward the employee, accruing every year. The employee may then decide that such debt is paid out by the employer year after year by contributing an equal amount to the private pension scheme, whereas such further contribution will be totally tax exempt subject to no limits.

§15.3.2 Tax Treatment of Accumulation and Investment

Since the public pension system is "unfunded," there is no investment of resources and, consequently, there is no financial income and returns in composing the pension

14. Article 51, para. 2(a), of the Income Tax Code.
15. Article 95 of the Income Tax Code.
16. Article 8, para. 4, of Legislative Decree No. 252/2005. For employees starting their working activity, there is also a mechanism through which, over a twenty year period, they may increase the maximum amount of deductible private pension contributions, should they not be able, during their first five years of work, to reach the payment of the maximum deductible amount (Art. 8, para. 6, of Legislative Decree n. 252/2005).
17. Article 11, para. 6, and Art. 8, para, 4, of Legislative Decree No. 252/2005.
18. Article 8, para. 7, of Legislative Decree No. 252/2005.
19. Article 2120 of the Civil Code.

position accruing to the employee. The accumulation stage is, therefore, exempt from any income taxation.

However, as anticipated earlier, private pension schemes are "funded" systems and operate on the basis of the capitalization of the resources collected through the employees' and employers' contributions. Private pension schemes may only invest such resources in financial instruments, and the financial returns thus gained are subject to taxation at a rate of 20%.[20] Such rate is lower than the one generally applicable to financial income, which currently is 26%. As financial income from government bonds (issued by EU Member States) is generally taxed at the lower 12.5% tax rate, there is a mechanism, thanks to which the component of income of pension funds corresponding to government bonds will also be taxed at the 12.5% rate (rather than at the 20% rate).[21] The justification for such lower 20% tax rate on the accumulation of financial income by pension funds is generally deemed to be based upon the longer time constraint to which pension savings are subject to. However, it is to be considered that the financial income of pension funds is determined on an accrual basis, following a mark-to-market mechanism, and it also allows to carry forward losses. Instead, regular financial income, subject to the 26% tax rate, is determined on a cash realization basis.

§15.3.3 Tax Treatment of Pension Benefits

The payment of pensions always constitutes income for the pension recipient, and it is therefore subject to personal income taxation.[22]

Public pensions are always paid as annuities, and, hence, they are subject to progressive taxation for their entire amount.[23]

Private pension schemes may allow the pension recipient to opt for a partial payment of the pension as a lump sum, whereas the remaining part (at least half of the total pension position) must be paid out as annuity.[24]

The underlying principle for the taxation of private pensions is that they should be taxed only limited to the amounts corresponding to the contributions that enjoyed tax relief when they were paid in, thus avoiding any economic double taxation of income.[25] According to this principle, annuities and lump-sum payments will be

20. Article 17 of Legislative Decree No. 252/2005.
21. Article 1, para. 622, of Law No. 190/2014.
22. As mentioned earlier, public pensions are qualified as taxable income (the same way as employment income) under Art. 49 of the Income Tax Code and consequently subject to regular progressive taxation. Private pensions are also qualified as taxable income, under Art. 50, para. 1(h-bis), of the Income Tax Code; however, as it will be seen, they are excluded from regular progressive taxation.
23. Article 51 of the Income Tax Code.
24. Article 11, para. 3, of Legislative Decree No. 252/2005. There is an exception for private pension beneficiaries who started participating and accumulating their position before 1993 who may obtain their private pension benefit entirely as a lump-sum amount. Similar exception applies to any private pension beneficiary when their annuity would be particularly low (as compared to the minimum pensions paid under the public pension framework).
25. The principle is clearly expressed by Art. 11, para. 6, of Legislative Decree No. 252/2005, as it states that the taxable base for private pensions is their entire payment, net of any amount corresponding to income which was already taxed.

subject to taxation, but the component of the annuity or of the lump-sum payment corresponding to the financial returns accumulated by the pension fund or corresponding to the contributions that exceeded the tax relief threshold shall be excluded from any taxation.

Both the private pension annuities and the private pension lump-sum payments will be subject to the same special taxation and will not add up to general income subject to progressive taxation.[26]

The basic tax rate applying to private pension annuities and to private pension lump-sum payments will be 15%, which will then be diminished by 0.30% for each year of participation to the private pension scheme longer than fifteen years, down to a minimum tax rate of 9%.[27] Hence, the optimization of the tax rate, down to a very favorable 9%, will be reached when participating to the private pension scheme for at least thirty-five years.

It is a clear example of the use of the tax regime to enhance the pension function of the accumulation of savings, favoring the length in time of the accumulation and, consequently and presumably, given the capitalization mechanisms, the growth of the pension position.

§15.3.4 Cross-Border Pension Provisions

As for taxation of cross-border pension provisions, it is to be considered that Italian domestic legislation is subject to any existing Convention against double taxation.[28] In this respect, existing Conventions to which Italy is a party generally follow the directives of the OECD Model Convention, hence stating that pensions are taxed in the State where the pension recipient is a resident.[29]

Where no double taxation convention is in place, the general domestic rule is that both public and private pensions are taxed in the State where the pension scheme (be it public or private) is resident, regardless of the residence of the pension recipient.[30]

26. Article 11, para. 6, of Legislative Decree No. 252/2005. It is to be considered that major reforms to the taxation of pension funds and private pension benefits occurred in 1993, then in 2000 and, finally, in 2007. Each time a new taxation mechanism for private pension benefits was introduced, the law always envisaged specific transitionary adjustments leaving taxation unaltered in correspondence to the accumulation accrued. This means that a person who has been accumulating a private pension since 1990 (for example) will be subject to the taxation regime which was pending during the time of each segment of accumulation.
27. Article 11, para. 6, of Legislative Decree n. 252/2005.
28. Under Art. 10 and Art. 117, para. 1, of the Constitution, international law ranks higher than domestic law in the Italian legal system.
29. Article 18 of the OECD Model Convention states that "pensions and other similar remuneration paid to a resident of a Contracting State in consideration of past employment shall be taxable only in that State." However, it is to be noticed, especially with regard to private pensions, that the Italian tax administration generally does not consider lump-sum payments to be included in Art. 18 of the OECD Model Convention, but rather in Art. 15, which deals with employment income (ruling of the Italian tax administration No. 40/E of 2009). Under Art. 15 of the OECD Model Convention, taxing authority is generally granted to the State where the employment activity was performed (rather than to the State of residence).
30. Article 23, para. 2(a)(b), states that both public and private pensions, when paid by an entity resident in Italy, shall be subject to tax in Italy even when the pension beneficiary is a nonresident.

Restrictions may apply, however, when it comes to tax treatment of cross-border contributions or cross-border portability of pension positions with regard to private pension schemes.

Contributions to private pension schemes enjoy tax relief only if the pension scheme is Italian or if the pension scheme is established in an EU Member State and it is subject to the so-called IORP II Directive (EU Directive No. 2016/2341).[31] This limitation to tax relief, however, is only suffered by employees, whereas contributions paid by employers, even if to a non-EU pension fund, will anyhow be considered labor costs and hence will be deductible from revenues for tax purposes.

Similar restrictions apply to cross-border portability of the pension position. Tax neutrality of transfers from one pension scheme to another is only envisaged for domestic transfers and for transfers between EU pension schemes subject to the IORP II Directive, whereas the transfer of the position to (or from) a non-EU private pension scheme is, tax-wise, deemed to be receipt of a lump sum and hence subject to taxation accordingly.[32]

Hence, it should be considered that the rigidity envisaged for EU cross-border pension provisions, in terms of contributions and portability, does have a rational justification that must be taken into account in order to find a proper balance with the freedoms established by the EU Treaties. The rationale underlying the tax favor in place toward pension schemes is based upon the assumption that "today's relief" shall become "tomorrow's taxation." In principle, this assumption only works if the system is a closed system: when a person who has enjoyed tax relief in one State moves to another State, if the transfer of the pension position is neutral tax-wise, then the relief granted from the original State may become a unilateral "gift," unless, as it happens within the European Union, there is a general reciprocity regime. Therefore, from an EU point of view, the solution to the reciprocity regime, allowing for free and exempt transferability of private pension positions inside the European Union, may be founded upon the reciprocity regime that allows the exemption as the other EU countries equally allow exemption for transfers from its system to the other systems. The implementation of this reciprocity regime became possible once private pension systems found harmonization, thanks to the IORP II Directive.

Finally, one should also note that further harmonization of private pensions at the European level was pursued through the very recent pan-European Personal Pension Product (so-called PEPP), which found specific recognition with Regulation (EU) 2019/1238 of the European Parliament and of the Council of June 20, 2019. PEPPs are a typical "third pillar" individual pension product, aimed at favoring the common market for private pensions as a means to facilitate EU movement of labor. Their taxation, which the Regulation left to Member States for domestic implementation, is similar to the one applied to Italian private pension schemes.[33]

31. Article 15-ter, para. 4, of Legislative Decree No. 252/2005.
32. Article 15-ter, para. 4, of Legislative Decree No. 252/2005.
33. Legislative Decree No. 114/2022 adopted provisions to implement PEPPs in the Italian domestic legal system, in accordance with Regulation (EU) 2019/1238, including the taxation mechanisms.

§15.4 CONCLUSION

The review of the Italian pension system, and its taxation, brings about value judgments with regard to the structure of taxation which may not be considered completely positive.

As far as the public pension system is concerned, it must be acknowledged that it follows a pure E-E-T model, exempting from taxation all contributions entering the pension cycle, and then fully taxing, through the progressive personal income tax, the outcome of the pension benefits. The system seems quite straightforward in its application, although the strains that demographic factors continue to place on traditional public pension systems might encourage a greater use of the tax instrument in order to counter such demographic factors (e.g., reducing taxation should the employee voluntarily delay retirement age).

The situation seems to be much more complex (and altogether ambiguous) with regard to the private, supplementary, pension system. In fact, each of the stages of the pension cycle in the supplementary pension enjoys a peculiar tax treatment. As for the contribution stage, the tax exemption for contributions is limited to EUR 5,164.57, which is quite a low threshold for accumulating a private pension position (especially for higher-income individuals), also considering that such threshold has remained stable ever since 1995 (despite inflationary rebounds and economic growth). As for the investment stage, pension funds are certainly favored, as their returns on accumulation are subject to a 20% tax rate, lower than the ordinary 26% tax rate on regular investment income; however, despite such advantage in terms of tax rate, pension funds' accumulation is prejudiced as it is taxed on an accrual basis, whereas regular investment income is taxed on a cash realization basis. The taxation of the private pension system becomes seriously advantageous at the stage of payment of the pension benefits, which are taxed at a special 15% rate (which may even become as low as 9%). As mentioned, the 15%/9% tax rate is even lower than the minimum tax rate (23%) applying to progressive personal income tax. The taxation of private pension benefits at such low rate is totally inconsistent with the taxation of public pensions (and of any other item of income): this brings an element of irrationality to the system. At the same time, if the very low tax rate of private pension benefits is intended to be a measure of encouragement for employees to participate in private pension schemes, the incentive seems to be quite ineffective as, given the time horizons involved, the decision to participate in a private pension scheme is generally very far in time from the moment the pension benefits will be paid; hence, it is difficult to think that the pension benefit tax advantage may become clearly relevant in the decision-making process of the employee participating in the private pension scheme.

Part IV European Tax Law

CHAPTER 16

The EU (Direct) Tax Policy: Reflections on Current Trends

Adolfo Martín Jiménez

§16.1 INTRODUCTION: WHY A REFLECTION ON EU TAX POLICY?

As a professor and active politician, Peter Essers has always been a firm believer in democracy, human rights and the rule of law. In connection with this, he conceived taxes as means, not ends, to achieve social justice. Also, as an enthusiastic active promoter of cross-border cooperation (as his outstanding work with European Association of Tax Law Professors attests), his values were transferred to his thinking about EU direct tax harmonization. This chapter pays a tribute to Peter Essers by following up on his more recent analysis on EU direct tax policy, in a sort of constructive dialogue with him, to reflect some current trends he has also probably been thinking about.

§16.2 THE DEFICITS OF EU TAX POLICY FOR PETER ESSERS[1]

Peter Essers' works contrasted EU direct tax policy with the principle of no taxation without representation and Article 2 TEU to conclude that there are "democratic" and "material" deficits in EU tax policy.

For him, unanimity in Articles 113 and 115 TFEU is the most severe problem in terms of "democratic deficit." It permits situations where one single State can block initiatives wanted by the other 26 Member States (as the position by Poland and

1. *See*, for instance, Peter Essers, *Tax Justice and European Tax Law* 325 et seq. (StuW 4/2022); or Peter Essers, *History and Future of EU Taxation according to Frans Vanistendael: Inspiration for a Constructive and Critical Dialogue* 377 (World Tax Journal August 2022).

Hungary in the process of adoption of the Pillar 2 Directive[2] shows). Unanimity permits minority states to block what the majority wants and also allows results ("horse-trading") damaging for the rule of law. In the EU legislative process, the imperfect balance of powers between the Commission, the Council and EU Parliament is an issue since: (1) the Commission is not fully accountable to the Council or the Parliament; (2) in the Council, national interest plays a fundamental role; and (3) the EU Parliament has a weak—consultative—position, very different to the role of national Parliaments.

He recognized the major role the CJEU has played in direct taxes when applying the TFEU (the fundamental freedoms and State aid provisions) to the Member States' legislation. However, he also noted that the CJEU lacks democratic legitimation to take some of its decisions. Apart from the budgetary impact of many judgments, they are probably closer to positive integration than negative one and have led to uncertainty about how to implement them (*Mark & Spencer*, or *Bosal* are good examples).[3] For him, unanimity has brought not only more activism by the CJEU but also more reluctance to remove unanimity to avoid more intense budgetary consequences for the Member States.

As material deficits, he regretted the overemphasis at the international and EU level in fighting BEPS, being MNEs the scapegoats because of their allegedly "aggressive tax planning." After the financial crisis (2008), EU positive integration efforts have focused on fighting BEPS (ATAD 1[4] and 2,[5] CC(C)TB and BEFIT[6]) and have left behind the problems of companies or individuals caused by (nondiscriminatory) disparities or double taxation. The instrumental use by the Commission of Article 107 TFEU has also pushed in the same direction. In this context, the situation of taxpayers' rights is a concern, although he expressed moderate optimism for the future with, *inter alia*, BEFIT as a more pro-business proposal. Additionally, Peter Essers also referred to the absence after the European Monetary Union of a real EU Budget, independent from EU Member States' contributions.

§16.3 REFLECTIONS ON EU TAX POLICY

§16.3.1 Opening Remarks

While this author concurs with most of Peter Essers' diagnosis, it is also interesting to consider nuances deriving from recent EU legislation and proposals or the CJEU case

2. Council Directive (EU) 2022/2523, 14.12.2022, on ensuring a global minimum level of taxation for multinational enterprise groups and large-scale domestic groups in the Union, L 328/1, 22.12.2022 ("P2D").
3. C-446/03, *Mark & Spencer*, 13.12.2005 ECLI:EU:C:2005:763; C-168/01, *Bosal*, 18.09.2003 ECLI: EU:C:2003:479.
4. Council Directive (EU) 2016/1164, 12.07.2016, laying down rules against tax avoidance practices that directly affect the functioning of the internal market, L 193/1, 19.7.2016 ("ATAD").
5. Council Directive (EU) 2017/952, 29.05.2017 amending Directive (EU) 2016/1164 as regards hybrid mismatches with third countries, L 144/1, 7.6.2017 ("ATAD 2").
6. *See* on BEFIT s. 16.3.2.2 below.

law. Due to space limits, this chapter will focus on the paradoxes of unanimity, the goals of the EU tax policy and the role of the CJEU.[7]

§16.3.2 The Proliferation of EU Tax Rules Despite Unanimity

§16.3.2.1 The (Sometimes) Blocking or Petrifying Effect of Unanimity

Unanimity (Articles 113 and 115 TFEU) has prevented the adoption by the EU of many business-oriented rules, but it also has a "petrifying effect" with regrettable consequences. Examples of it are the Interest and Royalty Directive,[8] ATAD and, more recently, the P2D.[9]

First, although the elimination of withholding taxes for certain intragroup payments of interest and royalties deprived the Member States of one of the most effective techniques to fight aggressive tax planning, achieving unanimity to reform the IRD (the proposals to adopt a subject-to-tax-clause in Article 1) proved impossible over the years. This moved the Member States to design more complex tools (i.e., "interest and royalty barriers"[10]) with disproportionate effects in purely domestic transactions and for third parties. Later, the interest barrier was "upgraded" in ATAD, a Directive with no evident connections with internal market goals (it only regulates minimum anti-avoidance standards), too hastily approved, and probably in need of a relevant fine-tuning to adapt it to the CJEU's case law.[11] Changing it, however, is difficult due to unanimity.

On top of the IRD and ATAD, the P2D was passed without waiting to have the final OECD P2 rules released, but with similar "blocking effects" as its predecessors, and no coordination with ATAD measures (i.e., anti-hybrid rules, interest-barrier, CFC rules). The P2D not only may condition the Member States' position in the context of future OECD/Inclusive Framework initiatives but also tights their hands to move on (collectively or individually) to another system if they wish, makes it more difficult to react to unforeseen problems that may arise once P2 rules are rolled out, and makes doing business in the EU more difficult (also overlapping with other rules[12]). The effects are regrettable for taxpayers and tax authorities alike: rules that may need to be

7. For instance, the funding of the EU budget is another fundamental topic not dealt with here. *See* Adolfo Martín Jiménez, *Los recursos propios y los tributos en el presupuesto de la UE en la recuperación post-covid* (Nueva Fiscalidad N° 2 2022).
8. Council Directive 2003/49/EC, 3.06.2003, on a common system of taxation applicable to interest and royalty payments made between associated companies of different Member States, L 157/49, 26.6.2003 ("IRD").
9. Wolfgang Schön, *International Tax Rules for Unruly Times* (Max Planck Institute for Tax Law and Public Finance Working Paper 2023) (also citing his previous works on this).
10. The scope of both IRD and the interest barrier in ATAD differs, but the connection of both rules is clear for those affected by them simultaneously.
11. For instance, Art. 7.1.a) ATAD is not in line with the free movement of capital case law (C-135/17, *X GmbH/Finamzamt Stuttgart*, 26.02.2019, ECLI:EU:C:2019:136). *See* Alexander Rust, *Controlled Foreign Company Rule (Articles 7 and 8 ATAD)* in Werner Haslehner et al., A Guide to the Anti-Tax Avoidance Directive (Edgar 2020).
12. *See* on this, Schön, *supra* n. 9.

changed (i.e., to eliminate unnoticed flaws, simplify or adapt to new circumstances) may remain carved in stone.

Although some solutions have been proposed to relax unanimity and facilitate "exit" by the Member States from EU tax directives,[13] there is another angle of unanimity worth considering: if after some years it was clear that the IRD did not work, why did the Commission pursue and the Member States accept the strategy of adding up new rules (i.e., interest barrier) in ATAD that may be less efficient than simply reforming the IRD? Why was not ATAD also reformed with the P2D to avoid the application to MNL groups of older rules (e.g., CFC, interest barriers, anti-hybrid rules) that are probably unnecessary with the P2D? After all, the same unanimity of the Member States is required to reform the previous Directives as to approve new ones. This suggests that unanimity works with paradoxical dynamics. Sometimes, it is an obstacle to approve, reform or derogate tax Directives. Sometimes it is not and works in the direction of producing too many overlapping and uncoordinated rules.

§*16.3.2.2* *The Paradox of Unanimity*

Although business-friendly (direct) tax measures have been hampered frequently by unanimity at the EU Council, in the last years, it seems as though unanimity was easy to achieve to enact tax Directives pursuing tax transparency and fighting "aggressive tax planning" (whatever it means) ("Unshell" and "Safe" draft proposals go in the same direction).[14] Thus, besides its blocking or petrifying effect, unanimity has also allowed the EU legislator to approve rules in almost the exclusive interest of the Member States, without being evident what they added in terms single market goals or EU competitiveness.[15] In this process, "momentum" – the opportunity to approve at EU-level directives to appease public claims or discomfort in the wake of the 2008 financial crisis and scandals (i.e., the Pandora or Panama papers) – seems to have played for the Commission and the Council a more important role than pondering the consequences of the measures for the EU.[16] Momentum also probably moved the EU Commission to (unduly) use Article 107 TFEU to fight "aggressive tax planning" of MNEs and Member States' tax rulings, with the consequence of still ongoing protracted litigation and damage to legal certainty and the rule of law.

The absence (also in the post-Covid, Next Generation context) of a truly EU Budget funded with real EU taxes that permitted the EU to pursue its own policy goals, without being dependent on Member States' contributions, also facilitates that the EU

13. *See* Schön, *supra* n. 9.
14. Council Directive (EU) 2017/1852, 10.10.2017 on tax dispute resolution mechanisms in the European Union, L 265/1, 14.10.2017, has been an exception in this trend.
15. *See* Adolfo Martín Jiménez, *Towards Corporate Tax Harmonization in the EC* (Kluwer, 1999), Chapter 5.
16. The EU Commission itself recognized and complained about this. *See* Communication from the Commission to the European Parliament, the European Council and the Council Towards a More Efficient and Democratic Decision making in EU tax policy, COM(2019) 8 final, 15.1.2019, pp. 5-6.

legislative process is used, as happened in the last years, mainly to reinforce the Member States national revenue raising capacities (also to refund the EU loans).[17]

The outputs of the EU legislative process in the last years and the paradox of unanimity are easy to understand: in an EU legislative process almost fully dominated by the Member States, rules in their collective interest (or the interest of their tax administrations) have more potential to be approved than others. Even rules which may be difficult to pass at national level are more easily enacted in the EU (and, later, presented to the national legislatures as "rules to be followed," without much margin, by the national legislator). It is arguable to what extent some of these new Directives are really within the sphere of competences of the EU, really contribute to the goals of the internal market, or meet the requirements of the proportionality, subsidiarity principles (Article 5 TFEU)[18] or even the rule of law (Article 2 TEU). For instance, with all the options and disparities it permits, does ATAD improve or worsen the situation of disparity of legislations? Was a P2D really needed to attain single market goals in view of the OECD/Inclusive Framework model rules (and OECD peer review of P2 domestic legislation)? Is the accumulation of the existing rules and the compliance efforts required from taxpayers really necessary?

Paradoxically, one of the side-effects of this evolution is also the extraordinary reinforcement of the Commission's powers in the direct tax field. Not only the scope of Article 107 TFEU has broadened but also the EU direct tax system has grown dramatically, from a few rules with limited scope, to giving the Commission more visibility and leverage within the EU and internationally (this international dimension of EU law also has a certain lock-in effect also for third countries, which need to take into account what happens within the EU to define what is internationally acceptable[19]).

Fighting tax fraud and avoidance or limiting unfair tax competition are very laudable goals. It is incredible and commendable how much progress has been made in this area, thanks to the OECD, the EU Commission and the Council. However, tax policy is much more than simply having anti-tax avoidance, fraud and tax transparency rules. Tax policy is instrumental in achieving a society's preferences in terms of social and economic policies. In particular, corporate taxes have always been powerful instruments to achieve these goals, hence why Member States have opposed corporate tax harmonization for so long. It is time to wonder whether the current EU tax policy, as a consequence of the "filtering effect" of unanimity, is really instrumental in achieving EU goals and enhancing EU competitiveness and growth or, rather, it goes in

17. On the EU Own Resources policy, *see* Martín Jiménez, *supra* n. 7.
18. *See*, for instance, on the P2D, Sjoerd Douma et al., *The UTPR and International Law: Analysis From Three Angles*, 857 (Tax Notes International May 2023), expressing doubts about whether Art. 115 TFEU is a suitable legal basis for the P2D and its compatibility with the subsidiarity and proportionality principles. The argument of competence, however, is less persuasive after the CJEU concluded that Directives can also have as their goal regulating the exercise of fundamental freedoms "on a fair basis." See C-620/18, *Hungary v. EU Parliament / Council, 8 Dec. 2020,* ECLI:EU:C:2020:1001; and C-626/18, *Poland v. Parliament / Council, 8 Dec. 2020,* ECLI:EU:C:2020:1000.
19. *See* Werner Haslehner, *The Costs of Pillar 2: Legitimacy, Legality, and Lock-In,* 51 Intertax (2023) DOI: 10.54648/taxi2023066 Actions.

the opposite direction. The accumulation of new, difficult-to-interpret-and-apply EU tax transparency, anti-avoidance or anti-fraud rules without much guidance (for taxpayers and tax administrations) also raises very relevant issues in terms of legal certainty to do business in the EU.

This is the paradox of unanimity; the problem is not only that it blocks or petrifies EU direct tax rules but also that it has acted as a filter in favor of interest and values that may not always be fully aligned with the EU fundamental principles and goals.

Is it possible to rebalance the situation?[20] High-level representatives of the EU Commission[21] or EU Parliament Reports[22] have recognized some of the abovementioned problems. Because of this, the EU Commission is nudging some business-friendly proposals, i.e., FASTER[23] or the "BEFIT package," which consists of: (1) a BEFIT draft Directive[24] for P2 groups that abandons (temporarily?) formulary apportionment in favor of allocation of the EU MNE corporate tax base on the weighted share of the individual base of companies of the group in the last three years; (2) a draft EU Transfer Pricing Directive[25] that leverages on the OECD TP Guidelines (without being very concrete on fundamental issues), is a reaction to *FIAT* (where the CJEU ruled that there is no "UE arm's-length" principle)[26] and seeks more EU control on the corporate tax base; and (3) a draft Directive on an optional "head office tax system" for SMEs with PEs in other Member States.[27]

Despite aspirations of simplicity, legal certainty and willingness to improve the competitiveness of EU companies, the "package" will mean, if approved, that EU MNEs will have to live with three different systems (P2 and tax treaties for third countries, national corporate taxes, and BEFIT) in a period where the consequences of P2 will still be unfolding. Out-of-scope companies will also have their own problems, uncertainties and overlapping rules that are not much improved either by the BEFIT package, which does not seem to put forward more concrete specific proposals about simplification or providing more legal certainty (e.g., the BEFIT proposal is not clear about its relationship with ATAD, P2 or, if approved, Unshell or DEBRA, etc.). The EU Commission's goal of promoting EU growth and competitiveness with the BEFIT package may be a step in the right direction, but it is not totally clear yet to what extent the new proposals

20. *See*, on plans for simplification at the OECD level, Elodie Lamer, *Time to Declutter the Corporate Tax System, OECD Official Says* (Tax Notes International 111, 2023).
21. Elodie Lamer, *European Commission's Faster Proposal on Fast Track* (Tax Notes International 110, 2023), quoting the opinion of B. Angel, TaxUd Director for Direct Taxes at the European Commission.
22. *See* the study commissioned by the FISC Subcommittee of the European Parliament, *Removal of taxation-based obstacles and distortions in the Single Market in order to encourage cross-border Investment*, European Parliament, 2022.
23. Proposal for a Council Directive on Faster and Safer Relief of Excess Withholding Taxes, Brussels, 19.6.2023, COM(2023) 324 final.
24. Proposal for a Council Directive on Business in Europe: Framework for Income Taxation (BEFIT), Strasbourg, 12.9.2023 COM(2023) 532 final.
25. Proposal for a Council Directive on transfer pricing, Strasbourg, 12.9.2023 COM(2023) 529 final.
26. *See* C-885/19 P and C-898/19 P, *Fiat Chrysler Finance Europe e Ireland v. Commission*, 8.11.2022, ECLI:EU:C:2022:859 ("*FIAT*").
27. Proposal for a Council Directive establishing a Head Office Tax system for micro-, small- and medium-sized enterprises, Strasbourg, 12.9.2023 COM(2023) 528 final.

will contribute to fully achieve this goal (this is assuming that they are approved by the Member States, something that is not evident).

In a nutshell, unanimity has loosened the link between EU rules and the single market and allowed the enactment of Directives focusing on tax transparency and fighting "aggressive tax planning." In an EU legislative process where the Member States' executive branch interests are overrepresented, it is natural that the output may not always be in the interest of EU, companies and taxpayers, as such. This has also affected the (expansive) application of Article 107 TFEU by the Commission. Although the BEFIT package may represent an attempt at rebalancing the situation, its accumulation with other EU rules enacted may not mean that it will always be welcomed by EU companies or even the Member States, for whom the possibility of using corporate taxes as a tool of economic policy has been severely curtailed by P2 (more so if the effects of Article 107 TFEU are considered). New tools to grant more legal certainty with regard to existing rules are also missing in the more recent proposals, as well as initiatives to simplify ('declutter') the application of the current rules.[28]

§16.3.2.3 *"Overcoming Unanimity" and the Recent Examples of Majority Voting*

For years, it was claimed that a move toward majority voting would remove obstacles to (corporate) tax harmonization in the interest of the single market. For that purpose, the "passerelle clauses" in Articles 48 (7) TEU and 192 (2) TFEU are seen as the most pragmatical way of making that move (reforming the TEU/TFEU is more difficult, and the use of Article 116 TFEU is not a solid legal basis).[29]

Recent examples of the use of majority voting in the tax field do not suggest such a move will correct the paradoxes of unanimity. The solidarity contribution for the oil, gas, coal, and refining sectors of Articles 14-17 of Regulation (UE) 2022/1854 (approved by majority voting of the Council with Article 122 TFEU as a legal basis)[30] shares some of the most controversial problems of recent EU tax rules approved by unanimity. It not only may represent a misuse of Article 122 TFEU to circumvent Article 115 TFEU (and the case law of the CJEU) but seems a sort of alibi to back national equivalent measures, without really coordinating national windfall taxes or avoiding potential double taxation and gaps. Besides, it presents serious difficulties in terms of respecting EU fundamental rights and principles (e.g., nondiscrimination, subsidiarity, proportionality) or the rule of law (Article 2 TFEU).[31,32]

28. It seems though that the Commission's work plan for 2024 anticipates the intention to review Directive 2011/16/EU and look at the potential for rationalization of the reporting obligations arising from the Directive to inform proposals to reduce the reporting burden. *See* Initiative 16 of the Annex 1 to the Commission Work Program 2024, COM(2023) 638 final, Strasbourg, 17.10.2023.
29. COM(2019) 8 final, 15.1.2019, pp. 6-7.
30. OJ L 261, 7.10.2022, pp. 1-21.
31. *See*, for instance, the arguments against Regulation 2022/1854 in case T-802/22, *ExxonMobil and Mobil Erdgas-Erdöl v. Council* (not yet decided).

Would more involvement of the European Parliament in the tax policymaking (with equal footing to the Council) contribute to sorting out the problems? Some of the positions of the EU Parliament on already enacted or draft Directives rules may not invite to optimist. Still, upgrading the role of the EU Parliament may help counterbalance the Member States' interest and make the Commission and Council more politically accountable, although a reform of the TFEU in this direction is not an easy task. However, even within the current EU institutional layout, there is room for more control of the EU institutions to render them more accountable, improve their proximity to the taxpayers or the formulation of tax policy, and limit the most pernicious effects of unanimity, as well as to implement solutions that may provide more tax and legal certainty.[33]

In conclusion, it is not that clear that only with a shift to majority voting the outcomes of the EU legislative procedure in tax terms would be far better unless there are also reforms in the mentioned directions: more accountability, better tax policies and more legal certainty.

§16.4 THE ROLE OF THE CJEU

§16.4.1 Preliminary Remarks

As Peter Essers indicated, the role of the CJEU in the direct tax field has mainly been connected with assessing the compatibility of the Member States' legislation with the TFEU (fundamental freedoms) and reinforcing the powers of the EU Commission under Article 107 TFEU. In view of the proliferation of EU direct tax legislation in favor of the Member States' interest, has the role of the CJEU changed? Is the CJEU in a position to control some of the "rule of law" emerging issues in terms of competences and respect for fundamental EU principles and rights? Some recent cases are interesting in this respect.

§16.4.2 The Control by the CJEU of the EU Legislator and the Commission

Traditionally, the CJEU, also in tax cases, has exerted a great degree of deference toward the EU legislator. The "manifest error" standard in view of the goals pursued by EU regulations/directives was the yardstick used by the CJEU, with the consequence that the EU legislator has a broad discretion to pursue its economic, social and political goals. In this context, only very rarely were EU (tax) rules declared void.[34] However, things may be changing, probably as a consequence of the *PSPP* judgment by the

32. Directive (EU) 2021/2101 on public-country-by-country-reporting, adopted with Art. 50.1. TFEU as legal basis is another example where the benefits for EU companies of going beyond the OECD BEPS Action 13 standards are dubious.
33. *See*, for example, Bertil Wiman, *Who Should Be in the Driver's Seat in Developing International Tax Norms—Civil Servants or National Parliaments?*, 77 Bulletin for International Taxation (2023). Other solutions can also be developed.
34. *See* the CJEU (Grand Chamber) judgments, C-390/15, *RPO*, 7.03.2017, ECLI:EU:C:2017:174 (a VAT case), or, the nontax cases, C-491/01, *British American Tobacco (Investments)*, 10.12.2002,

German Constitutional Court of 5.05.2020, which directly challenged, as ultra vires, the decisions of the ECB and the CJEU, questioning their competences, the proportionality of their acts, the judicial review of EU acts by the CJEU, and the supremacy of EU law.[35] After *PSPP*, the CJEU seems to be engaging in a more in-depth review of the compatibility of EU legislation and acts with general principles of EU law. Only in 2022, several judgments annulled EU law acts to reinforce the effectiveness of EU general principles and rights vis-à-vis the EU legislature (two of them affecting respectively EU legislation on public beneficial ownership registries and DAC 6).[36] More cases are waiting to be decided,[37] and more will come as a consequence of recent decisions. Moreover, in *FIAT*, the CJEU limited the expansion of the Commission's State aid competences in connection with national corporate taxes (transfer pricing legislation) to reclaim the importance of the principle of legality for tax purposes at the EU level.

This strand of judgments shows more willingness to rein in the Council and Commission (although other cases have shown a certain degree of deference to admit the use of the legislative procedure to regulate 'fair market' goals)[38]. In view of how EU tax policy has evolved in the last years, it may also herald a new phase of EU integration in which, besides Member States' tax legislations, also EU tax Directives and acts will be scrutinized more closely by the CJEU through the lens of EU fundamental principles, rights and competences. This would be a welcomed development since the same rule of law controls to which the Member States are submitted[39] should also apply to EU institutions, in particular, to limit the most undesirable effects of "the paradox of

---

EU:C:2002:741; C-127/07, *Arcelor Atlantique*, 16.12.2008, EU:C:2008:728; C-203/12, *Billerud Karlsborg*, 17.10.2013, EU:C:2013:664, or C-628/18, *Poland v. Parliament and Council*, ECLI: EU:C:2020:1000.

35. In this judgment, the German Constitutional Court declared that the CJEU judgment in *Weiss* (C-493/17, *Weiss*, 11.12.2018, ECLI:EU:C:2018:1000, a decision based on the "manifest error standard") and the ECB acts were ultra vires and not applicable in Germany because they breached the proportionality principle. For an English version of the judgment, *see* https://www.bundesverfassungsgericht.de/SharedDocs/Entscheidungen/EN/2020/05/rs20200505_2bvr085915en.html;jsessionid=635E13439C44CD0E904D12A900579CAE.internet971. *See*, on *PSPP*, for instance, Josep Weiler, *Why Weiss? The I.Con Symposium: Preface*, 19 International Journal of Constitutional Law (2021).
36. C-181/20, *VYSOČINA WIND a.s.*, 25.01.2022, ECLI:EU:C:2022:51 (the Grand Chamber declared invalid an article of Directive 2012/19/EU because of its retroactive effects and breach of the legal certainty principle); C-37/20 and C-601/20, CJEU, *WM y Sovim SA*, 22.11.2022, ECLI: EU:C:2022:912 (the Grand Chamber declared an article of Directive (EU) 2018/843, on beneficial ownership registries, in breach of Arts 7 and 8 of the EU Charter of Fundamental Rights); and C-694/20, *Orde van Vlaamse Balies, IG, Belgian Association of Tax Lawyers*, 8.12.2022, ECLI:EU:C:2022:963 (the Grand Chamber concluded that Art. 8ab(5) of DAC 6 is invalid in the light of Art. 7 of the EU Charter of Fundamental Rights).
37. *See*, for instance, the fundamental questions raised by the Belgian Constitutional Court in case C-623/22 (not yet decided) in connection with DAC 6 and some of its non-defined concepts. Moreover, direct appeals by energy companies against the solidarity contribution in Regulation UE 2022/1854 will be heard by the GCEU (e.g., T-802/22, ExxonMobil, not yet decided; or C-391/23, *Braila Winds*).
38. See C-620/18, *Hungary v. EU Parliament / Council, 8 Dec. 2020,* ECLI:EU:C:2020:1001; and C-626/18, *Poland v. Parliament / Council, 8 Dec. 2020,*ECLI:EU:C:2020:1000, concluding that Directive can have as their goal not only the removal of obstacles to EU freedoms but also the regulation of a "fair market."
39. *See* the judgments (Full Court), C-156/21, *Comisión / Hungría*, 16.02.2022, ECLI:EU:C:2022:97, and *Comision / Polonia*, C-157/21, 16.02.2022, ECLI:EU:C:2022:98, 16.02.2022.

unanimity." Although obviously the CJEU cannot design the right EU tax policy, a closer judicial review may contribute to indicating the right path to take.

In this line, a relevant nontax CJEU decision regarding international treaties may further enhance this trend. Many authors have focused their attention on the compatibility of EU direct tax directives, including ATAD and P2D, with tax and international investment treaties and whether those treaties can block the rolling out of those Directives. Basically, they rely on an extended (*per analogiam*) interpretation of Article 351.1 TFEU to defend that (tax and investment) treaties cannot be overridden by later-in-time Directives.[40] The CJEU (Grand Chamber) has, with clear and strong language, closed the viability of these arguments in *HF* when it instructed the national court that if the US-Germany 1978 extradition treaty could not be interpreted in line with EU law, it should disapply any provision of the treaty which could be incompatible with EU law having direct effect, without waiting for the specific Member State (Germany) to renegotiate the international treaty.[41] Therefore, the CJEU interpreted Article 351.1 TFEU very strictly: it only grandfathers pre-accession international treaties.

The practical effects of *HF* for tax purposes are that tax or investment treaties concluded by the Member States with third countries after accession to the EU but prior to EU tax directives (i.e., P2D) cannot block the application of the latter within the EU (as a consequence, the Member States will have to renegotiate such treaties if incompatible with them). This decision suggests that the only judicial review of EU (tax) Directives implementing new international tax standards (BEPS, P2) should be based on EU fundamental principles and rights, which may fuel new legal actions and preliminary rulings on these grounds against recent tax Directives.

Therefore, in this new stage of EU (tax) law, it appears that the CJEU may have a very relevant role to play, which is very different to the one previously displayed: instead of strictly controlling the Member States, the CJEU may feel the need to enforce EU fundamental rights and principles vis-à-vis EU acts, may be also acting as a catalyzer toward institutional reforms of the EU legislative procedure in tax matters.

§16.5 A FINAL REFLECTION

The dynamics of the EU tax legislative procedure and unanimity, in view of the developments of the last years, probably require more than simply replacing unanimity with majority voting. As Peter Essers has longed for, more democracy, accountability, solidarity and impulse of the rule of law is needed, with improvements in how EU tax policy is formulated. There is a need to counterbalance the natural inclination of the current legislative procedure to (over) protect the Member State's interest and also to provide more legal certainty while fostering economic growth.

Although a reform of the existing institutional set-up may be desirable to more closely connect taxes and democratic control, more modest reforms are also possible to

40. *See*, for instance, with regard to the P2D and the UTPR rule, Douma et al., *supra* n. 18.
41. C-435/22 PPU, *HF v. Generalstaatsanwaltschaft München*, 28.10.2022, ECLI:EU:C:2022:852, paras. 108 and 110.

improve the process of defining the EU tax policy. In this context, the role of the CJEU in the field of EU direct taxation may slightly be shifting from controlling the Member States' legislation toward more activism to enforce EU fundamental principles and rights vis-à-vis the Commission or the Council (although it is probably too soon to say if, as happened before in EU history, the CJEU will be the promoter of those reforms).

In essence, by pointing at the EU democratic and material deficits, Peter Essers taught us that there is much room to improve EU tax policy. This chapter can only but subscribe to his words and acknowledge that his wisdom and experience make him a truly fundamental asset to enlighten the way forward.

CHAPTER 17

Should We Veto the Proposed Abolition of the Unanimity Rule in EU Taxation?

Cees Peters

§17.1 INTRODUCTION

Undoubtedly, the EUCOTAX Wintercourse was one of the biggest joys in the academic life of Peter Essers. The well-known success formula of this project is that students from twelve different countries perform a comparative research and then propose a harmonized solution of tax law. That recommendation of the students does not have to take into consideration the harsh political realities of arriving at that solution.

Needless to say that the political reality in the European Union (EU) is a different one. There is the power of veto of all Member States in between the student's dream and the real world. After all, the relevant legal bases for tax harmonization (i.e., Articles 113 and 115 Treaty on the Functioning of the European Union (TFEU)) provide for unanimous decision-making on the basis of the so-called special legislative procedure. This procedure deviates from the "ordinary legislative procedure" that entails qualified majority voting (QMV). Peter was very critical of this unanimity rule, describing it as "(t)he most significant democratic deficit in EU tax law."[1] He concurred with his Belgian friend Vanistendael that it is about time to switch to QMV.[2]

Interestingly, this academic call for a transformation from the unanimity rule to QMV is slowly starting to gain traction in the political domain. The fact that the German Bundeskanzler Olaf Scholz is consistently repeating that the use of vetoes in the areas

1. Peter Essers, *Tax Justice and European Tax Law* volume 99, issue 4, pp. 325-328 (326) (Steuer und Wirtschaft 2022) DOI: 10.9785/stuw-2022-990408. *See also*: Peter Essers, *Shifting Power Relationships and the (Un)democratic EU-Unanimity Rule for Tax Measures*. In *Verschuivende machtsverhoudingen in de fiscaliteit* pp. 47-53 (Peter Essers et al. eds., Kluwer Deventer 2022).
2. Peter Essers, *History and Future of EU Taxation According to Frans Vanistendael: Inspiration for a Constructive and Critical Dialogue* volume 14, issue 3, pp. 377-405 (World Tax Journal 2022).

of taxation and foreign policy will paralyze the enlarged EU in the future should be considered as a meaningful signal.[3] These pleas will certainly sound like music to the ears of the European Commission which did a proposal back in 2019 to establish a step-by-step abolition of the unanimity rule and to move to QMV.[4] The plan is to make use of the so-called general "passerelle clause" in Article 48(7) of the Treaty on European Union (TEU) in order to gradually introduce QMV in the area of taxation.[5] Unsurprisingly, some of the smaller Member States, like Ireland[6] and the Netherlands,[7] are strongly opposed to this curtailment of tax sovereignty.

It is the purpose of this chapter to analyze the proposed introduction of QMV in the domain of taxation. The research question is whether and to what extent there are convincing arguments to veto the proposed abolition of the unanimity rule in EU taxation. For this matter, §17.2 describes some aspects of the EU institutional framework to illustrate the context of the unanimity rule. Section 17.3 elaborates on arguments in favor of and against the unanimity rule, after which these arguments will be balanced in §17.4 on the basis of an exercise of institutional balancing. Section 17.5 brings this chapter to an end with the conclusion.

§17.2 THE INSTITUTIONAL CONTEXT OF THE UNANIMITY RULE

The first step of the analysis is to place (the limitations of) the unanimity rule in the context of the institutional framework of the EU. For this matter, it is useful to build on the work of the political scientist Fritz Scharpf. This scholar studied collective decision-making processes and the situation in the EU in particular. One of his main claims in this context was that the EU is struggling with a so-called joint-decision trap.[8] This phenomenon implies, simply put, that the institutional framework of the EU blocks progress, or change more in general, in some policy areas given the fact that all Member States take part in a bargaining style decision-making process in the Council of the European Union ("Council") that requires unanimity in order to establish results.

It goes without saying that the decision-making processes about personal and corporate income taxation constitute classical situations of a joint-decision trap since the Member States ruthlessly defend their own divergent interests in negotiations at the

3. https://www.reuters.com/world/europe/eu-needs-majority-voting-foreign-tax-policy-scholz-2022-08-29/ and https://www.bundesregierung.de/breg-en/news/address-by-olaf-scholz-2189412.
4. European Commission, *Towards a more efficient and democratic decision making in EU tax policy* COM(2019) 8 final (Strasbourg 2019).
5. It is outside the scope of this chapter to deal with this clause in detail.
6. https://www.irishtimes.com/business/economy/ireland-rejects-brussels-plan-to-kill-national-vetoes-on-tax-1.3759027.
7. The official stance of the Dutch government is a negative one since it respects the will of the Dutch House of Representatives (*Tweede Kamer*) to adhere to the unanimity rule. *See* letter of the Dutch State Secretary of Finance of July 2, 2020 as published in V-N 2020/41.9.
8. *See* Fritz Scharpf, *The Joint-Decision Trap: Lessons from German Federalism and European Integration* volume 66, pp. 239-278 (Public Administration 1988), Fritz Scharpf, *The Joint-Decision Trap Revisited* volume 44, issue 4, pp. 845-864 (Journal of Common Market Studies 2006) and Fritz Scharpf, *The JDT Model: Context and Extensions*. In *The EU's Decision Traps: Comparing Policies* pp. 217-236 (Gerda Falkner ed., Oxford University Press 2011).

European level.[9] At the same time, it should also be acknowledged though that there are several "exit mechanisms" in place in the institutional framework of the EU to get round this joint-decision trap.[10] These mechanisms basically make it possible to circumvent the veto power of the Member States in order to establish effective solutions for European tax integration.

The fundamental freedoms and the framework of fiscal state aid control are certainly the most well-known examples of such "exit mechanisms" that can be found in the TFEU.[11] The Court of Justice of the European Union (CJEU) did not quite shy away from taking controversial decisions about these provisions in order to establish tax harmonization "through the backdoor" in the integration through law tradition.[12] There are, however, also some more voluntary modes of governance to be found in the institutional framework of the EU. Most of all, the enhanced cooperation provision makes it possible to leave the obstructionists behind to achieve cooperation between a more limited group of Member States.[13] The 2013 proposal for a Financial Transaction Tax and the 2022 joint declaration of France, Germany, Spain, Italy and the Netherlands about the implementation of the global minimum tax illustrate how this piecemeal approach to tax harmonization has an appeal to (some of) the Member States. At the same time, the Member States are less keen on the use of the so-called market distortion provision of Article 116 TFEU.[14] The critical point is that every individual Member State is eventually in control of the application of the enhanced cooperation provision, whereas this is not the case for the "market distortion provision."

The takeaway of this brief contextual overview is that there is an unsteady balance at the heart of the institutional framework of the EU. On the one hand, there is the unanimity rule that has the potential to obstruct the process of European tax integration as a result of the joint-decision trap. At the same time, there is a variety of mechanisms that make it possible to "escape" from this hurdle to realize the objective of an internal market which is explicitly laid down in Article 3(3) TEU. It is this very tension that is at the heart of the debate about the unanimity rule which will be discussed in the next sections.

9. *See* Philipp Genschel, *One Trap, Many Exits, but No Free Lunch: How the Joint-Decision Trap Shapes EU Tax Policy* in *The EU's Decision Traps: Comparing Policies* pp. 54-72 (Gerda Falkner ed., Oxford University Press 2011).
10. *Ibid.*, Genschel makes a distinction between "exit by bypass," "exit by nudging," and "exit by self-extrication." This concerns the respective power of the CJEU, the European Commission and the Council to "exit" from the joint-decision trap.
11. These mechanisms may also be described as the process of negative integration.
12. Think for example of the decisions of the CJEU in the Schumacker (279/93) and the Marks & Spencer (C-446/03) cases. Moreover, its interpretation of Art. 107 TFEU as a nondiscrimination test implies that fiscal state aid control has become a powerful tool to fight harmful tax competition.
13. *See* Art. 20 TEU. An exhaustive analysis of this mechanism can be found in Caroline Heber, *Enhanced Cooperation and European Tax Law* (Oxford University Press 2021).
14. *See, e.g.*, Joachim Englisch, *Article 116 TFEU—The Nuclear Option for Qualified Majority Tax Harmonization?* volume 29, issue 2, pp. 58-61 (EC Tax Review 2020) DOI: 10.54648/ecta2020 007.

§17.3 PROS AND CONS OF THE UNANIMITY RULE

§17.3.1 Arguments in Favor

The first question is then for what reasons we would adhere to the unanimity rule to decide about matters of taxation in the EU. The principal reason for this rule is undoubtedly the aspiration of the Member States to preserve tax sovereignty in order to be completely in control over their tax revenues. This argument is closely related to considerations of legitimacy. The basic point is, as explained by Jaakkola, that "(n)o Member State should be subject to a tax statute that it has not agreed to."[15] In this view, national parliaments should exercise full democratic control over their taxing systems to guarantee their legitimacy. This also implies that only the Member States themselves dictate the desirable level of tax integration for the benefit of their own citizens.

This position on the unanimity rule should be linked to claims about the need to protect the minority group of Member States. Heber takes, for example, the view that the stability of the European Union would be at risk in case the minority of Member States would need to comply with a decision that is forced upon them by a majority of Member States.[16] She argues that the Member States should be able to rely on their taxing system to "follow their intrinsic interests and national values."[17] In case "the EU" would force the Member States to act against these interests and values, they might, in her view, cease to be cooperative members of the EU.[18]

Heber's position also illustrates how the debate on the unanimity rule is infused with (implicit) positions on the political economy of taxation in the EU. Arguably, the European founders had a balancing act between a European internal market and national social market economies in mind.[19] In this view, it would indeed be the case that the Member States should be fully autonomous to decide what taxing system is most suitable to the particular design of their social market economy so that the unanimity rule is indeed a prerequisite for tax harmonization at the European level.

These arguments can also be linked to a final group of claims about the need to stick to the unanimity rule. This concerns the views about the "quality of a decision" that is being made in case all Member States have the possibility to use the veto to defend national interests and values. Heinemann, for example, refers to the well-known economist Knut Wicksel to support the already-mentioned claim that the "losers" of a decision might pose a threat to the stability of the EU.[20] He writes how

15. Jussi Jaakkola, *A Democratic Dilemma of European Power to Tax: Reconstructing the Symbiosis Between Taxation and Democracy Beyond the State?* volume 20, issue 5, pp. 660-678 (675) (German Law Journal 2019) DOI: 10.1017/glj.2019.55.
16. Heber, *supra* n. 13, pp. 37-42.
17. *Ibid.*, p. 42.
18. *Ibid.*
19. *See* Agustín José Menéndez, *Neumark Vindicated: The Three Patterns of Europeanisation of National Tax Systems and the Future of the Social and Democratic Rechtsstaat*. In *The End of the Eurocrats' Dream* pp. 78-126 (81) (Damian Chalmers et al. eds., Cambridge University Press 2016).
20. Friedrich Heinemann, *Majority Voting on Taxation Could Prove Explosive for European Integration* opinion 18 (EconPol May 2019) available at https://www.econpol.eu/opinion_18.

"(o)nly unanimity guarantees that a new tax harmonization step is really a win-win project and not part of a selfish majority agenda."[21] This position therefore clearly explains how the advocates of the unanimity rule in the EU are eventually concerned about the need to protect the minority position. The underlying standpoint is that only the explicit consent of a Member State serves as an appropriate mechanism to protect the minority of Member States from the majority.[22]

§17.3.2 Arguments Against

This conclusion leads to the other side of the coin. Why would we bother to let go of the unanimity rule of Articles 113 and 115 TFEU? The most inclusive argument is probably that the unanimity rule hampers the effectiveness of European tax integration.[23] Also, the European Commission stresses how the unanimity rule hindered "progress on important tax initiatives" that would be needed to reinforce the internal market.[24] In this regard, it also insists that a switch to QMV would lead to "better decisions" since the unanimity rule hampers the decision-making process in several ways.[25] The European Commission claims that the threat of a veto has several undesirable consequences, including the difficulty of reaching a compromise at all and the risk of making a deal at the lowest level of common ground.[26] As a matter of fact, this last point is just one of the "conflict-minimizing" methods that the Member States rely on in order to "extricate" themselves from the unanimity rule.[27]

These claims about the effectiveness of European tax integration should be distinguished from more institutional arguments about the question of who should be making the decisions about this process. Peter was, for example, very critical of the fact that a minority of Member States (i.e., Poland and Hungary) could hijack the decision-making process about the adoption of the Directive on minimum effective taxation for large multinationals.[28] In his view, this constituted "a sort of horse-trading with the protection of the rule of law as bet", which "has nothing to do with democratic

21. *Ibid.* Obviously, it would be outside the scope of this chapter to study Wicksel's views on this topic and the relevant tradition of scholars that was influenced by his position including Musgrave and Buchanan and Tullock.
22. Compare (in the national context of the protection of the individual taxpayer): Wolfgang Schön, *Taxation and Democracy* vol. 72 no. 13 (Max Planck Institute for Tax Law and Public Finance Working Paper 2018).
23. Compare, for example, Eric Kemmeren, *Sources of EU Law for European Tax Integration: Well-Known and Alternative Legal Instruments*. In *Traditional and Alternative Routes to European Tax Integration* pp. 29-49 (33) (Dennis Weber ed., IBFD Amsterdam 2010).
24. European Commission, *supra* n. 4, p. 3.
25. *Ibid.*, p. 7.
26. *Ibid.*, p. 8.
27. *See* Genschel, *supra* n. 9, p. 65. Genschel (at p. 66) distinguishes this method from a "conflict-concealing mode of agreement," such as the reliance on soft law. The example of the Code of Conduct for Business Taxation clearly illustrates how soft law is basically another way to accomplish (nonbinding) forms of European tax integration despite of the unanimity requirement.
28. Essers, *supra* n. 1, p. 326. Also compare Vanistendael who wrote how the unanimity rule is "utterly undemocratic, because it allows representatives of Liliput states to block the political will of the overwhelming majority of European voters." *See* Frans Vanistendael, *A Window of*

decision-making."[29] In this context, it is obviously useful to add that also a small group of more powerful Member States can take advantage of this kind of bargaining in order to put a knife to the throat of the less powerful ones.[30]

A related issue concerns the ascertainment that the CJEU has obtained such a decisive role in the process of European tax integration and that this crucial position is very much related to the unanimity rule.[31] Section 17.2 already made clear how the process of negative integration should be regarded as an "exit mechanism" from the joint-decision trap in the current institutional framework of the EU. Peter,[32] and many others, of course,[33] was critical of this pivotal role for the CJEU since—in Vanistendael's crisp words—its decisions "lack the democratic legitimacy of statutory law approved by the parliament; and ... are an imprecise instrument to establish clear and certain tax rules."[34] Consequently, in this view, the unanimity rule is at the basis of legitimacy concerns that are caused by the far-reaching decisions of the CJEU.

A final institutional concern about the unanimity rule is the view that the European Parliament should be having a more decisive role in the European legislative process. It is after all well known that the European Parliament has a negligible (consultative) role in the special legislative procedure of Articles 113 and 115 TFEU. This implies that the Council basically lacks appropriate political accountability in relation to this European Parliament.[35] It is therefore this concern about the faltering democratic legitimacy that has become increasingly relevant over the years in the academic debate about the unanimity rule.[36] Also, the European Commission is concerned about the "democratic deficit" as a result of the limited role of the European Parliament—and therefore of the European citizens—in the current institutional setting.[37] It therefore explicitly mentions that a switch to QMV would ensure that the European Parliament has "equal weight in deciding the final shape of EU tax policy

Opportunity for the Making of Europe: Member States Cannot Have Their National Cake and Eat the European One volume 12, issue 1, pp. 2-3 (2) (EC Tax Review 2003) DOI: 10.54648/ecta2003001.

29. *Ibid.*
30. Compare Frans Vanistendael, *Memorandum on the Taxing Powers of the European Union* volume 11, issue 3, pp. 120-129 (126) (EC Tax Review 2002) DOI: 10.54648/5093536.
31. Compare Pasquale Pistone, *A Plea for Qualified Majority Voting and the Ordinary Legislative Procedure in European Tax Law*. In *CFE Tax Advisers Europe 60th Anniversary—Liber Amicorum* para. 2.1. (Servaas van Thiel et al. eds., IBFD Amsterdam 2019) and Peter Essers, *supra* n. 1, p. 327.
32. Essers, *supra* n. 1, p. 327.
33. The case law of the CJEU stirred criticism as from the second part of 1990s when the reach of its decision-making power became clear. *See, e.g.*, David Williams, *Asscher: The European Court of Justice and the Power to Destroy* volume 6, issue 1, pp. 4-10 (EC Tax Review 1997) DOI: 10.54648/ecta1997002.
34. Frans Vanistendael, *On Democratic Legitimacy of European Tax Law and the Role of the European Parliament*. In *European Tax Integration: Law, Policy and Politics* pp. 99-121 (111) (Pasquale Pistone ed., IBFD Amsterdam 2018).
35. *See* Vanistendael, *The Limits to the New Community Tax Order* volume 31, issue 2, pp. 293-314 (296) (Common Market Law Review 1994).
36. *See, e.g.*, Vanistendael, *supra* n. 34, p. 111, Pasquale Pistone, *supra* n. 31, para. 2.1. and Essers, *supra* n. 1, pp. 326-327.
37. European Commission, *supra* n. 4, p. 2.

initiatives."[38] Moreover, it stresses how the explicit consent of the European Parliament would improve the political accountability of these initiatives.[39]

§17.4 ANALYSIS OF THE ARGUMENTS FOR AND AGAINST THE UNANIMITY RULE

§17.4.1 Institutional Balancing

The overview of arguments for and against the unanimity rule leads to the question of how these grounds should be assessed.[40] My methodological choice in this chapter to deal with this challenge is to resort to Maduro's work on institutional balancing.[41] His starting point is basically that we should be careful to assume that an alternative institutional setting will function necessarily better than the current defective setting.[42] In other words, an idealized institutional setting of QMV in combination with a stronger role for the European Parliament will not necessarily function better than the current (possibly dysfunctional) reality of the unanimity rule. Maduro's approach basically implies that "institutional choices should be made by comparing the different alternative institutions and not solely on the ground that a particular institution suffers from serious institutional malfunctioning."[43]

Following this approach, it is crucial to look in a critical way at the institutional alternative of QMV in combination with a stronger role for the European Parliament. Maduro makes clear that it cannot simply be taken for granted that the decision of a (qualified) majority of states is a "more democratic" one than an unanimous decision.[44] Needless to say that Vanistendael and Peter were completely correct to be concerned about the undemocratic nature of the horse-trading between the Member States in the current institutional setting.[45] However, the catch of QMV is that "the cumulative benefit it gives to the majority of states is lower than the cumulative costs burdening the minority of states."[46] This implies, in other words, that the smaller Member States may have, for example, more to lose from a harmonized corporate income tax system than the bigger ones might gain from such an alternative.

38. *Ibid.*, p. 8.
39. *Ibid.*, p. 11.
40. *See* R. de la Feria, *Pillar 2, Fiat, and the Unanimity Rule on Tax Matters* volume 32, issue 1, pp. 2-8 (EC Tax Review 2023) DOI: 10.54648/ecta2023001.
41. *See* Miguel Poiares Maduro, *We the Court: The European Court of Justice & the European Economic Constitution—A Critical Reading of Article 30 of the EC Treaty* (Hart Publishing Oxford and Portland, Oregon 2002) (original: 1998) and Miguel Poiares Maduro, *Europe and the Constitution: What If This Is as Good as It Gets?* In *European Constitutionalism Beyond the State* pp. 74-102 (Marlene Wind & Joseph Weiler eds., Cambridge University Press 2003).
42. Maduro, *supra* n. 41, p. 88. Maduro's position is strongly influenced by Neil Komesar who described this problem of legal analysis as "single institutionalism." *See* Neil Komesar, *Imperfect Alternatives: Choosing Institutions in Law, Economics, and Public Policy* (The University of Chicago Press, Chicago and London 1996).
43. Maduro, *supra* n. 41, p. 88. Maduro explicitly points at Komesar for this insight.
44. Maduro, *supra* n. 41, pp. 89-90.
45. *See* §17.3.2.
46. Maduro, *supra* n. 41, p. 90.

Consequently, the unanimity rule comes with a justified fear of the majority of Member States for the minority, but a decision on the basis of QMV also co-occurs with a legitimate uneasiness about the majority on the side of the minority of Member States.[47] Nevertheless, it should also not be underestimated that the new voting methodology for the Council that was introduced in the Lisbon Treaty truly acknowledges this concern. Arguably, the introduction of the so-called double-majority voting rule[48] in combination with the rule on the blocking minority[49] truly improved the balance between both fears since it finds a reasonable equilibrium between the competing maxims of one-citizen-one-vote and one-state-one-vote.[50] Consequently, a change to QMV in the domain of taxation would probably truly result in a more balanced consideration of the different interests of the various groups of Member States than the current unanimity rule.[51]

This leads to the respective roles of national parliaments and the European Parliament since these responsibilities are substantially different in both alternative institutional settings. It would be tempting to claim, as, for example, the Dutch government does, that the democratic legitimacy of European decisions may very well be *exclusively* based on the consent of national parliaments.[52] Such a position is, however, not convincing for several reasons.[53] Most of all, this view does not take into consideration that "national political processes no longer control many decision-making processes which impact on the national polity but take place outside its borders," such as tax competition.[54] Moreover, this standpoint also does not consider that national parliaments may be captured by special interests that, for example, do not properly take into consideration the effects of national policy decisions on the other Member States.[55]

It is therefore exactly for these kinds of reasons that the legitimacy of the EU political and legal order as such *should* be based on its ability to correct national democratic failures.[56] Within the current institutional framework of the EU, it is

47. This may be labeled as "the fear of the few and the fear of the many." *See* Maduro, *supra* n. 41, p. 86 who refers to Komesar in this context.
48. *See* Art. 16(4) TEU: "a qualified majority shall be defined as at least 55% of the members of the Council, comprising at least fifteen of them and representing Members States comprising at least of 65% of the population of the Union."
49. *See* Art. 16(4) TEU: "A blocking minority must include at least four Council members, failing which the qualified majority shall be deemed attained."
50. Compare Paul Magnette & Kalypso Nicolaïdis, *Coping with the Lilliput Syndrome: Large vs. Small Member States in the European Convention* volume 11, issue 1, pp. 85-104 (European Public Law 2005).
51. *See* Pistone, *supra* n. 31, para. 2.1.
52. Letter of the Dutch Minister of Foreign Affairs, February 15, 2019, Tweede Kamer der Staten-Generaal 22112 (*Nieuwe Commissievoorstellen en initiatieven van de lidstaten van de Europese Unie*), nr. 2772, Fiche: *Mededeling voor meer efficiënte en democratische besluitvorming bij EU-belastingzaken*, p. 8.
53. *See* Cees Peters, *Global Tax Justice: Who's Involved?* In *Ethics and Taxation* pp. 172-173 (Robert van Brederode ed., Singapore, Springer 2020).
54. Miguel Poiares Maduro, *Where to Look for Legitimacy* in *Institutional Challenges in Post-constitutional Europe* pp. 43-70 (62) (Catherine Moury & Luis de Sousa eds., Routledge 2009).
55. *Ibid.*, p. 63.
56. This line of thinking evolved in my Ph.D. research. *See* Cees Peters, *On the Legitimacy of International Tax Law* para. 8.4.2 (IFBD Amsterdam 2014).

therefore only logical to rely on the European Parliament to establish a counterbalance to these kinds of deficiencies. Unquestionably, there are certainly reasons to be concerned about the democratic quality of the current functioning of the European Parliament, such as the large distance between this institution and the European citizens and the related risk that this parliament is captured by a minority position.[57] It is my view though that these disadvantages are, on balance, less discomforting than the stressed concerns about the exclusive reliance on national parliaments.

§17.4.2 Overall Assessment of the Unanimity Rule in EU Taxation

This careful institutional balancing of the two alternative settings makes it possible to weigh the arguments for and against the unanimity rule.

Either way, the starting point of the overall assessment would be that the proponents of the unanimity rule are actually somewhat overtaken by reality. Indeed, in spite of this unanimity rule, it cannot be denied that the process of European tax integration is more and more arriving at somewhat effective solutions anyway. This is particularly true ever since the OECD's work on BEPS and the global minimum tax have been driving the rapid introduction of European Directives. In fact, the OECD's work is therefore basically serving as a new "exit mechanism" that makes it possible to get round the veto power of the Member States in order to establish effective solutions for European tax integration.

In my view, it is persuasive to argue that this latest development is actually undesirable. It is undoubtedly true that it is a very important objective of European tax cooperation to make sure that the Member States regain control over the market forces of tax competition. Such de facto control over the taxpayer is after all, like also the European Commission recognizes,[58] a crucial condition for the Member States in order to make autonomous choices about the particularities of the taxing system that is most suitable to the design of its social market economy.[59] That end does, however, not necessarily justify the means, and therefore I struggle with the establishment of, in particular, Pillar Two.[60] That project clearly illustrates that the precarious link between the democratic consent of national parliaments and the need for an effective resolution of a global collective action problem cannot be expanded endlessly. It is therefore unfortunate that this imbalance does not quite benefit the legitimacy of the EU minimum tax directive that was indeed—after some bargaining—adopted on the basis of unanimity.

It would be incorrect though to regard this criticism as a legitimate reason to put the corks of sovereignty and unanimity back in the bottle. We cannot close our eyes and pretend that there is no "post-national constellation"[61] of states and that therefore

57. Compare Maduro, *supra* n. 41, pp. 91-92.
58. European Commission, *supra* n. 4, pp. 6-7.
59. *See* §3.1.
60. *See* Cees Peters, *The Legitimacy of the OECD's Work on Pillar Two: An Analysis of the Overconfidence in a "Devilish Logic"* volume 51, issue 8&9, pp. 554-571 (Intertax 2023) DOI: 10.54648/taxi2023057.
61. This is a terminology used by Jürgen Habermas.

it is not necessary to arrive at a "deep, effective reorganization of the relationship between existing national and global institutions."[62] Consequently, it is not sufficient for the EU to focus its tax policy exclusively on the recapturing of "de facto sovereignty", as the OECD is currently doing. It is precisely the supranational framework of the EU that makes it possible to work *also* on the more ambitious goal of correcting national democratic failures instead.[63] The EU should therefore seriously go about the job of improving the legitimacy of European tax integration by strengthening the role of the European Parliament in this domain.[64]

It is therefore my view that the work of the EU in this context can and should be functioning better than the current fixation on unanimity is bringing us. As explained, it should indeed not simply be assumed that a future change to QMV in combination with a stronger role for the European Parliament is necessarily better than the current reliance on the unanimity rule. Nonetheless, it is my strong opinion that the time has really come to reshape this artefact of the EU institutional framework. A change to QMV with co-decision by the European Parliament will ensure more input legitimacy at the EU level. Such a direct involvement of the European citizens in the process of European tax integration is certainly more desirable than the traditional focus on output legitimacy of the described "exit mechanisms" and the CJEU's extensive interpretation of the legal instruments of negative integration in particular. Consequently, it is certainly desirable to establish a more equal relationship between the Council and the European Parliament. Moreover, such a change to QMV will also result in a better equilibrium between "the fear of the few and the fear of the many" within the Council itself. After all, it was exactly the introduction of the "double majority rule" and the rule on the blocking minority in the Lisbon Treaty that established a more balanced weighing of different interests in the Council. These reasons therefore definitely lead to the conclusion that the ordinary legislative procedure should be preferred over the special legislative procedure. That ordinary legislative procedure is certainly not perfect but no doubt better than the current exceptionalism for taxation.

§17.5 CONCLUSION

My final assessment at the end of this chapter is that there are no proper academic grounds to veto the plans of the European Commission to abolish the unanimity rule in EU taxation. The ongoing process of EU tax integration cannot do without better guarantees about the democratic legitimacy of the decisions taken at the EU level. As a matter of fact, the European institutional framework is actually very well equipped to achieve this result ever since November 1, 2014 when the new system of QMV laid

62. *See* Max Pensky, *Postnational.* In *The Cambridge Habermas Lexicon* 324 (Amy Allen & Eduardo Mendieta eds., Cambridge University Press 2019).
63. This is obviously the major distinction between the EU, on the one hand, and the OECD and the United Nations, on the other hand. It is outside the scope of this chapter to reflect on the question of how somewhat democratic forms of global tax governance can be realized in these two international organizations.
64. It is my assumption, following Jürgen Habermas, that there is an evolving transnational public sphere in the EU and that national citizens are also capable of being a European citizen.

down in the Treaty of Lisbon became effective. These new QMV rules in combination with the co-decision procedure with the European Parliament will therefore certainly promise progress. It is simply really about time now to move beyond the special position for decisions about taxation and to count on the "ordinary legislative procedure" instead. This "ordinary" procedure is clearly superior to the "special procedure" in terms of democratic legitimacy at the EU level and effectiveness.

It is, of course, another question whether our political leaders will follow this academic plea. One veto from a Member State is sufficient to make the proposal of the European Commission disappear in a drawer again. Nevertheless, it is my conviction that at some point not far from the present, things will start moving in the EU since the EU project is always making progress in times of crisis. Moreover, the power of ideas is eventually always stronger than the raw cynicism and pragmatism of the political process. That is also exactly how we should characterize Peter's attitude toward academic life. I am therefore convinced that there will be countless future Winter-course students who will continue to work on the joint responsibility of European tax integration. These students will all follow in Peter's footsteps.

CHAPTER 18

More EU Law and Less Prozac: Revisiting Pescatore's *The Law of Integration* in 2023

Ricardo García Antón

§18.1 INTRODUCTION

I met Peter during the ceremony of my EATLP award for my dissertation in Munich 2016, at the outset of my academic career. Later in 2018, when I started working at the Fiscal Institute Tilburg (FIT), I realized that he is more than a simple Co-Head of our Department. He represents the soul of the FIT, and thus an irreplaceable figure. In academic terms, I am very grateful to have written with my friend Cesar Martínez the Spanish Report for the EATLP book on 'History and Taxation' edited by him in 2022.[1] I will always remember his inspirational conversations on the future of the Union and the need for more democracy, human rights, and the rule of law in the EU. I really enjoy his extraordinary sense of humour, humbleness, and kindness. Peter is a truly academic mind far from *TikTok/Twitter* and academic noise. Peter's work in the Dutch Senate (*Eerste Kamer*) makes him strongly believe in the power of dialogue and democracy to shape tax policy.[2] Peter is '*een eerlijke man*', someone who cares about others, especially in difficult times like the pandemic showed.

1. Ricardo García & Cesar Martínez, *National Report – Spain*, in *History and Taxation: The Dialectical Relationship Between Taxation and the Political Balance of Power* 607-632 (Peter Essers ed., IBFD 2022).
2. Peter Essers, *International Tax Justice Between Machiavelli and Habermas*, 68 Bull. Intl. Taxn. 2 (2014), [Electronic Resource]; Peter Essers, *History and Future of EU Taxation according to Frans Vanistendael: Inspiration for a Constructive and Critical Dialogue*, 14 World Tax J. 3 (2022), [electronic resource].

Peter's well-known interest in history, and especially in the role of scholars in shaping tax law,[3] has inclined me to choose this topic for his *liber amicorum*. This chapter aims to revitalize the seminal work of Pierre Pescatore's *The Law of Integration*, on the integration process, currently under stress due to innumerable challenges (war in Ukraine, pandemic, rule of law backsliding).[4] The choice of this topic for the *liber amicorum* is multiple. First, both Peter and Pierre Pescatore worked in different capacities, and not only as academics. Their life experience contributed to frame their thinking. Second, both authors shared a strong support for the rule of law, as a key element of our democratic societies. Third, the bulk of Pescatore's analysis in *The Law of Integration* is still relevant today to solve EU crucial challenges.

In this short chapter, the research question can be formulated as follows: What can we learn from *The Law of Integration* today? *The Law of Integration* puts the focus on the EU integration process as a legal phenomenon. Section 18.2 revisits the legal implications derived from *The Law of Integration* in the current stage of the integration process, as well as connect them with Peter's work. Such exercise surprisingly reveals that Pescatore's worries, predictions, and concerns are still valid today. Section 18.3 briefly stresses the menaces to the Community legal order, as Pescatore conceived the European Communities. Finally, the epilogue makes a call for revitalizing the work of lawyers in EU studies.

§18.2 PIERRE PESCATORE AND *THE LAW OF INTEGRATION*

Pierre Pescatore was born in Luxembourg on 20 November 1919 and died on 2 February 2010 in Luxembourg.[5] After obtaining his Ph.D. in Law in 1946, he worked as a diplomat, law professor and judge at the Court of Justice of the European Communities (currently, Court of Justice of the European Union, 'CJEU'). The different capacities exercised throughout his life made him a prominent legal scholar and one of the founding fathers of EU legal studies. As a diplomatic at the Luxembourg Ministry of Foreign Affairs (1946-1952), he played a crucial role in the negotiations and signature of the Treaty of Rome (1957).[6] As a professor at the University of Luxembourg (1954-1960 and 1968-1982), and the University of Liege (1952-1982), he taught courses and lectured on introduction to law, community law, international law, and legal theory. As a judge at the CJEU (1967-1985), his contribution was crucial in seminal

3. Peter Essers, *Opkomst en Ondergang van Drie Eminente Duitse Fiscaliste nuit de Weimartijd'*, in *Taxes Crossing Borders (and Tax Professors too): Liber Amicorum Prof. Dr Rainer Prokisch*, (Jasper Korving, Narin Kerinc & Fernando Souza de Man, eds, Maastricht University Press, 2022).
4. Pierre Pescatore, *Le droit de l'intégration: emergence d'un phénomène nouveau dans les relations internationales selon l'expérience des Communautés Européennes* (Sijthoff, 1972).
5. The bibliographical data of Pierre Pescatore are obtained from Francesco Capotorti et al. (ed.), *Du droit international au droit de l'intégration: Liber Amicorum Pierre Pescatore* (Nomos *Verlagsgesellschaft*, 1987) and the website of the *Societé Française pour le droit international*. Available at https://www.sfdi.org/internationalistes/pescatore/#: ~ :text = Pierre%20Pescatore%20est%20 professeur%20de,droit%20international%20et%20relations%20internationales.
6. The Treaty of Rome signed on 25 March 1957 refers to the Treaty establishing the European Economic Community (EEC) and the Treaty establishing the European Atomic Energy Community (EAEC or Euratom).

cases wherein he was Reporting Judge (*Simmenthal*,[7] *AETR*,[8] Opinion 1/78[9]). Pescatore was the mind behind the creation of the preliminary reference procedure (ex-Article 177 Treaty CEE – current Article 267 TFEU), which is the basis of the judicial dialogue between national courts and the CJEU.[10]

In a nutshell, *The Law of Integration* presents the EU (former *European Communities*) as an autonomous legal order, independent from the legal systems of the Member States and from international law. In Chapter 2, Pescatore questioned the idea of 'indivisible sovereignty', which '*blinds men's minds to the phenomenon of integration*'.[11] Sovereignty must be refashioned and divided. As argued by Pescatore, supranationality thus recognizes: (i) common values; (ii) the creation of an effective power placed at the service of these values (i.e., take decisions that are binding for the states and the possibility of imposing sanctions against recalcitrant states) and (iii) the autonomy of this power (i.e., the power must be autonomous from the power of the participant states).[12]

Surprisingly, Pescatore's vision enshrined in *The Law of Integration* is still contemporary and his thought-provoking analysis helps us to understand the current challenges in the Union. In the next lines, shortly, this author addresses the relevant insights of the book that are still debated.

§18.2.1 A Union Based on Objectives

Pescatore noted that the Union has three objectives.[13] The immediate one is the custom union. The intermediate one is the economic union, and the distant one is the political union. The classification into objectives shows the journey to the unknown that the EU integration process means. In his book, Baquero recalls three anecdotes told by Pescatore during their conversations. The first anecdote, which is quite relevant to the discussion of a Union based on objectives, 'is a story about how the physical copy of the Treaty of Rome, which was to be signed on 25 March 1957 in a formal ceremony at the *Campidoglio*, was not ready because of a delay at the *Zecca dello Stato*, the Italian state printing works. What the representatives of the six Member States ended up signing was a stack of white pages, with the first printed pages on top. "*Vous voyez?*" Pescatore added. He didn't need to say more for me to understand that the story was a telling metaphor of the journey to an unknown (or not totally known) destination,

7. CJEU, Case C-243/78, *Simmenthal*, 5 March 1980.
8. CJEU, Case 22/70, *Commission of the European Communities v. Council of the European Communities. – European Agreement on Road Transport*, 31 March 1971.
9. CJEU, Opinion 1/78 of the Court of 4 October 1979 (International Agreement on Natural Rubber).
10. On Pescatore's contributions to the preliminary reference procedure, *see* Julio Baquero Cruz, *What's Left of the Law of Integration? Decay and Resistance in European Union Law* (Oxford University Press, 2018).
11. Pierre Pescatore, *supra* n. 4, pp. 30-31.
12. Pierre Pescatore, *supra* n. 4, pp. 50-51.
13. Pierre Pescatore, *supra* n. 4, pp. 19-22.

which those states (and their peoples) had decided to start for reasons they understood very well, and which many other states were to join later on'.[14]

The economic and political union are not yet completed. Despite having the euro as the currency of the European Union as of 1 January 2002 (Monetary Union), the economic policy remains largely in the Member States. The EU constitutional architecture of economic governance is still incomplete, and the Union lacks fiscal capacity (centralized budget funded by its own resources).[15] The euro-crisis (2009-2012) showed the inefficiencies of an asymmetric Economic and Monetary Union (EMU). While the economic policy is decentralized in the Member States, the Union could only impose fiscal rules upon the Member States within a 'surveillance model'.[16] Examples thereof are the Six Pack,[17] the Two Pack,[18] and the request to the Member States to submit their draft budget bills to the Commission for review.

One may think that the Union's reaction in relation to the Covid-19 pandemic, namely the Recovery Fund called 'Next Generation EU' (NGEU) and EU Own Resources Decision (ORD, Council Decision 2020/2053 of 14 December 2020 on the system of own resources of the European Union), paves the way towards a fiscal federalism model where the EU acquires autonomous taxing power, its own independent sphere of fiscal capacity, and thus its own fiscal tools for macroeconomic stabilization.[19] However, the initial optimism towards an EU autonomous fiscal

14. Julio Baquero Cruz, *supra* n. 10, p. 2.
15. *See* Federico Fabbrini, *EU Fiscal Capacity*, (Oxford University Press, 2022); Tomasz P. Wozniakowski, *Fiscal Unions: Economic Integration in Europe and the United States* (Oxford University Press, 2022).
16. Federico Fabbrini, *supra* n. 15, pp. 11 ss; Alicia Hinarejos, *Fiscal Federalism in the European Union*, 50 Common Market Law Review 6, 1621-1642 (2013); Miguel Poiares Maduro, *A New Governance for the European Union and the Euro: Democracy and Justice*, Report for the European Parliament published as a Robert Schuman Centre for Advanced Studies Policy Paper 2012/11 (Florence: European University Institute, 2012).
17. *See* Regulation (EU) No. 1173/2011 of the European Parliament and of the Council of 16 November 2011 on the effective enforcement of budgetary surveillance in the euro area [2011] OJ L306/1; Regulation (EU) No. 1174/2011 of the European Parliament and of the Council of 16 November 2011 on enforcement measures to correct excessive macroeconomic imbalances in the euro area [2011] OJ L306/8; Regulation (EU) No. 1175/2011 of the European Parliament and of the Council of 16 November 2011 amending Council Regulation (EC) No. 1466/97 on the strengthening of the surveillance of budgetary positions and the surveillance and coordination of economic policies [2011] OJ L306/12; Regulation (EU) No. 1176/2011 of the European Parliament and of the Council of 16 November 2011 on the prevention and correction of macroeconomic imbalances [2011] OJ L306/25; Council Regulation (EU) 1177/2011 of 8 November 2011 amending Regulation (EC) No. 1467/97 on speeding up and clarifying the implementation of the excessive deficit procedure [2011] OJ L306/33; Council Directive 2011/85/EU of 8 November 2011 on requirements for budgetary frameworks of the Member States [2011] OJ L306/41.
18. *See* Regulation (EU) No. 473/2013 of 21 May 2013 of the European Parliament and the Council on monitoring and assessing draft budgetary plans and ensuring the correction of excessive deficits in euro-area Member States [2013] OJ L140/11; Regulation (EU) No. 472/2013 of 21 May 2013 of the European Parliament and the Council on enhanced surveillance of euro-area Member States experiencing or threatened with serious difficulties with respect to their financial stability [2013] OJ L140/1.
19. Federico Fabbrini, *supra* n. 15; Bruno De Witte, *The European Union's COVID-19 Recovery Plan: The Legal Engineering of an Economic Policy Shift*, 58 Common Market Law Review 3, 635-682 (2021).

capacity, a sort of '*Hamiltonian Moment*' derived from NGEU, can be easily frustrated. First, the NGEU is a temporary exceptional budget to strengthen the Member States' budgets hit by the pandemic. It is not clear now whether in the long term, the Union would provide European public goods to European citizens that require new own resources to match the EU expenditure side. Second, the new EU own resources for the period 2021-2027 seem to be insufficient to pay back the massive resources borrowed from the financial markets, and some resources like the non-recycled plastic packaging waste are designed in the ORD as a Member State contribution rather than a proper autonomous tax levied at the Union level.[20]

In relation to the distant objective, the political union, Pescatore rightly observed: 'It must be admitted that, contrary to what has sometimes been hoped, economic integration has not always led us by a natural progression to political union.'[21] However, 'the building of Europe would lose its future prospects if it renounced in advance the possibilities of political unification [...] they [the Members States] must be questioned also about their intentions as regards the chances of an ultimate evolution towards political union'.[22] Indeed, in the author's view, this statement is true. The progression towards an economic union with an autonomous fiscal power would likely result in the major involvement of the EU Parliament ('no taxation without representation') and redistribution of resources (solidarity) but not automatically a unification process.[23] Peter is strongly convinced that EU taxes will create more EU solidarity and the achievement of a more democratic EU.[24]

§18.2.2 The Union Forms a Legal System

Pescatore's background as a lawyer pervades the book and justifies the strong belief in the rule of law to foster integration.[25] Accordingly, Chapter 3 is devoted to the institutional sketch of the Communities and the law decision-making (Council, European Parliament, Commission). Pescatore wisely conceptualizes the legislative process in the Communities as a phenomenon of osmosis and symbiosis between the Member

20. Adolfo Martín Jimenez, *The EU Own Resources and Budget after the Covid Pandemia: Still Far from a Closer European Union*, in *The Roadmap to an EU Budget* (Frans Vanistendael & Gianluigi Bizioli eds, EU Law Live Press, 2023); Claudio Sciancalepore, *The Reform of EU Own Resources under the Next Generation EU Program: A Suitable Moment for the Introduction of a European Tax?*, in *The Power to Tax in Europe* (Johan Lindholm & Anders Hultqvist eds, Hart, 2023).
21. Pierre Pescatore, *supra* n. 4, p. 23.
22. Pierre Pescatore, *supra* n. 4, p. 24.
23. Ricardo Garcia Antón, *Does the EU Have a Legitimate Power to Enact Direct Taxes?* in *The Power to Tax in Europe* (Johan Lindholm & Anders Hultqvist eds, Hart, 2023); Ricardo García Antón, *Building up the Revenue Side... But What Is a EU Tax?*, 11 Politics and Governance 4, 17-27, (2023)
24. *See* Peter Essers et al., *European Solidarity Requires EU Taxes* (2020) EU law live, Long read. 24 April 2020.
25. *See, for example,* Pierre Pescatore, *supra* n. 4, p. 2: 'I am a lawyer by training and temperament. This does not prevent me from acknowledging the debt of recognition which I owe to the economists and political scientists, a study of whom can broaden our legal perspectives considerably.'

States and European institutions (Commission, Council and European Parliament).[26] In doing so, Pescatore rejects the idea of the EU as a technocracy. The representatives of the Commission negotiate face to face with the members of the Council, as representatives of the governments, who bear responsibilities towards their national parliaments.

The dynamism of the Union and its law 'form a system, that is to say, a structured, organized and finalized whole'.[27] Pescatore's strong defence of a flawless legal system of sharing competence and powers together with the potential of law to lead the integration process is clearly influenced by the Kelsen's pure theory of law.[28] However, the reality presents more 'grey areas' and 'impurities', as Baquero pointed out. The EU legal system currently presents a complex interaction between the EU and national powers which triggers discrepancies between the formal allocation of power in the treaties and the actual legal practice.[29]

Pescatore pinpointed two main problems of the EU legislative decision-making. On the one hand, the unanimity rule introduces a veto power[30] and on the other hand, the limited role of the European Parliament in the EU legislative process.[31] The 'Empty Chair Crisis', which ended up with the 'Luxembourg compromise' on 29 January 1966 showed that the Member States do not easily agree to replace the unanimity rule for the majority decision-making. Throughout the successive reform of the treaties, the majority voting in the Council has been expanded. For example, Article 18 of the Single European Act amended Article 100 of the EEC Treaty to introduce qualified majority. The Treaty of Lisbon introduced the *pasarelle clause* (Article 48.7 TEU) to shift from unanimity to qualified majority. Unanimity is a hurdle to European integration and is used for the Member States to block initiatives and obtain compensations in exchange.[32] The initial veto of Hungary approval of the Pillar 2 Directive,[33] only lifted when financial aid was secured, is a perfect example of the perverse effects of the unanimity rule. To prevent the vetoes, some commentators have argued that qualified majority in Article 116 TFEU could be used as legal basis for tax harmonization.[34]

Regarding the involvement of the European Parliament on the EU decision-making, commentators stress that the role of the European Parliament is merely consultative.[35] The Council is still the essential EU decision-maker. The European Parliament does not have the legislative initiative, as, for example, the national

26. Pierre Pescatore, *supra* n. 4, p. 61.
27. Pierre Pescatore, *supra* n. 4, p. 41.
28. *See* this opinion in Julio Baquero Cruz, *supra* n. 14, p. 6.
29. In terms of competence, *see* Loic Azoulai, *Introduction*, in *The Question of Competence, in the EU* (Loic Azoulai ed., Oxford University Press, 2014).
30. Pierre Pescatore, *supra* n. 4, p. 12.
31. Pierre Pescatore, *supra* n. 4, p. 69.
32. Frans Vanistendael, *Unanimity in Taxation and Human Rights*, 103 Tax Notes International, 19 July 2021 (2021).
33. Council Directive (EU) 2022/2523 of 14 December 2022 on ensuring a global minimum level of taxation for multinational enterprise groups and large-scale domestic groups in the Union.
34. *See* Joachim Englisch, *Article 116 TFEU – The Nuclear Option for Qualified Majority Tax Harmonization*, 29 EC Tax Review 2 58-61 (2020) DOI: 10.54648/ecta2020007.
35. On the limited role of the European Parliament and EU democracy, *see* Dieter Grimm, *The Constitution of European Democracy* (Oxford University Press, 2017); Richard Corbett, *The*

parliaments traditionally do. Under the ordinary legal procedure (Article 294 TFEU), for example, the European Parliament cannot reject the Commission's proposal at the first reading, and only can make amendments. Such consultative role of the Parliament deepens the democratic deficit of the Union. Therein probably lies the strong disaffection of European citizens with the EU as reflected, for example, in Brexit and the rise of Eurosceptic parties.[36]

In his academic career, Peter has also insisted on the democratic deficit in the EU, which undermines the principle 'No taxation without representation'.[37] Together with other scholars like Professor Vanistendael,[38] Peter has criticized the limited role of the European Parliament and the unanimity rule. Using his sharp sense of humour, Peter affirmed the EU decision-making 'has nothing to do with democratic decision-making, it seems rather a sort of horse-trading with the protection of the rule of law as bet'.[39]

§18.2.3 A Community of Rights Preserved by the Court

In *Van Gend en Loos*,[40] the CJEU confirmed that the Union constitutes a new legal order, wherein the Member States have given up their sovereign rights. Since the Preamble of the treaty refers to people and not only to governments, the preliminary reference procedure (Article 267 TFEU, ex Article 177) becomes the suitable mechanism to ensure the protection of the fundamental rights/EU freedoms of EU individuals.[41] Commenting *Van Gend en Loos*, Pescatore remarked: 'There has rarely been a legal argumentation as well developed as this one, and presented to individuals and their judges with such elegance and persuasive power.'[42]

The extraordinary role attributed to the European Judicial Power to ensure the fundamental rights of the EU citizens is the core message in Chapter IV of *The Law of Integration*. Such defence of fundamental rights/EU freedoms of circulation is anchored in judicial dialogue. Pescatore insisted that the real innovation of the treaties was to build up a relationship based on jurisdiction and powers between the CJEU and

---

Evolving Roles of the European Parliament and of National Parliaments, in *EU Law after Lisbon*, 249-261 (Andrea Biondi, Piet Eeckhout & Stefanie Ripley eds, Oxford University Press 2012).

36. Amitai Etzioni, *Closing the Community Deficit in the EU* (9 September 2008) CEPS Policy Brief No 169, available at: ssrn.com/abstract = 1333531 or dx.doi.org/10.2139/ssrn.1333531; Enrique Hernandez and Hanspeter Kriesi, *Turning Your Back on the EU: The Role of Eurosceptic Parties in the 2014 European Parliament Elections*, 44 Electoral Studies 515 (2016) DOI: 10.1016/j.electstud.2016.04.013.
37. Peter Essers, *Tax Justice and European Tax Law, Steuer und Wirtschaft*, num. 4, pp. 325-328 (2022); Peter Essers (2022), *supra* n. 2.
38. Frans Vanistendael, *No European Taxation without European Representation*, 9(3) EC Tax Review 142-143 (2000) DOI: 10.54648/276470.
39. Peter Essers, *supra* n. 37, p. 326.
40. CJEU, Case 26/62, *Van Gen den Loos*, 5 February 1963.
41. This idea is developed in depth in Ricardo Garcia Antón, *La Cuestión Prejudicial y La fiscalidad Directa* (European University Institute, 2015).
42. Pierre Pescatore, *Van Gend en Loos, 3 February 1963 – A View from Within*, in *The Past and Future of EU Law: The Classics of EU Law Revisited on the 50th Anniversary of the Rome Treaty* 3-8 (Loic Azoulai & Miguel Poiares Maduro eds, Hart, 2010).

the national judicial bodies that goes beyond a mere consultation procedure.[43] As stated earlier, Pescatore was one of the minds behind the preliminary reference procedure (Article 177 TFEU). In Peter's work, we can appraise the extraordinary role attributed to the CJEU in the progress of steering tax integration.[44]

An important reform of the preliminary reference procedure is currently under discussion. The request to transfer to the General Court jurisdiction to hear and adjudicate questions for preliminary rulings in specific areas under Article 267 TFEU (Value Added Tax – 'VAT', excises and Customs, compensation and assistance to passengers, and the scheme for greenhouse gas emission allowance trading) leads the path towards an EU-decentralized judicial power.[45] If the reform is eventually approved, the CJEU ensures its position as a court to develop EU principles and national courts to apply the principles to solve the case at stake. If Pescatore were alive, he would likely have supported the reform since it deepens dialogue in the EU judicial power.

§18.3 THE MENACES FOR A 'COMMUNITY LEGAL ORDER'

As stated earlier, *The Law of Integration* exudes a strong faith in the role of EU law: 'It is that we are working here within the framework of a coherent system, and this system in itself involves resources highly superior to those normally inherent in an isolated international act. On this point, lawyers might usefully draw upon the teaching of political science.'[46] The EU legal system is referred by Pescatore as the 'Community System' or the 'Community Legal Order'. Reading *The Law of Integration*, one has the impression that without the law, the EU would not exist. Recently, some commentators pointed out in the same direction. As Marzal puts it, law not only is the substance for Europe's emerging community but also provides the impetus for a gradual realization of the Political Union, the third distant objective stressed by Pescatore.[47] In this brief chapter, I would like to sketch recent menaces for the 'Community Legal Order'.

§18.3.1 The Threats to the Rule of Law

The 'Community Legal Order' has a specific constitutional recognition in Article 2 TUE, which states that the Union is founded on the rule of law. Member States must comply

43. Pierre Pescatore, *supra* n. 4, p. 91.
44. Peter Essers (2022), *supra* n. 2, section 4.3.2.
45. *See* Draft Amendment to Protocol No. 3 on the Statute of the Court of Justice of the European Union, presented by the Court of Justice on 30 November 2022. Further comments on the reform of the preliminary reference procedure, *see* Ricardo Garcia Antón, *Op-Ed: Reframing the Reform to Transfer Preliminary Rulings to the General Court with the Meaning of Judicial Cooperation: a Look into Recent VAT Preliminary Rulings*, EU law live, 12 May 2023; Chiara Amalfitano, *The Future of Preliminary Rulings in the EU Judicial System* (2023) EU law Live, Weekend Edition, 4 March 2023; Sara Iglesias, *Preliminary Rulings Before the General Court* (2023) EU law Live, Weekend Edition 17 December 2002.
46. Pierre Pescatore, *supra* n. 4, p. 107.
47. Toni Marzal, *Between Integration and the Rule of Law: EU Law's Culture of Lawful Messianism*, 24(4) German Law Journal 718-734 (2023) DOI: 10.1017/glj.2023.43.

with the rule of law in their legal systems. The rule of law backsliding in several countries of the EU (Poland or Hungary) has posed serious challenges. Both countries have been enacting legislation that jeopardizes the principle of separation of powers, the independence of the judiciary, and media pluralism.[48] The threats can also be found in decisions of constitutional courts that questioned the groundings of the EU legal order and especially the supremacy of EU law. The Polish Constitutional Court's Decision (Case K3/21) set aside EU Primary law because it violated the national constitution.[49] Fortunately, EU law is reacting positively against such menaces. Not only does the CJEU verify the independence and impartiality of the national judiciary[50] but also the Rule of Law Conditionality Regulation constitutes a powerful legal framework to suspend payments to Member States if breaches of the rule of law are detected.[51]

In the field of taxation, namely in state aid, there have been important controversies related to the rule of law. In the famous cases solved by the General Court (*Amazon,*[52] *Apple,*[53] *Starbucks,*[54] *FIAT*[55]), the core question was to decide whether the Commission could consider some Advance Pricing Agreements granted by the Member States as selective advantages within the meaning of illegal state aid in Article 107 TFEU. In these transfer pricing cases, the Commission handled the so-called EU arm's length derived from Article 107 TFEU, which basically required the Member States to treat equally standalone companies and group companies. Such EU arm's length under Article 107 TFEU was autonomous from the OECD framework and regardless of the national implementation of the arm's length (i.e., Ireland did not incorporate the arm's length into domestic legislation).[56] Although the General Court initially endorsed the Commission's approach, the CJEU in the *FIAT* case rejected the sui generis EU arm's

48. *See for example* in relation to Hungary, the Commission Staff Working Document SWD (2023) 817, 2023 Rule of Law Report, available at https://commission.europa.eu/system/files/2023-07/40_1_52623_coun_chap_hungary_en.pdf.
49. For further analysis of the Polish Constitutional judgement, *see* EU Law Live Symposium on the primacy of EU law and the implications of the Polish Constitutional Court's Decision in case K 3/21. Available at https://eulawlive.com/op-ed-the-rule-of-law-breach-and-consequence-by-paul-craig/.
50. CJEU, C-204/21, *Commission v. Poland,* 5 June 2023.
51. Regulation (EU, Euratom) 2020/2092 of the European Parliament and of the Council of 16 December 2020 on a general regime of conditionality for the protection of the Union budget. https://eur-lex.europa.eu/legal-content/EN/TXT/?uri = uriserv:OJ.LI.2020.433.01.0001.01.EN G&toc = OJ:L:2020:433I:TOC.
52. General Court, Case T-816/17 and T-318/18, *Grand Duchy of Luxembourg and Amazon v. European Commission,* 12 May 2021.
53. General Court, Joined Cases T-778/16 and T-892/16, *Ireland and Apple v. European Commission,* 15 July 2020.
54. General Court, Joined Cases T-760/15 and T-636/16, *Kingdom of the Netherlands and Starbucks v. European Commission,* 24 September 2019.
55. General Court, Joined cases T-755/15 and T-759/15, *Grand Duchy of Luxembourg and Fiat v. European Commission,* 24 September 2019.
56. On the autonomy of the EU arm's length, *see, for example,* Fausta Todhe, *The Rise of an Autonomous Arm's Length Principle in EU State Aid Rules?,* 18(3) European State Aid Law Quarterly 249-263 (2019) DOI: 10.21552/estal/2019/3/5; Cees Peters, *Critical Analysis of the General Court's 'EU Arm's Length Tool': Beware of the Reflexivity of Transfer Pricing Law,* 31 EC Tax Review 1 30-49 (2022) DOI: 10.54648/ecta2022004.

length under 107 TFEU.[57] The CJEU ruled that the identification of the reference framework in state aid should be based on the analysis of national law. Otherwise, the Commission would encroach upon Member State's autonomy in tax matters, which has not yet been harmonized.[58] Some commentators have labelled *FIAT* as a clear victory of the rule of law and the Member States' sovereignty in tax matters.[59] The previous discussion on the state aid saga shows the importance of preserving the equilibrium between the Member States and the EU 'Community Legal Order'.

§18.3.2 Bad Legislative Inflation

One of the most recent threats to the 'Community Legal Order' derives from the so-called bad legislative inflation by Kuzniacki.[60] An example thereof is the field of tax abuse. Bad Legislative inflation in tax abuse means the proliferation and overlapping of EU legislative initiatives which are: (i) not well coordinated among them; (ii) drafted using a poor legal technique; (iii) disproportionate in balancing the interest of the taxpayer versus the tax administration.[61] As Kuzniacki put it, the increase in the amount of law is translated into a decrease in the quality of legal norms.[62]

In recent years, the Union has extensively harmonized anti-abuse legislation through the Anti-Avoidance Directives ('ATAD 1 and ATAD 2').[63] One may wonder whether the Union is competent to harmonize such an area. Such harmonization on the legal basis of Article 115 TFEU has been subject to criticism in the literature.[64] In the Preamble of the latter directives, the Commission made vague references to the need to

57. CJEU, Joined Cases C-885/19 P and C-898/19 P, *Fiat Chrysler Finance Europe v. Commission*, 8 November 2022.
58. On the rule of law implications of the FIAT judgment, *see* Nieves Bayon & Ricardo Garcia, *Op-Ed Final Judgment in Fiat: The Answers (Not) Provided by the Court of Justice in Its Second Chapter of the Tax Rulings Saga*, EU law live, 2 December 2022.
59. *See, for example*, Ruth Mason, *Ding-Dong! The EU Arm's-Length Standard Is Dead*, Virginia Law School, Public Law and Legal Theory Research Paper Series 2022-79 (2022), available at: http://www.ssrn.com/link/U-Virginia-LEC.html.
60. Blazej Kuzniacki, *Aggressive Tax Planning in Light of the Securing the Activity Framework of Enablers Initiative: A Path to Inflation of Anti-Tax Avoidance Rules in the EU Law* (IBFD International Tax Studies, 2023).
61. *See* Kuzniacki, *supra* n. 60, p. 3; the references to the proliferation, overlapping, and poor quality of EU anti-avoidance legislation were also made in the Seminar 'Countering tax avoidance in the European Union and beyond' chaired by Prof. Martín Jimenez in the IFA Regional Meeting, 5-7 July 2023, Amsterdam (for a summary of the main findings of the panel, see www.ifa.nl).
62. *See* Kuzniacki, *supra* n. 60, p. 3.
63. Council Directive (EU) 2016/1164 of 12 July 2016 laying down rules against tax avoidance practices that directly affect the functioning of the internal market ('ATAD 1') (2016). Official Journal of the European Union, L 193. https://eur-lex.europa.eu/legal-content/EN/TXT/?uri=celex%3A32016L1164; Council Directive (EU) 2017/952 of 29 May 2017 amending Directive (EU) 2016/1164 as regards hybrid mismatches with third countries ('ATAD 2'). (2017). Official Journal of the European Union, L 144.
64. Rita Szudoczky, *The Sources of EU Law and Their Relationships: Lessons for the Field of Taxation* (IBFD, 2014), p. 361; Werner Haslehner, 'Anti-Hybrid Measures in the Parent Subsidiary Directive and the EU's Competence to Harmonise' (Kluwer International Tax Blog, 31 August 2015), available at: kluwertaxblog.com/2015/08/31/anti-hybrid-measures-in-the-parent-subsidiary-directive-and-the-eus-competence-to-harmonise/; and Werner Haslehner, 'The Commission Proposal for an Anti-BEPS Directive: Some Preliminary Comments' (Kluwer International

strengthen the average level of protection against aggressive tax planning and achieve resilience in the internal market. Yet, as commentators argue, anti-avoidance legislation protects the domestic tax bases of the Member States against abusive tax practices.[65] Under Article 115 TFEU, it seems that there are no limits to the power of the Union to legislate in direct taxation. The principles of subsidiarity and proportionality (Article 5 TFEU and EU Protocol No 2 on the application of the principles of subsidiarity and proportionality to the TFEU), which should constrain the legislation action of the Union, play an insignificant role in the EU legislative process.[66]

Despite the reasonable doubts on the legal basis selected to harmonize anti-avoidance legislation, the Union has continued to launch initiatives in this area: (1) the Commission's draft directive to prevent misuse of shell entities (ATAD 3 Proposal);[67] (2) Securing the Activity Framework of Enablers (SAFE), which aims to prohibit enablers who design, market and/or assist in the creation of tax arrangements or schemes in non-EU countries that lead to tax evasion or aggressive tax planning for the EU Member State.[68]

This chapter solely focuses on ATAD 3 to demonstrate that is a good example of this phenomenon of bad legislative inflation. The ATAD 3 Proposal sets up a series of indicators ('gateways') to deem a company as a shell. If so, the company will be first subject to stringent annual reporting obligation of 'minimum substance indicators' to the tax authorities (premises of the company, bank accounts, tax residency of the directors, etc.)[69] and second, it will not be able to access tax reliefs, tax benefits of the treaty network of its Member States, and tax benefits in the Parent-Subsidiary Directive and Interest Royalty Directive (Article 11 of the Directive Proposal).

Article 6 of the ATAD 3 Proposal enumerated the three gateways that a company must meet to be deemed as a shell. The first gateway is met if more than 75% of an entity's overall revenue in the previous two tax years consists of income such as interest from financial assets, royalties from IP and dividends, and income from disposal of shares or if more than 75% of its assets are real estate property or other private property of particularly high value. The second gateway requires a cross-border element (i.e., at least 60% of the undertaking's relevant income is earned or paid out

---

Tax Blog, 5 February 2016), available at: kluwertaxblog.com/2016/02/05/the-commission-proposal-for-an-anti-beps-directive-some-preliminary-comments/.

65. *See* further development of this argument in my contribution, Ricardo Garcia Antón, *Does the EU Have a Legitimate Power to Enact Direct Taxes*, in *The Power to Tax in Europe* 19-36 (Johan Lindholm & Anders Hultqvist eds, Hart, 2023).
66. The Commission is granted with a broad discretion to legislate. The CJEU has also endorsed the broad discretion of the Commission under the subsidiarity and proportionality analysis (*Czech Republic v. European Parliament and Council of the European Union*, 2019; Vodafone and Others, 2010, paras 52 and 77).
67. Proposal for a Council Directive laying down rules to prevent the misuse of shell entities for tax purposes and amending Directive 2011/16/EU. Available at https://taxation-customs.ec.europa.eu/system/files/2021-12/COM_2021_565_1_EN_ACT_part1_v7.pdf.
68. Proposal for a Council Directive to tackle the role of enablers that facilitate tax evasion and aggressive tax planning in the European Union (Securing the Activity Framework of Enablers - SAFE) (6 July 2022).
69. *See* Art. 7 of ATAD 3 Proposal.

via cross-border transactions). The third gateway focuses on whether corporate management and administration services are performed either in-house or outsourced. Article 9 of the ATAD 3 Proposal compels the Member States to allow undertakings to rebut the presumption of being a shell. Article 11 of the ATAD 3 requires the Member States to impose penalties for not reporting or making false declarations.

The reasons why ATAD 3 Proposal falls within the label of bad legislative inflation are numerous. First, there is no reflection on the overlapping of ATAD 3 Proposal with previous anti-abuse devices, such as the EU GAAR in Article 6 ATAD 1. If a taxpayer meets the hallmarks, this does not prevent tax authorities from applying other anti-abuse devices like SAARs and GAARs.[70] Second, the drafting of the ATAD 3 Proposal uses a poor legislative technique. For example, there is no definition of a shell in the ATAD 3 Proposal.[71] Third, ATAD 3 Proposal reversed the burden of proof in terms of abuse, which is clearly disproportionate.

Prof. Martín Jimenez observed the ATAD 3 Proposal presumes that all shell companies are used for tax evasion and avoidance purposes and thus requires the taxpayer to prove they are not, with a considerable burden of proof and potential penalties.[72] Such reverse burden of proof contradicts the allocation of the burden of proof within the Principal Purpose Test (PPT) in Article 29 (9) of the OECD Model Convention (2017). Interpreting the burden of proof in the PPT, many commentators have stressed that while tax authorities must provide evidence of the abuse (*'one of the principal purposes'*), the taxpayer must demonstrate that granting a benefit was in accordance with the object and purpose of the Convention.[73] Shifting the burden of proof in tax abuse may also contradict the case law of the CJEU in relation to the general principle of abuse of EU law (*SGI, Deister, Eqiom*).[74] As Nogueira stated: 'In applying the EU general principle, Member States have no such margin of appreciation. The CJEU has a more stringent approach by (i) considering the fight against abuse as an obligation of Member States and, (ii) placing the \burden of the proof of abuse on the side of tax authorities. Accordingly, any domestic provision or administrative regulation aimed at shifting the burden back to the taxpayer in this realm appears to be inadmissible.'[75]

70. Adolfo Martín Jiménez, *Is There an International Minimum Standard on Tax Treaty Shopping after BEPS Action 6? Some Recent Divergent Trends*, 14 World Tax J. 3 (2022) [electronic resource].
71. On further analysis of the critical issues regarding the drafting of the ATAD 3 Proposal, *see* P. Pistone et al., Abuse, *Shell Entities and Right of Establishment: A Plea for Refocusing Current Proposals and Achieving Deeper Coordination Within the Internal Market*, 14 World Tax J. 2 (2022) [electronic resource].
72. *See* Adolfo Martín Jiménez, *supra* n. 70.
73. See Stef van Weeghel, *A Deconstruction of the Principal Purposes Test*, 11 World Tax J. 1 (2019), [electronic resource]; Luc De Broe & Joris Luts, *BEPS Action 6: Tax Treaty Abuse*, 43 Intertax 2, p. 132 (2015) DOI: 10.54648/taxi2015011.
74. CJEU, C-311/08, *SGI*, 21 January 2010, para. 73; CJEU, Joined cases C-504/16 and C-613/16, *Deister Holding*, para. 62; CJEU, C-6/16, *Eqiom*, 7 September 2017, para. 32.
75. Joao Nogueira, *Abuse, Proportionality and the Burden of Proof in CJEU's Case Law on Direct Taxation, Taxes Crossing Borders (and Tax Professors Too): Liber Amicorum Prof. Dr R.G. (Rainer) Prokisch.* (Jasper Korving, Narin Kerinc & Fernando Souza de Man eds, Maastricht University Press, 2022).

The distribution of the burden of proof under the general principle of abuse of EU law has also pervaded domestic law. In a hallmark judgment (*Global Noray*),[76] the Spanish Supreme Court overturned its previous case law to fully endorse the allocation of the burden of proof requested under the general principle of abuse of EU law. In previous case law before *Global Noray*, the Supreme Court demanded the taxpayer to give precise evidence of the economic rationale of the arrangements to avoid the scheme being qualified as abusive.[77] Yet, in *Global Noray*, the Supreme Court applied the *Danish cases*,[78] particularly the well-known abuse indicia in paragraphs 100-106 of *T Denmark*, to clearly require the tax administration to prove the existence of tax abuse.

In *Global Noray*, the Supreme Court dealt with a classical 'Directive-shopping' case. The arrangement consisted of a payment of dividends from a Spanish company to an intermediate holding company located in Luxembourg owned by a Canadian Investment Pension. The main legal framework at stake was the exemption for the distribution of dividends laid down in the Parent-Subsidiary Directive (P-S)[79] and implemented in Article 14.1.h) of the Spanish Non-resident Income Tax law.

Global Noray is thus a landmark decision that interprets EU law correctly and allocates the burden of proof of abuse exclusively in the hands of the tax administration. The shift in the Supreme Court's jurisprudence tallies with the allocation of the burden of proof in abuse within civil law. In Spanish Private law, Article 7 of the Spanish Civil Law prescribes that rights must be exercised in accordance with the good faith standard; thereby, the law does not support abuse of rights which exceeds the normal limits to exercise a right with damage to a third party. In horizontal relations between private parties, the Spanish Supreme Court has constantly ruled that the party that alleges the existence of abuse in a transaction must bear the burden of proof and demonstrate that the conduct of the counterparty was in breach of good faith.[80]

ATAD 3 Proposal is a good example of bad legislative inflation in anti-abuse legislation. Despite reasonable doubts raised about the competence of the Union to harmonize anti-abuse legislation, the Union has continued to launch initiatives in this field (ATAD 3 and SAFE). Turning to ATAD 3, there is a lack of reflection on how it interacts with previous GAARs and SAARs, a poor legislative technique, and it is disproportionate since it dramatically reversed the burden of proof.

76. ES: *Global Norey*, num 771/2023, 8 June 2023.
77. *Global Noray* explicitly overturned the previous case law: case ES: Supreme Court, num. 3312/2008, 4 April 2012; ES: Supreme Court, num. 5448/2018, 3 March 2020.
78. CJEU, Joined C-116/16 and C-117/16, *T-Danmark*, 26 February 2019; CJEU, Joined cases C-115/16, C-118/16, C-119/16 y C-299/16, *N Luxembourg 1*, 26 February 2019.
79. Council Directive 90/435/CEE 23 July 1990 and amended by Council Directive 2015/121/EU).
80. *See, for example*, Spain: Spanish Supreme Court, num. 1992/3281, 17 March 1992; Spanish Supreme Court, num. 1996/2231, 21 March 1996; further comments of the burden of proof in, *see* A. Carrasco Perera, *Tratado del Abuso de Derecho y del Fraude de Ley* 119 and ss (Thompson, 2016).

§18.4 EPILOGUE: THE NEED FOR EU LAW IN THE EU INTEGRATION JOURNEY

The Law of Integration is a seminal work to discover the powerful role of law in the integration process. Pescatore visualized the integration process as a phenomenon of osmosis and symbiosis between the EU institutions and the Member States channelled by EU law.[81] This brief contribution has sketched several threats to the EU legal system. On the one hand, the rule of law problems (backsliding problems in Hungary and Poland and the State Aid saga), and, on the other hand, bad legislation inflation in tax avoidance. Although the EU legal system is reacting positively to rule of law backsliding problems, there is still much to do to face the problems associated with bad legislative inflation. The Union is currently facing many political challenges: enlargement of the Union, construction of an EU autonomous power to tax and the progression towards a more democratic Union under 'No Taxation without Representation', etc. In the journey to a Political Union, as described by Pescatore, we cannot neglect the role of EU law in shaping the process. I am completely sure that Peter would be happy to be engaged in these exciting times for European integration.

81. Pierre Pescatore, *supra* n. 4, p. 61.

CHAPTER 19

A Wishful Thinking Towards a European Tax Agency

Giuseppe Marino

§19.1 INTRODUCTION

During the preparation of my General Report *New Exchange of Information Versus Tax Solutions of Equivalent Effect* for the EATLP Istanbul Congress in 2014, I discussed several times with Peter Essers this topic as a dream, and it is, thanks to his thoughts, towards I am grateful, that became a vision, hopefully happy ending in reality.[1]

On the official website of the European Union,[2] there is a list of over thirty agencies that cover various areas, from education and culture (EACEA) to fisheries control (EFCA), and from chemicals (ECHA) to railways (ERA). On the other hand, there are entities being explicitly defined as 'authorities' or being endowed with full independence.

The European phenomenon of 'agencification' emerged in the 1970s to address the deficiency of the Community legal system in the executive-administrative field. Agencies serve as an institutional mechanism to achieve the goal of common administrative action without altering the balance of powers between the European Union and its Member States. Moreover, they provide a way to create networks of national and supranational entities in sectors where the aim is generally to strengthen the degree of harmonization of certain services. This is achieved not so much through regulation (a power most agencies lack) but through studies and measures aimed at increasing the qualitative level of performance. This solution represents a kind of

1. I started to research on the topic through various essays, the last of which was for the *Accademia dei Lincei* with the title: Autori Vari, *Verso un'Agenzia delle entrate europea?* in *Una nuova politica economica e tributaria per l'Unione Europea*, pp. 203 et seq. (Bardi edizioni, Roma 2022).
2. *See* https://european-union.europa.eu/institutions-law-budget/institutions-and-bodies/search-all-eu-institutions-and-bodies_en.

compromise between the European Commission and national authorities, within a perfect game of political-institutional equilibrium. The agencies are European entities, but they lack binding powers and a position of superiority over national entities. They trigger a series of operational relationships that allow for the development of a genuine practice of interdependence and functional complementarity. The agencies primarily perform functions related to information gathering, mainly at the request of the Commission or other European institutions. This activity is of an instructive nature and never translates into the exercise of administrative discretion or, more generally, into regulatory power. This profile adheres to the so-called Meroni principle, which states that bodies not provided for in the treaties cannot be assigned tasks that involve the exercise of discretionary powers.

The guarantee of independence represents the main dividing line between the agency model and the model of authorities. In certain sectors characterized by the protection of fundamental interests or strong economic relevance and interdependence, the main objective is precisely to achieve this through bodies endowed with high discretionary and impartial powers, with respect to not only governments but also parliaments. As purely illustrative examples, mention can be made of the European Banking Authority (EBA) and the European Securities and Markets Authority (ESMA), which are governed by Article 298(1) of the Treaty on the Functioning of the European Union. This article states that 'in carrying out their missions, the institutions, bodies, offices and agencies of the Union shall have the support of an open, efficient and independent European administration'.[3]

§19.1.1 The Lack of a European Tax Governance

However, it is strikingly evident on the aforementioned website of the European Union that there is no European Tax Agency, let alone a European Tax Authority. This absence is well known and has been debated for quite some time. Taxation is a politically sensitive and unpredictably media-driven matter despite being instrumental in achieving the objectives that the European Union aims to accomplish. For better or worse, taxation has always influenced human history, and Member States are reluctant to abandon the decision-making process that exclusively relies on the unanimity of the special legislative procedure outlined in Articles 113 and 115 of the Treaty on the Functioning of the European Union. Not even the plea of Jean-Claude Juncker, President of the European Commission, who, in his '*State of the Union 2017, Catching the Wind in our Sails*' (EU Speech/17/3165), proposed a move towards qualified majority voting on certain tax matters (or the recent Communication from the European Commission by President Ursula von der Leyen on 15 January 2019 (COM(2019) 8 final) titled *Towards a More Efficient and Democratic Decision-Making*

3. *See* on the matter Edoardo Chiti, *Le trasformazioni delle Agenzie europee*, in *Rivista trimestrale diritto pubblico*, pp. 57 et seq. (1/2020); Edoardo Chiti, *European Agencies' Rulemaking: Powers, Procedures and Assessment*, in *European Law Journal*, pp. 93 et seq., (1/2013); Edoardo Chiti, *An Important Part of the EU's Institutional Machinery: Features, Problems and Perspectives of European Agencies*, in *Common Market Law Review*, pp. 1395 et seq. (5/2009).

Process in the EU Tax Policy), has been able to undermine the political resilience of Member States. Meanwhile, the pandemic before, and the Russo-Ukrainian war now, should hopefully contribute to consolidating the European values identity, even from a financial perspective.

Despite these premises, it must be acknowledged that European taxation, as well as the legal framework of international taxation with which it is closely linked, has evolved since 1997. It has transitioned from a period of excessive and unregulated tax competition to a period of administrative cooperation aimed at fighting tax fraud, evasion, and avoidance, which is unprecedented in the history of the discipline. This period was initiated with a package of measures (including a Code of Conduct) proposed by the European Commission under President Prodi, at the initiative of Commissioner Monti, and approved by the European Council on 1 December 1997.[4] A few months later, in March 1998, the international community, driven by the United States, also adapted to this change with the publication of the recommendation *'Harmful Tax Competition: An Emerging Global Issue'* by the OECD.

§19.1.2 International Tax Governance in Doctrine

In this particular context, it is necessary to recall some reflections that now sound like precursors to the topic under discussion. In 1999, Professor Vito Tanzi, Director of the Fiscal Affairs Department at the International Monetary Fund, advocated for the establishment of a World Tax Organization to complement other international institutions (such as the IMF, OECD, WTO and WB) in the governance of globalization. This organization would have been responsible for monitoring the evolution of tax systems in its Member States, including through statistical analysis, providing technical assistance in determining their tax policies, and serving as a competent arbitration forum for resolving disputes that bilateral treaties to eliminate double taxation (and, today, double non-taxation) could not resolve.[5]

In a perspective broader than tax law, in 2006, Italian Professor Sabino Cassese, former Judge at the Italian Constitutional Court, highlighted that economic globalization does not correspond to legal globalization but rather to an increasing global legal order composed of approximately two thousand international organizations, also referred to as the global legal space.[6] This global legal order does not have a higher authority or a vertical hierarchy that characterizes national public powers. However, this order exists and operates horizontally between national authorities and global agencies, as well as among global agencies. In other words, Cassese observes the growth of a legal system largely based on cooperation, both at the interstate level and in a narrow global sense, which, within the supranational sphere closest to us, has led to the establishment of a European administrative space.

4. *See* 'The Conclusions of the Ecofin Council Meeting on 1 December 1997, concerning taxation policy', published in the Official Journal on 6 January 1998.
5. *See* Vito Tanzi, *Is There a Need for a World Tax Organization?* in Assaf Razin & Efraim Sadka (eds), *The Economics of Globalization*, pp. 173 et seq. (Cambridge University Press 1999).
6. *See* Sabino Cassese, *Oltre lo Stato*, pp. 3 et seq. (Laterza, Bari 2006).

The proactive synchrony between the EU and the OECD, albeit with different legal instruments, has been destined to mark the evolution of tax cooperation up to the present day, with significant accelerations on occasions of events that exert strong public pressure, such as the fall of the Twin Towers on 11 September 2001, the global financial crisis triggered by the collapse of American subprime mortgages in 2008, and some highly publicized tax scandals (e.g., UBS, HSBC, LuxLeaks, Panama Papers). At a historical moment when the US Congress approved the Foreign Account Tax Compliance Act (FATCA) in 2010, proposed by the Obama Administration as a model for the automatic exchange of financial information (AEOI) in response to the urgent need to rebuild the US public finance post-crisis, the European Council approved Directive 2011/16/EU on administrative cooperation in the field of taxation (DAC) on 15 February 2011, which repealed the previous Directive of 19 September 1977, limited to mutual assistance between the competent authorities of the Member States in the field of direct taxes. The directive came into force on 11 March 2011, the date of its publication in the Official Journal, but became binding on the Member States on 1 January 2013 (with the exception of provisions on the automatic exchange of tax information, which became binding on 1 January 2015). Following suit, in 2014, the OECD recommended that all signatory States of the Multilateral Convention on Mutual Administrative Assistance in Tax Matters adopt the Common Reporting Standard (CRS), an information standard that has now become customary for the automatic exchange of information on financial accounts to combat international tax fraud, evasion, and avoidance.[7]

§19.1.3 Final Remarks

In conclusion, focusing solely on the European Union, there is an apparent contradiction between the lack of political sensitivity towards tax harmonization and the extensive administrative cooperation in tax matters that has filled the void. For the Member States, the political awareness of fighting fraud, evasion, and excessive tax competition has prevailed over reluctance to work together towards a true European tax system. To put it cynically, the embarrassment of losing portions of national revenue before the eyes of public opinion has compelled Member States to overcome the discomfort of potentially losing long-term political manoeuvrability over their respective tax systems, even though EU tax policy should not depend on public protests in order to effectively address shortcomings and progress towards common objectives.

7. *See* on the rise of AEOI, Giuseppe Marino, *International and European Measures for De-Offshoring: Global Ambitions and Local Hypocrisies*, in *Intertax*, pp. 527 et seq. DOI: 10.54648/taxi2017044 (8&9/2017).

§19.2 THE RISE OF ADMINISTRATIVE COOPERATION IN TAX MATTERS

Never before has there been such a rapid evolution in international and European tax law as the one that has affected administrative cooperation, prompting reflection within the European Union on the most appropriate response in terms of administrative and organizational tax law.

Directive No. 2011/16 has undergone six significant amendments in just a few years, namely:

(i) Directive of 9 December 2014, No. 2014/107 (DAC 2), which focuses on the integration of the EU system with the Common Reporting Standard developed by the OECD and extends the automatic exchange of information on financial accounts held by non-resident individuals, establishing a framework for such global exchange.[8]

(ii) Directive of 8 December 2015, No. 2015/2376 (DAC 3), which extends the automatic exchange of information to cross-border advance tax rulings (following the LuxLeaks scandal).[9]

(iii) Directive of 25 May 2016, No. 2016/881 (DAC 4), which extends the mandatory automatic exchange of information among the financial administrations of the Member States to the 'glocally' prepared reporting by multinational enterprises concerning transfer pricing.[10]

(iv) Directive of 6 December 2016, No. 2016/2258 (DAC 5), which requires Member States to provide Tax Authorities with access to anti-money laundering information resulting from customer due diligence procedures applied by financial intermediaries in accordance with the Fourth Anti-Money Laundering Directive.[11]

(v) Directive of 25 May 2018, No. 2018/822 (DAC 6), which is one of the instruments of the so-called transparency package launched by the European Commission following the work carried out at the OECD/G20 on the Base Erosion and Profit Shifting (BEPS) project, in line with the Final Report of Action 12 on Mandatory Disclosure Rules.[12] It imposes an obligation on any intermediary (i.e., a person registered with a professional association providing legal, tax, or consultancy services in a Member State) who designs, markets, organizes, makes available, or manages the implementation of a cross-border arrangement in the interest of a relevant taxpayer, to report it to

---

8. The directive was published in the Official Journal on 16 December 2014 and entered into force twenty days later, with the first exchanges becoming mandatory on 30 September 2017.
9. The directive entered into force on 18 December 2015, the date of its publication in the Official Journal, with the first exchanges becoming mandatory on 30 September 2017.
10. The directive entered into force on 30 June 2016, the date of its publication in the Official Journal, with the first exchanges becoming mandatory on 30 June 2018.
11. The directive entered into force on the date of its adoption.
12. *See* the *OECD/G20 Base Erosion and Profit Shifting Project 'Mandatory Disclosure Rules' Action 12: 2015 Final Report*, OECD (Paris 2015).

their own Tax Administration at an early stage, i.e., before it is effectively implemented.[13]

(vi) Directive of 22 March 2021, No. 2021/514 (DAC 7), which will extend, starting from 1 January 2023, the automatic reporting obligation to all digital platform operators regarding their customer sellers, whether individuals or legal entities, to the Tax Authorities of the Member States where they are resident.[14]

It is worth noting that on 17 October 2023, the European Council adopted a directive concerning the reporting and automatic exchange of information on revenues from transactions in crypto-assets and on advance tax rulings for the wealthiest (high-net-worth) (DAC 8).[15] This will help Tax Authorities to track the trade of crypto-assets and the proceeds gained, thereby reducing the risk of tax fraud and evasion. The directive also puts forward a series of (smaller) changes to improve the existing exchange of tax-related information.

§19.2.1 The TFEU Sources for Tax Cooperation

The remarkable evolution of administrative tax cooperation reflects the prism of politics that has characterized the European Union, parallel to the evolution of international taxation governed by the OECD, emanating from the G20.[16] This has resulted in a different and more effective articulation of tax administrative power, as an alternative to the inertia of any coordination between taxing powers at both the global and European levels. While the process of tax harmonization has always been limited by the need for unanimous deliberations in the European Council, within the special

13. The directive was published in the Official Journal on 5 June 2018 and entered into force twenty days later, with the first exchanges becoming mandatory on 31 October 2020. The bibliography of DAC 6 is wide, *see* Marco Greggi, *Shades of Transparency: DAC 6 and the Client-Attorney Privilege*, in *EC Tax Review*, pp. 67 et seq. (2/2023) DOI: 10.54648/ecta2023012; Andrea Purpura, *DAC 6: Some (Potential) Incompatibility Profiles with Article 6 ATAD*, in *Intertax*, pp. 51 et seq. (1/2023) DOI: 10.54648/taxi2023003; Dennis Weber & Jorn Steenbergen, *The (Absence of) Member State Autonomy in the Interpretation of DAC 6: A Call for EU Guidance*, in *EC Tax Review*, pp. 254 et seq. (5&6/2021) DOI: 10.54648/ecta2021026; Andrea Ballancin & Francesco Cannas, *The DAC 6 and Its Compatibility with Some of the Founding Principles of the European Legal System(s)*, in *EC Tax Review*, pp. 117 et seq. DOI: 10.54648/ecta2020038 (3/2020); Brin Rajathurai, *DAC 6: the UK's Proposals for Implementation*, in *British Tax Review*, pp. 1 et seq. (5/2019).
14. *See* Nevia Cicin-Sain & Joachim Englisch, *DAC 7: An Entire New Framework for Joint Audits in the EU: How Do the Taxpayers Fare?* in *Intertax*, pp. 7 et seq. (1/2022) DOI: 10.54648/taxi2022002, S.A. Stevens & J.T. van Wamelen, *The DAC 7 Proposal and Reporting Obligation for Online Platforms*, in *EC Tax Review*, pp. 24 et seq. (1/2021) DOI: 10.54648/ecta2021003.
15. DAC 8 proposal is dated 18 September 2023, 10215/23, FISC 115, ECOFIN 566, Interinstitutional File: 2022/0413 (CNS), *see* https://data.consilium.europa.eu/doc/document/ST-10215-2023-INIT/en/pdf), This directive has been adopted on 17 October 2023, *see* https://www.consilium.europa.eu/en/press/press-releases/2023/10/17/council-adopts-directive-to-boost-cooperation-between-national-taxation-authorities-dac8/.
16. The interpretation that AEOI is indeed a new international tax custom is interesting, *see* Roberto Codorniz Leite Pereira, *The Emergence of Transparency and Exchange of Information for Tax Purposes on Request as an International Tax Custom*, in *Intertax*, pp. 624 et seq. (6&7/2020) DOI: 10.54648/taxi2020057.

legislative procedure provided for in Articles. 113 and 115 of the TFEU, administrative cooperation stands out as a new shape of European solidarity. This has been made possible, especially through the legislative changes introduced by the Lisbon Treaty of 2007: on the one hand, by introducing the competence of the Union to *'take action to support, coordinate, and supplement the action of the Member States'* in accordance with Article 6 of the TFEU, and, on the other hand, with Article 197, paragraph 1, of the TFEU, which established the new principle that *'the effective implementation of Union law by the Member States, essential for the functioning of the Union, is considered a matter of common interest'*. Therefore, the Union can now *'support the efforts of the Member States to improve their administrative capacity to implement Union law'*.

Article 197 and, to some extent, Article 114 of the TFEU provide for the application of the ordinary legislative procedure and, therefore, the qualified majority quorum for their deliberations. This assumption has found concrete confirmation in EU Regulation No. 2013/1286 establishing the *'Fiscalis 2020'* Program that, along with the *Multiannual Work Programme 2023-2025 for Customs* of 30 January 2023 [C(2023) 725 final], constitutes the telematic architecture for European information. Its legal basis has been explicitly referred to in Article 197 of the TFEU by the European legislator. However, since a part of this program also deals with the IT development capacity of the EU, specifically in the context of measures supporting the exchange of information between Member States for administrative cooperation in the tax field, the legal basis has also been identified in Article 114 of the TFEU.

§19.2.2 A New Identity for Tax Cooperation

Administrative cooperation has thus acquired a distinct legal and solidarity dimension compared to tax harmonization, positioning itself in a complementary, if not superior, relationship with it, towards the achievement of the Union's objectives, and particularly to ensure the proper functioning of the internal market. All the legal prerequisites have been established to facilitate the strengthening of operational capacities of National Tax Administrations, which are increasingly called upon to cooperate in a coordinated manner to effectively implement European law. Cooperation, without directly affecting the sensitivity of Member States in matters of non-harmonized taxes, has emerged as the most suitable choice to promote wider participation of National Administrations in the implementation of European law, in line with the principles of solidarity, subsidiarity and proportionality. All this is intended to promote a common administrative tax culture that directly affects Tax Administrations, under the increasingly strong leadership of the Commission through the TAXUD Directorate, which now formulates legislative proposals for the establishment and improvement of information exchange between Member States, monitors the implementation of legislation in Member States, and provides mechanisms and electronic interfaces to coordinate the exchange of information itself. National Tax Administrations, despite their heterogeneity, appear to integrate on a legal-functional level, according to the forms and dynamics dictated by cooperation, operating in the interest of the Union or limited to the pursuit of common and general supranational objectives. There is no doubt that this rapid expansion of European administrative tax law, from simple assistance to bilateral cooperation, with the aim of achieving true multilateral integration, has contributed to strengthening studies and stimulating jurisprudence on the right to good administration,[17] as written and detailed in Article 41 of the Charter of Fundamental Rights of the European Union.

§19.2.3 Tax Cooperation and Technology

A fundamental factor that has driven this evolution, which seemingly has nothing to do with law, is information and communication technology, particularly artificial intelligence, which enables us to understand what a Tax Administration is and, more importantly, what it can become with its decisions, services and access to its databases. Digitalization and the right to good administration become two sides of the same coin, where information, databases, blockchain and interoperability of computer systems in the tax administrative sector undoubtedly provide the prerequisites for their 'entification'. Unfortunately, it is equally true that information and communication technology often overlays procedures that have not fundamentally changed but have been somewhat adapted, without resulting in a homogeneous step forward across various levels of Public Administration, including Tax Administration (a sort of wardrobe that never gets empty).[18] In other words, digital evolution must always be accompanied by an organizational process analysis and, in this regard, the support of the *'Fiscalis 2021-2027'* programmes and the Multi-Annual Strategic Plan for Taxation Systems (MASP-T) proposed by the EU Commission will be crucial.[19]

§19.3 THE CURRENT CHALLENGES OF ADMINISTRATIVE COOPERATION

As briefly mentioned, administrative cooperation presents significant challenges at the intersection of law, technology, and politics. These challenges have been highlighted by European institutions themselves, starting with the EU Commission, which emphasized in its Report to the European Parliament and Council on 18 December 2017 (COM (2017) 781 final) that the implementation of the DAC has led to a significant increase in the amount of data that Tax Administrations have to manage, even though their capacity to manage them has not increased proportionally. Therefore, it is necessary to obtain qualitatively better and more understandable data on the implementation of the DAC and its related benefits. The European Court of Auditors has also expressed its views in an interesting report titled *'Exchange of Tax Information in the EU: Solid*

17. The last but not least is Tobias Lock, *Article 41 CFR Right to Good Administration*, in Manuel Kellerbauer et al. (eds), *The EU Treaties and the Charter of Fundamental Rights: A Commentary*, Oxford, 2019.
18. A very interesting essay on how to solve this issue is *Tax Administration 3.0: the Digital Transformation of Tax Administration*, OECD, pp. 65 et seq. (Paris, 2020).
19. Regulation 20 May 2021 No. 2021/847 concerning the programme *Fiscalis 2021-2027* was published in the Official Journal on 28 May 2021.

Foundations, but Cracks in Implementation', which assesses the state of the art ten years after the implementation of EU Directive 2011/16.[20] After conducting careful auditing activities in five Member States (Cyprus, Italy, the Netherlands, Poland, and Spain), the Court concluded that the EU Commission's TAXUD Directorate has established an adequate framework for the exchange of tax information but is not proactive in providing guidance and does not sufficiently measure the effects and impact resulting from the use of the exchanged information. In particular, the Court concluded that the exchanged information is deficient in terms of quality, completeness, and accuracy, and is not widely utilized, and that Member States do not sufficiently monitor the effectiveness of the system. The EU Commission should take direct and effective actions to address the poor quality of data transmitted by Member States, propose legislative measures to ensure the exchange of all relevant income-related information, and expand monitoring activities while providing additional guidance to Member States. In the same vein, the European Parliament Resolution of 16 September 2021, No. 2022/C 117/13, titled *'Implementation of EU Requirements on the Exchange of Tax Information: Progress Made, Lessons Learned, and Overcoming Obstacles'*, recognizes the added value of sharing best practices and the ongoing support from the Commission in terms of strengthening the powers of National Tax Administrations. The Parliament takes note of the observations made by the European Court of Auditors, namely that more can be done in terms of monitoring, ensuring data quality, and using received information to make the exchange of tax information more effective. Additionally, the Parliament expresses deep regret over the fact that the Commission and all Member States have refused to grant access to relevant data for assessing the implementation of DAC provisions. It believes that the Parliament has effectively been hindered in exercising its political control function over the Commission, as provided for in Articles 14 and 17(8) of the Treaty on European Union (TUE). Furthermore, the Parliament is aware that the DAC, being related to tax matters, represents an intergovernmental dimension of European integration and deplores the Council's position on successive revisions of the DAC, based on repeated mitigation of the Commission's proposals and a lack of interest in the Parliament's positions. It calls on the Council to allow access to relevant information regarding the implementation of the DAC to ensure adequate democratic control by the Parliament.

§19.3.1 The New EU Custom Agency

The emerging picture is one of a lack of technical coordination, which translates into institutional political deafness regarding administrative cooperation. It is clear that the topic clashes with the politically hypersensitive issue of 'sovereignty' and the different *Weltanschauungen* in tax matters, which leads to limiting any ambitions for European tax policy to only harmonized taxes (or future own resources if they were to materialize).

20. *See* European Court of Auditors, Special Report No. 03/2021.

Furthermore, it must be noted that only last 17 May 2023 the EU Commission announced that it would put forward an initiative for Revision of the Union customs legislation, as the EU customs code is facing situations for which it was not conceived, notably e-commerce.[21] The key part of the reform is the proposal for a set-up of a new EU Customs Agency, which should oversee an EU Data Hub. Customs data will only need to be submitted to the EU Customs Data Hub, as opposed to the multiple interfaces from the many separate systems in place across the EU Member States today, saving Member States up to EUR 2 billion a year in operating costs. The new Custom Agency will deliver on an improved EU approach to risk management and customs checks. A small group of traders, known as 'Trusts & Checks' traders, will also benefit from simplifications. Subject to certain conditions, the Trusts & Checks traders will be able to import goods without any need for active customs intervention. From 2032, Trusts & Checks will have one single Customs Administration as a partner while operating across the EU. The proposal is subject to the ordinary legislative procedure, requiring support in both the European Parliament and the Council.

Regarding taxes, it is therefore easier to hope that programs like VIES (the electronic system for the exchange of VAT data owned by the European Commission) or entities like the Standing Committee on Administrative Cooperation (SCAC) that supports the EU Commission in the implementation of the legal framework governing administrative cooperation in the field of VAT[22] will continue to improve. The Court of Justice, for its part, does not seem inclined to impose European standards on administrative action, and it also appears cautious when it comes to fundamental rights [as exemplified in cases like Sabou (C-276/12) and Berlioz (C-682/15)]. Finally, it must also take into account the resistance from the European bureaucracy, as well as from the Member States, who believe that the horizontal cooperation governed by the DAC directives is a sufficient legal framework for cross-border tax assessment activities.

§19.4 CONCLUSIONS: THE POLITICAL PERSPECTIVE OF A EUROPEAN TAX COOPERATION AGENCY

For all these reasons, while acknowledging the increasingly urgent need to fight European tax fraud, evasion and tax avoidance, the most effective rational step, with the least political impact, could be to convince the EU Council to establish a European Tax Cooperation Agency (in a visionary scenario, ETCA). This agency would concentrate advisory and investigative activities to support, on the one hand, the policy direction of the Commission, and, on the other hand, the joint audits regulated by Article 12b of Directive 2021/514/EU (DAC 7). These joint audits involve administrative investigations conducted jointly by competent authorities of two or more Member

21. Communication from the Commission to the European Parliament, the Council and the European Economic and Social Committee on the Customs reform: Taking the Customs Union to the next level, of 17 May 2023, COM/2023/257 final. See for a preliminary comment Martijn L. Schippers, *Proposals to Reform the EU Customs Union*, in *EC Tax Review*, pp. 253 et seq. (6/2023) DOI: 10.54648/ecta2023031.
22. *See* Council Regulation (EU) No. 904/2010 of 7 October 2010 on administrative cooperation and combating fraud in the field of value added tax (recast).

States, linked to one or more individuals of common or complementary interest to the competent authorities of those Member States. In particular, certain strategic functions could be centralized, such as the preventive analysis of information flows and databases aimed at the selection and better management of fraud, evasion, and tax avoidance risks. This would apply not only in the European context but especially in the international context, in close connection with the OECD for monitoring the relationship between DAC and automatic exchange of information through CRS between EU Member States and non-EU countries. Naturally, these tasks require adequate and highly qualified personnel, divided into categories of taxpayers, legal entities, and individuals, starting with those with the highest tax dimensions.

The political ambition could go so far as to transfer to the European Tax Cooperation Agency the investigative and even the tax assessment powers of larger cross-border groups (those with a turnover exceeding EUR 750 million) currently involved in the *European Trust and Cooperation Approach* (ETACA) pilot project for the construction of enhanced European cooperation.[23] In the future, they could also be subject to the European implementation of OECD Pillar 2 on global minimum taxation. The purpose of this cooperation is to provide the parties involved with the certainty that, based on the collected information and subsequent measurements of tax risks, the examined operations (starting from transfer pricing to the application of the global minimum tax) are low risk, thus avoiding the need for further investigative resources for the tax year in question and the following two years, unless there is a change in facts and circumstances. With the same political objective, the Agency could also be entrusted with monitoring: (i) the rules to prevent the improper use of shell entities for tax purposes, as modified by the Council Proposal COM(2021) 656 final of 22 December 2021; and (ii) High Net Worth Individuals (HNWI) and their related family offices, mentioned in recital AD of European Parliament Resolution No. 2022/C 117/13.[24] This would be a further step towards a true European Tax Cooperation Authority.

§19.4.1 The OLAF Example

The reference model could be the European Anti-Fraud Office (OLAF) established by the European Commission (President Prodi) with Decision No. 352 of 28 April 1999, aimed at fighting fraud, corruption, and any illicit activity detrimental to the financial interests of the European Union. It would be even better to study, from a tax

23. *See* the Communication from the Commission to the European Parliament and the Council *An Action Plan for Fair and Simple Taxation Strategy Supporting the Recovery Strategy*, of 15 July 2020, COM(2020) 312 final.
24. The recital AD of the Resolution states that: 'Considering that "family offices" often hold large cross-border activities through direct ownership of companies or through investment entities controlled by a restricted group; that such financial institutions can be subject to conflicts of interest contributing to unreliable communication of tax information; that unrealized capital gains held abroad by individuals in low-tax entities are difficult to regulate under national tax systems; that both these conditions allow individuals with significant assets to accumulate wealth based on low-tax income, while the middle class can only do so on fully taxed income.'

administrative perspective, Regulation No. 2017/1939 of 12 October 2017, concerning the implementation of enhanced cooperation on the establishment of the European Public Prosecutor's Office (EPPO), which represents one of the most significant achievements of European legislation from 2014 to 2019 and a decisive step forward in the construction of the '*Area of Freedom, Security, and Justice*' governed by Articles 67-89 (Part Three-Title V) of the TFEU. It follows shortly after the adoption, based on Article 83, paragraph 2, of the TFEU, of Directive No. 2017/1371 of 28 July 2017, on the fight against fraud to the Union's financial interests through criminal law, which precisely aims at defining 'minimum rules' on offences and criminal sanctions related to fraud harmful to the financial interests of the European Union.[25] The only comparable precedent of such a wide transfer of powers from the national level to a European Union institution is constituted, albeit broadly, by Regulation No. 2013/1024, which provided for the transfer of supervisory functions over the main banks of the nineteen eurozone Member States from their central banks to the European Central Bank.

The institutional aspects of the EPPO's functioning concern: (a) the applicable substantive and procedural criminal legislation; (b) judicial remedies, i.e., the regime for challenging acts issued by European prosecutors in the exercise of their functions conferred by the Regulation; (c) the procedure for resolving conflicts of jurisdiction that will inevitably arise between the European Public Prosecutor's Office and the prosecutors of the Member States.

Not that some contradictions are lacking in this context either. For example, according to Article 22, paragraph 4, of Regulation No. 2017/1939, offences related to national direct taxes, including offences closely linked to them, are excluded from the competence of the European Public Prosecutor's Office. Therefore, if during the same investigation, possible evasion of both corporate income tax and value added tax (VAT) is discovered, the entire file will be transmitted to the national prosecutor's office and not to the European Public Prosecutor's Office, thus largely undermining the transferred competences under Article 22, paragraph 1, of Regulation No. 2017/1939.

§19.4.2 The Needs for an ETCA

A European Tax Cooperation Agency (ETCA) as a tool for tax governance requires investment in human resources and training by the individual Tax Administrations of the Member States, as highlighted in the aforementioned report by the EU Commission COM (2017) 781 final, perhaps with the support of the Fiscalis 2021-2027 programme, still in the proposal phase. Unfortunately, it seems that the number of officials trained in the EU perspective still appears excessively low when compared to the total number of officials operating in the tax field.[26] This indicates a limited investment by the Member States of the European Union in administrative cooperation in the tax area.

25. *See* Enrico Traversa, *I tre principali aspetti istituzionali della Procura Europea ('EPPO'): legge applicabile, rimedi giurisdizionali e conflitti di competenza*, in *Riv. dir. com. sc. int.*, pp. 487 et seq. (3-4/2020).
26. *See* the Report of the Commission to the European Parliament and the Council on the final evaluation of the Fiscalis 2020, of 14 December 2022 SWD(2022) 406 final.

All these considerations are consistent with the picture of administrative cooperation activity that can be inferred at the Italian national level from the decision of the Italian Court of Auditors dated 1 April 2019, No. 6/2019/G, that confirms that Italy's position does not appear dissimilar to that of other States. The overall staffing of the International Cooperation Office within the Revenue Agency, which encompasses multiple activities, was only thirty-two employees as of September 2018, out of a total of over thirty-two thousand employees. However, it is not possible to ascertain the resources available to the Department of Tax Policies of the Ministry of Economy and Finance, where the Central Liaison Office is located, specifically the Directorate for International Relations, which acts as the main responsible authority for administrative cooperation with the Member States, in coordination with the Central Directorate for Assessment – International Sector of the Revenue Agency and the General Command of the Tax Police (*Guardia di finanza*) – II Department for Analysis and International Relations.

This Office includes not only the service for information exchange with the Member States, assistance in the notification of acts, and coercive collection of tax credits (C.L.O.) but also the allocation and monitoring of multilateral controls or simultaneous audits; management of requests for collection of credits arising in other States; management of requests for collection of taxes from and to foreign countries within the framework of international law relations; management of activities related to the introduction of the MOSS regime (Directive No. 2008/8/EC); administrative mutual assistance with foreign Tax Administrations; the service for information exchange with any other state, including the sending and receiving of Country-by-Country reports; analysis of exchanged information for subsequent use by the competent central authorities.

Furthermore, the Agency has acknowledged the development of a dedicated database called INDACO (Information from Abroad for National Taxpayers), designed to collect information received as a result of DAC 1, 2, 3, and 4, and that a procedure is being implemented to extract the information contained in INDACO and channel it into a specific section of SERPICO (Taxpayer Information Service, available to the Revenue Agency and the Tax Police), where the presence of automatic information exchange for each taxpayer will be displayed, detailed by tax year and type of exchange.[27]

In short, the Revenue Agency seems to be ready to engage with a European Tax Cooperation Agency, and the hope is that this will happen as soon as possible, with the training support of the National School of Administration in Italy as well as in all other European Member States.

27. *See* Fabio Saponaro, *L'attuazione amministrativa del tributo nel diritto dell'integrazione europea*, Cedam, Padova, 2017; Andrea Buccisano, *Assistenza amministrativa internazionale dall'accertamento alla riscossione dei tributi*, Cacucci (Bari 2013).

CHAPTER 20
Tax Cooperation Between the European Union and China

Diheng Xu

§20.1 INTRODUCTION

The European Union and China have close business ties. In 2020-2021, China surpassed the United States to become the European Union's largest trading partner.[1] The two parties concluded negotiations on a European Union-China Comprehensive Agreement on Investment (CAI or Agreement) on 30 December 2020.[2] This Agreement aims to ensure that EU investors obtain better access to the fast-growing consumer market in China and that they compete on a level playing field in China. Both the European Union and China have made commitments in the CAI. The Agreement is just the starting point; both parties hope to establish an institutional framework in two years to promote implementation. It signals both parties' willingness to further trade relations with each other.

Along with the CAI, China's Belt and Road Initiative (BRI) (2015)[3] is another project that is intended to facilitate trade and investment between the European Union

1. In 2021, China was the European Union's largest trading partner, amounting to 16.2% of the European Union's total trade. China was the largest partner in terms of EU imports of goods and the third largest partner regarding EU export of goods. *See* Eurostat, *China–EU International Trade in Goods Statistics* (11 June 2023), https://ec.europa.eu/eurostat/statistics-explained/index.php?title=China-EU_-_international_trade_in_goods_statistics#Recent_developments China-EU – international trade in goods statistics – Statistics Explained (europa.eu).
2. *EU-China Comprehensive Agreement on Investment, The Agreement in Principle* (11 June 2023), https://policy.trade.ec.europa.eu/eu-trade-relationships-country-and-region/countries-and-regions/china/eu-china-agreement/eu-china-agreement-principle_en.
3. In 2015, the National Development and Reform Commission, Ministry of Foreign Affairs and Ministry of Commerce jointly released Vision and Actions on Jointly Building Silk Road Economic Belt and 21st Century Maritime Silk Road (28 March 2015). *See Visions and Actions on Jointly*

and China. The main objective of the BRI is to connect China and the East Asian economic circle with the European Union. The main business activities involved in the BRI are cooperation on infrastructure building, maritime and land connectivity, trade of goods and services and other economic cooperation. It is often considered to be the largest infrastructure project in the decades to come, with total investment anticipated to be in the trillions of US dollars.[4] By 2022, 149 countries and 32 international organizations had joined the BRI.[5] Eighteen EU Member States have also participated in the BRI (Austria, Bulgaria, Croatia, Cyprus, the Czech Republic, Estonia, Greece, Hungary, Italy, Latvia, Lithuania, Luxemburg, Malta, Poland, Portugal, the Slovak Republic, Slovenia and Romania). In general, the BRI is intended to facilitate the entry of Chinese investors into the EU market, and the CAI can assist EU investors to further access the Chinese market.

Tax cooperation can be an excellent starting point for further business cooperation. Under the BRI, China has started initiatives on tax cooperation between the participating members. In April 2019, China established the Belt and Road Initiative Tax Administration Cooperation Mechanism (BRITACOM), a non-profit official mechanism for tax administration cooperation among the jurisdictions that have joined the BRI. It is a multilateral platform for greater tax cooperation between BRI members, focusing on tax administration.[6] Six EU Member States have become observer members of this new tax cooperation framework (Cyprus, Germany, Greece, Hungary, Italy and Spain).[7] The CAI does not have separate tax cooperation proposals but sets up a common platform for tax cooperation, namely a level playing field for EU investors and transparency rules for subsidies.[8] Nevertheless, the CAI is still pending signature, as the European Union has concerns.[9] The main concern is that whether China can ensure fair access for European businesses to the Chinese market. This chapter provides insights on further tax cooperation opportunities between the EU and China. The research question of this chapter: what is the feasibility of corporate tax cooperation between the EU and China, and how can both parties further the tax cooperation? Section 20.2 introduces the EU's direction for tax cooperation. Section 20.3 analyses China's direction for tax cooperation. Section 20.4 summarizes the common base for tax cooperation between the two parties. Section 20.5 concludes.

Building Silk Road Economic Belt and 21st Century Maritime Silk Road, Xinhua News (28 March 2015) (11 June 2023), http://www.xinhuanet.com//world/2015-03/28/c_1114793986.htm.

4. *Ibid.*
5. An Overview of Countries that Have Signed a Memorandum of Understanding with China (7 February 2022) (11 June 2023), www.yidaiyilu.gov.cn/xwzx/roll/77298.htm.
6. Na Li, *The Belt and Road Initiative Tax Administration Cooperation Mechanism (BRITACOM): Where Is It Heading?*, 75 Bull. Intl. Taxn. 11/12, 740 (2021).
7. The list of observing members of BRITACOM is available at https://www.britacom.org/jzgk/council (14 June 2023).
8. European Commission, Key Elements of the EU-China Comprehensive Agreement on Investment (30 December 2020) (14 June 2023), https://ec.europa.eu/commission/presscorner/detail/en/IP_20_2542.
9. Theresa Fallon, *The Strategic Implications of the China-EU Investment Deal: The EU-China Comprehensive Agreement on Investment Is a Win for China, and a Blow to Transatlantic Relations*, The Diplomat (4 January 2021).

§20.2 THE EU'S DIRECTION FOR TAX COOPERATION

In 2020, the European Union launched a new tax package that aims to address economic recovery following the pandemic.[10] In this package, the European Union emphasizes its objective to boost tax fairness by intensifying the fight against tax abuse, combating unfair tax competition and increasing tax transparency. Accordingly, it will reform its standard of tax good governance and seek its application to third countries.[11] The standard mainly includes transparency, fair tax competition, exchange of information and internationally agreed standards on BEPS.[12]

§20.2.1 Fair Tax Competition

By issuing different regulations and documents to maintain fair tax competition, the European Union aims to create a level playing field for tax competition between EU Member States and third countries. The creation of a level playing field is the requirement for free trade and investment within the internal market.[13] Thus, the understanding of fair tax competition in the European Union is grounded in the idea of fair trade from a business perspective.[14] Although there could be a different interpretation of fair tax competition from a political, philosophical or social perspective, the European Union gives priority to the economic approach to interpreting fair tax competition.[15] This justifies the Member State governments' intervention in the market to combat harmful tax measures that distort fair tax competition. A typical example is the widespread application of state aid law to tax rulings in EU Member States. Since 2015, the European Commission has started investigating the tax rulings of different Member States. Large multinational companies like Apple, Starbucks, Google and Amazon have all been involved in state aid cases initiated by the European Commission.[16] In general, the Commission has claimed that the tax rulings of Member States grant specific tax advantages to these companies that result in a lower tax burden, and

10. European Commission, Press Release IP/20/1334, *Fair and Simple Taxation: Commission Proposes New Package of Measures to Contribute to Europe's Recovery and Growth* (15 July 2020), https://ec.europa.eu/commission/presscorner/detail/en/ip_20_1334.
11. European Commission, *Communication from the Commission to the European Parliament and the Council on Tax Good Governance in the EU and beyond* (15 July 2020), COM(2020) 313 final, https://ec.europa.eu/taxation_customs/sites/taxation/files/2020_tax_package_tax_good_governance_communication_en.pdf.
12. Irma J. M. Valderrama, *The EU Standard of Good Governance in Tax Matters for Third (Non-EU) Countries*, 47 Intertax 5, 454-467 (2019) DOI: 10.54648/taxi2019046.
13. Article 26 TFEU.
14. Alice Pirlot, *The Vagueness of Tax Fairness: A Discursive Analysis of the Commission's 'Fair Tax Agenda'*, 48 Intertax 4, 410-412 (2020) DOI: 10.54648/taxi2020036.
15. Irene Burgers & Irma J.M. Valderrama, *Fairness: A Dire International Tax Standard with No Meaning?*, 45 Intertax 12, 780-781 (2017) DOI: 10.54648/taxi2017067.
16. For an overview of all state aid case decisions (15 June 2023), *see* the website of the European Commission, https://competition-policy.ec.europa.eu/state-aid/tax-rulings_en#guidance.

this is not fair for other undertakings in the internal market.[17] Therefore, as a part of competition policy, state aid law is a powerful tool adopted by the European Union to combat harmful tax competition.

§20.2.2 Transparency

The European Union has a stringent requirement on tax transparency for corporations. In 2021, the European Union officially published the Public CbCR Directive (2021/2101).[18] It requires qualified companies to publish their tax information publicly within the European Union. This means that, besides tax authorities, civil society can have access to large multinational companies' tax information as well. The aim is to increase tax transparency and strengthen public scrutiny. Multinational companies must pay attention to paying their fair share of taxes, as they bear the reputational risk vis-à-vis the public.[19] Compared to the OECD's standard of CbC reporting, the European Union goes one step further, i.e., making the report public. This reveals the European Union's strong stance towards multinational companies in terms of tax transparency. In addition, besides following the OECD's standard on exchange of information, the European Union also has higher requirements on the exchange of information of tax rulings, tax planning cross-border arrangements and intermediaries via the Directive on Administrative Cooperation (2011/16) (DAC).[20]

Therefore, tax transparency is strengthened by including administrative cooperation regarding the exchange of information within the European Union.

§20.2.3 Promotion of the EU Tax Good Governance Standards with Third Countries

It is the European Union's objective to help developing countries build robust tax systems and to strengthen the European Union's international position with third countries.[21] To implement the standards on tax good governance, the European Union

17. DG Competition Working Paper on State Aid and Tax Rulings, Background to the High Level Forum on State Aid of 3 June 2016, https://competition-policy.ec.europa.eu/system/files/2021-04/specific_aid_instruments_working_paper_tax_rulings.pdf.
18. Directive EU 2021/2101 of the European Parliament and of the Council of 21 November 2021 amending Directive 2013/34/EU as regards disclosure of income tax information by certain undertakings and branches, OJ L 429/1 (1 December 2021), available at https://eur-lex.europa.eu/legal-content/EN/TXT/PDF/?uri=CELEX:32021L2101&from=EN.
19. Willemien Netjes & Dominik Freyer, *Tax Transparency Is Here to Stay: An Analysis of the Public CbCR Directive*, 50 Intertax 8/9, 612 (2022) DOI: 10.54648/taxi2022060.
20. Council Directive 2011/16/EU of 15 February 2011 on Administrative Cooperation in the Field of Taxation and Repealing Directive 77/799/EEC, OJ L 64 (2011), Primary Sources IBFD. There are eight Directives on Administrative Cooperation (DAC) so far. They require different information to be exchanged. *See* European Commission, Administrative Cooperation in (Direct) Taxation in the EU, https://taxation-customs.ec.europa.eu/taxation-1/tax-co-operation-and-control/general-overview/enhanced-administrative-cooperation-field-direct-taxation_en (15 June 2023).
21. COM(2020) 313 final, *supra* n. 11.

needs the cooperation of third countries to export this norm.[22] For instance, the European Union relies on certain standards to determine the list of non-cooperative jurisdictions. This means that if jurisdictions aim to be removed from the list, they have to check the European Union's standards and amend their domestic tax rules and measures accordingly.[23] Another example is that the European Union has signed bilateral trade and investment cooperation agreements with different countries, including China. These agreements contain the European Union's tax good governance standards. By signing these agreements with the European Union, the third countries demonstrate that they will adopt these standards.[24] This process not only exports norms to third countries but also is evidence of the transformation of the European Union's soft law into hard law globally. In summary, the European Union is becoming a norm maker not only for EU Member States but also for third countries, especially developing countries with business activities with the European Union.

§20.3 CHINA'S DIRECTION FOR TAX COOPERATION

§20.3.1 BRI: Tax Good Governance

China initiated the BRI tax cooperation mechanism BRITACOM in 2019. Although it is still in the beginning stages, it evidences China's aim to strengthen tax cooperation with members of the BRI. The BRITACOM has five policy objectives, namely: following the rule of law and increasing tax certainty, expediting tax dispute resolution, enhancing tax administration capacity, streamlining tax compliance and digitalizing tax administration.[25] As the mechanism is still in the initial stages, there are no concrete implementation actions regarding these policy objectives. The main activities are holding meetings and workshops for members online to exchange opinions and experiences.[26] However, between 2019 and 2021, the BRITACOM conducted surveys on tax administrations and enterprises among BRI members to first discover specific problems relating to these five aspects, which culminated in the publication of reports. This will allow it to provide further suggestions on how to achieve its goals.[27] This demonstrates that China does not promote its own ideas on how to formulate tax cooperation unilaterally but adopts multilateral means to reflect major concerns from different parties. These task forces concentrate more on the capacity building of tax administrations, such as improving the capacity of tax collection and regulating discretionary behaviour in terms of tax enforcement by local governments. With regard to the rule of law and tax certainty, the report presents suggestions including improving the tax system through sound tax policy design and simplified tax legislation, as well as

22. Valderrama, *supra* n. 12, 458-459.
23. Alexandra Koutsouva, *The European Union's List of Non-cooperative Jurisdictions for Tax Purposes*, 29 EC Tax Rev. 4, 194-195 (2020) DOI: 10.54648/ecta2020045.
24. Valderrama, *supra* n. 12, 461-462.
25. *See supra* n. 7.
26. *See supra* n. 6, 744.
27. The BRITACOM released five final reports for the five policy goals in 2021, available at https://www.britacom.org/gkzljxz/Documents (accessed 20 June 2023).

optimizing mechanisms to prevent tax disputes, etc.[28] Moreover, the surveys show that enterprises have concerns regarding the lack of transparency of tax laws and regulations. Thus, it is also important to increase the transparency of tax rules to increase tax certainty. All of these efforts rely on following the rule of law, especially clear guidance on procedural law. The report refers to the international understanding of the rule of law, which can embody basic legal principles of accountability, just laws, open government, accessibility, impartial dispute resolution and fair treatment.[29] The interpretation here may not represent China's complete interpretation of the rule of law with respect to tax measures, but it sends a signal that China aims to integrate the international standard on the rule of law under the tax cooperation framework. A further focus is on procedural and institutional elements. In summary, China is moving towards its own outlook of tax good governance in the context of tax cooperation under the BRI.

§20.3.2 CAI: The Creation of a Level Playing Field

The European Union and China concluded the CAI in 2020, which is considered the European Union's most ambitious agreement ever concluded with a third country.[30] The CAI benefits the European Union mainly in three respects: better market access for EU companies to China, a level playing field for EU investors by disciplining state-owned enterprises (SOEs) and increasing transparency for subsidies, and sustainable development, including corporate social responsibility, labour and environmental norms.[31] Signature of the CAI is still pending by both the European Union and China, especially ratification by the European Parliament.[32]

A major concern for foreign investors with regard to fair tax competition in Chinese markets is Chinese SOEs, namely whether Chinese SOEs benefit from a more favourable tax treatment, thus causing unfair tax competition. To further tax cooperation with China, it is necessary to understand the position of SOEs in China and the current reforms. SOEs have undergone reforms under several phases since China's opening. The trend is to reduce the number of SOEs and to introduce more private and mixed ownership, thus letting the market play a more decisive role.[33] Currently, SOEs are classified as commercial SOEs and public-interest SOEs. Commercial SOEs include commercial strategic SOEs and commercial non strategic SOEs. Commercial strategic SOEs relate to industries concerning national security and the lifeline of the national economy. In this scenario, the state still is a majority owner, but is open to private and

28. Following Rule of Law and Raising Tax Certainty, Wuzhen Action Plan (2019-2021) Final Report, September 2021 (accessed 30 June 2023), https://www.britacom.org/gkzljxz/Documents.
29. *Ibid.*, 3.
30. European Commission, *supra* n. 8.
31. *Ibid.*
32. Julien Chaisse & Matthieu Burnay, *Introduction – CAI's Contribution to International Investment Law: European, Chinese, and Global Perspectives*, 23 J. World Invest. Trade 4, 507-509 (2022) DOI: 10.1163/22119000-12340258.
33. Qunhui Huang, *How 'New SOEs' Come of Age: Four Decades of China's SOEs Reform*, 13 China Economist, 58-72 (2018).

mixed ownership. Commercial non-strategic SOEs should be fully open to mixed ownership and compete directly in the market. Public-interest SOEs perform the function of providing public goods and services and may decide themselves whether to introduce diversified ownership.[34] Until 2021, the number of mixed-ownership enterprises that were central SOEs was over 70%. The percentage is 54% for local SOEs with mixed ownership. The number of SOEs has decreased from 117 to 98.[35] Accordingly, with the increase in mixed ownership SOEs, the level of fair competition should also improve. Foreign investors can have greater access to China's domestic market by purchasing shares in SOEs and investing in fields that used to be merely open to SOEs. The reform has further opened market access to private and foreign investors in China and has contributed to the efficiency and governance of SOEs.[36] Under the increasing reforms, SOEs, especially commercial SOEs, are being required to compete with other enterprises in the market and accept the results in terms of competition. Under the CAI, SOEs should act according to commercial considerations and behave as any private business would.[37] No tax incentives will be allowed to be granted specifically to certain commercial SOEs. The direction of the reform is to let all enterprises compete fairly in the domestic market without the involvement of a different tax treatment. Moreover, the reform has tremendously increased mixed ownership of SOEs, including private and foreign ownership. As a result, private and foreign shareholders can enjoy tax benefits equivalent to those granted to SOEs. Empirical studies also show that the reform regarding mixed ownership should curb the tax avoidance behaviour of firms. An SOE with a high level of mixed ownership should engage in less tax avoidance.[38]

§20.3.3 Transparency of Tax Subsidies

According to the CAI, the transparency of subsidies will be improved. This also applies to subsidies in the form of tax incentives. China has an obligation to increase the transparency of tax incentives in respect of industrial goods and the services sectors, including those for SOEs. China joined the WTO in 2001 and has consistently faced compatibility challenges relating to tax subsidies.[39] Although China has reformed

34. The current reform began with the 18th Party Congress in 2013. *See Art. 2* Guiding Opinions of the Chinese Communist Party Central Committee and the State Council on Deeping the Reform of State Owned Enterprises (24 August 2015) (Guiding Opinions).
35. China Youth Daily, *At Present, the Number of Mixed Ownership Enterprises of Central Enterprises Exceeds 70%* (17 June 2022) (25 November 2022) https://baijiahao.baidu.com/s?id=1735860771812508359&wfr=spider&for=pc.
36. Jiangyu Wang & Tan Cheng-Han, *Mixed Ownership Reform and Corporate Governance in China's State-Owned Enterprises*, 53 Vand. J. Transnat'l L, 1100-1105 (2020).
37. European Commission, *Q&A: EU-China Comprehensive Agreement on Investment (CAI)* (30 December 2020) (3 December 2022), https://ec.europa.eu/commission/presscorner/detail/en/qanda_20_2543.
38. Wei Wang, Hua Wang & Ji Wu, *Mixed Ownership Reform and Corporate Tax Avoidance: Evidence of Chinese Listed Firms*, 69 Pac. Basin Finance J. 1016-1048 (2021) DOI: 10.1016/j.pacfin.2021.101648.
39. Diheng Xu, *Prospects on the Relationship Between Chinese Direct Tax Incentives and Subsidy Rules of the World Trade Organization*, 44 Intertax 6/7, 539-540 (2016) DOI: 10.54648/taxi2016043.

tremendously with regard to its tax incentives, due to inadequate notification in the WTO, the transparency of subsidies to Chinese SOEs is still considered insufficient from the WTO's perspective.[40] Under the CAI, China must provide more information on tax subsidies for domestic enterprises on the basis of a specific consultation mechanism. Therefore, the CAI can compensate for the WTO's subsidy rules to increase the transparency of tax subsidies. To guarantee enforcement, the CAI also provides a dispute resolution mechanism. If it fails to do so, the European Union will retain its right to adopt autonomous measures to address any distortions in the European Union's market.[41] If the CAI can be implemented, there will be a comprehensive set of transparency rules for regulatory and administrative measures to enhance legal certainty.[42]

§20.4 COMMON BASE FOR TAX COOPERATION

§20.4.1 Common Objectives

The previous analysis shows that the European Union and China share common objectives for further tax cooperation, which are mainly in the fields of fair tax competition, tax transparency and tax dispute resolution. A major concern of the European Union is that China cannot ensure a level playing field for foreign investors. However, the analysis in this chapter, on new developments in terms of China's domestic and international tax mechanisms, demonstrates that there are no substantive conflicts or huge differences regarding tax cooperation between the two parties. In contrast, the European Union and China currently share more in common in terms of how to realize tax good governance and promote sustainable development. Both the European Union and China aim to create a level playing field. The understanding of this level playing field is the same, namely ensuring fair tax competition by combating harmful tax measures. The European Union relies on state aid law, the ATAD, and other codes of conduct to achieve this goal, while China has made great progress on SOE reforms, the establishment of a national unified market and is strictly controlling the granting of tax incentives, etc. To increase transparency, the European Union is stricter regarding public CbC reporting, while China specifically aims to increase the transparency of tax incentives for SOEs. Although there are numerous options available to realize the objectives of the parties, the two can start to become common norm makers to establish a tax cooperation framework.

40. Weihuan Zhou et al., *China's SOE Reform: Using WTO Rules to Build a Market Economy*, 68 Int. Compar. Law Q. 4, 1002 (2019) DOI: 10.2139/ssrn.3209613.
41. *See supra* n. 2, at s. V.
42. EU-China Comprehensive Agreement on Investment – The Agreement in Principle – Factsheet (30 December 2020), available at https://circabc.europa.eu/ui/group/09242a36-a438-40fd-a7af-fe32e36cbd0e/library/6b4e0ec7-5ff0-4872-a4cf-54717b881d90/details (25 June 2023).

§20.4.2 Multilateralism

The fundamental basis for cooperation is that both the European Union and China are supporters of multilateralism. In the area of international tax coordination, multilateralism is increasing. In order for tax coordination to be considered multilateral, the governments of three or more countries must participate.[43] Against the background of the BEPS Project and the subsequent series of actions initiated by the OECD/G20, countries are relying more on multilateral actions to solve common tax challenges. Multilateralism is considered a requirement of international tax justice.[44] In substance, the different parties need to reach a consensus on universal and binding rules to overcome the insufficiencies of bilateral measures.[45]

The European Union is good at practising tax multilateralism. It has actively implemented the international tax standards under the BEPS Project. Moreover, the European Union, itself, is a multilateral union that contributes to the progress of multilateralism within the internal market. The EU standard of tax good governance is a typical example of the European Union's aim to improve the tax environment internally through multilateral means, but its intention is also to expand multilateralism to third countries.[46]

China is an advocate of multilateralism as well. Although not an OECD member, China has actively participated in the BEPS Project and is relying on multilateral processes to become a norm-shaker.[47] It believes it is practising true multilateralism.[48] The BRITACOM is also a multilateral mechanism promoted by China to achieve better tax cooperation. If the CAI becomes effective, it can advance both China and the European Union's practice of regional multilateralism. Although the BRITACOM and CAI are at the beginning stages, both certainty and stability could be encouraged if China were to initiate multilateral conventions and encourage more parties to participate.

§20.4.3 Concerns

The European Union's response to further tax cooperation with China under the BRI and the CAI is impacted by the need to preserve the political autonomy of the

43. Ricardo Garcia Anton, *Substantive Multilateralism in the Context of the MLI*, in *International and EU Tax Multilateralism: Challenges Raised by the MLI*, p. 15 (A. Dourado ed., IBFD 2020).
44. Ana Paula Dourado, *International Tax Multilateralism or Reinforced Unilateralism?*, in *International and EU Tax Multilateralism: Challenges Raised by the MLI*, p. 3 (Ana Paula Dourado ed., IBFD 2020).
45. Gracia Anton, *supra* n. 43, 16.
46. Richard Lyal, *The EU and Tax Good Governance in a Multilateral Environment*, in *International and EU Tax Multilateralism: Challenges Raised by the MLI*, pp. 53-66 (Ana Paula Dourado ed., IBFD 2020).
47. For instance, China has made proposals on allocating profits according to location specific advantages, which means fairer tax allocation for developing countries. *See* Diheng Xu, *The Convergence and Divergence Between China's Implementation and OECD/G20 BEPS Minimum Standards*, 10 World Tax J. 3, 474-479 (2018).
48. Jinyan Li, *China's Rising (and the United States' Declining) Influence in Global Tax Governance? Some Observations*, 75 Bull. Intl. Taxn. 11/12, 738 (2021).

individual Member States. Individual Member States have different interests regarding tax cooperation with China. More information on China's objectives and progress, with regard to the tax cooperation framework, may lead to a better understanding between the parties. Nevertheless, it is unsure how long it will take for the European Union, as a whole, to fully embrace tax cooperation with China.

Meanwhile, the implementation of all of the tax measures in these two framework agreements may also trigger concerns in China. Although China has undergone a dramatic reform in many aspects of taxation, whether China can guarantee implementation of all the measures in a consistent and stable way remains uncertain. In the past, China had a state-oriented attitude towards taxation, always viewing taxation as an instrument to achieve governmental goals.[49] At present, it is now relying more on the rule of law to safeguard the enforcement of its actions while retaining its own features and means to achieve the rule of law.[50] Moreover, China is, in general, fiscally centralized at the central government level. Most tax policies are designed at the central government level but are implemented at the local government level. There is a distribution of spending powers, however, between the central and local governments, which is somewhat characteristic of decentralization.[51] Due to imbalanced economic development between the regions and the impact of the pandemic, local governments may have an incentive to deviate from the central government's decisions to prioritize local needs, although this is prohibited. In addition, although China has announced that it would like to increase transparency of tax information, the means to realize this raises more concerns. Turning policy goals into actions is a key step. The potential success will depend on how determined China is to embrace reform and integrate international standards.

§20.5 CONCLUSION

The European Union and China can become common norm makers within the corporate tax cooperation framework. To realize this, both parties should work on the establishment of a conceptual framework by consistently expanding the common understanding on fairness, legal certainty and the rule of law, which will provide a foundation of values for further tax cooperation.

For the European Union, the cooperation framework is providing an opportunity to rethink its approach to China. Starting from a common base, the European Union

49. Diheng Xu, *Why Does China Have a State-Oriented Attitude Towards Tax Incentives?*, 33 Aus. Tax Forum, 805-809 (2018).
50. China does not have the typical Western liberal democratic rule of law, which is based on free market capitalism, multiparty democracy, and a liberal interpretation of human rights. China has socialist rule of law with its own characteristics, which is closer to the thin rule of law. *See* Randall Peerenboom, *China's Long March toward Rule of Law*, 103-109 (Cambridge University Press 2002) and Wei Cui, *Pivoting Away from the Rule of Law*, in *The Administrative Foundations of the Chinese Fiscal State (Cambridge Tax Law Series)*, 254-268 (Cambridge University Press 2022) DOI: 10.1017/9781108868648.010.
51. Wei Cui, *The Forgotten Reform*, in *The Administrative Foundations of the Chinese Fiscal State (Cambridge Tax Law Series)*, 26-58 (Cambridge University Press 2022) DOI: 10.1017/9781108 868648.002.

will have more opportunities to further tax cooperation with China, such as updating its tax treaties with China by adopting the MLI, increasing participation in the BRI and BRITACOM, and further discussing and approving the CAI.

China, considering the concerns mentioned before, should introduce more legal certainty to guarantee the implementation of all the tax measures agreed to. This will depend also on the practice of the rule of law in China, especially for tax administrations. To achieve true multilateralism, the next step is to promote a transition from soft law to hard law through a multilateral convention.

CHAPTER 21

Ne bis in Idem: Article 4 of Protocol No. 7 to the European Convention on Human Rights*

Philip Baker

It might seem a little strange to focus a chapter on the principle *ne bis in idem* (or the principle of double jeopardy, as it is often known) and taxation in a festschrift for a leading tax academic and policymaker. However, recent case law before the European Court of Human Rights and the Court of Justice of the European Union has illustrated how important this principle has become in practice in European countries. An interest in aspects of human rights and non-discrimination in European law has also been a theme of Peter Essers' work.[1]

The focus of this chapter is on Article 4 of the Seventh Protocol to the European Convention on Human Rights (ECHR) and its impact on taxation, especially tax procedures in Europe.[2] Since the early 1950s, there have been a number of protocols added to the ECHR, some of them procedural, some of them adding new rights. The Seventh Protocol arose out of the International Covenant on Civil and Political Rights (ICCPR) which was drafted by the UN, at the worldwide level, in the 1960s. After the ICCPR was drafted, the Council of Europe noted that there were certain rights in the

---

* This chapter is based on a lecture delivered in Strasbourg.

1. See, for example, Peter Essers, *Tax Justice and European Tax Law*, 99 Steuer und Wirtschaft 2022 DOI: 10.9785/stuw-2022-990408.; Peter Essers, *International Tax Justice Between Machiavelli and Habermas (Klaus Vogel Lecture 2013)*, 68 Bulletin for International Taxation, 54 (2014); as well as a large number of related contributions in Dutch on European law.
2. There are now some 16 protocols to the European Convention. It has been a continuously developing instrument since it was signed in the 1950s. For example, the right to property was never in the original Convention; it was always in the First Protocol because at the time that it was drafted in the 1950s, it was thought that perhaps the communist countries of Eastern Europe would sign the Convention, but they would never sign up to a right to property. Hence, the right to property was put into the First Protocol rather than in the Convention.

ICCPR which were not in the ECHR and that might be added. This is where the Seventh Protocol came from; the Seventh Protocol adds a number of rights that are in the ICCPR but were not in the original ECHR. One of those rights is the principle *ne bis in idem*, which is the prohibition of double jeopardy. The protocol was unveiled in 1984, and all countries of the Council of Europe have signed it, except one. The one and only country that has not signed it is the United Kingdom. Two other countries, Germany and the Netherlands, have signed the protocol but never ratified it. With the exception of those three countries, forty-three countries have ratified it, and it has been in force since 1988.

The wording of Article 4, with some comments, is as follows: '*No one shall be liable to be* ***tried*** *or* ***punished*** – so it is prohibition of double trial or double punishment - ***again*** *in* ***criminal proceedings*** – so there must be two sets of criminal proceedings – *under the jurisdiction of the same State* – so it is a one country rule; it doesn't apply if you've been tried in one country and then you are tried again in another country – *for an offence for which he has* ***already been finally acquitted or convicted*** *in accordance with the law and penal procedure of that State*.'

Article 4 applies, therefore, to the scenario where a person[3] has been charged with a criminal offence, tried, and either acquitted or convicted, and the government then attempts to bring another trial or punish them again, in addition to the trial that has already been held or the punishment already imposed, in another round of criminal proceedings.

The double jeopardy principle has a very long history.[4] In the United Kingdom, it goes back certainly to the seventeenth century. At the time, the British Government was sometimes oppressive, and if there was a political opponent, they would charge him with a criminal offence. But often, the jury at the trial would be sympathetic, would refuse to convict, and they would acquit the person. As the person would walk out of the Court, the authorities would bring him before another court in the hope that another jury would convict him. There developed a rule that if you were brought to trial a second time, you could put in a plea of 'autrefois convict' or 'autrefois acquit'. You could say you had previously been convicted or acquitted, and that was a bar to you being tried again. The Fifth Amendment to the US Constitution also has the double jeopardy principle. So, the principle that you should not be tried twice for the same offence has been recognised nationally by some countries for several centuries.

Before getting into the tax aspects of the application of the principle, it is worth asking oneself what are the human rights concerns that one might have. Why should there be a prohibition on double jeopardy? If somebody has been charged with a criminal offence and if the jury cannot reach a verdict then (certainly in the UK), you can have a second trial if the jury cannot reach a conclusion. Why should we not be able to charge somebody twice for the same offence (even if acquitted a first time) if the evidence looks very strong against the person?

3. There is nothing that expressly limits Article 4 to individuals and not legal persons as well, and some of the reported cases involve legal persons.
4. *See, for example*, Jay Sigler, *A History of Double Jeopardy*, 7 American Journal of Legal History 283 (1963) DOI: 10.2307/844041.

There are a number of reasons why there is a double jeopardy principle. One of them goes back to that seventeenth-century situation in the UK: to prevent persecution of political opponents or people that the government does not like by repeated trials or punishment for the same offence. However, it is relatively unlikely that this reason would arise in a tax context. Protecting the finality of criminal prosecutions: one can see this as a good reason if somebody has been tried and the prosecution has presented its evidence and there has been a decision, there should be finality. A person cannot go through the rest of their life with this hanging over them. Again, this does not immediately have a great deal to do with tax. Excessive punishment for the same offence: the danger that if somebody is punished twice, then the overall cumulative punishments may be excessive. One can see how excessive punishment can be a rationale, and that may include excessive taxation and tax-related penalties. The excessive and duplicative gathering of evidence: one can imagine how oppressive it can become if a person is asked repeatedly to explain why, for example, a particular deduction was included in a tax return. The person may say 'but I've already explained it' to the tax authorities. The response might be, 'Yes, but we are the prosecution authorities. Explain it to us again', and then have another meeting. So, excessive gathering of evidence could become somewhat repressive. That may arise on the tax context.

It is quite appropriate that in the general criminal context, one might have a double jeopardy principle. However, in the tax context, it is not immediately obvious how double jeopardy ties in with tax. Some of the concerns set out above do not seem to be ones that are immediately relevant to tax. So why is it that this has become such an issue in the tax world? The reason is that in many tax systems around the world (and this is not just a European issue), a taxpayer can end up facing both an administrative penalty if they have made errors in their tax return and also if the matter is serious, they could face a criminal prosecution. The author is not aware of any country that does not have that type of scenario. In the United Kingdom, certainly if a taxpayer has submitted a careless tax return, they can face a penalty (generally up to 100% of the tax not reported in the tax return). In addition, the papers could be referred to the Public Prosecution Department, and they could (though it is not very common in the UK) face a criminal charge as well. They could end up before a judge and jury in a criminal court and could face a larger fine or imprisonment.

It is not unusual in many countries, therefore, to have both an administrative penalty (typically at a percentage of the tax – e.g., 10%, 20% or 30% of the tax) and the possibility of a criminal charge.

The reason why this engages Article 4 of the Seventh Protocol is that, for purposes of the European Convention, administrative penalties are normally regarded as 'criminal' for convention purposes. Administrative penalties of 20% or 30% of the tax are usually regarded as criminal for convention purposes; that arises most frequently under Article 6 ECHR (right to a fair trial). There is a long line of cases going back at least to *Bendenoun v. France*,[5] where the European Court of Human Rights

5. Application number 12547/86.

(ECtHR) has held that a substantial administrative penalty designed to penalise comes within the scope of a criminal charge for Article 6 purposes. The Court applies a set of criteria set out in a non-tax case, the *Engel* case, and three criteria for determining whether an administrative penalty is regarded as criminal. First, is it regarded as criminal under the national law? The national law may say it is not; it is an administrative penalty, but that is not the end of the matter. Second, one looks at the nature of the conduct of the offence and what is the penalty for. If it is for dishonesty, and it is designed to discourage the activity, it will be criminal. Finally, the severity of the punishment. The Court has said that even a 10% administrative penalty can be very severe because 10% of a large amount of tax is a large penalty, so even as low as a 10% administrative penalty can be regarded as criminal for this purpose.

For Article 4 of the Seventh Protocol, the same definition has been lifted across so that the administrative penalty (that is often imposed first) is regarded as criminal, then the papers go to the criminal prosecution department, and the criminal prosecution department then is looking to send somebody to prison or have a larger penalty. This creates the scenario of somebody being charged and brought to trial twice for essentially the same conduct; that is where the problem has arisen from this conjunction of administrative penalty and criminal penalty at the same time.

This is not a new problem. The problem began to be highlighted in the early 2000s where in cases like *Carlberg v. Sweden*[6] the taxpayer faced both a tax penalty and prosecution. All arose out of a bookkeeping offence, and the Court had to say if that was double jeopardy. The answer given in that case was that the constituent's facts were slightly different. There was a failure to pay the tax, and there was a separate bookkeeping offence. Those were not the same conduct, so it was not the same facts being punished.

Subsequent cases concluded that if it was fundamentally the same factual background that is leading to the administrative penalty – for example, the deliberate non-inclusion of an item in a tax return – and to the criminal charge, that engages the *ne bis in idem* principle.[7] The Court in *Ruotsalainen*[8] dealt with a penalty for having fuel that was only to be used for certain purposes and was low taxed, but was being used in Mr Ruotsalainen's car. It should not have been used that way, so he was subject to a fuel charge, payment of the tax and a penalty as well.

Those cases led to a run of cases that came to Strasbourg where the approach that was being taken was a very simplistic, procedural-timing approach.[9] The ECtHR asked whether the taxpayer had been subject to an administrative penalty or criminal charge

6. Application number 9631/04.
7. The requirement that the underlying factual matrix should be the same for the two penalties was emphasised by the General Court in *Sergey Zolotukhin v. Russia* [GC] (Application number 14939/03), 10 February 2009.
8. Application number 13079/03.
9. These cases included: *Kiiveri v. Finland* (Application number 53753/12); *Rinas v. Finland* (Application number 17039/13); *Osterlund v. Finland* (Application number 53197/13); *Alasippola v. Finland* (Application number 39771/12); *VP-Kuljetus Oy v. Finland* (Application number 15396/12); *Lucky Dev v. Sweden* (Application number 7356/10); *Svensson v Sweden* (Application number 51469/11); *Ask v. Sweden* (Application number 8167/11); and *Kapetanios v. Greece* (Application numbers 3453/12, 42941/12 and 9028/13).

which had become final. If, after it became final, proceedings for a further administrative penalty or criminal charge were brought or continued, that was double jeopardy. So the sole question was a time one – had the taxpayer been charged, and it had become a final penalty? If so, then a subsequent criminal charge would breach *ne bis in idem*.

To take an example: in *Kiiveri v. Finland*,[10] the taxpayer underdeclared their tax. They were liable to a tax penalty. The penalty was imposed, and they did not appeal against the penalty, so it became final. Then, the criminal prosecution started a new case. There was a final decision on a penalty; to commence criminal proceedings was a breach of the double jeopardy principle. The case went to the ECtHR in Strasbourg, and the Court confirmed that the person had been conclusively found liable for a penalty; there could not be proceedings for a second penalty in that case.

One can speculate from these cases that what was happening was that tax advisers were telling their clients to game the system. If a client had underdeclared tax and was caught out, the client should get a penalty imposed as quickly as possible and pay it and not appeal. Then, when the prosecutors come along, the taxpayer could say to them: 'you can't prosecute me; I've already been liable for the penalty'.[11]

One can review the cases and see that the taxpayer did not bother to appeal the penalty. By not appealing the penalty, the taxpayer literally received a 'get out of jail free' card. One can see that people were obviously gaming the system by accepting the first penalty.

This was obviously an unsustainable position. It was not at all surprising to find that a case eventually had to go to the Grand Chamber to determine if this approach was right or not. The Grand Chamber case is *A and B v. Norway*.[12] A and B had both deliberately failed to include certain items of income in their tax return. The Norwegian SKAT caught up with them and imposed on them a tax assessment for the tax that they should have paid, plus a 30% administrative penalty. A and B paid the penalty, and they did not appeal. Then, the file went to Økokrim (economic crime unit in Norway). Økokrim wanted to prosecute them for aggravated tax fraud, and A and B argued they could not be prosecuted as they had already paid the 30% penalty – i.e., *ne bis in idem*. The Norwegian Courts disagreed and said it must be possible to proceed with the prosecution, so eventually the case ended up in the Grand Chamber in Strasbourg.

By way of background to this case: in certain non-tax areas, there was already established case law that the same conduct might in certain circumstances give rise to more than one proceeding, which could lead to more than one penalty or adverse consequence, so long as it was appropriate and it was part of an overall integrated approach. For example, if you were a doctor and you acted with gross negligence and your patient died. You might be subject to a professional procedure which struck you off as a doctor, but then if your negligence was so extreme you might be subject to a

10. Application number 53753/12.
11. In some cases, the taxpayer encouraged a criminal prosecution, in which they were successful because of the higher burden of proof. The taxpayer could then use that acquittal to prevent even an administrative penalty being imposed.
12. Application numbers 24130/11 and 29758/11 – Grand Chamber, judgment of 15 November 2016.

criminal prosecution as well. It was felt that that was perfectly appropriate because this was part of an integrated approach; you do not want to have doctors who are dangerous still in practice. Or, for example, a company director who might have defrauded the company might be liable to a criminal prosecution penalty or a fine, but they may also be subject to a procedure that disqualified them as a director for the future. Or, for example, if you are a dangerous driver, you might be subject to a penalty for your driving and you might also have your licence taken away. The Court has held in those areas that, so long as it is part of an appropriate, integrated approach to the consequences of the conduct, then it is appropriate to have more than one procedure.

Essentially, that is what the Court concluded in *A and B v. Norway*. In this case, the Grand Chamber of the Court abandoned the approach which one saw in the earlier cases and said that as a matter of principle there is no prohibition in duplicated proceedings in Article 4 of the Seventh Protocol. There is not an absolute ban on being charged or tried twice as long as they are part of an integrated approach. The Grand Chamber said as follows:

> 123. It cannot be the effect of Article 4 of Protocol No. 7 that the Contracting States are prohibited from organising their legal systems so as to provide for the imposition of a standard administrative penalty on wrongfully unpaid tax (albeit a penalty qualifying as 'criminal' for the purposes of the Convention's fair-trial guarantees). This also holds true in those more serious cases where it may be appropriate to prosecute the offender for an additional element present in the non-payment, such as fraudulent conduct, which is not addressed in the 'administrative' tax-recovery procedure. The object of Article 4 of Protocol No. 7 is to prevent the injustice of a person being prosecuted or punished twice for the same criminalised conduct. *It does not, however, outlaw legal systems which take an 'integrated' approach to the social wrongdoing in question, and in particular an approach involving parallel stages of legal response to the wrongdoing by different authorities and for different purposes.*

As long as there is an integrated approach (whatever that might mean: that is what one has to have ask of this decision), then the fact that a taxpayer is facing both an administrative penalty and criminal prosecution is not of itself a breach so long as the two together are part of an integrated process.

Carrying on with the judgment:

> 130. On the basis of the foregoing review of the Court's case-law, it is evident that, in relation to matters subject to repression under both criminal and administrative law, *the surest manner of ensuring compliance with Article 4 of Protocol No. 7 is the provision, at some appropriate stage, of a single-track procedure* enabling the parallel strands of legal regulation of the activity concerned to be brought together, so that the different needs of society in responding to the offence can be addressed within the framework of a single process … .

That recommendation of having a single-track procedure has had an impact in a number of European countries where, after this judgment came out, the government reviewed the procedure which they had in serious tax cases. Instead of having the tax authorities doing one thing and the criminal prosecutions doing another, for the first time, they brought them together and required them to act in an integrated fashion. The single-track procedure may lead to both a penalty and a prosecution, but they are worked together on the same track rather than two parallel procedures:

> Nonetheless, as explained above (see notably paragraphs 111 and 117-20), Article 4 of Protocol No. 7 does not exclude the conduct of dual sets of proceedings, even to their term, provided that certain conditions are fulfilled. In particular, for the Court to be satisfied that there is no duplication ('bis') of trial or punishment as proscribed by Article 4 of Protocol No. 7, the respondent State must demonstrate convincingly that the dual sets of proceedings in question have been *sufficiently closely connected in substance and in time* ... .

The Court has been applying this approach since then. It has been looking at the proceedings and asking if the administrative penalty and the criminal prosecution were sufficiently closely connected in substance. Was the gathering of the evidence all a single process, and was the taxpayer given the same protections. Were the proceedings sufficiently closely connected in time: one cannot have an administrative penalty and then five years later the criminal prosecution. They must be in close proximity to one another. The test is whether the proceedings are sufficiently closely connected in substance and in time:

> In other words, it must be shown that they have been *combined in an integrated manner so as to form a coherent whole.* This implies not only that the purposes pursued and the means used to achieve them should in essence be complementary and linked in time, but also that the possible consequences of organising the legal treatment of the conduct concerned in such a manner should be *proportionate and foreseeable for the persons affected.*

The Grand Chamber has brought into the assessment also proportionality and foreseeability. Could the taxpayer, when they left this item out of their tax return, have foreseen that they could face both a penalty and criminal prosecution? Was it foreseeable and proportionate that they might face both?

The Court gave some additional guidance by identifying material factors for determining *whether there is a sufficiently close connection in substance*:

> First, whether the different proceedings *pursue complementary purposes* and thus address, not only in abstracto but also in concreto, different aspects of the social misconduct involved.

The Court asks if this is an appropriate response to what the taxpayer has done there - *whether the duality of proceedings concerned is a foreseeable consequence*, both in law and in practice, of the same impugned conduct (*'in idem'*):

> 132. ...- whether the relevant sets of proceedings are conducted in such a manner as to avoid *as far as possible any duplication in the collection and in the assessment of the evidence*, notably through adequate interaction between the various competent authorities to ensure that the establishment of the facts in one set of proceedings is replicated in the other;
>
> - and, *above all, whether the sanction imposed in the proceedings which become final first is taken into account in those which become final last, so as to prevent the situation where the individual concerned is in the end made to bear an excessive burden*, this latter risk being least likely to be present where there is in place *an*

offsetting mechanism designed to ensure that the overall quantum of any penalties imposed is proportionate.

Thus, if the taxpayer has had to pay a 30% administrative fine, that should be taken into account by the criminal courts, so the criminal court says, 'we would have sent you to prison for five years and made you pay €500,000 fine but because you've already paid €300,000 we will send you to prison for five years and will only make you pay €200,000'. Or, 'we will only send you to prison for four years rather than five years because you've already acknowledged that you had a liability, and you paid the tax, and you have had a penalty, so the court must make certain that overall the total penalties are not excessive'.

It is appropriate to summarise where we are after *A and B Norway*. The *Engel* test determines whether the administrative penalty is characterised as a criminal charge. One looks at the facts to see if it is the same conduct that is being penalised. Duplicated proceedings are permitted if they form 'an integrated system of sanctions' and 'there is a sufficiently close connection, both in substance and in time, between the decision on the tax penalties and the subsequent criminal conviction ... '. There are various safeguards, including no overall excessive burden.

Subsequent to *A and B*, there has been a series of cases before the ECtHR on the application of *A and B* which show that it is not so easy to apply in practice. Determining whether there has been a sufficiently integrated set of proceedings is actually quite hard.

In *Johannesson v. Iceland*,[13] the proceedings were not sufficiently close in time to constitute a single, integrated procedure. On the one hand, in *Ingvarsdottir v. Iceland*,[14] the taxpayer faced a single, integrated procedure, so they brought the two together there. On the other hand, in *Thorisson v. Iceland*,[15] there was not a single, integrated procedure – there was an independent collection of evidence; the tax authorities and the criminal prosecution carried out separate gathering of evidence.[16]

The most recent case of *Goulandris and Vardinogianni v. Greece*[17] is not a tax case, but it applies to *A and B*. The Court again emphasised the need for an integrated approach to the different penalties.

The Grand Chamber has established the approach to double jeopardy in tax cases, but exactly what it means in practice remains unclear. We know that it is very

13. Application number 22007/11.
14. Application number 22779/14.
15. Application number 52623/14.
16. Subsequent cases have included *Armannsson v. Iceland* (Application number 72098/14) (not a single, integrated procedure); *Kristjansson v. Iceland* (Application number 12951/18) (not a single, integrated procedure – double collection of evidence; criminal case went on for two extra years); *Milosevic v. Croatia* (Application number 12022/16) (not a single, integrated procedure; a minor offence fine followed by 100x surcharge – no account taken of fine); *Rinas v. Finland* (Application number 17039/13) (tax fraud proceedings concluded, but tax penalty appeal continued – breach); *Osterlund v. Finland* (Application number 53197/13) (tax fraud proceedings concluded, but tax penalty appeal continued – breach); *Alasippola v. Finland* (Application number 39771/12) (parallel proceedings but taxpayer failed to raise *ne bis* issue); *VP-Kuljetus Oy v. Finland* (Application number 15396/12) (fuel fee proceedings and tax fraud proceedings did not arise from same facts).
17. *Goulandris and Vardinogianni v. Greece* (App no. 1735/13) Judgment of 16.6.2022.

clearly the right side of the line if the tax authorities and the criminal prosecution have a single, one-track approach. If they gather the evidence once and they bring the matter forward as quickly as possible within the same timeframe, that should satisfy the principle. However, once there is a separate gathering of evidence and, in particular, if there is a gap in time between the administrative penalty proceedings and the criminal proceedings, there may well be an issue with Article 4 of the Seventh Protocol. This raises the question as to whether this issue needs to go back to the Grand Chamber for a reexamination. Though one sees the principle in *A and B*, exactly how that works out in practice is not immediately clear.

Meanwhile, in Luxembourg, *ne bis in idem* is also found in Article 50 of the European Union Charter of Fundamental Rights.[18] Recently, we have been seeing a number of cases coming to the Court of Justice in Luxembourg on the same issue as was coming to the ECtHR in Strasbourg. The leading CJEU case in this area is probably *Menci*.[19] The case concerned VAT (hence, it came within the scope of European law).[20] The taxpayer faced an administrative penalty for non-declaration and non-payment of VAT and then a prosecution. The CJEU referred to the ECtHR decision in *A and B*. However, the CJEU applied a slightly different approach from the ECtHR. It accepted that there is no absolute ban on duplication of proceedings. However, the rights in the Charter of Fundamental Rights are subject to an explicit justification provision in Article 52.[21] The focus of the European Court in Luxembourg has been on the justification for the breach.[22] The CJEU asks whether the duplication was necessary.

18. Article 50 provides:

> Article 50 – Right not to be tried or punished twice in criminal proceedings for the same criminal offence
>
> 'No one shall be liable to be tried or punished again in criminal proceedings for an offence for which he or she has already been finally acquitted or convicted within the Union in accordance with the law.'

19. Case C-524/15 – 20 March 2018 (Grand Chamber).
20. The earlier case of *Akerberg Fransson* (Case C-617/10 – 26 February 2013 Grand Chamber) (VAT and income tax – tax surcharge and criminal prosecution – Article 50 did not preclude duplication if first proceedings are not criminal) confirmed that the provision in the Charter might apply as, in imposing VAT, the Member State is implementing the VAT Directives and hence applying EU law.
21. Article 52 – Scope and interpretation

> 1. Any limitation on the exercise of the rights and freedoms recognised by this Charter must be provided for by law and respect the essence of those rights and freedoms. Subject to the principle of proportionality, limitations may be made only if they are necessary and genuinely meet objectives of general interest recognised by the Union or the need to protect the rights and freedoms of others.

22. This is seen in the more recent cases on the principle *ne bis in idem* before the CJEU:

> *BV v. Haute Savoie* (C-570/20) – 5th May 2022 (VAT – administrative penalty and criminal penalty in cases of serious offences – French law only looked at financial sanctions to check if penalty is excessive – potential breach).
>
> *Dual Prod* (C-412/21) – 23rd March 2023 (Excise duty – warehouse – authorisation suspended for 8 months – then criminal prosecution and suspension pending outcome (already over 3 years) – also potential breach of presumption of innocence)

Was it in accordance with the law? Did it achieve an acceptable social purpose, and did it have a result that was not disproportionate?

The European Court has taken a slightly different approach to the ECtHR and is coming to not exactly the same landing point as the ECtHR. The approach is similar in that it also allows duplicate procedures, but the CJEU asks whether the procedures produced a disproportionate interference with the rights of the taxpayer which could not be justified. Thus, the current position is a somewhat nuanced difference between the approach in Strasbourg of *A and B*, which is giving problems in practice, and the Court of Justice in Luxembourg.

All this leads to the ultimate question: does the whole issue of *ne bis in idem* in relation to tax matters need to be reconsidered? If one were to ask what are the real human rights/taxpayer rights concerns with duplicated proceedings, the major issue would seem to be that the overall penalty should not be excessive. In most tax cases, the broader concerns for duplicated criminal proceedings – potentially oppressive and discriminatory treatment – are not present. It may be unpleasant for a taxpayer who has committed (or been charged) with a serious tax offence to have to answer questions from the tax authorities and the police/prosecution authorities, but it is hardly a major breach of the taxpayer's rights. Equally, proceedings that continue in time because of the two sets of proceedings may be unpleasant but again hardly a major issue. Once duplicated proceedings are seen to be compatible with the *ne bis in idem* principle, they should be integrated as far as possible. However, so long as they do not together result in an excessive overall penalty, one may say that the major protection of the double jeopardy principle in respect of tax matters has been achieved.

Vinal AD (C-820/21) – 14th Sept 2023 (Excise duty – warehouse – withdrawal of authorization and financial penalty (c. 130,000 Euros) – duplication may be justified if not disproportionate).

CHAPTER 22

Tax Whistleblowing in a Digitalized Taxation Model: The Need for Legal Protection of the Whistleblowing Tax Official

Bruno Peeters & Sylvie De Raedt

§22.1 INTRODUCTION

For several years, the European Court of Human Rights (ECtHR) has been prepared to qualify the public reporting of wrongdoing as an aspect of the right to the freedom of expression enshrined in Article 10 of the European Convention of Human Rights (ECHR).[1] Dismissals or even criminal convictions resulting from this type of public reporting (or 'whistleblowing') are considered interferences with this right. This allows the Court to assess the proportionality of these interferences.[2] In the recent *Halet* case,[3] the ECtHR had to judge on whistleblowing in the tax context. In this case, an offshoot of the so-called Lux Leaks scandal, the Court had to rule on the public disclosure of highly advantageous tax rulings negotiated between a tax consultancy firm and the Luxembourg tax authorities. The whistleblower was an employee of the tax consultancy firm, and the Grand Chamber of the ECtHR ultimately considered the criminal conviction of the (former) employee a violation of Article 10 of the ECHR.

In the European Union, the European Parliament and the Council recently adopted the Whistleblowing Directive,[4] which provides legal protection for people

1. European Court of Human Rights, *Fact Sheet – whistleblowers and the freedom to impart and receive information*, February 2023, 9 p.
2. Article 10 §2 ECHR.
3. ECtHR, 14 February 2023, Halet/Luxembourg (Grand Chamber).
4. Directive (EU) 2019/1937 of the European Parliament and of the Council of 23 October 2019 on the protection of persons who report breaches of Union law.

working for (or in contact with) a public or private organization who are aware of threats or harm to the public interest and wish to report it. The Directive explicitly refers to corporate tax law violations or tax abuse as examples of such threats to the public interest, as these practices can have a negative impact on the proper functioning of the internal market.[5] It seems clear that the European legislator mainly had harmful corporate practices in mind when referring to tax-related malpractices.

However, in the light of the increasing use of artificial intelligence (AI) by public authorities, including tax authorities,[6] and the risks associated with the use of AI, the question arises whether society could benefit from the protection of public servants including tax officials in case of (public) reporting of wrongdoing related to the use of AI (tax) tools. Public scandals such as the Dutch childcare benefits scandal or the Australian *Robodebt* case clearly demonstrate the risk that careless use of AI by public authorities can pose to citizens' fundamental rights, including their right not to be discriminated (*see* §22.2).

This chapter first explores the need for such a legal protection (*see* §22.2) and will then examine the current legal protection of (tax) officials seeking to report harmful AI practices (*see* §22.3). We conclude with legislative suggestions (*see* §22.4).

§22.2 THE RISK OF AI TOOLS IN TAX PRACTICE AND THE NEED FOR PROTECTING THE WHISTLEBLOWING TAX OFFICIAL

§22.2.1 The Risk of AI Tools in Tax Practice

Society is increasingly aware of the damage AI can cause. In many cases, this harm is unintentionally caused by the careless use of AI. Public coverage of cases of harmful effects caused by careless use of AI contributes to public awareness of this problem.

In 2019, newspapers reported on the gender bias in the Goldman Sachs' AI-driven credit scoring system used for Apple Card credit lines, as huge differences in credit scores between male and female customers were discovered.[7] Although the credit scoring system was not based on gender data, according to the company, the system still discriminated against women. Stories were made public about married couples, filing a joint tax return in which the man received a credit line 20 times higher than the woman's. A few years earlier, several news media reported on a similar gender bias in Amazon's AI recruitment tool.[8] This recruiting tool used AI to give candidates scores ranging from one to five stars. In 2015, the company realized that the tool favoured male candidates for software developer jobs simply because the AI models were trained

5. Directive (EU) 2019/1937, Preambule nmbr 6.
6. AI Taxadmin.EU University of Antwerp (3 October 2023) https://www.uantwerpen.be/en/projects/aitax/.
7. Taylor Telford, *Apple Card Algorithm Sparks Gender Bias Allegations Against Goldman Sachs*, The Washington Post (11 November 2019) https://www.washingtonpost.com/business/2019/11/11/apple-card-algorithm-sparks-gender-bias-allegations-against-goldman-sachs/.
8. Jeffrey Dastin, *Amazon Scraps Secret AI Recruiting Tool That Showed Bias Against Women*, Reuters (11 October 2018) https://www.reuters.com/article/us-amazon-com-jobs-automation-insight-idUSKCN1MK08G.

on resumes in the tech industry that came primarily from men, which is no surprise in a male-dominated industry like technology. Thus, the AI model taught itself that male candidates were preferred, which was caused by the overrepresentation of resumes of male employees used in the AI model. Only recently, newspapers reported on a Belgian man who ended his life following a six-week-long conversation with an artificial intelligent chatbot about the climate crisis.[9] The man, who was extremely eco-anxious, was encouraged by the chatbot to put an end to his life after he proposed sacrificing himself to save the planet. The media coverage of these cases was clearly a revelation to the public and forced the companies involved to adapt their systems.

Similar stories exist for AI used by public authorities. Both the childcare benefits scandal in the Netherlands and the *Robodebt* scandal in Australia show how blind reliance on AI systems to underpin legal decisions of public authorities can lead to tragedies for citizens. In the Netherlands, an AI system used to detect childcare benefit fraud wrongly identified low-income families as fraudsters, forcing them to repay large sums of legally obtained benefits. One of the causes of the tragedy was the illegal use of (dual) nationality data to feed the AI model, leading to racial profiling.[10] A similar scandal took place in Australia with a system designed to automatically recover allegedly overpaid welfare benefits. The system was inaccurate and led to heavy public criticism. As with the Dutch scandal, the Australian government was slow to respond to the troubling signals,[11] and it took public notice to force them to action.

Today, research shows that AI is used by the majority of tax authorities in the European Union, and little is known about how these authorities deal with the unwanted risks that AI can bring.[12]

§22.2.2 The Need for Protecting Whistleblowers in the Field of AI Tools for Taxation

From a legal point of view, the European Commission tries to mitigate the risks from the use of AI with a Regulation that is in its final stages at the time this text was submitted for publication.[13] This Proposal for a Regulation, known as the 'AI Act',

9. La Libre, 'Sans ces conversation avec le chatbot Eliza, mon mari serait touours là', 28 March 2023.
10. D. Hadwick and S. Lan, 'Lessons to Be Learned from the Dutch Childcare Allowance Scandal: A Comparative Review of Algorithmic Governance by Tax Administrations in the Netherlands, France and Germany', *World Tax Journal*, 2021, 13:4; D. Hadwick, S. De Raedt and A. Van de Vijver, 'De toeslagenaffaire in Nederland. Aanleiding tot evaluatie van het fiscaal algoritmisch bestuur in België', *Tijdschrift voor Fiscaal Recht*, 2023, pp. 387-405.
11. Report of the Royal Commission into the Robodebt Scheme, 7 July 2023, https://robodebt.royalcommission.gov.au/publications/report (accessed 6 October 2023); Question O-000028/2022 of the European Parliament to the European Commission, 28 June 2022 on the Dutch childcare benefit scanda, institutional racism and algorithms: https://www.europarl.europa.eu/doceo/document/O-9-2022-000028_EN.html (accessed 3 October 2023).
12. *Supra* n. 6.
13. Proposal for a regulation of the European Parliament and of the Council on laying down harmonized rules on artificial intelligence (Artificial Intelligence Act) and amending certain Union legislative acts, 21 April 2021 (COM(2021) 206 final – C9-0146/2021 – 2021/0106(COD)) (https://eur-lex.europa.eu/legal-content/EN/TXT/HTML/?uri=CELEX:52021PC0206).

establishes a set of quality standards applicable to providers and users of AI. To enforce these standards, the Proposal for the AI Act combines different systems, depending on the risk of the AI system. For so-called high-risk applications, such as AI used for law enforcement (Article 6 of the Proposal of a Regulation for AI, referring to Annexe III.6), the Proposal for the AI Act provides for *ex ante* conformity assessment audits with possible *ex post* supervision by the competent authorities. However, due to consideration 38 *in fine* to the Proposal for a Regulation on AI, AI used by tax and customs authorities for administrative proceedings should not be considered high-risk AI systems used by law enforcement authorities.

However, AI tools used by tax authorities to detect, for example, tax fraud, are in any case subject to the requirements of the General Data Protection Regulation (GDPR) which focuses on the processing of personal data, including data processing through AI (Article 2.1 of the GDPR). Similar enforcement mechanisms apply under the GDPR. As with the Proposal for the AI Act, there is a strong emphasis on accountability (*see* Article 5.2 of the GDPR). Several provisions in the GDPR aim to force the data processor to verify compliance with the data protection principles through *ex ante* compliance assessments and document this self-assessment (*see* Articles 24 to 43 of the GDPR). Although data processing can also be monitored retrospectively and competent authorities can impose sanctions (Articles 51 to 59 and Article 83 of the GDPR), including heavy fines for violations of the GDPR principles, enforcement of the latter principles still relies heavily on the strength of self-assessment. This is especially true for the processing of personal data by public authorities since the mechanism of fines, which are related to the turnover of the companies that breach the GDPR (Article 83.4 of the GDPR), is clearly designed for the private sector.

Public disclosures by whistleblowers are considered as an upstream component of law enforcement, as the information disclosed by whistleblowers can feed legal enforcement systems, leading to effective detection, investigation and prosecution of the law.[14] In the enforcement context described in the previous paragraphs, with a high reliance on self-assessment, whistleblowing can help to enforce the principles of both the GDPR and the Proposal for the AI Act. Legal protection of whistleblowers in the field of technology (so-called tech whistleblowers) could therefore ensure compliance with existing legal principles for the careful use of AI. Moreover, public disclosure of malfunctioning AI systems has historically forced companies and governments to adjust their models (as was discussed in section 22.2.1 of this §22.2), even before legal action was taken. This is important because in some cases it is not always clear why AI caused an undesirable outcome, let alone which legal provision was violated. In the childcare benefits scandal, for example, a thorough investigation was needed to find out what caused the wrongful childcare benefits reimbursement decisions. In this case, the Dutch Data Protection Authority ultimately decided that using nationality to feed the fraud detection algorithm violated several provisions of the GDPR.[15] In many cases,

14. *See* Directive (EU) 2019/1937, Preambule nmbr 2.
15. Autoriteit Persoonsgegevens, *Belastingdienst – Verwerking van persoonsgegevens in de Fraude Signale Voorziening, Rapport nr. z2020-04615* 61 (2021); D. Hadwick and S. Lan, *Lessons to Be Learned from the Dutch Childcare Allowance Scandal: A Comparative Review of Algorithmic*

the undesirable outcome of the AI model is not caused by a clear violation of the law,[16] and data scientists are even puzzled as to why a complex AI model generates a specific outcome. Legal protection of whistleblowers who alert society on unwanted or unethical outcomes of AI models could therefore also contribute to a more careful and ethical use of AI in general.

Companies are critical of public reporting on the malfunctioning of AI and fear overreporting by employees who are afraid of losing their jobs and being replaced by AI.[17] This argument seems not strong enough to argue against the legal protection of tech whistleblowers. However, the risk of overreporting seems to be an element to be taken into account in a balanced legal protection of these tech whistleblowers, as will be discussed in §22.3.

§22.3 THE LEGAL PROTECTION OF TAX OFFICIALS REPORTING HARMFUL AI PRACTICES

The aforementioned Whistleblowing Directive sets common minimum standards for the protection of whistleblowers (Article 2.1 Whistleblowing Directive). However, the scope of the Directive is limited to persons reporting certain breaches of EU law (Article 2.1 a, b and C Whistleblowing Directive).[18] As discussed in the previous §22.2, the cause of malfunctioning AI is not always clear, especially when complex AI models are used, nor is the breach of any legal provision. Therefore, it is doubtful that a whistleblower who reports on harmful AI practices will find legal protection in the Whistleblowing Directive.

The legal protection provided in Article 10 ECHR is not limited to whistleblowing about violations of law. It extends to the freedom to provide information in general. Therefore, we will examine below the extent to which the tax official who wishes to report the malfunctioning of AI tools is protected by the right to freedom of expression enshrined in Article 10 of the ECHR.

Governance by Tax Administrations in the Netherlands, France and Germany, 13:4 World Tax Journal (2021); D. Hadwick, S. De Raedt and A. Van de Vijver, *De toeslagenaffaire in Nederland. Aanleiding tot evaluatie van het fiscaal algoritmisch bestuur in België*, Tijdschrift voor Fiscaal Recht 387, 405 (2023).

16. *See, for example,* the case discussed in section 22.2.1 of this §22.2 on the gender bias in the Goldman Sachs' AI-driven credit scoring system used for Apple Card credit lines, where no gender data was used to build the AI model.
17. Makenzie Holland, *Whistleblower Risk Rises with AI Policy Adoption*, TechTarget (28 October 2022) https://www.techtarget.com/searchcio/news/252526681/Whistleblower-risk-rises-with-AI-policy-adoption.
18. The only 'exception' to that rule can be found in the tax field, where the legal protection of whistleblowers extends not only to acts that breach the rules of corporate tax law but also to tax abuse (Article 2.1.c of the Whistleblowing Directive). Whistleblowers reporting on arrangements the purpose of which is to obtain a tax advantage that defeats the object or purpose of the applicable corporate tax law (but do not breach the applicable corporate tax law provision as such) can therefore also benefit from the legal protection provided by the Whistleblowing Directive. However, in these cases, there will in general be an anti-abuse provision in place that is then breached.

As mentioned in the introduction (§22.1), the ECtHR considers public reporting of wrongdoing as an aspect of the right to the freedom of expression enshrined in Article 10 of the ECHR. Dismissals or other forms of retaliation resulting from whistleblowing activities are therefore qualified as interferences with this right. If the Court assesses that these interferences do not meet the requirements of Article 10 § 2 ECHR (being: the requirement of legality, necessity and legitimacy), it will conclude that the right to freedom of expression has been violated. The whistleblower can then seek legal redress under the rules of the applicable national legal system. This whistleblower protection is fragmented across Member States and uneven across policy areas,[19] but the recognition of an interference in the whistleblowing activities, such as a criminal conviction or a dismissal, as disproportionate is at least an important starting point in the legal protection of whistleblowers.

The ECtHR developed clear and specific criteria to assess whistleblowing activities in the well-known *Guja* judgment of 2008.[20] Since this ruling, however, there have been several developments regarding the place whistleblowers now occupy in democratic societies and the leading role they can play by uncovering information of public interest, and regarding the European and international legal framework (such as the 2019 Whistleblower Directive).[21] Therefore in the recent *Halet* case,[22] the Court took the opportunity to confirm and refine its existing criteria. The *Halet* judgment therefore provides an ideal legal framework to assess the legal protection of tax officials involved in the problematic use of AI by tax authorities.

In short, Mr Halet was an employee of a large tax consulting firm. Between 2012 and 2014, several hundred tax rulings and tax returns prepared by this firm were published in various media. These publications drew attention to a practice of highly advantageous tax agreements concluded between the firm, acting on behalf of its client (multinational companies) and the Luxembourg tax authorities. An initial internal investigation revealed that a colleague of Mr Halet had copied and handed these documents over to a journalist and that Mr Halet had contacted the same journalist and offered to hand over additional documents revealing the same practice that his colleague had previously revealed. The publication of the documents was later dubbed '*Luxleaks*'. As a result of these publications, the firm had a difficult year. After this year, however, the company posted an increased turnover which was accompanied by a significant expansion of its workforce. Mr Halet and his colleague were convicted by a Luxemburg criminal court of theft, breach of professional secrecy and some other offences and sentenced to a (suspended) term of imprisonment, a fine of EUR 1.000 and a token amount of one euro to the company as compensation for damages. Mr Halet and his colleague appealed and invoked Article 10 of the ECHR as a legal ground for their request to the Luxemburg Court to grant them the 'whistleblower' status.

19. *See* Directive (EU) 2019/1937, Preambule nmbr 4.
20. ECtHR 12 February 2008, Guja/Moldova.
21. ECtHR, 14 February 2023, Halet/Luxembourg, cons. 120.
22. ECtHR, 14 February 2023, Halet/Luxembourg, cons. 120.

After assessing the ECtHR's Guja criteria, the Luxembourg Court of Appeal concluded that the applicant was *not* entitled to the full protection of Article 10 of the ECHR but only to the recognition of mitigating circumstances because Mr Halet acted in good faith and from honourable motives. For these reasons, Mr Halet was exempted from imprisonment, but the fine and sentence ordering him to pay the sum of one euro as compensation for damages suffered by the company were upheld. The ECtHR, in a judgment of 11 May 2021, found that the national courts in Luxembourg had fairly balanced the interests involved and concluded, five votes to two, that there was *no* violation of Article 10 of the ECHR. However, the applicant requested the referral of the case to the Grand Chamber. In its judgment of 14 February 2023, the Grand Chamber assessed the case against the confirmed and refined Guja criteria and came to the opposite conclusion and decided, twelve votes to five, that there *has* been a violation of Article 10 of the ECHR. In the following paragraphs, we discuss the elements of the Court's assessment that are relevant to assessing the legal status of the tax official who wishes to publicly report on malfunctioning AI tools.

A first important element relates to the fact that the Court emphasizes that the whistleblowers' freedom of speech protection regime is likely to be applied when the employee or civil servant in question is the only person, or part of a small category of persons, aware of what is happening at work and thus is best placed to act in the public interest by alerting the employer or the general public.[23] This is particularly the case for the tax officials dealing with AI tools. Where a large group of tax officials, including the management of the tax authorities, is not involved in the AI practice, only a small group of data scientists will work with AI on a daily basis and thus may be aware (first) of undesirable outcomes resulting from the use of AI. However, the Court also takes into account the duty of loyalty, restraint and discretion employees and officials have towards their employer when trying to find a fair balance between the right to the freedom of expression and the reciprocal rights and obligations specific to employment contracts and the professional environment.[24] In some cases, this duty of loyalty includes the obligation to comply with a statutory duty of secrecy,[25] as was the case in the *Halet* judgment, but will definitely also be the case for whistleblowing tax officials. This duty of loyalty, reserve and discretion and in some cases even a duty of secrecy is coupled with one of the Guja criteria for assessing the proportionality of the interference with the right to freedom of expression (such as any form of retaliation), namely, the availability of alternative channels or other effective means for the employee or official to report or remedy the alleged wrongdoing (such as reporting to the person's superior or another competent authority or body).[26]

This brings us to a second element of the *Halet* case that is important in assessing the legal position of the whistleblowing tax official who wishes to report publicly on harmful AI, and at the same time, the first criterion used by the Court to assess

23. ECtHR, 14 February 2023, Halet/Luxembourg, cons. 116; ECtHR 12 February 2008, Guja/Moldova, cons. § 72; ECtHR 21 July 2011, Heinisch/Germany, cons. 63.
24. ECtHR, 14 February 2023, Halet/Luxembourg, cons. 116.
25. ECtHR 14 February 2023, Halet/Luxembourg, cons 119.
26. ECtHR 14 February 2023, Halet/Luxembourg, cons. 117.

whistleblowing activities in the light of Article 10 of the ECHR: *the availability of internal reporting channels*. The Court emphasizes that – in principle – priority should be given to these internal reporting channels, such as the person's superior or other competent authorities or bodies. Internal reporting is considered the best way to reconcile an employee's or public servant's duty of loyalty with the public interest served by disclosure.[27] Applied to the context of tech whistleblowers, this criterion seems to be an important safeguard against companies' fear of overreporting AI risks as a method of preventing AI replacement of employees by AI. At the same time, this criterion implies an obligation for companies and public authorities using AI to have these internal reporting mechanisms in place and to ensure that they are functioning properly. The Court accepts that whistleblowers may use 'external reporting' if internal reporting mechanisms do not exist or are clearly impracticable, unreliable or ineffective.[28] Thus, the tax official who becomes aware of the harmful effects of AI will need to ascertain whether internal reporting mechanisms exist within the tax administration. Information about malfunctioning AI tools can only be disclosed to the public as a last resort if these channels do not exist or are not functioning properly. However, if a tax official is aware of the existence of internal disclosure channels and fails to use them, it is sufficient that he can provide a convincing explanation for this.[29] If a whistleblower is likely to be exposed to retaliation, the Court will accept that the whistleblower does not use these internal channels.[30] Internal channels should therefore be used only if they seem 'appropriate' to the Court.[31] Against the background of the recent history with examples of malfunctioning AI used by public authorities and their enormous impact on a large number of citizens (as was the case in the child benefits scandal and the *Robodebt* case) and the highly sensitive nature of these scandals from a political perspective (as was the case in the Netherlands where the prime minister had to resign because of the scandal caused by this careless use of AI), it seems very difficult for a tax official faced with an undesirable outcome due to the use of AI tools to assess the appropriateness of the internal channels.

A second criterion to assess whistleblowing activities relates to the *authenticity of the disclosed information*. Anyone who chooses to disclose information must carefully consider, as far as circumstances permit, whether that information is accurate and reliable.[32] Fortunately, however, the ECtHR accepts that a person may enjoy whistleblowing protection when information is subsequently found to be inaccurate if that whistleblower has diligently taken steps to verify the authenticity of the disclosed

27. ECtHR 14 February 2023, Halet/Luxembourg, cons. 121.
28. ECtHR 12 February 12, 2008, Guja/Moldova, cons. 73; ECtHR 21 July 2011, Heinisch/Germany, cons. 73-74; ECtHR 12 February 2008, Guja/Moldova, cons. 82-83.
29. ECtHR 14 February 2023, Halet/Luxembourg, cons. 121, with reference to ECtHR 12 October 2010, Bathellier/France and ECtHR 22 November 2011, Stanciulescu/Romania.
30. ECtHR 14 February 2023, Halet/Luxembourg, cons. 122.
31. ECtHR 14 February 2023, Halet/Luxembourg, cons. 123.
32. ECtHR 12 February 2008, Guja/Moldova, cons. 75; *see also* ECtHR 16 February 2021, Gawlik/Liechtenstein, where a doctor publicly raised suspicion of euthanasia taking place in the hospital he worked for. The Court considered that the doctor had been negligent in verifying the information.

information to the extent possible.[33] Thus, if a tax official has serious reasons to believe that an AI model is functioning inaccurately or appears to have discriminatory effects, that tax official cannot lose the protection of Article 10 of the ECHR merely because, after investigation, it turns out that the model is functioning properly after all. The ECtHR will therefore test the criterion of the authenticity of the disclosed information against the criterion of the whistleblower's good faith,[34] which is another important criterion assessed by the Court in this type of whistleblowing cases. Provided that the whistleblower is not pursuing unlawful or unethical objectives, the ECtHR seems even willing to consider any whistleblower as having acted in good faith if he or she had reasonable grounds to believe that the disclosed information was true, even if it later turns out that it was not.[35]

Returning to the *good faith criterion* assessed by the Court, this appears to be another safeguard against excessive reporting of malfunctioning AI tools. According to the ECtHR, the motive behind the actions of the reporting employee determines whether or not a particular disclosure should be protected.[36] If the whistleblower was motivated by a desire for personal gain, or harboured a personal grievance against his or her employer, the protection of Article 10 of the ECHR cannot be granted.

The Court also assesses the *public interest in the disclosed information* as a criterion for deciding the proportionality of the interference in whistleblowing activities. In cases where AI used by tax authorities unfairly targets certain (categories of) citizens and government decisions are blindly based on this biased AI outcome, the public interest in the disclosed information seems undeniable. Information pertaining to the proper functioning of public authorities will generally be considered information of public interest, as acts or omissions of the government should be closely monitored not only by legislative and judicial authorities but also by public opinion.[37] While information about illegal acts or practices is considered by the Court as undeniably of particularly high public interest,[38] the information disclosed need not necessarily relate to violations of the law, as is the case in the Whistleblowing Directive. In the *Halet* case, for example, the advantageous tax rulings between the Luxembourg tax authorities and the multinationals represented by the tax consultancy firm in question did not violate any (tax) legislation. Therefore, cases of malfunctioning AI that lead to unethical outcomes, such as singling out certain (groups of) citizens for tax audits as a result of, for example, the overrepresentation of data on these groups in the AI model, can be considered as information with public interest.

The public interest in the information disclosed must be weighed against *the caused detriment* to the public government involved.[39] In this regard, the Court has already accepted that disclosure may harm the government for a loss of public

33. ECtHR 14 February 2023, Halet/Luxembourg, cons. 126.
34. ECtHR 14 February 2023, Halet/Luxembourg, cons. 126.
35. ECtHR 16 February 2021, Gawlik/Liechtenstein, cons. 76.
36. ECtHR 12 February 2008, Guja/Moldova, cons. 77.
37. ECtHR, 14 February 2023, Halet/Luxembourg, cons. 127, 138 en 139 with reference to ECtHR 8 July 1999, Sürek and Özdemir/Turkey.
38. ECtHR 14 February 2023, Halet/Luxembourg, cons. 141.
39. ECtHR 14 February 2023, Halet/Luxembourg, cons. 145.

confidence[40] or citizens' trust in the fairness and justice of States' fiscal policies.[41] Malfunctioning AI tools that influenced government decisions, including tax decisions, can have a serious negative effect on public confidence in the tax administration and the public government as a whole. This negative effect may be weighed against the public interest, in this case, the negative impact of the malfunctioning AI on citizens.

A final criterion taken into account by the Court in assessing whistleblowing activities is *the severity of the sanction* imposed on the whistleblower. A dismissal without notice of the whistleblowing employee is qualified by the Court as the most severe sanction possible under labour law,[42] which also has a deterrent effect on other employees and discourages them from reporting inappropriate behaviour.[43] The Court makes the same observation with respect to the imposition of criminal sanctions[44] and is also willing to consider a person's conviction in some cases more important than the minor nature of punishment imposed,[45] as was the case in the *Halet* judgment, in which the Luxembourg Court upheld only the penalty of a limited fine of EUR 1.000. On the other hand, very severe sanctions, such as imprisonment, have been considered as a disproportionate measure for making public accusations even though these accusations contained insufficient evidence, were defamatory for the accused person, and undermined the accused person's right to be presumed innocent.[46]

§22.4 CONCLUSION AND LEGISLATIVE SUGGESTIONS

Whistleblower protection for tax officials who want to report on harmful AI tools used by the tax administration seems beneficial for a more careful use of AI in taxation. Several examples show how public governments adapt their AI models as a result of public disclosure of unwanted or unethical outcomes. Moreover, the current legal framework regulating the use of AI relies heavily on self-assessment by the provider and user of AI to comply with the legal principles that seek to mitigate the risks of AI. In such a law enforcement system, whistleblowing activities can be helpful to detect wrongdoing and force governments to fix the problem, even before legal action is taken. The tax official willing to report malfunctioning AI can find legal protection under Article 10 of the ECHR. Although the criteria for assessing the degree of protection are clearly formulated by the ECtHR, in practice – as always – the application of these criteria will depend heavily on the specific circumstances of the case. Moreover, recognition of the disproportionate nature of any form of retaliation against a whistleblowing tax official will only be the starting point in the search for legal

40. ECtHR 8 January 8, 2013, Bucur and Toma/Romania, cons. 115 (with regard to a loss of public confidence in the State's Intelligence Services).
41. ECtHR 14 February 2023, Halet/Luxembourg, cons. §147.
42. ECtHR 14 February 2023, Halet/Luxembourg, cons. §149 and ECtHR 16 February 2021, Gawlik/Liechtenstein, cons. 84.
43. ECtHR 14 February 2023, Halet/Luxembourg, cons. §149.
44. ECtHR 14 February 2023, Halet/Luxembourg, cons. §150.
45. ECtHR 14 February 2023, Halet/Luxembourg, cons. 151 with references to ECtHR 8 January 2013, Bucur and Toma/Romania, cons. 119, and *Marchenko v. Ukraine*, no. 4063/04, § 53, 19 February 2009.
46. ECtHR 19 February 2009, Marchenko/Ukraine.

redress at the applicable national level. The Whistleblowing Directive aims to provide a minimum standard of legal protection throughout the entire Union but seems insufficient to provide legal protection for tech whistleblowers. Obviously, it would be helpful if the scope of the Directive were expanded in the future to include breaches of the AI Act, combined with effective reporting channels and clear legal protection for whistleblowing of unethical or undesirable outcomes of AI use in national law.

CHAPTER 23

Sliding Scales of Review in State Aid Control of Fiscal Aid Measures

Joachim Englisch

§23.1 INTRODUCTION

With this chapter on fiscal State aid control, I would like to express my gratitude to *Peter Essers* for many inspiring conversations and publications. In light of the extraordinary breadth of his academic oeuvre, one can be confident of meeting Peter's interest with almost any subject matter of domestic, European, or international taxation; most notably, he has also consistently researched the broader constitutional, philosophical, historical and political context of taxation. Specifically on fiscal State aid, Peter has written not only several articles but also indeed an entire book offering an interdisciplinary analysis of the *Starbucks* case and its many ramifications.[1] I, therefore, hope that this small chapter, which also touches on core aspects of fiscal federalism in the European Union, will be an adequate contribution to this publication in his honor.

The chapter is based on the premise that the notion of selective aid has become the crucial factor for State aid control because it marks a pivotal boundary between the remaining fiscal autonomy of the Member States and the Commission's authority to enforce the interests of the internal market, as well as other public welfare objectives defined by Union law. The criteria for determining selectivity are therefore politically sensitive and highly controversial. In practice, they are developed and tested by the European Commission and ultimately fixed by the Court of Justice of the European Union (CJEU). The case law of the CJEU in this regard is still fluid, as it seeks to strike an adequate balance between the conflicting principles. While this state of flux renders the application of Article 107(1) TFEU to tax measures less certain, it is arguably not the

1. Peter Essers, *De Starbuckszaak en haar dilemma's: Heerlijke koffie met een bittere nasmaak* (Kluwer 2020).

main source of legal uncertainty in the review of potential fiscal aid. In addition, all the delimitation criteria that are currently relied on in fiscal State aid control require value judgments, which provide the Commission and the European Courts with considerable latitude in their assessment. This, in turn, causes considerable fuzziness in the application of the concept of fiscal aid, and a lack of predictability of the outcomes of State aid litigation. This is also reflected in the unusually high degree of divergence between judgments of the General Court and contrary findings in subsequent appeal proceedings before the CJEU in recent fiscal State aid proceedings.

The hypothesis of this chapter is that the lack of bright-line rules for determining the selectivity of fiscal aid is a direct consequence of the aforementioned federalist conflict, which is reflected in the definitional elements of the selectivity concept as it currently stands. In view of this quasi-constitutional dimension of those interpretational issues, it would seem illusory to assume that margins of appreciation could simply be defined away by further refining the relevant criteria. Instead, this chapter proposes to enhance them with a sliding scale of review of fiscal aid schemes, in function of the degree to which the conflicting national and Union interests are presumably affected by the tax measure at issue. While this approach would not eliminate grey areas of the notion of fiscal State aid, it should improve the rationality of the State aid review and thereby also increase legal certainty for the affected undertakings and national governments. The chapter does not concern the review of individual aid, however; as has already been explained elsewhere, a number of other considerations suggest that the Commission and the CJEU should qualify only *manifestly* unlawful tax assessments, rulings or settlements as selective aid.[2]

The remainder of this chapter is structured as follows. The second section explores the fuzzy edges of the current concept of selective fiscal aid. The third section analyzes the underlying causes and elaborates on a flexible mechanism of devolution of the necessary value judgments to the Member State level, effectively resulting in a sliding scale of review for fiscal aid schemes. Section four concludes.

§23.2 THE CHALLENGES IN ASSESSING SELECTIVITY

§23.2.1 General Observations on the Selectivity Criterion

According to the settled case law of the CJEU, the classification of a national measure as "State aid," within the meaning of Article 107(1) TFEU, requires all the following conditions to be fulfilled. First, there must be an intervention by the State or through State resources. Second, the intervention must be liable to affect trade between the Member States. Third, it must confer a selective advantage on the beneficiary. Fourth,

2. *See* CJEU, Case C-256/97, *DMT*, 29.06.1999, ECLI:EU:C:1999:332, at paras. 25 and 30; Opinion of AG Kokott, Case C-454/21 P, *Engie Global LNG Holding*, 04.05.2023, ECLI:EU:C:2023:383, paras. 93 and 96; Richard Lyal, *Transfer Pricing Rules and State Aid*, 38 Fordham Int'l Law Journal 1017, 1042 (2015); K.P.E. Lasok, *State Aids and Remedies under the EEC Treaty*, 7 E.C.L.R. 53, 58 (1986).

it must distort or threaten to distort competition.[3] Unless the tax benefit at issue, including its selective effects, is required or authorized by secondary Union law, the "State" aid element of the definition is usually present in a case of potential fiscal aid.[4] As to the second and fourth criteria of State aid, the CJEU routinely assumes them to be fulfilled where the tax measure under scrutiny confers a selective advantage upon undertakings that are active in liberalized markets with—at least potential—intra-Community trade.[5] It is therefore quintessentially the latter concept of selective aid that determines the scope of fiscal State aid control.

In general, the CJEU does no longer properly distinguish between the favorable "advantage" conferred by the tax system and its selectivity, despite occasional statements to the contrary.[6] Instead, the two concepts are usually conflated into a single nondiscrimination test: Pursuant to the case law, to establish that a tax measure confers a selective advantage, it is first necessary to identify the reference system, that is, the "normal" tax system applicable in the Member State concerned. It must then be determined whether the measure at issue constitutes a beneficial derogation from that reference system. This will be assumed by the CJEU in so far as it differentiates between operators who, in the light of the objective pursued by the tax system at issue, are in a comparable factual and legal situation.[7] Any such discrimination indicates both prima facie (or a priori) selectivity and the presence of an advantage.[8] The selectivity of the latter can then only be ruled out if the Member State concerned is able to demonstrate that the problematic differentiation is justified in the sense that it flows from the "nature or general structure" of the system of which those measures form part.[9]

It should be noted that the aforementioned comparability test required by the CJEU as part of the selectivity assessment does not go beyond the analysis of whether the favorable tax regime can be regarded as a consistent implementation of the

3. *See* CJEU, Joined Cases C-855/19 P and C-898/19 P, *Fiat Chrysler Finance Europe/Commission*, 08.11.2022, ECLI:EU:C:2022:859, at para. 66.
4. For a detailed analysis, *see* Joachim Englisch, *EU State Aid Rules Applied to Indirect Tax Measures*, 22 EC Tax Review 9, 14 et seq. (2013) DOI: 10.54648/ecta2013002, with references to CJEU case law. For a slightly broader understanding of imputability to the Member State, *see* Commission Notice (EU) C/2016/2946, *on the notion of State aid as referred to in Article 107(1) of the Treaty on the Functioning of the European Union*, 19.07.2016, at paras. 44-45; Sjoerd Douma, *State Aid and Direct Taxation*, in Terra/Wattel—European Tax Law, Vol. I, para. 15.2.3 (Douma et al. eds, 8th ed., 2023).
5. *See, e.g.*, CJEU, Case C-148/04, *Unicredito Italiano*, 15.12.2005, ECLI:EU:C:2005:774, at paras. 56 et seq.; C-74/16, *Congregación de Escuelas Pías Provincia Betania*, 27.06.2017, ECLI:EU:C:2017:496, at para. 80.
6. *See, e.g.*, CJEU, Case C-831/21 P, *Fachverband Spielhallen*, 21.09.2023, ECLI:EU:C:2023:686, at para. 35.
7. *See, e.g.*, CJEU, Joined Cases C-78/08 to C-80/08, *Paint Graphos*, 08.09.2011, ECLI:EU:C:2011:550, at para. 49; Joined Cases C-855/19 P and C-898/19 P, *Fiat Chrysler Finance Europe/Commission*, 08.11.2022, ECLI:EU:C:2022:859, at para. 68.
8. *See* CJEU, Case C-831/21 P, *Fachverband Spielhallen*, 21.9.2023, ECLI:EU:C:2023:686, at paras. 48 and 40.
9. *See, e.g.*, CJEU, Case C-52/19 P, *Banco Santander*, 06.10.2021, ECLI:EU:C:2021:794, at para. 28; Joined Cases C-855/19 P and C-898/19 P, *Fiat Chrysler Finance Europe/Commission*, 08.11.2022, ECLI:EU:C:2022:859, at para. 68, with further references.

fundamental objective of the tax system.[10] As the CJEU has clarified, the comparable factual and legal situation of the taxpayers who benefit from the beneficial tax regime and of those who do not must be determined "in the light of the objective pursued by the tax system."[11] Ultimately, the comparability test is thereby rendered redundant; it is sufficient to find a derogation from the reference system to establish prima facie selectivity.

Different from earlier case law,[12] it is now generally regarded as irrelevant by the CJEU whether the tax benefit is limited to a particular, privileged category of undertakings, which are "selectively" favored by the measure concerned and which can be distinguished by reason of specific properties, common to them and characteristic of them.[13] Under this modern approach, any tax relief measure that cannot be characterized as a consistent implementation of the rationale and the guiding principles of the allocation of the respective tax burden is qualified as selective, regardless of how broadly accessible it is. While the CJEU still pays lip service to the idea that favorable "general measures" are not prohibited by Article 107(1) TFEU,[14] this concept therefore no longer effectively limits the scope of State aid control.[15] The expansionist jurisprudence of the CJEU has been met with skepticism by some Advocate Generals,[16] and it has been criticized by many scholars,[17] including the author of this chapter.[18] However, the CJEU has so far not been impressed, but instead it has consolidated its position.[19]

10. *See, e.g.*, Opinion of AG Pikamäe, Case C-898/19 P, *Ireland/Commission*, 16.12.2021, ECLI:EU:C:2021:1029, at para. 53.
11. *See* CJEU, Joined Cases C-855/19 P and C-898/19 P, *Fiat Chrysler Finance Europe/Commission*, 08.11.2022, ECLI:EU:C:2022:859, at para. 69, with further references.
12. *See, e.g.*, CJEU, Case C-156/98, *Germany/Commission*, 19.9.2000, ECLI:EU:C:2000:467, at para. 22. *See also* Commission, *First survey on state aids in the European Community* (1989) point 10.5 of the Technical Annex: "[some] departures from the benchmark system are on the borderline between aid within the meaning of Article 92(1) and general measures."
13. *See, e.g.*, CJEU, Case C-20/15 P, *World Duty Free Group*, 21.12.2016, ECLI:EU:C:2016:981, at paras. 71 et seq.
14. *See, e.g.*, CJEU, Case C-705/20, *Fossil (Gibraltar)*, 15.09.2022, ECLI:EU:C:2022:680, at para. 58.
15. *See* Joachim Englisch, *Das Beihilfenverbot im Steuerrecht*, in Europäisches Steuerrecht, § 9 para. 18 (Schaumburg/Englisch eds., 2nd ed. 2020).
16. *See* Opinion of AG Kokott, Case C-66/14, *Finanzamt Linz*, 16.04.2015, ECLI:EU:C:2015:242, at paras. 85 and 109 et seq., 113; Joined Cases C-236/16 and 237/16, *ANGED*, 09.11.2017, ECLI:EU:C:2017:854, at para. 84; Opinion of AG Saugmandsgaard Øe, Case C-374/17, *A-Brauerei*, 19.09.2018, ECLI:EU:C:2018:741, at paras. 123 et seq.
17. *See, e.g.*, Raymond Luja, *The Selectivity Test: The Concept of "Sectoral Aid"*, in State Aid and Tax Law 107, 111 (Rust/Micheau eds., 2012); Claire Micheau, Tax Selectivity in State Aid Review: A Debatable Case Practice, 17 EC Tax Review 276, 280 et seq. (2008) DOI: 10.54648/ecta2008083; Emily Forrester, *Is the State Aid Regime a Suitable Instrument to Be Used in the Fight Against Harmful Tax Competition?*, 27 EC Tax Review 19, 26 (2018) DOI: 10.54648/ecta2018003.
18. *See* Joachim Englisch (*supra* n. 15) at § 9 paras. 28 and 30.
19. *See, e.g.*, CJEU, Case C-20/15 P, *World Duty Free Group*, 21.12.2016, ECLI:EU:C:2016:981, at paras. 70 et seq., Case C-374/17, *A-Brauerei*, 19.12.2018, ECLI:EU:C:2018:1024, at paras. 25 et seq.

§23.2.2 The Need for Value Judgments in the Application of the Traditional Three-Step Test

Against this backdrop, the crucial question in the assessment of whether a tax relief scheme constitutes fiscal State aid is therefore now usually whether the tax measure can be regarded as a mere manifestation or concretization of the fundamental objectives of the tax system at issue, as opposed to a derogation from this benchmark.[20] As is well known, in many cases, this assessment is not a straightforward exercise:[21]

(a) It requires, first, to determine the fundamental "objective pursued by the tax system" of which the disputed measure forms part. Obviously, the purpose of generating revenue that is inherent to every tax is irrelevant in this regard. Instead, it is necessary to identify the distributional or regulatory objective that is underlying the choice of a particular—personal and substantive—scope of the tax, the tax base and the tax rate. This general or "internal" objective informs the overall structure and effects of the tax, as opposed to "external" objectives that are pursued only sporadically within the framework of the relevant tax. External objectives merely constitute the *ratio legis* of certain tax relief measures, but they are not underlying and shaping the tax system as a whole, nor do they flesh out such fundamental tax design principles. They therefore do not define the "normal" level of taxation.

The identification of these core tax principles is context-sensitive; one and the same policy objective can constitute a fundamental principle of tax design for a particular kind of tax and an external objective within the framework of another tax. For example, the climate protection objective to reduce carbon emissions can form the guiding principle of a carbon tax, but as the rationale for an income tax incentive for the purchase of electric vehicles, it constitutes an external objective that cannot be traced back to the ability-to-pay principle underlying the income tax.

Some scholars have objected that this approach of identifying a reference system of "normal" taxation is generally unfeasible and leads to arbitrary results because they are of the view that it is generally not possible to distinguish the guiding principles of a particular tax system from "external" objectives.[22] However, this criticism is too strong and thus unfounded in its generality. In most cases, the overarching objective of a tax can be identified

20. *See also* CJEU, Joined Cases C-855/19 P and C-898/19 P, *Fiat Chrysler Finance Europe/Commission*, 08.11.2022, ECLI:EU:C:2022:859, at paras. 93 and 95: Member States remain free to define "the specific detailed rules for the application" of their fundamental taxation principles and "fix the criteria" that reflect them; any eventual beneficial effects of such "clarification" (*see* para. 99) do not, in principle, constitute selective aid.
21. *See also* Opinion of AG Saugmandsgaard Øe, Case C-374/17, *A-Brauerei*, 19.09.2018, ECLI: EU:C:2018:741, at para. 119.
22. *See* Michael Lang, *Die Auswirkungen des gemeinschaftsrechtlichen Beihilferechts auf das Steuerrecht*, in Österreichischer Juristentag (2009), pp. 25 et seq.; Michael Lang, *State Aid and Taxation: Selectivity and Comparability Analysis*, in State Aid Law and Business Taxation, 27 (Richelle/Schön/Traversa eds., 2016).

with sufficient confidence.[23] It might be explicitly stated in the very tax statute itself, or it might be constitutionally predefined, as it is, for instance, the case in many Member States regarding the need to align taxes on income with the ability-to-pay principle. Absent such unequivocal findings, the provisions on the taxable person and the taxable event, as well as the generally applicable provisions on the determination of the tax base, together with other core design elements, often permit conclusions as to the fundamental objectives underlying the tax system. This inductive approach is also practiced and advocated by the CJEU itself.[24] It can be particularly conclusive where those design features reflect stated legislative intentions, historical regulatory or distributional concerns, or internationally shared taxation principles. In fact, national courts as well as tax law scholars tend to be able to clearly and unambiguously identify the fundamental objectives and guiding principles of most mainstream business taxes. In the case of certain excise duties or transaction taxes with a conceivable but not clearly identifiable regulatory (e.g., environmental or healthcare) objective, however, even this first step of the selectivity analysis may cause certain difficulties and give rise to doubts.

(b) Usually, the challenge of the selectivity analysis will lie in determining whether a favorable tax regime can still be regarded as a mere *concretization* of the reference system, or whether it cannot be reconciled with the latter and must thus be regarded as a *derogation*. Conformity with the reference system requires that the beneficial tax provisions at issue substantiate, operationalize or concretize either the fundamental objective of the tax system itself or a more specific tax design principle that fulfils this function.[25] In essence, this can be qualified as a consistency test,[26] and it is often not a bright-line test.[27]

For example, in the context of a tax on business income, rules on straight-line depreciation of fixed assets can normally be assumed to constitute a consistent element of the tax accounting regime that seeks to measure taxpaying capacity in line with the ability-to-pay principle. It can, however, be doubtful whether rules that fix time periods for the calculation of the depreciation amount for specific assets are also consistent with the aforementioned rationale underlying the overall depreciation regime. This will depend on whether they can be regarded as being based on a reasonable estimate of

23. Likewise Sjoerd Douma (*supra* n. 4) at para. 15.2.4.
24. *See* CJEU, Joined Cases C-855/19 P and C-898/19 P, *Fiat Chrysler Finance Europe/Kommission*, 08.11.2022, ECLI:EU:C:2022:859, at para. 72.
25. *See* Wolfgang Schön, *Taxation and State Aid Law in the European Union*, 36 Common Market Law Review 911, 926 (1999) DOI: 10.54648/239680.
26. *See, e.g.*, Roland Ismer & Sophia Piotrowski, *The Selectivity of Tax Measures: A Tale of Two Consistencies*, 43 Intertax 559, 563 (2015) DOI: 10.54648/taxi2015055; Rita Szudoczkiy & Balazs Karolyi, *The CJEU's Approach to the Objectives of Progressive Turnover-Based Taxes: Respect for the Member States' Fiscal Sovereignty or Authorization for Circumventing EU Law?*, 50 Intertax 82 (2022) DOI: 10.54648/taxi2022007; Richard Lyal, *State Aid, Tax Integration and State Sovereignty*, in Research Handbook on European Union Taxation Law 410, 422-423 (Panayi et al. eds, 2020).
27. *See* Wolfgang Schön (*supra* n. 25), at 927.

the useful life of those assets, or systematically underestimate the latter.[28] In a similar vein, it was long disputed whether national rules on arm's-length transfer pricing adjustments for intragroup transactions of multinationals should be considered a consistent subsystem of the corporation tax system that concretizes the territorial nexus of taxable profits, even where those rules do not (fully) attribute an amount of profits to the domestic group entity that it could have earned with comparable transactions as an independent company under conditions of free competition. In the notorious tax ruling cases, the EU Commission in particular had argued that it was the core objective of every ordinary corporation tax system to tax incorporated enterprises based on the difference between profits and losses as they arise when an undertaking carries on its activities "under normal market conditions."[29] In the Commission's view, a national transfer pricing regime could therefore only be regarded as a consistent part of the reference system if "it leads to a reliable approximation of a market-based outcome."[30] It took a grand chamber ruling of the CJEU[31] to—convincingly[32]—refute this position.

(c) Similar difficulties are encountered where a beneficial tax provision appears to be aligned with the fundamental objective or a core design principle of the tax system as a whole, but at the same time derogates from a more specific regime that is embedded in this system. A well-known example from the CJEU jurisprudence is the *Andres* case,[33] which concerned the German corporation tax regime on the forfeiture of the loss carry-forward upon the acquisition of a substantial shareholding in the loss-bearing company. An exception was provided for in the case of an acquisition for the purpose of restructuring a company in difficulty; this exception thus reverted the tax treatment to the general rule of an unlimited carry-forward of losses irrespective of the composition of the shareholder base (separate entity principle of corporate taxation). The EU Commission had argued that the special regime on the forfeiture of a loss carry-forward constituted the reference system, in itself, and that the exception for companies in difficulties was therefore a derogation that implied the presence of a selective aid scheme.[34] While the General Court

28. For a similar problem regarding a legally fixed period until the decommissioning of nuclear power plants for the purposes of determining the provisions for deconstruction liabilities, *see* GC, Case T-92/02, *Stadtwerke Schwäbisch Hall*, 26.01.2006, ECLI:EU:T:2006:26.
29. *See, e.g.*, Commission Decision (EU) C(2014) 3627 final, *Luxembourg—Alleged aid to FFT*, 11.06.2014, at para. 60.
30. *See* Commission Decision (EU) C(2015) 7152 final, *Luxembourg—State aid granted to Fiat*, 21.10.2015, at paras. 226 et seq.
31. *See* CJEU, Joined Cases C-855/19 P and C-898/19 P, *Fiat Chrysler Finance Europe/Kommission*, 08.11.2022, ECLI:EU:C:2022:859.
32. *See* Joachim Englisch (*supra* n. 15), at para. 9.27, with further references.
33. *See* CJEU, Case C-203/16 P, *Andres*, 28.06.2018, ECLI:EU:C:2018:505; and also Case C-219/16 P, *Lowell Financial Services/Commission*, 28.06.2018, ECLI:EU:C:2018:508.
34. *See* Commission Decision (EU) C(2011) 275 final, *Germany—Scheme for the carry-forward of tax losses in the case of restructuring of companies in difficulty*, 26.01.2011, at para. 66.

endorsed this view,[35] the CJEU later rejected it. The CJEU argued that the isolated assessment on the basis of the special regime had "artificially" ignored the broader legislative framework and thus defined the reference system too narrowly.[36]

So far, the CJEU has not elaborated upon the criteria that should determine whether an assessment in the light of only the provisions of the disadvantageous subsystem should be regarded as "artificial." Arguably, a distinction between different categories of subsystems needs to be made: On the one hand, those that seek to implement or safeguard the fundamental objective, overall logic, or guiding principles of the tax system, and, on the other, those that pursue complementary or external objectives. In the former case, which typically concerns special anti-avoidance rules (SAAR), the reference system is indeed made up of the layer of fundamental principles of the tax system. But even if ostensibly aligned with those principles, the "exception from the exception" should then still be regarded as a derogation from the reference system if it is not targeted at situations with low or no avoidance risk but instead selectively tolerates abuse opportunities that the SAAR seeks to curb.[37] The rule must then be held to compromise the fundamental tax objectives that the SAAR is designed to protect and thus to effectively derogate from them. By contrast, where the subsystem follows a—complementary or external—logic of its own, it should be assumed to constitute the relevant reference system for any derogations from it.

It is obvious that all the aforementioned delineation criteria will often require intricate assessments and leave room for value judgments.

(d) Finally, the possibility to justify a priori selective measures if the apparent derogation flows from the "nature or the overall structure of the system of charges of which they are part"[38] can raise similarly vexing qualification issues.

This third step of the selectivity analysis refers back to the rationale and underlying logic of the tax system as such. The nature and general structure of the system would appear to constitute the very reference system that should already have informed the prima facie selectivity test. The two steps of the analysis would then be interchangeable. This is sometimes indeed how the CJEU proceeds.[39] Under this approach, the justification analysis appears erratic, and its implications for the

35. *See* General Court, Case T-287/11, *Heitkamp BauHolding/Commission*, 04.02.2016, ECLI:EU:T:2016:60, at paras. 106 et seq.

36. *See* CJEU, Case C-203/16 P, *Andres*, 28.06.2018, ECLI:EU:C:2018:505, at para. 103.

37. *See* Edoardo Traversa/Pierre Sabbadini, *Anti-avoidance Measures and State Aid in a Post-BEPS Context: An Attempt at Reconciliation*, in State Aid Law and Business Taxation 85, 104 et seq. (Richelle/Schön/Traversa eds., 2016); Luc de Broe, *The State Aid Selectivity-Test in Corporate Tax Matters*, 27 EC Tax Review 285, 297 et seq. (2018) DOI: 10.54648/ecta2018031; Lyal (*supra* n. 26), at 422.

38. *See* CJEU, landmark Case C-88/03, *Portugal/Commission*, 06.12.2006, ECLI:EU:C:2006:511, at para. 53.

39. *See* CJEU, Case C-233/16, *Asociación Nacional de Grandes Empresas de Distribución (ANGED)*, 26.04.2018, ECLI:EU:C:2018:280, at paras. 37 et seq. and at paras. 47 et seq.

distribution of proof[40] are arbitrary. In any event, the difficulties in identifying the relevant guiding principles of the tax system are then the same as described above.

However, the Commission and the CJEU also admit "technical" reasons as justification for an a priori selective provision. They need not be fully congruent with the core objective of the tax but instead can seek to enhance or safeguard it or facilitate its implementation.[41] In the words of the CJEU, what is admitted, in principle, are rules that are "necessary for the functioning and efficiency" of the reference system,[42] "necessary for the achievement" of the guiding principles of the tax system,[43] or "related to the proper functioning of the general tax regime at issue."[44] More specifically, this covers objectives such as tax simplification, proportionality and efficiency of tax collection, and legal certainty of taxation, e.g., through generalizations, bright-line thresholds, *de minimis* exceptions. Moreover, the European Courts and the Commission have also acknowledged that the abstention from imposing a tax liability or a waiver of such liability may be justified on the grounds of avoidance of international double taxation,[45] or more generally speaking, as a limitation of excessive double burdens.[46]

In this context, too, the required delineations, namely to "extrinsic" objectives that are not inherent to the reference system, may become fuzzy. To give some examples: Are generous *de minimis* thresholds that determine the applicability of exemptions, or are beneficial simplifying regimes, still motivated by proportionality and efficiency concerns? Should they rather be qualified as an element of economic policy in favor of (local) small business owners? Are double burdens really excessive so that their avoidance corresponds to the "nature of the system"? Or are they merely an inherent consequence of the tax design so that their mitigation in certain scenarios must be qualified as the pursuit of "external" economic policy goals?[47] To what extent is the avoidance of mere "virtual" international double taxation also a valid justification?[48]

Moreover, the challenge of proper classification is further amplified by the fact that the Commission[49] and also the CJEU[50] will only consider an a priori selective tax

40. *See, e.g.*, CJEU, Joined Cases C-106/09 P and C-107/09 P, *Government of Gibraltar and UK/Commission*, 15.11.2011, ECLI:EU:C:2011:732, at para. 146.
41. *See also* the overview by Sjoerd Douma (*supra* n. 4) at para. 15.2.5.
42. *See* CJEU, Case C-74/16, *Congregación de Escuelas Pías Provincia Betania*, 27.06.2017, ECLI:EU:C:2017:496, at para. 72.
43. *See* CJEU, Case C-88/03, *Portuguese Republic/Commission*, 06.09.2006, ECLI:EU:C:2006:511, at para. 81.
44. *See* CJEU, Case C-374/17, *A-Brauerei*, 19.12.2018, ECLI:EU:C:2018:1024, at para. 50.
45. *See* Commission Decision C (2012) 4217 final, *on Container Terminal Port of Piraeus & Cosco Pacific Limited*, State aid SA.28876, 11.07.2012, at paras. 179-180; *see also—e contrario*—GC, Case T-131/16 RENV, Belgium/Commission, 20.09.2023, ECLI:EU:T:2023:561, at paras. 143 et seq.
46. *See* CJEU, Case C-374/17, *A-Brauerei*, 19.12.2018, ECLI:EU:C:2018:1024, at para. 50.
47. This could very well have been argued in the aforementioned Case C-374/17, *A-Brauerei* (*supra* n. 46), considering that the German RETT design at issue is not firmly rooted in considerations of ability to pay.
48. This has been answered in the negative by the GC, Case T-131/16 RENV, Belgium/Commission, 20.09.2023, ECLI:EU:T:2023:561, at paras. 143 et seq.
49. *See* Commission Notice (*supra* n. 4), at para. 140.

provision to be justified if the relevant "intrinsic" objective is pursued in conformity with the proportionality principle. A proper proportionality test will always involve value judgments. It can be doubtful, for example, if a lump-sum deduction that can imply significant—favorable—deviations from a more exact implementation of the guiding principles of the tax system is still proportionate.

§23.2.3 Further Grey Areas under the De Facto Selectivity Test

The complexities of the selectivity analysis are further exacerbated by the fact that according to what is now settled CJEU case law, "in order for a tax to be established as being selective, it is not always necessary that it should derogate from a tax system considered to be an ordinary tax system."[51] This goes back to the (in-)famous *Gibraltar* judgment of the CJEU, where it held that a "general tax regime" may be, in itself, "in practice" discriminatory and thus selective if it favors a "privileged category" of undertakings which can be distinguished from other undertakings "by virtue of the properties which are specific to them."[52]

The scope and criteria for this exceptional de facto selectivity test remain elusive, however. The overall reasoning in the *Gibraltar* ruling suggested that it was—or that at least some of the justices conceived it to be—a mere variation of the classical three-step analysis. *In concreto*, the CJEU explicitly objected to the fact that the stated objective of the tax at issue was to introduce a general system of business profit taxation for all companies established in Gibraltar, but this system was—inconsistently—designed in a way that inherently excluded offshore companies from its scope.[53] This conservative interpretation of the ruling would be in line with the mantra of the CJEU that selectivity must be established based on regulatory effects rather than regulatory techniques.[54] It would not interfere with the sovereignty of Member States to make fundamental tax policy choices also with their broader economic effects in mind.[55] However, in the subsequent *World Duty Free* decision, the CJEU explained that it followed from its *Gibraltar* ruling that "the selectivity of a tax measure can be established even if that measure does not constitute a derogation from an ordinary tax system, but is an integral part of that system."[56] The CJEU thus pushed the boundaries of the nondiscrimination standard that it reads into Article 107(1) TFEU, by including also instances of indirect discrimination through facially neutral tax rules that however have a

50. *See* CJEU, Case C-78/08, *Paint Graphos*, 08.09.2011, ECLI:EU:C:2011:550, at para. 75.
51. *See* CJEU, Case C-233/16, *Asociación Nacional de Grandes Empresas de Distribución (ANGED)*, 26.04.2018, ECLI:EU:C:2018:280, at para. 32; Joined Cases C-855/19 P and C-898/19 P, *Fiat Chrysler Finance Europe/Commission*, 08.11.2022, ECLI:EU:C:2022:859, at para. 70.
52. *See* CJEU, Joined Cases C-106/09 P and C-107/09 P, *Government of Gibraltar and UK/Commission*, 15.11.2011, ECLI:EU:C:2011:732, at paras. 103-104.
53. *See* CJEU, Joined Cases C-106/09 P and C-107/09 P, *Government of Gibraltar and UK/Commission*, 15.11.2011, ECLI:EU:C:2011:732, at paras. 101-102.
54. *See, e.g.*, CJEU, Case C-487/06 P, *British Aggregates*, 22.12.2008, ECLI:EU:C:2008:757, para. 85; *see* also Commission Notice (*supra* n. 4) at para. 129.
55. This interpretation has therefore also been endorsed by the author of this chapter, *see* Joachim Englisch (*supra* n. 15) at para. 9.26.
56. *See* CJEU, Case C-20/15 P, *World Duty Free*, 21.12.2016, ECLI:EU:C:2016:981, at para. 76.

disparate impact on distinct groups of market operators.[57] Later, the CJEU suggested that this de facto selectivity analysis should focus on an eventual "intention to circumvent" EU State aid law,[58] and thereby converted the approach into a "substance over form" doctrine[59] that should take into account legislative intent.[60] However, in the most recent *Fiat Chrysler* decision, the CJEU apparently reverted to the indirect discrimination perspective.[61]

Obviously, the ambiguous and controversial nature of the *Gibraltar* test of de facto selectivity gives rise to considerable legal uncertainty. In particular, the exact bearing of legislative intent on the analysis, if any, and the requirements for establishing such intent remain murky. Moreover, under the apparently predominant understanding as an extension of the nondiscrimination standard to indirect discrimination, it must be determined how specifically the group of beneficiaries must be delimited and to what extent disparate effects must be present. So far, the CJEU has not elaborated on this matter.

§23.3 CONTEXT-SPECIFIC LEVELS OF REVIEW OF FISCAL AID SCHEMES: A BALANCING ACT

§23.3.1 The Federalist Conflict Underlying the Grey Areas of Selectivity

The blurred edges and grey areas of the CJEU's understanding of the concept of selective aid, as described above, reflect the difficulty of striking a proper balance between the tax sovereignty of the Member States, on the one hand, and undistorted competition within the EU internal market, on the other.

The principle of prohibition of State aid and the corresponding competences of the Commission are situated in a chapter of the TFEU that concerns "rules on competition." The wording of all three paragraphs of Article 107 TFEU furthermore underlines the internal market dimension of State aid control. More specifically, the objective to ensure undistorted competition within the internal market can be inferred from both the first and the third paragraph of Article 107 TFEU. The CJEU and the Commission therefore rightfully regard the protection of undistorted competition and the establishment of a level playing field as the core rationale underlying State aid

57. *See also* CJEU, Case C-374/17, *A-Brauerei*, 19.12.2018, ECLI:EU:C:2018:1024, at para. 32.
58. *See* CJEU, Case C-562/19 P, *Commission v. Poland*, 16.03.2021, ECLI:EU:C:2021:201, at para. 43; Case C-596/19 P, *Commission v. Hungary*, 16.03.2021, ECLI:EU:C:2021:202, at para. 49.
59. Likewise Wolfgang Schön, *Tax Legislation and the Notion of Fiscal Aid*, in State Aid Law and Business Taxation 3, 10 (Richelle/Schön/Traversa eds., 2016). *See also* Richard Lyal (*supra* n. 26), at 426: "hypothetical general framework"; likewise—and critical—Edoardo Traversa/Alessandra Flamini, *Fighting Harmful Tax Competition through EU State Aid Law*, 14 EStAL 323, 329 (2015).
60. *See* the criticism by Michael Lang, *Taxation and State Aid—Recent Case Law on Progressive Turnover Taxes*, 61 European Taxation 515, 521 (2021).
61. *See* CJEU, Joined Cases C-855/19 P and C-898/19 P, *Fiat Chrysler Finance Europe/Kommission*, 08.11.2022, ECLI:EU:C:2022:859, at para. 70.

control.[62] This is also reflected in the recently adopted Foreign Subsidies Regulation, which complements State aid control vis-à-vis third countries and seeks to "address distortions caused, directly or indirectly, by foreign subsidies, with a view to ensuring a level playing field."[63] While the principle of prohibition of State aid might be construed so as to safeguard additional aspects of economic efficiency in the internal market,[64] this does not call into question its primary function as an instrument of EU competition law.

In the light of the above, it stands to reason that fiscal State aid control, too, primarily aims to achieve the fundamental objective of establishing a level playing field for businesses in the internal market.[65] It is moreover obvious that national tax measures cannot be a priori exempt from such control.[66] Direct subsidies and tax expenditures have similar economic effects[67] and are equally liable to distort competition if granted selectively. This notwithstanding, a significant difference exists between those two categories of aid: The advantageous effects that direct subsidies have for their recipients are implicit in the interference of the State with normal market conditions. The constraint of Member States regarding their economic or regulatory policy choices that potentially results from qualifying such an interference as selective aid is therefore inherent to the system of State aid control established by Articles 107 et seq. TFEU. A reconciliation of the conflicting national and Community interests has been (almost) entirely entrusted with the Commission, by virtue of the discretion that it enjoys under Article 107(3) TFEU.

By contrast, in the context of fiscal measures, it is the imposition of a tax that constitutes the original "market intervention" by the State. This creates the risk of a potential over-reach of State aid control: In areas that are not harmonized through Union tax legislation, there exists no commonly agreed baseline level of business taxation in the EU which would automatically limit the concept of fiscal aid to specific national derogations from a European taxation framework that result in a lower tax burden. As a consequence, any national tax policy choice regarding the tax mix and tax law design that has favorable effects for certain categories of businesses or branches could theoretically be characterized as fiscal State aid within the meaning of Article 107(1) TFEU. But under such an approach, the national tax sovereignty of the Member

62. *See, e.g.*, CJEU, Joined Cases C-622/16 P to C-624/16 P, *Scuola Elementare Maria Montessori*, ECLI:EU:C:2018:873, at para. 43; Commission, *State Aid Action Plan: Less and better targeted State aid: a roadmap for State aid reform 2005-2009*, 07.06.2005, COM(2005) 107 final, at para. 9.
63. *See* Art. 1(1) of Regulation (EU) 2022/2560.
64. For an overview, *see* Roland Ismer, *Umgang mit dem unionsrechtlichen Beihilfeverbot—aktuelle Herausforderungen*, in Festschrift für den Bundesfinanzhof 845 (Drüen/Hey/Mellinghoff eds., Vol. I, 2018).
65. Likewise, e.g., Conor Quigley, *European State Aid Law and Policy* 128 (4th ed., 2022); Juliane Kokott, *Das Steuerrecht der Europäischen Union* (2018) § 3 at para. 137.
66. *See* CJEU, Case C-173/73, *Italian Republic/Commission*, 02.07.1974, ECLI:EU:C:1974:71, at paras. 12-13; Henk van Arendonk, The European Cooperation Project, Tax & Sovereignty, 25 EC Tax Review 214, 245 (2016) DOI: 10.54648/ecta2016026.
67. *See* CJEU, Case C-30/59, *De gezamenlijke Steenkolenmijnen in Limburg/High Authority*, 23.02.1961, ECLI:EU:C:1961:2; Case C-69/69, *Commission/France*, 10.12.1969, ECLI:EU:C:1969:68.

States would not merely be constrained; it would be fundamentally compromised. Through its powers under Article 107(3) TFEU, the Commission could then make the fundamental policy choices for business taxation instead of Member States.[68]

Arguably, such a far-reaching interference would be at odds with the emphasis that the European treaties still place on the fiscal autonomy of Member States. Pursuant to Articles 113, 114(2) and 115 TFEU, taxation is one of the few (shared) competences of the EU where unanimity is still required in the Council for European Legislation to be adopted. Moreover, while direct subsidies are a policy option that need not be exercised by Member States, no modern liberal market economy can dispense with the imposition of taxes, including taxes on business. Even broadly implemented tax design choices typically have certain distortive or selective adverse effects that affect some categories of businesses more than others. In the case of unfettered fiscal State aid control, Member States could thus not avoid the de facto harmonization of this key policy area[69] through guidance or decision practice of the EU Commission based on Article 107(3) TFEU. However, this would not be compatible with the requirement of sufficient democratic legitimacy of fundamental tax policy choices:[70] Even when assuming that the Commission, in exercising its discretion under Article 107(3) TFEU, always acts benevolently in the interest of European citizens, such "output legitimacy" cannot fully compensate for a lack of sufficient input legitimacy by the ultimate sovereign, i.e., the peoples of the Member States.[71] This classical understanding of the democracy principle is also clearly underlying the European Union, as is apparent from Articles 9 et seq. TEU.[72]

It is therefore broadly, albeit not universally, accepted that a balance needs to be struck between the objective of protection of undistorted competition within the internal market, on the one hand, and national tax sovereignty, on the other.[73] The approach of the CJEU to generally shield the fundamental tax policy choices of a

68. *See*, in this regard, Cees Peters, *Tax Policy Convergence and EU Fiscal State Aid Control: In Search of Rationality*, 28 EC Tax Review 6, 8 (2019) DOI: 10.54648/ecta2019002.
69. *See also* Dimitrios Kyriazis, *From Soft Law to Soft Law Through Hard Law: The Commission's Approach to the State Aid Assessment of Tax Rulings*, 15 EStAL 428, 436 (2016): "stealthy tax harmonization."
70. *See* Francesco Nanetti & Giovanni Mameli, *The Creeping Normative Role of the EC Commission in the Twin-Track Struggle Against State Aids and Harmful Tax Competition*, 11 EC Tax Review 185, 191 (2002) DOI: 10.54648/5104394; Thomas Jaeger, *Tax Incentives under State Aid Law: A Competition Law Perspective*, in State Aid Law and Business Taxation 39, 43 (Richelle, Schön & Traversa eds., 2016).
71. For a different opinion, *see* in general terms Fritz Scharpf, *Governing in Europe: Effective and Democratic?*, 6 (1999); and with similar tendencies for State aid control this is discussed in Cees Peters, *The Legitimacy of EU Fiscal State Aid Control: What Is Your Legitimate Narrative?*, in New Perspectives on Fiscal State Aid 5, 10 (De Pietro ed. 2019).
72. The above analysis should therefore not be discounted as a "mere legal one." In particular, from a normative perspective it cannot be replaced by a "political" understanding of how State aid review should be construed to address "present day challenges," because the democratically legitimized Treaty text and context establish clear limits to such an approach. For a different opinion, *see* Cees Peters (*supra* n. 71), at 29.
73. *See, e.g.*, Wolfgang Schön (*supra* n. 25), at 915; Sophia Piotrowski, *Selectivity in Corporate Tax Matters After World Duty Free: A Tale of Two Consistencies Revisited*, 46 Intertax 156, 158 (2018) DOI: 10.54648/taxi2018016; Juliane Kokott (*supra* n. 65) at paras. 139 and 182; Paul-John Loewenthal, *Fiscal Selectivity: A Notion in Need of Clarity*, in New Perspectives on Fiscal State

Member State from State aid control and take them as a "starting point"[74] for a mere consistency test, but exceptionally permit the Commission to object to the de facto selectivity of the tax system itself under the *Gibraltar* formula, constitutes such a balancing exercise.[75] The CJEU has indeed repeatedly emphasized that the remaining fiscal autonomy of Member States in designing their tax systems must not be undermined through State aid control.[76]

From this perspective, the occasional changes in the case law of the CJEU regarding the notion of selectivity represent a shift in its position on the *domaine reserve* of national tax sovereignty, i.e., on the essential core of national fiscal autonomy that Member States can still exercise without being subject to State aid review.[77] There has been a general tendency in the past decades to place greater emphasis on the Union interest, at the expense of national tax sovereignty. The most obvious manifestations of this trend are, first, the de facto abandonment of the concept of out-of-scope "general measures" that derogate from the reference system but are accessible to all market operators alike, and second, the invention of the *Gibraltar* test for the overall tax law design. The CJEU has counterbalanced this expansion in the enforcement of Union interests only to a limited degree by admitting additional justifications under the "nature and general structure" test in the third step of the selectivity analysis. This notwithstanding, the CJEU has now also clearly indicated its unwillingness to accept an even further encroachment on the Member State's fiscal autonomy through State aid control, as advocated by the Commission in the tax ruling cases.[78]

The CJEU's current position on the scope of the Member States' *domaine réservé* in the exercise of their sovereign right to design the national system of business taxation according to their tax policy preferences is highly controversial. However, this discussion is beyond the scope of the present analysis.[79]

Aid 31, 41 (De Pietro ed. 2019). *See also* the clear statements to this effect in the Opinion of GA Pikamäe, Case C-898/19 P, *Ireland/Commission*, 16.12.2021, ECLI:EU:C:2021:1029, paras. 103 et seq.

74. *See* CJEU, Joined Cases C-855/19 P and C-898/19 P, *Fiat Chrysler Finance Europe/Kommission*, 08.11.2022, ECLI:EU:C:2022:859, at para. 71. *See also, e.g.*, CJEU, Case C-562/19 P, *Commission/Poland*, 16.03.2021, ECLI:EU:C:2021:201, at para. 38.
75. Likewise Opinion of AG Darmon, Joined Cases C-72/91 and C-73/91, *Sloman Netptun*, 17.03.1992, ECLI:EU:C:1992:130, at para. 55 (regarding the classical derogation test).
76. *See* CJEU, Joined Cases C-855/19 P and C-898/19 P, *Fiat Chrysler Finance Europe/Kommission*, 08.11.2022, ECLI:EU:C:2022:859, at paras. 73 and 94.
77. *See also* Liza Lovdahl Gormsen, *European State Aid and Tax Rulings* 112 (2019): "hard core of the Member States' competences." As a caveat, the notion of *domaine réservé* in this context is without prejudice to the possibility that the exercise of such competences could still be restrained by other provisions of Union law.
78. Some scholars have also supported the use of "external" benchmarks for the assessment of a selective advantage; *see, e.g.*, Roland Ismer & Sophia Piotrowski (*supra* n. 26) at 568-569; and the overview provided by Cees Peters (*supra* n. 71) at 18-19.
79. Regarding the author's position, *see* Joachim Englisch (*supra* n. 15) at § 9 paras. 28 et seq.

§23.3.2 A Sliding Scale of Review Informed by the Conflicting Interests

§23.3.2.1 General Considerations

What matters here is the acknowledgment that the CJEU's selectivity test, as well as its critical reception in academic literature, fundamentally strives to establish a proper balance between competing Union interests and national interests. On this basis, it is possible to conceive the grey areas of the selectivity concept—discussed above at 23.2—as a built-in flexibility mechanism rather than as an undesirable shortcoming of the case law of the CJEU.

Conceptually, the prohibition of State aid according to Article 107(1) TFEU does not provide for the possibility to strike a concrete and proportionate balance between national tax sovereignty and the Union interest in undistorted competition. None of the defining elements of State aid inherently requires to carry out an analysis to this effect. Nor is national fiscal autonomy a concern that is explicitly mentioned in Article 107(2) and (3) TFEU as a criterion which requires or permits the EU Commission to declare aid compatible with the internal market, apart from the fact that granting the Commission full discretion in this regard would seem inadequate for the reasons mentioned above.

This gap can be filled, however, through the case-specific concretizations and value judgments required by the notion of selectivity since the latter quintessentially delineates potentially objectionable national tax policy choices from those that are not subject to Commission scrutiny from a State aid perspective. The relevant margins of interpretation and assessment could be leveraged upon for a case-specific analysis of the relative importance of national tax sovereignty, on the one hand, and the degree of interference of the tax measure at issue with the internal market objective of undistorted competition, on the other.

In the following, this idea is developed based on the case law of the CJEU as it currently stands. Arguably, this approach could nevertheless and *mutatis mutandis* also be brought to fruition under alternative conceptions of the selectivity test that would draw a different, abstract line between fiscal State aid control and a *domaine réservé* of national fiscal autonomy. Since such alternative approaches still need certain delineation criteria, they, too, will normally feature "grey areas" that are not readily susceptible to bright-line testing.

§23.3.2.2 Application under the Consistency Test of the Three-Step Selectivity Analysis

Regarding the consistency test of the classical three-step selectivity analysis, this chapter quintessentially proposes a sliding scale in review—by the EU Commission and the CJEU—of the Member State's submissions on the relevant criteria, i.e., regarding the guiding principles of their tax law design and the conformity of the measure at issue with those principles.[80]

The CJEU has indeed already indicated that substantiated declarations of the Member States to this effect need to be solicited and considered by the EU Commission.[81] Moreover, the concession of a margin of appreciation to the respective Member State, which is then to be respected by the EU Commission and the CJEU, is not alien to the Court's case law, either.[82] But the CJEU has so far not elaborated on the abstract conditions for relaxing the review of the consistency requirement or on the criteria that should influence the degree of review.

In line with the above considerations, it is suggested here that these aspects should be guided by an assessment of the likelihood and gravity of the distortions of competition that the measure is liable to cause, as well as the degree to which national tax autonomy is potentially impaired by State aid control. To facilitate the corresponding analysis, it is furthermore proposed to rely on two proxies for the respective criteria.

The first proxy should be the degree of competition between the potential beneficiaries of the tax measure at issue and the undertakings or sectors of the economy that do not qualify for its use, including—but not limited to—the degree of competition between onshore and offshore operators. This proxy reflects the internal market dimension of the gliding scale of review. As a side effect, this would also counterbalance, to a certain degree, the preference of the CJEU for a very low threshold[83] regarding the separate State aid criterion whereby the aid measure must "distort or threaten to distort competition."

The second proxy should be the degree of homogeneity and specificity, if any, of the potential beneficiaries. This second proxy is based on the assumption that targeted tax relief measures for a clearly defined and relatively small group of undertakings are less likely to embody fundamental tax policy preferences; their scrutiny is therefore also less likely to amount to an interference with the essence of national tax autonomy. It is furthermore justified by the—generalizing—assumption that such targeted relief measures are more likely to be motivated by "extra-fiscal" or "external" policy considerations that are unrelated to the core objectives and fundamental principles of the tax system at issue, and therefore merit a closer review. In this context, a tax measure should be considered to target "specific" undertakings if it is contingent upon criteria that an existing undertaking has no influence on fulfilling or that it can only

80. This idea has already been partially developed in Joachim Englisch (*supra* n. 15) at para. 9.30. A sliding scale in review is also proposed by Juliane Kokott (*supra* n. 64) § 3 paras. 181 et seq.; however, this proposal relies on other aspects than it is suggested here; and it moreover tends to conflate the selectivity criteria and the standard of review criteria.
81. *See* CJEU, Joined Cases C-855/19 P and C-898/19 P, *Fiat Chrysler Finance Europe/Kommission*, 08.11.2022, ECLI:EU:C:2022:859, at para. 72.
82. *See* CJEU, Joined Cases C-234/16 und C-235/16, *ANGED*, ECLI:EU:C:2018:281, at para. 48: "The determination of [whether the relevant criterion of differentiation, which implies an advantage for certain taxpayers, is consistent with the overall objective of the levy at issue] comes within the discretion of the national legislature and is based on technical, complex assessments that the Court only has limited powers to review."
83. *See, e.g.*, CJEU, Case C-148/04, *Unicredito Italiano*, 15.12.2005, ECLI:EU:C:2005:774, at paras. 57-58; Case C-518/13, *Eventech*, 14.01.2015, ECLI:EU:C:2015:9, at paras. 64 et seq.

fulfil by changing its business model, operational structure or form of organization.[84] A precise delineation would not be necessary, however, since this assessment would not, in itself, determine the outcome of the selectivity analysis, but it would merely constitute a factor to consider in choosing the standard of review.

As to the precise graduation of the scale of review, a strict scrutiny would require that there is no plausible alternative explanation other than the one submitted by the Member State concerned. An intermediate scrutiny would merely ask whether, based on such a submission, it can be reasonably assumed that the disputed tax measure is consistent with fundamental principles of tax law design. Under the most lenient approach, where there is little competition between the beneficiaries of the tax measure and other operators in the single market and where the measure is also broadly accessible to a variety of undertakings, it should be sufficient that the Member State's claim of consistency with core taxation principles is not manifestly unreasonable or implausible.[85]

§23.3.2.3 *Application under the Justification Test of the Three-Step Selectivity Analysis*

For the above reasons, and based on the same proxies, a similarly sliding scale of review should also apply in the context of the third step, i.e., the analysis of a possible justification for a priori selective tax measures.

A strict review of the arguments put forward by the respective Member State regarding the conformity of the tax measure at issue with the "nature and general structure" of the relevant tax system is warranted if the tax relief is ring-fenced to a specific and homogenous group of taxpayers and its beneficiaries compete intensely with other market operators who are not eligible to benefit. Otherwise, an intermediate or lenient standard of review should apply. This concerns both the assessment of whether the rationale allegedly underlying the disputed tax measure is inherent to the "structure" of the system instead of a mere "external" motive and the eventual follow-up question as to whether the measure is indeed motivated by such a qualifying justification.

In a similar vein, the degree of discretion conceded to the national legislator regarding the proportionality of the measure, which the CJEU now assesses as part of the justification analysis, should also depend on the aforementioned proxies. This implies a range of reviews, from a strict proportionality test to a reasonableness test to a mere test of arbitrariness.

---

84. *See also* General Court, Case T-219/10, *Autogrill España*, 07.11.2014, ECLI:EU:T:2014:939, at para. 56; and—in the context of *Gibraltar*-type de facto selectivity—Commission Notice (*supra* n. 4) at para. 121.
85. *See also*—in the context of individual aid—the Opinion of AG Kokott, Case C-454/21 P, *Engie Global LNG Holding and Others/Commission*, 04.05.2023, ECLI:EU:C:2023:383, at para. 92, where the AG suggests that under a lenient standard of review ("manifest error"), selectivity should be assumed if the derogation from the reference framework "cannot be plausibly explained."

Under no circumstances should it be permissible for Member States, however, to justify derogations from the benchmark system where they are unequivocally based on "external" objectives that are unrelated to the overall structure of the tax system or tax enforcement concerns.[86] This would undermine the competences of the Commission under Article 107(3) TFEU.

§23.3.3 Consistency with the De Facto Selectivity Test

According to the position adopted here, the establishment of a "de facto selectivity" test based on the CJEU *Gibraltar* ruling as an alternative, autonomous test besides the classical three-step analysis of selectivity goes a step too far. Arguably, this approach—endorsed in subsequent case law, as discussed above at 23.2.3—infringes on the essence of national tax sovereignty. It instrumentalizes State aid control so as to prohibit a Member State from making certain fundamental tax policy choices on account of their disparate impact on different groups of undertakings. However, where the system of business taxation as a whole causes such distortions of competition, the respect for national tax sovereignty and sufficient democratic legitimacy of fundamental tax policy choices requires a resolution through the political processes of Articles 113, 115 TFEU.[87]

By contrast, if the *Gibraltar* decision of the CJEU were understood as an extensive application of the three-step analysis—as it should be—it would be consistent with the flexible review standard that is advocated in this chapter: If the design of a corporate income tax is such that it excludes from its scope a clearly defined, specific group of undertakings and thereby causes significant distortions of competition within the internal market, a strict review of the coherence of this design and its consistency with the taxation principles that the national legislator claims to pursue is appropriate. This should then be sufficient to identify any attempts to "circumvent" the prohibition of fiscal State aid.

Notwithstanding the above criticism of an independent "de facto selectivity" test as it is now propagated by the CJEU and the Commission, such an approach can still be reconciled with the suggestion that a sliding scale of review should be guided by the criteria discussed above.

The CJEU has set high hurdles for characterizing a tax measure as selective even though it is consistent with taxation principles of a general nature, and thus with fundamental tax policy preferences of the respective Member State. First, the privileged group of undertakings must be "characterized" by "specific" features that set it apart from other undertakings.[88] Moreover, according to some more recent judgments, this

86. For a different opinion, *see* Juliane Kokott (*supra* n. 64) § 3 para. 189; Rita Szudoczky, *Convergence of the Analysis of National Tax Measures under the EU State Aid Rules and the Fundamental Freedoms*, 15 EStAL 357, 374 (2016) DOI: 10.21552/estal/2016/3/6.

87. *See* also Andrea Biondi, *The Rationale of State Aid Control: A Return to Orthodoxy*, 12 Cambridge Yearbook of European legal Studies 25, 43-44 (2010) DOI: 10.5235/152888712802636139.

88. *See* CJEU, Joined Cases C-106/09 P and C-107/09 P, *Government of Gibraltar and UK/Commission*, 15.11.2011, ECLI:EU:C:2011:732, at para. 107; Case C-20/15 P, *World Duty Free*, 21.12.2016, ECLI:EU:C:2016:981, at paras. 72 and 74.

disparate impact to the benefit of a clearly defined and homogeneous group must result in "manifestly" discriminatory treatment.[89] Finally, in the original *Gibraltar* ruling, which is so far still the only one where the CJEU actually qualified a measure as selective aid under this approach, the tax law design at issue clearly had a significant effect on competition in the internal market because it facilitated "aggressive" tax planning on a large scale.

Altogether, the CJEU has made clear that it will—and the Commission may—only exceptionally carry out a "de facto selectivity" analysis, namely when the two conditions are met that, under the approach proposed here, would justify a strict review of the tax measure under the classical three-step test. And yet, the CJEU will even then only object to a "manifestly" discriminatory arrangement of the tax system; i.e., the CJEU practices a lenient standard of review in the sense of an "abuse" of the political discretion that a Member State enjoys. The CJEU thereby acknowledges that the "de facto selectivity" approach is significantly more intrusive with respect to national tax sovereignty than the traditional derogation analysis[90] and therefore requires particular judicial restraint.

§23.4 CONCLUSION

The State aid control of tax measures needs to establish a proper balance between the tax sovereignty of the Member States, on the one hand, and the Union's objective of an internal market with equal conditions of competition, on the other. The recently reaffirmed approach of the CJEU to generally shield the fundamental tax policy choices of a Member State from State aid control and take them as a "starting point" for a consistency test, but exceptionally permit the Commission to object to the de facto selectivity of the tax system itself, constitutes such a balancing exercise. To operationalize this approach in the application of Article 107(1) TFEU, the CJEU relies on several definitional elements of the concept of selective aid, in particular in the context of the so-called three-step derogation analysis. The relevant delineation criteria all require value judgments relating to an assessment of the national tax system and the role of the tax measure at issue within this system. In practice, this gives rise to considerable legal uncertainty.

This chapter proposes to rationalize the review of selectivity of fiscal aid schemes and thereby increase legal certainty through a sliding scale of review that is based on factors reflecting the underlying federalist conflict. More specifically, it is argued that Member States should be conceded a broad margin of appreciation as to the consistency of the disputed tax measure with core taxation principles if there is little competition between the beneficiaries of the tax measure and other operators in the

89. *See* CJEU, Case C-562/19 P, *Commission v. Poland*, 16.03.2021, ECLI:EU:C:2021:201, at paras. 42-44; Case C-596/19 P, *Commission v. Hungary*, 16.03.2021, ECLI:EU:C:2021:202, at paras. 48-50. *See also* Opinion of AG Kokott, Case C-562/19 P, *Commission/Poland*, 15.10.2020, ECLI:EU:C:2020:834, at para. 46; Case C-596/19 P, *Commission/Hungary*, 15.10.2020, ECLI:EU: C:2020:835, at para. 53.
90. *See also* Conor Quigley (*supra* n. 65) at 127 and 140.

single market, and if the measure is also broadly accessible to a variety of undertakings. Conversely, where the tax relief is ring-fenced to a specific and homogenous group of taxpayers and its beneficiaries compete intensely with excluded (onshore or offshore) market operators, a strict scrutiny of the Member State's submissions is warranted. Between these extremes, an intermediate level of review should apply. This approach can also be reconciled with the exceptional analysis of the de facto selectivity of the tax system as a whole.

CHAPTER 24

From the Proposed EU Transfer Pricing Arbitration Directive to the Proposed EU Transfer Pricing Directive: A Guided Path Through Half a Century of History of Tax Law in the European Union

Pasquale Pistone

Over the past thirty years, Peter Essers has been a model EU tax law scholar and a learned friend to me. The title of my contribution to this book in his honour, on the occasion of this academic retirement, shows my intention to focus on both areas of European tax law within which his research has been mostly visible, namely corporate tax law and the history of tax law. However, the title should not create too high expectations in the readers: for how my own life and trajectory as a European tax law scholar permeates across the lines of this chapter, transfer pricing is neither my core area of specialisation, nor described as an exact science.[1]

§24.1 INTRODUCTION

The focus of this chapter on transfer pricing in taxation is an opportunity to have a concrete reference framework for examining the direction of travelling of EU tax law during almost half a century of its history. Two proposed Directives – namely the one put forward in 1976 on the establishment of an arbitration procedure in the field of transfer pricing[2] and the one released on 12 September 2023 on the regulation of

1. As per the oft-cited remark included in the OECD Transfer Pricing Guidelines. *See Transfer Pricing Guidelines*, Chapter IV, para. 4.8 (2022).
2. The proposed Directive was released on 29 November 1976 and published in OJ 21 December 1976 C 301, pp. 4 ff.

transfer pricing in the European Union[3] – constitute the starting and arrival point of this analysis across time. This choice to look at the evolution of EU tax law between two proposed Directives – none of which has binding value – might be emblematic: it reflects the ambitions of positive integration of EU tax law, which must face the reality of the practical barriers that have limited such development until present.

The line that unites the two proposals is the need to approximate national tax laws of EU Member States with a view to enhancing the functioning of the EU internal market. Such need was already clearly visible at the time that the first proposal was made and has become exponentially more important in the current scenario, especially if one considers that tax integration in the European Union has made considerable progress in the past half a century[4] and that a strong mutual dependence binds national economies of EU Member States without a corresponding coordinated tax policy approach.

This short chapter examines the invisible thread that links the measures of positive European tax integration proposed and approved half a century ago with the latest developments, making an assessment not only of selected technical issues from a legal perspective but also of the evolutionary trend from a policy perspective, with a view to extracting the direction of travelling of European tax law.

After reviewing some features of the measures on cross-border tax dispute settlement applicable to transfer pricing,[5] the analysis of the merits and shortcomings connected with addressing such issues by means of primary EU law[6] will make it possible to address the importance and selected technical matters of the rules contained in the proposed EU Transfer Pricing Directive.[7]

§24.2 EU POSITIVE INTEGRATION ON TAX DISPUTE SETTLEMENT

The introduction of a dispute settlement mechanism on cross-border tax disputes in the field of transfer pricing took place almost fourteen years after the publication of the proposed EU Directive, but by means of an international multilateral convention, made available for signature to EU Member States only.

This sui generis legally binding instrument of coordination[8] was the outcome of a political compromise, reached in July 1990, which transferred the rules initially

3. European Commission, Proposal for a Council Directive on Transfer Pricing, 12 September 2023, COM(2023) 529 final.
4. This development has produced various implications for transfer pricing within the EU. Besides the possibility to conduct joint audits under Art. 12a of the Mutual Assistance Directive (DAC), mandatory automatic exchange of information was extended by Directive 2011/16/EU (DAC 3) to advance cross-border rulings and advance pricing agreements (Directive 2015/2376/EU of 8 December 2015, published in OH 18 December 2015, L 332, pp. 1 ff.), and the so-called ETACA (European Trust and Cooperation Approach) has experimented a pilot project common framework for high-level risk assessment in the field of transfer pricing by EU tax authorities.
5. *See* §24.2.
6. *See* §24.3.
7. *See* §24.4.
8. I consider it as an expression of acquis of the Union (*see*: Pasquale Pistone, *The Settlement of Cross-Border Tax Disputes in the European Union*, in: *European Tax Law*, 8th ed. 730 (Pasquale

contained in the proposed Directive into the said multilateral convention.[9] That compromise was hard to question from an EU law perspective, considering that at that time, the primary law of the European Union still included a safeguard clause to preserve the rights of EU Member States to regulate matters connected with cross-border double taxation in the European Union.[10] Reconciling a multilateral international convention with the existing bilateral tax treaty network possibly made things easier than it would have been the case in the presence of an EU Directive. The broad alignment between the rules contained in such conventions did the rest, giving associated enterprises within the EU an additional legal instrument to achieve a single solution to their cross-border tax disputes on transfer pricing.

However, the choice to approve such rules by means of an international binding legal instrument of coordination produced the important consequence of preventing the development of secondary law of the European Union in an area of cross-border taxation that was already regulated at the national level by most Member States through international convention. Moreover, being contained in the EU Tax Arbitration Convention, those rules were thus also subtracted from the jurisdiction of the Court of Justice, which, already at that time, was giving clear signals that direct taxation did not constitute a reserved domain for EU Member States, but an area in which the exercise of their powers at the national level had to comply with the supremacy of EU law.

From a historical perspective, it is interesting to note that it was not until the introduction of the EU Cross-Border Tax Dispute Settlement Directive in 2017 that secondary law could be issued in this area. The overlap in the scope with the 1990 EU Tax Arbitration Convention as to cross-border transfer pricing disputes affecting tax treaties is evident, just like the fact that the Convention constituted a reference framework for the Directive to overcome some procedural issues that have prevented the Convention from fully deploying its settlement potential. However, the Directive did not put an end to such Convention but allows for its parallel functioning.

The evolution of European and international tax law in the quarter of a century following the entry into force of the Convention has meanwhile shown that the adoption of an EU Directive with such a content and formulation does not necessarily deprive EU Member States of their power to continue applying rules agreed in the framework of international conventions that operate at the national level. Leaving aside the regulatory complexity that arises in the presence of several legal instruments that are applicable in parallel and that operate in different legal scenarios, the key to make them all compatible is that they can be activated upon the initiative of the affected taxpayer.

Pistone et al. eds, Wolters Kluwer Law & Business 2018)), but Harm M. Pit does not (*see*: Harm M. Pit, *Dispute Resolution in the EU: The EU Arbitration Convention and the Dispute Resolution Directive* 188 (IBFD 2018)).

9. Convention 90/436/EEC of 23 July 1990, on the elimination of double taxation in connection with the adjustment of profits of associated enterprises, in OJ L 225, 20 August 1990, p. 10.
10. This clause was included in Art. 220, 2nd indent of the Treaty of Rome. Despite lacking a direct effect, as the CJEU would have then indicated in CJEU, 12 May 1998, Case C-336/96, Gilly, ECLI:CU:C:1998:221, para. 17.

A common element between the two normative texts is that the taxpayer remains always in the background. This shows a trend that characterised EU tax law in 2017 no differently from what it did back in 1990, especially in respect of cross-border tax disputes between States, such as the ones that arise in the field of transfer pricing. However, the legal instrument makes the difference for the taxpayer. Judicial interpretation by the Court of Justice has meanwhile clarified that the obligation to comply with EU primary law applies also in the presence of secondary law, including when the latter does not contain specific rules that secure consistent exercise of powers in the framework of tax procedures with the general principles of EU law. Considering, in particular, the implications of the *Berlioz* judgment for mutual administrative cooperation in the field of tax law,[11] it is therefore possible to hold that taxpayers not only have a right in respect of the situations expressly enshrined in Article 13 of the EU Tax Dispute Settlement Directive[12] but are also obliged to exercise their powers in conformity with the requirements of the Rule of Law and that the affected taxpayers have legal standing to obtain, with the active involvement of the judiciary, that this occurs in practice. Similar conclusions may be reached in respect of all the clauses contained in the Directive that include deadlines and the application of actual remedies under domestic law of the Member States involved to avoid possible procedural *impasses*.

A notable difference is that the Convention requires the agreement to eliminate double taxation,[13] but the Directive only refers to an agreement on how to resolve the cross-border tax dispute.[14] This might be regarded as a step back in the evolution of positive integration of tax rules applicable to transfer pricing. However, the recently proposed Directive might not confirm this conclusion, showing instead that the EU Commission has changed its strategy. Before addressing that, it might be meaningful to observe further developments in European tax law that have affected transfer pricing.

§24.3 THE IMPACT OF PRIMARY EU LAW ON TAXATION AND TRANSFER PRICING

The impact of primary EU law on taxation has significantly developed across the years by means of judicial interpretation, starting with the one on fundamental freedoms and then gradually spreading also through to that on State aids and EU fundamental rights.[15]

11. CJEU, 16 May 2017, Case C-682/15, Berlioz, EU:C:2017:373, para. 49.
12. The fact that the title of Art. 13 refers to 'information, evidence and hearings' and that the wording of such clause refers to the fact that the affected persons 'may' provide them is by its own nature not incompatible with the existence of actual rights in this respect, which is required by contextual interpretation of such clauses in line with the requirements established by the general principles of EU law.
13. *See* Arts 1 and 7 of the 1990 EU Tax Arbitration Convention. Moreover, Art. 14 contains detailed rules that determine when the double taxation is eliminated.
14. *See* Art. 15 of the 2017 EU Tax Dispute Settlement Directive.
15. A separate analysis of the impact of CJEU case law on EU fundamental rights is not required for the purposes of this chapter, given its negligible specific impact on transfer pricing, which is usually the consequence of the application of more general principles, such as in the case of the right to participate in dispute settlement procedures.

The specific developments concerning transfer pricing have also been significantly influenced by the attempts of the EU Commission to steer the panoply of national tax rules towards a coordinated exercise in line with the EU competition policy.

Whether or not such attempts have been successful is a matter that this chapter will not evaluate on a final basis, also considering that there are still pending cases before the Court of Justice and the Tribunal.[16] However, such ongoing developments should not prevent from recording some ongoing trends and assessing the existing criticalities at the intersection between an existing supranational competition policy of the EU and taxation, besides the reiterated attempts of the EU Commission to introduce elements of coordination across the different national tax policies of EU Member States.

The interpretation of fundamental freedoms allowed negative integration of direct taxes to remove various obstacles and to achieve a level-playing field by using the non-discrimination principle. The line of reasoning adopted by the Court has acknowledged the factual relevance of the arm's-length standard in connection with the application of EU justification. In particular, in the *SGI* case,[17] the Court, on the one hand, regarded the existence of 'fully competitive conditions', i.e., arm's length, as not requiring further evidence of the absence of potential avoidance schemes, and, on the other hand, admitted a reversal of the burden of proof for all situations in which the conditions agreed between associated enterprises diverted from such standard. By doing so, it also considered the arm's length as a relevant benchmark for determining the so-called balanced allocation of taxing powers.[18]

However, negative integration is by its own nature neither sufficient nor able to achieve a consistent tax treatment across the Union. The fragmentation of national tax policies across the Member States activated a parallel process of creating cross-border disparities by means of unilateralism, which the interpretation of EU law cannot address.

The difficulties also arise when applying the prohibition of State aids to matters of taxation,[19] which spread from the identification of the national reference framework to the existence of selective advantages in connection with the exploitation of cross-border tax disparities.

When addressing the first type of issue, the Court has eventually rejected the direct relevance of arm's length for EU law beyond its potential validity as a standard aggregating consensus among OECD countries.[20] What matters is instead the existence

16. For example, CJEU, *Commission v. Ireland and Others (Apple)*, case C-465/20 *P & Commission v. Amazon.com and Others*, case C-457/21 P.
17. CJEU, 21 January 2010, case C-311/08, SGI, paras 71-73.
18. CJEU, 31 May 2018, case C-382/16, *Hornbach-Baumarkt*, paras 43-45.
19. *See* further on this topic the comprehensive analysis developed by Jérôme Monsenego, *Selectivity in State Aid Law and the Methods for the Allocation of the Corporate Tax Base* (Kluwer Law International 2018) and Alexandra Miladinovic, *Selectivity and the Arm's Length Principle in EU State Aid* (IBFD 2022).
20. *See* CJEU, 8.11.2022, joined cases C-885/19 P and C-898/19 P, *Fiat and Luxembourg v. Commission*, para. 96. *See also*, Ruth Mason, *Ding-Dong! The EU Arm's Length Standard Is Dead*, Tax Notes International (5 December 2022), retrievable at the following link: https://www.taxnotes.com/featured-analysis/ding-dong-eu-arms-length-standard-dead/2022/12/02/7

of its binding relevance in the national systems, which was rejected by the Court in the absence of specific national rules requiring its application as a violation of the principle of legality in taxation.[21] Therefore, if one Member State introduces arm's length in its national legislation and another one does not, significant repercussions will arise from competition across the borders within the internal market.

The repercussions of unilateralism on competition within the internal market allow the creation of tax advantages from the exploitation of cross-border tax disparities, which are hard to address along the lines of State aids. This is, for instance, the case of the Belgian excess profit ruling system. Such measures replaced relief of cross-border economic double taxation between associated enterprises with a preventive approach that presupposes consistency with the arm's-length standard and applies regardless of whether the other State involved complies with such standard. The schedular application of such advantages is theoretically compliant with an international standard but nevertheless allows MNEs to obtain advantages that would not be available in purely domestic situations.[22]

The status quo of European taxation generates disparities that just nurture distortions across the national borders. The absence of a policy-based approach to tax issues connected with transfer pricing, combined with a significant development of judicial interpretation on primary law, might prevent consistency of tax treatment at both national and supranational levels.

However, the need for unanimous consent by all EU Member States creates structural difficulties in introducing common rules in the field of taxation but is not suitable to endorse the preservation of national tax rules without any coordination at EU level.

§24.4 THE PROPOSED EU TRANSFER PRICING DIRECTIVE: SELECTED ISSUES FROM A LEGAL AND POLICY PERSPECTIVE

§24.4.1 General Issues

Shortly before the end of its mandate, the EU Commission published a package of measures on direct taxation of MNEs, which include proposals for EU Directives on the

fd35. For a critical analysis of the General Court's acceptance of the European Commission's reconstruction, both later overturned by the Court of Justice, *see* Cees Peters, *Critical Analysis of the General Court's 'EU Arm's Length Tool': Beware of the Reflexivity of Transfer Pricing Law!*, 31 EC Tax Review 1, 30 (2022) DOI: 10.54648/ecta2022004.

21. In her Opinion delivered on 8.6.2023, case C-457/21, *Commission v. Luxembourg and Amazon*, para. 72, AG Kokott expressly recalled the relevance of this principle for determining the binding value of a given measure in a Member State.

22. The cases on Belgian excess profit ruling system have not been conclusively addressed by CJEU, which in some of them has referred the case back to the General Court, indicating some precise conclusions as to the de facto selective advantages of such measures. *See* for instance: CJEU, 16 September 2021, case C-337/19 P, *Commission v. Belgium and Magnetrol.*

corporate tax base (BEFIT)[23] and on the introduction of the arm's-length standard for the relations between associated enterprises.[24]

The latter proposal shows a fundamental change of strategy, which overcomes the repeated attempts to achieve such goal by using soft law first and primary law then. This change of strategy goes in the right direction, as it reflects the awareness of having tax policy decisions steering the convergence of cross-border tax disparities of business taxation towards a common mould. This development might make tax competition within the internal market more transparent and fairer.

The introduction of supranational tax rules on transfer pricing requires addressing a selection of critical issues raised by the proposal of the EU Commission. In particular, these issues relate to the legal basis of the proposed Directive;[25] the legal relevance of the OECD Transfer Pricing Guidelines for its application;[26] as well as the meaning, scope and determination of arm's length according to its clauses.[27] Even though all such issues have been selected for reasons connected with the criticalities that they present, this chapter will also put forward possible proposals to address them in a satisfactory way.

§24.4.2 The Legal Basis of the Proposed Directive

First and foremost, the proposed regime must find the unanimous consensus required for the introduction of secondary law under Article 115 TFEU. This might be a challenge in itself.

From a theoretical perspective, the fact that arm's length is endorsed as an international standard by EU countries within the OECD and is consistent with Article 9 of most bilateral tax treaties might pave the way for a smooth approval in the framework of the EU Council.

However, external factors have hampered (or slowed down) the approval of other measures of tax harmonisation related to good tax governance even though they had been the object of coordination under the auspices of the OECD. The main factor is that unanimity ends up prompting single Member States to subordinate their consent to concessions in other fields, where majority voting makes their single vote irrelevant.

Moreover, recent litigation on State aids shows that the failure to adopt arm's length in the domestic legislation of some Member States was the main reason to exclude the existence of a selective advantage for State aid purposes. The obligation to introduce the arm's-length standard for transactions between associated enterprises

23. European Commission, Proposal for a Council Directive on Business in Europe: Framework for Income Taxation (BEFIT), 12 September 2023, COM(2023) 532 final and *see* for a study that elaborately comments on this proposed Directive: Pasquale Pistone et al., *Proposal for a Council Directive on BEFIT: An Initial Assessment* (IBFD 2023).
24. *Supra* n. 2, at 529.
25. *See* §24.4.2.
26. *See* §24.4.3.
27. *See* §24.4.4.

would therefore deprive such countries of an important tool to enhance the competitiveness of their systems as opposed to the ones of other EU Member States. Nevertheless, this argument can also be used to justify the need for secondary law in this field. Accordingly, the unwillingness of those countries to abide by this widely accepted international standard might prove the need to intervene with positive integration in the form of tax harmonisation in order to make a consistent progress towards the elimination of the cross-border tax disparities that would otherwise distort business within the EU internal market. This argument is also important to stress that even if free competition is of major importance within the EU internal market, the shortcomings of cross-border tax disparities require limiting national autonomy in this context with the introduction of regulatory measures by means of secondary EU law.

Time will tell whether the EU Commission will manage to aggregate the unanimous consensus in the EU Council that is required for the approval of the proposed Directive and, in the affirmative, whether the proposed regime might be approved without major amendments to its current structure and content.

§24.4.3 The Relevance of the OECD Transfer Pricing Guidelines from a Legal Perspective

A second critical point may arise as to the rules that govern the amendments to the proposed Directive. When Article 3 n. 18 of the proposed Directive defines the meaning of the expression 'OECD Transfer Pricing Guidelines', it includes a kind of dynamic clause, which refers primarily to the 2022 version of such document, as included in Annex I of the proposed Directive, and then adds an express reference to 'any further amendments…that the Union approved in the context of the OECD Committee on Fiscal Affairs via the adoption of a Union position under Article 218 (9) TFEU'.

This kind of clause is an absolute première in the realm of supranational tax law[28] and requires some closer analysis. The choice of the proposed EU Directive to apply Article 218(9) TFEU is clear as to its object and purpose: achieving a dynamic alignment of the EU arm's-length standard to the boundaries of the one resulting from the OECD Transfer Pricing Guidelines. By contrast, the content and legal implications of this choice might leave room for discussion from various legal perspectives. Neither of such clauses contains any express reference to tax law nor to general domains that could justify its potential application to tax matters. This conclusion may not change if one considers that Article 207 TFEU also includes a reference to agreements with international organisations.

It is doubtful that Article 218 TFEU might apply outside of the boundaries of the common commercial policy. This clause belongs to a cluster of provisions that regulates the common commercial policy with other countries and international organisations: this context differs significantly from that in which tax law operates.

28. Some countries foresee in their domestic legislation the possibility to align the domestic framework with later updates to the OECD Transfer Pricing Guidelines; however, this process of dynamic adaptation is typically mediated by administrative practice. *See, inter alia*, in this sense, Art. 9 of Ministerial Decree 14 May 2018 (Italy).

International taxation keeps exclusive taxing powers at the national level for all purposes other than the ones that are specifically regulated within EU Directives. In such context, it should be noted that the introduction of an EU Directive in tax matters does not per se deprive Member States of their own taxing powers but confine them within the boundaries of the implementation of the Directive. This means that Member States will preserve leeway as to how they implement the Directive, provided that they fully include its content in their national legislation. Leaving aside those criticalities and even for those who could put arguments to overcome them, more issues would therefore arise as to whether the competence of the EU would be an exclusive or mixed one.[29]

Further critical issues arise in connection with the legal nature of the OECD Transfer Pricing Guidelines, which are nothing but a technical international regulatory document. Even though the content of the OECD Transfer Pricing Guidelines makes them very authoritative at the global level from a technical perspective, they remain an expression of international regulatory soft law.[30] The circumstance that the development of the arm's-length standard has been mainly prompted by the OECD and that the OECD has nudged the development of the so-called OECD Transfer Pricing Guidelines in the form of soft law, hardened at the level of the various States,[31] are something different from the existence of an agreement with an international organisation, which is presupposed by Article 218 TFEU. Neither the proposed Directive enshrines an agreement with the OECD nor can its proposed amendments comply with the OECD Transfer Pricing Guidelines by allowing the EU Commission to preserve an alignment with them. Therefore, until the OECD Transfer Pricing Guidelines are implemented by a multilateral international agreement, they lack an international binding dimension.

The situation does not change if one considers that Article 3 n. 18 of the proposed Directive refers to 'the adoption of a Union position'. Adopting a position of the Union under Article 218(9) TFEU is something that can be done in respect of a body set up by an agreement, which is missing in this case. In such circumstances, the absence of such agreement would make it very difficult to determine, from an international law perspective, the actual legal implications of this adopted position, which would remain instead mostly at the level of the regulatory effects of this expression of international soft law.

---

29. The existence of an external power of the Union in the specific areas governed by the proposed Directive might nevertheless be argued along the line of reasoning adopted by the CJEU on 31 March 1971, case 22/70, *Commission v. Council*, ECLI:EU:C:1971:32, also known as the *ERTA* doctrine, which secures a parallel development between internal and external powers of the Union. The application of the reasoning included in para. 17 of this judgment should nevertheless not go as far as to produce the effect of depriving EU Member States of their power to (co-)regulate the matters object of the proposed Directive in their relations with third countries.
30. *See* further on this point Alberto Vega, *International Governance Through Soft Law: The Case of the OECD Transfer Pricing Guidelines*, Working Paper of the Max Planck Institute for Tax Law and Public Finance No. 2012-05, Accessible on SSRN at the following link: https://papers.ssrn.com/sol3/papers.cfm?abstract_id=2100341.
31. On such dynamics, in connection in particular to the earlier cited high-profile State Aid cases, *see also* Dimitrios A. Kyriazis, *From Soft Law to Soft Law Through Hard Law: The Commission's Approach to the State Aid Assessment of Tax Rulings*, 15 European State Aid Law Quarterly 3 (2016) DOI: 10.21552/estal/2016/3/10.

More doubts arise as to whether Article 218 TFEU could apply to such context, namely as to the fact that the conclusion of an agreement would bind the EU and its Member States towards the OECD not only in the absence of an international agreement but also without a corresponding obligation for other countries to do the same. This means that such other countries could informally decide to withdraw or weaken in practice their support to the OECD Transfer Pricing Guidelines, while the EU would be unilaterally bound to abide by it. From this perspective, it is submitted that the envisaged dynamic adaptation to the OECD Transfer Pricing Guidelines might require a prior signature of an international multilateral agreement hardening this expression of international regulatory soft law.

Given the frequent amendments to its content, from a policy perspective, the issue arises as to whether such hardening would be desirable at all. Even though a positive answer might not be excluded, it would certainly require setting up a flexible mechanism for adjusting its content on a periodical basis, which might be very complex in practice.

Last but not least, Article 207(4) TFEU indicates that the Council decides on the negotiation of the agreements with third countries and international organisations by a qualified majority. Even though Article 218 TFEU is *lex specialis* in respect of Article 207 TFEU, nothing indicates different rules for the adoption of the position enshrined in Article 218(9) TFEU. Therefore, for how flexibility might be highly desirable to amend technical rules, absolute clarity is required as to the fact that the unanimity on the introduction of the proposed Directive also implies the right for the EU Council to adopt qualified majority voting as to the amendments of the rules contained in the EU Directive with a view to adjusting them to the developments of the content of the OECD Transfer Pricing Guidelines.

The introduction of qualified majority voting is in fact very meaningful in tax matters[32] and might be regarded as a pragmatic way to achieve sound policy decisions with a correspondingly suitable content. Besides, it would remove the need for political compromises that often undermine technical consistency and that often reflect a vision of national tax sovereignty that no longer corresponds to the substance of the limits that States currently accept when pursuing global tax governance goals by means of international and supranational regulatory measures.

§24.4.4 The Meaning, Scope and Determination of Arm's Length

This section focuses on the meaning, scope and determination of arm's length in the proposed EU Transfer Pricing Directive.

The definition of Article 3 n. 1 of the proposed Directive contains the core substance of the introduction of arm's length within the secondary law of the European Union.

32. Pasquale Pistone, *A Plea for Qualified Majority Voting and the Ordinary Legislative Procedure in European Tax Law*, in: *CFE Tax Advisers Europe – 60th Anniversary Liber Amicorum* 11-34 (Servaas van Thiel et al. eds, IBFD 2019).

Interestingly, the definition describes 'arm's length principle' as an international standard, thus implicitly qualifying it in line with its real nature. The difference between principles and standards might be merely theoretical. The validity and recognition of principles from the perspective of justice beyond their posited dimension are certainly more than an agreed set of rules which constitute a standard. Further insight on such difference might have limited relevance in this context, besides that of stressing the excessive inclination to refer to principles even in the absence of their typical features.

The wording of Article 3 of the proposed Directive limits the relevance of its definitions to the sole purposes of this Directive. This means that they may not express an immediate relevance in the context of other EU law instruments that also address similar issues. *Inter alia*, this means that it does not bind the interpretation of the EU Directive on Administrative Cooperation when tax authorities conduct joint audits on transfer pricing, that of the proposed BEFIT Directive in respect of the determination of the taxable base, as well as that of the EU Tax Dispute Settlement Directive when it addresses transfer pricing issues. Establishing a clearer coordination between the scope of the proposed EU Transfer Pricing Directive and the other pieces of EU secondary legislation affecting transfer pricing, as well as with the EU Tax Arbitration Convention might thus be a meaningful option for possible amendments to the proposed Directive.[33]

It is also unclear whether this definition may also produce repercussions on tax treaties, including in particular on Article 9, which shares the common substance with the definition contained in the proposed Directive, except for the fact that the letter is formulated in a more specific manner. This might also raise the issue as to whether the Commentary on Article 9 of the OECD Model Convention might be relevant to clarify the meaning and scope of arm's length[34] under the proposed Directive, also considering the express reference to the OECD Transfer Pricing Guidelines contained in Article 3, n. 18 of the proposed Directive.

The meaning, scope and determination of arm's length in the context of the proposed Directive raise several difficulties in connection with the establishment of a dynamic link with the OECD Transfer Pricing Guidelines that have been outlined earlier; the question might arise as to whether, from a policy perspective, such link is necessary and desirable.

The view of the author is that, for how such link might be desirable from a perspective of global tax governance, it is in fact not necessary, as the definition of Article 3 n. 1 of the proposed Directive leaves leeway for achieving some form of alignment with the international standard at the level of interpretation. Moreover, the absence of a binding obligation to comply with the OECD Transfer Pricing Guidelines will also allow to preserve consistency with the overall framework established by EU

33. This might occur by adding a final clause in the final text of the Directive clarifying that the value of the definitions also applies to the other legal instruments of EU law that address issues related to arm's length.
34. On the interplay between the OECD Transfer Pricing Guidelines and the OECD Commentary to Art. 9 of the OECD Model Convention, *see* Michael Kobetsky, *The Status of the OECD Transfer Pricing Guidelines in the Post-BEPS Dynamics*, 3 Int. Tax. Stud. 2 (2020).

law. Accordingly, it would turn the international standard into a source of technical inspiration and a non-exclusive principle of interpretation for determining the actual meaning under EU law, which would instead have to be determined by the Court of Justice in line with the wording of Article 3, n. 1 of the proposed Directive, in its context as an instrument of secondary EU law, and in line with its object and purpose.

Adjusting the wording of Article 3, n. 18 of the proposed Directive with the removal of the powers of amendment linked to Article 218(9) TFEU[35] would in fact not produce major repercussions on the technical relevance of the OECD Transfer Pricing Guidelines, given their authoritative content and their validity across the countries. However, it might make it meaningful to intervene also with an amendment to the wording of Article 14 of the proposed Directive, which would reflect the opportunity of restructuring the relevance of the OECD Transfer Pricing Guidelines as an external source of secondary EU law.

The current wording of Article 14(1) of the proposed Directive refers to an obligation of transposition of the rules contained in Chapter II of the Directive, adding that they should 'ensure that those transfer pricing rules are applied in a manner consistent with the OECD Transfer Pricing Guidelines'. This clause creates an open-ended obligation under EU law to comply with an international technical regulatory document, which might prevent the judiciary from achieving other solutions at the interpretative level and thus, in the current content, turn an instrument of international regulatory soft law into a binding measure, hardened at supranational level of the European Union. Therefore, any failure to do so, even at the level of interpretation, would turn into a violation of the primacy of EU law.

This argument should also be seen from the perspective of the powers of the EU judiciary to interpret its own law. In this specific context, the question might arise as to whether the binding value of the OECD Transfer Pricing Guidelines is compatible with the power of the CJEU to be the single judicial body to interpret its own law. When addressing this question, it should be noted that, in other similar circumstances, the Court of Justice has opposed solutions that would deprive it of such power. Practically speaking, removing the renvoi clause of Article 14(1) of the proposed Directive might be a meaningful amendment to preserve the power of the CJEU to determine the meaning of 'arm's length' under EU law.

Moreover, it would also prevent possible issues from arising in respect of the powers of the Council enshrined in Article 14(2) of the proposed Directive, according to which further rules may be introduced to ensure tax certainty and mitigate the risk of double taxation. In the absence of Article 14(1) of the proposed Directive, the CJEU would have full interpretative powers as to the determination of whether the EU Council is acting consistently, i.e., taking into account, with the source of inspiration of the rules contained in the EU Directive.

35. In particular, the author suggests removing the following words from Art. 3, n. 18 of the proposed Directive: ', and any further amendments to these OECD Transfer Pricing Guidelines that the Union approved in the context of the OECD Committee on Fiscal Affairs via the adoption of a Union position under 218(9) TFEU'.

Based on these arguments, it might be meaningful to amend the text of the proposed Directive by excluding the dynamic renvoi to an external legal source from its final text.

§24.5 CONCLUSIONS

The developments of secondary EU law on transfer pricing show an important evolution of tax harmonisation, which reflect the awareness of the need for common supranational rules applicable to large enterprises within the EU internal market.

The package presented by the EU Commission on 12 September 2023 by the EU Commission makes an important shift towards the removal of cross-border tax disparities and might contribute to the establishment of a real supranational coordination of corporate tax policies within the European Union. The goals pursued by the proposed EU Transfer Pricing Directive presuppose a parallel intervention at the level of the establishment of common rules on the taxable base for corporate entities, which is what the proposed EU BEFIT Directive wants to achieve. From this perspective, the two proposals are the arms joint to the same trunk and presuppose a parallel introduction into the EU legal system.

The expected reduction of disparities in corporate taxation within the EU will remove the sources of intended and unintended advantages and distortions across the borders. This outcome will prevent disputes from arising, rather than addressing them at the sole settlement level, as the EU Commission had proposed with the EU Tax Arbitration Directive on Transfer Pricing back in 1976.

Much has changed in the field of direct taxation during the past half a century, but the ambitions of the EU Commission to push forward tax harmonisation with the package of measures proposed on 12 September 2023 regain speed in the direction of introducing measures that remove cross-border tax obstacles. And this is all very encouraging.

From a policy perspective, this change of direction also helps overcome the notable complexity imported from the OECD international tax coordination projects into EU law with the ATAD and GMT Directives. It might also be a lesson for international tax coordination, which continues along the lines of highly complex rules, such as the ones recently released in the multilateral convention implementing the so-called Pillar 1, and the dynamics of keeping wide discretionary margins for tax authorities that might address critical issues mainly at the level of settlement.

Insofar as the final text of the EU Transfer Pricing Directive will address the critical issues of legal interpretation outlined earlier in this chapter and will make it to obtain the unanimity required for the introduction, it can mark a new era for the taxation of multinational enterprises in the European Union.

CHAPTER 25

The Impact of CJEU Decisions in Preliminary Ruling Proceedings on German Tax Law with Particular Focus on Procedural Law

Steffen Lampert

§25.1 INTRODUCTION

Peter Essers of the Fiscal Institute of Tilburg University and the Institute for Financial and Tax Law at the University of Osnabrück, now part of the Institute for Constitutional, Administrative and Economic Law, have always maintained a close relationship already under my predecessors Prof. Jörg Manfred Mössner and Prof. Heike Jochum, particularly through the EUCOTAX Wintercourse, which the jubilarian continues to shape to this day. With the following chapter, I would like to thank Peter for his commitment to this great program of international understanding. The following chapter is devoted to the domestic effect of decisions of the CJEU in preliminary ruling proceedings. It is intended to make a small contribution to a better understanding, particularly of the administrative framework for the implementation of CJEU decisions in taxation proceedings in Germany and possibly to provide suggestions for the discussion of similar regulatory regimes in other Member States.

§25.2 CONSIDERATION OF DECISIONS OF THE CJEU IN TAXATION PROCEEDINGS

§25.2.1 Obligation to Refer

If a tax court or the Federal Fiscal Court (*Bundesfinanzhof* (BFH)) considers a preliminary ruling on the interpretation of the Treaties to be necessary for the issuance of its judgment, it must suspend the proceedings by order pursuant to Article 267 of the Treaty on the Functioning of the European Union (TFEU)[1] and address the substantiated question for a preliminary ruling to the CJEU.[2] The courts are not only obliged to do this under Article 267(3) TFEU; moreover, the German Constitution supports this obligation to refer questions under European Union law: if a tax court fails to make a referral despite its obligation to do so under EU law, this violates the right to the lawful judge guaranteed in Article 101(1) sentence 2 of the German Constitution (*Grundgesetz* (GG)). This can be challenged by a constitutional complaint.[3] The Federal Constitutional Court (*Bundesverfassungsgericht* (BVerfG)) assumes a violation if the German court has unjustifiably exceeded its discretion by failing to submit the case. This is the case, for example, if the case law of the CJEU is incomplete, but the fiscal court assumes a legal situation to be clear or clarified beyond doubt, without providing a factually plausible justification for this.[4] For instance, the 3rd Chamber of the Second Senate of the Federal Constitutional Court decided on March 4, 2021, that the Federal Fiscal Court had violated the complainant's right to a lawful judge. In the opinion of the Federal Constitutional Court, the Federal Fiscal Court had unreasonably assumed that an *acte clair* or an *acte éclairé* existed in the *Hornbach-Baumarkt* case of the CJEU regarding the correction of income under tax law due to the structuring of loans between companies belonging to the same group with their registered offices in different EU Member States.[5] The ruling was therefore overturned, and the case was referred back to the Federal Fiscal Court.

§25.2.2 Binding Effect of the Decision

The referring court and the other courts dealing with the same subject of the proceedings are then bound by the interpretation made by the CJEU (effect *inter partes*).[6] Regarding a binding effect *erga omnes*, it must be noted that a national legal provision which contradicts EU law according to a judgment of the CJEU[7] may not be applied due to the primacy of the application of EU law.[8] According to the case law of the CJEU, other national institutions are also obliged to "take the general or particular measures necessary to ensure that Community law is complied within that state, in particular ensure that national law is changed so as to comply with Community law as

1. In connection with section 74 of the German Finance Courts Code (*Finanzgerichtsordnung* (FGO)).
2. Consolidated version of the Treaty on the Functioning of the European Union—Protocol (No. 3) of the Statute of the Court of Justice of the European Union, Art. 23(1), OJ C 202/210, 7.6.2016.
3. German Federal Constitutional Court (*Bundesverfassungsgericht* (BVerfG)), order of 22.10.1986—2 BvR 197/83 (Solange II) (mn. 49 ff.).
4. BVerfG, order of 28.01.2014—2 BvR 1561/12, 2 (mn. 185); BVerfG, order of 19.12.2017—2 BvR 424/17 (mn. 43).
5. BVerfG, order of 4.3.2021—2 BvR 1161/19 (mn. 44).
6. Case C-29/68, *Milch- Fett- und Eierkontor v. Hauptzollamt Saarbrücken* [1969], ECLI:EU:C:1969:13.
7. To be exact, the CJEU does not conclude that the national law is contrary to EU law, but only that EU law takes precedence over national laws as interpreted by the CJEU.
8. Case C-6/64, *Costa v. E.N.E.L.* [1964] (mn. 3), ECLI:EU:C:1964:51; Case C-106/77 *Finanzverwaltung v. Simmenthal* [1978], ECLI:EU:C:1978:31 (mn. 17 f.).

soon as possible and that the rights which individuals derive from Community law are given full effect."[9]

For this reason, even before the legislator takes action, the German authorities must ensure that national law is interpreted and applied in conformity with EU law by administrative orders or other similar procedures.[10] The establishment of conditions in conformity with EU law by means of administrative instructions[11] is only an immediate measure, not a permanent solution. According to the established case law of the CJEU, a definitive remedy of the violation of EU law is only possible through mandatory national provisions which have the same legal effect as the provision to be amended, which means that in German tax law this is regularly done through a federal law.[12]

§25.2.3 Effects on the Taxation Procedure

§25.2.3.1 Cases of Already Issued Tax Assessment Notices

The binding effect erga omnes of CJEU decisions described above raises the legal question of whether and how CJEU decisions can be taken into account in German taxation proceedings. The consideration of decisions—for example, the non-application of a German tax law provision or the interpretation of a provision that deviates from the previous administrative interpretation—in tax assessment notices that have *already been issued* conflicts with the principle of legal certainty that is derived from the fundamental principle of the rule of law under Article 20(3) of the German Constitution, according to which citizens should be able to rely on a consistent and foreseeable application of the law.

In the following, the questions will be addressed as to how decisions of the CJEU affect cases in which a tax assessment has already been issued on the basis of an application of a tax law that is contrary to EU law, and what the impact is if there is uncertainty about the application of a tax law during the taxation proceedings because a preliminary ruling procedure is held before the CJEU that relates to the applicable norm. In this context, the question also arises as to how to proceed if the proceedings relate to a provision of foreign law that is similar to a domestic regulation.

§25.2.3.2 Brief Overview of the Taxation Procedure and the Amendment of Tax Assessments

Before addressing these issues, it is necessary to take a look at the German taxation procedure: the taxpayer is obliged to file a tax return (e.g., income tax return/corporate

9. Cases C-231/06–233/06, *Office national de pension v. Jonkman, Vercheval, Permesaen* [2007], ECLI:EU:C:2007:373 (mn. 38).
10. Grabitz/Hilf/Nettesheim/Karpenstein, *Das Recht der Europäischen Union* Art. 267 TFEU (mn. 106) (79th ed., Beck 2023).
11. These are generally regulations issued by higher-level authorities which are binding within the administration but do not have any binding effect on taxpayers or courts in external relations.
12. Case C-151/94, *Commission v. Luxembourg* [1995] (mn. 18 with further evidence), ECLI: EU:C:1995:357.

income tax return/sales tax return) to the competent tax authority.[13] The tax authority then reviews the information and issues a tax assessment based on it.[14] After the tax assessment has been issued, the taxpayer has one month to appeal the assessment by filing a so-called objection.[15] In the following objection procedure, the tax authority itself reviews the legitimacy of the tax assessment. The objection procedure must be distinguished from the lawsuit, which is only admissible against the so-called objection decision that is issued by the tax authority after the objection procedure has been (partially) unsuccessful. If the taxpayer does not file an appeal, he or she can no longer take action against the assessment after the deadline for filing an appeal has expired, even if the content of the assessment is incorrect (so-called formal validity). The formal validity is to be distinguished from the so-called material validity, which expresses a general binding effect of the authorities on their decisions once they have been made. Thus, once a tax assessment notice has been issued, the tax authority is generally bound by its content.

With regard to the question of whether the tax authority can amend a tax assessment on its own initiative, a distinction must be made: on the one hand, the tax authorities can break through this binding effect in accordance with so-called correction provisions,[16] which allow a subsequent amendment in special cases (e.g., in the event of the existence of new facts or obvious inaccuracies). Although the amendment of tax assessments concerning consumption taxes is possible without further requirements, it is limited by the statute of limitations,[17] which is the limitation period after whose expiry a remission/amendment/revocation of a tax assessment is no longer possible even if there are generally possibilities for amendment.[18] However, with regard to direct taxes, no correction provision that would allow decisions of the CJEU to be considered is regularly applicable. Moreover, a tax assessment notice cannot be amended under more favorable conditions than would be the case in the event of a violation of domestic law since the correction system of the German Fiscal Code[19] conclusively regulates the enforcement of claims arising from EU law without a violation of EU law.[20]

In addition, sections 164 and 165 of the German Fiscal Code are of considerable importance. They have in common that they allow a tax assessment even in cases in which a final tax assessment cannot yet be made because the case has not yet been conclusively examined (section 164) or because there is a current uncertainty of fact or law that cannot be remedied (section 165).[21] Both provisions prevent the material validity of the decision and therefore do not make a change or cancellation subject to

13. *See* section 149 of the German Fiscal Code.
14. *See* section 155(1) sentence 1 of the German Fiscal Code.
15. *See* sections 347(1) and 355(1) of the German Fiscal Code.
16. Especially sections 172-177 of the German Fiscal Code; *note* that section 129 Fiscal Code, which permits the amendment of administrative acts due to obvious incorrectness, is not applicable here.
17. *See* sections 169 f. of the German Fiscal Code.
18. *See* section 172(1) sentence 1 no. 1 of the German Fiscal Code.
19. *See* sections 172 f. of the German Fiscal Code.
20. German Federal Fiscal Court (BFH), judgment of 16.09.2010—V R 57/09 (mn. 43 ff.)
21. BFH, judgment of 06.03.1992—III R 47/91.

the requirements of the above-mentioned correction provisions.[22] Section 164 typically applies to constellations in which the tax authority cannot make a final decision on the tax case for internal administrative reasons, whereas section 165 relates to obstacles to a decision that lie outside the sphere of the tax authority.

§25.2.3.3 The Significance of the Provisional Tax Assessment for the Impact of CJEU Rulings

Given the limited possibilities for correction, the "keeping open" of a tax assessment through the order of a reservation subject to review (section 164 Fiscal Code) or the provisional tax assessment (section 165 AO) is of decisive importance. The legislator has regulated the consideration of ongoing and completed (preliminary ruling) proceedings before the CJEU in section 165 Fiscal Code.[23] This includes cases in which the incompatibility of a tax law with EU law is claimed before the CJEU. It thus requires that the "model case proceedings" before the CJEU[24] were already pending at the time of the tax assessment and are not obviously without a prospect of success.[25] This way, the legislator avoids that taxpayers file appeals against tax assessments purely as a precautionary measure in order to benefit from a possible later finding that a tax law is contrary to EU law. The provision is thus in the interest of the taxpayer, who does not have to file an appeal, and conserves resources of the tax authorities and courts.[26] Pursuant to section 165(2) sentence 2 Fiscal Code, the provisional character ends when the uncertainty has been cleared up, which in cases of proceedings before the CJEU[27] should regularly be with the decision of the CJEU.[28]

Depending on the circumstances, the provisionality of the tax assessment may be to the benefit or detriment of the taxpayer and may mean that legal certainty in the form of a final tax assessment does not occur for an indefinite period of time—because since the provisionality only keeps the material validity open to the extent specified in the tax assessment notice,[29,30] the provisional tax assessment suspends the expiry of the assessment period.[31] It thus prevents the material validity of the assessment, even though the assessment period has (actually) expired. The Federal Fiscal Court considers this acceptable[32] under the principle of the rule of law since this legal consequence

22. Sections 172-177 of the German Fiscal Code.
23. Specifically: section 165(1) sentence 2 no. 2a and no. 3 var. 1.
24. Proceedings before the European Court of Human Rights (ECtHR) are not included given the clear wording "before the Court of Justice of the European Union."
25. Ingo Oellerich, *AO/FGO*, § 165 (mn. 75) (Dietmar Gosch, Andreas Hoyer ed., Stollfuß 2023).
26. Reinhart Rüsken, *Klein Abgabenordnung*, § 165 (mn. 24) (16th ed., Beck 2022).
27. *See* section 165(1) no. 3 var. 1 of the German Fiscal Code.
28. However, this may be followed by a provisional ruling, if due to a decision by the CJEU a new legislative provision must be adopted, *see* section 165(1) sentence 2 no. 2a of the German Fiscal Code.
29. *See* section 165(1) sentence 3 of the German Fiscal Code.
30. *Rüsken*, § 165 Rn. 1.
31. In accordance with section 171(8) of the German Fiscal Code.
32. BFH, order of 19.10.2011—IV B 24/10; BFH, judgment of 26.10.2005—II R 9/01.

is justified by "objectively plausible" reasons and is mitigated by the legal institution of forfeiture.[33]

However, a declaration of provisionality[34] may not be issued (or is not applicable) if the proceedings before the CJEU have already been concluded when the tax assessment notice is issued. In order to ensure that any new statutory provisions that may follow from this also apply to the case affected by the violation of EU law, section 165 has been extended by a further provision.[35] An uncertainty justifying the provisional tax assessment already exists if it is possible and not entirely unlikely that a new regulation will be adopted.[36] The possibility of provisional assessment[37] does not only include activities of the legislator that are a consequence of rulings of the CJEU that directly affected German law, but generally also actions of the legislator as a consequence of rulings that related to foreign regulatory complexes comparable to German law.[38]

§25.3 SUBMISSION PRACTICE OF THE TAX COURTS

Considering the scope left to the courts with regard to requests for preliminary rulings in individual cases by Article 267(3) TFEU, the effectiveness of the preliminary ruling procedure also especially depends on how willing tax courts are to submit questions of law. So, what is the situation of the German fiscal jurisdiction in this respect? To answer this question, it is important to know that the German fiscal jurisdiction has only a two-level structure and that the fiscal administration itself plays a significant role in the system of legal protection: The eighteen fiscal courts set up at the level of the federal states[39] act as instances of fact, while the Federal Fiscal Court, as the highest federal court, is exclusively a court of appeal. Prior to the stages of appeal of the tax courts, there is an opposition procedure as an out-of-court appeal procedure.[40] In the opposition procedure, the tax authority—and thus the administration itself—initially reviews the legality of the issued tax assessment itself. Before an action can be filed with the responsible tax court, it is mandatory that the opposition procedure has first been completed. The vast majority of objections to the legality of tax assessments are thus already remedied at the level of the administration; in 2022, only 1.6% of the completed objections resulted in a lawsuit.[41]

33. BFH, judgment of 26.10.2005—II R 9/01 with reference to BVerfG, order of 29.06.1981—1 BvR 154/81.
34. Pursuant to section 165(1) sentence 2 no. 3 of the German Fiscal Code.
35. BestVModG, law of 18.07.2016, BGBl. I 2016, 1679 (1691).
36. Roman Seer, *Tipke/ Kruse AO/FGO*, § 165 mn. 14 (Otto Schmidt Verlag Cologne 2023).
37. Pursuant to section 165(1) sentence 2, no. 2a of the German Fiscal Code.
38. Oellerich, 165 (mn. 65.5).
39. Not every federal state has a fiscal court: Berlin and Brandenburg have a joint fiscal court, while North Rhine-Westphalia and Bavaria, the most populated states, have three and two fiscal courts, respectively.
40. *See* sections 347 f. of the German Fiscal Code.
41. Statistics of the Federal Ministry of Finance (*Bundesministerium der Finanzen* (BMF)) on the processing of objections in tax offices in 2022.

The practice of preliminary rulings by the fiscal courts can be traced back to the mid-1960s and initially related exclusively to turnover taxation. Since these beginnings, the Federal Fiscal Court has regularly requested preliminary rulings from the CJEU—until 2022, a total of 356 times and thus far more often than any other highest court in Germany.[42] The situation is similar for the tax courts of the federal states, which had submitted 519 requests for preliminary rulings to the CJEU by the end of November 2017.[43] The fact that primarily the respective senates for VAT have requested preliminary rulings from the CJEU is hardly surprising, given the degree of harmonization in this area. Recently, however, the number of requests for preliminary rulings in procedural and data protection law has increased significantly.[44]

§25.4 IMPULSES OF THE PRELIMINARY RULING PROCEDURES ON THE LEGISLATION OF INCOME TAX LAW

A detailed discussion of the question of whether and how the German legislature reacted to CJEU rulings in preliminary ruling proceedings would go beyond the scope of this chapter. Nevertheless, this aspect should not be left out but is limited in this chapter to the fundamental freedoms concerning the income tax and corporate income tax. On the one hand, a brief look reveals how the legislator eliminated situations that were contrary to EU law—for instance, by extending the favorable regulatory content to situations relating to EU/European Economic Area (EEA) Member States or—conversely—by placing domestic persons or situations at a disadvantage. Furthermore, it can be shown whether the implementation of CJEU rulings had a rather selective effect or provided reason for a reorganization of the regulatory area altogether. Finally, it is of interest whether and how the German legislator reacted to decisions of the CJEU on preliminary rulings of foreign courts in tax matters.

§25.4.1 Implementation of Decisions in Preliminary Ruling Proceedings on German Law

Looking at the preliminary ruling proceedings that dealt with the compatibility of German law with EU law, it can be stated on the one hand that the legislator evidently remedied the unlawfulness of a provision by extending the scope of application of favorable provisions to situations or persons with a connection to EU/EEA Member

42. For comparison, the referrals from the other German Federal Courts: Federal Supreme Court (BGH): 284, Federal Administrative Court (BVerwG): 164, Federal Labor Court (BAG): 67, Federal Social Court (BSozG): 77, according to statistics from the CJEU, https://curia.europa.eu/jcms/jcms/Jo2_7032/de/ accessed on October 10, 2023.
43. Hans-Friedrich Lange, *100 Jahre Steuerrechtsprechung in Deutschland 1918-2018: Praxis der Vorabentscheidungsersuchen in der Finanzgerichtsbarkeit* 870 (Otto Schmidt Verlag Cologne 2018).
44. Thomas Sendke, *Aktuelle Verfahren des EuGH im Bereich des Steuerverfahrensrechts* 40 (ISR 2022).

States.[45] On the other hand, the scope of application of disadvantageous provisions was limited to third countries, such as in the case of the consideration of foreign losses (section 2a of the Income Tax Act)[46] as a result of CJEU ruling in the case *Rewe Zentralfinanz eG*.[47]

The legislator took a completely different approach with regard to shareholder debt financing. Section 8a of the German Corporation Tax Act[48] (*Körperschaftsteurgesetz* (KStG)), which was submitted to the CJEU by the Finance Court of Münster for a preliminary ruling in the case *Lankhorst-Hohorst*, provided that interest on loans paid by a domestic corporation to its foreign parent company qualified as (hidden) profit distributions and could therefore not be claimed by the domestic company as operating expenses to reduce its tax burden. The CJEU found this to be a restriction of the freedom of establishment. The Court held that this could not be justified on the grounds of combating tax avoidance, as section 8a was not specifically tailored to these constellations; rather, the provision disproportionately applied in general to any situation in which the parent company had its registered office outside Germany.[49] The legislator initially eliminated this situation, which was in violation of EU law, by extending the deduction restriction also to payments made to parent companies located in Germany.[50] Subsequently, the legislator created a general restriction on the deductibility of interest, especially for large companies, which was to become the blueprint for the limitation of the deductibility of interest payments under Article 4 of the ATAD.[51]

Therefore, the implementation of the requirements resulting from the rulings of the European Court of Justice -just as in national law in the case of violations of the fundamental principle of equal treatment—is not always carried out by extending the favorable legal consequences to other groups of persons.

§25.4.2 Implementation of Decisions in Preliminary Ruling Proceedings on Foreign Law

Since the regulatory structures of corporate taxation in the Member States of the European Union are often similar, decisions of the CJEU on preliminary rulings in tax matters initiated by foreign courts often also have an impact on the German legal system. The fact that the reasons for the CJEU's decisions cannot be directly applied to

45. For example, the deductibility of donations (section 10b German Income Tax Act) by the EU VorgabenG of April 8, 2010, BGBl. I 2010, 386 (387) as a result of the ruling of the CJEU in the case *Persche* (Case C-318/07, *Persche v. Finanzamt Lüdenscheid* [2009], ECLI:EU:C:2009:33) or the deductibility of certain expenses for limited taxpayers (section 50(2) sentence 2 no. 5 German Income Tax Act) by the JStG 2009 of December 19, 2008, Federal Law Gazette I 2008, 2794 (2804) as a result of the ruling of the CJEU in the case *Gerritse* (Case C-234/01, *Gerritse v. Finanzamt Neukölln-Nord* [2003], ECLI:EU:C:2003:340).
46. Jahressteuergesetz 2009 of 19.12.2008, BGBl. I 2008, p. 2794.
47. Case C-347/04, *Rewe v. Finanzamt Köln-Mitte* [2007], ECLI:EU:C:2007:194.
48. Section 8a KStG dated 1.1.1996, BGBl. I 1996, p. 346.
49. Case C-324/00, *Lankhorst-Hohorst v. Finanzamt Steinfurt* [2002], ECLI:EU:C:2002:749.
50. ProtErklG of 22.12.2003, BGBl. I 2003, p. 2841.
51. Steffen Lampert et al., *Art. 4 of the Draft EU Directive on Implementation of the BEPS Action Plan, in Light of the Questionable Constitutionality of the German "Interest Barrier" Rule* 323-327 (European Taxation 2016).

similar provisions of German tax law[52] opens up room for interpretation, which the German legislator uses in very different ways. This can be illustrated by the example of the exit taxation of individuals and the consideration of "final losses" (of a foreign permanent establishment or subsidiary) for tax purposes: while on the one subject the legislator has been permanently active to date with reference to CJEU rulings, on the other issue, the legislature has done nothing so far.

As far as the taxation of capital appreciation is concerned, the German legislator recognized an urgent need for action as a result of the CJEU's ruling in the case of *Hughes de Lasteyrie du Saillant*,[53] in which the French regulation on exit taxation of natural persons had been found to be incompatible with the freedom of establishment. As a result, the corresponding German laws on the taxation of capital appreciation, which had remained almost unchanged since the 1970s, were largely mitigated in section 6 of the German External Tax Relations Act (*Außensteuergesetz* (AStG)) by granting an indefinite interest-free deferral for exit taxpayers—but only if they were EU/EEA nationals who took up residence in an EU/EEA Member State. Although the legislator could have argued, not without good reason, that the regulatory purposes (and thus the justifications) of the German and French regulations are not entirely identical, the decision of the CJEU in the case *N*[54]—issued upon the request of a Dutch court and immediately before the publication of the government draft—indicated that the CJEU generally set high standards for the justification of "exit taxation," which section 6 of the External Tax Relations Act did not fulfill. Moreover, the focus of section 6 has always been on relocations to Switzerland; since third countries were excluded from the above-mentioned amendment of section 6, it apparently seemed acceptable to the legislator to reduce the legal consequences to EU/EEA nationals and Member States only. However, the legislator used (the not entirely clarified) statements of the CJEU in the preliminary ruling proceedings in the case *Commission/Portugal* as an opportunity to replace the previously unlimited deferral by a deferral that decreases proportionally—and this without distinction for EU/EEA and third-country situations.[55]

A completely different situation emerged with regard to the problem of considering "final losses" of foreign subsidiaries and foreign (tax-exempt) permanent establishments. German treaty law also generally does not allow foreign losses to be considered by the German parent company or the German parent company of a foreign permanent establishment if the corresponding profits are taxed outside of Germany

52. David Hummel, *Auch im Verhältnis zur Schweiz gibt es keine Wegzugsbesteuerung ohne Stundungsmöglichkeit, wenn im Inland erst bei Realisierung der stillen Reserven besteuert wird*, 436-438 (ISR 2019).
53. Case C-9/02, *de Lasteyrie du Saillant v. Ministère de l'Économie, des Finances et de l'Industrie* [2004], ECLI:EU:C:2004:138.
54. Case C-470/04, *N v. Inspecteur van de Belastingdienst Oost/kantoor Almelo* [2006], ECLI:EU:C:2006:525.
55. Section 6 AStG dated 1.7.2021, amended by ATAD-Umsetzungsgesetz of 3.6.2021, BGBl. I 2021, p. 2035; the decision of the CJEU in the case *Wächtler* (Case C-581/17, *Wächtler v. Finanzamt Konstanz* [2019], ECLI:EU:C:2019:138) on the Agreement on the Free Movement of Persons with Switzerland, on the other hand, did not lead the legislator to a different conclusion.

(so-called symmetry thesis). To this day, there is no legal regulation of this problem.[56] Overall, the legislator therefore left it to the tax courts to meet the requirements of the CJEU by interpreting double tax treaties in conformity with EU law; the resulting teleological interpretation of the treaty provision by the tax courts stretches the methodological limits of the application of the norm to the utmost—or to achieve clarification through preliminary ruling proceedings.

§25.5 CONCLUSION

The preliminary ruling procedure has gained considerable importance in Germany, also due to the comparatively low admissibility requirements both in the harmonized area of consumption taxes and in the much less harmonized area of direct taxes. A contributing factor is that the German fiscal jurisdiction has proven to be particularly eager to make submissions since the early days of the common market—and thus for the most part meets the constitutional requirements for the lawful judge. Procedural law makes it possible to take CJEU rulings into account by requiring the tax authorities to keep taxation proceedings "open" because of an expected CJEU ruling. In this way, the CJEU has been able to exert significant influence on the German tax law system, although this influence is not uniform. Instead, the reactions of the German legislator reveal a broad spectrum, in terms of both the scope of legislation and the technique used to eliminate unequal treatment.

56. Steffen Lampert, *Das Vorabentscheidungsverfahren in Deutschland und Polen* p. 175 (Lukanko/Thiele eds., Mohr Siebeck 2023).

CHAPTER 26

Controversy Regarding the Subject-to-Tax Requirement in the EU Parent-Subsidiary Directive (2011/96) and in the Polish Corporate Income Tax Act

Hanna Litwińczuk

§26.1 INTRODUCTION

The problem regarding the subject-to-tax condition in the EU Parent-Subsidiary Directive (2011/96),[1] hereinafter referred to as the Directive, and in the Polish Corporate Income Tax Act (CITA),[2] relies on answering the question of whether this condition means that the company of a Member State will not benefit only from the subjective exemption covering all of its income but also from the objective exemption, that means that the company receiving the dividend should effectively pay tax in its residence country.

The Polish tax practice knows cases where a company that is a Polish tax resident and meets the conditions of the Directive pays dividends to a company being resident in another Member State that benefits there from special tax regimes which grant its objective exemption. It happens that as a result of such an exemption, a company does not pay any tax. In this situation, the Polish tax authority refuses to grant the tax exemption on dividends paid to such a recipient by a Polish company. The reason for the refusal is the fact that the recipient of dividends is not subject to effective taxation.

1. Council Directive 2011/96/EU of November 2011 on the common system of taxation applicable in the case of parent companies and subsidiaries of different Member States Official Journal of European Union L 345/8.
2. Ustawa z dnia 15 lutego 1992 r. o podatku dochodowym od osób prawnych (Dz.U. z 2022 r. poz.2587) z późniejszymi zmianami (Act of 15 February 1992 on Corporate Income Tax); consolidated text Journal of Laws of 2022 item 2587 as amended.

According to the tax authority, the provisions of the Directive establish a positive qualifying criterion, namely being subject to a given tax, and a negative criterion, namely the lack of exemption from this tax.

§26.2 PROVISIONS OF THE DIRECTIVE AND PROVISIONS OF THE POLISH ACT

Pursuant to Article 2(a) (iii) of the Directive:

> For the purposes of this Directive, the following definitions shall apply:
>
> (a) 'company of a Member State' means any company which:
> (i) takes one of the forms listed in Annex I, Part A;
> (ii) according to the tax laws of a Member State is considered to be resident in that Member State for tax purposes and, under the terms of a double taxation agreement concluded with a third State, is not considered to be resident for tax purposes outside the Union;
> (iii) moreover, *is subject to one of the taxes listed in Annex I, Part B, without the possibility of an option or of being exempt*, or to any other tax which may be substituted for any of those taxes;

Before the amendment of the Directive and giving it the new reference number – 2011/96/EU – the definition of a company of a Member State was regulated by Directive 90/435/EEC in Article 2(1), and the condition regarding the exemption was listed under letter c, which is why judgments and doctrine also refer to the older (original) reference number of the Directive.

The Polish CITA does not introduce the definition of a company of a Member State as such, but specifies the conditions that the parent company and the subsidiary must meet, and from the point of view of the discussed problem, attention should be paid to two conditions for the parent company: it must be a tax resident of Poland or an EU/European Economic Area (EEA) country (i.e., must be subject to income tax on all of his income, regardless of where it is earned) and cannot benefit from exemption from income tax on all of his income, regardless of where it is earned.[3]

As can be seen from the above, Polish regulations are not an exact transposition of the provisions of the Directive. However, they formulate two requirements for the application of the Directive: the requirement to be subject to taxation on all income and the requirement not to benefit from the exemption from income tax on all income, regardless of the source of its achievement (subject-to-tax).

Further considerations will be devoted first to the interpretation of Article 2 a (iii) of the Directive made in the CJEU judgment in the *Wereldhave* case[4] and then the possibility of its application under Article 22(4) of CITA.

3. Article 22(4) CITA.
4. Case C-448/15, *Wereldhave*, ECLI:EU:C:2017:180.

§26.3 INTERPRETATION OF THE PROVISION OF ARTICLE 2(A) (III) OF THE DIRECTIVE BY THE CJEU IN THE *WERELDHAVE* JUDGMENT

As the CJEU points out at the outset, in order to interpret Article 2 of the Directive containing the definition of a company of a Member State, it is necessary to take into account not only the wording of this provision but also the objectives and scheme of the Directive. The CJEU further states that the subject of interpretation should be the third condition of the definition of a company of a Member State, specified in Article 2 letter (c) of the Directive, according to which that company must be liable, without option or exemption, to one of the taxes specified in that provision or to another tax which may replace any of those taxes. The CJEU interprets this provision in such a way that it establishes a positive qualifying criterion, namely being subject to a given tax, and a negative criterion, i.e., not being exempt from this tax and not having the option to choose. The dispute over this premise arises from the fact that in the *Wereldhave* case, the company is subject to such tax at a zero rate, provided that all its profits are distributed to its shareholders. The CJEU further states that although, formally, a company which is subject to tax at a zero rate, provided that all of its profits are paid to its shareholders, is not exempt from that tax, it is, in practical terms, in the same situation as the one which Article 2(c) of the Directive seeks to exclude, that is to say, a situation in which it is not liable to pay that tax. The aim of the Directive, which is beyond doubt in the light of both the preamble and the wording of its provisions, is to prevent double taxation of profits paid to parent companies by subsidiaries. The CJEU refers to the scheme of the Directive, in particular to Articles 4 and 5, the first of which eliminates double taxation by imposing on the country of residence of the parent company the obligation to apply the tax exemption or tax credit method to these profits, and Article 5 eliminates double taxation by prohibiting the country of residence of the subsidiary from collecting withholding tax. Ultimately, the CJEU expresses the view that if the parent company under the provisions of the country of its residence is not covered by the exemption, but uses a different tax structure that gives an effect equivalent to the exemption and thus the risk of double taxation is eliminated, this effect makes illegitimate application of the provisions of the Directive. The aim of the Directive, as mentioned above, is to eliminate double taxation, and this will not occur in this case. Consequently, a company benefiting from a tax structure, the effect of which is equivalent to an exemption, is not a company of a Member State as defined in the Directive. The method of interpretation made by the CJEU indicates a departure from the wording of the provisions of the Directive and the use of a purposive interpretation, and the purpose of the Directive will be achieved, according to the Court, when any other tax structure leading to an equivalent effect is treated equally with the exemption mentioned in the provision, i.e., the lack of effective taxation. The reasoning is supported by J. Kokott who stated 'Such interpretation is consistent with the broad logic of the Parent Subsidiary Directive and the objective of ensuring the neutrality, from the tax point of view, of the distribution of profits established in one Member State to its parent company established in another Member State. That rationale does not cover the described zero tax situation as there the risk of double taxation on the part of that parent company of profits which were distributed to it by its subsidiary is ruled out.'[5]

§26.4 VIEWS OF THE DOCTRINE ON THE NATURE OF THE SUBJECT-TO-TAX REQUIREMENT IN THE DIRECTIVE

Long before the *Wereldhave* judgment was issued, many authors pointed out that the subject-to-tax requirement in the Directive raises a number of interpretative doubts.[6] Also after this judgment was issued, critical comments regarding its theses appeared in the literature. For example, P. Arginelli, who made a very thorough assessment of the CJEU judgment in the *Wereldhave* case and the interpretation used therein, states that various tax structures leading to a lack of effective taxation should be analysed and it should be considered whether all of them, if used by the parent company, deprive it of the status of a company of a Member State.[7] First, he distinguishes between subjective exemptions and objective exemptions. Subjective exemptions usually (although not always) apply to the taxpayer's entire income, while objective exemptions generally cover only part of his income. However, it may happen that in a given tax year or years, a taxpayer only obtains income that is covered by objective exemptions; i.e., he is not effectively taxed. It may also happen that a taxpayer takes advantage of the subjective exemption from all income only for a strictly defined period of time. According to this author, while companies benefitting from full exemption schemes fall outside the scope of application of the Directive, partial exemption as well as reduced taxation should not disqualify a company for purposes of the Directive. The wording of the Directive is, in this respect, clear, and both the system and the telos of the Directive concur with this construction.[8] In other words, linguistic, teleological and systemic interpretation leads to a consistent result. In the case of reduced taxation, P. Arginelli refers to the views of other authors who claim that the application of special tax schemes or tax rulings to the parent company still qualifies the company as a company of a Member State within the meaning of the Directive.[9] He also quotes the view of G. Maisto, who claims that even a subjective exemption from all income, but granted for a strictly defined period, does not exclude the company from the scope of the

5. Juliane Kokott, *EU Tax Law* 375-376 (Bloomsbury Publishing 2022).
6. For example, Guglielmo Maisto, *Shaping EU Company Tax Policy: Amending the Tax Directives*, 42 European Taxation 288 (2002); Fred C. de Hosson, *The Parent-Subsidiary Directive*, 44 Intertax 429 (1990) DOI: 10.54648/taxi1990068.
7. Paolo Arginelli, *The Subject-to-Tax Requirement in the EU Parent-Subsidiary Directive*, 57 European Taxation 338 (2017).
8. Arginelli, *supra* n. 7, at 338-339.
9. For example, Peter H. Schonewille, *Some Questions on the Parent-Subsidiary Directive and the Merger Directive*, 20 Intertax 16 (1992) DOI: 10.54648/taxi1992003, stated 'that companies whose taxable profits are significantly reduced because of the application of special tax schemes, or tax rulings, still qualify as companies of a Member State, under the clear wording of (current) art. 2(a)(iii) of the Directive'; similarly Guglielmo Maisto, *Current Issues on the Interpretation of the Parent-Subsidiary Directive*, 9 EU Income Tax Law: Issues for the Years Ahead (2013).

Directive.[10] P. Arginelli citing F.C. de Hosson points out to the provision in the protocol preceding the first version of the Directive from 1990, which stated that only the company which is, in principle, liable to tax but which, in effect, does not pay any tax because of the existence of a regime that exempts all of its income was to exclude from the scope of application of the Directive.[11] For the purposes of further considerations, it is important to point out that in the context of the division into subjective and objective exemptions, P. Arginelli distinguishes between companies that, from a legal point of view, are exempt from tax on all of their profits and companies that benefit only from the exemption of a certain part of their profits. For the sake of completeness of the argument, Arginelli distinguishes between de jure exemption and de facto absence of tax liability and states that the absence of taxation, e.g., due to obtaining exempt income in specific years or as a result of incurring losses has no impact on the status of the company regarding its recognition as tax-exempt. Only a subjective de jure exemption relating to all income excludes the company from the Directive.[12] Finally, it is worth adding that P. Arginelli also formulates *de lege ferenda* conclusions because in the light of all these doubts, he states that the subject-to-tax requirement should be removed from the Directive and replaced with other mechanisms. He also notes that this requirement currently applies to both the subsidiary (paying the dividend) and the parent company (recipient of the dividend), but from the perspective of the purpose of the Directive, this condition only makes sense if it applies to the subsidiary, while in the case of the parent company, it is sufficient if it meets a condition to be liable to tax. Meeting the subject-to-tax condition by a subsidiary ensures that the dividend paid will not avoid taxation within the EU.[13] Therefore, P. Arginelli is critical of the *Wereldhave* judgment on the grounds that it sacrifices the principles of consistency and proportionality in favour of simplicity.[14]

§26.5 GENERAL PRINCIPLES OF INTERPRETATION OF DOMESTIC TAX LAW AND INTERPRETATION IN CONFORMITY WITH EU LAW (CONSISTENT INTERPRETATION)

The question arises whether the application of the *Werldhave* judgment's conclusions in the light of the wording of the Polish provision (Article 22(4) of the CITA) was correct.

In the beginning, the principles of interpretation of domestic tax law and the principles of interpretation in conformity with EU law (consistent interpretation) which are widely recognized and accepted in Polish case law and doctrine will be briefly presented.

10. It has been argued in the literature that full exemptions granted for a limited number of years could be regarded as not disqualifying the relevant company (Guglielmo Maisto, *Il regime tributario dei dividendi nei rapporti tra 'società madri' e 'società figlie'*, Giuffré editore 27 (Giuffré editore 1996)).
11. Arginelli, *supra* n. 7, at 339.
12. Arginelli, *supra* n. 7, at 339-340.
13. Arginelli, *supra* n. 7, at 337.
14. Arginelli, *supra* n. 7, at 337.

When it comes to the principles of interpretation of national law, first of all, the basic importance of linguistic interpretation should be pointed out. It is not only the starting point for any interpretation but also outlines its boundaries within the possible meaning of words. The meaning of words and phrases is an insurmountable barrier to interpretation processes, and breaking it inevitably leads to a *contra legem* interpretation. The principle of primacy of linguistic interpretation is clearly declared in the tax jurisprudence of administrative courts.[15] This is due to the fact that language is a carrier of information about the will of the legislator, and the understandability of this message by the addressees of legal norms is a condition for their compliance with the content of these norms.[16] The taxpayer, as the addressee of these standards, should be sure that his rights and obligations will result from the content of the tax act, from the words and phrases used therein, which should be understandable to him.

The primacy of linguistic interpretation is also related to the principle of collecting tax on the basis of self-calculation of its amount by the taxpayer, who should read the legal norms regarding his situation on the basis of the relevant provisions of tax law.[17] Departing from the results of linguistic interpretation is possible only in two situations: when it does not provide clear results or when these results are clear but are in fundamental contradiction with the hierarchy of values observed by the interpreter (they are absurd, unfair, harmful, violate constitutionally protected values). Due to the primacy of linguistic interpretation, the role of other methods of interpretation may be limited to confirming its results or denying them, which, as indicated, may exceptionally be the basis for ignoring its results. However, there are situations when this is not possible. Attention should be paid to the most important of them from the point of view of taxpayer protection. If an interpretation other than the linguistic one is unfavourable to the taxpayer, the results of the linguistic interpretation should be accepted. The taxpayer has the right to expect that he is bound by the norms resulting from the linguistic meaning of the text. When it comes to systemic interpretation, it involves determining the meaning of a provision by reference to the legal system, i.e., locating the interpreted provision within the legal order. Attention should be paid to the role of directives of systemic interpretation as directives of choice (second degree), which allow the selection of one of several possible interpretation hypotheses. Among these directives (thus Polish guidelines for interpretation), it is worth mentioning the directive of interpretation consistent with the Constitution, which involves examining the meaning of a provision in the light of constitutional norms that express the most important values underlying the legal system, as well as the directive to resolve interpretation doubts in favour of the taxpayer which since 2016 has been regulated in Article 2a of the Tax Ordinance.[18] In turn, purposive interpretation involves linking the wording of a legal provision with its meaning and purpose, while the limit of interpretation is always the possible meaning of the words, reflecting the will of the

15. Bogumił Brzeziński *Prawo podatkowe*, Zagadnienia teorii i praktyki Toruń (2017), 517.
16. Bogumił Brzeziński, *Wykładnia prawa podatkowego* 24 (2013).
17. Brzeziński, *supra* n. 16, at 25.
18. Ustawa z dnia 29 sierpnia 1997 r. Ordynacja podatkowa Dz.U. z 2022 r. poz.2651 z póź.zm. (Act of 29 August 1997 on Tax Ordinance; consolidated text Journal of Laws of 2022 item 2651 as amended).

legislator. Generally, there is consensus that purposive interpretation is of an auxiliary nature and should primarily serve to confirm and supplement the results of linguistic interpretation when they are not clear. Knowledge of the purpose of the legal regulation will allow, in cases of doubt, to ensure the correctness of the linguistic interpretation.[19] Of course, the most desirable situation in the interpretation process occurs when linguistic, systemic and teleological interpretation provide consistent results.

When it comes to the principles of interpretation in conformity with EU law (consistent interpretation), it is emphasized that this interpretation, aimed primarily at ensuring the effectiveness of EU law, has its own specificity in that the principles of EU law play a more important role than the linguistic interpretation.[20] There is also a view that, in the light of the rules of interpretation adopted in Polish legal culture, the obligation of consistent interpretation can be reconstructed, in particular, as a prohibition to limit oneself to the linguistic interpretation, even if it provides a clear result. Moreover, the obligation to apply systemic interpretation occurs from the very beginning of determining the meaning of a tax provision and not only as a consequence of an ambiguous result of linguistic interpretation.[21] It is also pointed out that purposive interpretation is perceived as the most effective interpretation of EU law, and this particular effectiveness is caused by the nature of this law and its texts and the nature of the Directive as a source of law setting specific goals that are implemented by the provisions of national tax law. The jurisprudence of the ECJ (currently the CJEU) indicates that the most effective instrument for the interpretation of EU law is the search for the purpose of regulation.[22]

As can be seen from the above, there is a different approach to the interpretation of national and EU law, especially when it comes to the role and order of application of individual types of interpretation. Therefore, questions began about the limits of consistent interpretation.[23] In particular, this concerned the possibility of a conflict between the provisions of EU law and the provisions of the Constitution.[24] In the latest literature, this issue was most fully described by R. Wiatrowski, who summarized the previous case law in this regard scope; therefore, it will be advisable to refer to this author.[25] R. Wiatrowski distinguishes and analyses four types of limits of consistent interpretation, but for the purposes of this chapter, the focus will be on *contra legem* interpretation.

19. Brzeziński, *supra* n. 16, at 25.
20. Andrzej Gomułowicz, Dominik Mączyński, *Podatki i prawo podatkowe* 206 (Wolters Kluwer Polska 2022).
21. Roman Wiatrowski, *Wykładnia prounijna Naczelnego Sądu Administracyjnego w zakresie przepisów dotyczących podatku od towarów i usług* 97–99 (Wolters Kluwer Polska 2021).
22. Dobrosława Antonów, *Wykładnia prawa podatkowego po wstąpieniu Polski do Unii Europejskiej* 236 (Wolters Kluwer Polska 2009).
23. Artur Mudrecki, *Granice wykładni prounijnej w orzecznictwie Naczelnego Sądu Administracyjnego*, in: *Stanowienie i stosowanie prawa podatkowego w Polsce* (Michalina Duda et al. eds, KUL 2011).
24. Gomułowicz & Mączyński, *supra* n. 20, at 214-218.
25. Wiatrowski, *supra* n. 21: ... In particular, the author relied on the judgments of the Supreme Administrative Court: judgment from 13.05.2008 r. I FSK 600/07; judgment from 25.06.2008 r. I FSK 743/07, judgment from 20.01.2015 r., I FSK 2102/13.

R. Wiatrowski points out that '... The Supreme Administrative Court respects the limits of a consistent interpretation, concluding that a consistent interpretation should not be used if it leads to results inconsistent with the effects of the linguistic interpretation, as this could lead to an unacceptable *contra legem* interpretation. The Supreme Administrative Court justifies its position that a consistent interpretation of national tax provisions, which would lead to a *contra legem* interpretation of these provisions by extending the scope of taxation (tax obligation) resulting from them, also refers to the provision expressed in Art. 217 of the Constitution of the Republic of Poland, the principle of statutory exclusivity in tax matters, requiring a clear and understandable definition of the scope of application of the tax norm in a statutory tax provision that is understandable to the addressees. As stated by the Supreme Administrative Court, the subject of taxation (activities giving rise to tax liability) cannot be presumed and determined by applying a purposive or consistent interpretation, leading to the extension of tax liability to activities which, in the light of the interpreted provisions, are not covered by such an obligation.' Next, R. Wiatrowski stated that this position of the Supreme Administrative Court had been approved in the literature, which emphasizes that a consistent interpretation cannot go beyond the linguistic content of the Polish provision (which is more favourable to the taxpayer)'[26] (the quote omitted the footnotes – HL). R. Wiatrowski also adds that the prohibition of *contra legem* interpretation applies to situations when the result of the interpretation of national law is clear and does not violate the general principles of EU law.[27]

§26.6 CONCLUSION

The aim of the study was to try to answer the question of whether the interpretation of the subject-to-tax condition made by the CJEU in *Wereldhave* judgment may also apply to the provision of Article 22 (4) CITA. The general thesis of this judgment is as follows: a company benefiting from a tax construction (in the case from zero tax rate), the effect of which is equivalent to an exemption is not a company of a Member State as defined in the Directive because it effectively pays no tax.

As stated above, there is a certain difference in defining this condition between the Directive and the Polish Act. The Directive stipulates the requirement to be subject to one of the taxes listed in Annex I, Part B, without the possibility of an option or exemption, while the Polish Act clearly defines the nature of this exemption. This is the exemption from income tax on all its profits, regardless of the source of its achievement.

The term used by the Polish legislator, i.e., a company is exempt from tax on all of its profits, means a subjective exemption from the entire income. Under Polish tax law, subjective exemption and objective exemption are also different.

There is no doubt that in accordance with the principles of interpretation of tax law in the Polish legal system, an interpretation leading to the result that a subjective

26. Wiatrowski, *supra* n. 21, at 120.
27. Wiatrowski, *supra* n. 21, at 120.

exemption is equivalent to an objective exemption goes beyond the limits of the possible meaning of the words used by the legislator.

The question should be asked whether such a change in the possible meaning of words is justified by the interpretation in conformity with EU law (consistent interpretation). However, in accordance with the jurisprudence of the Supreme Administrative Court and Polish doctrine, the application of consistent interpretation has its limits. It cannot go beyond the wording of the Polish provision (which is more favourable to the taxpayer), i.e., to the interpretation *contra legem*. It may be doubted whether it is justified to strive for such a reading of Article 22 section 4 point 4 CITA, so that the scope of the exemption resulting from this provision is consistent with the scope of the Directive.

Since the Polish legislator in the provisions of Article 22(4)(4) has expanded the scope of its application in comparison with the Directive by excluding only companies that benefit from the exemption from all their income, it is not, in my opinion, justified to interpret this provision in accordance with the Directive, the scope of which is narrower as it does not cover companies that are subject to taxation but are generally exempt from it (without the possibility to be exempt).

Most likely, the Supreme Administrative Court will comment on this matter, and it is currently unclear which interpretation of Article 22(4) CITA the Court will adopt.

CHAPTER 27

Some Comments from a Tax Standpoint on the Italian Implementing Provisions of Directive No. 2019/2112/EU on Cross-Border Conversions, Mergers and Divisions

Giuseppe Melis & Alessio Persiani[*]

§27.1 INTRODUCTION

Legislative Decree no. 19 of 2 March 2023 implemented Directive no. 2019/2121/EU adopted on 27 November 2019 regarding cross-border conversions, mergers and divisions.

The absence of a legal framework for the mentioned transactions has been considered a cause of legal fragmentation and uncertainty, leading to barriers to the exercise of the freedom of establishment. In this sense Directive no. 2019/2121/EU provides for harmonised rules for cross-border conversions and divisions in the EU and reinforces the protection of shareholders, employees and creditors in case of cross-border mergers.[1]

Unlike the current rules applicable to cross-border mergers, Directive no. 2019/2121/EU requires to include additional information in the common draft terms

* Sections 27.1 and 27.2 have been written by Giuseppe Melis, while sections 27.3 and 27.4 have been written by Alessio Persiani. The conclusions have been written by both the authors.

1. The rules applicable to cross-border conversions and divisions involve almost identical steps and information requirements as is the case for cross-border mergers. They include: (i) the publication of the draft terms of the operation; (ii) the issuance of a report for the shareholders and employees; (iii) the issuance of an independent expert report; (iv) the approval by the general meeting; and (v) the issuance of a certificate from a competent authority confirming compliance with legal obligations.

and in the report of the management body of the company for its shareholders and employees related to the impact of the transaction on such persons. Shareholders and employees will have the opportunity to present their observations to the general meeting in charge of the decision on the transaction. The common draft terms should also inform on the safeguards offered by the companies to their creditors, such as guarantees or pledges. If such safeguards are deemed insufficient by the creditors, they can apply before the competent administrative or judicial authority within three months of the publication of the draft terms. Member States can also require that financial statements reflecting the current financial situation of the companies are published at the same time as the draft terms of the transaction. Directive no. 2019/2121/EU also requires EU Member States not to issue the confirmatory certificate regarding compliance with legal obligations if it is established that the transaction has been set up for abusive or fraudulent purposes.

The provisions of Directive no. 2019/2121/EU have a crucial – if not historical – relevance: while they are aimed at regulating the private international and company law aspects of the mentioned cross-border transactions, the same provisions are also relevant from a tax standpoint.

The complexity that has traditionally characterised the tax aspects of cross-border transactions, in fact, is essentially due to their 'horizontal' dimension, since they involve provisions pertaining to multiple branches of law, primarily private international law and EU law. On this 'slippery' terrain the tax rules then come into play, with the ensuing technicalities and interpretative difficulties.

§27.2 THE CJEU JURISPRUDENCE ON THE MOBILITY OF COMPANIES AND ITS RELEVANCE IN THE TAX AREA

The interplay between legal and tax aspects of cross-border conversions, mergers and divisions is appropriately summed up in the expression used by the Court of Justice of the EU (CJEU) in its well-known *Daily Mail* judgment: 'unlike natural persons, companies are creatures of the law and, in the present state of Community law, creatures of national law. They exist only by virtue of the varying national legislation which determines their incorporation and functioning'.[2]

The legal issues arising from the fact that the company is not a natural person, being a creature of the law, connect to the application of the 'incorporation theory' ('*Gründungstheorie*') – according to which the *lex societatis* should be identified in the law of the State in which the incorporation procedure of the entity took place – and of the 'real seat theory' ('*Sitztheorie*'), according to which commercial companies should be regulated by the law of the place where the administration is actually located.[3]

The main risk deriving from the application of these different approaches is that the cross-border transaction could result in the 'discontinuity' of the legal entity

2. CJEU, 27 September 1988, C-81/87, *Daily Mail*, ECLI:EU:C:1988:456, para. 19.
3. *See* Giuseppe Melis, *Trasferimento della residenza fiscale ed imposizione sui redditi*, Milan, 2008, pp. 162 and ff.

involved, with the ensuing tax consequences arising from such a 'deemed liquidation' of the entity.

Over the years, the CJEU jurisprudence on the mobility of companies, however, has progressively raised the level of protection of companies' rights, although such protection has never been full and, in any case, limited to intra-EU transactions.

The first relevant case is the mentioned *Daily Mail*, concerning a UK tax provision that subjected the transfer of tax residence to another State to the Treasury authorisation. In the case at hand, the Treasury made the authorisation to the transfer conditional on the payment of the tax on the unrealised capital gain on the participation held by the company. We were before a procedural (rather than substantive) exit tax, with similar effects.

Leveraging on the statements that: (i) unlike natural persons, companies are entities created in a national legal order, and are therefore not subject to any restriction on the right of establishment; and (ii) the laws of each EU Member State widely differ with respect to both the connecting factors to the national territory required for the incorporation of a company and the ability of a company incorporated under such laws to subsequently alter that connecting factor, the CJEU concluded that 'Articles 52 and 58 of the Treaty cannot be interpreted as conferring on companies incorporated under the law of a Member State a right to transfer their central management and control and their central administration to another Member State while retaining their status as companies incorporated under the legislation of the first Member State.'[4]

While the subsequent cases *Centros*[5] and *Inspire Art*[6] are not relevant for our purposes as they relate to secondary establishment, the *Überseering* case[7] is relevant as it concerns the primary right of establishment, and the CJEU addressed the continuity of a company transferring from a state applying the incorporation principle to one applying the real seat principle.

In *Überseering*, the CJEU denied the applicability of the conclusions reached in the *Daily Mail* judgment: while *Daily Mail* regarded the relationships between the company and the State of its origin, the *Überseering* case involved the different perspective of the State of destination and ignoring the personality attributed to the company by the State of its origin was not possible. While Member States may determine – absent any ad hoc rule – the loss of nationality of a company transferring its seat abroad, the same Member States, when 'receiving' a transferring company, cannot disregard the personality recognised by another Member State and cannot oblige the company to re-establish itself in the Member State of destination.

The judgment solved one of the aspects related to the continuity of a transferring company but left open the issue of a transfer from a state adopting the real seat criterion and the potential dissolution effects deriving from it.

4. *Supra* n. 2, para. 24.
5. CJEU, 9 March 1999, C-212/97, *Centros*, ECLI: ECLI:EU:C:1999:126.
6. CJEU, 30 September 2003, C-167/01, *Inspire Art*, ECLI:EU:C:2003:512.
7. CJEU, 5 November 2002, C-208/00, *Überseering BV*, ECLI:EU:C:2002:632.

On these aspects a further opening of the CJEU occurred in the *Cartesio* judgment,[8] concerning a Hungarian limited partnership willing to transfer its effective seat (i.e., the management centre of its business) to Italy, while remaining registered in Hungary. The Hungarian Court refused the transfer requiring the company to first dissolve in Hungary and then reincorporate under the Italian law.

In spite of the Advocate General's opinion – who concluded that any restriction in the State of departure was incompatible with EC law – the CJEU adopted an intermediate position, stating that a given Member State has 'the power to define both the connecting factor required of a company if it is to be regarded as incorporated under the law of that Member State and, as such, capable of enjoying the right of establishment, and that required if the company is to be able subsequently to maintain that status. That power includes the possibility for that Member State not to permit a company governed by its law to retain that status if the company intends to reorganize itself in another Member State by moving its seat to the territory of the latter, thereby breaking the connecting factor required under the national law of the Member State of incorporation'.[9]

Anyway, while regulations hindering a transfer 'without change of applicable law' do not encounter any limit under EU law, the same cannot be said for transfers implying a 'change of applicable national law', i.e., transfers in which the company converts into a company subject to the national law of the destination Member State: in such a case, the Member State of incorporation cannot require the liquidation of the relevant company.

As a consequence, if no obstacle can be placed by the State of origin to the conversion into a company of another Member State – provided that the latter allows such conversion – also the issues arising in case of a transfer from a state that adopts the principle of the real seat to one that adopts the principle of the place of incorporation should be deemed as solved, at least insofar as the new company adopts the statutes laid down for companies of the destination State. Thus, only a few cases remained unprotected at the EU freedoms level, namely those connected with a transfer to a state adopting the principle of the real seat in which the destination State does not allow such a conversion.

The latter conclusion is supported by the tax case *National Grid Indus* where the CJEU stated that 'a Member State is able, in the case of a company incorporated under its law, to make the company's right to retain its legal personality under the law of that State subject to restrictions on the transfer abroad of the company's place of effective management'[10] and that where such a status ceases to exist, it cannot rely on the freedom of establishment, while in the opposite case the company can 'rely on its rights under Article 49 TFEU, in particular for challenging the lawfulness of a tax imposed on it by that Member State on the occasion of the transfer of its place of effective management to another Member State'.[11]

8. CJEU, 16 December 2008, C-210/06, *Cartesio*, ECLI:EU:C:2008:723.
9. *Supra* n. 8, para. 110.
10. CJEU, 29 November 2011, C-371/10, *National Grid Indus*, ECLI:EU:C:2011:785, para. 27.
11. *Supra* n. 10, para. 32.

The *Cartesio* judgment was followed by the *Vale* judgment, regarding an Italian company willing to self-convert into a Hungarian company, whose registration was refused by Hungarian authorities. After having confirmed that 'a Member State has the power to define both the connecting factor required of a company if it is to be regarded as incorporated under its national law and as such capable of enjoying the right of establishment, and the connecting factor required if the company is to be able subsequently to maintain that status', the CJEU further stated that 'any obligation, under Articles 49 TFEU and 54 TFEU, to permit a cross-border conversion neither infringes the power, referred to in the preceding paragraph, of the host Member State nor that State's determination of the rules governing the incorporation and functioning of the company resulting from a cross-border conversion'.[12]

The CJEU's latest judgment has been issued in the *Polbud* case,[13] in which a Polish company had transferred its registered office in legal continuity – as expressly provided for by Polish law – to Luxembourg and subsequently asked to be cancelled from the Polish commercial register. The Polish authority, however, refused such cancellation and required the prior liquidation, being it necessary to protect the interests of creditors, minority shareholders and employees. Thus, while Polish law allowed the survival (i.e., legal continuity) of the company in case of transfer, it nevertheless required its prior liquidation. After stating – differently from the *Vale* case – that freedom of establishment covers cross-border conversions regardless of whether the company had transferred its effective establishment in the new country (thus implying that the establishment could be maintained in the State of origin), the CJEU held that this set of rules was not proportionate, since, on the one hand, an obligation to liquidate a company while keeping the legal person alive could never be considered a measure proportionate to the purpose, and, on the other hand, the actual risk of harming those interests had not been taken into account, being possible to adopt less restrictive measures to safeguard the same interests. Thus, based on the principle of proportionality, the right to change the *lex societatis* cannot be subject to liquidation measures.

Since the *Daily Mail* case, the CJEU stated that 'certain States require that not merely the registered office but also the real head office, that is to say the central administration of the company, should be situated on their territory, and the removal of the central administration from that territory thus presupposes the winding-up of the company with all the consequences that winding-up entails in company law and tax law'[14] and that 'the legislation of other States permits companies to transfer their central administration to a foreign country but certain of them, such as the United Kingdom, make that right subject to certain restrictions, and the legal consequences of a transfer, particularly in regard to taxation, vary from one Member State to another'.[15]

12. CJEU, 12 July 2012, C-378/10, *Vale*, ECLI:EU:C:2012:440, paras 29-30.
13. CJEU, 25 October 2017, C-106/16, *Polbud*, ECLI:EU:C:2017:804.
14. *Supra* n. 2, para. 20.
15. *Supra* n. 2, para. 20.

The CJEU further added that no convention on mutual recognition of companies had been concluded pursuant to Article 220 of the EEC Treaty.[16]

This basic principle has essentially remained firm, with only its gradual loosening in the terms outlined above.

Anyway, we should clearly keep the case of unfavourable tax effects deriving from private and corporate international law distinct and separate from the case in which such tax effects are autonomous from private international law rules. Only in the first case it is possible to rely upon factors external to tax law in order to justify the restrictions – as affirmed in the *National Grid Indus* judgment – whereas in the second case, the restrictions directly derive from tax provisions and should be only dealt with having regard to tax law principles.

Based on the above and according to the principles developed by the CJEU so far, the qualification of the transfer of seat as a liquidation on the basis of private international law rules should be deemed as a legitimate consequence of the lack of harmonisation of the same rules and, therefore, unprotected at the level of the TFEU.

The ensuing contradiction, however, clearly emerges.

If the company transferring its place of administration (and, therefore, its tax residence) belongs to a state applying the real seat principle, there will not be a restriction within the meaning of Article 49 TFEU since a liquidation at the civil law level of the transferring entity generally occurs. This, however, with the exception of certain States, which admit the continuity of the transferring entity in a state applying the place of incorporation principle, and without prejudice to cases in which conversion into a company governed by the law of the destination State, is possible, in accordance with the principles set out in *Cartesio*.

If, however, the company transferring its residence for tax purposes belongs to a state applying the place of incorporation principle, since there is no liquidation at the civil law level and, therefore, no break in the continuity of the transferring entity, a restriction within the meaning of Article 49 of the TFEU may occur with respect to the provisions that attribute relevance to such a transfer for tax purposes.

In short, if the State of origin adopts the real seat principle, it may decide the civil law regime of the company transferring its seat of administration, requiring the liquidation of the company – unless the State of destination allows the company to be converted into a type of company envisaged by its own law – and, consequently, may attribute tax relevance to that transfer without that giving rise to a restriction within the meaning of Article 49 of the TFEU; however, the destination State must accept the foreign entity if it complies with the connecting factors which that State requires in order for a company to be regarded as incorporated under its national law.

§27.3 THE 'HISTORICAL' RELEVANCE OF DIRECTIVE NO. 2019/2121/EU FOR TAX PURPOSES

Considering the scenario illustrated above, the 'historical' relevance of Directive 2019/2121/EU becomes clear, as it eventually provides a multilateral regulation to

16. *Supra* n. 2, para. 21.

cross-border conversions, mergers and divisions, being all EU Member States are required to adopt the same rules in a coordinated manner. This will also result in a more aligned tax framework across the EU, as the tax regimes of the different EU Member States will no longer be affected by the lack of coordination among national regulations.

Until now, the objective of an intra-EU transfer of seat could be achieved through an intra-EU merger under Directive no. 2005/56/EC. While the result was similar, we cannot ignore that only Directive no. 2019/2121/EU provides for a full-scope regulation of cross-border transactions, going well beyond the rules laid under Directive no. 2005/56/EC, even considering its amendments adopted through Directive no. 2017/1132/EU. In this respect, Directive no. 2019/2121/EU applies not only to cross-border conversions – intended as transfer of the registered office with a change of applicable law and adoption of one of the legal forms envisaged by the destination Member State[17] – but also to cross-border divisions, even in the form of 'division by separation'.[18]

Furthermore, the scope of application of Directive no. 2019/2121/EU is rather wide, being applicable also to: (i) corporations that, although subject to the *lex societatis* of another EU Member State, do not have their statutory seat, central administration or place of business in the territory of the EU; and to (ii) purely 'international transactions', i.e., transactions concerning companies governed by the law of non-EU Member States, provided that the principles of international private law on the *lex societatis* are observed. As a consequence, the risk of 'discontinuity' from a corporate law standpoint – with the ensuing tax consequences – is considerably reduced not only in the EU area but also in respect of non-EU Member States.

The harmonised rules resulting from Directive no. 2019/2121/EU are also relevant for the shareholders of the companies involved in the cross-border transaction.

Legislative Decree no. 199 of 2007 introduced paragraph 2-*ter* within Article 166 of the Italian Income Tax Code (hereinafter, IITC),[19] providing that 'the transfer of tax residence abroad by a company does not give rise per se to the taxation of the shareholders of the transferred company'. This provision implemented Article 10d of Directive no. 2005/19/EC, according to which 'the transfer of the registered office of an SE or of an SCE shall not, of itself, give rise to any taxation of the income, profits or capital gains of the shareholders'. The underlying rationale of this provision is that, since the transaction takes place on a private international level outside any dissolving logic, any effect on the shareholders should be excluded.

17. Thus avoiding the need to adopt the *escamotage* of the cross-border reverse merger in a company incorporated in the destination Member State.
18. Article 160(b), para. 4, let. c) of Directive no. 2019/2121/EU regulates the 'division by separation', i.e., when the company being divided transfers part of its assets and liabilities to one or more recipient companies, in exchange for the issue to the company being divided (instead of its shareholders) of securities or shares in the recipient companies.
19. The IITC is provided by Presidential Decree no. 917 of 22 September 1986.

The circumstance that the transfer does not give rise per se to the taxation of the shareholders, however, leaves the door open to certain cases in which such taxation under Article 47, paragraph 7 of the IITC may occur.

This would be the case where the legal system of the destination State does not recognise the Italian company moving its residence abroad, thus requiring its liquidation pursuant to the private international law provision of Article 25, paragraph 3 of Law no. 218 of 1995: in this case, the rules on the tax regime of sums attributed to the shareholders would apply, in combination with Article 166 of the IITC.

Apart from this specific case (and except, of course, for the case of partnerships taxed on a transparency basis), any immediate effect of the transfer of residence on the shareholders should be ruled out.

In this respect, as the implementing rules of Directive no. 2019/2121/EU significantly reduce the cases of legal discontinuity, they also benefit the company's shareholders by reducing the frequency with which the above-illustrated case of taxation of the shareholders may occur.

At the same time, the alternative of conversion now available under the provisions of Directive no. 2019/2121/EU makes the alignment of the tax residence of the companies with the *lex societatis* possible, thus reducing the 'hybrid' situations of foreign-law companies that, being unable to 'abandon' the law of the State of origin, only transfer the place of effective management to another State in order to be considered tax resident therein on the basis of double tax conventions.

Lastly, Directive no. 2019/2121/EU also addresses the case of companies that, despite the change of seat, wish to continue to be governed by the law of their State of origin. In such case, however, the Directive provides for stringent requirements, as companies may establish a registered office abroad only for the purpose of holding shareholders' meetings and filing of documents referred to the company, provided that the registered office is maintained in the territory of the State.

The newly introduced Article 2510-*bis* of the Italian Civil Code further specifies that 'the right of companies to establish their place of management, main purpose or tax residence outside the territory of the State is unaffected': as the place of management must necessarily be maintained in Italy, also one of the elements provided for by Article 73, paragraph 3, IITC for the purpose of determining the tax residence of companies continues to be located in Italy. Thus, the 'tax residence' to which Article 2510-*bis* refers can only be the one also attributed by the State of destination: as in most of the cases also the place of effective management would be located in the State of destination, the tax residence of the company will be located there insofar as the applicable double tax convention provides for the place of effective management as the applicable tie-breaker rule.[20]

20. As from 2017, in fact, the OECD Model Convention no longer provides for the place of effective management as the sole *tie-breaker rule* for entities other than individuals. Indeed: (a) Art. 4, para. 3 of the OECD Model provides that: 'where by reason of the provisions of paragraph 1 a person other than an individual is a resident of both Contracting States, the competent authorities of the Contracting States shall endeavour to determine by mutual agreement the Contracting State of which such person shall be deemed to be a resident for the purposes of the

§27.4 THE INTERPLAY BETWEEN DIRECTIVE NO. 2019/2121/EU AND THE PROTECTION OF TAX CLAIMS

One of the main innovations of Directive no. 2019/2121/EU regards the rules aimed at protecting the creditors.

Article 30, paragraph 1 of Legislative Decree no. 19 of 2023 states that when the cross-border merger results in a company subject to the law of another State, the Italian company taking part in the merger, upon request of the pre-operation certificate, has to prove, through the relevant certificates, that it has no debts towards public administrations or bodies or that it has satisfied or guaranteed them in accordance with Article 31. Tax debts certified by the Italian Revenue Agency or the Italian tax collection agent are relevant in this respect.

The subsequent paragraph 2 of Article 30 clarifies that the obligation to satisfy or guarantee tax debts can only be admitted in limited cases, in which the legislator assumes that the transaction may be aimed at circumventing guarantees in favour of tax authorities or other public bodies.[21] This implies that the existence of tax debts does not constitute per se an obstacle to the performance of the transactions and to the issuance of the pre-operation certificate, except for the above-mentioned limited cases. From a tax standpoint, such a scenario is fully in line with the limits traditionally set by the CJEU to the possibility for EU Member States to claim the risk of international tax evasion (or avoidance) as a possible justification for the infringement of EU freedoms.[22]

Another aspect referred to the protection of tax claims deserving a specific attention regards the rules on exit taxation laid under Article 166 IITC.

Further to the implementation of the ATAD Directive, the Italian legislator eliminated the possibility to defer the payment of the exit tax until the actual realisation of the gains on the assets. The sole alternative to the immediate payment of the exit tax, in fact, is the instalment payment, whose applicability is limited to EU Member States

---

Convention, having regard to its place of effective management, the place where it is incorporated or otherwise constituted and any other relevant factors ...'; and (b) para. 24.1 of the Commentary to Art. 4 para. 3 of the OECD Model provides that 'competent authorities having to apply paragraph 3 would be expected to take account of various factors, such as where the meetings of the person's board of directors or equivalent body are usually held, where the chief executive officer and other senior executives usually carry on their activities, where the senior day-to-day management of the person is carried on, where the person's headquarters are located, which country's laws govern the legal status of the person, where its accounting records are kept ... '.

21. Reference is to: (i) the existence of significant doubts as to the company's ability to continue as a going concern; (ii) the existence of a state of liquidation or its revocation in the three years preceding the date of publication of the merger plan; (iii) a negative net equity or an amount of net equity below the legal minimum; and (iv) the failure to file one (or more than one) financial statements in the last three years.
22. Please refer to the following CJEU judgments: 16 July 1998, C-264/96, *Imperial Chemical Industries*, ECLI:EU:C:1998:370; 21 September 1999, C-307/97 *Saint Gobain*, ECLI:EU:C:1999:438; 6 June 2000, C-35/98 *Verkooijen*, ECLI:EU:C:2000:294; 8 March 2001, C-397/98 and C-410/98 *Metallgesellshaft*, ECLI:EU:C:2001:134; 12 September 2006, C-196/04 *Cadbury Schweppes*, ECLI:EU:C:2006:544; 7 September 2017, C-6/16, *Eqiom*, ECLI:EU:C:2017:641; 20 December 2017, C-504/16 and C-613/16, *Deister Holding and Juhler Holding*, ECLI:EU:C:2017:1009.

and EEA Member States.[23] Such approach - grounded on the provisions of the ATAD Directive - derives from an evolution of the jurisprudence of the CJEU which raises some doubts, also considering the more recent judgments.

In the *National Grid Indus* judgment, the CJEU stated that 'a national legislation offering a company transferring its place of effective management to another Member State the choice between, first, immediate payment of the amount of tax, which creates a disadvantage for that company in terms of cash flow but frees it from subsequent administrative burdens, and, secondly, deferred payment of the amount of tax, possibly together with interest in accordance with the applicable national legislation, which necessarily involves an administrative burden for the company in connection with tracing the transferred assets'[24] constitutes a measure less harmful to the freedom of establishment than the immediate payment of the tax. Then, with respect to the risk of non-recovery of the tax, the CJEU for the first time affirmed that 'measures such as the provision of a bank guarantee'[25] could represent a reasonable and legitimate path.

Further to *National Grid Indus*, the CJEU ruled on the Portuguese,[26] Dutch,[27] Spanish[28] and Danish[29] exit tax provisions, all being considered to infringe the TFEU insofar as they only provided for the immediate payment of the exit tax, without the possibility of deferring such payment until the realisation of capital gains. Other EU Member States (i.e., Italy, UK and Belgium) applying similar tax rules were not brought before the CJEU as, further to the opening of the infringement proceeding, they committed to amend the applicable tax rules.

The judgment on the Danish exit tax constituted the turning point in the CJEU jurisprudence. While concluding for the contrast between the immediate payment of the exit tax and the fundamental freedoms, the CJEU dealt with the argument of the Danish Government challenging the general applicability of the deferral of the tax payment until the actual realisation of the gains. In the opinion of the Danish Government, the case of exit tax on financial assets - i.e., participations, not subject to obsolescence and for which a realisation event always occurs - had to be distinguished from tangible assets (whose value decreases with obsolescence) and intangible assets, whose value decreases with the shortening of the period of protection: companies could decide to use such tangible and intangible assets until the end of their life cycle without ever realising them. Hence, the need - in the opinion of the Danish Government - to provide for an immediate payment of the exit tax, without the possibility of deferring such payment until the realisation of the assets. In response to this, the CJEU simply stated that EU Member States have the power to identify, for the purposes of such taxation, a taxable event other than the actual realisation of the assets in order to

23. In case of EEA Member States, the payment in instalments is limited to States that entered into an agreement on mutual assistance in the collection of tax debts comparable to the regime provided under Directive no. 2010/24/EU.
24. *Supra* n. 10, para. 73.
25. *Supra* n. 10, para. 74.
26. CJEU, 6 September 2012, C-38/10, *Commission v. Portuguese Republic*, ECLI:EU:C:2012:521.
27. CJEU, 31 January 2013, C-301/11, *Commission v. Kingdom of the Netherlands*, ECLI:EU:C:2013:47.
28. CJEU, 25 April 2013, C-64/11, *Commission v. Kingdom of Spain*, ECLI:EU:C:2013:264.
29. CJEU, 18 July 2013, C-261/11, *Commission v. Kingdom of Denmark*, ECLI:EU:C:2013:480.

ensure the taxation of assets that are not intended to be transferred, and less detrimental to freedom of establishment than the immediate payment of the tax.[30]

In the subsequent *DMC* judgment,[31] the Court reiterated this statement on the applicability of the exit tax at a time other than the realisation of the assets, making it conditional on the verification of the actual loss of the power to tax the assets by the State of departure and considering as proportional a five-year instalment scheme. Then, in the *Verder LabTec* judgment,[32] CJEU's attention progressively shifted to the assessment of exit tax instalment schemes from a proportionality standpoint, affirming that a ten-year instalment scheme was in line with such principle.

Indications of a *revirement* by the CJEU can be derived from the *A Oy* judgment,[33] in which the Court dealt with the transfer of a permanent establishment of a resident company to a non-resident company, governed by Article 10, paragraph 2 of Directive 90/434/EEC.[34] The CJEU reiterated the statements of *National Grid Indus* on the choice between immediate and deferred payment of tax: as the Court deals with the deferred payment of tax explicitly mentioning the administrative burdens for the taxpayer in connection with tracing the transferred assets, this clearly refers to the deferral until the actual realisation of the gains, rather than to a mere instalment payment, for which such administrative burdens do not come into play.[35]

The *revirement* has been further confirmed in the more recent *Wächtler* judgment,[36] where the CJEU considered not proportional the German regime that denied the deferral of the exit tax until realisation of the gains owed by a German taxpayer who sold shares in a Swiss company and transferred his residence to Switzerland while allowing such a deferral in a purely domestic situation. In the *Wächtler* case, the CJEU not only censured the German legislation on the grounds that the instalment payment was not provided as a general rule but also added that instalment payment is in any case more burdensome from a financial standpoint rather than deferring the payment of tax until realisation of the assets.[37]

30. *Supra* n. 29, para. 37. The judgment is available only in Danish and French. In the French version, the CJEU states: '*en effet, les États membres étant en droit d'imposer les plus-values qui ont été générées alors que les actifs en cause se trouvaient sur leur territoire ont le pouvoir de prévoir, pour cette imposition, un fait générateur autre que la cession effective, afin de garantir l'imposition des actifs qui ne sont pas destinés à être cédés, et moins attentatoire à la liberté d'établissement que le prélèvement au moment du transfert*'.
31. CJEU, 23 January 2014, C-164/12, *DMC*, ECLI:EU:C:2014:20.
32. CJEU, 21 May 2015, C-657/13, *Verder LabTec*, ECLI:EU:C:2015:331.
33. CJEU, 23 November 2017, C-292/16, *A Oy*, ECLI:EU:C:2017:888.
34. Article 10, para. 2 of Directive 90/434/EC (now recasted in Directive no. 2009/133/EC) states that: 'where the Member State of the transferring company applies a system of taxing worldwide profits, that Member State shall have the right to tax any profits or capital gains of the permanent establishment resulting from the merger, division or transfer of assets, on condition that it gives relief for the tax that, but for the provisions of this Directive, would have been charged on those profits or capital gains in the Member State in which that permanent establishment is situated, in the same way and in the same amount as it would have done if that tax had actually been charged and paid'.
35. *Supra* n. 33, paras 35-37.
36. CJEU, 26 February 2019, C-581/17, *Wächtler*, ECLI:EU:C:2019:138.
37. It has also to be noted that in March 2021, Germany amended its exit tax rules by eliminating the tax deferral until realisation for all transfers of residence, including transfers to other EU Member States. *See* William Hoke, *German Cabinet OKs Bill Implementing Anti-Avoidance Directive*, in

Thus, the *A Oy* and *Wächtler* judgments demonstrate that according to the CJEU the concept of deferral of tax payment should be referred to the deferral until the realisation of the assets. If this is the case, the statement included in the Explanatory Memorandum to the ATAD proposal according to which 'this Directive also addresses the EU law angle of exit taxation by giving taxpayers the option for deferring the payment of the amount of tax over a certain number of years and settling through staggered payments'[38] seems to be not in line with the CJEU jurisprudence.

Considering the relevant doubts of compliance with the EU fundamental freedoms raised by the current version of Article 166 IITC, we should also note that the rules of Article 30 of Legislative Decree no. 29 of 2023 regarding the protection of tax claims do not affect the payment of exit tax, being applicable only in very specific and limited circumstances. Thus, the payment of the exit tax cannot constitute a condition for the issuance of the pre-operation certificate.

§27.5 CONCLUSIONS

Directive no. 2019/2121/EU and its implementing provisions in the Italian corporate law system should be welcomed both from a civil and private international law standpoint and for tax law purposes.

With respect to civil and private international law, the Directive at hand finally renders these transactions easier through the provision of detailed rules and the illustrated extension of their scope of application.

From a tax law standpoint, the Directive significantly reduces the issues related to the possible 'dissolving' effect of such cross-border transactions and provides for a solution to certain issues linked to private international law rules.

Although not specifically deriving from the Directive, some issues remain still in place, among which the opportunity to amend the current version of Article 166 of IITC in order to comply with the most recent CJEU jurisprudence and allowing taxpayers to opt for the deferral of the payment of the exit tax until the actual realisation of the assets.

Tax Notes Today International, 26 March 2021; William Hoke, *Proposed German Exit Tax Revisions Are Subject of Controversy*, in *Tax Notes Today International*, 27 April 2021.

38. European Commission, 28 January 2016, COM (2016) 26, p. 8.

Part V International Tax Law

CHAPTER 28

International Tax Treaty Law and the Renewed Role of the *Pacta Sunt Servanda* Rule

Carla De Pietro

§28.1 INTRODUCTION: THE DIFFICULT BALANCE BETWEEN THE *PACTA SUNT SERVANDA* RULE AND NATIONAL TAX SOVEREIGNTY

One of the most critical issues characterizing international tax treaty law and its progressive development concerns the search of an acceptable balance between national tax sovereignty and its consequent limitations as deriving from an international agreement. This issue is particularly acute in the field of taxation, given its high budgetary relevance. Therefore, when concluding tax treaties to avoid double taxation following the OECD Model Tax Convention—whose functioning is based on the limitation of tax liability as arising under domestic law—States are torn between different interests, i.e., avoiding double taxation by limiting tax liability and preserving their national tax sovereignty. This conflict is made even more striking by the fact that—exactly because of their functioning—tax treaties may favor tax abuse at both treaty and domestic level.[1] Therefore, within the context of international tax treaty law, one of the most difficult debates concerns the role of the *pacta sunt servanda* rule[2] vis-à-vis the protection of national tax sovereignty.

1. *See*, for example, OEÇD, *Preventing the Granting of Treaty Benefits in Inappropriate Circumstances* (Action 6: 2015 Final Report), 2015, p. 17.
2. Article 26 of the Vienna Convention on the Law of Treaties, entitled "Pacta sunt servanda," establishes: "Every treaty in force is binding upon the parties to it and must be performed by them in good faith."

In the author's Ph.D. thesis, dedicated to Tax Treaty Override, and of which Peter was one of the supervisors, different perspectives were taken into consideration within the context of tax treaties based on the OECD Model Tax Convention, in order to evaluate the effectiveness of the *pacta sunt servanda* rule vis-à-vis national tax sovereignty. One of these perspectives concerned the relationship between domestic anti-abuse rules and tax treaty provisions. The analysis showed—in light of the 2003 OECD Commentary on Article 1—an approach substantially relying on national tax jurisdictions in order to curb abuse of tax treaties. The Commentary acknowledged and—in fact—allowed a position on the basis of which each Contracting State could decide unilaterally the approach to be taken when transactions effecting abuse of the provisions of a treaty were entered into. According to some States, the occurrence of an instance of tax treaty abuse, with consequent denial of tax treaty benefits, resulted from the interpretation of the relevant tax treaty provisions. However, at the opposite, many States considered tax treaty abuse as amounting to abuse of domestic law. Therefore, the occurrence of an instance of tax treaty abuse was unilaterally evaluated on the basis of domestic law and applied for treaty purposes. Thus, the 2003 OECD Commentary on Article 1 gave strong emphasis to national tax sovereignty with detrimental effects, as will be illustrated below, to the *pacta sunt servanda* rule.

The most recent academic interests of Peter concern the effects of tax reforms in an evaluation connecting past, present and future. Certainly, one of the most crucial recent reforms affecting international tax treaty law has been adopted, within the framework of the OECD BEPS initiatives, in terms of tax treaty abuse. While the principal purpose of tax treaties based on the OECD Model Tax Convention remains the elimination of double taxation,[3] the function consisting in curbing tax avoidance has been significantly strengthened. This is also the result of the minimum standard agreed upon within the framework of BEPS Action item 6. This minimum standard includes first of all an express statement according to which the common intention of the Contracting States is to eliminate double taxation without creating opportunities for non-taxation or reduced taxation through tax evasion or tax avoidance, including through treaty-shopping arrangements. Furthermore, this common intention must be implemented through one of the following approaches: (i) the combined application of an LOB (limitation on benefits rule) and PPT ("principal purpose test") rule (included in Article 29(9) of the OECD Model Tax Convention); (ii) the exclusive application of the PPT rule; or (iii) the LOB rule applied together with a mechanism targeting conduit financing arrangements not already addressed in tax treaties.[4]

The Final Report on BEPS Action item 6 also explains that the incorporation of anti-abuse provisions, including the PPT rule, in the treaty text is not sufficient to address tax avoidance risks because there are also situations in which there is no abuse of tax treaty provisions as such, but the granting of tax treaty benefits favors the abuse of domestic law. The report points out the need that – in these situations – the application of domestic anti-abuse rules is not prevented by tax treaty provisions.

3. OECD, Commentary on Art. 1, 2017, para. 54.
4. OECD, *Preventing the Granting of Treaty Benefits in Inappropriate Circumstances* (Action 6: 2015 Final Report), 2015, p. 19.

Consequently, the agreement on a minimum standard within the framework of BEPS Action item 6 has been accompanied by important changes to the OECD Commentary on Article 1. According to the OECD, these changes are intended to guaranteeing a proper functioning of domestic anti-abuse rules vis-à-vis tax treaty provisions notwithstanding the possible introduction of the PPT rule in the treaty text.[5]

This chapter will be developed on the basis of an interpretative analysis of the position expressed in the 2017 OECD Commentary on Article 1 in order to evaluate to what extent this renewed Commentary represents a step forward toward the recognition of the *pacta sunt servanda* rule and, consequently, the effectiveness of international tax treaty law. Within this framework, this chapter aims at answering the following main research question: "To what extent do the changes affecting the OECD Commentary on Article 1, as resulting from BEPS Action item 6, strengthen the role of the *pacta sunt servanda* rule when evaluating the occurrence of an instance of tax treaty abuse compared with the previous position expressed in the 2003 version of the same Commentary?"

Regardless of the different relevance attributed to the OECD Commentaries as interpretative tools both in literature and by national courts,[6] the objective of this chapter is to demonstrate an important change of perspective at OECD level compared with the position expressed in the 2003 Commentary on Article 1. Exactly as recommended by the author in her Ph.D. thesis,[7] the OECD has finally developed a theory in terms of tax treaty abuse on the basis of which the relevant agreement between the Contracting States is the starting point when evaluating the possible occurrence of an instance of tax treaty abuse.

This chapter will be developed by conducting—in the following paragraph—an interpretive analysis that will compare the 2003 OECD Commentary on Article 1 with the 2017 version of the same Commentary. The final paragraph will close this analysis with some conclusive remarks.

§28.2 THE *PACTA SUNT SERVANDA* RULE AND ITS RENEWED ROLE WITHIN THE CONTEXT OF TAX TREATY ABUSE

§28.2.1 The 2003 OECD Commentary on Article 1

The 2003 version of the Commentary on Article 1, in its part concerning the "Improper use of the Convention," was articulated around two fundamental questions:[8]

5. OECD, *Preventing the Granting of Treaty Benefits in Inappropriate Circumstances* (Action 6: 2015 Final Report), 2015, p. 10 and pp. 78-80.
6. *See*, for example, David A. Ward et al., *The Interpretation of Income Tax Treaties with Particular Reference to the Commentaries on the OECD Model* (2005), and the different positions indicated there.
7. Carla De Pietro, *Tax Treaty Override*, 40 EUCOTAX Series on European Taxation 161-162 (2014).
8. Notwithstanding the changes to the Commentary on Art. 1, in fact these remain the two fundamental questions addressed also in the 2017 version.

- "whether the benefits of tax conventions must be granted when transactions that constitute an abuse of the provisions of these conventions are entered into [...]; and
- whether specific provisions and jurisprudential rules of the domestic law of a Contracting State that are intended to prevent tax abuse conflict with tax conventions [...]".[9]

Two different national positions were acknowledged and—in fact—allowed in order to answer the first question. More specifically, it was pointed out that, according to some States, treaty abuse actually amounts to abuse of domestic law. Taxes are levied on the basis of domestic law and, therefore, in case of treaty abuse, there is a domestic loss.[10] On the opposite, other States distinguish between treaty abuse and abuse of domestic law. Therefore, according to the position of these States, the occurrence of an instance of treaty abuse is established by interpreting the relevant treaty provisions.[11]

The application of domestic anti-abuse rules for treaty purposes determined the need of addressing the question of whether tax treaty provisions can limit the application of domestic anti-abuse rules. Therefore, for those States considering treaty abuse as amounting to abuse of domestic law, the answer to the first question was turned into an issue concerning the relationship between domestic anti-abuse rules and tax treaty provisions. The approach of the 2003 Commentary on Article 1 was based on the exclusion of the possibility that a conflict arises between these two orders of provisions. According to paragraph 22.1 of the 2003 Commentary on Article 1, domestic anti-abuse rules, including "substance-over-form," "economic substance" and general anti-abuse rules,[12] "are part of the basic domestic rules set by domestic tax laws for determining *which facts give rise to a tax liability; these rules are not addressed in tax treaties and are therefore not affected by them. Thus, as a general rule and having regard to paragraph 9.5, there will be no conflict" [emphasis added].*

The 2003 version of the Commentary on Article 1 already contained the so-called guiding principle. It was indicated in paragraph 9.5, according to which "[...] *it should not be lightly assumed* that a taxpayer is entering into the type of abusive transactions referred to above. *A guiding principle is that the benefits of a double taxation convention should not be available where a main purpose for entering into certain transactions or arrangements was to secure a more favourable tax position and obtaining that more favourable treatment in these circumstances would be contrary to the object and purpose of the relevant provisions" [emphasis added].* However, notwithstanding the indication of this guiding principle, the 2003 Commentary allowed States to apply their domestic anti-abuse rules without taking into consideration the possibility that these domestic rules could be based on a concept of abuse differing from that

9. OECD, Commentary on Art. 1, 2003, para. 9.1.
10. OECD, Commentary on Art. 1, 2003, para. 9.2.
11. OECD, Commentary on Art. 1, 2003, para. 9.3.
12. *See also*, OECD, Commentary on Art. 1, 2003, para. 22.

expressed through the guiding principle.[13] States were allowed to characterize treaty abuse on the basis of domestic law and to apply this result for treaty purposes on the basis of the argument according to which the possibility of a conflict between domestic anti-abuse rules and tax treaty provisions was excluded.

Already within the context of the 2003 Commentary on Article 1, the author of the present chapter had expressed disagreement on the OECD position that excluded a priori the possibility of a conflict between domestic anti-abuse rules and tax treaty provisions.[14] In brief, according to the author, there was an intrinsic contradiction in a position that pretended to characterize treaty abuse exclusively on the basis of domestic law. The determination concerning the occurrence of an instance of treaty abuse is a complex interpretative process[15] that includes not only the evidence on the occurrence of objective facts and circumstances, but also their characterization as abusive.[16] The position expressed in the 2003 Commentary implied that this characterization in terms of treaty abuse could be conducted exclusively on the basis of domestic law with the consequent application, for example, of a recharacterization of income or redetermination of the taxpayer for treaty purposes.[17] However, according to the author, a correct application of the *pacta sunt servanda* rule implies that any evaluation concerning the possible abusive character of the obtainment of treaty benefits should necessarily start from the interpretation of the relevant tax treaty provisions. Therefore, if the starting point is that the characterization as abusive of the obtainment of certain treaty benefits necessarily takes treaty provisions as relevant parameters, a conflict can indeed arise between domestic anti-abuse rules and treaty provisions when the concept of abuse on which domestic provisions are based (including the specific features characterizing domestic-specific anti-abuse rules) differ from the concept of abuse as resulting from the interpretation of the relevant treaty

13. *See also*, Brian J. Arnold & Stef van Weeghel, *The Relationship Between Tax Treaties and Domestic Anti-abuse Measures*, in Guglielmo Maisto (ed.), *Tax Treaties and Domestic Law*, 2 EC and International Tax Law Series 91-97 (2006).
14. Carla De Pietro, *Tax Treaty Override*, 40 EUCOTAX Series on European Taxation 107-113 (2014). *See also*, Luc De Broe, *International Tax Planning and Prevention of Abuse: A Study under Domestic Tax Law, Tax Treaties and EC Law in Relation to Conduit and Base Companies*, 14 IBFD Doctoral Series 386 et seq. (2008); Brian J. Arnold & Stef van Weeghel, *The Relationship Between Tax Treaties and Domestic Anti-abuse Measures*, in Guglielmo Maisto (ed.), *Tax Treaties and Domestic Law*, 2 EC and International Tax Law Series 91-97 (2006). For case law, *see* Luc De Broe & Joris Luts, *BEPS Action 6: Tax Treaty Abuse*, 43 Intertax 135 and fn. 136 (2015) DOI: 10.54648/taxi2015011. For a different position, *see* Michael Lang, *CFC Regulations and Double Taxation Treaties*, 57 Bulletin for International Taxation 54 (2003); Supreme Administrative Court (Korkein Hallinto-oikeus), 20 March 2002, KHO: 2002:26. *See Re A Oyj Abp – KHO:2002: 26*, 4 International Tax Law Reports, 1009-1076 (2002) (with note of Philip Baker).
15. The expression “interpretative process” is used in a broad sense and does not deal with the distinction between “factual approach” and “interpretative approach.” *See* Frederick Zimmer, *Domestic Anti-Avoidance Rules and Tax Treaties: Comment on Brian Arnold’s Article*, 59 Bulletin for International Fiscal Documentation 25-26 (2005).
16. *See also*, Frederick Zimmer, “General Report”, in *Form and Substance in Tax Law*, LXXXVIIa Cahiers de droit fiscal international 2002 Oslo Congress 31 (2002): “there is a difference of principle between establishing the facts on the basis of rules of evidence and deciding whether the legal conditions for declaring tax avoidance are fulfilled.”
17. OECD, Commentary on Art. 1, 2003, para. 22.1.

provisions. According to the author, this position was also coherent with the indication of the guiding principle[18] mentioned above.

As far as international treaty law is concerned, the Vienna Convention on the Law of Treaties (VCLT) expressly establishes that treaty provisions must be interpreted (Article 31) and performed (Article 26) in good faith. Article 26 of the VCLT directly connects the obligation to perform the treaty in good faith with the respect of the *pacta sunt servanda* rule. Therefore, an application in good faith of a treaty necessarily implies the respect of the common will expressed by the parties.

According to the author, this also implies that, in the absence of treaty abuse (even when there is abuse of domestic law), the application of domestic anti-abuse rules may be limited by conflicting tax treaty provisions, unless the treaty expressly excludes this possibility.[19]

Furthermore, allowing countries to characterize tax treaty abuse on the basis of autonomous positions[20] had the concrete consequence of fragmenting[21] the notion of treaty abuse and determining an unbalanced treatment of taxpayers even under the same tax treaty. In fact, the treatment of taxpayers in substantially similar situations could differ depending on the specific position of the Contracting State characterizing the situation at issue.[22]

It can, therefore, be concluded that in the 2003 OECD Commentary on Article 1, the approach concerning the fight against tax treaty abuse was substantially based on the autonomy of national tax jurisdictions. The alleged absence of conflict between domestic anti-abuse rules and tax treaty provisions, by allowing a unilateral determination of tax treaty abuse on the basis of domestic law, in fact, produced the consequence of relegating the *pacta sunt servanda* rule, as expression of the common will of the Contracting States, to a rather marginal position.[23,24]

18. On the controversial nature and scope of the guiding principle within the framework of the 2003 OECD Commentary on Art. 1, *see*, for example, Brian J. Arnold & Stef van Weeghel, *The Relationship Between Tax Treaties and Domestic Anti-abuse Measures*, in Guglielmo Maisto (ed.), *Tax Treaties and Domestic Law*, 2 EC and International Tax Law Series 92-97 (2006).
19. For example, with reference to CFC rules, *see* Carla De Pietro, *The GloBE Income Inclusion Rule and Its Global Character: Complexities Underlying Its Fully Effective Application*, 30 EC Tax Review 222-227 (2021) DOI: 10.54648/ecta2021023; Carla De Pietro, *Tax Treaty Override*, 40 EUCOTAX Series on European Taxation 144-158 (2014).
20. Within the framework of the 2003 OECD Commentary on Art. 1, the application of different notions of tax treaty abuse by the Contracting States under the same tax treaty could derive: (i) from the interpretation of treaty provisions vis-à-vis the application of domestic anti-abuse rules; (ii) the application of domestic anti-abuse rules expressing different notions of abuse; (iii) different interpretative positions on similar domestic anti-abuse rules.
21. *See also*, Luc De Broe, *International Tax Planning and Prevention of Abuse: A Study under Domestic Tax Law, Tax Treaties and EC Law in Relation to Conduit and Base Companies*, 14 IBFD Doctoral Series 392-393 (2008); Brian J. Arnold & Stef van Weeghel, *The Relationship Between Tax Treaties and Domestic Anti-abuse Measures*, in Guglielmo Maisto (ed.), *Tax Treaties and Domestic Law*, 2 EC and International Tax Law Series 92 (2006).
22. For a concrete example, *see* Carla De Pietro, *Taxpayer's Mobility in the Context of Tax Treaty Law: The Need for a Renewed Balance Between Favouring the Movement of Persons and Tackling Treaty Abuse*, in Edoardo Traversa (ed.), *Corporate Tax Residence and Mobility*, 16 EATLP International Tax Series 83-84 (2018).
23. *See also*, Robert L.H. IJzerman, "Netherlands," in *Form and Substance in Tax Law*, LXXXVIIa Cahiers de droit fiscal international, 2002 Oslo Congress 466 (2002); Luc De Broe, *International*

§28.2.2 The 2017 OECD Commentary on Article 1

The Final Report on BEPS Action item 6 includes under the concept of "treaty abuse" or "the granting of treaty benefits in inappropriate circumstances"[25] both: (1) "cases where a person tries to circumvent limitations provided by the treaty itself" and (2) "cases where a person tries to circumvent the provisions of domestic tax law using treaty benefits."[26] According to the report, it would be inappropriate to apply the provisions of a tax treaty when their application would lead to the abuse of domestic law. It is, therefore, further explained that the introduction in the treaty text of a general anti-abuse rule incorporating the guiding principle (the PPT rule) will not modify the conclusions already reached in the Commentary on Article 1 concerning the relationship between domestic anti-abuse rules and treaty provisions "in particular with respect to treaties that do not incorporate the new general anti-abuse rule."[27,28]

The OECD seems, therefore, to pretend that not much has changed in the Commentary on Article 1 about the relationship between domestic anti-abuse rules and tax treaty provisions as a result of BEPS Action item 6. However, according to the author and as will be demonstrated below, an interpretative analysis of the new Commentary on Article 1 actually shows substantial changes, acknowledging a stronger role of the *pacta sunt servanda* rule, compared to the position expressed in the 2003 Commentary.

In paragraph 57 of the 2017 Commentary on Article 1, introducing the part of the Commentary that focuses on the fight against tax avoidance through tax treaties, it is specified that, when these treaties do not include anti-abuse provisions, it may be

---

Tax Planning and Prevention of Abuse: A Study under Domestic Tax Law, Tax Treaties and EC Law in Relation to Conduit and Base Companies, 14 IBFD Doctoral Series 387–388 (2008); Brian J. Arnold & Stef van Weeghel, *The Relationship Between Tax Treaties and Domestic Anti-abuse Measures*, in Guglielmo Maisto (ed.), *Tax Treaties and Domestic Law*, 2 EC and International Tax Law Series 97 (2006).

24. Very interestingly, these aspects had been considered also from a political science's perspective. *See* Thomas Rixen, *The Political Economy of International Tax Governance* 196 (2008): "[s]ophisticated methods of tax arbitrage such as hybrid entities and corporate inversions are examples of the increasing internal tension within an international tax system built on the notion of sovereignty-preserving cooperation. These cannot be tackled effectively with unilateral anti-avoidance measures ... [This approach] will ultimately lead to conflict among governments ... What one OECD country considers undue double-non taxation another considers the desired outcome of its policies. If conflicts of this kind increase in number and intensity, the implicit consensus may break down. If they should in the future be forced to craft an explicit consensus, governments would have to address the current incoherence of the international tax regime head on. Either they drop the ambition to counteract 'tax arbitrage' and continue to have purely national tax systems or they come to harmonize at least certain features of their tax systems—that is, share legislative sovereignty with others—in order to be able to define and counteract 'tax arbitrage'."
25. *See, for example*, OECD, *Preventing the Granting of Treaty Benefits in Inappropriate Circumstances* (Action 6: 2015 Final Report), 2015, p. 13.
26. OECD, *Preventing the Granting of Treaty Benefits in Inappropriate Circumstances* (Action 6: 2015 Final Report), 2015, p. 17.
27. OECD, *Preventing the Granting of Treaty Benefits in Inappropriate Circumstances* (Action 6: 2015 Final Report), 2015, p. 79.
28. In general, *see* OECD, *Preventing the Granting of Treaty Benefits in Inappropriate Circumstances* (Action 6: 2015 Final Report), 2015, pp. 78-80.

necessary to consider whether treaty benefits should be granted in case of abuse of treaty provisions. After this premise, the Commentary on Article 1 distinguishes between the position of those States according to which the abuse of tax treaty provisions also amounts to abuse of domestic law[29] and the position of those States that characterize tax treaty abuse through the interpretation of tax treaty provisions.[30] Thus, for the first category of States, it is necessary to consider whether the tax treaty provisions may limit the application of domestic anti-abuse rules. Within this context, the 2017 Commentary on Article 1, reiterating the 2003 position, states that "as a general rule" there will be no conflict between domestic anti-abuse rules and tax treaty provisions.[31] However, in the 2017 version of the Commentary, the expression "as a general rule" refers directly to the explanations given in paragraphs 66 to 80 of the Commentary on Article 1, concerning the fight against tax avoidance through domestic anti-abuse rules and judicial doctrines. In fact, the interpretation of these paragraphs, as conducted below, shows that the previous position excluding a priori the possibility of a conflict between domestic anti-abuse rules and tax treaty provisions is now abandoned.

First of all, this is expressly confirmed in paragraph 70 of the 2017 Commentary on Article 1, which states: "*[g]enerally, where the application of provisions of domestic law and of those of tax treaties produces conflicting results, the provisions of tax treaties are intended to prevail. This is a logical consequence of the principle of "pacta sunt servanda" which is incorporated in Article 26 of the Vienna Convention on the Law of Treaties.* Thus, if the application of specific anti-abuse rules found in domestic law were to result in a tax treatment that is not in accordance with the provisions of a tax treaty, this would conflict with the provisions of that treaty and the provisions of the treaty should prevail under public international law" *[emphasis added]*.[32]

Although this paragraph is included in the part of the Commentary concerning specific legislative anti-abuse rules, the first part of the text "*generally … provisions of domestic law*" has a general scope, also in consideration of the subsequent express reference to "*specific anti-abuse rules.*" The fact that, in case of conflict between tax treaty provisions and domestic-specific anti-abuse rules, the firsts must prevail is a consequence ("thus") of the principle expressed in the first part of paragraph 70 generally concerning "*the application of provisions of domestic law.*"

Very importantly, paragraph 70 also refers to situations when tax treaty provisions are not abused in themselves, but facilitate the abuse of domestic law.[33] Therefore, according to the author, paragraph 70 also implies that, in the absence of treaty abuse, tax treaty provisions limit the application of domestic rules addressing the abuse of domestic law when a conflict arises between these rules and the relevant tax treaty provisions.

29. OECD, Commentary on Art. 1, 2017, para. 58.
30. OECD, Commentary on Art. 1, 2017, para. 59.
31. OECD, Commentary on Art. 1, 2017, para. 58.
32. OECD, Commentary on Art. 1, 2017, para. 70.
33. OECD, Commentary on Art. 1, 2017, paras. 66 and 67.

This conclusion has to be considered also in connection with paragraph 74 of the 2017 Commentary on Article 1. In fact, this paragraph concretely addresses the possibility that domestic specific anti-abuse rules conflict with tax treaty provisions. In order to explain this concrete possibility, the paragraph gives the following example: an individual taxpayer realizes gains upon the alienation of property situated in a third State after transferring her/his tax residence from State A to State B. However, State A applies a domestic rule that leads to taxation in that State as the taxpayer was resident there when the property was acquired as well as for at least seven of the ten years prior to the alienation. The Commentary explains that the application of such a domestic rule would be prevented by Article 13(5) of tax treaties based on the OECD Model Tax Convention, unless—on the basis of the specific circumstances of the case—an instance of tax treaty abuse occurs by virtue of Article 29(9) of the OECD Model Tax Convention or the principles expressed in paragraphs 60 and 61 of the 2017 Commentary on Article 1, including the guiding principle.

In light of this position, when a domestic rule is an expression of a concept of abuse that is broader than the concept of abuse as determined at treaty level, the application of domestic law can be limited by a tax treaty provision when a conflict arises. According to the author, and notwithstanding the explanation given in the Final Report on Action item 6 on the role of domestic anti-abuse rules in order to address situations in which tax treaty provisions favor abuse of domestic law, this position confirms that, in the absence of treaty abuse, a conflict can arise between domestic anti-abuse rules and tax treaty provisions. In fact, this position is in accordance with what was maintained by the present author already within the context of the 2003 Commentary on Article 1 and addressed above. In light of the structure and functioning of the OECD Model Tax Convention, the application of domestic law and tax treaty provisions are complementary to each other. Tax liability arises under domestic law, and treaty provisions restrict this tax liability. In light of this complementarity, and in the absence of abuse as determined at treaty level, a conflict can arise between domestic anti-abuse rules and tax treaty provisions.

The 2017 Commentary on Article 1 also explains that, in any case, conflicts will "often" be avoided.[34] It is indicated that, in the first instance, this will be the case if a tax treaty, even when the existence of a conflict is acknowledged, expressly allows the application of domestic-specific anti-abuse rules or if it is expressly stated in the tax treaty that there is no conflict.[35] Very importantly, according to the author, although these passages are meant to explain that—in concrete terms—a conflict will be avoided, they actually confirm a position giving priority to the common will of the Contracting States. This emphasis on the agreement is—indeed—again an acknowledgment of the *pacta sunt servanda* rule.

According to the author, the same conclusion can be reached with regard to the explanation according to which—due to the fact that the functioning of the OECD Model Tax Convention—also through Article 3(2)—is often based on the application of domestic law, in fact domestic-specific anti-abuse rules may determine the way in

34. OECD, Commentary on Art. 1, 2017, para. 71.
35. OECD, Commentary on Art. 1, 2017, para. 72.

which the treaty applies instead of conflicting with it. Also in this case, it is the treaty (i.e., the agreement between the Contracting States) that allows the application of domestic law.[36]

With reference to domestic judicial doctrines and principles of interpretation, paragraphs 75 and 78 of the 2017 Commentary on Article 1 explain that these doctrines and principles can be applied to the interpretation of tax treaty provisions to the extent that there is no conflict with the rules of interpretation of treaties. More specifically, "there will be no conflict with the treaty provisions if the benefits of the treaty are denied under both a proper interpretation of the treaty and as result of the application of domestic specific [and general] anti-abuse rules."[37] However, it is clear that the interpretation of tax treaty provisions will necessarily imply taking into consideration Article 29(9) of the OECD Model Tax Convention when it is formally introduced in the treaty text. Therefore, in this case, it will not be possible to apply domestic judicial doctrines and principles of interpretation leading to the identification of a concept of abuse differing from the notion of abuse expressed in Article 29(9). Furthermore, according to paragraph 61 of the 2017 Commentary on Article 1, Article 29(9) merely confirms the guiding principle, which applies regardless of the formal adoption of Article 29(9). Therefore, a coherent unitary interpretation of the 2017 Commentary on Article 1 necessarily implies that, when interpreting a treaty provision, especially in order to verify its possible abuse, the guiding principle must be taken into consideration.[38] Therefore, there will be no conflict with tax treaty provisions, and it will be possible to deny the relevant treaty benefits in light of domestic judicial doctrines and principles of interpretation, only to the extent that the interpretative results consequent to the application of the domestic interpretative approach do not lead to the application of a notion of abuse differing from that expressed in the guiding principle.

The same conclusion is expressly reached in paragraph 77 of the 2017 Commentary on Article 1 with reference to the application of domestic general legislative anti-abuse rules. A conflict will be avoided only to the extent that the notion of abuse on which the domestic rule is based coincides with the treaty notion of abuse as applicable under Article 29(9) or the guiding principle. Alternatively, a conflict will be avoided through tax treaty provisions expressly allowing the application of domestic anti-abuse rules or expressly excluding the occurrence of a conflict, or when the interpretation and application of the treaty is based on the application of domestic law.

Thus, paragraph 79 of the 2017 Commentary on Article 1 concludes that, on the basis of the conducted analysis, as a general rule and in light of the guiding principle, judicial anti-abuse doctrines and general domestic anti-abuse rules will not conflict with tax treaty provisions. Paragraph 79 substantially reiterates paragraph 22.1 of the 2003 Commentary on Article 1. However, and very importantly, it is now deleted the

36. OECD, Commentary on Art. 1, 2017, para. 73.
37. OECD, Commentary on Art. 1, 2017, para. 75.
38. This conclusion expresses a position exclusively based on the interpretation of the 2017 Commentary on Art. 1, regardless of the different relevance attributed to the OECD Commentaries as interpretative tools both in literature and by national courts. *See supra* n. 6. It is also beyond the scope of this chapter to assess the position expressed in the 2017 Commentary on Art. 1 on the full coincidence between the guiding principle and the PPT rule.

part according to which domestic anti-abuse rules "are part of the basic domestic rules set by domestic tax laws for determining which facts give rise to a tax liability; these rules are not addressed in tax treaties and are therefore not affected by them."

Therefore, according to the author, and contrary to the position indicated in the Final Report on BEPS Action item 6, through the 2017 Commentary on Article 1, the OECD approach concerning the relationship between domestic anti-abuse rules and tax treaty provisions has been substantially changed compared to the 2003 version of the same Commentary. More precisely, the position excluding a priori the possibility of a conflict between these two orders of provisions has been abandoned. In light of the renewed Commentary on Article 1, a conflict between domestic anti-abuse rules and tax treaty provisions is indeed possible although—in practice—it can be avoided through treaty provisions expressly allowing the application of domestic law. This renewed position is the consequence of the development of an anti-abuse theory based on the idea that an assessment in terms of tax treaty abuse should necessarily have—as a starting point—the relevant tax treaty provisions in light of Article 29(9) of the OECD Model Tax Convention or the guiding principle indicated in paragraph 61 of the 2017 Commentary on Article 1. Thus, in the absence of tax treaty abuse as determined at the treaty level, a conflict can arise between domestic anti-abuse rules and tax treaty provisions.[39] According to the author, these conclusions do not necessarily contradict the position maintained in the Final Report on BEPS Action item 6 to the extent that the report has considered inappropriate the application of tax treaty provisions when their application leads to the abuse of domestic law. The position maintained in the 2017 Commentary on Article 1 is the expression of an important acknowledgement of the *pacta sunt servanda* rule. Therefore, even in the absence of tax treaty abuse, the obtainment of treaty benefits can be denied when an instance of abuse of domestic law occurs, but exclusively on the basis of the common will of the Contracting States. This is, for example, confirmed by the inclusion in Article 1(3) of the OECD Model Tax Convention, in light of the OECD BEPS Action item 6, of a saving clause expressly stating that tax treaties do not affect the taxation, by a Contracting State, of its residents (with some indicated exceptions).[40]

§28.3 CONCLUSIONS: *PACTA SUNT SERVANDA* RULE AND THE EFFECTIVENESS OF INTERNATIONAL TAX TREATY LAW

An interpretative analysis of the 2017 Commentary on Article 1 of the OECD Model Tax Convention has shown a renewed role of the *pacta sunt servanda* rule within the

39. *See also*, Luc De Broe & Joris Luts, *BEPS Action 6: Tax Treaty Abuse*, 43 Intertax 136-137 (2015) DOI: 10.54648/taxi2015011; Andrés Báez Moreno, *GAARs and Treaties: From the Guiding Principle to the Principal Purpose Test—What Have We Gained from BEPS Action 6?*, 45 Intertax 434-435 (2017) DOI: 10.54648/taxi2017036.

40. According to para. 81 of the 2017 OECD Commentary on Art. 1, the principle expressed in Art. 1(3) of the 2017 OECD Model Tax Convention applies regardless of the inclusion of this provision in the treaty text. However, in this regard, *see* Carla De Pietro, *The GloBE Income Inclusion Rule and Its Global Character: Complexities Underlying Its Fully Effective Application*, 30 EC Tax Review 225-227 (2021) DOI: 10.54648/ecta2021023.

framework of tax treaty abuse. This renewed OECD position is an expression of the central role of the agreement between the Contracting States. The 2003 Commentary on Article 1 excluded a priori the possibility of a conflict between domestic anti-abuse rules and tax treaty provisions on the basis of the position according to which domestic anti-abuse rules "are part of the basic domestic rules set by domestic tax laws for determining which facts give rise to a tax liability; these rules are not addressed in tax treaties and are therefore not affected by them." Already within the context of the 2003 Commentary on Article 1, the present author had pointed out the intrinsic contradiction in a position that allowed the Contracting States to characterize an instance of tax treaty abuse exclusively on the basis of domestic law. The determination concerning the occurrence of an instance of tax treaty abuse is a complex interpretative process that includes not only the evidence on the occurrence of objective facts and circumstances, but also their characterization as abusive. According to the author, a correct application of the *pacta sunt servanda* rule implies that any evaluation concerning the possible abusive character of the obtainment of tax treaty benefits should necessarily start from the interpretation of the relevant tax treaty provisions. Therefore, according to the author, this also implies that, in the absence of treaty abuse (even when there is abuse of domestic law), the application of domestic anti-abuse rules may be limited by conflicting tax treaty provisions, unless the treaty expressly excludes this possibility.

In line with this position, the 2017 Commentary on Article 1 now explicitly addresses the possibility of a conflict when domestic law is the expression of a concept of abuse that does not fully coincide with the concept of abuse as adopted at treaty level through Article 29(9) of the OECD Model Tax Convention or, when the PPT rule is not included in the treaty text, the guiding principle. The amended Commentary also refers to situations when tax treaty provisions are not abused in themselves, but their application facilitates the abuse of domestic law. Exactly in light of these situations, the Final Report on Action item 6 emphasizes the important role of domestic anti-abuse rules. Therefore, the relevance of the changes to the 2017 Commentary on Article 1 goes beyond the express incorporation of anti-abuse provisions, including the PPT rule, in the treaty text. However, as demonstrated above, when—in the absence of tax treaty abuse—a conflict arises between domestic anti-abuse rules and tax treaty provisions, the application of domestic law can only derive from express treaty provisions. Therefore, in the absence of tax treaty abuse, the obtainment of treaty benefits can be denied when an instance of abuse of domestic law occurs, but exclusively on the basis of the common will of the Contracting States.

This chapter has, therefore, demonstrated an important change of perspective at OECD level. Through the renewed Commentary on Article 1, it has been developed a position on the basis of which the relevant agreement between the Contracting States is considered to be the starting point when evaluating the possible occurrence of an instance of tax treaty abuse. Although the OECD seems to downplay these results in the Final Report on BEPS Action item 6, this position represents a substantial step forward toward a stronger role of the *pacta sunt servanda* rule and, consequently, the effectiveness of international tax treaty law, at least within the framework of tax treaty abuse. In fact, because the OECD has developed a theory on tax treaty abuse that is based on the reciprocity between the Contracting States, its renewed position on the relationship between domestic anti-abuse rules and tax treaty provisions, in turn, strengthens the recognition of the effectiveness of the anti-abuse provisions incorporated in the treaty text, including the PPT rule. These treaty anti-abuse provisions are common parameters for the definition of tax treaty abuse, limiting the application of domestic anti-abuse rules.

CHAPTER 29

Subsequent Practice and Tax Treaties

Michael Lang[*]

§29.1 THE REPORT OF THE ILC

Peter Essers is one of the most outstanding tax law scholars, known and active far beyond the Netherlands. For many years, I have had a professional collaboration with him, which over time has also become a very good friendship. We share not only a passion for European tax law but also an interest in international tax law and in particular double taxation treaties. Peter Essers is also very concerned about the rule of law and – related to this – the separation of powers. Especially in the area of international tax law, the executive branch often has a predominant position. In contrast, the importance of legislation and jurisdiction often recedes into the background.

This is particularly evident in the case of subsequent practice, which is decisive for the interpretation of international treaties according to Article 31(3) lit b Vienna Convention on the Law of Treaties (VCLT): Subsequent practice is mostly shaped by the administrative authorities. In this way, the administrative authorities influence the content of the norms of international treaties and thereby compete with the competence of the legislature, which, at least in the area of double taxation agreements, is reserved in most states for the approval of these international treaties.[1] However, they also encroach on the jurisdiction of the courts, insofar as the 'subsequent practice'

* I completed this manuscript on 31 August 2023. I wish to express my sincere thanks to Dominik Hemmelmeyer for the critical review and his support in literature research, in drafting the annotations, and proofreading.

1. *See* in general Stefan Kadelbach, *The International Law Commission and Role of Subsequent Practice as a Means of Interpretation under Articles 31 and 32 VCLT*, QIL, Zoom-in 46 (2018), 5 (15); *see also* Stefan Kadelbach, *Domestic Constitutional Concerns with Respect to the Use of Subsequent Agreements and Practice at the International Level*, in: Georg Nolte (ed.) Treaties and Subsequent Practice (2013), 145 (153).

shaped by the administrative authorities is to be taken into account as part of the context of the international treaty when interpreting it. In the final analysis, this could lead to the courts adopting views of the administration instead of performing their very own task, namely reviewing administrative decisions.[2] Especially tax law scholars and tax courts, who are committed to the principle of separation of powers, are therefore often sceptical about the 'subsequent practice' according to Article 31(3) lit b VCLT.

The International Law Commission (ILC) has given new impetus to this topic: After long preparatory work – in particular by its Special Rapporteur *Georg Nolte* – the ILC adopted a report in its 70th session in 2018, which in its Chapter IV deals in detail with the topic 'Subsequent agreements and subsequent practice in relation to the interpretation of treaties'.[3] The ILC has reproduced, summarized and attempted to reconcile the views that have emerged on the interpretation of Article 31(3) lit b VCLT, and has naturally also set its own accents. Chapter IV of the report, including the 'Draft Conclusions' contained therein, became the subject of a separate resolution, which was adopted by the UN General Assembly on 20 December 2018.[4] I will not go into the significance of this resolution and the report of the ILC in terms of international law here, but there is no question that the work of the ILC will have a considerable influence on the further practice of international law and the jurisprudence on Article 31(3) lit b VCLT.[5] For this reason, I would like to pick out some of the considerations put forward by the ILC and examine what significance they might have, in particular, for the interpretation of tax treaties.

§29.2 IMPORTANCE OF 'SUBSEQUENT PRACTICE' IN THE CONTEXT OF DTA INTERPRETATION

In its 'Conclusion 2', the ILC emphasizes right at the beginning of its report that Articles 31 and 32 VCLT are also applicable as customary international law. In the Commentary, the ILC states:[6] '... the rules contained in articles 31 and 32 apply as treaty law in relation to those States that are parties to the 1969 Vienna Convention, and as customary international law between all States, including to treaties which were concluded before the entry into force of the Vienna Convention for the States parties concerned'. However, this does not necessarily apply to all rules of interpretation of the VCLT:[7] 'The Commission nevertheless decided not to address ... the question of how far article 33 reflects customary international law.'

2. *See* in that respect the Letter of the German Ministry of Finance of 19 April 2023 (BStBl I 2023, 630) in which the Ministry took the view that the most recent OECD Commentaries should be regarded as 'subsequent practice' for the interpretation of German tax treaties; in more detail Michael Lang, *Die Auffassung des BMF zur Bedeutung des OECD-Kommentars für die Auslegung von DBA*, IStR 2023, 549 et seq.
3. Report of the International Law Commission, Seventieth session 2018, UN Doc. A/73/10, 11 et seq.
4. Resolution of the UN General Assembly, 20 December 2018, UN Doc. A/RES/73/202.
5. *See, e.g.*, Danae Azaria, *'Codification by Interpretation': The International Law Commission as an Interpreter of International Law*, EJIL (2020), Vol. 31 No. 1, 171 (188 et seq.).
6. Report of the International Law Commission, Seventieth session 2018, 19 (para. 4 Conclusion 2).
7. Report of the International Law Commission, Seventieth session 2018, 19 (para. 5 Conclusion 2).

The significance of Articles 31 and 32 VCLT for the interpretation of a specific international treaty is not yet clear: As an international treaty, the VCLT is not superior to other international treaties - such as the tax treaties - but is on the same level. This also applies to customary international law. Articles 31 and 32 VCLT are therefore also a component of customary international law on the same level with the tax treaties. Therefore, each international treaty can also regulate its own interpretation, which in the field of tax treaties is evidenced by the provision modelled on Article 3(2) OECD Model Convention (OECD MC). Even if there is no explicit provision, international treaties could regulate their own interpretation if this results from the subject matter of the treaty.[8] Therefore, it is not excluded that for individual treaties the provisions of Articles 31 and 32 VCLT are applied in a modified form, which may also be relevant with regard to Article 31(3) lit b VCLT. Particularly in the area of tax treaties, where the provisions modelled on Article 3(2) OECD MC explicitly provide a separate interpretation provision, the question arises as to what extent this provision leaves room for Article 31(3) lit b VCLT. This is a question not only of the relationship between Articles 31 and 32 VCLT and Article 3(2) OECD MC but also of the interpretation of Article 3(2) OECD MC itself: If one assumes that this provision requires the primacy of the interpretation from the context of the tax treaty, and only in the second place the consideration of mutual agreements and in the third place that of the domestic law of the application state,[9] the question arises whether under the 'context' Articles 31 and 32 VCLT as a whole is to be understood, or, for instance, Article 31(3) VCLT is to be excluded.[10] Since the ILC does not address these questions, they will not be dealt with in depth here but only briefly addressed in this way.

The ILC emphasizes the primacy of Article 31 VCLT resulting from Article 32 VCLT:[11] 'Whereas article 31 sets forth the general rule and article 32 the recourse to supplementary means of interpretation, these rules must be read together as they constitute an integrated framework for the interpretation of treaties. Article 32 includes thresholds between the application of the primary means of interpretation according to article 31, all of which are to be taken into account in the process of interpretation, and "supplementary means of interpretation" set forth in article 32. Recourse may be had

8. For more details, *see* Michael Lang, *Can Law Regulate Its Own Interpretation? Relevance and Meaning of Articles 31-33 of the Vienna Convention on the Law of Treaties (VCLT) and Article 3 Para. 2 of the Model Convention of the Organisation for Economic Co-operation and Development (OECD MC) for the Interpretation of Double-Taxation Conventions*, in: Yariv Brauner, Research Handbook on International Taxation, 174 et seq.
9. On this subject in detail Michael Lang, *Tax Treaty Interpretation: A Response to John Avery Jones*, Bulletin for International Taxation 2020 (Vol. 74, no. 11), 660 et seq.; *see also* Michael Lang, *Die Bedeutung von Verständigungsvereinbarungen nach Art 3 Abs 2 OECD-Musterabkommen 2017*, in *FS Moris Lehner* 209 et seq. (Roland Ismer et al. (eds), 2019).
10. *See, e.g.*, Jasper Bossuyt, *The Legal Status of Extrinsic Instruments for the Interpretation of Tax Treaties* (2021), 1328: 'The "context" should not be interpreted as broadly as generally advocated in doctrine but refers to (i) the position that a term has in a phrase; (ii) the position that a phrase has in a paragraph; or (iii) the position that a paragraph has in an article, i.e. the mutual consistency of sentences and parts of sentences in a treaty, including the preamble and annexes. It additionally includes agreements concluded by both contracting states at the moment of treaty conclusion.'
11. Report of the International Law Commission, Seventieth session 2018, 17 et seq. (para. 3 Conclusion 2).

to the supplementary means of interpretation, either in order to confirm the meaning resulting from the application of article 31, or to determine the meaning when the interpretation according to article 31 leaves the meaning of the treaty or its terms ambiguous or obscure or leads to a result that is manifestly absurd or unreasonable.' This distinction is particularly important with regard to 'subsequent practice': According to Article 31(3) lit b VCLT, 'any subsequent practice in the application of the treaty which establishes the agreement of the parties regarding its interpretation' may be relevant. In certain cases, however, Article 32 VCLT may also come into consideration:[12] '... subsequent practice in the application of the treaty, which does not establish the agreement of all parties to the treaty, but only of one or more parties, may be used as a supplementary means of interpretation. This was stated by the Commission, and has since been recognized by international courts and tribunals, and in the literature'. The ILC attaches great importance to considering 'subsequent practice' as relevant under certain conditions, at least according to Article 32 VCLT.

Regarding the relationship of the individual means of interpretation mentioned in Article 31 VCLT, the ILC states the following in its Commentary:[13] 'The characterization of subsequent agreements and subsequent practice of the parties under article 31, paragraph 3 (a) and (b), as "authentic means of interpretation" does not, however, imply that these means necessarily possess a conclusive effect. According to the chapeau of article 31, paragraph 3, subsequent agreements and subsequent practice shall, after all, only "be taken into account" in the interpretation of a treaty, which consists of a "single combined operation" with no hierarchy among the means of interpretation that are referred to in article 31 ... .'

In addition, the ILC has stated:[14] 'Domestic courts have sometimes explicitly recognized that subsequent agreements and subsequent practice under article 31, paragraph 3 (a) and (b), are "authentic" means of interpretation. They have, however, not always been consistent regarding the legal consequences that this characterization entails. Whereas some courts have assumed that subsequent agreements and practice by the parties under the treaty may produce certain binding effects, others have rightly emphasized that article 31, paragraph 3, only requires that subsequent agreements and subsequent practice "be taken into account".'

Thus the ILC makes it clear that the importance of 'subsequent practice' must not be overestimated: it is *one* of the 'means of interpretation'. It is by no means more important than other means of interpretation.[15] Therefore, the interpretation can also lead to a completely different result than subsequent practice suggests at first glance.[16]

12. Report of the International Law Commission, Seventieth session 2018, 20 et seq. (para. 9 Conclusion 2).
13. Report of the International Law Commission, Seventieth session 2018, 24 (para. 4 Conclusion 3).
14. Report of the International Law Commission, Seventieth session 2018, 26 (para. 8 Conclusion 3).
15. *See also* Artur Kozlowski, *Comment on the ILC Draft Conclusions on Subsequent Agreements and Subsequent Practice in Relation to the Interpretation of Treaties*, Polish Review on International and European Law 2021, Vol. 10, Issue 1, 121 (124).
16. *See* Rahim Moloo, *When Actions Speak Louder than Words: The Relevance of Subsequent Party Conduct to Treaty Interpretation*, Berkeley Journal of International Law 2013, 39 (76).

§29.3 CONDUCT OF TAX AUTHORITIES MAY CONSTITUTE SUBSEQUENT PRACTICE

The ILC also addresses an issue that is particularly relevant in the area of tax treaties:[17] 'Subsequent practice of States in the application of a treaty may certainly be performed by the high-ranking government officials mentioned in article 7 of the 1969 Vienna Convention. Yet, since most treaties typically are not applied by such high officials, international courts and tribunals have recognized that the conduct of lower authorities may also, under certain conditions, constitute relevant subsequent practice in the application of a treaty.'

In fact, tax treaties are generally applied by local tax authorities all over the world. In addition, there are courts that are called upon to review the decisions of the local tax authorities. But none of the officials mentioned in Article 7 VCLT - Heads of State, Heads of Government and Ministers for Foreign Affairs as well as heads of diplomatic mission - apply the provisions of the DTAs. This is also true for the representatives accredited by states to an international conference or to an international organization or one of its organs mentioned in Article 7(2) lit c because this applies only 'for the purpose of adopting the text of a treaty in that conference, organization or organ'. The Ministers of Finance and their authorities, which are not explicitly mentioned in Article 7 VCLT, apply the DTAs only in special situations, as in the case of Article 26 or Article 27 OECD MC or Article 29(8) lit c OECD MC. The application of Article 25 OECD MC is also reserved for the 'competent authorities' but only serves the conclusion of mutual agreements, which in turn may have significance for the interpretation as 'subsequent agreements'.[18]

The ILC even mentions, by way of illustration, an example from international tax law concerning the tax treatment of pensions by local tax authorities:[19] 'And in the case of *Tax regime governing pensions paid to retired UNESCO officials residing in France*, the Arbitral Tribunal accepted, in principle, the practice of the French tax administration of not collecting taxes on the pensions of retired UNESCO employees as being relevant subsequent practice. Ultimately, however, the Arbitral Tribunal considered some contrary official pronouncements by a higher authority, the French Government, to be decisive.' The ILC Report then summarizes as follows:[20] 'The practice of lower

17. Report of the International Law Commission, Seventieth session 2018, 38 (para. 6 Conclusion 5); *see also* Irina Buga, *Subsequent Practice and Treaty Modification*, in: Michael J. Bowman & Dino Kritsiotis (eds) *Conceptual and Contextual Perspectives on the Modern Law of Treaties* (2018), 363 (368).
18. *See also* Rahim Moloo, *When Actions Speak Louder than Words: The Relevance of Subsequent Party Conduct to Treaty Interpretation*, Berkeley Journal of International Law 2013, 39 (69 et seq.): '[...] with respect to customs exemptions in a treaty, the actions of border customs agents may be relevant [under Article 31 (3) lit b VCLT], though that same customs agent would not be able to represent the state in entering an agreement on the interpretation of the same treaty for the purposes of Article 31(3)(a)'.
19. Report of the International Law Commission, Seventieth session 2018, 38 (para. 6 Conclusion 5).
20. Report of the International Law Commission, Seventieth session 2018, 38 (para. 7 Conclusion 5); *see also* Irina Buga, *Subsequent Practice and Treaty Modification*, in: Michael J. Bowman & Dino Kritsiotis (eds) *Conceptual and Contextual Perspectives on the Modern Law of Treaties* (2018), 363 (368).

and local officials may thus be subsequent practice "of a party in the application of a treaty" if this practice is sufficiently unequivocal and if the Government can be expected to be aware of this practice and has not contradicted it within a reasonable time.'

Therefore, according to the ILC Report, the practice of the competent local authorities, i.e., as a rule, the tax offices, is decisive for the determination of a 'subsequent practice'. In such cases, statements by the government or another 'higher authority' cannot themselves establish a 'subsequent practice'. They can – if the government takes a view contrary to the practice of the competent local authorities – only *prevent* this practice from becoming a 'subsequent practice' according to Article 31(3) lit b VCLT.[21]

A judgment of the Austrian Supreme Constitutional Court (Verfassungsgerichtshof) goes in a similar direction:[22] 'A later practice within the meaning of Article 31 (3) of the Vienna Convention on the Law of Treaties that is to be taken into account in the context of treaty interpretation can only be spoken of if the authorities entrusted with the application of the law hold a uniform opinion that has remained undisputed, i.e. has not been challenged before the courts or confirmed by the appellate court (cf. also *Lang*, ÖStZ 2006, 208 f.).' The authorities entrusted with the application of the law, whose conduct may constitute a 'subsequent practice', are also in Austria primarily the local tax authorities.[23] Decisions of the local tax authorities can only be considered a 'subsequent practice' if they have remained uncontested, i.e., have not been challenged before the courts or have even been confirmed by them. However, if a court disagrees, no 'subsequent practice' can arise.[24]

Recently, the Swiss Federal Supreme Court (Bundesgericht) referred to the above-mentioned ruling of the Austrian Supreme Constitutional Court, among others, and also made statements along the same lines.[25] In particular, the Swiss Federal Supreme Court also rejected the argument that the OECD Commentaries could be an expression of a 'subsequent practice':[26] 'In the literature, it was rightly pointed out that the OECD MC itself does not yet embody a consistent application practice and that the tax offices and tax judicial authorities – and not, for example, the representatives of the Member States in the Fiscal Committee of the OECD or the supreme tax authority of the Member States – are typically entrusted with the application of the DTAs (cf. MICHAEL

21. In this regard also already Michael Lang, *Die Auffassung des BMF zur Bedeutung des OECD-Kommentars für die Auslegung von DBA*, IStR 2023, 549 (554).
22. VfSlg. 20005/2015; on this also Michael Lang in Georg Kofler et al., *Steuerpolitik und Verfassungsrecht*, 2023, 135 (160 et seq.).
23. More closely Michael Lang, *Wer hat das Sagen im Steuerrecht? Die Bedeutung des OECD-Steuerausschusses und seiner Working Parties*, ÖStZ 2006, 203 (207); *see also* Rahim Moloo, *When Actions Speak Louder than Words: The Relevance of Subsequent Party Conduct to Treaty Interpretation*, Berkeley Journal of International Law 2013, 39 (69), who points out that in interpreting customs exemptions in international treaties, the 'practice' is shaped by the customs authorities.
24. In this regard also Michael Lang, *Die Auffassung des BMF zur Bedeutung des OECD-Kommentars für die Auslegung von DBA*, IStR 2023, 549 (551).
25. In addition also Michael Lang, *Schweizer Bundesgericht zur Bedeutung des OECD-Kommentars*, SWI 2023, 418 et seq.
26. Swiss Federal Supreme Court, 23 June 2023, 9C_682/2022 (para. 9.4.4.).

LANG, Die Bedeutung des OECD-Kommentars und der Reservations, Observations und Positions für die DBA-Auslegung, in FS Dietmar Gosch, 235 (239); cf. also judgment of the Austrian Supreme Constitutional Court V 41/2015 of September 25, 2015, para. 2.2.3; contrary view judgment of the Supreme Court of Canada of November 26, 2021 Canada v Alta Energy Luxembourg S.A.R.L., 2021 SCC 49 para. 41; LINDERFALK/HILLING, op. cit, p. 45 f.; cf. for the identification of the application practice of a State Party UN International Law Commission, Yearbook of the International Law Commission 2018, Vol. II, Part Two, Text of the draft conclusions on subsequent agreements and subsequent practice in relation to the interpretation of treaties, commentary on Conclusion 5 paras. 6 f. and 9 and on Conclusion 6 paras. 7 and 22).'

According to the standard set by the Austrian Supreme Constitutional Court and now also by the Swiss Federal Supreme Court, it is difficult at all to prove a practice that is significant under Article 31(3) lit b VCLT: For such a practice arises 'when the authorities entrusted with the application of the law' take 'a uniform view' in their decisions. As a rule, taxpayers have no knowledge of how the authority responsible for them and the other authorities in their country have proceeded in cases of other taxpayers involving the same legal issue. However, the authorities are also prevented from granting taxpayers insight into other tax files for reasons of tax secrecy. The proof of an undisputed practice is therefore practically hardly possible.[27] More realistic, however, is the proof of a practice – at least considered relevant by the Austrian Supreme Constitutional Court –[28] confirmed by the appellate courts. Therefore, if courts unanimously confirm the opinion of the local tax authorities on a certain question of interpretation of tax treaties, this can rather establish a 'practice'.[29]

In the case of the tax regime governing pensions paid to retired UNESCO officials residing in France referred to by the ILC in its report, the group of taxpayers concerned was manageable from the outset. This made it easier to provide evidence. In addition, the proof of a uniform practice was not decisive in this case because the assumption of a 'subsequent practice' within the meaning of Article 31(3) lit b VCLT was ruled out in any case due to the government's contradiction to this legal interpretation.

In this context, the requirements explicitly mentioned by the ILC in Conclusion 9 are interesting:[30] 'The weight of a subsequent agreement or subsequent practice as a means of interpretation under article 31, paragraph 3, depends, *inter alia*, on its clarity and specificity. ... In addition, the weight of subsequent practice under article 31, paragraph 3 (b), depends, *inter alia*, on whether and how it is repeated.' According to the Commentary of the ILC, this does not exclude that there are constellations in which even a single act can be considered as 'subsequent practice'.[31] In the context of tax treaties, one might think of constellations in which only in one single case a court was

27. In this regard also Michael Lang, *Die Auffassung des BMF zur Bedeutung des OECD-Kommentars für die Auslegung von DBA*, IStR 2023, 549 (551).
28. VfSlg. 20005/2015.
29. Michael Lang, *Die Auffassung des BMF zur Bedeutung des OECD-Kommentars für die Auslegung von DBA*, IStR 2023, 549 (551).
30. Report of the International Law Commission, Seventieth session 2018, 70.
31. Report of the International Law Commission, Seventieth session 2018, 73 et seq. (para. 11 Conclusion 9).

involved in the review of the legal issue, and the court confirmed the opinion of the local tax authorities. However, the ILC also points out that the WTO Appellate Body, for example, regularly sets higher standards:[32] 'subsequent practice in interpreting a treaty has been recognized as a "concordant, common and consistent" sequence of acts or pronouncements which is sufficient to establish a discernible pattern implying the agreement of the parties regarding its interpretation'.

For the purposes of Article 31(3) lit b VCLT, a concurrent practice in both states is required. According to the ILC, a 'parallel practice' is sufficient.[33] It would therefore have to be proven in both states that the local tax authorities or, if applicable, the courts have taken the same legal view. If the proof can only be provided in one of the two states, this unilateral subsequent practice is not completely irrelevant in the opinion of the ILC: It can still be taken into account according to Article 32 VCLT.[34] However, this is only possible under the conditions stated there, either to confirm the interpretation obtained under Article 31 VCLT or if the interpretation under Article 31 VCLT leaves the meaning of the treaty or its terms ambiguous or obscure or leads to a result that is manifestly absurd or unreasonable.

§29.4 SUBSEQUENT PRACTICE AND INTERPRETATION OF TREATY TERMS AS CAPABLE OF EVOLVING OVER TIME?

According to the ILC, subsequent practice – just like subsequent agreements – is also relevant to the question of whether and to what extent a provision of an international treaty carries with it the possibility of its further development. Conclusion 8 reads as follows:[35] 'Subsequent agreements and subsequent practice under articles 31 and 32 may assist in determining whether or not the presumed intention of the parties upon the conclusion of the treaty was to give a term used a meaning which is capable of evolving over time.'

The ILC clearly differentiates here: The ILC does not say that when it comes to expressions that have a 'meaning which is capable of evolving over time', there is more room for subsequent practice in the interpretation of these expressions. Subsequent practice can merely help to determine whether an expression is to be given a more dynamic or more static understanding. 'Subsequent practice' can therefore also show that a more contemporaneous approach is appropriate for the interpretation of an

32. Report of the International Law Commission, Seventieth session 2018, 33 (para. 25 Conclusion 4); *see also* Georg Nolte, *Subsequent Practice as a Means of Interpretation in the Jurisprudence of the WTO Appellate Body*, in: Enzo Cannizzaro (ed.) The Law of Treaties Beyond the Vienna Convention (2011), 138 (143 et seq.).
33. Report of the International Law Commission, Seventieth session 2018, 50 (para. 23 Conclusion 6).
34. Report of the International Law Commission, Seventieth session 2018, 75 (para. 15 Conclusion 9).
35. Report of the International Law Commission, Seventieth session 2018, 64.

expression. According to the Commentary of the ILC, this is also not at all unlikely:[36] 'The conclusion should, however, be understood as indicating the need for some caution with regard to arriving at a conclusion in a specific case whether to adopt an evolutive approach.' The ILC therefore urges caution in adopting an 'evolutionary approach' in a particular case.

On the question of which understanding is appropriate in which cases, the ILC then refers to the case law of the International Court of Justice (ICJ):[37] 'The International Court of Justice, in particular, is seen as having developed two strands of jurisprudence, one tending towards a more "contemporaneous" and the other towards a more "evolutionary" interpretation, as Judge *ad hoc* Guillaume pointed out in his Declaration in *Dispute regarding Navigational and Related Rights*. The decisions that favour a more contemporaneous approach mostly concern specific treaty terms ("water-parting"; "main channel or Thalweg"; names of places; and "mouth" of a river). On the other hand, the cases that support an evolutive interpretation seem to relate to more general terms. This is true, in particular, for terms that are by definition evolutionary, such as "the strenuous conditions of the modern world", "the well-being and development of such peoples", and "sacred trust" in article 22 of the Covenant of the League of Nations. The International Court of Justice, in its *Namibia* Advisory Opinion gave "sacred trust" an evolving meaning so as to conclude "that the ultimate objective of the sacred trust was the self-determination and independence of the peoples concerned."'

A decision in which the ICJ arrived at an evolving meaning is quoted in detail in the Commentary of the ILC to Conclusion 8:[38] 'The judgment of the International Court of Justice in *Dispute regarding Navigational and Related Rights* illustrates how subsequent agreements and subsequent practice of the parties can assist in determining whether a term has to be given a meaning that is capable of evolving over time. Interpreting the term "comercio" in a treaty of 1858, the Court held:

> On the one hand, the subsequent practice of the parties, within the meaning of article 31 (3) (b) of the Vienna Convention, can result in a departure from the original intent on the basis of a tacit agreement between the parties. On the other hand, there are situations in which the parties' intent upon conclusion of the treaty was ... to give the terms used ... a meaning or content capable of evolving, not one fixed once and for all, so as to make allowance for, among other things, developments in international law.

The Court then found that the term "comercio" was a "generic term" of which "the parties necessarily" had "been aware that the meaning ... was likely to evolve over

36. Report of the International Law Commission, Seventieth session 2018, 67 (para. 10 Conclusion 8); *see also* Sean D. Murphy, *The Relevance of Subsequent Agreement and Subsequent Practice for the Interpretation of Treaties*, in: Georg Nolte (ed.) Treaties and Subsequent Practice (2013), 82 (87).
37. Report of the International Law Commission, Seventieth session 2018, 65 (para. 6 Conclusion 8); *see also* Bruno Simma, *Miscellaneous Thoughts on Subsequent Agreements and Practice*, in: Georg Nolte (ed.) Treaties and Subsequent Practice (2013), 46 (48).
38. Report of the International Law Commission, Seventieth session 2018, 67 et seq. (para. 12 Conclusion 8); *see also* Marcelo G. Kohen, *Keeping Subsequent Agreements and Practice in Their Right Limits*, in: Georg Nolte (ed.) Treaties and Subsequent Practice (2013), 34 (41).

time" and that "the treaty has been entered into for a very long period", and concluded that "the parties must be presumed ... to have intended" this term to "have an evolving meaning". Judge Skotnikov, in a Separate Opinion, while disagreeing with this reasoning, ultimately arrived at the same result by accepting a more recent subsequent practice of Costa Rica related to tourism on the San Juan River "for at least a decade" against which Nicaragua "never protested" but rather "engaged in consistent practice of allowing tourist navigation" and concluded that this "suggests that the parties have established an agreement regarding its interpretation."'

The latter example in particular gives rise to the question of whether we are really dealing with two different 'strands of jurisprudence'. For apparently there was no tourism on the San Juan River in 1858. From the perspective of the year 1858, this is a new phenomenon. However, it is part of the daily routine of any legal interpretation to clarify which facts that have only newly arisen since the entry into force of the law or the conclusion of the contract are covered by the provision and which are not. In the present case, it has been shown that tourism is still covered by 'comercio'. However, if the decision had been on a completely different service and the ICJ had ruled that this service was not covered by 'comercio', this would probably not have led to the term 'comercio' no longer having an evolving meaning.[39] The boundaries are fluid in interpretation. It is a matter of continuum: some provisions are more, others less, likely to cover new phenomena as well.

The Swiss Federal Supreme Court recently had to rule on how to proceed in this tension in the interpretation of terms contained in tax treaties:[40] 'The terms "salaries", "wages" and above all "similar remuneration" would be open in themselves and a dynamic interpretation autonomous of the treaty would therefore not be excluded from the outset. However, according to practically unanimous doctrine, they are to be interpreted in accordance with Art. 3 para. 2 OECD MC and Art. 3 para. 2 of the tax treaty Switzerland – United Arab Emirates, respectively, with recourse to the law of the applicable state, in order to enable a complete coverage of taxable employment income ... . In any case, the new explanations in the OECD commentaries are not intended to define "salaries, wages and similar remuneration". Rather, they are intended to help identify the specific consideration of a remuneration so that it can be determined whether or, if so, to what extent it was received for the performance of work in the State in which the work was performed ... . Consequently, this addition concerns the interpretation of Art. 15, para. 1, sentence 2 of the tax treaty Switzerland – United Arab Emirates and of the OECD MC, respectively, where the connection between remuneration and work performed is presupposed (...; in the original French and English versions: "Si l'emploi y [i.e.: dans l'autre État contractant] est exercé, les rémunérations reçues à ce titre sont imposables dans cet autre État."; "If the employment is so [i.e.: in the other Contracting State] exercised, such remuneration as is derived therefrom may be taxed in that other State."). In this respect, however, no open terms are apparent, the meaning of which would foreseeably change in the course of time and

39. Critical also Malgosia Fitzmaurice, *Subsequent Agreement and Subsequent Practice*, ICLR 22 (2020), 14 (31).
40. Swiss Federal Supreme Court, 23 June 2023, 9C_682/2022 (para. 10.1.).

the dynamic interpretation of which the Contracting States of the tax treaty Switzerland – United Arab Emirates could have intended.'

The Swiss Federal Supreme Court agrees that in the context of Article 15 OECD MC – and presumably also in the context of the other distribution norms of the tax treaties – there is no indication that these are open terms which would support a dynamic interpretation. In the case of the terms 'salaries, wages and similar remuneration' in Article 15 OECD MC, the situation is indeed different. These words serve the same purpose as the words 'profits', 'payments' or 'income' in the other distribution standards: They ensure that each distributive rule of a tax treaty is linked to the tax base of the domestic tax law of the Contracting States so that then the distributive rule – either alone or in combination with the method article – restricts accordingly, if necessary. Tax treaties distribute taxation rights between the Contracting States and must therefore be based on domestic tax law not only from the perspective of its personal scope – by the 'resident person' – but also from the perspective of its substantial scope. From this point of view, the tax treaty provision modelled on Article 3(2) OECD MC can only be relevant to the extent that the context of the treaty requires the use of the tax base under domestic law, i.e., by way of an autonomous interpretation.[41] It is absolutely correct that with all these mentioned expressions ('salaries, wages and similar remuneration'), the respective domestic tax base at the time when the facts occur is decisive.

§29.5 SUMMARY

In my opinion, the work of the ILC, whose conclusions were even the subject of a resolution of the UN General Assembly, contributes significantly to eliminating concerns about the meaning of 'subsequent practice' in Article 31(3) lit b VCLT from the perspective of the rule of law. At first sight, the possibilities granted by Article 31(3) lit b VCLT to the executive branch to change the content of the tax treaties by means of subsequent practice for which it is responsible and thus to interfere with the prerogative of the legislative branch and, in addition, to eliminate the control of the judicial branch by assuming a binding effect of subsequent practice are oppressive. However, the Conclusions and the Commentaries of the ILC make it clear that 'subsequent practice' according to Article 31(3) lit b VCLT is only relevant if it is consistent in both states. Unilateral subsequent practice could only be relevant under Article 32 VCLT and therefore only under very limited conditions. But also, in the context of Article 31 VCLT, subsequent practice is only a means of interpretation, which stands on an equal footing with the other means of interpretation. Therefore, there is no question of a 'binding effect' of subsequent practice. If the other means of interpretation suggest a different direction, subsequent practice recedes into the background. However, it is hardly verifiable because it is usually the practice of the local tax authorities that is at issue. It will be difficult to prove that a consistent practice exists throughout the entire

41. *See also* Michael Lang, *Schweizer Bundesgericht zur Bedeutung des OECD-Kommentars*, SWI 2023, 418 (425).

country if only because of tax secrecy. It is only considered subsequent practice if it has remained undisputed. If courts or even the Ministry of Finance itself then take a completely different view, it is no longer possible to speak of a 'subsequent practice'. Conversely, the opinion of the Ministry of Finance alone cannot justify a subsequent practice.

The ILC Report has also made clear that a 'subsequent practice' to a provision of a tax treaty is not an indication that this provision is to be understood in an evolutionary way. Rather, only 'subsequent practice' can even help to determine whether a more 'contemporaneous' or a more 'evolutionary' interpretation should be applied. Subsequent practice may also indicate that a more 'contemporaneous interpretation' is appropriate. The ILC also advocates a cautious approach in this regard. There is much to be said for requiring a more 'contemporaneous interpretation', especially in the area of tax treaties.

CHAPTER 30

Notes on the Application of Article 4(1) OECD Model Convention to Territorial Tax Systems

Guglielmo Maisto

§30.1 INTRODUCTION

An IFA conference on the treaty relations between Panama and Italy[1] suggests some reflections on the Italy-Panama treaty for the avoidance of double taxation,[2] its interaction with domestic law and the treaty definition of 'resident' reflecting Article 4 OECD Model Convention. The subject may rightly be offered as a tribute to Peter Essers who contributed for many years to the progress of tax study and research, including his contribution to the very successful series of events and collective work series on tax treaty case law around the world.[3]

The Italy-Panama treaty was negotiated before the start of the Base Erosion and Profit Shifting (BEPS) project that led to the conclusion of the Multilateral Convention in 2016.[4] It is an example of 'tax treaty pioneering' because some of its provisions

1. IFA Panama, 'Tax talks between Panama and Italy based on the Double Taxation Treaty application' held in Panama on 10 May 2023.
2. Convention between the Government of the Republic of Panama and the Government of the Italian Republic for the avoidance of double taxation with respect to taxes on income and the prevention of fiscal evasion signed on 30 December 2010 and ratified in Italy through Law 3 November 2016, No. 208. The Convention entered into force on 1 June 2017 following the exchange of ratification instruments between the two Contracting States (*see* Italian Official Gazette No. 60 of 16 March 2018).
3. Michael Lang et al. (eds), *Tax treaty case law around the globe - 2011* (Wien: Linde, 2011). Published for the first time in 2011 and then annually (lastly published in 2022).
4. Multilateral Convention to Implement Tax Treaty Related Measures to Prevent Base Erosion and Profit Shifting (MLI) signed on 7 June 2017.

remarkably rely on principles which in later years have been reflected in the multilateral instrument and the OECD Model Convention.[5]

The most significant feature of the treaty stems, however, from the territorial system adopted by Panama (so exempting foreign source income[6,7]) and for this reason presents interesting interpretative issues relating to the definition of 'resident of a Contracting State' laid down by Article 4 of the treaty, which mirrors Article 4(1) OECD Model Convention.

§30.2 RESIDENCE OF PERSONS FOR TAX TREATY PURPOSES AND 'COMPREHENSIVE TAX LIABILITY'

As mentioned earlier, Article 4 of the treaty reflects Article 4(1) OECD Model Convention, pursuant to which the expression 'resident of a Contracting State' includes:

> any person who, under the laws of that State, is liable to tax therein by reason of his domicile, residence, place of management or any other criterion of a similar nature

and

> does not include any person who is liable to tax in that State in respect only of income from sources in that State or capital situated therein.

How can such provision be consistent with the tax regime applicable to companies residing in Panama, which are subject to a tax regime exempting foreign source income?[8]

The issue relates to the literal meaning of Article 4 OECD Model Convention and must be considered in accordance with the canons of interpretation laid down by Article 3(2) OECD Model Convention – which provides a special rule of interpretation of terms not otherwise defined[9] – and Articles 31 and 32 of the Vienna Convention on the Law of Treaties (VCLT).

---

5. This is so, for instance, for Art. 4(3) relating to dual residence of companies which reflects Art. 4 of the MLI and Art. 4(3) OECD Model Convention (2017).
6. The existence of special regimes is the origin of its inclusion in the list of non-cooperative tax jurisdictions drawn up by the European Union, *see* Official Journal of the European Union (C 64/19), The EU List of non-cooperative Jurisdictions for tax purposes, Annex I to Council conclusions on the revised EU list of non-cooperative jurisdictions for tax purposes (2023/C 64/06), 21 February 2023.
7. In 2019, the Group on the Code of Conduct set up by the EU Council in 2016 listed the criteria for the assessment of territorial tax systems. While they do not represent in principle harmful tax regimes – insofar as they wish to eliminate double taxation of income – a conflict may exist where the definition of foreign source income: (i) includes income other than business income (e.g., income from capital) and exempts such income with no conditions; (ii) does not provide for a definition of source (nexus) complying with the principles laid down by the OECD Model Convention (such as the existence of a permanent establishment for business income).
8. Article 694 of the Panamanian Fiscal Code states that the object of income tax is 'the taxable income that is produced, from any source, within the territory of the Republic of Panama whichever may be the place where it is received' (author's translation).
9. I agree that Art. 3(2) OECD Model Convention is a special rule of interpretation on terms not otherwise defined and therefore must be given priority over other canons of interpretation. *See*

In making this exercise, I support the view that the terms used in the first sentence of Article 4(1) ('residence', 'domicile', 'place of management') have to be interpreted pursuant to domestic law, although the context (especially the Commentary to the OECD Model Convention) may come into play because the treaty requires the domestic law residence to cause the 'liability to tax'; for some scholars and case law,[10] worldwide taxation would by itself satisfy the treaty residence test (so-called functional approach), while others support a territorial approach and opine that a domestic law residence to fit treaty residence must also satisfy a personal territorial nexus between the liability and the person. This view would be confirmed not only by the reference made by Article 4(1) OECD Model Convention to personal-based criteria such as 'residence' or 'domicile', but also by the residual reference to 'any other criterion of a similar nature'.

Therefore, a unitary interpretation of the terms is required and resort to the Commentary may be helpful.[11,12,13] In other words, the meanings of 'residence', 'domicile' and 'place of management' rely on domestic law but are affected by the

---

Philippe Martin, *L'interpretation des conventions fiscales internationales*, 24 Revue de Droit Fiscal 320 (2013), No. 4 quoted by Marc Pelletier, *La notion de resident: le Conseil d'État à contre-sens*, 49 Revue de Droit Fiscal 664 (2015).

10. Most recently, the UK Upper Tribunal ([2023] UKUT 00146 (TCC)) applied a functional interpretation where the 'other criterion' is viewed as a comparator to the effect that such criteria determines (liability to tax) so that the personal nexus would no longer matter if the person is fully liable to tax. For a comment *see* John Avery Jones, *GE Financial Investments v. HMRC: a novel point of treaty interpretation*, 5 British Tax Review (2023), pp. 574 et seq. The same view is shared by Michael Lang, Taxation of Income in the Hands of Different Taxpayers from the Viewpoint of Tax Treaty Law, 55 Bulletin for International Taxation 12 (2001), p. 598 who states that '[p]ersons subject to unlimited tax liability are therefore covered in any case'. Under a contrary view, such full liability to tax must rely on a strong personal attachment with the territory of the State (*see* Roland Ismer & Katharina Blank, *Art. 4*, in Ekkehart Reimer & Alexander Rust (eds), *Klaus Vogel on Double Taxation Conventions* (Alphen aan den Rijn: Kluwer Law International, 2022), para. 61).
11. On the mix between domestic law and the context, *see* Roland Ismer & Katharina Blank in Ekkehart Reimer & Alexander Rust (eds), *Klaus Vogel on Double Taxation Conventions* (Alphen aan den Rijn: Kluwer Law International, 2022) at para. 53 of the Commentary to Art. 4 OECD Model Convention who use the expression 'semi-autonomous contextual interpretation'; Robert Couzin, *Corporate Residence and International Taxation* (Amsterdam: IBFD, 2002), pp. 134 et seq.; Michael Lang, *Taxation of Income in the Hands of Different Taxpayers from the Viewpoint of Tax Treaty Law*, 55 Bulletin for International Taxation 12 (2001), p. 597; Klaus Vogel, *Klaus Vogel on Double Taxation Conventions: A Commentary of the OECD, UN and US Model Conventions for the Avoidance of Double Taxation of Income and Capital* (London: Kluwer Law International, 1997), p. 230; John Avery Jones et al., *Dual Residence of Individuals: The Meaning of the Expressions in the OECD Model Convention*, 1 British Tax Review (1981), pp. 19 et seq. who says that 'an individual's tax status (referred to below as "residence") under paragraph 1 is clearly to be determined under internal law initially'.
12. Material may include the OECD Model Double Taxation Conventions on Estates and Inheritances and on Gifts which were concluded in 1966 and 1982 and their Commentaries. The Commentary to the 1966 Draft Convention confirms the intention to interpret the criteria laid down by the first sentence of Art. 4(1) with reference to domestic law as well as the reference to other criteria as criteria which operate as a test of liability. This criterion of liability, which is expressed in the domestic laws by such terms as domicile, home, residence, or all other similar terms, does not refer solely to the meaning given to the word 'domicile' in private civil law, but also to the circumstance of habitual abode or any other situation of this kind. This situation is characterized in certain laws by special expressions, such as *Inländer* in the law of the Federal Republic of Germany, *habitant du Royaume* in Belgian law, etc. Moreover, the concept of

meaning of 'liable to tax', a connection which suggests a move from domestic law to the context of the provision.

The context including the Commentary plays an equally important role in interpreting the second sentence of Article 4(1) OECD Model Convention which refers again to a 'liability to tax' in a Contracting State (no longer using the qualification 'under the laws of that State' included in the first sentence[14]) and to 'source',[15] a term which is defined solely under other provisions of the Model relating to certain categories of income.

In making preliminary remarks on the meaning of treaty residence, the Commentary to Article 4 OECD Model Convention states that:

> generally, the domestic laws of the various States impose a comprehensive liability to tax – 'full tax liability' – based on the taxpayers' personal attachment to the State concerned (the 'State of residence')[16]

and that:

> This liability to tax is not imposed only on persons who are 'domiciled' in a State in the sense in which 'domicile' is usually taken in the legislations (private law). The cases of full liability to tax are extended to comprise also, for instance, persons who stay continually, or maybe only for a certain period, in the territory of the State.[17]

The Commentary marks three fundamental points relating to the interpretation of Article 4(1).

First, it clarifies that the tax treaty definition of residence is based on the domestic laws which determine a 'comprehensive tax liability'. The expression dates to the

domicile – or any other concept standing for it – which is employed as a test of liability to estate tax varies according to the domestic laws (para. 1 of the Commentary to Art. 4 of the 1966 Draft Convention).

13. One example of the issue of conformity of the domestic law residence with the treaty may be found in the Italian domestic law definition of tax residence which includes individuals who are listed in the Register of the Resident population which is a requirement provided for individuals having their habitual abode in a Municipality of the Italian Republic (the enrolment in such Register makes the individual becoming a tax resident regardless of whether or not he or she had or continued to maintain the habitual abode in the taxable period, a situation which might be found not to satisfy the treaty territorial link). For a comment *see* Guglielmo Maisto, *Residence of Individuals and the Italy–France Tax Treaty*, 99 European Taxation 2 (1999), pp. 42 et seq.
14. The issue which does arise is whether the liability to tax covered by the second sentence needs to be assessed having regard to domestic law only and not to treaties concluded with other States (*see inter alia* Christo J.A.M. van Gennep, *The Second Sentence of Article 4(1) of the OECD Model Convention 1977*, 31 European Taxation 5 (1991), pp. 141 et seq., contra *see* Roland Ismer & Katharina Blank, *Art. 4*, in Ekkehart Reimer & Alexander Rust (eds), *Klaus Vogel on Double Taxation Conventions* (Alphen aan den Rijn: Kluwer Law International, 2022), para 48).
15. On the meaning of 'source', *see* Kees Van Raad, *2008 OECD Model: Operation and Effect of Article 4(1) in Dual Residence Issues under the Updated Commentary*, 63 Bulletin for International Taxation 5 (2009), pp. 187 et seq.; Hans Pijl, *The Excluded Resident and the Term 'Law'/'Laws' in Article 4 of the OECD Draft (1963) and OECD Model (1977/2010)*, 66 Bulletin for International Taxation 1 (2012), pp. 4 et seq. DOI: 10.33278/sae-2012.plenary.
16. Paragraph 3 of the Commentary to Art. 4 OECD Model Convention.
17. Paragraph 3 of the Commentary to Art. 4 OECD Model Convention.

preparatory work done by the OEEC[18,19] for the drafting of the OECD Model Convention, which originally was focused on a definition of residence relying on 'full tax liability' in accordance with domestic law. The absence of a definition of 'full tax liability' - not surprising as the definition of residence relies on domestic law - is the primary source of interpretative issues relating to paragraph 1 of Article 4 OECD Model Convention.[20]

The difficulty of interpretation is echoed by the use - by the working documents which belong to the history of the provision and by the current Commentary and its previous versions - of similar terms and expressions such as 'more comprehensive liability to tax'[21] or 'full tax liability'[22] or 'fully liable to tax'[23] or 'unlimited liability to taxation'.[24] All these terms were and yet are not defined and furthermore have been subject to revisions which may be viewed as the intention to either use synonymous terms or change a meaning which may have evolved over time (the final report adopted in 1958 by the Working Party set up by the Fiscal Committee of the OEEC and the 1963 version of the Commentary to the OECD Model Convention use the expression 'more comprehensive taxation'[25]). In the intention of the drafters, the expression 'more comprehensive liability to tax' adopted in the preparatory work of the OEEC was always related to the domestic legislation of the Contracting States. It is reiterated in the current Commentary to Article 4(1) through the expression 'comprehensive liability to tax' which, however, provides no guidance.

The Commentary then acknowledges that the listing of several connecting criteria in the treaty definition of residence is therefore the consequence of the policy decision to rely on domestic law and so covers the several ways the personal nexus was formulated under domestic laws of the Contracting States (residence, domicile, etc.).[26,27]

18. Working Group 2 was set up in 1956 by the Fiscal Committee of the OEEC.
19. For a comprehensive review of the history of the provision, *see* Richard Vann, *'Liable to Tax' and Company Residence under Tax Treaties*, in Guglielmo Maisto (ed.), *Residence of Companies under EC Law and Tax Treaties* (Amsterdam: IBFD, 2009), p. 253.
20. The expression 'fully liable to tax' may be found however in some treaties such as the Australia-China treaty (1988).
21. FC/WP2(58)1.
22. WP No. 2 of the OEEC Fiscal Committee, FC/WP2(56)1.
23. WP No. 2 of the OEEC Fiscal Committee, FC/WP2(56)1.
24. WP No. 2 of the OEEC Fiscal Committee, FC/WP2(57)2.
25. *See* Michael Dirkis, *The expression 'Liable to Tax by reason of his domicile, residence' under Article 4(1) of the OECD Model Convention*, in Guglielmo Maisto (ed.), *Residence of Individuals under Tax Treaties and EC Law* (Amsterdam: IBFD, 2010), p. 142 and Richard Vann, *'Liable to Tax' and Company Residence under Tax Treaties*, in Guglielmo Maisto (ed.), *Residence of Companies under EC Law and Tax Treaties* (Amsterdam: IBFD, 2009), p. 233.
26. Paragraph 3 of the Commentary to Article 4 OECD Model Convention.
27. The Working Party set up by the OEEC Tax Committee in 1956 for drafting the provision of the Model Convention relating to tax residence (Working Party No. 2) recognized from the outset of its studies that '[f]or determining the taxpayers who come under the scope of the Agreement, a reference to the internal concept of domicile of the countries has been found quite sufficient' (FC/WP2(57(1), p. 9). Similarly, the Tax Committee concluded that 'it was essential to try not to rely on the concept of 'full liability' but to refer instead to national concepts' (FC/M(57)2, VI, p. 5).

The Commentary finally states that the criteria listed by Article 4 to illustrate the domestic law tax residence personal nexus present different degrees of connection with the territory of the State so that the treaty residence does not require the closest domestic tax residence nexus if the person is 'liable to tax' in the State ('the cases of full liability to tax are extended …'[28]). The 'full liability to tax' seems to prevail therefore on the nexus listed by paragraph 1 of Article 4, a conclusion which influenced the functional approach mentioned earlier[29] that treaty residence is always satisfied where the person is subject to 'full taxation' no matter on whether such liability derives from residence, domicile, or a similar criterion.

§30.3 THE EXCLUSION LAID DOWN BY THE SECOND SENTENCE OF ARTICLE 4(1) OECD MODEL CONVENTION

I will now address more specifically the second sentence of Article 4(1) OECD Model Convention which I report again for ease of reference:

> This term, however, does not include any person who is liable to tax in that State in respect only of income from sources in that State or capital situated therein.

The history of the Model Convention – notably the revision of the 1963 version occurred in 1977 – indicates that this is a clarification of the general rule laid down by the first sentence of Article 4(1). The second sentence was originally included in the Commentary of the 1963 version of the Model Convention and then elevated to a Model provision in the 1977 revision.[30]

The literal meaning of the opening of the sentence ('However') could suggest the intention to include an exception to the general definition of 'resident of a Contracting State', as other provisions of the OECD Model providing exceptions use the same term to express a derogation to a general rule (*see*, for instance, Article 11(5) relating to the exception to the concept of source where the interest is related to indebtedness connected to a PE situated in the source State[31]). This is not true for Article 4(1) because the term 'however' was included in the 1995 version of the OECD Model

28. Paragraph 3 of the Commentary to Art. 4 OECD Model Convention.
29. Paragraph II and *supra* n. 11.
30. On the clarifying nature of the second sentence, *see* Roland Ismer & Katharina Blank, *Art. 4*, in Ekkehart Reimer & Alexander Rust (eds), *Klaus Vogel on Double Taxation Conventions* (Alphen aan den Rijn: Kluwer Law International, 2022), para. 41; Alexander Rust, *Chapter 15 – Germany*, in Guglielmo Maisto (ed.), *Residence of Individuals under Tax Treaties and EC Law* (Amsterdam: IBFD, 2010), p. 380; Moris Lehner, *Art. 4*, in Klaus Vogel & Moris Lehner (eds), *Doppelbesteuerungsabkommen* (Munich: C.H. Beck, 2008), para. 120; Veronika Daurer, *Chapter 11 – Austria*, in Guglielmo Maisto (ed.), *Residence of Individuals under Tax Treaties and EC Law* (Amsterdam: IBFD 2010), p. 263 quoting Edgar Huemer, *Die unbeschränkte Steuerpflicht natürlicher Personen* (Vienna: Linde, 1996), pp. 106 et seq.
31. Interest shall be deemed to arise in a Contracting State when the payer is a resident of that State. Where, however, the person paying the interest, whether he is a resident of a Contracting State or not, has in a Contracting State a permanent establishment in connection with which the indebtedness on which the interest is paid was incurred, and such interest is borne by such permanent establishment, then such interest shall be deemed to arise in the State in which the permanent establishment is situated.

Convention and follows a re-drafting due to the revision of Article 4(1) designed to comprise States and their political and administrative subdivisions in the general definition of treaty residence.[32] The treaty practice and case law confirm this view and indicate the practical implications for treaties which do not include the second sentence of Article 4(1) OECD Model Convention.

The German Federal Tax Administration, for instance, in its guidelines relating to the tax treaty regime of employment stated that:

> Residence according to Art. 4 Para. 1 OECD ... presupposes an unlimited tax liability under the respective domestic law. This also applies to agreements that do not contain the declaratory addition of Article 4 Paragraph 1 Sentence 2 OECD.[33]

I therefore disagree with the argument that the second sentence is an exception to the general rule laid down by Article 4(1). Indeed, under the general rule, the treaty residence is satisfied if the person is a resident under domestic law *and* if it is liable to tax. If this 'liability' is intended not to comprise a taxation limited to income from sources derived from only one Contracting State, then the second sentence is a mere clarification.

A different interpretation views the second sentence of Article 4(1) as a provision governing situations where taxation is based solely on source and therefore where the liability is not related to a personal connection. This view was expressed by a French Court decision[34] dealing with the application of the treaty between France and Israel to a person domiciled in Israel who benefited from the special regime available to foreign aliens moving residence to Israel for a period of ten years. The Court held that the second sentence of Article 4(1) applies solely if the income from sources within one Contracting State is disconnected from domicile, residence or other criterion of a similar nature and concluded for the individual's treaty entitlement.

The argument put forward by the Court was supported by the fact that the taxation of domestic source income applied by Israel's domestic law under the special regime derived from the domicile of the person and not merely from the source of the income. In other words, in the Court's view, the general rule laid down by Article 4(1) would cover all forms of tax liability by reason of a personal criterion so that the second sentence would govern the different situations where source taxation is not based on a personal connection.[35]

The judgment suggests the consideration that the original wording of the second sentence of Article 4(1), which was proposed by the WP20 in 1971,[36] intended to

32. Paragraph 1 was previously amended on 21 September 1995, by adding to the first sentence the words 'and also includes that State and any political subdivision or local authority thereof' and by replacing in the second sentence the words 'But this term' with 'This term, however', by the report entitled 'The 1995 Update to the Model Tax Convention', adopted by the OECD Council on 21 September 1995.
33. BMFv. May 3, 2018 – IV B 2 – S 1300/08/10027 BStBl 2018 I p. 643.
34. Court of Toulouse, 13 October 2022, no. 20TL22832.
35. In this sense Roland Ismer & Katharina Blank, *Art. 4*, in Klaus Vogel & Moris Lehner (eds), *Doppelbesteuerungsabkommen* (Munich: C.H. Beck, 2021), para. 120.
36. CFA/WP1(71)7 of 23 December 1971.

establish a causal link between the person and the liability to tax that may have supported the conclusion advocated by the judgment. The text read as follows:

> But the term does not include any individual who is liable to tax in that Contracting State *for the sole reason that* he derives income from sources therein' (relevant departure from current wording of the Model is in italicized).

However, the draft provision was later reviewed and amended by the Fiscal Committee with no stated reasons.[37]

As the second sentence is not an exception, there is no room for a restrictive interpretation. Turning to the exclusion indicated by the second sentence of Article 4(1), the Commentary states that:

> 8.1 In accordance with the provisions of the second sentence of paragraph 1, however, a person is not to be considered a 'resident of a Contracting State' in the sense of the Convention if, although not domiciled in that State, he is considered to be a resident according to the domestic laws but is subject only to a taxation limited to the income from sources in that State or to capital situated in that State. That situation exists in some States in relation to individuals, e.g., in the case of foreign diplomatic and consular staff serving in their territory.[38]

The exclusion applies to persons who have a weaker territorial nexus and notwithstanding this are regarded to be residents in a Contracting State in accordance with domestic law.

Indeed, the Commentary to the second sentence of Article 4(1) OECD Model Convention indicates that the examples of persons liable to tax listed in paragraph 1 exclude persons: (i) who do not have a permanent territorial nexus (defined by the Commentary as 'domicile') and (ii) who are subject to tax solely on income sourced in one Contracting State, unlike other persons having a stronger territorial nexus.[39]

§30.4 THE APPLICATION OF TAX TREATIES TO PERSONS RESIDING IN STATES ADOPTING TERRITORIAL SYSTEMS

The Commentary continues with the clarification that the exclusion must be construed in accordance with its object and purpose, which is to carve out:

> Persons who are not subjected to comprehensive taxation (full liability to tax) in a State, because it might otherwise exclude from the scope of the Convention all

37. CFA/WP1(73)1 of 3 January 1973.
38. Paragraph 8.1 of the Commentary to Article 4 OECD Model Convention.
39. This interpretation is consistent with remittance-based taxation regimes whereby persons who qualify as resident persons but do not have a permanent link with the State are only taxed on income derived from sources outside the State to the extent that such income is remitted. This regime is found not to fall within the scope of the second sentence of Art. 4(1) as foreign source income is not exempt and the special regime is limited to a deferral of taxation (*see* para. 108 of the Commentary to Art. 1 which includes an alternative provision for States wishing to restrict the scope of application of the treaty to such situations).

residents of countries adopting a territorial principle in their taxation, a result which is clearly not intended.[40]

Notwithstanding the literal meaning of the second sentence of Article 4(1), the Commentary states that territorial systems are not caught by that sentence so that persons who are liable to tax solely from sources within such States are eligible for treaty application.

The conclusion deserves some consideration.

The Commentary seems to conclude that the second sentence of Article 4(1) excludes persons who enjoy an exception to the general domestic regime of 'full tax liability' where such exception amounts to a limited tax liability confined to income sourced within the State.

This interpretation is confirmed by the examples illustrated by the Commentary which include a diplomat who is a resident of a Contracting State but unlike other residents is liable to tax solely on income sourced in that State.[41,42]

As the exclusion applies to special regimes (exceptions to the general tax regimes applied to resident persons under domestic law), persons who are subject to tax solely on domestic source income by reason of the general application of the territorial system of income taxation are eligible for treaty protection under Article 4 OECD Model Convention.[43]

The conclusion is consistent with the 'full tax liability' or 'comprehensive tax liability' mentioned in the Commentary. Article 4 OECD Model Convention lists the criteria which determine the 'full tax liability'. The provision also applies to persons who are liable to tax by reason of 'other criteria', i.e., criteria which determine 'full tax liability'. In the territorial systems, the expression 'full tax liability' or 'comprehensive liability to tax' must be interpreted as the widest tax liability applicable under domestic income tax rules so that the liability to domestic source income fits into Article 4 to the extent that such limited taxation reflects the general and widest tax liability of a person under domestic law. It would therefore be odd to conclude that full tax liability equals worldwide taxation.[44]

It is also worth noting that territorial systems of taxation may differentiate between residents and non-residents, a distinction which may apply for the purpose of determining the tax rate (e.g., proportional or progressive) or the taxable base. Had the meaning of 'liable to tax' included solely worldwide taxation, the second sentence of Article 4(1) would have been redundant.

This interpretation finds additional support in the circumstance that treaties concluded by countries adopting territorial systems include in the 'taxes covered' provision taxes which have a territorial scope of application and so apply solely to

40. Paragraph 8.3 of the Commentary to Art. 4 OECD Model Convention.
41. Paragraph 8.1 of the Commentary to Art. 4 OECD Model Convention.
42. In this sense Franz Wassermeyer & Christian Kaeser, *Art. 4*, in Franz Wassermeyer, Christian Kaeser, Michael Lang & Josef Schuch (eds), *Doppelbesteuerung* (Wien: Linde, 2015), para. 45.
43. In this sense Roland Ismer & Katharina Blank, *Art. 4*, in Klaus Vogel & Moris Lehner (eds), *Doppelbesteuerungsabkommen* (Munich: C.H. Beck, 2021), para. 120.
44. *See also* Michael Lang, *Taxation of Income in the Hands of Different Taxpayers from the Viewpoint of Tax Treaty Law*, 55 Bulletin for International Taxation 12 (2001), p. 598.

income from sources within a Contracting State. On the contrary, the argument that territoriality reflects Article 23A OECD Model Convention as a method to eliminate double taxation is less relevant because certain territorial systems clearly exempt foreign source income regardless of any strong foreign source nexus and irrespective of any taxation borne by such foreign source income.

Finally, historical reasons indicate that a territorial system does not prevent treaty residence, as during the 1950s several countries represented in the Fiscal Committee of the Organisation for European Economic Co-operation (OEEC) and OECD adopted territorial systems, and concluded bilateral treaties either between themselves or with countries adopting the worldwide system which accepted the principle of reciprocity insofar as treaty eligibility and 'full liability to tax' was concerned.

§30.5 CONCLUSION

The interpretation of the second sentence of Article 4(1) OECD Model Convention remains obscure and is largely affected by the general definition of tax treaty residence which is interpreted as: (i) worldwide income taxation only; (ii) full taxation (the widest available taxation in the country) by reason of a personal nexus; or (iii) taxation by reason of a personal nexus, regardless of the magnitude of the liability to tax.

The history of Article 4(1) indicates the purpose of defining treaty residence and the intention to differentiate between residence and source States to provide a preference criterion. The distinction was made based on personal nexus as applied under domestic law. Once the personal nexus is ascertained, then treaty rules may operate and apply the preference criterion in the allocation of taxing rights.

Under the view endorsed by the French Court case mentioned earlier, the second sentence of Article 4(1) would exclude solely persons who are subject to source taxation under domestic law having no regard to a personal nexus.[45]

Following this path, the reference to diplomats made by the Commentary would – according to the above-mentioned view – apply where a provision other than domestic law (Vienna Convention on diplomatic relations or customary international law relating to diplomatic immunity) makes the person liable solely to domestic source income notwithstanding a personal nexus. However, this view is contradicted by the preparatory work of Article 4 (WP20 suggesting a wording indicating source as the sole reason for taxing income from sources in a Contracting State) and by the 2008 revisions to the Commentary to Article 4 where it is said that no treaty residence is available to persons who are subject to special domestic tax regimes made available under domestic law such as exemption of foreign source income granted to foreign-held companies.[46]

45. This view is endorsed by Stéphane Austry in *Art. 4: Résident*, in Robert Danon, Daniel Gutmann, Xavier Oberson & Pasquale Pistone (eds), *Modéle de Convention Fiscale OCDE concernant le revenue et la fortune. Commentaire* (Bale: Francis Lefebvre, 2014) paras. 33-46, pp. 155-160.
46. Paragraph 8.2 of the Commentary to Art. 4 OECD Model Convention.

CHAPTER 31

Taxation of Cross-Border Remote Workers: A *Smörgåsbord** of Possibilities

Katia Cejie

§31.1 INTRODUCTION

§31.1.1 Problem and Purpose

The COVID-19 pandemic made teleworking (work from home, WFH), remote work, and the gig economy accessible to many employees. Closed borders, quarantine requirements, and lockdowns forced employers and employees as well as countries to adapt to new situations. The OECD[1] and the EU[2] provided recommendations and guidance on how to handle the changes during the pandemic, but as of June 2022, most of the temporary agreements between countries in this regard have ceased to apply.

In this new digitalized world, labour can be as mobile as capital, and countries compete to attract not only passive income but also active income.[3] They have started adopting policies to attract individuals to move to or at least invest in their countries

* A *smörgåsbord* could probably best be described as a buffet, starting off with a table of cold dishes, followed by warm dishes, and ending with the table of desserts. The author is connected to Centre for Tax Law in Uppsala, which is supported by Deloitte, EY, KPMG, Mannhemier Swartling, PWC, Skeppsbron Skatt and Svalner. The present research has been financed by the Torsten Söderberg Foundation as part of the research project Taxes and Contributions in Cross-Border Situations (R13/18).

1. OECD, *OECD Secretariat Analysis of Tax Treaties and the Impact of the COVID-19 Crisis*, Version 3 April 2020 and OECD, *Updated Guidance on Tax Treaties and the Impact of the COVID-19 Crisis*, 21 January 2021.
2. EU Commission, 2020/C 102I/03, European Labour Authority's (ELA), *Impact of Teleworking during the COVID-19 Pandemic on the Applicable Social Security*, July 2021.
3. *See for example* Georgio Beretta, *Cross-Border Mobility of Individuals and the Lack of Fiscal Policy Coordination among Jurisdictions (Even) after the BEPS Project* in Intertax, Vol. 47, Issue 1, pp. 91-112 (2019) DOI: 10.54648/taxi2019006, with further references.

and to become residents there. Whereas such policies were once only found in countries like Bahamas and Barbados, they are now found in countries within the EU, for example, Austria, Estonia, Malta, the Netherlands, Spain, and Portugal.[4]

Competing for tax bases is not a new phenomenon. Pillars 1 and 2 of the Base Erosion and Profit Shifting (BEPS) Project are examples of joint work by the OECD, G20 and EU to address this type of competition and prevent profit shifting to low tax jurisdictions within the business sector. It is now time to focus similar effort on the area of employment income, since personal income tax (PIT) and social security contributions (SSC) are often very important sources of income for states.[5] In the past few years, this topic has aroused interest, and several organizations and academics are seeking solutions to the problems raised.[6] The purpose of this chapter is to summarize some of this discussion and provide a starting point for further discussion of how remote work should or could be taxed in this new digitalized world.

§31.1.2 Concepts, Situations and Delimitations

There is enormous variation in the nature of cross-border work and in the terminology used when speaking of it. Historically, different types of situations have been distinguished in the international tax context. In the OECD Model,[7] for example, different allocation rules apply to different varieties and categories of cross-border work.[8] Before the pandemic, cross-border work was usually discussed in terms of two main situations: posted workers and frontier workers.

Now that digitalization has advanced, the popularity of remote work is increasing. *Remote working* is a type of flexible working arrangement that allows employees to work from a remote location outside of corporate offices. Because of the pros and cons

4. For example, Estonia has issued e-residency certificates since 1 December 2014, and several other countries within the EU have launched CIP regimes (Citizenship by Investment Programmes). *See* Anton van Zantbeek, *Tax-Driven Relocation of High Net Worth Individuals: Where to Run To?*, Vol. 50, Issue 5, European Taxation (2010). The golden visa programme used by Portugal also attracts non-EU investors, leading to opening up the EU to non-EU citizens. See, for example, Owen Parker, *Commercializing Citizenship in the Crisis EU: The Case of Immigrant Investor Programmes*, in JCMS Vol. 55, Issue 2, pp. 332–348 (2017) DOI: 10.1111/jcms.12462.
5. In Sweden, for example, tax on employment income (PIT) is estimated to be SEK 740 billion plus 710 billion in employers' contributions (SSC). This can be compared with VAT of 735 billion and tax on capital and business profits of 345 billion all in all. *See* Government Bill (prop.) 2022/23:1 p. 65. *See also* Rita de la Feria & Giorgia Maffini, *The Impact of Digitalisation on Personal Income Taxes*, in BTR 2, 154-168 (2021) DOI: 10.2139/ssrn.3835095.
6. Several conferences addressing this topic were held in 2022-2023, including MoveS Seminar Denmark/Sweden, *Cross-Border Work and Social Security Protection in the Öresund Region: Challenges and Solutions for High Mobility, Telework and Platform Work*, Copenhagen 9 May 2022; IFA Europe, *Mobility of Work, Capital, IP and Business in Changing European Tax Environment*, Milan May 19-20 2022; WU Vienna, *Mobility of Work*, Rust 7-9 July 2022; ITLR Network, *International Tax Challenges Raised by Mobility of Individuals/Work Forces as a Result of Digitalization*, Belgrade 6-7 October 2022; and the public hearing of the European Economic and Social Committee (EESC): *Taxation of Cross-Border Teleworkers: Possible Solutions*, Tallinn 4 July 2023.
7. OECD Model on Income and on Capital (2017).
8. *See, for example,* §31.2.1 below.

of remote work,[9] some companies have policies that allow employees to work from anywhere (WFA),[10] whereas others have policies that make it possible for employees to work for a few weeks remotely. For example, an employee may WFH, which is sometimes referred to as *teleworking*.[11] If an employee is working in a third country or a country other than the country where his employer and family reside, for example, from a co-working office or a summer residence abroad, it is sometimes referred to as a *workcation*. Remote workers also include *digital nomads*, that is, people whose work, study or leisure are not attached to any single geographical location and whose mobility is enabled by the internet and mobile connections.[12]

It is possible that all these different varieties of workers need different solutions rather than a one-size-fits-all solution.[13] Various options have been discussed in the literature.[14] Before summarizing some of this discussion and presenting a *smörgåsbord* as a starting point for further discussion (§31.3-§31.4, warm dishes) on how remote work should or could be taxed, some of the problems with today's rules are highlighted (§31.2, cold dishes). In §31.5 a few concluding comments are made (the dessert table).

Four delimitations on the scope of this chapter have been made. First, I will restrict the focus to persons employed by privately held companies, and thus will not be dealing with issues relating to self-employed persons or government officials. Second, although the problems raised by this type of employment also relate to social security, this chapter will cover only possible solution in regard to income tax. However, I will comment briefly on social security issues given that there can be no doubt that the preferred solution would be one that minimizes administrative burdens and makes it possible for the employee and the employer to pay PIT and SSC to one state only. Third, immigration law and employment law are highly relevant but will not be dealt with here. Finally, the question if the employer is having a permanent establishment in the state where the work is performed by the employee is not discussed.[15]

---

9. Prithwiraj Choudhury, *Our Work-from-Anywhere Future*, Harvard Business Review, November-December 2020, pp. 61-66; Beverly Yuen Thompson, *The Digital Nomad Lifestyle: (Remote) Work/Leisure Balance, Privilege, and Constructed Community*, in International Journal of the Sociology of Leisure, Vol. 2, pp. 27–42 (2019) DOI: 10.1007/s41978-018-00030-y.
10. For example, Spotify and Airbnb.
11. This term is often used when frontier workers start to work from home, *see* EESC, Opinion: *Taxation of Cross-Border Teleworkers and Their Employers*, ECO/585. *See* a brilliant article by Hannelore Niesten, *Revising the Fiscal and Social Security Landscape of International Teleworkers in the Digital Age*, in Intertax, Vol. 49, Issue 2, pp. 120–143 (2021) DOI: 10.54648/taxi2021 013.
12. Leonard Thomaz Pignatari, *The Taxation of 'Digital Nomads' and the '3 W's': Between Tax Challenges and Heavenly Beaches*, in Intertax, Vol. 51, Issue 5, pp. 384-396 (2023) DOI: 10.54648/taxi2023033; Svetislav V. Kostić, *In Search of the Digital Nomad: Rethinking the Taxation of Employment Income under Tax Treaties*, WTJ, Vol. 11, Issue 2, pp. 189-225 (2019).
13. It has been held that the variation and the complexity in this area are greater than when it comes to business taxation. Presentation held by David Rosenbloom at the conference ITLR Network, *International Tax Challenges Raised by Mobility of Individuals/Work Forces as a Result of Digitalization*, Belgrade 6-7 October 2022.
14. Literature and other publications up until 6 July 2023 have been taken into account when writing this summary.
15. Instead *see for example* Svetislav V. Kostić, *A Plea for a Workforce Presence PE Concept in a Post-Covid Digitalized World*, in Intertax, Vol. 49, Issue 10, pp. 758-770 (2021) DOI: 10.54648/ taxi2021078.

§31.2 NEW PROBLEMS: OLD SOLUTIONS?

§31.2.1 The Guiding Principles of Today

In domestic tax law, many jurisdictions base tax liability on the residence principle and the source principle. The *residence principle*, leading to unlimited tax liability, often contains a criterion of domicile/residency. In addition, many states have a rule on physical presence (183-day rule or habitual abode) to constitute the same.[16] In Sweden, these two grounds are complemented with a rule constituting a deemed residency principle; that is, if a person moves from Sweden but still has essential ties to Sweden, they will be deemed resident. All three criteria constitute unlimited tax liability in Sweden.[17] A few countries use citizenship as a decisive factor for unlimited tax liability. Limited tax liability is based on the *source principle* in Sweden as well as in many other jurisdictions.[18] The rationale behind the source principle is that the income has a strong connection to the country.[19]

These different principles used in domestic law often lead to double taxation. A starting point in the OECD Model[20] is that only one of the two states can be the resident state (Article 4 OECD). Depending on the classification of the income, different allocation rules apply.

The main rule for employment income is that the resident state (R) has the right to tax; hence, if the employment[21] is exercised in the other state (S), such remuneration as is derived therefrom may be taxed in the source state (Article 15.1 OECD). Similarly, income derived from entertainment or by sportspersons is divided between state S and R (Article 17.1 OECD). These allocation rules are often explained as using the *physical presence* of the employee as a decisive factor for source taxation.[22]

Physical presence is also the main rule when it comes to social security law (Article 11.3.a EU Regulation).[23] Exceptions exist regarding posted workers and persons who normally work in two or more states (multistate workers).

In addition to the role of physical presence in source state taxation, the *resident principle* is also relied upon in international taxation, for example, in situations of short term visits (Article 15.2 OECD) or for highly mobile workers such as persons

16. *See, for example,* in Sweden, Chapter 3 §3 paras 1-2 ITA (Income Tax Act). *See also* Kostić, *supra* n. 12, p. 201.
17. Chapter 3 §3 and §8 ITA.
18. Chapter 3 §§17-18 ITA.
19. Martin Berglund & Katia Cejie, *Basics of International Taxation: From a Methodological Point of View* (Iustus 2018), p. 25.
20. The OECD Model on Income and on Capital (2017) is here used as an example of an applicable tax treaty. Different tax treaties have different content.
21. *See* Kostić, *supra* n. 12, for a critical analysis of the concept of employment and reasons why we should abandon these concepts and perhaps return to the 'dependent personal service' approach, esp. pp. 208, 212-223. *See also* the initiative and the proposal of 12 June 2023 of the Council on a directive on platform workers, https://www.consilium.europa.eu/en/policies/platform-work-eu/.
22. Kostić, *supra* n. 15, 193.
23. Regulation (EC) No. 883/2004 of the European Parliament and of the Council of 29 April 2004 on the coordination of social security systems.

working on a ship or aircraft in international traffic (Article 15.3 OECD). In these situations, state R has the right to tax.

Director's fees may be taxed in both states if the director and the company have their tax treaty residency in different states (Article 16 OECD) according to the POEM principle.

In situations where double taxation arises, the resident state is obliged to mitigate or eliminate the double taxation (Article 23 OECD).

§31.2.2 Problems That Need to Be Addressed

The principles of residency and source taxation have worked because we have been able to rely on the concept of employment and the static nature of individuals leading them to remain in the same country for long periods of time. However, in the changing landscape brought about by digitalization, nomadic lifestyles are increasing and the quest for new solutions has just begun. In addition, countries have started to compete to levy taxes on employment income.

Some of the main problems identified so far are the risk of double taxation, the regulatory burden on both the employer and the employee to comply with two separate tax declarations (possibly at different times) as well as the need to struggle with calculations of tax expenses, credits, and deductions for the generation of income in both jurisdictions. Within the EU one also needs to take the Schumacker doctrine[24] into account when addressing these issues. A remote worker may very well miss out on personal and family tax benefits, depending on the length of the stay in another jurisdiction.[25] Other problems identified include the difficulty of foreseeing where and how taxes and contributions are to be paid, and the risk of employees constituting a PE in another country. Even though the Court of Justice of the European Union has ruled that international double taxation is not in conflict with the Treaty of the Functioning of the European Union (TFEU), these difficulties and problems may lead to less mobility within the EU and globally.[26]

These problems are not getting smaller with the impact of digitalization. A core principle when discussing these situations is to find simplified solutions with as few compliance burdens as possible for the employee and the employer. An outcome of this principle would be that taxes and contributions are coordinated and levied by one state only. The rationale behind this is that the (dis)coordination between taxes and contributions is a large administrative burden for taxpayers and employers.[27] Another

24. Case C-279/93 *Schumacker* and subsequent case law.
25. *See* Niesten, supra n. 11, at 133.
26. *See* Commission Communication on Removing Cross-Border Tax Obstacles for EU citizens, COM(2010) 769 final, p. 3 (2010).
27. Frans Pennings & Marjon Weerepas, *Towards a Convergence of Coordination in Social Security and Tax Law?*, in EC Tax Review, Vol. 15, Issue 4, pp. 215-225 (2006) DOI: 10.54648/ecta2006039; Bernhard Spiegel et al., *Analytical Report 2014: The Relation Between Social Security Coordination and Taxation Law*, FreSsco, European Commission, (2015); Niesten (*supra* n. 11).

problem mentioned from an employer perspective is the impact on transfer pricing structures.[28]

§31.3 NEW SOLUTIONS: A *SMÖRGÅSBORD* OF PRINCIPLES

§31.3.1 Introduction

The fact that countries have started to compete for individual taxpayers by offering beneficial regimes (e.g., golden visas and e-residence status) and that taxpayers can now work remotely to a greater extent (with or without the consent of their employers) leads to the conclusion that the nexus for the taxation of employment[29] income has to be discussed and updated.[30] In this section, a summary of several suggestions presented in literature is given – as a starting point for further research.

§31.3.2 Residency and Citizenship: Outdated or Revisited?

Historically, reliance on the resident principle has been important, both in domestic tax law and in international taxation. However, in recent years this principle has been questioned and said to be outdated.[31] One main argument for this is the fact that residency today is more or less for sale.[32] Another argument is that workers like digital nomads may no longer have deep personal links with any specific country.[33] Similar problems arise with the citizenship principle, since citizenship can be acquired (bought) by investing in a country.[34]

While admitting that residency and citizenship may not be ideal grounds for taxation, it remains true that if a country of residence can be identified, that country still has the best possibility of taking the ability-to-pay principle into account. Even though in the past, I have been very critical of the deemed residence principle used in Sweden,[35] this approach might deserve further discussion. To prevent double non-taxation, persons leaving a country could, for example, have the burden of proof to

28. Monique van Herksen (UN) as well as David Bradbury (OECD) at the Public Hearing (*supra* n. 6) organized by EESC in Tallinn, 4 July 2023.
29. In addition, the concept of employment itself needs to be discussed further. *See* Kostić, *supra* n. 12; Savvas Kostikidis, *Nexus for Source Taxation of Mobile Individual Service Providers in Tax Treaties*, BTR 2, pp. 164-192 (2023) DOI: 10.2139/ssrn.4021974.
30. Discussions are being conducted at the UN and European Social Services Commission (ESSC), and will be intensified during the fall within the OECD. *See* the Public Hearing (*supra* n. 6) and Hans Peter Larsson, *Svensk bolagsbeskattning*, in SvSkT 2023 pp. 289-304. *See also Annual Report on Taxation 2023*, Directorate-General for Taxation and Customs Union, European Commission, Publications Office of the European Union, Luxembourg, p. 5 (2023).
31. Kostić, *supra* n. 15, 196; Beretta, *supra* n. 3, at 99–102.
32. *See* Beretta, *supra* n. 3 and Van Zantbeek, *supra* n. 4.
33. Kostić, *supra* n. 15, 224.
34. Beretta, *supra* n. 3, at 93-99; Kostić, *supra* n. 15, 198.
35. Katia Cejie, *Den utsträckta hemvistprincipen – reglerna om väsentlig anknytning* (Iustus 2015).

show that they have taken up residency in another country. If not, they will be deemed to be resident in the exit state.[36]

§31.3.3 Physical Presence by Using Geo-Localization Technologies: Source State Taxation

Beretta's (2021) proposed physical presence test offers an alternative to the outdated concepts of residency and citizenship.[37] He suggests a new nexus based on the physical presence of an individual in the territory of a state, determined using geo-localization technology. His proposal would result in a proportional allocation of taxing rights among the countries involved, applied through a fractional allocation on a pro rata and pro tempore basis, levied on both the worldwide income and the allowances of an individual.[38] He argues that the Schumacker doctrine would be considered in doing this. This proposal requires intense cooperation among tax agencies, regardless of whether this is legislated through tax treaties, a multilateral instrument (MLI) or by an EU directive.

Niesten is probably not in favour of Beretta's somewhat radical proposal as regards physical presence when it comes to teleworking, in particular in WFH situations, since the fragmentation would lead to heavy administrative burdens for tax agencies, employees and employers.[39]

§31.3.4 A Tolerance Rule for Teleworkers Working from Home

Niesten (2021) argues that taxes and social security rules should be coordinated, and accordingly discusses the possibility of linking taxing rules to social security rules when it comes to establishing the source state for teleworkers. After a detailed discussion of the pros and cons of the POEM[40] and residence principles,[41] she proposes a tolerance rule. Unlike Beretta, as I have understood it, she focuses on the pure situation where an employee (a frontier worker) is teleworking from home to some extent, with the employer in the other state. Inspired by a mutual agreement between Belgium and Luxembourg, she suggests that a tolerance rule of sixty-nine days could be included in Article 15.1 of the OECD Model to cover work performed in the resident state or in a third state. If the threshold of days is not exceeded, the employment income will be taxed only in the source state (POEM).[42] A similar proposal of ninety-six days is mentioned by the European Economic and Social Committee (ESSC).[43]

36. *See also* suggestions by Kostić, *supra* n. 15.
37. Beretta, *supra* n. 3, at 107-111 with reference to other scholars as well.
38. Kostić, *supra* n. 15.
39. Niesten, *supra* n. 11, at 129. Please note that Niesten does not comment directly on Beretta's suggestion.
40. Niesten, *supra* n. 11, at 134-137.
41. Niesten, *supra* n. 11, at 137-139.
42. Niesten, *supra* n. 11, at 139-141. Interestingly, Niesten refers to the POEM principle as source taxation.
43. EESC, *supra* n. 11, at 4.2.

This proposal is interesting, especially if one reflects on the new Framework Agreement regarding social security that came into force on 1 July 2023 in those states that have signed it.[44] If an agreement is reached, SSCs would only be paid in the state where the employer has his registered office (place of business), provided that the cross-border telework in the state of residence is less than 50 % of the total working time.[45] In contrast to Niesten's proposal, the Framework Agreement covers only the situation of teleworking (aka WFH) and does not cover work performed in third states.

§31.3.5 Monetary Threshold

Kostikidis (2023) discusses the nexus for source taxation of *service providers*.[46] He suggests a new provision in tax treaties (the Models) according to which services performed within the source state will be taxable in that state if they exceed a monetary threshold. He argues that such a rule, which would apply to all mobile individual service providers (artists, consultants, influencers, digital nomads, etc.), would fulfil the criteria of appropriateness. As I understand this proposal, it could probably be discussed in conjunction with the physical presence principle proposed by Beretta.

§31.3.6 A Few Other Principles

In his publication on digital nomads, Kostić discusses the principle of origin, the destination principle, and the benefit principle, none of which are applicable as the law stands today.[47] However, this does not mean that we cannot discuss them for the future, and so I will comment on them briefly.

In his dissertation, Kemmeren suggests the concept of taxation according to the *principle of origin*.[48] The essence of the principle is that taxing rights should be allocated to the jurisdiction within which the income was created. The origin of income is intimately related to the intellectual element that is provided by the activities of individual human beings. Only individuals can create income; things in themselves cannot.[49] The principle of origin has similarities with how the source principle is used today; hence, it can be seen as a tool of interpretation when interpreting the term 'source'. This approach also gives interesting input to the discussion on capital and labour import and export neutrality (CLIN, CLEN), with preference to CLIN.[50]

44. Framework Agreement on the application of Art. 16(1) of Regulation (EC) No. 883/2004 in cases of habitual cross-border telework.
45. Article 3 in the Framework Agreement. *See also* the Explanatory Memorandum to the agreement, and the definitions of teleworker, digital connection (IT link), for example.
46. Kostikidis, *supra* n. 29.
47. Kostić, *supra* n. 15, at 210-211.
48. Eric C.C.M. Kemmeren, *Principle of Origin in Tax Conventions: A Rethinking of Models*. Tilburg University (2001).
49. Eric C.C.M. Kemmeren, *Source of Income in Globalizing Economies: Overview of the Issues and the Plea for an Origin-Based Approach*, in BFIT, pp. 430-452 (2006).
50. Kemmeren, *supra* n. 49, at 439-441.

The *destination principle* stands in contrast to the principle of origin. It focuses on the demand side of income production and asserts that the taxing right ought to be given to the state where the goods and services produced are brought to the market (business output). If this principle were adopted, it might be possible to stop levying PIT and SSC and instead increase the VAT rate.

The *benefit principle* states that tax should be paid where the benefits from government are received. Schwartz (2022) evaluates the allocation rules in the OECD Model against the benefit principle in regard to remote work. He concludes that the current rules favour resident state taxation in regard to remote work (WFH) and says that if amendments are to be made in favour of the state of employment – in light of the benefit principle – it should be done carefully.[51] Here, as well as with the other suggestions, it appears that one has to look at different situations separately. In this case, one would need to be able to establish where the benefits are really received.

§31.3.7 Brief Comment: Choosing a Warm Dish

Before deciding which of the proposed principles to elaborate on, we should note that this discussion still strongly reflects the basic principles of residency and source taxation.

Looking at the suggestions more or less influenced by the source principle, it would be beneficial to have further research analysing the solutions presented by Beretta, Kostikidis and Kemmeren and their views on physical presence, a monetary threshold and the content of the principle of origin.[52]

If one considers the pure situation of teleworkers (WFH), much of the administrative burden would be solved if the state of the employer had the taxing right (POEM) since this state will still levy the SSC according to the new Framework Agreement if applicable. However, this solution would probably not reflect the benefit principle since the resident state would have to supply major parts of the welfare system. This problem could be solved by adding a compensation regime, as will be discussed in §31.4.

§31.4 NEW SOLUTION FROM A MORE ADMINISTRATIVE PERSPECTIVE

§31.4.1 Introduction

If one were to choose a principal starting point from the *smörgåsbord* presented in §31.3, the choice might be heavily influenced by a desire to reduce the administrative

51. Christian Schwartz, *Taxation of Remote Workers: Is the Allocation of Taxation Rights in Line with the Benefit Principle?* pp. 72-98, in Lic. Dissertation, *Cross-Border Taxation of Workers: New Ways of Working*, Lund University (2022).
52. A comparison could also be made to the discussion of market jurisdiction and value creation in business taxation, *see* Svitlana Buriak, *A New Taxing Right for the Market Jurisdiction: Where Are the Limits?* in Intertax, Vol. 49, Issue 3 (2020) DOI: 10.54648/taxi2020026.

burden on the taxpayers (employees and employers). However, these options might not necessarily be the fairest or most appropriate principles when allocating taxing rights. So, two more examples will be mentioned in this section: compensation regimes and an one-stop-shop (OSS).

§31.4.2 Compensation Regimes

Compensation regimes are sometimes included in bilateral treaties in frontier regions. Such regimes exist, for example, between Sweden and Denmark, and between Germany and France.[53] The direction of the compensation is, of course, dependent on which state has the primary right to tax the income in the first place. In its essence, a compensation regime means that one country levies the taxes and contributions and then uses some apportioning formula to transfer some of the taxes and contributions to the other country.

§31.4.3 One-Stop-Shop: An Administrative Solution

An alternative that is sometimes mentioned is influenced by the OSS VAT rule.[54] This rule was put in place by the EU to ease the burden on businesses selling to consumers (B2C) in other EU Member States. The rule permits businesses to submit a single VAT return declaring sales in multiple EU Member States rather than having to register for VAT in each country. The tax agency of the company's home jurisdiction transfers the VAT paid in the countries of the consumers.

Similarly, an OSS system especially developed for cross-border remote workers might allow taxpayers a reduced administrative burden and reduce disputes between states while at the same time ensuring that taxes are levied correctly.

§31.5 CONCLUDING COMMENTS

I have presented a *smörgåsbord* of possible principles on which the increasing number of remote workers can be taxed. I have also added a few solutions to ease the administrative burdens on taxpayers. But a *smörgåsbord* is always a bit boring and can lack flavour and style. However, it can be used as a starting point for preparing a more delicious a la carte menu. The *smörgåsbord* can be divided into smaller pieces, and one can take one bite at a time and chew it well. The same principle can apply in regard to taxing the different situations of remote workers.

This chapter has brought an overall approach to the table, with a mix of different possibilities derived from different situations. Future research needs to focus on

53. *See* Katia Cejie, *New Problems Caused by the COVID-19 Pandemic: Income Taxes and Social Security Contributions (An Overview)*, in European Taxation, pp. 188-189 (2021), for the regime between Sweden and Denmark; and Niesten (*supra* n. 11) 141-142 regarding Germany and France.

54. EESC, *supra* n. 11, at 4.7.

smaller pieces, and also needs to address the question of how future changes are to be implemented. Should countries change their domestic law, should the OECD Model/UN Model or its commentaries be updated, should a specific article on remote work be included, should an MLI be drafted, should a Directive or Regulation be put in place within the EU, or would a communication (soft law) from the Commission be enough?

One thing is certain: we cannot put off trying to solve these problems simply because they are complex and the variations in situations are enormous. While a global solution would be preferable, we should probably take only one plate at a time at the *smörgåsbord,* and so we should probably start at the EU level and try to coordinate or harmonize ourselves.[55]

Myself, I always prefer desserts, and I am looking forward to continuing to dig into the creamy chocolate batter that will produce the most perfect tax cake.

55. For a similar opinion, *see* EESC, *supra* n. 11, at 1.7.

CHAPTER 32

Legal Form Neutrality and the Mitigation of Double Taxation of Income Earned by Entertainers and Sportspersons

Eric Kemmeren

§32.1 INTRODUCTION

My journey with Peter Essers started in 1987. I met Peter when I became a board member of the 'Foundation Tax Legal Assistance De Smeetskring' of which he already was a board member representing the Fiscal Institute Tilburg (FIT).[1] In 1991, Peter, knowing that I was eager to work in academia and to do a Ph.D. study, asked me to apply for a position as a lecturer/researcher at the FIT. Surprise: they hired me. Since then, Peter and I made together as entrepreneurial academics a lot of inspiring and challenging journeys, especially in the fields of European and international taxation. Just to mention a few of them. We started together the 'EUCOTAX Wintercourse'.[2] Together with the always energetic, inspiring and out-of-the-box thinking Frans Vanistendael, we started the European Tax College (ETC), of which the Leuven 'International and European Tax Moot Court' is a part of the legacy.[3] Whereas the ETC stopped, it was a source of inspiration for the current international Tilburg LLM 'International Business Taxation'.[4] We also internationalized the staff of the FIT.[5] But

1. In Dutch: *Stichting Fiskale Rechtshulp "De Smeetskring"*. The day-to-day operations are run by tax law and tax economic students. They provide for free tax consultancy services, predominantly filling out tax returns regarding personal income tax for people with low-income and low net equity.
2. *See* https://www.tilburguniversity.edu/students/studying/additional-education/eucotax-wintercourse (consulted on 21 October 2023).
3. *See* https://www.law.kuleuven.be/taxmootcourt (consulted on 21 October 2023).
4. *See* https://www.tilburguniversity.edu/nl/onderwijs/masteropleidingen/international-business-taxation (consulted on 21 October 2023).

for me, the most precious is not only that Peter is one of my closest colleagues, if not the closest, but also that we have become very good friends, and that is true for our spouses as well. Peter's retirement will end our professional relationship, at least to a certain extent, but it will not stop our warm friendship.

As many people know, the academic Peter Essers has a wide range of interests. Just consult his very long list of publications.[6] In those publications, I found inspiration for the topic of this chapter. Peter has published on legal form-neutral taxation.[7] This was predominantly in the area of business taxation. But he also led a publication on taxation of top sportspersons.[8] The combination of both topics triggered me because of a Dutch Supreme Court ruling in which an entertainer claimed for personal income tax (PIT) purposes an additional ordinary tax credit under tax treaties to the extent that his star company could not fully realize its ordinary tax credit, because of insufficient taxes due.[9] The Supreme Court ruled that the entertainer and his star company could not be identified. Thus, the legal form matters, also regarding the mitigation of double taxation through a tax credit mechanism. In this case, it was even more complex than the regular issue of legal form-neutral taxation, i.e., performing activities as a natural person or by means of an entity, because in this case, the entertainer performed the activities both as a natural person and by means of an entity. Under tax treaties, entertainers, sportspersons and the relevant entities are normally covered by the same provision, i.e., a provision similar to Article 17 OECD Model Tax Convention (OM) 2017 (OM 2017).[10] Therefore, this ruling can easily be connected with the two research fields of Peter to develop the research questions of this chapter:

> Can mitigation of double taxation of income earned by entertainers and sportspersons by means of an ordinary tax credit be done in a legal form-neutral manner, and if not, how should legal form-neutral mitigation of double taxation of this income be realized?

I think that this question is relevant from an academic point of view because, as far as I know, the mitigation of double taxation of income earned by entertainers and sportspersons has never been addressed before from the perspective of legal form neutrality.[11] I also believe that it is of societal relevance because the answer to the question might prevent an excess tax credit which cannot be credited. This seems to be

5. *See* https://www.tilburguniversity.edu/about/schools/law/departments/fit/staff (consulted on 21 October 2023).
6. *See* https://research.tilburguniversity.edu/en/persons/peter-essers/publications/ (consulted on 21 October 2023).
7. *See, e.g.*, Peter H.J. Essers, *Rechsvormneutraliteit*, 112/113 Tijdschrift Fiscaal Ondernemingsrecht (2011).
8. *See*, Peter H.J Essers et al., *Topsport en fiscaliteit, een onderzoek naar de fiscale positie van topsport vanuit nationaal en Europees perspectief* 195 (1999).
9. *See* Hoge Raad (HR) 24 September 2021, No. 20/01875, ECLI:NL:HR:2021:1352, Beslissingen in belastingzaken Nederlandse Belastingrechtspraak (BNB) 2022/7. Compare also Hoge Raad 8 July 2022, No. 21/04627, ECLI:NL:HR:2022:1048, Vakstudie-Nieuws (V-N) 2022/37.9.
10. *See* Art. 17 OECD Model Tax Convention on Income and Capital (2017) and earlier versions.
11. For example, while the Editor of V-N in his annotation to HR 24 September 2021, No. 20/01875, *supra* n. 9, V-N 2021/39.5 refers to a legal form-neutral business profit tax, he does not elaborate on it or on a legal form-neutral mitigation of double taxation.

in the interest of entertainers and sportspersons. This might result in less tax costs. If so, this might also be in the interest of persons who contract an entertainer or a sportsperson because lower tax costs might enable them to buy the services at lower prices.

To answer the research questions, benchmarks will be developed (§32.2). In §32.3, the Supreme Court ruling will be discussed. Research on alternative methods of legal form-neutral mitigation of double taxation, based on the benchmarks, will be presented in §32.4. This chapter ends with the main conclusions (§32.5).

The allowed number of words sets inevitable restrictions. Therefore, for example, this chapter will not address which persons qualify or should qualify as entertainers or sportspersons. I do neither go into the question which income is or should be connected with an entertainer or a sportsperson nor will discuss whether a specific provision for entertainers and sportspersons is justified. The focus is on the method of mitigating double taxation of such income.

The applied research methodology is the traditional doctrinal legal methodology.[12] This methodology makes it possible to acquire a more complete understanding of the mitigation of double taxation of income earned by entertainers and sportspersons. It also enables to assess, based on the developed benchmarks, whether positive law should be improved, and if so, how this should be done. Therefore, I think that the application of the doctrinal legal methodology is appropriate to discuss the legal form-neutral mitigation of double taxation of income earned by entertainers and sportspersons.

§32.2 BENCHMARKS[13]

The key benchmark for this chapter is legal form-neutral taxation. One dimension is that it should not matter for tax purposes whether an economic activity, such as business activities or activities of an entertainer or a sportsperson, which can also be business activities, is performed as natural person or through an entity, often a company. Another dimension in an international context is that it should not matter for tax purposes of whether a business activity is carried on through a permanent establishment or a subsidiary.[14] The focus of this chapter is on the first dimension.

12. *See, e.g.*, Jan B.M. Vranken, *Wij weten wel wat wij doen – Over juridisch-dogmatisch onderzoek in het privaatrecht, maar wel een slag anders*, 26 Nederlands Juristenblad (NJB)8 (2014). Doctrinal legal research covers positive law, as contained in written and unwritten international, European and national rules, treaties, court decisions, policies, principles, concepts, doctrines and articles in the commentary literature.
13. For a more detailed discussion *see, e.g.*, Eric C.C.M. Kemmeren, *Principle of Origin in Tax Conventions, A Rethinking of Models* 18-55 and 413-421 (2001) (also available on https://pure.uvt.nl/ws/portalfiles/portal/439888/87428.pdf); Eric C.C.M Kemmeren, *If We Need a Destination-Based Corporate Income Tax, Do We Also Need a Production-Based Consumption Tax?* in: Jérôme Monsenego & Jan Bjuvberg (eds), *International Taxation in a Changing Landscape – Liber Amicorum in Honour of Bertil Wiman* 147-164 (Kluwer Law International 2019), and Eric C.C.M. Kemmeren, *Taxing Interest in the Debtor State as an Alternative to DEBRA* 32 EC Tax Review 47-47 (2023) DOI: 10.54648/ecta2023010.
14. *See, e.g.*, Essers, *supra* n. 7.

However, entities are normally not ignored for tax purposes. For example, corporate tax is levied on entities. The legal basis of this tax has been wrestled with since its existence.[15] In my view, corporate tax is the systematic consequence of the recognition in our legal system of entities alongside natural persons. A legal person, or an entity assimilated with it for tax purposes, can be an independent bearer of rights and obligations as a result of the fiction devised by lawyers.[16] A legal person is thus in principle equated but not identified with a natural person. Thereby, in principle, each legal person is recognized individually, regardless of whether it is part of a group or not.[17]

Based on this equivalence, both natural persons and legal persons are independent bearers of rights and obligations. Both are also clothed with ability-to-pay taxes.[18] In this context, I understand ability-to-pay to mean a person's wealth that provides him with the capacity (means) to pay taxes. Both a natural person and a legal person generating income from activities as an entertainer or sportsperson increase their wealth and thus also have individual capacity to pay tax. If then legal persons concerning those corporate profits were to be excluded from taxation, it would be contrary to the ability-to-pay principle. After all, this principle also implies that natural persons and legal persons in comparable economic circumstances should be treated equally (horizontal equality) and that natural persons and legal persons in not-comparable economic circumstances should be treated differently according to the degree of inequality (vertical equality).

Based on the direct benefit principle, whoever directly benefits from the public expenditure made in a State should also contribute to that expenditure. This means that a person who produces income (including capital gains), i.e., increases his individual ability-to-pay taxes, benefits from that public expenditure (public goods and services). That public expenditure allows him to produce income. Consequently, he should contribute to the financing of this public expenditure, i.e., pay taxes. In a comprehensive tax system, taxes on production, property, consumption and renunciation of wealth should be aligned because a taxpayer's total wealth should be taxed only once.

Tax jurisdiction on income should therefore be based on the economic link to the State in question. In this context, taxation based on the principle of origin justifies taxation of income by a State if the income is created within the territory of that State; i.e., the cause of the income is within the territory of that State.[19] That State makes the

15. *See, e.g.*, Jan Verburg, *Vennootschapsbelasting* 1-15 (Wolters Kluwer 2000), and Frank J. Elsweier & Stan A. Stevens, *Hoofdzaken vennootschapsbelasting* 13-25 (Wolters Kluwer 2023).
16. Hereafter, for the sake of convenience, only the term 'legal person' will be used for all relevant bodies.
17. *See, e.g.*, HR 8 May 1957, no. 12.931, ECLI:NL:HR:1957:AY2274, BNB 1957/208 and Verburg, *supra* n. 15, at 393-396.
18. *See also, e.g.*, CJEU 14 February 1995, Case C-279/93 (*Schumacker*), points 10, 32-33, and CJEU 12 June 2018 Case C-650/ 16 (*Bevola*), points 39, 49-50, and 59. That there are also different views on this in the context of the wrestling over the legal basis of corporate tax may be clear. For an overview, *see, e.g.*, Elsweier & Stevens, *supra* n. 15, at 15-16.
19. *See also, e.g.*, Irene J.J. Burgers, *'Waardecreatie': nieuw(e) mantra, concept, standaard of beginsel,* Nederlands Tijdschrift voor Fiscaal Recht 1-6 (2018) on value creation from the perspective of different stakeholders, such as shareholders, subordinates and customers.

yield or the acquisition of wealth possible. The basic principle is that income is only produced if an individual uses the production factor of labour, whether or not supplemented by the production factor of capital. The *intellectual element* of a natural person is the key component for the production of income. Therefore, the allocation of tax jurisdiction over income should correspond, at least as far as possible, to this use of labour and thus also to the place (the territory) where these production factors are employed (the territorial principle). There is a close link between the territorial principle and the direct benefit principle; i.e., taxes should be regarded as contributions to the direct benefits enjoyed by a natural person or legal person as a result of government activities. Thus, in my view, the direct benefit principle is also part of the ability-to-pay principle.

The origin of income from entertainment or sport is: the individual human performance activity of the entertainer or sportsperson. The performance is considered to be essential and significant for the production of this income. All income functionally linked with the performance involved should be attributed to the performance State. The place where such a performance has been prepared is immaterial. Preparations themselves do not produce income, but the performance does. Nonetheless, it is clear that preparations, e.g., rehearsals and training sessions, are a prerequisite for income-producing performance. Therefore, expenses which are incurred for the purposes of each performance should be attributed to the performance concerned and should be deductible regardless of where they were incurred. To the extent that the expenses cannot be attributed to a single performance, the expenses should be attributed *pro rate parte*. Consequently, tax jurisdiction on income regarding entertainers and sportspersons should be attributed to the performance State, i.e., the State in which the entertainer or sportsperson performs or has performed as such.

The territoriality principle is a narrower application of the territorial principle. It implies that the extent of a State's taxing rights is determined only by the income earned in that State. Unlike the universality principle, where the tax level of the State of residence prevails, under the territoriality principle, the tax level of the State of origin is decisive. Exclusive taxation by the State of origin implies a tax-base exemption, also called objective exemption, in the State of residence of the income recipient. This thus avoids double taxation. In my view, the ability-to-pay principle and the direct benefit principle are the strongest arguments for giving precedence to a tax-base exemption and the territoriality principle as method for mitigation of double taxation and not to an (ordinary) tax credit which is a reflection of the universality principle.[20]

Next to the above tax-legal benchmarks, I distinguish economic benchmarks. The efficiency of the global economy would be maximized if production factors were allocated where they produce the highest returns. In this way, global prosperity increases. As part of that efficiency, tax neutrality should prevail as much as possible

20. Both are rooted in capital and labour neutrality: an income recipient should pay the same total (domestic plus foreign) tax, irrespective of whether he derives a given amount of labour or investment income from foreign or from domestic sources.

in open markets; i.e., taxes should not unintentionally counteract an efficient allocation of the factors of production of labour and capital. The highest possible level of neutrality should be pursued.[21]

One perspective of neutrality is international tax neutrality. In my view, this implies that the relation between taxes (burdens) and public goods (benefits) should not be disrupted to the disadvantage of transnational (economic) activities, but, however, they should neither be favoured. This is because the effect of taxation cannot be isolated from the overall effects of all other State-induced transaction and production costs and benefits. In this way, fair competition between foreign and domestic persons who carry on the same genuine economic activities under the same market conditions and using the same public goods to the same extent in the same State is promoted. Taxation on the basis of residence is incompatible with this neutrality approach since no State can ensure that foreign activities carried out by its residents are subject to the same transaction and other State-induced costs and benefits.

In my view, international tax neutrality is also in line with capital and labour import neutrality (CLIN). An efficient allocation of factors of production is best achieved with a CLIN economic policy: labour and capital funds originating in different States should compete on an equal footing in the respective labour and capital markets of each State regardless of the residence of the worker or investor. Opposite of CLIN is capital and labour export neutrality (CLEN): an income recipient should pay the same total (domestic plus foreign) tax, irrespective of whether that recipient derives a given amount of labour or investment income from foreign or domestic sources. The aim of this policy is to tax residents equally. I cannot see that CLEN is consistent with international tax neutrality. I think that, in the context of activities as an entertainer or a sportsperson, a tax based on the universality principle creates a non-neutral and consequently an inefficient system because of the differences in the residence State taxes of competitors in the relevant market. Entertainers and sportspersons compete with entertainers and sportspersons, not residents with residents. Therefore, the allocation of tax jurisdiction and mitigation of double taxation based on the territoriality principle should be encouraged. In this way, entertainers and sportspersons, whether active as a natural person or through a legal person, are enabled to compete with each other on an equal footing because all competitors are presumably treated the same way for tax purposes.

A taxation of income from activities as an entertainer or a sportsperson will be neutral only if it does not alter the market conditions. Differences in taxation by the States of which entertainers or sportspersons are residents will affect the market conditions under which the entertainer or sportsperson operates. This is also true if entertainers or sportspersons are able to transfer their State of residence tax burden to the person with whom they contract (the contractor).[22] This leads to the conclusion

21. In my view, tax competition can be sound as long as it involves measures aimed at increasing the 'economic cake' that can then be shared and not at luring activities carried out at neighbours, which only relocates economic activities and does not increase the 'cake' per se. *See* for a more detailed discussion, e.g., Carlo Pinto, *Tax Competition and EU Law* 1-52 (2003).
22. Whether such a transfer is actually possible in an individual case will always depend on the concrete market conditions.

that a system based on the universality principle is not neutral and affects not only the position of the entertainers and sportspersons, respectively, the contractor, but also the functioning of entertainment or sports markets. However, a system based on the territoriality and origin principles will be neutral with regard to their tax position because income earned by entertainers and sportspersons will be taxed only by the State in which they perform their activities as entertainers or sportspersons. In this way, it is also possible to achieve tax neutrality between natural persons and legal persons carrying out activities as entertainers or sportspersons. This can be done in the performance State by imposing the same effective tax rate on the income irrespective of whether the income is earned by a natural person or a legal person. This means that the taxation of income earned by legal persons should be aligned with the taxation of income earned by a natural person or the other way around.

In conclusion, international tax neutrality and CLIN imply that income should be taxed only in the State to which it can be economically linked. Therefore, creating a level playing field, establishing international tax neutrality, CLIN, satisfying the recognition of legal persons alongside natural persons, the ability-to-pay principle, and establishing an origin-based allocation of tax jurisdiction on income go hand in hand. Below, I will research in more detail whether these goals can be achieved in a legal form-neutral manner regarding the mitigation of double taxation of income earned by entertainers and sportspersons.

However, I will also research whether a legal form-neutral mitigation of double taxation can be realized when applying the universality principle and in line with this principle an (ordinary) tax credit because such a case was decided by the Dutch Supreme Court which will be discussed in the next section.

§32.3 DUTCH SUPREME COURT: THE STAR COMPANY AND THE STAR ARE NOT INTERCHANGEABLE REGARDING MITIGATION OF DOUBLE TAXATION[23]

Considering the limited words available for this chapter, I will only discuss the essentials of the ruling as far as necessary to answer the research questions.

§32.3.1 Facts of the Case

X was a Dutch Disk Jockey (DJ) and a tax resident of the Netherlands. He was a director and sole shareholder of a holding company, which also was a tax resident of the Netherlands. This holding company in turn held all the shares in an operating company (the star company), which was a tax resident of the Netherlands as well.

In connection with performances by X, the star company concluded contracts with principals. The star company received the fees for those performances and paid the associated costs. The star company also paid a management fee to the holding

23. *See* HR 24 September 2021, No. 20/01875, *supra* n. 9.

company. The income of the holding company consisted of the management fee paid by the star company, royalties, sponsorships, and other fees.

X was subject to the Dutch PIT tax in respect of salary received from the holding company.

In 2015, foreign withholding taxes were withheld from the fees paid to the star company by foreign principals in respect of foreign performances. The star company's corporate income tax (CIT) return for 2015 included an amount of EUR 247,493 in creditable foreign withholding taxes. These withholdings took place in Argentina, Austria, Belgium, Brazil, Canada, Chile, India, Japan, and the United Kingdom.

Of the amount of withholding tax of EUR 247,493, EUR 70,807 was offset against the CIT payable by the star company for the year 2015 and EUR 3,725 was offset against CIT payable by the holding company for that year. Thus, EUR 172,961 remained unsettled for CIT for the year 2015.

X requested the Inspector to set off part of the amount of EUR 172,961, i.e., in the amount of EUR 39,609, against the PIT assessment imposed on it for the year 2015. He also requested to issue a rolling-over decision as referred to in Article 14 of the Dutch Unilateral Decree Avoidance of Double Taxation 2001 (UDADT) in his name for the remainder of EUR 133,352 in order to be able to set off this amount against the PIT in future years. The Inspector rejected these requests.

§32.3.2 The Supreme Court's Decision

The relevant tax treaties all contain an artist and sportsman article which (as far as relevant here) is identical to Article 17 OM 2010 and its predecessors.[24] With respect to mitigation of double taxation on Article 17-income, all treaties provide for an ordinary tax credit referred to in Article 23B OM 2010 and its predecessors. In the case for the fees from Chile, Article 13 UDADT also provides for an ordinary tax credit.

The Court holds that from Articles 17 and 23B OM, it does not follow that the artist and his star company must be identified and that, consequently, the withholding tax levied at the expense of the star company must be capable of being credited by the artist. According to the Court, the Commentaries to the OM (OC) do neither compel such identification.[25] It has been noted that Article 17(2) OM does not interfere with the person of the recipient of the Article 17-income. The star company remains the recipient and not the artist or sportsmen if no 'look-trough' approach is applied by the performance State.[26]

Furthermore, the Court argues that the relevant tax treaties do not provide legal rules that differ from the laws of the Contracting States on the basis of which the person

24. As from 2014, the OECD has converted the terms 'artistes' and 'sportsmen' into 'entertainers' respectively 'sportspersons'.
25. The Court refers to the sections 4.6 to 4.12 of the Advocate General (AG) Wattel's Opinion who refers to the Commentaries of 1977 (paras 4 and 11 to Art. 17 OM), and 1992 (para. 8 to Art. 17 OM).
26. A 'look-trough' approach means that the income is not allocated to the star company but to the artist or sportsman who personally performs the entertainment respectively sport.

from whom a tax is levied should be assessed. The foreign taxes relevant to this litigation were levied only on the star company and not on the DJ personally.[27]

Next to this, the Court decides that it cannot be inferred from paragraph 11.5 OC 2014 to Article 17 OM 2014 that the State of residence is obliged to allow a tax credit with both the DJ and the star company. The comments concern the manner in which the source State exercises its taxing right. From the contents of that passage, already for that reason, no inference can be drawn regarding the right of a tax credit in the State of residence claimed by the DJ.[28]

The Court also rejected the claim that it follows from its previous case law that the granting of double taxation relief to a sportsman or artist cannot be subject to the condition that the foreign income in question should also have been specifically taxed there.[29] Contrary to the tax treaties in this litigation, the tax treaties in those previous cases included a tax-base exemption and not an ordinary tax credit as a method for mitigation of double taxation. When avoiding double taxation by applying the exemption method, it is not required that the income in question has actually been taxed abroad, and therefore it is not required whether tax has been levied there from the taxpayer in question. That is different in the case of a tax credit. This involves crediting of the tax actually levied on the taxpayer abroad, and it is therefore relevant whether, and if so from whom, this foreign tax was levied. Therefore, still according to the Supreme Court, the conclusion cannot be drawn from the fact that the manner in which the fees were taxed in the source State is not important in this case.

Also, with respect to the withholding tax levied from the star company on the gages in Chile, a country with which the Netherlands has no tax treaty, the DJ cannot claim credit for that tax. Also, the UDADT provides no basis for doing so, according to the Court.

27. This interpretation cannot be tested for correctness in cassation. The interpretation is reserved for the fact-finding court, such as a court of appeals.
28. The Court does not indicate which OC it refers to. However, it is likely that it is the OC 2014 because both the Court of Appeals whose decision is challenged in this litigation and the AG Wattel refer to this OC (*see* sections 1.7, 2.14, 4.12, 4.15, 4.16 and 9.1 of his opinion). It should be noted that this OC is an OC of a later date than the relevant tax treaties were concluded. Later, case law learns that a treaty-posterior amendment to the OC may be of importance if the text of the relevant tax treaty provision is aligned as much as possible with the OM and if it is a 'precision or clarification' of that provision or treaty antecedent commentary. It is a supplementary means of interpretation (Art. 32 Vienna Convention of the law of treaties) and of limited significance when interpreting a previously concluded tax treaty. *See* HR 14-10-2022, no. 21-00747, ECLI:NL:HR:2022:1436, BNB 2023/33. I think that Supreme Court's reasoning is consistent with this later case law because para. 11.5 does not deal with the position of the State of residence but only with the position of the State of source and 'already for that reason', this paragraph should not be considered. It is not 'precision or clarification' regarding the obligation of the State of residence to provide a tax credit.
29. *See* HR 9 February 2007, nos 40.465, 40.604 and 41.478, ECLI:NL:HR:2007:AU3571, ECLI:NL:HR:2007:AU3577 respectively ECLI:NL:HR:2007:AU3578, BNB 2007/142-144.

§32.3.3 Comments

How should this ruling be assessed based on the benchmarks?[30]

The result is not that the mitigation of double taxation by means of an ordinary tax credit is legal form neutral. It matters whether activities of an entertainer or a sportsperson are performed as natural person or through a legal person. However, I think that this is an inevitable consequence of the basic system of recognizing legal persons alongside natural persons, also for tax purposes. This is not only a juridical but also an economic reality. Both are independent bearers of rights and obligations. Therefore, they (in this case, the star company and the DJ) cannot be identified, as the Supreme Court ruled.[31]

Both the star company and the DJ are individually clothed with ability-to-pay taxes. Whereas both increase individually their wealth by performing economic activities as an artist, i.e., earn income, both should individually pay tax on the income they earn, unless a specific rule would treat them as one taxable unit. Consequently, this distinction should also be taken into account when applying an ordinary tax credit because the obligation of paying taxes (both withholding taxes in the performance States and CIT and PIT in the Netherlands as the State of residence) is one of the obligations of the star company and the DJ as the case may be, unless a specific rule allows using a tax credit of other persons. Therefore, I think that the Court's ruling is also consistent with the ability-to-pay principle.

When earning income in performance States, the star company and the DJ benefit individually from the public expense of these States. Therefore, I think that is also in line with the direct benefit principle that performance States distinguish between the star company and the DJ for withholding tax purposes. They do not consider them as one tax unit, e.g., by applying a look-through approach. Consequently, the Netherlands as State of residence should also follow this approach when applying an ordinary tax credit.[32]

However, the application of an ordinary tax credit is, in my view, inconsistent with the ability-to-pay and the direct benefit principles. The wealth of the star company and the DJ has not been increased by means of artist activities in the Netherlands, but only in the performance States. The public goods and services of the Netherlands have not been used to create that wealth. Therefore, in my view, any additional tax levied in the Netherlands because of the ordinary tax credit mechanism cannot be justified based on the ability-to-pay and direct benefit principles.

Maybe of all allocation rules of the OM, Article 17 OM best reflects the principle of origin by allocating tax jurisdiction on the income earned through the individual human performance activity of the entertainer or sportsperson in the performance

30. *See* for the benchmarks §32.2 of this chapter.
31. *See also, e.g.*, Peter Kavelaars in his annotation to BNB 2022/7, *supra* n. 9, at paras 1-2. *See* for dissenting opinions, e.g., Dick Molenaar, *DJ en dubbele belastingheffing*, 194 Weekblad Fiscaal Recht (WFR) (2021), and Otto C.R. Marres in his annotation to this ruling in FED 2021/147, para. 4.
32. *See also, e.g.*, AG Wattel's Opinion to HR 24 September 2021, No. 20/01875, *supra* n. 9, at section 4.7, and Marres, *supra* n. 32, at para. 4.

State. The income is not produced in the State of residence of the star company or the entertainer or sportsperson. Therefore, the ruling is also inconsistent with the principle of origin. However, the Supreme Court is not to blame for that, simply because it must apply the ordinary tax credit because it has been included in the relevant tax treaties and the UDADT. As a result, additional tax may be levied in the Netherlands inconsistent with the principle of origin.

The result of the ruling does neither satisfy the territoriality principle. Because of the ordinary tax credit mechanism, the universality principle and thus the tax level of the Netherlands as State of residence prevails. A tax-base exemption would satisfy not only the territoriality principle but also the ability-to-pay and direct benefit principle.

A tax-base exemption would also be consistent with the international tax neutrality principle. The ordinary tax credit mechanism does not satisfy this principle, because a State of residence, in the present case the Netherlands, cannot ensure a fair competition between foreign and domestic persons who carry on the same genuine economic entertainment or sports activities under the same market conditions and using the same public goods to the same extent in the performance States.

The application of the ordinary tax credit reflects CLEN, which policy aim is to tax Netherlands residents equally, and not CLIN which would result in a tax-base exemption. In my view, the Netherlands contributes to a non-neutral and an inefficient system of allocation of the factors of production of labour and capital in the context of entertainment and sports activities.

In conclusion, the mitigation of double taxation by means of an ordinary tax credit as applied by the Supreme Court is consistent with the basic system of recognizing legal persons alongside natural persons, also for tax purposes. The star company and the DJ cannot be identified. This distinction is also consistent with the ability-to-pay and direct benefit principles. On the other hand, however, the application of an ordinary tax credit by the Netherlands is inconsistent with both principles. This is also inconsistent with legal form neutrality, the principle of origin, the territoriality principle, the principle of international neutrality and CLIN. Again, the Supreme Court is not to blame for these inconsistencies simply because it must apply the ordinary tax credit because it has been included in the relevant tax treaties and the UDADT.

§32.4 ALTERNATIVE METHODS OF MITIGATION OF DOUBLE TAXATION BASED ON LEGAL FORM NEUTRALITY

In this section, I will briefly research whether it is possible to develop methods of mitigation of double taxation which are legal form neutral and whether based on the benchmarks it is possible to rank the various methods if more than one method could be applied. It is not claimed that the six researched methods constitute an exhaustive list of possible methods.

First, all 17-income earned by a star company or a natural person could exclusively be allocated to the State of residence of these persons.[33] This State should impose the same effective tax rate on the income irrespective of whether the income is earned by a legal person or a natural person. This means that the taxation of income earned by legal persons should be aligned with the taxation of income earned by natural persons or the other way around. However, this alignment becomes problematic, for example, if the State of residence of the star company differs from the one of the natural person. Although such a system would be consistent with the basic system of recognizing legal persons alongside natural persons, also for tax purposes, and that this distinction is also in line with the ability-to-pay and direct benefit principles, it is, at the same time, inconsistent with the ability-to-pay and direct benefit principles, the principle of origin, the territoriality principle, the principle of international neutrality and CLIN. The income is not earned in the State of residence, so the wealth has not been created there. The public goods and services of this State have not been used to create the income. The entertainers or sportspersons do not perform their income-producing activities in that State. Therefore, such an allocation is also inconsistent with the territoriality principle. Furthermore, it is also inconsistent with the international tax neutrality principle and CLIN. A taxation based on the residence principle creates a non-neutral and consequently an inefficient system because of the differences in the residence State taxes of competitors in the entertainment or sports markets.

Second, a look-through approach could be applied by State of residence of the star company and the natural person.[34] I think that such an approach would be inconsistent with the basic system of recognizing legal persons alongside natural persons, also for tax purposes, and, that non-recognition would also not be in line with the ability-to-pay and direct benefit principles. However, it could also be argued that they should be considered as one unit for tax purposes, and, consequently, this would justify a deviation from the juridical basic recognition of legal persons and natural persons in case of, for example, a star company and the entertainer or sportsperson concerned. However, I think that for the rest, the same arguments against such a system apply as to the first alternative. An additional problem arises if, for example, the State of residence of the star company differs from the one of the natural person and only one of the States applies a look-through approach. That will make an alignment of the taxation of Article-17-income earned by legal persons and by natural persons even more problematic. However, if the performance State would apply a look-through approach and the States of residence should follow this approach, this additional problem would not arise.

33. *See, e.g.*, Dick Molenaar, *Taxation of International Performing Artistes* 353-361 (2005), Dick Molenaar, *Artiesten en sporters niet in het verdrag met België*, 229 WFR (2023), and Kavelaars, *supra* n. 31, at para. 7.

34. Compare also, e.g., Kavelaars, *supra* n. 31, at para. 6.

Third, the State of residence of the star company and the natural person could allow any non-deductible foreign withholding tax to be transferred to another taxpayer.[35] Again, I think that the same arguments against such a system can be upheld as against the first alternative. However, I believe that additional arguments can be put forward. The tax credit would be uncoupled with the income. The credit would be granted to another person than the person who earned the income. In my view, this would be inconsistent with the basic system of recognizing legal persons alongside natural persons, also for tax purposes. This separation would also be inconsistent with the ability-to-pay principle because, as a basic rule, I think that the taxes on income should be borne by the one who has earned the income. This is also true for Article-17 income.[36] Furthermore, the risk may arise of an undesired or abusive trade in tax credits. To prevent such a trade, complex (anti-abuse) rules may be necessary.[37]

Fourth, the star company and the natural person could be given an option in the State of residence to allocate the income of the star company to the natural person. The star company would be considered transparent.[38] In substance, this is a look-through approach as discussed under the second alternative. Therefore, the same arguments against this approach apply here. Furthermore, giving an option may in itself conflict with the principle of equal treatment. Similar economic positions may be treated differently.

Fifth, the star company and the natural person could be given the option in the performance State instead of the State of residence to allocate the income of the star company to the natural person. The star company would be considered transparent in the performance State. This also is a look-through approach. To certain extent, similar arguments against a look-through approach apply here: inconsistent with the basic system of recognizing legal persons alongside natural persons, which would also be inconsistent with the ability-to-pay and direct benefit principles. Also, here, it could be held that a star company and the entertainer or sportsperson concerned should be considered as one unit for tax purposes. Furthermore, it could also be held here that this option is inconsistent with the principle of equal treatment. There are also differences compared to the fourth alternative. For example, the performance State is more or less in the driver's seat instead of the State of residence. As a consequence, the additional problems arising if the State of residence of the star company differs from the one of the natural may not arise, or to a lesser extent, assuming that the States of residence should follow the performance State's look-through approach. Maybe this would make an alignment of the taxation of Article-17-income earned by legal persons and by a natural person easier.

35. Compare HR 24 September 2021, No. 20/01875, *supra* n. 9, at section 3.1, referring to the decision of Court of Appeals which held that such a rule has been included in none of the relevant tax treaties. *See also, e.g.*, Kavelaars, *supra* n. 31, at para. 5.
36. It may be true that economically such a person is able to pass on the burden to another person. Whether such a transfer is actually possible in an individual case will always depend on the concrete market conditions.
37. Compare, e.g. Art. 46 UDADT.
38. Compare to a certain extent, e.g., Art. 1(2) OM 2017 concerning the allocation of income in case of hybrid entities.

Sixth, a tax-base exemption could be granted in the State of residence of the star company and the natural person. This seems to me the most promising method to realize mitigation of double taxation of income earned by entertainers and sportspersons in a legal form-neutral manner. Such a system would also best satisfy the other benchmarks. It would be consistent with the basic system of recognizing legal persons alongside natural persons, also for tax purposes. This recognition would also be in line with the ability-to-pay and direct benefit principles. It would also solve the problems mentioned above under a residence-based mitigation of double taxation if the State of residence of the star company differs from the one of the natural person: both States would apply a tax-base exemption.[39] Furthermore, this system would also be consistent with the ability-to-pay and direct benefit principles, the principle of origin, the territoriality principle, the principle of international neutrality and CLIN. The income is earned in the performance State. The wealth has been created there. The public goods and services of this State have been used to create the income. The entertainers or sportspersons perform their income-producing activities within the territory of that State. A tax-base exemption creates a neutral and, consequently, an efficient system because the competitors in the entertainment or sports markets face the same tax burden, i.e., only the tax burden of the performance State.[40] Furthermore, it seems to me that the arguments that the performance State may lack sufficient information to realize its tax jurisdiction[41] and that a tax credit is necessary instead of tax-base exemption to guarantee that Article-17-income is taxed once[42] are, at least, out of date. Such a reasoning seems to underestimate the impact of the current dense network of rules regarding the international exchange of information.[43] Nowadays, the performance State can be well informed. Furthermore, I think that the notion of single taxation[44] is not convincing either because it completely disregards where the Article-17-income has been created and from which State's public goods and services the star company and the entertainers and sportsperson have benefited in order to

39. Compare to a certain extent also HR 24 September 2021, No. 20/01875, *supra* n. 9, at para. 4.4.
40. The legal form-neutral taxation of Art. 17-income could be made more complete by this State if it would align the taxation of income earned by legal persons with the taxation of income earned by a natural person, or the other way around. Furthermore, this State should only tax on a net basis, i.e., all relevant costs to produce the Art. 17-income should be taken into account. *See* §32.2 of this chapter.
41. *See, e.g.*, OECD, *The Taxation of Income Derived from Entertainment, Artistic and Sporting Activities* (1987), paras 18-23, 99-101, and 105-109; Daniel Sandler, *The Taxation of International Entertainers and Athletes* (1995), at 311-312, 322, 342-347, Molenaar, *supra* n. 33, at 179-185, 187, 196-197, and 348-351, and Kavelaars, *supra* n. 31, at para. 4.
42. *See, e.g.*, para. 12 OC 2017 to Art. 17 OM 2017 and para. 35 OC 2017 to Arts 23A and 23B OM 2017.
43. *See, e.g.*, the often amended an extended European Union Council Directive 2011/16/EU, Art. 26 OECD MC 2017, and the Convention on Mutual Administrative Assistance in Tax Matters (1988).
44. I would like to emphasize that I do not consider single taxation to constitute a principle, but only a notion, because under this notion, it does not matter where the income is taxed, as long as it is taxed. So this premise, as far as I am concerned, is not based on any choice of principle. *See* for a more detailed discussion, e.g., Eric C.C.M. Kemmeren & Francesco De Lillo, *International Single Taxation: A Misguiding Notion*, in: Joanna Wheeler (ed.), *Single Taxation?* 219-235 (IBFD 2018).

produce their wealth. Therefore, this notion is also inconsistent with the ability-to-pay and direct benefit principles, the principle of origin, the territoriality principle, the principle of international neutrality and CLIN.

§32.5 CONCLUSIONS

I have taken you on a journey inspired by two elements of the incredibly rich national, European and international journey that Peter has made during his academic career (legal form-neutral taxation and the taxation of top sportspersons) and a Dutch Supreme Court case on the mitigation of double taxation by means of an ordinary tax credit. The research questions of this chapter are:

> Can mitigation of double taxation of income earned by entertainers and sportspersons by means of an ordinary tax credit be done in a legal form-neutral manner, and if not, how should legal form-neutral mitigation of double taxation of this income be realized?

The answer to these questions has been given based on the following benchmarks: the recognition in our legal system of legal persons alongside natural persons, the ability-to-pay and direct benefit principles, the principle of origin, the territoriality principle, the principle of international neutrality and CLIN.

The answers to the research question are:

(1) Mitigation of double taxation of income earned by entertainers and sportspersons by means of an ordinary tax credit cannot convincingly be done in a legal form-neutral manner.
(2) It can best be done by means of granting a tax-base exemption of Article-17-income in the State(s) of residence of the star company and the natural person.

Of course, I hope that I can convince the academic in Peter with these answers, but we are certainly not always in agreement. This is also at the core of academic freedom which is priceless and which Peter always defends with great passion and consistently. As a full-time academic, we will miss him at the FIT and Tilburg University, in the Netherlands and in the European and international tax arenas. However, I am very happy that I will not have to miss his warm personal friendship!

EUCOTAX Series on European Taxation

(1) Peter HJ Essers, Guido JME de Bont & Eric CCM Kemmeren (eds), *The Compatibility of Anti-Abuse Provisions in Tax Treaties with EC Law*, 1998 (ISBN 90-411-9678-1).
(2) Gerard TK Meussen (ed.), *The Principle of Equality in European Taxation*, 1999 (ISBN 90-411-9693-5).
(3) Michael Lang (ed.), *Tax Treaty Interpretation*, 2001 (ISBN 90-411-9857-1).
(4) Pasquale Pistone, *The Impact of Community Law on Tax Treaties: Issues and Solutions*, 2002 (ISBN 90-411-9860-1).
(5) René Offermanns, *The Entrepreneurship Concept in a European Comparative Tax Law Perspective*, 2002 (ISBN 90-411-9887-3).
(6) Michael Lang & Mario Züger, *Settlement of Disputes in Tax Treaty Law*, 2002 (ISBN 90-411-9904-7).
(7) Carlo Pinto, *Tax Competition and EU Law*, 2003 (ISBN 90-411-9913-6).
(8) Michael Lang, Hans-Jörgen Aigner, Ulrich Scheuerle & Markus Stefaner, *CFC Legislation, Tax Treaties and EC Law*, 2004 (ISBN 90-411-2284-2).
(9) Mattias Dahlberg, *Direct Taxation in Relation to the Freedom of Establishment and the Free Movement of Capital*, 2005 (ISBN 90-411-2363-6).
(10) Michael Lang, Judith Herdin & Ines Hofbauer, *WTO and Direct Taxation*, 2005 (ISBN 90-411-2371-7).
(11) Dennis Weber, *Tax Avoidance and the EC Tray Freedoms: A Study of the Limitations under European Law for the Prevention of Tax Avoidance*, 2005 (ISBN 90-411-2402-0).
(12) Félix Alberto Vega Borrego, *Limitations on Benefits Clauses on Double Taxation Conventions*, 2005 (ISBN 90-411-2370-9).
(13) Michael Lang, Josef Schuch & Claus Staringer, *ECJ-Recent Developments in Direct Taxation*, 2006 (ISBN 90-411-2509-4).
(14) Reuven S. Avi-Yonah, James R. Hines Jr. & Michael Lang, *Comparative Fiscal Federalism. Comparing the European Court of Justice and the US Supreme Court's Tax Jurisprudence*, 2007 (ISBN 978-90-411-2552-1).
(15) Christiana HJI Panayi, *Double Taxation, Tax Treaties, Treaty-Shopping and the European Community*, 2007 (ISBN 978-90-411-2658-0).
(16) Dennis Weber, *The Influence of European Law on Direct Taxation: Recent and Future Developments*, 2007 (ISBN 978-90-411-2667-2).
(17) Michael Lang & Pasquale Pistone, *The EU and Third Countries: Direct Taxation*, 2007 (ISBN 978-90-411-2665-8).
(18) Oskar Henkow, *Financial Activities in European VAT: A Theoretical and Legal Research of the European VAT System and Preferred Treatment of Financial Activities*, 2007 (ISBN 978-90-411-2703-7).
(19) Michael Lang (ed.), *Tax Compliance Costs for Companies in an Enlarged European Community*, 2008 (ISBN 978-90-411-2666-5).

(20) Michael Lang (ed.), *Source versus Residence. Problems Arising from the Allocation of Taxing Rights in Tax Treaty Law and Possible Alternatives*, 2008 (ISBN 978-90-411-2763-1).
(21) Ioanna Mitroyanni, *Integration Approaches to Group Taxation in the European Internal Market*, 2008 (ISBN 978-90-411-2779-2).
(22) Rolf Eicke, *Tax Planning with Holding Companies. Repatriation of US Profits from Europe: Concepts, Strategies, Structures*, 2008 (ISBN978-90-411-2794-5).
(23) Peter Essers et al. (ed.), *The Influence of IAS/IFRS on the CCCTB, Tax Accounting, Disclosure and Corporate Law Accounting Concepts: 'A Clash of Cultures'*, 2008 (ISBN 978-90-411-2819-5).
(24) Tonny Schenk-Geers, *International Exchange of Information and the Protection of Taxpayers*, 2009 (ISBN 978-90-411-3142-3).
(25) Raymond Adema, *UCITS and Taxation: Towards Harmonization of the Taxation of UCITS*, 2009 (ISBN 978-90-411-2839-3).
(26) Michael Lang, Jianwen Liu & Gongliang Tang (eds), *Europe–China Tax Treaties*, 2010 (ISBN 978-90-411-3216-1).
(27) Michael Lang, Pasquale Pistone, Josef Schuch & Claus Staringer (eds), *Procedural Rules in Tax Law in the Context of European Union and Domestic Law*, 2010 (ISBN 978-90-411-3376-2).
(28) Sjaak J.J.M. Jansen, *Fiscal Sovereignty of the Member States in an Internal Market: Past and Future*, 2011 (ISBN 978-90-411-3403-5).
(29) Dennis Weber & Bruno da Silva, *From Marks & Spencer to X Holding: The Future of Cross-Border Group Taxation*, 2011 (ISBN 978-90-411-3399-1).
(30) Claus Bohn Jespersen, *Intermediation of Insurance and Financial Services in European VAT*, 2011 (ISBN 978-90-411-3732-6).
(31) Sabine Heidenbauer, *Charity Crossing Borders: The Fundamental Freedoms' Influence on Charity and Donor Taxation in Europe*, 2011 (ISBN 978-90-411-3813-2).
(32) Michael Lang, et al., *The Future of Indirect Taxation: Recent Trends in VAT and GST Systems around the World*, 2012 (ISBN 978-90-411-3797-5).
(33) Harm van den Broek, *Cross-Border Mergers within the EU: Proposals to Remove the Remaining Tax Obstacles*, 2012 (ISBN 978-90-411-3824-8).
(34) Michael Lang, et al. (eds), *Tax Treaty Case Law around the Globe 2011*, 2012 (ISBN 978-90-411-3876-7).
(35) Dennis Weber (ed.), *CCCTB: Selected Issues*, 2012 (ISBN 978-90-411-3872-9).
(36) Daniël Smit, *EU Freedoms, Non-EU Countries and Company Taxation*, 2012 (ISBN 978-90-411-4041-8).
(37) Rita de la Feria, *VAT Exemptions: Consequences and Design Alternatives*, 2013 (ISBN 978-90-411-3276-5).
(38) Karin Simader, *Withholding Taxes and the Fundamental Freedoms*, 2013 (ISBN 978-90-411-4842-1).
(39) Madeleine Merkx, *Establishments in European VAT*, 2013 (ISBN 978-90-411-4554-3).
(40) Carla De Pietro, *Tax Treaty Override*, 2014 (ISBN 978-90-411-5406-4).

(41) G.K. Fibbe & A.J.A. Stevens (eds), *Hybrid Entities and the EU Direct Tax Directives*, 2015 (ISBN 978-90-411-5942-7).
(42) Gerard Staats, *Personal Pensions in the EU*, 2015 (ISBN 978-90-411-5953-3).
(43) Michael Lang & Ine Lejeune (eds), *VAT/GST in a Global Digital Economy*, 2015 (ISBN 978-90-411-5952-6).
(44) Massimo Basilavecchia, Lorenzo del Federico & Pietro Mastellone (eds), *Tax Implications of Environmental Disasters and Pollution*, 2015 (ISBN 978-90-411-5611-2).
(45) Cristina Trenta, *Rethinking EU VAT for P2P Distribution*, 2015 (ISBN 978-90-411-6137-6).
(46) Marie Lamensch, Edoardo Traversa & Servaas van Thiel (eds), *Value Added Tax and the Digital Economy: The 2015 EU Rules and Broader Issues*, 2016 (ISBN 978-90-411-6612-8).
(47) Raffaele Petruzzi, *Transfer Pricing Aspects of Intra-Group Financing*, 2016 (ISBN 978-90-411-6732-3).
(48) Mario Grandinetti (ed.), *Corporate Tax Base in the Light of the IAS/IFRS and EU Directive 2013/34: A Comparative Approach*, 2016 (ISBN 978-90-411-6745-3).
(49) Bruno da Silva, *The Impact of Tax Treaties and EU Law on Group Taxation Regimes*, 2016 (ISBN 978-90-411-6905-1).
(50) Michael Lang, Alfred Storck & Raffaele Petruzzi (eds), *Transfer Pricing in a Post-BEPS World*, 2016 (ISBN 978-90-411-6710-1).
(51) Marta Papis-Almansa, *Insurance in European VAT: Current and Preferred Treatment in the Light of the New Zealand and Australian GST Systems*, 2017 (ISBN 978-90-411-8360-6).
(52) Wolfgang Speckhahn, *Real Estate Investment Trusts In Europe: Europeanising Tax Regimes*, 2017 (ISBN 978-90-411-8360-6).
(53) Frank J.G. Nellen, *Information Asymmetries in EU VAT*, 2017 (ISBN 978-90-411-8837-3).
(54) Erik Ros, *EU Citizenship and Direct Taxation*, 2017 (ISBN 978-90-411-8584-6).
(55) Werner Haslehner, Georg Kofler & Alexander Rust (eds), *EU Tax Law and Policy in the 21st Century*, 2017 (ISBN 978-90-411-8815-1).
(56) Claudia Sanò, *National Legal Presumptions and European Tax Law*, 2018 (ISBN 978-90-411-6613-5).
(57) Christoph Marchgraber, *Double (Non-)Taxation and EU Law*, 2018 (ISBN 978-90-411-9410-7).
(58) Dennis Weber & Jan van de Streek (eds), *The EU Common Consolidated Corporate Tax Base: Critical Analysis*, 2018 (ISBN 978-90-411-9233-2).
(59) Werner Haslehner (ed.), *Investment Fund Taxation: Domestic Law, EU Law, and Double Taxation Treaties*, 2018 (ISBN 978-90-411-9669-9).
(60) Jérôme Monsenego, *Selectivity in State Aid Law and the Methods for the Allocation of the Corporate Tax Base*, 2018 (ISBN 978-90-411-9413-8).
(61) José Manuel Almudí Cid, Jorge A. Ferreras Gutiérrez & Pablo A. Hernández González-Barreda (eds), *Combating Tax Avoidance in the EU: Harmonization and Cooperation in Direct Taxation*, 2019 (ISBN 978-94-035-0154-3).

(62) Werner Haslehner, Georg Kofler & Alexander Rust (eds), *Time and Tax: Issues in International, EU, and Constitutional Law*, 2019 (ISBN 978-94-035-0354-7).

(63) Nathalie Wittock, *Sales Promotion Techniques and VAT in the EU*, 2019 (ISBN 978-94-035-0861-0).

(64) Carla De Pietro (ed.), *New Perspectives on Fiscal State Aid: Legitimacy and Effectiveness of Fiscal State Aid Control*, 2019 (ISBN 978-94-035-1415-4).

(65) Giorgio Beretta, *European VAT and the Sharing Economy*, 2019 (ISBN 978-94-035-1435-2).

(66) Claudio Cipollini, *Special Tax Zones and EU Law: Theory, Implementations, and Future Challenges*, 2020 (ISBN 978-94-035-1885-5).

(67) Gianluigi Bizioli, Mario Grandinetti, Leopoldo Parada, Giuseppe Vanz & Alessandro Vicini Ronchetti (eds), *Corporate Taxation, Group Debt Funding and Base Erosion: New Perspectives on the EU Anti-Tax Avoidance Directive*, 2020 (ISBN 978-94-035-1170-2).

(68) Ronald Hein & Ronald Russo (eds), *Co-operative Compliance and the OECD's International Compliance Assurance Programme*, 2020 (ISBN 978-94-035-1951-7).

(69) Jeffrey Owens & Jonathan Leigh Pemberton, *Cooperative Compliance: A Multi-stakeholder and Sustainable Approach to Taxation*, 2021 (ISBN 978-94-035-3193-9).

(70) Christina Pollak, *Platforms in EU VAT Law: A Legal Analysis of the Supply of Goods*, 2022 (ISBN 978-94-035-1026-2).

(71) Shu-Chien Chen, *Towards a Neutral Formulary Apportionment System in Regional Integration*, 2023 (ISBN 978-94-035-3276-9).

(72) Maria Júlia Ildefonso Mendonça, *International Juridical Double Taxation from an Ability-to-Pay Perspective under EU Law*, 2024 (ISBN 978-94-035-0298-4).

(73) Carla De Pietro, Cees Peters & Eric Kemmeren, *A Journey Through European and International Taxation: Liber Amicorum in Honour of Peter Essers*, 2024 (ISBN 978-94-035-3197-7).

www.ingramcontent.com/pod-product-compliance
Lightning Source LLC
Chambersburg PA
CBHW071236230926
51849CB00001B/124
* 9 7 8 9 4 0 3 5 3 1 9 7 7 *